# THE WRITER'S WORKPLACE

## with Readings

## Building College Writing Skills

### SEVENTH EDITION

## SANDRA SCARRY

Formerly with the Office of Academic Affairs
City University of New York

## JOHN SCARRY

Hostos Community College
City University of New York

WADSWORTH
CENGAGE Learning™

Australia • Brazil • Canada • Mexico • Singapore • Spain • United Kingdom • United States

**The Writer's Workplace with Readings:
Building College Writing Skills,
Seventh Edition**
Sandra Scarry, John Scarry

Publisher: Lyn Uhl

Acquisitions Editor: Annie Todd

Development Editor: Laurie Dobson

Assistant Editor: Janine Tangney

Editorial Assistant: Melanie Opacki

Media Editor: Emily Ryan

Marketing Manager: Kirsten Stoller

Marketing Coordinator: Ryan Ahern

Marketing Communications Manager:
Martha Pfeiffer

Content Project Manager: Aimee
Chevrette Bear

Art Director: Jill Ort

Print Buyer: Susan Spencer

Senior Rights Acquisition Account Manager:
Katie Huha

Production Service: Elm Street Publishing
Services

Photo Manager: Robyn Young

Compositor: Integra Software Services Pvt. Ltd.

For product information and technology assistance, contact us at
**Cengage Learning Customer & Sales Support, 1-800-354-9706**
For permission to use material from this text or product,
submit all requests online at **www.cengage.com/permissions**
Further permissions questions can be emailed to
**permissionrequest@cengage.com**

Library of Congress Control Number: 2009929903

Student Edition ISBN-10: 1-439-08210-3

Student Edition ISBN-13: 978-1-439-08210-2

**Wadsworth Cengage Learning**
20 Channel Center Street
Boston, MA 02210
USA

Cengage Learning is a leading provider of customized learning solutions with office locations around the globe, including Singapore, the United Kingdom, Australia, Mexico, Brazil and Japan. Locate your local office at international.cengage.com/region

Cengage Learning products are represented in Canada by Nelson Education, Ltd.

For your course and learning solutions, visit **www.cengage.com**

Purchase any of our products at your local college store or at our preferred online store **www.ichapters.com**

**FOR OUR STUDENTS**

What shall I do this year? What shall I become? What shall I learn—truly learn and know that I have learned by the time I look at these pages next year?

*Lorraine Hansberry*
*Journal entry of August 23, 1962*

Printed in the United States of America
1 2 3 4 5 6 7 13 12 11 10 09

# CONTENTS

## CHAPTER 22　DEVELOPING PARAGRAPHS: COMPARISON/CONTRAST　427

## CHAPTER 23　DEVELOPING PARAGRAPHS: CAUSE AND EFFECT　451

CHAPTER **24**

# DEVELOPING PARAGRAPHS: DEFINITION AND ANALYSIS                    471

CHAPTER **25**

# DEVELOPING PARAGRAPHS: CLASSIFICATION                    485

## PART 6     Further Readings for the College Writer     612

# Rhetorical Table of Contents

# PREFACE

I t has been said that the person who has the plan has the power. While this is true in many areas of human endeavor, it is never more true than in the area of writing. Both *The Writer's Workplace* and *The Writer's Workplace with Readings* contain a foundational plan that instructors and their students can follow to produce more powerful writing. These textbooks come out of more than twenty years of classroom use and nationwide adoptions in two-year and four-year colleges. This completely grounded approach to the teaching of grammar skills and composition development has served the needs of more than **half a million** students in colleges throughout the United States and Canada, establishing itself as a time-tested leader in the field. The book has helped students not only in their English classes but also in courses in many other fields. Because of the deliberate inclusion of many topics related to the world of work, students who use *The Writer's Workplace* or *The Writer's Workplace with Readings* feel connected to their career goals as they study for lifetime vocations.

One of the authors' major goals was to organize the material in a way that would provide the greatest flexibility for the users. Today's students and teachers need a textbook that offers them flexibility. Because of the book's careful organization, it works equally well in the classroom, in the writing lab, in collaborative groups, with a tutor, or even at home. In fact, when the wealth of ancillary material available online is considered, the result is a total support system for virtually any developmental need.

## Customize *The Writer's Workplace* to Fit Your Course

Once again, this edition of *The Writer's Workplace* offers a custom edition. Instructors who discover that a one-semester course cannot utilize all the contents of the book are able to select exactly those chapters that would be appropriate for their semester's work. Such a customized text will provide students with only those parts of the book that the instructor plans to teach, thereby saving on textbook costs.

## Features of Part 1: An Invitation to Writing

### THE PROCESS WRITING APPROACH

The two chapters that make up the opening section of *The Writer's Workplace with Readings* establish an inviting tone for the book, which immediately introduces the idea that writing is a process. From the very start, students engage in short skill-building activities that give them opportunities to practice all the actual techniques and concepts taught in these chapters. Whether the skill is freewriting, brainstorming, or revising for coherence and unity, students will directly participate in these important stages of the writing process.

# Features of Part 2: Creating Effective Sentences

## THE COMPREHENSIVENESS OF A GRAMMAR HANDBOOK

Students come to college writing classes from a wide range of educational backgrounds. Many of these students expect that any gaps they might have in their knowledge of grammar will be addressed in their developmental English classes. This textbook satisfies those expectations. Almost alone among the many writing textbooks in the field, *The Writer's Workplace with Readings* contains an exceptionally comprehensive language development section. Carefully crafted definitions, charts, and rules provide visual aids for students as they learn the underlying elements of sentence structure and punctuation. A careful sequencing of topics builds from less complex to more complex concepts as the student proceeds from nouns and verbs, to phrases and fragments, to coordination and subordination. After students have absorbed this material, they will be better able to discuss, analyze, and edit their own writing, as well as better understand the comments made by instructors on returned papers. Instructors who have concentrated on this sentence-building section of the book report that our text provides the most comprehensive and easy-to-follow presentation they have encountered.

## CAREFULLY CONSTRUCTED PRACTICES, EXERCISES, AND MASTERY TESTS TO ADDRESS DIFFERENT RATES OF LEARNING

Because every student learns at a different rate, some students need more practice opportunities than others in order to fully absorb a particular concept. Whether the concept is subordination or parallel structure, our textbook offers multiple opportunities to address that need. The quality and quantity of these exercises are seldom encountered in a textbook of this kind. Students are grateful for the additional practice opportunities, and by using the answer key to selected exercises, students will be able to judge their need for further work.

## CONTINUOUS DISCOURSE

Whenever possible, exercises teaching grammar skills use continuous discourse. Building a foundation in sentence skills while reading fresh and surprising information that often contains touches of humor and human interest makes grammar much less tedious.

## EDITING TESTS

The "Editing Student Writing" feature appears from Chapters 4 through 13 and serves as a cumulative review. Each of these exercises asks students to analyze student writing by locating errors and correcting them through the use of editing symbols.

When students become familiar with the use of editing symbols, they will more readily interpret the corrections that instructors or peers make when evaluating student work. Finally, we have included these editing exercises to remind students of the importance of editing their own papers before they hand them in; the errors they find in these exercises are the types of errors they must learn to find in their own writing.

# Features of Part 3: Understanding the Power of Words

## FOCUS ON WORD CHOICE

All writing is made stronger when a more careful attention is paid to word choice. These choices can range from deciding on the correct form of *its* and *it's*, to understanding why the word *kid* not appropriate in formal writing. The two chapters that make up this section contain challenging and enjoyable lessons that demonstrate the need for precise and appropriate language.

# Features of Part 4: Creating Effective Paragraphs

## PATTERNS OF RHETORICAL DEVELOPMENT

Strong paragraphs are the solid blocks of any good piece of writing, and students need to build on such a foundation to produce successful college essays. The chapters of Part 4 are organized around the classical rhetorical modes, the most commonly accepted method of introducing developmental students to the discipline of college writing. Each chapter explains the basic elements needed to develop a paragraph using a particular rhetorical pattern. Students study and then practice the specific elements of each mode. Then, students are guided using a step-by-step method to construct basic paragraphs or essays. Finally, with the confidence they have gained, accessible professional models followed by a list of writing topics will encourage students to compose their own creative paragraphs that demonstrate their skill in each particular mode. Many instructors who have used previous editions of the text have judged this section the heart of the book.

## STEP-BY-STEP APPROACH

Following the study and practice of the elements of a particular mode, students will follow a step-by-step guide to construct their own paragraphs. This will ensure a focus on each element whether it be the topic sentence, a supporting detail, or the use of a transitional expression. This section keeps developmental students on task and builds confidence.

## PROFESSIONAL WRITING MODELS WITH CHALLENGING CONTENT

The engaging professional models in each chapter have the primary goal of demonstrating a rhetorical mode. Each example, however, has also been chosen to enrich our students' lives and increase their love of reading. Mature individuals deserve to be challenged by stimulating and sometimes provocative content. With the confidence students will have gained from the study and practice of each modal element, these short professional paragraphs will inspire students to produce thoughtful and creative pieces of writing of their own. A list of carefully related writing topics is provided for consideration after each model paragraph.

## ENCOURAGEMENT OF COLLABORATIVE WORK

Whenever possible, students are encouraged to collaborate. Most developing writers need input from their peers and instructors. In the prewriting stages, in-class brainstorming and discussion of ideas for specific writing topics are especially productive to help students get started. Collaborative work is again useful during the stages of editing and revision.

# Features of Part 5: Structuring the College Essay

## FOLLOWING THE PROGRESS OF A STUDENT ESSAY

This feature gives students a unique opportunity to develop an essay of their own, as they follow each part of a model student essay on the same topic. The structure provided by this activity has one major advantage over other approaches. Students can compare the quality of their own work at each stage with the work of the model student.

## FOCUS ON THESIS STATEMENT

Because the ultimate goal of *The Writer's Workplace* is to enable students to construct the complete college essay, a focus on writing a strong thesis statement is critical for student success. Students have great difficulty narrowing the topic, finding the controlling idea, and indicating the strategy of development. Therefore, much effort is placed on learning this skill.

## MODEL INTRODUCTIONS AND CONCLUSIONS

Students are often at a loss to know how an introduction can be constructed or what to include in a conclusion. This text presents a variety of introductory and concluding strategies used by professional writers. Students can study these examples and consider using these strategies in their own writing.

## DEVELOPMENT OF THE CLASSIC ARGUMENT

One of the most difficult challenges for a writer is developing the essay of argument or persuasion. This is a challenge that demands logical and critical thinking. Instructors will find several short arguments that will be accessible to student experience and provide opportunity for debate. Students will be able to grasp the classic elements of the argument before writing an argument on their own.

## THE RESEARCH PAPER

The goal of this feature is to teach the skills of quoting, paraphrasing, and summarizing. Students at this level need these skills before they can hope to be successful at writing a research paper. The importance of avoiding plagiarism is stressed, and basic MLA documentation examples are provided.

## THE ESSAY EXAM

Students have the opportunity to analyze typical essay exam questions and develop strategies for tackling the answers while under the pressures of a time constraint.

# Features of Part 6: Further Readings for the College Writer

## ACTIVE READING APPROACH

While *The Writer's Workplace with Readings* is a book that depends heavily on student participation in the process of writing, no successful writing is produced without significant attention being paid to reading and study skills. The section that begins Part 6, "Strategies for the Active Reader," emphasizes the importance of active reading for the developmental writing student. One of the essays, "How to Mark a Book" by Mortimer Adler, makes the case for active reading. Students are encouraged to become more engaged in the texts they are reading and to place more emphasis on their critical thinking skills. These are skills that will take students far beyond the experience of a particular writing class, and will enrich many other parts of their lives.

## FURTHER READINGS ILLUSTRATING RHETORICAL MODES

In addition to the carefully chosen professional models used throughout the first five parts of *The Writer's Workplace with Readings*, twenty high-interest essays support the work of the book, with each reading giving the student further opportunity for study and enjoyment. Each reading illustrates a particular rhetorical mode, thus reinforcing the work of previous chapters. Brief introductory notes help students understand and appreciate the background and context of each reading. Finally, two sets of questions guide the instructor through classroom work. The first set, "Questions for Critical Thinking," concentrates on the structure of each piece, while the second set, "Writing in Response," stimulates critical reaction to the themes and leads to a number of challenging writing opportunities.

# Other Features

## THE UNIQUE *WORKING TOGETHER*

At the end of every chapter, the "Working Together" activity provides the instructor with an additional or alternative lesson plan that encourages critical thinking and collaborative learning. These activities tend to stress job-related issues such as integrity in the workplace (Chapter 12) or sexual harassment (Chapter 30). The skill might focus on brainstorming, peer editing, or class discussion to help students gather information for writing. Each of these Working Together projects is designed to provide an engaging full instructional class period that will stimulate class discussion and individual thinking.

## PORTFOLIO SUGGESTIONS

The portfolio feature at the conclusion of each chapter encourages students to gather and save all their writing efforts, not only for evaluation purposes, but also for ongoing and future writing projects. Students are encouraged to save journal entries, brainstorming lists, paragraphs, and drafts for essays. All these materials have real potential for development later in the term or in other courses throughout the student's college career.

## EXPLORING ONLINE

Students can now access the website for *The Writer's Workplace* and *The Writer's Workplace with Readings* to find additional help with the topics covered in each chapter. At the website, students will find a chapter-by-chapter glossary, along with quizzes, and other suggested activities.

## FIVE APPENDICES

The five appendices offer a wealth of pertinent and useful reference material. This section is an especially valuable resource for speakers of English as a Second Language. The first appendix deals with specific issues for ESOL, while the other appendices include material on parts of speech, irregular verbs, spelling, and transitions. All of these sections together serve as a resource for students who find themselves in a variety of other courses that require coherent writing.

## AN ANSWER KEY TO PRACTICES AND SELECTED EXERCISES

The answer key at the end of the book provides answers to all the practices and approximately one-third of the exercises in the book. For instance, where three exercises are given on a topic, the answers to the first exercise will always be given. This answer key allows students to work more independently. Of course, answers to the Mastery Tests are given only in the Annotated Instructor's Edition.

## INSIDE FRONT AND BACK COVER CHARTS

The inside front and back cover charts provide material on two important subjects for easy reference: options for coordination and subordination and a comprehensive list of common editing symbols.

## HUNDREDS OF SUGGESTIONS FOR WRITING TOPICS

Throughout the text, numerous writing topics are suggested. These topics are always related to and suggested by the content at hand. The authors repeatedly incorporate discussion and collaboration in the brainstorming stages so students can expand their thinking and learn to question their assumptions. Students are encouraged to take notes during discussions and save not only their own paragraphs but other classmates' ideas and any other material they may have gathered for future writing assignments.

# New to this Edition

We have been gratified by the enthusiastic response to the features added in the sixth edition of *The Writer's Workplace with Readings.* This new seventh edition retains all of these features while updating content, expanding selected topics, and adding many refinements. We are confident that both teacher and student will continue to find this latest edition engaging, flexible, and comprehensive, a supportive resource for developing writers everywhere.

- **More than 40 new practices and exercises provide fresh content** for this edition, notably the inclusion of such current topics as student credit card debt or serious head injuries among young people playing sports; national issues such as the problem of childhood obesity; and international concerns such as global warming and the need for more fuel-efficient cars. The exploration of these and many other human interest pieces will spark classroom discussions that give students a springboard for their writing. This new material also keeps the book relevant to current social concerns so important to our developmental students.

- **Twelve new model paragraphs** include accessible examples of outstanding writing from such well-known names as E. B. White ("The Three New Yorks"), Colin Powell ("The Dominant Figure of My Youth"), and Deborah Tannen ("Comparing Men and Women").

- **Two newly constructed chapters (Definition/Analysis, Chapter 24, and Classification, Chapter 25)** more fully develop the rhetorical modes. Each mode now has a chapter of its own with expanded activities and new model paragraphs.

- **Chapter 26 (Moving From the Paragraph to the Essay)** has been revised to include **more opportunities for student interaction.** New exercises require **more analysis of introductory patterns.**

- **Chapter 27 (Following the Progress of a Student Essay)** has been **revised and expanded** to include a more effective approach to the step-by-step work of the chapter.

- **Chapter 32 (Writing an Essay Using Persuasion)** has been revised to contain **four new model arguments** that are shorter and easier for students to analyze. These topics include the use of cell phones while driving, laptops in the classroom, and the legal drinking age.

- **Chapter 33** has been updated to encorporate **the newest MLA Guidelines** for documenting sources. In addition, **more emphasis has been placed on the issues of plagiarism** and how to avoid plagiarism by summarizing, paraphrasing and using quotations correctly.

- The **six new readings** in the "Further Readings" section include Lee Herrick's essay "What Is This Thing Called Family?" This piece reinforces themes introduced in the definition chapter. Molly Ivins' lively essay "Get a Knife, Get a Dog, but Get Rid of Guns" will provide provocative ideas for classroom debate and persuasive writing assignments.

- **The book's four-color design with a greater number of color photographs** will add to students' enjoyment as they work with the text.
- **A rhetorical table of contents** has been added, which will enable instructors and students alike to locate any particular paragraph or essay with ease.
- **Many refinements have been made throughout the book:** tightened definitions, more clearly designed presentations of concepts, expanded explanations and examples where needed, rewritten questions, new writing topics, and numerous other small and some not-so-small improvements. For many of these refinements, we must thank our users and reviewers for their thoughtful suggestions.

# Ancillaries

*The Writer's Workplace* is supported by a wide range of instructional materials, each one designed to aid the teacher's classroom work. These materials include the following:

## Annotated Instructor's Edition

This book provides answers to the practices and exercises for the student editions.

## Instructor's Resource Manual

The Instructor's Resource Manual, prepared by Siobhán Scarry of State University of New York at Buffalo, supports teachers who are using *The Writer's Workplace*, Ninth Edition, and *The Writer's Workplace with Readings*, Seventh Edition. The variety of materials in this manual will enhance, reinforce, and complement the material presented in the primary text.

This manual has been revised to support the new editions of *The Writer's Workplace*, with a view toward integrating ancillary materials more closely with the objectives, chapter content, and readings in the textbook. Instructors will find comprehensive support for planning and organizing their courses in Part 1, including specific sample syllabi. This section also includes in-depth discussion on incorporating collaborative learning and the use of journals into the classroom, as well as a section on grading and responding to student writing. Teachers looking for additional assignments to give their students will benefit from the revised chapter guides in Part 2, which offer in-class activities, journal assignments, and responding to reading assignments designed with the goals of each chapter in mind. Instructional essays, drawn from respected colleagues in the field of composition studies, are included in Part 3 and cover such topics as the teacher-student conference or plagiarism in policy and pedagogy. Part 4 includes a full and revised set of handouts and transparency masters that complement the entire text. Part 5 provides a variety of evaluation handouts that may prove useful for both teachers and students. Two appendices complete the manual, offering sample student writings (including two newly added student research papers) and a compendium of the more than one hundred assignments presented in the manual.

## Test Book

Prepared by Siobhán Scarry of State University of New York at Buffalo, the Test Book includes 100 diagnostic, exercise, and mastery tests that include multiple choice, identify, fill-in-the-blank, correction, and revision.

## ExamView®

ExamView® features a user-friendly testing environment that allows you to not only publish traditional paper and computer based tests, but also Web-deliverable exams.

## Book Companion Web Site (www.cengage.com/devenglish/scarry/writersworkplace)

The Book Companion Web Site features a wealth of text-specific resources for students. For each chapter of the text, students have access to chapter objectives, an "Exploring Online" section that provides links to additional online resources, a glossary of important terms, online activities that build on chapter material by leveraging the depth and breadth of content available on the Web, and interactive online grammar quizzes.

## WriteSpace in Angel

WriteSpace is a flexible, interactive, and customizable program that assesses students of English at all skill levels. WriteSpace motivates and assists students with varying skill levels by providing tutorial support. WriteSpace includes the following: Diagnostic assessments in writing and grammar skills, Exercises and Writing Modules (tutorials), Plagiarism Prevention Zone, Personal Tutor, CL Interactives, an Online Handbook, and a Gradebook.

# Acknowledgments

With this new edition, once more we find ourselves indebted to a host of people, including those who have inspired us and those who have worked with us behind the scenes to make certain that our initial vision of the book remain realized. First of all, we thank some wonderful colleagues at Hostos Communiity College (Professors Vermell Blanding, Sue Dicker, and Cynthia Jones chief among them) and all the amazing students we have taught there. Their inspiration has been a constant source of energy and creativity to us. One of them in particular, Raluca Tanasescu, is to be thanked for her contribution to Chapter 27 of this edition. First and foremost, it is the hard work and courage of our students, and indeed of all the students who have used our textbook, that motivate us to constantly refine the text. We have come to realize that the skills taught in this book have the ability to empower people and change their lives. Our gratitude to our team at Cengage Learning is not easy to measure. Through the previous editions and including the present work, we have had the good fortune to benefit from the energy and talent of professionals who have patiently and attentively addressed the needs of the book. Our former publisher, Michael Rosenberg, was with us from the start, and we recall with pleasure all of our working collaborations. Thanks also to our current Senior Publisher, Lyn Uhl, for her support. We owe a genuine debt of gratitude to Annie Todd, Acquisitions Editor, whose faith in our work and guiding insights have made our rethinking and revision much less stressful than otherwise might have been; her presence and personality have been much appreciated. Our book has benefited tremendously because of the professionalism and expertise of these people. Another piece of our good fortune deserves special mention. We have had the benefit of the day-to-day problem solving accomplished by our Developmental Editor, Laurie Dobson. We could not have hoped for anyone with more careful attention to every detail. We will always be grateful for her total support and encouragement every step of the way. Every author should be as fortunate!

Other members of the Cengage Learning family have been supportive in so many other ways. We thank Aimee Chevrette Bear, our Cengage Content Project Manager, and Allison Campbell, of Elm Street Publishing Services, for their page-by-page expert attention. To Kirsten Stoller, our Marketing Manager, our gratitude for her responsiveness to our needs as they have arisen. We also have been fortunate to have had help in the selection of photographs and the securing of literary texts by Audrey Pettengill, Manager of Permissions Acquisition, Amber Hosea, Photo Editor, and Katie Huha, Senior Rights Acquisition Account Manager. We understand all too well the detailed work required for these tasks and how important such good work has been for the finished product. Emily Ryan, Media Editor, has directed the work of the vast technological support system which accompanies our book; we have only profound admiration for all this work. We also thank Janine Tangney, Assistant Editor and Melanie Opacki, Editorial Assistant, for their support of our books and ancillaries.

One other person has played a major role in the creation of materials that accompany our text, and to her we must express how much her work has meant to us and to instructors everywhere. Siobhán Scarry, State University of New York at Buffalo, has again updated the Instructor's Resource Manual. It is filled with a wealth of helpful material for instructors. We have never seen a better Instructor's Resource Manual. She has also undertaken the revision of the Exercise and Test Book. This should be very helpful to instructors who need additional material keyed to the grammar and mechanics chapters. Finally, a big thanks to Siobhán for all her efforts to find the most useful and best sites for our "Exploring Online" feature in the textbook. We could not have completed this edition in a timely fashion without all of her expertise.

We would not be achieving the degree of success with each new edition without the invaluable insights of our professional reviewers. The fruits of their many years of collective experience, and their individual perceptions for the needs of this latest revised manuscript, have made our efforts for this new edition possible. To each of them, our sincerest gratitude. They include:

Susan Achziger, *Community College of Aurora*

Patricia Bennett, *Roanoke Chowan Community College*

Michael Burns, *Spokane Community College*

Nancy Cheeks, *California State University at Northridge*

Wayne Christensen, *Florida Memorial University*

Molly Desjardins, *Cypress College*

Jennifer Ferguson, *Cazenovia College*

Rebecca Fournier, *Triton College*

Lesa Hildebrand, *Triton College*

Michelle Holt, *Carroll College*

Betsy Lawrence, *Spokane Community College*

Scott Reichel, *Community College of Aurora*

John Silva, *LaGuardia Community College*

Robin Takahashi, *Ohlone Community College*

Marian Teachey, *South Piedmont Community College*

Gayle R. Thomas, *College of Southern Nevada*

Karen Thompson, *Manatee Community College*

Lorie Thomsen, *Butte Community College*

Michele Wollenzier, *Kent State University*

# Part 1

# An Invitation to Writing

Part 1 invites you to explore the beginning stages of the writing process and examine the essential elements of any effective piece of writing. Begin your work in this writing course with the kind of spirit that spells success.

- **Begin with a positive attitude.** You know more than you think. You have unique life experiences, and your ideas are worth writing about. Fortunately, writing is a skill that can be developed. No matter what your present skills are, practice can greatly help you improve those skills.

- **Be receptive to new techniques and approaches.** As a student beginning this course, you undoubtedly have not yet explored all the various techniques writers use to generate ideas on paper, and you may still have to learn how to incorporate other people's ideas in your writing. Be willing to experiment with the techniques given in this section of the book. Once you practice these proven techniques, you will feel a new confidence as you tackle your own writing assignments.

- **Actively reach out and welcome help from others.** When we learn new skills, we are not expected to figure out everything by ourselves. Most students need help getting started, and because learning styles are different, students need to explore whatever methods work best for them. At every stage of the process, writers need each other to brainstorm, to read and comment on drafts, and to help revise, edit, and proofread each other's work. Part 1 of this book will help you extend your own thinking as you work beyond your first thoughts on a topic.

(continued on next page)

2

- **Respect the ideas of others.** Communication goes two ways. In the process of exploring and expressing your ideas, you must be open to other points of view, whether they come from your instructors, your classmates, or your own reading. You can debate opposing ideas without criticizing the people who hold those ideas.

- **Finally, practice, practice, practice.** This means being willing to put in the necessary time and effort to achieve the needed results.

# GATHERING IDEAS FOR WRITING

In this first chapter, you will practice several **prewriting techniques** used by professional writers as well as student writers as they gather material and generate ideas for writing.

**CHAPTER OBJECTIVES**

- journal writing
- focused freewriting
- brainstorming, clustering, and outlining
- conducting interviews and surveys

## OVERVIEW OF THE WRITING PROCESS

The following chart shows the stages a writer goes through to produce a finished piece of writing. Writers may differ slightly in how they approach a task, but for most of us the following steps are necessary.

---

### The Writing Process

**PREWRITING STAGES**

**1.** Choose the topic and consider what aspect of that topic interests you.

**2.** Gather ideas using prewriting techniques.

**WRITING AND REVISING**

**3.** Compose a first draft and then set it aside for a time.

**4.** Reread your first draft, and if possible, ask the instructor or classmates for input.

**5.** Revise the first draft by adding, cutting, and moving material. Continue to revise, correcting grammar errors and producing new drafts, until you are satisfied.

**PROOFREADING**

**6.** Proofread the final copy, looking especially for typographical errors (typos), misspellings, and omitted words.

---

## BEGINNING TO WRITE: CARING ABOUT YOUR TOPIC

Whether you are writing a college paper or a report at work, your belief in the importance of your topic and confidence in your own ideas will be major factors in your success as a writer. Sometimes a college writing assignment can seem to have little or no relevance beyond a requirement for a passing grade. In this course, however, you should consider each assignment as an opportunity to do the following:

- discover that you have ideas worth expressing
- explore topics that you care about
- incorporate the ideas of others into your own work

## PREWRITING TECHNIQUES: THE FIRST STEP IN THE WRITING PROCESS

> **Prewriting,** the earliest stage of the writing process, uses techniques such as brainstorming, clustering, and outlining to transform thoughts into words.

Very few writers ever sit down and start writing immediately. To produce effective work, most writers begin by using a variety of strategies called *prewriting techniques*. These techniques help writers generate ideas and gather material about topics that are of interest to them or that they are required to write about for their work. Prewriting techniques are a way to explore and give some order to what might otherwise be a confusing hodgepodge of different thoughts on a topic. These techniques reassure every writer who feels the stress of looking at a blank page or an empty computer screen, knowing it has to be filled. Not only will the writer have needed material but he or she can also plan how to develop that material: what the major ideas will be, what the order of those ideas will be, and what specific details will be used. The rest of this chapter will describe these prewriting techniques and provide opportunities to practice them.

## JOURNAL WRITING

> **Journal writing** is the written record of a person's observations, thoughts, reactions, or opinions. Kept daily, or nearly every day, the journal usually draws on everyday experiences.

At some point in their lives, many people keep a diary or a journal. They may keep a simple record of day-to-day events, or they may want to explore thoughts and opinions about a variety of topics. If the journal is a personal one, the writer does not have to worry about making a mistake or being misunderstood. The journal writer does not have to worry about handwriting or how thoughts are organized, because the writer is the only person who will be reading the pages of that journal. Personal journals allow us to be totally honest and to write about anything we wish.

If you keep a personal journal, you might want to record events that happen around you, focus on problems you are trying to solve, or note your personal reactions to the people you know. Until you actually put your thoughts into words, you may not be fully aware of all your feelings and opinions. Most writers are surprised and pleased with the results of their personal explorations in writing.

For some people, a journal is a kind of scrapbook of meaningful written expressions they find around them. These journals could include drawings, quotations from books and articles, snippets of overheard conversations, or information heard on the radio or television. Over time, journals help students grow as writers and add to their overall success in college.

Another type of journal is the one that will definitely have an audience, even if it is only an instructor. In many writing classes, instructors require students to keep a more public journal as part of a semester's work. In this more public journal, handwriting will be important and some topics might be considered inappropriate. Sometimes this journal contributes to the final grade for a course. Instructors who make a journal part of their semester's assignments understand how such writing, done frequently, gives students valuable practice in setting thoughts down on paper.

## ENTRY FROM *THE DIARY OF LATOYA HUNTER*

Keeping a journal is especially popular during adolescence, partly because these years are usually a time of uncertainty when young people try to discover themselves as individuals. The following selection is from the published diary of a junior high school student, Latoya Hunter, who kept a journal when she was only twelve years old. The diary reports on her growing need for independence and her changing perceptions of the world around her.

> Today my friend Isabelle had a fit in her house. It was because of her mother. She's never home and she expects Isabelle to stay by herself. Today she was extra late because she was out with her boyfriend. Isabelle was really mad. She called her father and told him she wanted to live with him because her mother only cared about one person—her boyfriend. She was so upset. She was throwing things all over the place and crying. I never saw her like that before. It was really sad to see. I felt bad when I had to leave her all by herself. I hope she and her mother work it out but all mothers are the same. They think that you're young and shouldn't have an opinion. It's really hard to communicate with my parents. They'll listen to me but that's about it. They hardly take me seriously and it's because of my age. It's like discrimination! If you do speak your mind, you end up getting beaten. The real pain doesn't come from the belt though, it comes from inside. That's the worst pain you could ever feel.

**ACTIVITY  1**

### Writing a Journal Entry of Your Own

In the selection you have just read, Latoya Hunter sadly observes a friend going through an emotional crisis. Latoya uses her journal to explore her own feelings about parent-child relationships and to express what she thinks are some of the common failings of parents.

Write a journal entry of your own. Report an incident in which you were successful or unsuccessful in communicating with someone you know. The person could be a family member or someone from outside your family. Looking back on the incident, think about what contributed to the success or failure of that communication. What part did each person play that led to the final outcome?

_____

_____

_____

_____

_____

_____

_____

_____

_____

_____

_____

_____

_____

_____

_____

_____

_____

_____

_____

_____

# FOCUSED FREEWRITING

Focused freewriting offers another way to explore writing topics. With this technique, the writer keeps on writing for a predetermined amount of time and does not stop, no matter what. The goal of this technique is to put words on paper, and even if nothing new comes to mind, the writer keeps going by repeating a particular idea. This approach is one way to free a writer from what is often called "writer's block," that moment in the writing process when a person runs out of words and becomes paralyzed by the blank page or computer screen.

> **Focused freewriting** is a prewriting technique in which the writer explores a topic by writing for a predetermined amount of time without stopping, even if it means repeating the same ideas.

Here, for example, is what one young man wrote when he was asked to write for five minutes on the topic of *keeping a journal:*

I'm supposed to write about journal writing. I've never kept a journal so how can I say anything about it? But I broke into my younger sister's diary once and found out about a boy she had kissed. It was one of those diaries with those little keys and I ruined the lock. She didn't speak to me for over a month and my parents were mad at me. I thought it was funny at the time. After that she didn't keep a diary anymore. So now what should I say? Now what should I say? I don't really know. I guess I might keep a journal to keep track of important things that happen to me, like the day my dad came home with a used car for me—now that was really cool. Of course, it had a lot of problems that we had to fix over the next year little by little, but that was really an awesome day.

**ACTIVITY 2**

### Focused Freewriting

For this exercise, consider the topic *My Attitude toward Writing* as an opportunity to practice focused freewriting. Write for at least five minutes without stopping, making sure that you keep going even if you have to repeat some thoughts.

_____

_____

_____

_____

_____

_____

_____

_____

_____

_____

# BRAINSTORMING, CLUSTERING, AND OUTLINING

## BRAINSTORMING

Of all the prewriting techniques, brainstorming is perhaps the most widely used. Brainstorming is an exercise in free association. You allow a thought or phrase to lead you from one idea to the next until you feel you have fully explored your topic. Many writers find brainstorming liberating because item order is unimportant and no special connection is needed between items. The main goal is to jot down everything while your mind explores different paths. Later, you can sort the items, grouping some and eliminating others. Unless you are doing outside research, brainstorming is probably the best way to discover ideas for writing.

> **Brainstorming** is a prewriting technique in which the writer uses free association to create a list of whatever words, phrases, or ideas come to mind on a given topic. It can be done alone or in a group.

The following list shows a college student's initial brainstorming on the topic of *parent-teen communication*.

. . . . . . . . . . . . . . . . . . . . . . . . . . . . . . . . . . . . . . . . . . . . . . . . . . . . . . . . . . . . . . . . . . . . . . . . . . . . . . . . .

Problems talking with my father
 Called me immature sometimes
 Occasionally shouted
 Too tense
 Seemed overly critical
Stacy's father.
 Seemed to have a sense of humor about everything, not so serious, easygoing
Guidance counselor
 Always calm, no hurry, always listened
What prevents a good talk with a parent?
 person's voice—loud, soft, angry, calm
 namecalling, putdowns
 words that hurt
 bad language
 body language—no eye contact, frowning, glaring
 authoritarian or controlling
 monopolizing the conversation
 tense
 withdrawal or the silent treatment
 disrespectful and rude
 rushed, not listening
 rigid, won't consider any other viewpoint
 sarcastic

. . . . . . . . . . . . . . . . . . . . . . . . . . . . . . . . . . . . . . . . . . . . . . . . . . . . . . . . . . . . . . . . . . . . . . . . . . . . . . . . .

Below is a revised brainstorming list showing how the student has reorganized the initial list.

. . . . . . . . . . . . . . . . . . . . . . . . . . . . . . . . . . . . . . . . . . . . . . . . . . . . . . . . . . . . . . . . . . . . . . . . . . . . . . . . .

Advice to Parents: How to Communicate with Your Teens
Choose your words carefully
 do not call people names
 do not belittle them—use example of my father
 do not use bad language
 do not be disrespectful
 do not be mean or sarcastic
 do not use the silent treatment or monopolize the talk

(continued on next page)

Listen to the way you sound, your tone, your attitude

    watch the volume of your voice—use example of Stacy's father

    wait until you have calmed down so you do not sound angry and tense

    don't sound rushed and hurried, as if you have no time to listen

    don't sound too controlling

Take a look at your body language

    work at being calm and relaxed

    do not withdraw; if possible give the person a hug or a pat on the shoulder

    no physical abuse—pushing, shoving, slapping

    what is your facial expression (frowning, glaring, smirking, no eye contact)?

## CLUSTERING

Clustering is another method of gathering ideas during the prewriting stage. Clustering is very similar to brainstorming, except that when you cluster, you produce a visual map of your ideas rather than a list. You begin by placing a key idea (usually a single word or phrase) in the center of the page. Then you jot down other words and phrases that come to mind as you think about this key idea. As you work, you draw lines, or branches, to connect the items.

Here is how the writer might have explored the topic using a clustering technique:

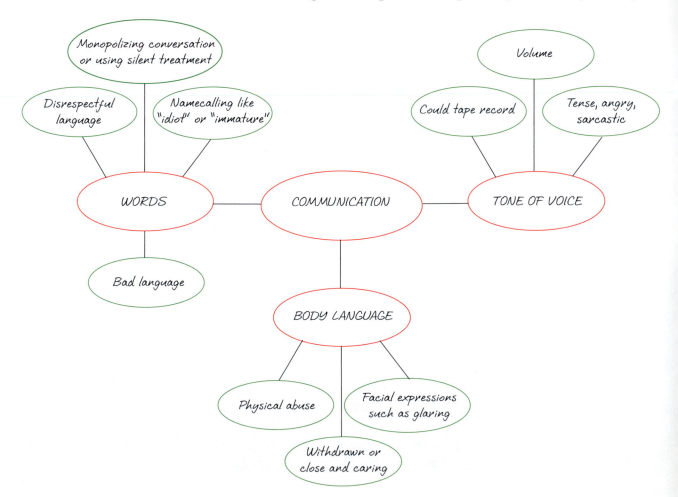

*Clustering* is a prewriting technique that emphasizes the connections among items on a brainstorming list. The topic is written in the middle of the page and has a circle drawn around it. As details or ideas are generated, they are circled and then lines are drawn to connect them to related details or ideas. This process continues until the topic has been fully explored. Variations of clustering are known as *mapping, webbing,* and *branching.*

**ACTIVITY** **3**

### Using Brainstorming or Clustering to Develop a Topic of Your Own

**Use either brainstorming or clustering to develop your ideas on one of the following topics:**

- communicating with teachers and classmates
- communicating on a cell phone
- communicating on the Internet (e-mail and chat rooms)

Create your brainstorming list or cluster on a separate sheet of paper.

## OUTLINING

Outlining is the most formal method of organizing ideas at the prewriting stage. It is more difficult than the other prewriting techniques and usually comes after considerable brainstorming and rearranging of ideas. In a formal outline you must distinguish between major headings and subheadings and list these points in the order in which you will present them. Because organization and order are so important in outlining, we follow a conventional system of numbers and letters. In the sample outline that follows, notice the use of roman capital numerals (I, II, III) for major headings, indented capital letters (A, B, C) for subheadings, and arabic numbers (1, 2, 3) to show the next level of subheadings.

*Outlining,* the most formal method of organizing prewriting ideas, uses numerals and letters to distinguish between major headings and subheadings of a planned piece of writing.

Here is how the student's outline of the material might have developed:

**Advice to Parents:**
**How to Communicate with Your Teens**

I.   Introduction

    Topic Sentence: Parents need to consider their words, tone, and body language when they talk to their teens.

II.  Choose your words carefully.

    A.  Do not call people names.

        1.  My father called me immature.

        2.  Parents sometimes use words like "idiot."

(continued on next page)

      B.  Do not use bad language.

      C.  Do not be disrespectful.

      D.  Do not monopolize the conversation.

      E.  Do not use the silent treatment.

III.  Listen to your tone.

      A.  Wait until you have calmed down so you do not sound angry and tense.

      B.  Watch the volume of your voice.

         1.  Stacy's father speaks softly.

         2.  Stacy's father speaks reassuringly.

      C.  Taping a conversation would reveal tone.

IV.  Observe your body language.

      A.  Notice your facial expression.

         1.  Are you glaring?

         2.  Are you full of rage?

      B.  Make eye contact.

      C.  Do not withdraw; if possible, give the person a hug or hold that person's hand.

      D.  Physical abuse is never appropriate.

V.  Conclusion

Parents who think about these three factors of communication will be able to avoid a lot of pain and heartache.

---

**ACTIVITY 4**

## Making an Outline

Using the title "Communication in the Twenty-First Century," make an outline for an essay that would describe modern forms of communication. You may want to consider the following items: Internet, e-mail, instant messaging, online courses, blogs, fax machines, printers, digital cameras, cell phones, and iPods.

_____

_____

_____

_____

_____

_____

_____

_____

_____

_____

## STUDENT ESSAY

Now we are ready to look at the student essay that evolved from the initial brainstorming list. Notice that the writer is not bound to follow the brainstorming list or the outline word for word. As the student wrote, a certain creative flow occurred.

### Advice to Parents:
### How to Communicate with Your Teens

*Introduction*

When parents and teens cannot sit down and talk together, parents should take a long hard look at themselves to see if part of the blame might lie with them. Parents need to consider three factors: the words they choose, the tone of voice they use, and the message their body language gives.

*Paragraph 1 of Development*

One usually thinks of words as being at the center of communication, and of course, words are important. The wrong words can unintentionally put people in a bad mood. Parents very often belittle their children or call them names. My father, for example, sometimes used the word "immature" to describe me when I made a mistake. I felt put down. It would probably have been better if he would have talked with me about the situation and explained why he thought I had made a bad choice. I have heard parents call their children "idiots" and even worse. Namecalling only makes teens angry and defensive. It is hard after being attacked to feel open to any discussion at all. I have heard teens and parents use bad language and speak disrespectfully to each other. Speaking in the heat of the moment, people often say things they really do not mean, but when they calm down, it is too late to take the words back. The harm is done. Then there is the parent who monopolizes the discussion, giving the teen no opportunity to explain his or her position. Finally, there is the complete opposite of the wrong words, and that is no words at all. Have you ever experienced the silent treatment? With this approach, everyone feels terrible and there is no chance to work out a problem.

*Paragraph 2 of Development*

A parent's tone of voice is a second factor in communicating with a teenager. Something said in a tense, harsh, or angry voice creates unnecessary bad feelings. The same words said with a firm but soft and reassuring voice can make for a completely different conversation. Even the volume of a person's voice can make a tremendous difference when people talk. My friend Stacy, for example, has a lot of disagreements with her father, but I have never heard their disagreements turn into angry arguments. Her father is from another country where people speak very softly. His voice is so calm and soft that I suppose this is one reason why Stacy never seems to get angry with him. He also uses a lot of humor, and they can laugh about her occasional outrageous behavior. It might be a good idea if some parents would tape themselves when they are talking with their teenagers. They might be very surprised to hear their tone. This might give them a better understanding of why their teenagers suddenly become upset or withdrawn.

*Paragraph 3 of Development*

Also, I wish some parents could see themselves when they are talking to their teens. Their body language really communicates, "I am angry at you!" Facial expressions can be glaring or even full of rage. To communicate

(continued on next page)

*Conclusion*

with your teen, you need to make eye contact and if possible even give an affectionate hug or hold the teen's hand; in other words, let your body language say that you care about him or her even though you are upset about your teen's behavior. Obviously, any kind of physical abuse is never appropriate. Slapping, hitting, or punching is absolutely unacceptable. If you cannot control your teen without physical restraint, you need to seek outside help.

If only parents would understand the importance of words, tone, and body language the next time they faced a conflict with their teens, much needless pain and heartache could be avoided.

# CONDUCTING INTERVIEWS AND SURVEYS

Journal writing, focused freewriting, brainstorming, and outlining are all techniques that you can use to explore your thoughts and ideas. Often, however, a writer needs to go further and obtain information from outside sources. An excellent way to obtain such information is to conduct an interview or prepare and distribute a survey or questionnaire. News reporters, marketing people, social workers, and government workers are only a few of the people who use these techniques in their everyday work.

## INTERVIEWS

Interviews are useful in many situations. Speaking to a single individual can provide information that you might not be able to get any other way. For example, you might want to interview an older family member to preserve stories of your family's past. You might want to talk to someone in a career that interests you. If you were considering a career in law, for example, speaking to a lawyer in your community might be more revealing than reading a book about the legal profession. An interview is also an excellent way to find information on very current topics, material you might have trouble finding in the library or even on the Internet.

The secret of a good interview lies in what happens before the interview. You must prepare properly. First of all, make an appointment with the person you want to interview. Let that person know how long the interview will take. If you intend to bring a tape recorder, be sure to ask for permission in advance. It is important for the person being interviewed to know what to expect so he or she can be relaxed and in a receptive frame of mind. Most importantly, the interviewer should always have a number of questions prepared beforehand. Few interviews go well without some structure and a sense of direction. This is not to say that every question must be asked in the way and order in which it was prepared; an interviewer is not restricted to a fixed set of questions. An interview can often take an interesting and unexpected turn with a single good question that leads to a surprising exploration of a subject.

When you prepare your questions, compose them in such a way that the answers require some thought. You do not want to ask questions that can be answered with a simple yes or no; such replies are not useful because they do not encourage any in-depth discussion of the answer.

**ACTIVITY** **5**

### Preparing Questions for an Interview

**The following five pairs of sentences could have been used in an interview in which a person was trying to learn about a lawyer's work. In each case, check which question would more likely lead to a thoughtful interview response.**

____ 1. What is a typical day at work like?

____    How many hours a day do you work?

____ 2. How much do you earn in a year?

____    What is the range of salaries that a person could expect to earn as a lawyer?

____ 3. What kind of law do you practice?

____    What are the different areas of law practice, and how did you choose which one you wanted to pursue?

____ 4. What is the most interesting case you have ever had?

____    Have you ever had an interesting case?

____ 5. Do you ever have a bad day?

____    What are some of your greatest challenges, and how do you handle them?

## SURVEYS

Taking a survey is an especially helpful prewriting technique when you want to write about a certain group's attitudes, practices, or experiences. For instance, you could do a survey on your classmates' attitudes toward binge drinking, your family's attitudes about how to share the household chores, or your community's attitudes about the need for a teen center. A survey is somewhat like an interview in that the person conducting it prepares a set of questions. However, an interview is conducted one-on-one, and the conversation has great flexibility. A survey, on the other hand, is usually written in advance. A number of participants agree to answer a set of questions. If they write their answers, the survey takes the form of a questionnaire. They may or may not complete the survey in your presence. What you will get will be the briefest answers to your questions—no more, no less. Obviously, you will run into difficulty if you realize later on that you should have asked different questions. Therefore, in a survey, most of the work lies in the preparation of the questions and in experimenting with different ways of presenting questions so as to get the best answers. Unlike the interview, the survey may include questions that can be answered with a yes or a no. You may also want to ask questions that call for precise facts and figures. Here are a few other considerations:

1. Will people give their names, or will they be anonymous?
2. How will the surveys be returned? Will you give people a deadline and collect the surveys yourself, or will you give them a self-addressed stamped envelope so that they can mail the survey to you?
3. Do not be surprised if some people fail to answer the survey's questions at all. If the survey is too long or too complicated, people may decide they do not have time to fill it out. After all, most people volunteer to answer a survey, and they will be completing it as a favor to you.

4. The more responses there are to a survey, the more valid the results of that survey will be. For example, if you want to know the attitudes of your classmates toward journal writing, the closer you come to having a 100 percent response, the more valid the survey will be.

5. How will you tally the answers? Will the results be presented as a chart, or will you write a report in which you explain the results?

**ACTIVITY 6**

## Composing Questions for a Survey

Several serious problems on college campuses today relate to the use of alcohol. Underage drinking, binge drinking, drunken fights, and vandalism of school property are some of the problems college administrations face. Compose five questions that could be included in a survey of your classmates to determine their drinking habits. Construct each question so that it asks for personal experience, not a person's opinion about what other students are doing. Here is an example:

Which of the following best describes how often you have an alcoholic drink?

a. never

b. only on holidays and other special occasions

c. two or three times a month

d. once or twice a week

e. three or more times a week

f. every day

1. _____

_____

_____

_____

2. _____

_____

_____

_____

_____

3. _____

_____

_____

_____

_____

4. _____

_____

_____

_____

_____

5. _____

_____

_____

_____

_____

## Exploring Online

Go to **www.cengage.com/devenglish/scarry/writersworkplace** to find the **Writer's Online Workplace,** a website designed for students using this book. You will find links to handouts, interactive quizzes, and other online resources as you explore the following topics:

- the writing process
- prewriting techniques
- journaling

# Working Together

## TAKING A SURVEY: STUDENT ATTITUDES ABOUT WRITING

Writers gather material for their work in a number of ways. One way is to conduct a survey, drawing on the experiences of people who have something in common. For this prewriting exercise, you will participate in a survey with all the students in your class. The survey asks students about their experiences with writing and their attitudes toward writing. As a class, you may add to or change the questions suggested here, but everyone should answer exactly the same questions.

Use the following procedure:

1. Remove the survey on page 19 from your textbook.
2. Put your name or an assigned number in the top right corner of the survey for purposes of identification.
3. Answer the survey questions as completely and honestly as possible.
4. Select two people who will collect all the surveys and lead the class in tallying the information. One person can read off the responses; the other person can put the information on a blackboard where everyone can view the information and take notes.

## PORTFOLIO SUGGESTION

A **portfolio** is a collection of materials representing a person's best work and is intended to help in the evaluation of that work, often for a grade in a course. A writer may also include materials to use in future work.

To start building your portfolio, take back your own page of responses to the survey and add it to any notes you took about the results of the class survey. Jot down any other ideas that might have come to you as you thought about the topic. Place all these in your portfolio and keep them for possible use in future writing assignments.

Consider using the interview and the survey as techniques for gathering material that can be transformed quite easily into an essay. Remember that people who write for a living—newspaper and magazine writers, for example—depend heavily on these techniques to work up their material.

## Student Survey

1. How would you describe the ideal place for a writer to work?

   _____

   _____

   _____

   _____

2. Where do you do your best writing—in the library, at home, or someplace else?

   _____

   _____

3. Is a certain time of day better for you than other times? When do you concentrate best?

   _____

4. How long can you write with concentration before you need a break?

   _____

5. What concerns do you have when you write?

   _____

6. Have you ever kept a journal?

   _____

7. Do you prefer composing on a computer or writing by hand?

   _____

8. In high school, how many of your classes included writing opportunities? How often were you required to write?

   _____

9. Keeping in mind that most people today use a telephone or e-mail to keep in touch, how often do you find yourself writing a letter?

   **a.** never     **b.** almost never     **c.** sometimes     **d.** often

10. At this point in your school career, which of the following best describes your attitude about writing?

    ____ I enjoy writing most of the time.

    ____ I occasionally like to write.

    ____ I usually do not like to write.

    ____ I don't have any opinion about writing at all.

# 2 RECOGNIZING THE ELEMENTS OF GOOD WRITING

In this chapter, you will learn how each of the following elements helps to create an effective piece of writing:

**CHAPTER OBJECTIVES**

- a carefully chosen **subject**
- a clear **purpose**
- a targeted **audience**
- a consistent and appropriate **voice**
- an overall **unity**
- a basic **coherence**

## THE SUBJECT: WHAT THE WRITING IS ABOUT

The *subject* of a piece of writing is also called the *topic* or the *central theme.* The subject can be chosen by the writer or assigned by someone else. We've all heard the student who complains, "I don't have anything to say." Not true! It may be that the student hasn't yet developed the skill to put ideas into writing, but we all know more than we think we do. We all know about our families, our homes, our friends, our opinions, and our experiences. We have childhood memories, interests, activities we participate in, and dreams. When we write, we need to tap into these life experiences and life lessons to find topics that interest us. We also need to remember that we can gather more information by consulting others.

Even with an assigned topic, a writer can often find an interesting aspect or approach to the subject. For example, on the subject of *binge drinking in college,* a writer might choose one of the following approaches:

**Topic: Binge Drinking in College**

| APPROACHES | EXAMPLES |
| --- | --- |
| Tell a personal story: | **The story of my friend Tom who flunked out of college last semester** |
| Discuss the effects: | **The effects of binge drinking on college campuses** |
| Explain how to do something: | **How to avoid substance abuse in college** |
| Show contrasts: | **Responsible use of alcohol contrasted to abusive use of alcohol** |

Take a stand on an issue:     **The need for colleges to enforce the laws on underage drinking**

**ACTIVITY 1**

### Providing Examples for Different Approaches to a Subject

Below are five possible approaches a writer might take, given the topic of *working while going to school.* Provide a possible example for each approach.

1. personal story

   _____

2. effects

   _____

3. how to do something

   _____

4. comparison/contrast

   _____

   _____

5. persuasion

   _____

# PURPOSE: THE WRITER'S INTENTION

In school, when a student hands in a writing assignment, that student's primary purpose may be to get a good grade. At work, an employee may produce a written document with the purpose of getting ahead in a job. These examples are not what we mean by *purpose.* In writing, *purpose* is what the piece of writing itself is intended to accomplish, apart from any other personal aims of the writer. The main purposes for writing are entertainment, information, and persuasion.

## ENTERTAINMENT

A writer may want to entertain an audience. One way to do this is by telling a good story. We all remember, as children, how much fun it was when someone read us a story. We were being entertained. Most of the stories we see on television are shown for the purpose of entertainment. The novels we buy in bookstores were written to entertain us. What we call *narrative writing* (the telling of stories) is mostly in this category.

## INFORMATION—PRESENTATION OF FACTS

Most of the writing you will do in school and in your future career will be informational in nature. In school, you will take written tests and write papers to explain what you know about a subject; at work, you might find yourself explaining why your company's profits have diminished or increased. In formal writing, these explanations can be developed in more than one way, depending on the type of information required. The methods of development that you will learn in this book include the following:

- illustration (giving examples)
- narration (telling a story)
- description (using sensory images)
- process (explaining how to do something)
- comparison and contrast
- cause and effect
- definition and analysis
- classification (putting material into mutually exclusive groups)

## PERSUASION OR ARGUMENTATION

Persuasive writing, or argumentation, tries to convince the reader to agree with the writer's point of view on a topic. In our daily lives, the newspaper editorial is the most common example of persuasive writing. Such writing gives facts and examples and uses logical reasoning to support the writer's claim. An argument seeks to change the reader's mind or confirm beliefs already there. Often, the conclusion pleads for a plan of action to be taken.

**ACTIVITY  2**

### Understanding Purpose in Writing

If your instructor told you that your assignment was to write an essay on some aspect of technology, each person in the class would most likely choose a slightly different topic. Below are five different topics concerned with some aspect of technology. For each topic, indicate what the writer's possible purpose (entertainment, information, or persuasion) could be.

| Topic | Purpose |
|---|---|
| 1. the cost of iPods | _____ |
| 2. my cell phone nightmare | _____ |
| 3. why everyone needs e-mail | _____ |
| 4. how to send a text message | _____ |
| 5. why our company should upgrade now | _____ |

## AUDIENCE: THE WRITER'S INTENDED READERS

Effective writers learn about their audience and then use what they have learned so that the audience will be receptive to their ideas. Several important questions need to be asked. For example, what do the readers already know about the subject? What are their attitudes toward the subject? Will they be in agreement with the writer's point of view? Will they be of similar age? Will they have a similar level of education? Will they have interests, tastes, or political points of view that agree?

Any number of factors could be important in determining how a writer chooses words and presents ideas. For example, if the readers are small children, the vocabulary and ideas of the piece will have to be age appropriate. On the other hand, if the readers are professionals who want to increase their knowledge in a certain field, the writer will be expected to know and use the terminology of that field. If the readers are likely to consider the subject a very sensitive one, the writer certainly will not want to treat the subject lightly.

**ACTIVITY 3**

### Identifying an Audience and a Purpose

Five possible writing subjects follow. In each case, choose a specific audience and imagine the writer's purpose. An example is done for you.

| Subject | Audience | Purpose |
|---|---|---|
| Description of two history courses | College students | Information to help students make course selections |

| Subject | Audience | Purpose |
|---|---|---|
| 1.  Instructions for CPR (cardiopulmonary resuscitation) | _____ | _____ |
| 2.  A proposal to set up a group home for emotionally disturbed adults in a neighborhood | _____ | _____ |
| 3.  Description of features on a new-model computer | _____ | _____ |
| 4.  A letter to a local newspaper arguing for a civilian police review board | _____ | _____ |
| 5.  My so-called job | _____ | _____ |

## VOICE: HOW THE WRITER'S ATTITUDE IS REVEALED

It is very difficult for a writer to be objective; writing almost always reveals conscious and unconscious attitudes. The voice of the writer comes through the text in the words that are chosen and the strategies that are used. In general, we can think of *voice* as revealing two different attitudes:

1.  **Voice reveals an attitude toward the subject matter**. A politician might write *passionately* about a subject. A comic writer could be *humorous* or *sarcastic* about a subject. A critic could reveal a *lighthearted* or *judgmental* attitude.

2.  **Voice reveals an attitude toward the audience**. The writer's attitude toward the audience ranges from very formal (such as the attitude of an expert submitting a research paper to an academic journal) to less formal (such as the attitude of a student writing a friendly e-mail to a classmate).

The skilled writer learns how to choose an appropriate and consistent voice, depending on the purpose of the writing. Cooking instructions on a box of rice, for example, are probably almost completely voiceless, with no indication of the writer's personality. The reporting of a news event should also be without any apparent voice, although sometimes the writer's personal attitude sneaks in through the choice of a word that carries a positive or negative connotation. Sometimes an attitude is revealed by the choice of facts to include or exclude. In general, writing that seeks to inform is usually more objective than writing that seeks to entertain or persuade.

Another way a writer expresses *voice* is by the personal pronoun chosen for a piece of writing. A writer chooses a pronoun that fits the subject and the audience. In a diary or a memoir, you would most likely talk about yourself, so the obvious choice would be the first person *(I or we)*. In a book about how to arrange flowers, the author might want to address readers in the informal second person *(you)*, the common choice for writing that gives directions or advice. For a business proposal that suggests how to market a new product, the third person *(he, she, it, or they)* would be the most appropriate. The third person is the most formal and objective. It is the expected voice for academic and professional writing. In short, the choice of personal pronoun is determined by the appropriate level of formality needed between the writer and the writer's audience.

Two additional points about voice need to be kept in mind. The first point is the importance of being consistent. Do not change your writing voice without a clear reason for doing so. In other words, if you begin by addressing your readers as *you*, do not switch to *we* later on in the same piece of writing. The second point is to be sincere. Do not try to be someone you are not. For instance, taking unfamiliar words from a thesaurus is not a good idea because these words could easily be used in the wrong way and will nearly always sound a little out of place compared to the rest of your writing. If English is your second language, you might have to be especially careful. You will most likely need a more complete understanding of words and their shades of meaning before you use them in your writing.

## FORMAL WRITING IN THE THIRD PERSON (*HE, SHE, IT,* OR *THEY*)

In formal writing, where there is a distance between the writer and the reader, the *third person* is generally used. This is the voice you would use for most college-level work as well as job-related work. Read the paragraph that follows and study the writer's use of the third person. (Each use of a third-person pronoun has been italicized.)

Many families feel lost trying to make sense of cyberspace. *They* become frustrated trying to find specific information such as the image of a skeleton for a child's science paper. *They* worry that a preteen daughter may not be safe when *she* is chatting online. Many parents are unsure how to navigate the web. The millions of pages of information on the net can make locating useful and enjoyable web pages seem more like work than play. How should families choose among them? Six exceptional web destinations will eliminate this uncertainty. As a group, these websites offer useful advice parents need and also provide fun features children want.

## LESS FORMAL WRITING IN THE SECOND PERSON (*YOU, YOUR*)

Here is the same material, but written in a less formal voice, using the second person (*you*) and more casual language. This choice is effective when the writer is giving instructions or speaking directly to the reader. (Each use of the second person has been italicized.)

Is *your* family lost in cyberspace? *You* know the feeling. Maybe it's the rush of frustration that comes after *your* son says he needs an image of a skeleton for a science paper but he can't find one on the Internet—and neither can *you*. Or perhaps it's that twinge of anxiety as *your* preteen daughter announces she wants to chat online, but *you* are not sure how she can do it safely. If *you* are unsure how to navigate the web, *you* are not alone. The millions of pages of information on the net can make locating useful and enjoyable web pages seem more like work than play. How can *you* choose among them? Consider six terrific web destinations. As a group, they offer the useful advice *you* need along with the fun features *your* children want.

**ACTIVITY 4**

### Voice: Rewriting a Paragraph Using First Person Singular (*I*)

Compose a new paragraph using the same content as in the two paragraphs you have just read, but now use the first-person singular (*I*). Remember that using the first-person singular results in the most informal voice in writing. The result is a more personal and casual tone, such as used in a diary or a memoir.

_____

_____

_____

_____

_____

_____

_____

_____

_____

_____

**ACTIVITY 5**

### Voice: Rewriting a Paragraph to Avoid the Second Person (*You*)

In many college courses, one important objective is for students to learn the proper standards for writing academic and work-related assignments. This involves the use of the more formal voice (not the second person *you*) in written work. Rewrite the following paragraph to avoid the use of the second person *you*. For instance, the opening words "Your world" could be rewritten as "The world," "This world," or "Our world."

Your world is getting smaller, and the pace of change is quickening. When you graduate you will change jobs as many as ten times over the course of your career, often moving in completely new directions. You will probably end up in a career that is fairly unrelated to what you studied in college and find yourself working with colleagues from many different nations and cultures. You will succeed if you think broadly. You should take courses that will give you the greatest range of opportunity. Your world has become much more interdependent. Health, law, business, and many other fields all operate in a world of permeable borders. You need an international outlook to prevent the spread of disease, to reduce the flow of illicit drugs, or to resolve environmental challenges. If you understand other societies and cultures, you will have a wider base of knowledge and have better communication skills than those who do not.

Your Rewrite:

_____

_____

_____

_____

_____

_____

_____

_____

_____

_____

_____

_____

# UNITY: ALL PARTS RELATING TO THE CENTRAL THEME

In a piece of good writing, every sentence serves the central theme, with every detail directly related to the main idea. All of the parts go together to make up a whole. The result is a sense of oneness or wholeness, so that by the end of the piece, the writing feels complete and the reader has no trouble grasping the writer's main point.

**ACTIVITY  6**

### Editing Student Writing for Unity

**The following paragraph lacks unity because some sentences do not contribute to the main idea. As you read the paragraph, cross out any sentences that do not contribute to the unity of the piece.**

Many parents fear the time when their children reach adolescence. When that time does come, some parents are afraid to give their children freedom to make choices. These same parents do not admit that their children have any ideas or feelings that are valid. Many adults like to look back on their own childhoods. Pets are often remembered fondly. Conflicts between parents and adolescents are bound to develop. Some conflicts, of course, are a sign of healthy development within the family. Psychologists say that parents should not be fearful when teenagers challenge authority. Challenging authority is a normal part of the maturing process. Adults without children have none of these concerns. The need for privacy is also normal during adolescence and should be respected rather than feared. On the other hand, when the right moment comes along and a teenager wants to talk, parents should not miss the opportunity to connect. Sometimes teenagers and their younger brothers and sisters fight continually over the most trivial things. Most important of all is the need for parents to be sensitive to the feelings of their teenagers. Remember, adolescence does not last for a lifetime, but a good relationship between parent and child can!

# COHERENCE: CLEAR AND LOGICAL PROGRESSION OF THOUGHT

A piece of writing needs careful organization of all its parts so that one idea leads logically to the next. To help all the parts relate to one another, writers use three important techniques: *repetition of key words, use of synonyms and pronouns to refer to key words*, and *careful choice of transitional expressions.*

All writers must continually work to achieve coherence. Even professional writers work on more than one draft because they see room for improvement as they move from one idea, one sentence, or one paragraph to the next. If something is unclear or lacks logical sequence, they revise. You too will be working on coherence in many of the chapters of this book.

The following paragraph is taken from a December 2000 article in the *Harvard Business Review*. The piece was intended to show people in business how to create "buzz" about a new fashion trend and thereby increase the sales of a product. The hot product in this case is the "hush puppy." The paragraph is a good example of how writers achieve coherence in their work by using *repetition of key words*, using *pronouns and synonyms to refer to these key words*, and choosing *transitional expressions* that will help the reader move from one thought to another.

> Sometimes even the most ordinary products can benefit from buzz. Remember Hush Puppies? When the company discovered that hip New York City kids were snapping up vintage pairs of its Hush Puppies at secondhand stores, it rushed into action. It began making its shoes in shades like Day-Glo orange, red, green and purple. Next, it sent free samples to celebrities, and not long after, David Bowie and Susan Sarandon were spotted wearing them. Then the company tightly controlled distribution, limiting the shoes to a handful of fashionable outlets. Soon high-end retailers like Saks, Bergdorf Goodman, and Barneys were begging for them. In just three years, from 1994 to 1996, Hush Puppies saw its annual sales of pups in North America skyrocket from fewer than 100,000 pairs to an estimated 1.5 million.

## REPETITION OF KEY WORDS

Notice that the key words "Hush Puppies" appear in the second sentence and again in the third sentence. In the last sentence, the words "Hush Puppies" occur for a third time and also a fourth time with a shortened, less formal name, "pups."

## USING SYNONYMS AND PRONOUNS TO REFER TO KEY WORDS

Writers often need to find other words or phrases to substitute for the key word so they will not have to repeat it over and over again. Notice in the paragraph how the author has twice used the common noun *shoes* to substitute for the proper noun *Hush Puppies*. Also *samples* is used in one instance to refer to Hush Puppies.

Even more common is the use of pronouns to refer to key words. Here the pronoun *them* is used twice to refer to the Hush Puppies. In addition, notice the five pronouns (its, it, it, its, it) that refer to the shoe company.

## USE OF TRANSITIONAL EXPRESSIONS

Finally, coherence is achieved through the careful use of *transitions*. Transitions are words and expressions used in a piece of writing to show how the different ideas relate to each other. In the paragraph on Hush Puppies, several transitional expressions (marked in yellow highlighting) help the reader move forward through a sequence of events: *next, then, soon,* and *in just three years*. If you turn to Appendix E at the back of this textbook, you will find a listing of many of these transitional words and expressions.

**ACTIVITY 7**

### Studying a Text for Coherence

Read the following paragraph to discover the techniques used by the writer to achieve coherence. Find (1) two examples of the repetition of key words, (2) three examples of pronoun reference, (3) one example of a phrase that is a synonym for *web pages* and (4) one example of a transitional word or expression. Label each of the examples that you find. (If necessary, refer to Appendix E for a list of transitional words and expressions.)

More than one billion web pages currently exist online and are accessible to the public. These pages are not numbered. They are not organized. They do not come with a table of contents or an index. It is as if people around the world took all their books and magazines, ripped out all the pages, and dumped them into one gigantic pile. In the past five years, that pile has grown bigger and bigger and bigger. So how do you find your way through this maze of information? The answer is search engines. As with any technology, some very smart people have devised new search engines for the Internet, based on the lessons of the previous generation. Names like Google, Yahoo!, and Alta Vista have become well known. They will likely be your best bet for quickly finding what you need on the web.

## Exploring Online

Go to **www.cengage.com/devenglish/scarry/writersworkplace** to find the **Writer's Online Workplace,** a website designed for students using this book. You will find links to handouts, interactive quizzes, and other online resources as you explore the following topics:

- subject
- purpose
- audience
- academic voice and the avoidance of the second person
- coherence
- transitional expressions

# Working Together

## KNOWING YOUR AUDIENCE

Every writer, when planning a piece of writing, must choose an approach to the topic, target the audience, and then keep that audience in mind as the work progresses. The following paragraph is from Patricia T. O'Conner's book on writing, *Words Fail Me*. In the passage, the author addresses the issue of a writer's audience and the importance of our awareness of audience in the writing process.

All writing has an intended audience, even the telephone book (it may be monotonous, short on verbs, and heavy on numbers and proper nouns, but it sure knows its readers!). Your audience probably won't be as wide as your area code, but it could be almost anyone—your landlord, a garden club, the parole board, Internet jocks, a college admissions director, fiction readers, the editorial page editor, the Supreme Court. Someone is always on the receiving end, but who? It's a big world out there, and before you write you have to narrow it down. Once you've identified your audience, everything you do—every decision you make about vocabulary, tone, sentence structure, imagery, humor, and the rest—should be done with this target, your reader, in mind.

After reviewing the text, divide into groups. The members of each group work together to fill in the following chart showing the relationship between audience, writer, topic, and voice. For example, who would write to a landlord, what might be the topic of such a letter, and would the writer use the first person (*I, we*), second person (*you*), or third person (*he, she, it, they*)?

| Audience | Possible Writer | Possible Topic | Appropriate Choice of Voice |
|---|---|---|---|
| the Supreme Court | lawyer for store owners | interpretation of gun laws as it applies to store owners | formal (third person) |
| an Internet chat room | | | |
| a college admissions director | | | |
| dear diary | | | |
| a parole board | | | |
| the editor of a newspaper | | | |
| fiction readers | | | |
| a landlord | | | |

If time permits, the class should come together to compare their charts. Choose one word that would describe the *tone* that should be set in each writing project.

## PORTFOLIO SUGGESTION

When writers for advertising agencies work up an ad campaign, they must know their target audience. These writers choose every word for their ads with the greatest care. Because we live in such a visual culture, they also make sure that the illustrations for their ads are compelling. Collect ads from magazines and newspapers that you find especially well designed and particularly effective. Study the words and pictures of these ads, noting the intended audience in each case. How does the ad target its audience? Preserve the ads and any notes for future writing projects that might interest you. A few possible topics could be audience in advertising, the careful choice of vocabulary in advertisement, and the psychology of advertising.

# Part 2

# Creating Effective Sentences

Many students need their college writing classes to include essential concepts that were not mastered during the students' foundational years in school. When students have papers returned with sentence-level errors corrected, they realize the corrections are valuable, but they do not always understand exactly what is wrong with their original word choice or structure. Without that understanding, an instructor's suggestions and corrections are to no avail. If students are to revise, edit, and proofread their work effectively, they will need to understand basic grammatical terms and concepts. Learning these terms and understanding sentence structure will give every student the confidence needed to work with the written word. Part 2 of this book carefully presents the foundational sentence-level concepts in a deliberately chosen sequence. Beginning with simple sentences and gradually building to more complex sentences, the material allows

(continued on next page)

students to achieve success at each step. When student writers find themselves in control of this material, they also find that the act of revising and editing any paper, especially the paper that has been returned with editing symbols, will become a much more meaningful activity.

# FINDING SUBJECTS AND VERBS IN SIMPLE SENTENCES

By the time you finish this chapter, you will understand what is essential in the construction of the most basic sentence, called the **simple sentence.** Your practice of the following skills will lay the foundation for the other chapters in Part 2.

**CHAPTER OBJECTIVES**

- finding the **subject** of a simple sentence, including sentences with **prepositional phrases** and **appositive phrases**
- finding the **verb** of a simple sentence
- identifying six **parts of speech** in a simple sentence

Ideas may be communicated in more than one way. In informal situations, we might shake our head to mean "Yes" or "No," or we might use a single slang expression, such as "Cool" to show our positive reaction to something. Such informal communication with friends is easy because we are with people who can see our gestures, can hear our tone of voice, and are familiar with our informal speech. When we write, however, we must express ourselves to an audience that cannot necessarily see us or know us. In this case, our words must be more deliberate and more precise. As writers, one important way we can be sure our ideas come across as clear and unmistakable is to use complete sentences.

# WHAT IS A COMPLETE SENTENCE?

As writers, we need to express ourselves in complete sentences so that our ideas will be fully understood. This need for completeness means that every writing student must have a clear understanding as to what makes up a sentence.

> A **complete sentence** is a group of words that contains a subject and a verb and also expresses a complete thought.
>
> **Avon lifts weights.**

# HOW DO YOU FIND THE SUBJECT OF A SENTENCE?

The most basic sentence is called the *simple sentence*. *Simple* in this case does not mean *easy*, but it does mean that the sentence has only one subject-verb group. For most simple sentences, you can find the subject by keeping in mind five generalizations. Use generalizations 1 and 2 to complete the practice exercise that follows.

GENERALIZATION

> In a sentence, the subject usually answers the question "Who or what is the sentence about?"

GENERALIZATION

> The subject often occurs early in the sentence.

**Practice**

In the following sentences, find the subject by asking yourself, "Who or what is the sentence about?"

1.  The gym seemed noisier than usual.

2.  Our coach was shouting last-minute instructions.

3.  He expected total concentration.

4.  Three athletes were doing push-ups.

5.  People were beginning to fill the bleachers.

GENERALIZATION

> The subject of a sentence is usually a noun or a pronoun.

## FINDING NOUNS

> A **noun** is a word that names a person, place, or thing. A noun can function as a subject, an object, or a possessive in a sentence.
>
> *Subject:*      *Avon* lifts weights.
> *Object:*       The coach trained *Avon*.
> *Possessive:*   *Avon's* coach always arrives early.

Nouns can be categorized in two different ways:

1. **Common nouns or proper nouns.** Most nouns in English are *common nouns*. They are not capitalized. *Proper nouns* name particular persons, places, or things. They are always capitalized.

| Common nouns | Proper nouns |
|---|---|
| aunt | Aunt Meriam |
| country | Nigeria |
| watch | Timex |

2. **Concrete nouns or abstract nouns.** A second way to categorize nouns is to identify them as concrete nouns or abstract nouns. *Concrete nouns* name all the things we can see or touch, such as *desk*, *car*, or *friend*. *Abstract nouns* name the things we cannot see or touch, such as *justice*, *honesty*, or *friendship*.

| Concrete nouns | Abstract nouns |
|---|---|
| face | loneliness |
| people | patriotism |
| jewelry | beauty |

**Practice**

**Underline every noun in each of the sentences below.**

1. The morning of June 27 was clear and sunny.

2. The flowers were blossoming profusely, and the grass was richly green.

3. The people of the village began to gather in the square.

4. The lottery was conducted by Mr. Sommers.

5. The jovial man had time and energy to devote to civic activities.

## FINDING PRONOUNS

> A **pronoun** is a word that takes the place of a noun. Like a noun, a pronoun can be a subject or an object in a sentence. It can also be used to show possession.
>
> **Subject:**      *He* lifts weights.
> **Object:**       The coach trained *him.*
> **Possessive:**   *His* coach always arrives early.

There are four different categories of pronouns. (To see the complete list of these pronouns, consult Appendix B.) The chart on the next page lists only those pronouns that function as the subjects of sentences.

**Practice**

**In each of the sentences below, replace the underlined word or words with a pronoun.**

1. The crowd arrived early.                    _____

2. The gym was noisy.                          _____

3. <u>People</u> waited eagerly. _____

4. <u>Coach Ann Bradway</u> had not lost a game yet this season. _____

5. <u>Steven and I</u> found the best seats in the front row. _____

6. <u>Not one person</u> could predict the outcome. _____

# Pronouns That Function as Subjects

| **Personal Pronouns That Can Be Subjects** | | |
| --- | --- | --- |
| | **Singular** | **Plural** |
| 1st person: | I | we |
| 2nd person: | you | you |
| 3rd person: | he / she / it | they |

**Relative Pronouns That Can Be Subjects**

who          what

**Demonstrative Pronouns That Can Be Subjects**

this          these
that          those

**Indefinite Pronouns That Can Be Subjects**

**Singular**

| | | | |
| --- | --- | --- | --- |
| anyone | everyone | no one | someone |
| anybody | everybody | nobody | somebody |
| anything | everything | nothing | something |
| each | another | either (of) | neither |
| one (of) | much | such (a) | (of) |

**Plural**

| | | | |
| --- | --- | --- | --- |
| both | few | many | several |

**Singular or plural depending on meaning**

| | | | |
| --- | --- | --- | --- |
| all | more | none | some |
| any | most | | |

GENERALIZATION **4**   Noun or pronoun subjects in a sentence can be modified by adjectives.

An ***adjective*** is a word that modifies (describes or limits) a noun or a pronoun. Adjectives usually come directly in front of the nouns they modify, but they can also appear later in the sentence and refer back to the noun or pronoun.

***young*** **Avon**          **He is** ***young.***

**Practice**    **Underline the adjectives in each of the following sentences. Then draw an arrow to the noun each adjective modifies.**

1. The swimmer was confident.

2. Her long and strenuous workouts would soon pay off.

3.   Several meters remained to reach the finish line.

4.   Suddenly, she felt a terrible cramp in one leg.

5.   A disappointing defeat would be the result.

GENERALIZATION          The subject of a sentence can be compound.

A **compound subject** is made up of two or more nouns or pronouns joined by one of the following: *and, or, either/or,* and *neither/nor.*

**Avon** and *his coach* lift *weights.*

**Practice**    **Underline the compound subject in each of the following sentences.**

1.  Exercise and diet are the secrets to good health.

2.  Mothers and fathers should help their children establish healthy lifestyles.

3.  Unfortunately, biological factors or environmental factors could cause health problems.

**Practice**    The following sentences illustrate the different kinds of subjects you will encounter in this chapter. Examine each sentence and decide who or what the sentence is about. Underline the subject of each sentence. Then, on the line to the right, write the kind of subject (for example, concrete noun or personal pronoun) you have underlined. Be as specific as possible.

1.   The young child played.                    _____

2.   Young Helen Keller played.                 _____

3.   She played.                                _____

4.   The park grew chilly.                      _____

5.   The leaves stirred.                        _____

6.   A thought suddenly struck her.             _____

7.   Her parents and teacher would
     be waiting.                                _____

**NOTE:** Not every noun or pronoun in a sentence is necessarily the subject of a verb. Remember that nouns and pronouns function as subjects, objects, and possessives. In the following sentence, which noun is the subject and which noun is the object?

**Helen drank the water.**

If you chose *Helen* as the subject and *water* as the object, you were correct.

In the exercises that follow, you will have the opportunity to practice finding subjects.

Refer to the definitions, charts, and previous examples as often as needed.

**EXERCISE  1**

## Finding the Subject of a Sentence

**Underline the subject in each of the following sentences. An example is done for you.**

The <u>loudspeaker</u> blared.

1.  The train stopped.

2.  Steven Laye had arrived.

3.  He was afraid.

4.  Everything looked so strange.

5.  The fearful man held his bag tightly.

6.  The tunnel led up to the street.

7.  Buses and cars choked the avenues.

8.  People rushed everywhere.

9.  The noise gave him a headache.

10.  Loneliness filled his heart.

**EXERCISE  2**

## Finding the Subject of a Sentence

**Underline the subject in each of the following sentences.**

1.  The road twisted and turned.

2.  A young boy hurried along briskly.

3.  He carried an important message.

4.  A red-winged blackbird flew overhead.

5.  Dark clouds and a sudden wind surprised him.

6.  His family would be elated.

7.  Someone was raking the leaves.

8.  His father called out his name.

9.   The old man tore open the envelope.

10.   The message was brief.

**EXERCISE 3**

### Finding the Subject of a Sentence

Underline the subject in each of the following sentences.

1.   The Chicago World's Fair opened.

2.   Americans had never seen anything like it.

3.   Architects had designed a gleaming white city.

4.   The buildings and grounds were unique.

5.   George Ferris designed an enormous wheel 264 feet high.

6.   It could carry sixty passengers per car.

7.   The inventor George Westinghouse designed the fair's electric motors and even the electric lights.

8.   Other fair inventors included Thomas Edison and Alexander Graham Bell.

9.   All played an important part.

10.   The future seemed bright.

**EXERCISE 4**

### Composing Your Own Sentences

Create ten sentences using a variety of subjects. If you wish, you may use the suggested nouns and the pronoun given below.

| | |
|---|---|
| **Proper noun:** | Whoopi Goldberg |
| **Common noun:** | entertainer |
| **Abstract noun:** | comedy |
| **Compound subject:** | actor and television personality |
| **Pronoun:** | she |

Exchange sentences with a classmate. For each sentence your classmate has written, underline and identify the subject to show that you understand the various terms.

## FINDING THE SUBJECT IN SENTENCES WITH PREPOSITIONAL PHRASES

The sentences in Exercises 1 and 2 were short and basic. If we wrote only sentences of that type, our writing would sound choppy. Complex ideas would be difficult to express. One way to expand a simple sentence is to add one or more prepositional phrases.

**He put his suitcase on the seat.**

*On* is a preposition. *Seat* is a noun used as the object of the preposition. *On the seat* is a prepositional phrase.

> A **prepositional phrase** is a group of words containing a preposition and an object of the preposition along with any modifiers. Prepositional phrases contain nouns or pronouns, but these nouns or pronouns are *never* the subject of the sentence.
>
> **on the train**
> **against the wall**
> **throughout his life**

In sentences with prepositional phrases, the subject may be difficult to spot. What is the subject of the following sentence?

**In the young man's apartment, books covered the walls.**

In the sentence above, what is the prepositional phrase? Who or what is the sentence about? To avoid making the mistake of thinking that a noun in the prepositional phrase could be the subject, a good practice is to cross out the prepositional phrase.

~~**In the young man's apartment**~~**, books covered the walls.**

With the entire prepositional phrase crossed out, it becomes clear that the subject of the sentence has to be the noun *books*.

> The subject of a sentence is *never* found within the prepositional phrase.

If you memorize the prepositions in the following list, you will be able to easily spot prepositional phrases in sentences.

## Common Prepositions

| | | | | |
|---|---|---|---|---|
| about | behind | except | onto | toward |
| above | below | for | out | under |
| across | beneath | from | outside | underneath |
| after | beside | in | over | unlike |
| against | between | inside | past | until |
| along | beyond | into | regarding | up |
| among | by | like | since | upon |
| around | concerning | near | through | with |
| as | despite | of | throughout | within |
| at | down | off | till | without |
| before | during | on | to | |

In addition to these common one-word prepositions, many other prepositions are composed of two-word, three-word, and four-word combinations. The following list provides a sampling.

## Common Prepositional Combinations

| | | |
|---|---|---|
| according to | for the sake of | in exchange for |
| ahead of | in addition to | in reference to |
| at the time of | in between | in regard to |
| because of | in care of | in search of |
| by means of | in case of | in spite of |
| except for | in common with | instead of |
| for fear of | in contrast to | on account of |
| for the purpose of | in the course of | similar to |

**EXERCISE 5**

### Recognizing Prepositions

**In the following paragraph, find ten different prepositions and circle them.**

A landmark study on shyness was conducted at Stanford University. The study questioned 10,000 American adults about their social anxiety. Surprisingly, 95% of the people in the study described themselves as sometimes shy. Many hold back for fear of making a mistake. According to Dr. Carducci, shy people are very self-focused. Shyness is a barrier to social contact. Without enough social contact, shy people may become depressed.

**EXERCISE 6**

### Recognizing Prepositional Phrases

**In the following paragraph, find ten prepositions. Circle each preposition and underline the entire prepositional phrase.**

People across the country are anxious about high heating costs. After the devastating Gulf Coast hurricanes of 2005, fuel prices spiked. On account of these higher fuel prices, many people are making changes to their homes. Some are turning their fears into actions. They have consulted with energy specialists for recommendations. They have plugged cracks, insulated attics, and crawled underneath warm blankets.

**EXERCISE 7**

### Finding Subjects in Sentences with Prepositional Phrases

**Remember that you will never find the subject of a sentence within a prepositional phrase. In each of the following sentences, cross out prepositional phrases. Then underline the subject of each sentence. An example follows:**

People paid for telegram messages by the word.

1. On Friday, January 27, 2006, Western Union sent its last telegram.

2. With the ascendancy of modern technology, the telegram is no longer needed.

3.  In 1851 in Rochester, New York, Western Union had its beginnings.

4.  Messages were transmitted by Morse code over the wires and delivered by couriers.

5.  Eventually, telegraph service drove the pony express out of business.

6.  Until the emergence of the telegraph, the average delivery time for a message by pony express took ten days.

7.  At the height of the telegram business, in 1929, two hundred million telegrams were sent around the world.

8.  Now for Western Union, money transfers, bill payment, and products such as telephone service and Internet access will form the core of their business.

9.  In the past, families sent messages of births, deaths, birthdays, and weddings by telegram.

10.  In the present era, e-mail and fax messages have taken the place of the telegram.

## FINDING THE SUBJECT IN SENTENCES WITH APPOSITIVE PHRASES

> An **appositive phrase** is a group of words within a sentence that gives us extra information about a noun or pronoun in that sentence. It is set off by commas.

**Example:**

**Martin Johnson, *the retired salesperson*, sat at his desk.**

In this sentence, the words *the retired salesperson* make up the appositive phrase. These words give extra information about Martin Johnson and are separated by commas from the rest of the sentence. If you were to leave out the appositive phrase, notice that what would remain would still be a complete sentence with the main idea undisturbed:

**Example:**

**Martin Johnson sat at his desk.**

Now the subject is clear: *Martin Johnson*

> The subject of a sentence is never found within the appositive phrase.

**Practice**   **In each of the following sentences, cross out the appositive phrase and then underline the subject.**

1.  Alex Harkavy, a high school senior, has an auditory-processing disorder.

2.  Marcia Rubinstein, an educational consultant, can help him find the right college.

3.  For instance, Landmark, a college in Putney, Vermont, specializes in programs for students with learning disabilities.

4.  A federal law, the Americans with Disabilities Act, was enacted in 1990.

5.  Now many colleges, both public and private ones, offer support for learning-disabled students.

6.  One particular guidebook, *Peterson's Colleges with Programs for Students with Learning Disabilities or Attention Deficit Disorder*, is especially helpful.

## OTHER PROBLEMS IN FINDING SUBJECTS

### Sentences with a Change in the Normal Subject Position

Some sentences begin with words that indicate a question is being asked. Such words as *why, where, how,* and *when* are adverbs, and they signal to the reader that a question will follow. These opening words are not the subjects. The subjects occur later in these sentences. The following sentences begin with words that signal a question:

**Why is *he* going away?**

**How did *he* find his sister in the city?**

**Where is her *office*?**

Notice that in each case the subject is not in the opening part of the sentence. However, if you answer the question or change the question into a statement, the subject becomes easier to identify.

***He* is going away because . . .**

***He* found his sister by . . .**

**Her *office* is . . .**

### Sentences Starting with *there* or *here*

Such words as *there* or *here* are adverbs. They cannot be the subjects of sentences.

**There is a new teacher in the department.**

**Here comes the woman now.**

Who or what is this first sentence about? This sentence is about a teacher. *Teacher* is the subject of the sentence. Who or what is the second sentence about? This sentence is about a woman. *Woman* is the subject of the second sentence.

### Commands

Sometimes a sentence contains a verb that gives an order:

**Go to Chicago.**

**Help your sister.**

In sentences that give orders, *you* is not written down, but *you* is understood to be the subject. This is the only case where the subject of a sentence may be left out.

**Practice**   **Underline the subject in each of the sentences below.**

1. Here in America the sale of human organs for transplant is against the law.

2. Unfortunately, there is a disturbing illegal market in the sale of these organs.

3. Where do some people desperately look for kidneys?

4. Why are so many donors exploited and unprotected?

5. Get involved.

6. Work toward a solution to this tragic social problem.

**EXERCISE  8**

## Finding Subjects in Simple Sentences

**In each of the following sentences, cross out prepositional phrases and appositive phrases. Then underline the subject. An example follows:**

In every car of the crowded train, passengers settled down for the night.

1. In the night train, the child slept.

2. Here the motion, of the railroad cars lulled the passengers.

3. The child's mother, a single parent, put a coat under the child's head for a pillow.

4. Outside the window, the lights from small towns and villages twinkled.

5. Sometimes passengers could look into people's windows.

6. There was a silence in the train.

7. Why do people travel in the middle of the night?

8. In most cases, children will rest quietly at night.

9. Will the woman with a young child and heavy suitcases have a difficult time at the end of the trip?

10. On the platform waits an elderly man, anxious for the first sight of his grandson.

**EXERCISE 9**

## Finding Subjects in Simple Sentences

In each of the following sentences, cross out prepositional phrases and appositive phrases. Then underline the subject. An example follows:

> Where ~~in the United States~~ can <u>we</u> find Lake Okeechobee?

1. Where can you find the only subtropical preserve in North America?

2. Look on a map at the southern tip of Florida.

3. Here lies the Everglades, a natural treasure.

4. At one time, this Florida peninsula was not habitable.

5. Now, five million people live there.

6. The Everglades, a national park since 1947, has been in constant danger of destruction.

7. Marjory Stoneman Douglas, author of the book *The Everglades: River of Crass*, became a national crusader for the Everglades.

8. With the expansion of new development, these marshes are shrinking fast.

9. Do we have a responsibility to nature?

10. In 2000, Congress approved a bill for the restoration of the marshland.

**EXERCISE 10**

## Finding Subjects in Simple Sentences

In each of the following sentences, cross out prepositional phrases and appositive phrases. Then underline the subject. An example follows:

> <u>Spinach</u> and <u>broccoli</u> are two well-known health foods.

1. Steven G. Pratt, ophthalmologist at Seripps Memorial Hospital in La Jolla, California, is an expert on the role of nutrition in health.

2. In his new book *Superfoods Healthstyle*, Dr. Pratt adds dark chocolate to his list of superfoods.

3. Here are some of the other superfoods: avocados, garlic, and honey.

4. Why are apples so beneficial?

5. They provide a great source of fiber, potassium, and disease fighting antioxidants.

6. Don't remove the peels.

7. The concentration of antioxidants is found in the apple's skin.

8. Throw an avocado into your salad.

9. It will increase the body's absorption of beta carotene from foods like carrots and tomatoes.

10. With exercise and weight control, the foods on Dr. Pratt's list can extend your life.

# HOW DO YOU FIND THE VERB OF A SENTENCE?

Verbs tell time.

Because a verb tells time (past, present, or future), you can test which word in a sentence functions as the verb of that sentence. Use the sentences below as models.

**Present tense: Today, the woman *dances.***

HINT

**Change the time to the *past* by beginning the sentence with *yesterday*.**

**Past tense: Yesterday, the woman *danced*.**

HINT

**Change the time to the *future* by beginning the sentence with *tomorrow*.**

**Future tense: Tomorrow, the woman *will dance*.**

**Practice**

Test the sentences below to determine which word functions as the verb in the sentence. Try three versions of each sentence: one beginning with *today*, one beginning with *yesterday*, and the third beginning with *tomorrow*. Which is the word that changes? Circle that word. This is the word that functions as the verb in the sentence.

1. The reason for his popularity is his foreign policy.

2. She has little control over the decision.

3. The test comes at a bad time.

Verbs fall into three classes: action verbs, linking verbs, and helping verbs.

## ACTION VERBS

An **action verb** tells us what the subject is doing and when the action occurs.

For example:

**The woman *studied* ballet.**

What did the woman do? She *studied*. What is the time of the action? The action took place in the *past* (*-ed* is the regular past-tense ending).

Most verbs are *action verbs*. Here are a few examples.

---

## Examples of Action Verbs

| | | | | | |
|---|---|---|---|---|---|
| arrive | despise | help | write | watch | wait |
| leave | learn | make | speak | fly | |
| enjoy | forget | open | teach | catch | |

---

**EXERCISE 11**

### Finding Action Verbs

Each of the following sentences contains an action verb. Cross out prepositional phrases and appositive phrases. Next, underline the subject. Finally, circle the action verb. Is the action in the present, past, or future? An example follows:

Many <u>people</u> (begin) hobbies ~~in childhood~~.

1. Collectors enjoy the search for unusual items.

2. Some people collect very strange objects.

3. A collection, like odd rocks or unique automobiles, will give a person some individuality.

4. One man saved the fortunes from fortune cookies.

5. A group in Michigan often trades spark plugs.

6. In Texas members of a club gather many types of barbed wire.

7. One person in New York kept handouts from the street.

8. Arthur Fiedler, the late conductor of the Boston Peps Orchestra, hung hundreds of fire hats on pegs around his study.

9. Tom Bloom finds "inspected by" tickets in the pockets of new clothes.

10. Collections will entertain us from childhood to old age.

**EXERCISE 12**

### Finding Action Verbs

Each of the following sentences contains an action verb. Cross out prepositional phrases and appositive phrases. Next, underline the subject. Finally, circle the action verb. Note that each verb you circle has a tense. Is the action in the past, present, or future? An example follows:

~~With the rise of literacy~~, the <u>demand</u> ~~for reading glasses~~ (increased.)

1.  Nero, an emperor of ancient Rome, gazed at gladiators in combat through a large emerald.

2.  The Chinese manufactured sunglasses seven hundred years ago.

3.  From quartz, monks carved the first magnifying glasses for reading.

4.  In the fourteenth century, with the rise of the Venetian glass industry, glass lenses replaced quartz lenses.

5.  In London in 1728, a man invented a pair of glasses with metal pieces and hinges.

6.  George Washington bought a pair of these new glasses.

7.  By 1939, movie producers in Hollywood devised colored contact lenses for special effects in horror movies.

8.  In 1948, an American technician developed the first pair of modern contact lenses.

9.  Now laser surgery repairs many eyesight problems.

10. Perhaps in the future nobody will need glasses or contact lenses.

## LINKING VERBS

> A **linking verb** is a verb that links the subject of a sentence to one or more words that describe or identify the subject.

The <u>child</u> (is) a constant dreamer.     <u>She</u> (seems) distracted.

<u>We</u> (feel) sympathetic.

In each of these examples, the verb links the subject to a word that identifies or describes the subject. In the first example, the verb *is* links *child* with *dreamer*. In the second example, the verb *seems* links the pronoun *she* with *distracted*. Finally, in the third example, the verb *feel* links the pronoun *we* with *sympathetic*.

## Common Linking Verbs

| | | | |
|---|---|---|---|
| act | become | look | sound |
| appear | feel | remain | taste |
| be (am, is, are, was, were, | get | seem | turn |
| has been, or have been) | grow | smell | |

**EXERCISE** **13**

### Finding Linking Verbs

Each of the following sentences contains a linking verb. Cross out prepositional phrases and appositive phrases. Underline the subject of the sentence. Then draw an arrow to the word or words that identify or describe the subject. Finally, circle the linking verb. An example follows:

<u>Dreams</u> (are) very important ~~in many cultures~~.

1. My dream last night was wonderful.

2. I had been transformed.

3. I looked young again.

4. The house was empty and quiet.

5. In a sunlit kitchen with a book in hand, I appeared relaxed and happy.

6. In the morning light, the kitchen felt cozy.

7. It seemed safe.

8. The brewing coffee smelled delicious.

9. The bacon, my usual Sunday morning treat, never tasted better.

10. In this dreamworld, life felt satisfying.

**EXERCISE** **14**

### Finding Linking Verbs

Each of the following sentences contains a linking verb. Cross out all prepositional phrases. Underline the subject of the sentence. Then draw an arrow to the word or words that identify or describe the subject. Finally, circle the linking verb. An example follows:

The <u>promise</u> ~~of easy credit~~ often (turns) sour.

1. Many college students are inexperienced about money matters.

2. Nearly every freshman is vulnerable to predatory offers.

3. To young adults, credit card offers look very helpful at first.

4. Many students get excited about their new purchasing power.

5. Unfortunately, they often become permanently trapped in debt.

6. Credit card companies appear satisfied with their offers of large amounts of credit to poor students.

7. Many colleges remain silent about the financial plight of their students.

8.  They seem content with their cut in the credit card profits.

9.  Shouldn't they feel guilty for the unregulated marketing of credit cards on their campuses?

10. The level of debt for American students grows more serious every year.

## HELPING VERBS (ALSO CALLED AUXILIARY VERBS)

> A **helping verb** is a verb that combines with a main verb to form a verb phrase. It always comes before the main verb and expresses a special meaning or a particular time.

In each of the following examples, a helping verb indicates what time the action of the verb *sleep* takes place.

| **Helping verbs** | **Time expressed by helping verbs** |
| --- | --- |
| He *is* sleeping. | right now |
| He *might* sleep. | maybe now or in the future |
| He *should* sleep. | ought to, now or in the future |
| He *could have been* sleeping. | maybe in the past |

## Common Helping Verbs

| | | **Forms of *be*** | | **Forms of *have*** | **Forms of *do*** |
| --- | --- | --- | --- | --- | --- |
| can | shall | being | are | has | does |
| could | should | been | was | have | do |
| may | will | am | were | had | did |
| might | would | is | | | |
| must | | | | | |

Remember that *be*, *do*, and *have* can also be used as the main verbs of sentences. In such cases, *be* is a linking verb and *do* and *have* are action verbs. The other helping verbs function only as helping verbs.

| ***Be*, *do*, and *have* used as helping verbs** | ***Be*, *do*, and *have* used as main verbs** |
| --- | --- |
| I *am teaching* this class. | I *am* the teacher. |
| He *does work* hard. | He *does* the homework. |
| I *have borrowed* the money. | I *have* the money. |

When we studied how to find the subject of a sentence, we learned that *nouns* and *pronouns* could be subjects and that *adjectives* could modify these nouns and pronouns. When we study how to find the verb of a sentence, we learn that the *adverb* is the part of speech that modifies a verb.

> **Adverbs** are words that modify verbs, adjectives, or other adverbs.

**An adverb modifying a verb:**

Dreams **often** frighten young children.

**An adverb modifying an adverb:**

Dreams **very** often frighten young children.

**An adverb modifying an adjective:**

Dreams often frighten **very** young children.

Watch out for an adverb that comes between the helping verb and the main verb. In the following sentence, the word *often* is an adverb between the helping verb *can* and the main verb *frighten*.

**Dreams can often frighten young children.**

For more on adverbs see Chapter 10. For a list of common adverbs, see Appendix B.

**EXERCISE 15**

## Finding Helping Verbs

Circle the complete verb in each sentence below. An example follows:

Lifelong learning has become essential for all adults.

1. Graduation from high school does not signal the end of one's learning.

2. In today's world, workers must adjust to many changes in the workplace.

3. They will need to understand new technologies.

4. Can they recognize the difference between facts and opinions in news articles?

5. All citizens would benefit from annual refresher courses in their fields.

6. Everyone should read a daily newspaper.

7. Senior citizens might take courses at local community colleges.

8. Also, they could keep their minds active with crossword puzzles and other games.

9.   Have people learned to try new recipes from television cooking programs?

10.   Do we take responsibility for keeping our minds curious and engaged?

**EXERCISE 16**

### Finding Helping Verbs

**Each of the following sentences contains a helping verb in addition to the main verb. In each sentence, cross out prepositional phrases and underline the subject. Then circle the complete verb. An example follows:**

~~In this country~~, <u>daycare</u> (has become) an important issue.

1.   How does a person start a daycare center?

2.   First, notices can be put in local churches and supermarkets.

3.   Then that person should also use word of mouth among friends.

4.   Many parents will need infant care during the day, after-school care, or evening and weekend care.

5.   With luck, a nearby doctor may be helpful with the local health laws and legal requirements.

6.   Of course, the licensing laws of the state must be thoroughly researched.

7.   Unfortunately, the director of a daycare center could have trouble finding an affordable place.

8.   Any child daycare center will depend on its ever widening good reputation.

9.   In good daycare centers, parents are never excluded from meetings or planning sessions.

10.   Finally, the center must be more interested in the character of its teachers than in the teachers' degrees.

## HOW DO YOU IDENTIFY THE PARTS OF SPEECH?

In this chapter, you have learned how most of the words in the English language function. These words can be placed into categories called *parts of speech*. You have learned to recognize and understand six of these categories: nouns, pronouns, adjectives, verbs, adverbs, and prepositions. (In later chapters, you will study the conjunction.) You can review your understanding of these parts of speech as you practice identifying them in the exercises provided here. You may also refer to Appendix B for a quick summary whenever you want to refresh your memory.

**EXERCISE 17**

### Identifying Parts of Speech

In the sentences below, identify the part of speech for each underlined word. Choose from the following list:

a. noun          c. adjective          e. adverb

b. pronoun          d. verb          f. preposition

\_\_\_\_  1.  When the Mali leader Konboro <u>fervently</u> converted to Islam,

\_\_\_\_  2.  he <u>asked</u> a holy man, "How may I please God?"

\_\_\_\_  3.  The <u>holy</u> man said, "Build a mosque."

\_\_\_\_  4.  The people will bless your name for <u>centuries</u>.

\_\_\_\_  5.  <u>Most</u> of the leaders of Mali were Muslims.

\_\_\_\_  6.  As a result, sometime <u>between</u> the years 1100 and 1300

\_\_\_\_  7.  a great mosque was built of <u>mud</u> bricks

\_\_\_\_  8.  <u>by</u> the people of Mali in the town of Djenne.

\_\_\_\_  9.  Djenne <u>became</u> a center for Islamic learning.

\_\_\_\_  10.  Today, the Great Mosque at Djenne is designated a world historic <u>site</u>.

**EXERCISE 18**

### Identifying Parts of Speech

In the sentences below, identify the part of speech for each underlined word. Choose from the following list:

a. noun          c. adjective          e. adverb

b. pronoun          d. verb          f. preposition

\_\_\_\_  1.  The *Grand Ole Opry* is a <u>famous</u> radio program.

\_\_\_\_  2.  It began more than seventy <u>years</u> ago in Nashville, Tennessee.

\_\_\_\_  3.  By the 1930s, the <u>program</u> was the best source of country music on the radio.

\_\_\_\_  4.  In 1943, the program <u>could</u> be heard in every home in the nation.

\_\_\_\_  5.  <u>Many</u> people traveled to Nashville.

\_\_\_\_  6.  In Nashville, <u>they</u> could hear the performers for themselves.

\_\_\_\_  7.  The existing old concert hall, <u>poorly</u> constructed in the nineteenth century, was not an ideal place for modern audiences.

\_\_\_\_  8.  Television came in <u>during</u> the 1950s, and with it the demand for a new hall.

\_\_\_\_  9.  Now the Nashville hall is <u>modern</u> and air-conditioned.

\_\_\_\_  10.  Three million people <u>visit</u> Nashville every year.

**EXERCISE  19**

## Identifying Parts of Speech

In the sentences below, identify the part of speech for each underlined word. Choose from the following list:

a. noun            c. adjective          e. adverb

b. pronoun         d. verb               f. preposition

____   1.  We all know the <u>gorgeous</u> smile of Soledad O'Brien, a news anchor on the CNN morning news.

____   2.  As a child, Soledad loved horses and <u>dreamed</u> of becoming a jockey.

____   3.  Her mother, who is Afro-Cuban, and her father, who is Irish-Australian, <u>always</u> believed in the American dream.

____   4.  <u>They</u> put all their hopes in education.

____   5.  Soledad and her five siblings all went <u>to</u> college.

____   6.  It was Soledad's <u>intelligence</u> and motivation that opened the first door into a career in television.

____   7.  Soledad started as an assistant to a writer, and in the <u>span</u> of three years, she became a producer.

____   8.  <u>She</u> was willing to work thirteen-hour days.

____   9.  Today, her <u>biggest</u> challenge is to be well read and well informed day in and day out.

____  10.  People magazine has placed her <u>among</u> America's 100 Most Beautiful People.

## MASTERY AND EDITING TESTS

**TEST  1**

### Finding Subjects and Verbs in Simple Sentences

In each of the following sentences, cross out prepositional phrases and appositive phrases. Then underline the subject and circle the complete verb. An example follows:

(Have) <u>you</u> (heard) of the first cyber athlete?

1.  Into this new century has burst the worldwide phenomenon of a new cyber sport.

2.  Jonathan Wendell, a teenager from Kansas City, Missouri, spends eight to ten hours a day at the computer.

3.  Is he doing his homework?

4.  In fact, Jonathan (his game name is Fatal1ty) is playing video games.

5.  Here in America, this young man has become the best video player.

6.  Our first professional cyber athlete has won forty-one tournaments and has pocketed three hundred thousand dollars in tournament prizes.

7.  Already, this teenager has become the world champion in five different video games.

8.  Around the world, thousands of people find video games very addictive.

9.  Now Jonathan "Fatal1ty" Wendell has launched his own Fatal1ty products.

10.  Imagine his surprised parents!

**TEST 2**

### Finding Subjects and Verbs in Simple Sentences

**In each of the sentences in the following paragraph, cross out prepositional phrases and appositive phrases. Then underline the subject and circle the complete verb. An example follows:**

(Has) <u>anything</u> strange ever (happened) in your life?

In 1999, a young boy was playing baseball. Suddenly he was hit by a baseball bat. He could not breathe. In fact, his heart had stopped. Who would help? There was a nurse at the game. She acted quickly and performed CPR on the boy. The boy lived. Seven years later, this same nurse was eating dinner in a Buffalo restaurant. Unfortunately, a piece of food stuck in her throat. A worker at the restaurant did not hesitate. He had learned the Heimlich maneuver and successfully used the technique. Can you guess the young man's identity? The restaurant worker was the young baseball player from seven years ago. Imagine everyone's amazement! What are the chances of such a coincidence?

**TEST 3**

### Student Writing: Finding Subjects and Verbs in Simple Sentences

**In each of the sentences in the following paragraph, cross out prepositional phrases and appositive phrases. Then underline the subject and circle the complete verb.**

In an unmarked grave at the edge of the woods (lies) <u>Marley</u>.

Here is a true story about a very bad dog. In rural Pennsylvania, John Grogan, a columnist for the *Philadelphia Inquirer*, lived with his wife Jenny. Soon they  would be ready for-children. In preparation, this young couple bought a Labrador retriever puppy. Into their home came the wildly energetic, highly dysfunctional Marley. Marley could chew door frames to the studs and  separate steel bars on his crate. Drool covered the legs of all visitors to the Grogan home. He was expelled from obedience school. Marley's owner wrote a memoir about his dog titled *Marley and Me.* Its great success has led to several children's books and even a movie. Why has this book become such a big success? Apparently, everyone loves a book about a bad but lovable-dog.

## Exploring Online

Go to **www.cengage.com/devenglish/scarry/ writersworkplace** to find the **Writer's Online Workplace**, a website designed for students using this book. You will find links to handouts, interactive quizzes, and other online resources as you explore the following topics:

• sentence subjects
• parts of speech
• action, linking, and helping verbs

# Working Together

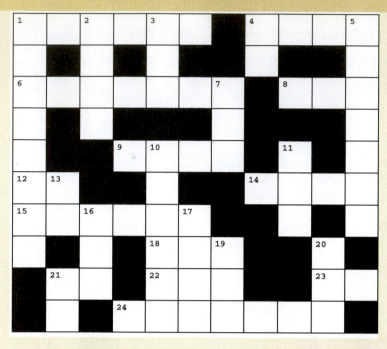

## CROSSWORD PUZZLE: REVIEWING THE TERMS FOR SENTENCE PARTS

Review the names for sentence parts by doing this crossword puzzle. Feel free to work in pairs. If necessary, look back in the chapter for the answers.

### Across

1. Verbs like *hop, sing,* and *play* are called _____ verbs.
4. Which of the following is a helping verb?
   *hear, when, will, only*
6. Every sentence has a _____ and a verb.
8. A helping verb
9. Which of the following is a preposition?
   *must, upon, they, open*
12. A preposition
14. *Word, witch, wall,* and *willow* are examples of the part of speech called a _____.
15. Most nouns are _____ nouns. They are not capitalized.
18. In the following sentence, which word is used as an adjective?
   *She has pet pigs for sale.*
21. Which of the following is a preposition?
   *he, be, by, if*
22. In the following sentence, which word is an abstract noun?
   *The era was not economically successful.*
23. A preposition
24. A word that can take the place of a noun

### Down

1. *Joy, confidence,* and *peace* are examples of this kind of noun (the opposite of a concrete noun).
2. Which word is the subject in the following sentence?
   *Here is the tube of glue for Toby.*
3. An indefinite pronoun
4. A plural pronoun
5. *Look, appear, feel,* and *seem* are examples of _____ verbs.
7. Which word is the object of the preposition in the following sentence?
   *The car must weigh over a ton.*
10. The opposite of a common noun is a _____ noun.
11. A personal pronoun
13. A preposition
16. In the following sentence, which word is a helping verb?
   *She may pay the fee for her son.*
17. Which of the following is a proper noun?
   *king, Nero, hero, teen*
19. In the following sentence, which word is an adjective?
   *Nan quickly ran toward the tan man.*
20. Which word is the verb in the following sentence?
   *Run down to the car for our bag.*
21. A common linking verb

# MAKING SUBJECTS AND VERBS AGREE

**4**

In this chapter, you will practice **making verbs agree with their subjects,** especially in cases where subject-verb agreement is not immediately obvious.

**CHAPTER OBJECTIVES**

Agreement when:

- the subject is a personal pronoun
- the verb is a form of *do* or *be*
- the subject is hard to find
- the subject is a collective noun
- the subject is an indefinite pronoun
- the subject is a compound subject
- the subject has an unusual singular or plural form

## WHAT IS SUBJECT-VERB AGREEMENT?

Subject-verb agreement means that a verb must agree with its subject in *number* (singular or plural).

> **When the subject is a singular noun, the verb takes an *-s* (or *-es*) in the present tense.**

The baby *sleeps.*

The baby *cries.*

> **When the subject is a plural noun, the verb does *not* take an *-s* (or *-es*) in the present tense.**

The babies *sleep.*

The babies *cry.*

Notice that when you add -*s* or -*es* to an ordinary noun, you form the plural of that noun. However, when you add -*s* to a verb in the present tense, you are forming a singular verb. This rule causes a lot of confusion for student writers, especially those whose first language is not English. It may also be confusing to students who already speak and write English but whose local manner of speaking does not follow this rule. Although no one way of speaking is correct or incorrect, society does recognize a standard form that is acceptable in the worlds of school and business. Because we all must master this standard form, the material contained in this chapter is of the greatest importance to your success in college and beyond.

## SUBJECT-VERB AGREEMENT WITH PERSONAL PRONOUNS

The following chart shows personal pronouns used with the verb *sleep*. After you have studied the chart, what rule can you state about the ending of a verb in the present tense?

### Personal Pronouns

|  | Singular | Plural |
|---|---|---|
| First person: | I *sleep* | we *sleep* |
| Second person: | you *sleep* | you *sleep* |
| Third person: | he ⎫<br>she ⎬ *sleeps*<br>it ⎭ | they *sleep* |

**Practice**

Circle the correct verb in each of the following sentences.

1.  The dog (bark, barks).

2.  It (wake, wakes) up the neighborhood.

3.  The neighbors (become, becomes) annoyed.

4.  They (deserve, deserves) a quiet Sunday morning.

5.  I (throws, throw) an old slipper at the dog.

## SUBJECT-VERB AGREEMENT WITH THE VERBS *DO* AND *BE*

Although you might have heard someone say, "It don't matter" or "We was working," these expressions are not considered standard English because the subjects do not agree with the verbs. Study the two charts that follow to learn which forms of *do* and *be* are singular and which forms are plural.

## The Verb *do*

| Singular | Plural |
|----------|--------|
| I *do* | we *do* |
| you *do* | you *do* |
| he ⎫ | they *do* |
| she ⎬ *does* | |
| it ⎭ | |

(Never use *he don't*, *she don't*, or *it don't*.)

## The Verb *be*

| Present Tense | | Past Tense | |
|---------------|---|------------|---|
| **Singular** | **Plural** | **Singular** | **Plural** |
| I *am* | we *are* | I *was* | we *were* |
| you *are* | you *are* | you *were* | you *were* |
| he ⎫ | they *are* | he ⎫ | they *were* |
| she ⎬ *is* | | she ⎬ *was* | |
| it ⎭ | | it ⎭ | |

(Never use *we was*, *you was*, or *they was*.)

**Practice**     Circle the verb that agrees with the subject.

1.  He (doesn't, don't) study in the library anymore.

2.  We (was, were) hoping to find him there.

3.  The library (doesn't, don't) close until eleven o'clock.

4.  (Was, Were) you late tonight?

5.  Irina (doesn't, don't) care if you stay until closing time.

**EXERCISE  1**     **Making the Subject and Verb Agree**

**In the blanks next to each sentence, write the subject of the sentence and the correct form of the verb.**

|  | Subject | Verb |
|---|---|---|
| 1. Mystery writers from around America (presents, present) an award called the Edgar, named after Edgar Allan Poe. | _____ | _____ |
| 2. They (nominates, nominate) several writers each year for the award. | _____ | _____ |
| 3. A successful mystery writer (lives, live) in our town. | _____ | _____ |
| 4. He (doesn't, don't) live too far from me. | _____ | _____ |
| 5. Sometimes we (sees, see) him out walking. | _____ | _____ |
| 6. He always (wears, wear) an old wide-brimmed hat. | _____ | _____ |
| 7. His books usually (centers, center) around a sports theme. | _____ | _____ |
| 8. His latest book (is, are) about a murder at the U.S. Open Tennis Tournament. | _____ | _____ |
| 9. He (was, were) nominated for the Edgar Award for best paperback of the year. | _____ | _____ |
| 10. We (doesn't, don't) know yet if he will win the award. | _____ | _____ |

**EXERCISE** ❷    ## Making the Subject and Verb Agree

**In the blanks next to each sentence, write the subject of the sentence and the correct form of the verb.**

|  | Subject | Verb |
|---|---|---|
| 1. Many companies today (tests, test) their workers for drugs. | _____ | _____ |
| 2. To many people, it (seems, seem) an invasion of privacy. | _____ | _____ |
| 3. Employers (worries, worry) that bus and train drivers are using drugs on the job. | _____ | _____ |
| 4. They (doesn't, don't) want the lives of their passengers at risk. | _____ | _____ |
| 5. Even operators of rides in amusement parks (undergoes, undergo) tests. | _____ | _____ |

6. Professional athletes on a team (has, have) special problems because of unwelcome publicity.   _____   _____

7. Some factories (installs, install) hidden video cameras for surveillance.   _____   _____

8. The General Motors Company (hires, hire) undercover agents as workers.   _____   _____

9. In Kansas City, drug-sniffing dogs (was, were) used in a newspaper office.   _____   _____

10. (Has, Have) you ever taken a drug test?   _____   _____

**EXERCISE  3**

## Making the Subject and Verb Agree

**In the blanks next to each sentence, write the subject of the sentence and the correct form of the verb.**

|  | Subject | Verb |
|---|---|---|

1. Many therapies (is, are) available today for people in need.   _____   _____

2. Talk therapy (encourages, encourage) troubled people to talk about problems to a trained therapist.   _____   _____

3. More recently, other treatments (has, have) become popular.   _____   _____

4. These (includes, include) music therapy, dance therapy, art therapy, and poetry therapy.   _____   _____

5. For example, professional writers (believes, believe) poetry has beneficial effects.   _____   _____

6. They (doesn't, don't) believe in repressing fear or anger.   _____   _____

7. Patients (creates, create) poetry as a form of self-healing.   _____   _____

8. A poem (gets, get) to the heart of a problem.   _____   _____

9. No invasive medical procedure (is, are) called for.   _____   _____

10. Poetry (allows, allow) these patients to explore emotions and organize thoughts.   _____   _____

# SUBJECT-VERB AGREEMENT WITH HARD-TO-FIND SUBJECTS

As you learned in Chapter 3, a verb does not always immediately follow the subject. Other words or groups of words called *phrases* (prepositional phrases or appositive phrases, for example) can come between the subject and the verb. Furthermore, subjects and verbs can be inverted when they are used in questions or in sentences beginning with *there* or *here*.

When looking for subject-verb agreement in sentences where the subjects are difficult to find, keep two points in mind:

- Subjects are *not* found in prepositional phrases or appositive phrases.
- Subjects can be found after the verb in sentences that are questions and in sentences that begin with the word *there* or the word *here*.

**EXERCISE 4**

## Agreement with Hidden Subjects

In each sentence below, cross out prepositional phrases, appositive phrases, and the word *there* or the word *here*. Then underline the subject. Finally, circle the correct verb.

1. Here (is, are) a plan about time management.

2. Too much busywork in your day (prevents, prevent) efficiency.

3. A period of time without interruptions (is, are) crucial.

4. People usually (does, do) too many things at once.

5. Why (is, are) frequent breaks important?

6. Constant clutter on people's desks (causes, cause) frustration.

7. Why (does, do) perfectionists have so much difficulty?

8. The habit of procrastination (is, are) another area of time management.

9. There (is, are) several other distracting activities, from watching television to playing video games.

10. Children in a family (needs, need) to help with chores.

**EXERCISE 5**

## Agreement with Hidden Subjects

In each sentence, cross out prepositional phrases, appositive phrases, and the word *there* or the word *here*. Then underline the subject. Finally, circle the correct verb.

1. Here (is, are) some basic medical supplies needed for every home.

2. A thermometer in the medicine chest (is, are) crucial.

3.  There (is, are) a box of bandages on hand for minor injuries.

4.  A vaporizer in the bedroom at night (relieves, relieve) bronchial congestion.

5.  Pads of sterile gauze often (helps, help) dress wounds.

6.  A small bottle of Coca Cola syrup (proves, prove) helpful for treating stomach upsets.

7.  A useful tool, a pair of tweezers, (removes, remove) splinters.

8.  In a home ready for emergencies, a list of emergency phone numbers (sits, sit) next to the telephone.

9.  Why (has, have) cold compresses been useful in treating sprains?

10. Every person with a sense of responsibility (needs, need) a resource book on first aid at hand.

## SUBJECT-VERB AGREEMENT WITH COLLECTIVE NOUNS

> **Collective nouns** name a group of people or things.

### Frequently Used Collective Nouns

| | | |
|---|---|---|
| assembly | couple | orchestra |
| audience | crowd | panel |
| board | faculty | public |
| class | family | senate |
| club | group | team |
| committee | herd | tribe |
| council | jury | troop |

> A *collective noun* (also called a *group noun*) is considered singular unless the meaning is clearly plural.

Usually, a collective noun takes a singular verb or requires a singular pronoun to refer to that noun. The reasoning is that the group acts as a single unit.

The class *was waiting* for *its* turn to use the gym.

The Cub Scout troop *is holding its* jamboree in July.

The orchestra *performs* in Cincinnati next week.

Sometimes a collective noun takes a plural verb or requires a plural pronoun to refer to that noun because the members of the group are clearly acting as individuals, with separate actions as a result. One clue that a group noun will be considered plural is if the verb shows a difference of opinion: *disagree, argue, debate,* or *differ.*

The class *were putting* on their coats.

*(Clearly, each member has his or her own coat.)*

The Cub Scout troop *were having* difficulty with *their* tents.

*(Here, the meaning is that each person is individually having trouble with his tent.)*

The orchestra *are debating* whether or not to go on tour.

*(Some individuals think they should go on tour; some think they should not.)*

**NOTE:** The word *number* is a collective noun that is governed by the following rule:

**If the definite article (*the*) is used with *number*, the meaning is singular.**

*The number* of reality shows on television *has* increased.

**If the indefinite article (*a, an*) is used with *number*, the meaning is plural.**

*A number* of reality shows on television *have* been canceled.

---

**EXERCISE** ⑥     ## Agreement with Collective Nouns

Collective nouns can sometimes be singular or plural depending on the writer's intention. After each sentence of the following exercise, the words in parentheses indicate the writer's intended meaning. Underline the subject and circle the correct verb in each sentence.

1.  The construction crew (is, are) being blamed for the accident. *(acting as a unit)*

2.  In this case, the union (accuses, accuse) the crew. *(acting as a unit)*

3.  A few days after the accident, the same group (files, file) charges. *(acting as a unit)*

4.  The crew's legal team (is, are) uncertain about their strategy. *(acting as individuals)*

5.  The public (voices, voice) their concerns to the media. *(acting as individuals)*

6.  The crowd (grows, grow) more and more impatient. *(acting as a unit)*

7.  The audience (interrupts, interrupt) the proceedings. *(acting as individuals)*

8.  The jury (hears, hear) the evidence. *(acting as a unit)*

9.   The group (has, have) very different opinions. *(acting as individuals)*

10.  The crowd (sits, sit) on the edge of their seats to hear the verdict. *(acting as individuals)*

**EXERCISE**  **7**

### Agreement with Collective Nouns

**Use the following general rule for collective nouns: A collective noun is considered singular unless the members of the group are acting as individuals with different ideas or separate actions. In the following exercise, underline the subject and circle the correct verb in each sentence.**

1.   The Spanish club (is, are) hiring a speaker for the meeting.

2.   The trio (performs, perform) mostly on weekends.

3.   The group (needs, need) a sponsor for its organization.

4.   The faculty (is, are) not in agreement about the new grading policy.

5.   The committee (was, were) undecided about who should be invited.

6.   The team (has, have) beaten its strongest opponent.

7.   A crowd usually (attends, attend) the competition.

8.   The board of directors (disagrees, disagree) about the proposed reorganization.

9.   The panel tonight (was, were) not all ready for the questions posed to them.

10.  The junior class (is, are) choosing their class rings this week.

# SUBJECT-VERB AGREEMENT WITH INDEFINITE PRONOUNS

Care should be taken to learn which indefinite pronouns are singular and which are plural.

## Indefinite Pronouns

**INDEFINITE PRONOUNS TAKING A SINGULAR VERB**

| | | | |
|---|---|---|---|
| everyone | someone | anyone | no one |
| everybody | somebody | anybody | nobody |
| everything | something | anything | nothing |
| each | another | either (of) | neither (of) |
| one (of) | much | such (a) | |

**Everyone *is expecting* a miracle.**

(continued on next page)

**INDEFINITE PRONOUNS TAKING A PLURAL VERB**

both          few          many          several

**The talks between the two countries failed. Both *were* to blame.**

**INDEFINITE PRONOUNS TAKING A SINGULAR OR PLURAL VERB
DEPENDING ON THE MEANING IN THE SENTENCE**

all          any          more          most

none          some

**The books are gone. All of them *were* very popular.**

**The sugar is gone. All of it *was* spilled.**

**EXERCISE**  **Agreement with Indefinite Pronouns**

**Underline the subject and circle the correct verb in each sentence.**

**HINT**: When a prepositional phrase follows an indefinite pronoun that is the subject, be sure the verb agrees with the indefinite pronoun subject.

1.  One of America's most talented regional artists (was, were) Walter Anderson of Mississippi.

2.  Each of his paintings (is, are) full of energy.

3.  Few (deny, denies) his greatness.

4.  Nobody (has, have) loved nature more than this artist.

5.  Many of his drawings (shows, show) vibrant plant life.

6.  Others (depicts, depict) animals in motion.

7.  Some of his animals (is, are) carved into wooden figures.

8.  Most of Walter Anderson's work (was, were) discovered after his death.

9.  All of us (was, were) saddened by the destruction of so much of his work in Hurricane Katrina and the subsequent flood.

10.  Anything from his studio (has, have) real value today.

**EXERCISE  9**

### Agreement with Indefinite Pronouns

Underline the subject and circle the correct verb in each sentence.

**Each** of these plants (grows), grow) in the rainforest.

1. Nobody (knows, know) how many drugs are contained in plants that grow in the rainforest.

2. Some (argues, argue) that wonderful drugs could be derived from many plants.

3. Most of the pharmaceutical experts (remains, remain) skeptical.

4. All of the research (is, are) expensive and often (proves, prove) fruitless.

5. Everybody (agrees, agree) that the tropical forest is a source of medicine.

6. One of the dangers (is, are) that if we wait, the tropical forest may disappear.

7. One of the two U.S. companies in Costa Rica (is, are) Merck and Company.

8. Each of the companies (has been, have been) paying the country for the right to search the rainforest.

9. Among scientists, some (recommends, recommend) that governments subsidize drug research.

10. Vincristine and vinblastine are two medicines found in the rainforest; both (is, are) used for cancer treatment.

## SUBJECT-VERB AGREEMENT WITH COMPOUND SUBJECTS

> **If the parts of a compound subject are connected by the word *and*, the verb is usually plural.**

**Alberto *and* Ramon *are* the winners.**

The exception to this rule occurs when the two subjects are thought of as a single unit.

> **If the parts of a compound subject connected by *and* are thought of as a single unit, the verb is singular.**

**Peanut butter *and* jelly *is* my favorite sandwich.**

The rule becomes more complicated when the parts of the compound subject are connected by *or, nor, either, either/or, neither, neither/nor,* or *not only/but also.*

---

When the parts of a compound subject are connected with *or, nor, either, either/or, neither, neither/nor,* or *not only/but also,* use the following rules:

1.   **If both subjects are singular, the verb is singular.**

     *Either* **Alberto** *or* **Ramon** *is* **at the concert.**

2.   **If both subjects are plural, the verb is plural.**

     *Either* **my friends** *or* **my two brothers** *are* **at the concert.**

3.   **If one subject is singular and one subject is plural, the verb agrees with the subject closer to the verb.**

     *Either* **my friends** *or* **my brother** *is* **at the concert.**

     *Either* **my brother** *or* **my friends** *are* **at the concert.**

---

**EXERCISE 10**

### Subject-Verb Agreement with Compound Subjects

**Underline the compound subject and circle the correct verb in each sentence.**

1.   Macaroni and cheese (is, are) my son's favorite supper.

2.   This meal and others like it (has, have) too much fat.

3.   My mother and father, on the other hand, often (enjoys, enjoy) a fruit salad for their main meal.

4.   For many of us, our shopping habits or cooking routine (needs, need) to be changed.

5.   Either a salad or a cooked vegetable with a sprinkling of cheese (is, are) a better choice than macaroni and cheese.

6.   Adults and children (does, do) need to watch their diets.

7.   Too many pizzas and sodas (is, are) a disaster for people's health.

8.   Either the lack of exercise or the eating of fatty foods (causes, cause) more problems than just weight gain.

9.   Neither potato chips nor buttered popcorn (is, are) a good snack choice.

10.  An apple or grapes (makes, make) a better choice.

**EXERCISE 11**     **Subject-Verb Agreement with Compound Subjects**

**In each sentence, underline the compound subject and circle the correct verb.**

1. Students and their teacher (meets, meet) at the University of Indiana to do marriage research.

2. Either Robert Levenson or John Gollman (uses, use) the video to examine how couples interact during arguments.

3. Neither body language nor the spoken words (is, are) unimportant.

4. Criticism, whining, or withdrawal (reveals, reveal) potential trouble.

5. Sweating, blood flow, and heart rate (is, are) also monitored during arguments.

6. Positive moments or good memories (needs, need) to outnumber the negative moments.

7. A man or a woman marrying someone with a different fighting style (risks, risk) an unhappy marriage.

8. Courtrooms or a baseball field (provides, provide) structured times and places for people to fight.

9. A particular time and a particular place (needs, need) to be set aside for talking about marital problems.

10. A happy husband and wife (gives, give) each other support and friendship.

# SUBJECT-VERB AGREEMENT WITH UNUSUAL NOUNS

Do not assume that every noun ending in *-s* is plural or that all nouns that do not end in *-s* are singular. There are some exceptions. Here are a few of the most common exceptions.

1. Some nouns are always singular in meaning but end in *-s:*

| | | |
|---|---|---|
| mathematics | diabetes | United States |
| economics | measles | Kansas |

   **Mathematics *is* my major.**

2. Some nouns are always plural in meaning.

| | | |
|---|---|---|
| clothes | tweezers | pants |
| scissors | fireworks | pliers |

   **My blue pants *are* ripped.**

3.  Some nouns change internally rather than add -s at the end:

| Singular | Plural |
|----------|--------|
| foot | feet |
| tooth | teeth |
| child | children |
| man | men |
| woman | women |
| mouse | mice |
| ox | oxen |
| goose | geese |

4.  Some nouns remain the same whether singular or plural:

| Singular | Plural |
|----------|--------|
| deer | deer |
| elk | elk |
| fish | fish |
| moose | moose |

5.  When some foreign words are used in English, they continue to form the plural by following the rules of their original languages. For example, here are four Latin words that follow the Latin rule (-um changes to -a to form the plural):

| Singular | Plural |
|----------|--------|
| bacterium | bacteria |
| datum | data |
| medium | media |
| stratum | strata |

# MASTERY AND EDITING TESTS

**TEST 1**

## Making the Subject and Verb Agree

In the blanks next to each sentence, write the subject of the sentence and the correct form of the verb. An example follows.

|  | Subject | Verb |
|--|---------|------|
| Everybody (has, have) heard of injuries suffered by young athletes. | Everybody | has |
| 1.  Many of these injuries (happens, happen) to football quarterbacks. | _____ | _____ |
| 2.  One of the most serious sports injuries (is, are) a concussion. | _____ | _____ |
| 3.  Many young people (thinks, think) nothing of a minor blow to the head. | _____ | _____ |
| 4.  Now scientists (understands, understand) these injuries much better than before. | _____ | _____ |

5. On impact, the arteries of the brain
   (is, are) constricted.                                    _____   _____

6. Some athletes unfortunately
   (suffers, suffer) a second concussion
   before healing from the first one.                        _____   _____

7. Several minor concussions often
   (leads, lead) to permanent brain
   damage or even death.                                     _____   _____

8. Medical doctors all over the country
   (wants, want) stricter guidelines
   for athletes with concussions.                            _____   _____

9. An athlete with one or more concussions
   (requires, require) a sufficient amount
   of rest.                                                  _____   _____

10. Today, nobody in contact sports
    (takes, take) a head injury lightly.                     _____   _____

**TEST  2**

### Making the Subject and Verb Agree

**Using your own words and ideas, complete each of the following sentences. Be sure the subject and verb agree. An example follows:**

The best place for wedding receptions is a restaurant with a view.

1. Our team _____

2. The box of chocolates _____

3. Both of my sisters _____

4. The effects of a pay cut on a family _____
   _____

5. Where are _____

6. Not only the teacher but also the students _____
   _____

7. The jury _____

8. Each of the contestants _____

9. There is _____

10. The table of contents in that book _____

**TEST  3**

### Editing Student Writing: Making the Subject and Verb Agree

**The following paragraph contains seven errors in subject-verb agreement. For each sentence, cross out prepositional phrases and appositive phrases, underline the subject, and circle the verb. Place a check over errors in agreement. On the lines following, list the subject and the correct form of the verb for each sentence.**

Bedbugs Are Back

[1] People in hotels and apartments around the country are complaining. [2]Gradually more and more places, including college dormitories, has bedbugs. [3]How does these pests get into a room? [4]International travel has been largely to blame. [5]Unfortunately, bedbugs have the ability to survive for over a year without a meal. [6]Furthermore, insecticides from a local hardware store is no longer effective. [7]Your new mattress sometimes arrive on a truck with an old mattress (filled with bedbugs) from another customer. [8]Also, a bedbug easily rides unseen from one place to another in a pants cuff or a jacket. [9]Either a crack in a wall or a ridge between the floor boards are enough room for a bedbug. [10]These invisible vampires of the night traumatizes their victims. [11]The number of them often grows quickly from only a few into several thounsands. [12]Unsightly, itchy red welts are left behind by this bloodsucking bug. [13]Nobody in my circle of friends knowingly visit a home with these invisible and nearly indestructible pests.

|  | Subject | Correct form of verb |
|---|---|---|
| 1. | _____ | _____ |
| 2. | _____ | _____ |
| 3. | _____ | _____ |
| 4. | _____ | _____ |
| 5. | _____ | _____ |
| 6. | _____ | _____ |
| 7. | _____ | _____ |
| 8. | _____ | _____ |
| 9. | _____ | _____ |
| 10. | _____ | _____ |
| 11. | _____ | _____ |
| 12. | _____ | _____ |
| 13. | _____ | _____ |

TEST **4**

## Editing Student Writing Using Editing Symbols

Instructors often use commonly accepted symbols to mark corrections in student writing. The editing symbol for subject-verb agreement is agr. (See the inside back cover for a list of common editing symbols.) The paragraph contains five subject-verb agreement errors. Write agr above each error you find, and then write the subject and the correct verb form on the lines

**provided. (In sentence 9, consider *audience* as a collective noun that acts as a unit.)**

¹Why don't everybody like a hair-raising horror movie? ²I don't see many of my college classmates at all the latest shows. ³My girlfriend doesn't like these kinds of movies, and neither do any of her friends. ⁴In fact, the theaters are filled almost exclusively with teenagers. ⁵My friends and I pays our eight bucks and anticipate a nightmare. ⁶Each of us hope for a thrill. ⁷Emotions like love, friendship, or kindness go by the wayside. ⁸The audience wants blood and guts! ⁹It don't matter if the plot is ridiculous and the acting is terrible. ¹⁰The typical horror movie with all its violent scenes appeal to our worst nature. ¹¹One of my favorite horror movies is *The Hills Have Eyes.* ¹²Fortunately for my friends and me, a popular horror movie these days usually has a sequel. ¹³We look forward to the next adrenaline rush.

**Five subject-verb agreement corrections**

| Subject | Correct form of the verb |
|---|---|
| 1. _____ | _____ |
| 2. _____ | _____ |
| 3. _____ | _____ |
| 4. _____ | _____ |
| 5. _____ | _____ |

## Exploring Online

Go to **www.cengage.com/devenglish/scarry/writersworkplace** to find the **Writer's Online Workplace**, a website designed for students using this book. You will find links to handouts, interactive quizzes, and other online resources as you explore the following topic:

• subject-verb agreement

# Working Together

## FOCUSED FREEWRITING: PRESERVING FAMILY HISTORY

Though it is more difficult to write about my father than about my mother, since I spent less time with him and knew him less well, it is equally as liberating. Partly this is because writing about people helps us to understand them, and understanding them helps us to accept them as part of ourselves. Since I share so many of my father's characteristics, physical and otherwise, coming to terms with what he has meant to my life is crucial to a full acceptance and love of myself.

Alice Walker, the well-known novelist and essay writer, expressed these thoughts in a journal that she kept for a time. She discovered that by writing down her thoughts and feelings about her father she felt liberated. We can all be liberated by a better understanding of the people who have shaped our lives. Obviously, we cannot know everything about another person, even a person with whom we have lived, but we can put together stories we have heard from relatives, along with memories that we have ourselves. When we write about family members, it is always good to remember that each person's perspective is colored by his or her own personality and by a memory that may not be entirely accurate. In this regard, you might want to create a portrait of a family member through the eyes of a person other than yourself, always keeping in mind that people's recollections can be distorted.

## Questions for Class Discussion

1.  On the basis of the Alice Walker quote above, can you explain why Alice Walker found writing about her father to be liberating?

2.  To what extent should we feel that our family members are "part of ourselves"? What if we do not like or accept everything about a family member? In that case, what should we do about including that family member in a memoir?

3.  What types of information might you be tempted to write in a journal entry about a family member? Are there any people who could provide you with stories that you would like to include in your entry?

4.  What would you like your grandchildren to know about you?

5.  What characteristics, both mental and physical, do you believe you have inherited? Do you like what you have inherited? What do you wish had been left out?

6.  Think about a person who has been adopted. How is preserving family history made more complicated for such a person? What advice could you offer?

7.  What are the most common obstacles people face that prevent them from accepting themselves?

## Freewriting

Freewrite for fifteen minutes. Share a story, a memory of some kind, or a description of a family member that you find worthy of recording. You might tell a story about yourself, one that you would like your family to remember. Think of your piece of writing as the beginning of a memoir that future members of your family would like to have.

## PORTFOLIO SUGGESTION

Save the freewriting you have done on your family's history. This is a topic that you may want to return to again and again. Children will appreciate all the stories and memories you can gather about your relatives. This may be one of the greatest gifts you can give your family.

# 5

# UNDERSTANDING FRAGMENTS AND PHRASES

Groups of words that go together are not necessarily sentences. In this chapter, you will learn to recognize the different sentence parts and distinguish between a phrase and a sentence. Your focus will be on three skills.

**CHAPTER OBJECTIVES**

- Distinguish a **fragment** from a sentence when one of the following elements is missing:
    - a subject
    - a verb
    - a complete thought
- Identify the **six kinds of phrases** in English:
    - noun phrases (includes appositive phrases)
    - prepositional phrases
    - verb phrases
    - infinitive phrases
    - participial phrases
    - gerund phrases
- Understand the three different functions of the **present participle:**
    - as part of a verb phrase
    - as an adjective
    - as a noun

The fragment is a major problem for many student writers. A thought may be clear in a writer's mind, but on paper the expression of this idea may be incomplete because it does not include a subject, a verb, or a complete thought. In this section, you will improve your ability to spot fragments (incomplete sentences), and you will learn how to correct them. This practice will help you avoid fragments in your own writing.

Here, for example, is a typical conversation between two people in a laboratory. It is composed entirely of fragments, but the two people who are speaking have no trouble understanding each other.

**Doug:**     Had any test results yet?
**Nelida:**   Nothing statistically significant.
**Doug:**     Not good.
**Nelida:**   Back to step one.

Rewritten in complete sentences, this brief conversation might go as follows:

**Doug:**     Have you had any test results yet?
**Nelida:**   The results were not statistically significant.
**Doug:**     That is not good.
**Nelida:**   We will have to go back to step one.

In the first conversation, misunderstanding is unlikely since the two speakers stand face to face. Seeing the other's gestures and hearing the intonations in the other's voice help each one grasp the other's meaning. These short phrases are enough for communication because the speakers are using more than just words to convey their thoughts. They understand each other because each one has no difficulty completing the thoughts in the other's mind.

In writing, however, readers cannot be present to observe tone of voice, gestures, or other signals for themselves. They cannot be expected to read the writer's mind. For a reader, only words grouped into sentences and sentences grouped into paragraphs can provide clues to the meaning. Because writing often involves thoughts that are abstract and even complex, fragments cause great difficulty and sometimes result in total confusion for the reader.

**EXERCISE**  **Putting a Conversation into Complete Sentences**

The following conversation could have taken place between two airline pilots. Rewrite the conversation in complete thoughts (or standard sentences). Remember the definition of a sentence:

> A ***complete sentence*** has a subject and a verb and expresses a complete thought.

**Nick:**       Got everything?
**Chandra:**    Everything but the new flight plan.
**Nick:**       Twenty minutes until takeoff.
**Chandra:**    Looks like nasty weather.
**Nick:**       Hopefully no flocks of birds in our flight path.
**Chandra:**    What about deicing?
**Nick:**       Done!
**Chandra:**    A full plane today.
**Nick:**       Ready?
**Chandra:**    Good to go.

**Conversation rewritten in standard sentences**

**Nick:**  _____

**Chandra:**  _____

**Nick:**  _____

**Chandra:**  _____

**Nick:**  _____

**Chandra:**  _____

**Nick:**  _____

**Chandra:**  _____

**Nick:**  _____

**Chandra:**  _____

Remember that when you write in complete sentences, the results may differ from the way you would express the same ideas in everyday conversation with a friend.

Although you will occasionally spot incomplete sentences in professional writing, you may be sure the writer is using these fragments intentionally. In such cases, the fragment may be appropriate because it captures the way a person thinks or speaks or because it creates a special effect. A student developing his or her writing skills should be careful to use only standard-sentence form so that every thought will be communicated effectively. Nearly all the writing you will do in your life—business correspondence, papers in school, or reports in your job—will demand standard-sentence form. Fragments will be looked upon as a sign of ignorance rather than evidence of a creative style!

## WHAT IS A FRAGMENT?

> A **fragment** is a piece of a sentence.

A group of words may appear to be a sentence, but if one of the following elements is missing, the result is a fragment.

a. The subject is missing:

   **is setting the trap**

b. The verb is missing:

   **the hunter in the woods**

c. Both the subject and the verb are missing:

   **in the woods**

d. The subject and verb are present, but the group of words does not express a complete thought:

   **The hunter set**

# HOW DO YOU CORRECT A FRAGMENT?

1. **Add the missing part or parts.**

   | | |
   |---|---|
   | **Fragment:** | **across the lake** |
   | **To be added:** | **subject and verb** |
   | **Complete sentence:** | **I swam across the lake.** |

   The prepositional phrase *across the lake* is a fragment because a prepositional phrase cannot function as the subject or the verb in a sentence. Furthermore, the words *across the lake* do not express a complete thought.

2. **Join the fragment to the sentence where it belongs.**

   If you look at the context in which a fragment occurs, you will often find that the complete thought is already present. The writer did not recognize that the fragment belonged to the sentence that came just before or to the sentence that immediately followed. Therefore, another way to correct a fragment is to join the fragment to the sentence that precedes it or to the sentence that immediately follows it. Which sentence you choose depends on where the information in the fragment belongs. Study the example below.

   | | |
   |---|---|
   | **Incorrect:** | **In the middle of the night, I swam. Across the lake. The water was cool and inviting.** |
   | **Correct:** | **In the middle of the night, I swam across the lake. The water was cool and inviting.** |

Fragments can exist in a writer's work for a number of reasons. A writer may become careless for a moment or may not fully understand how all the parts of a sentence work. If the writer does not have a clear idea of what he or she is trying to say, fragments and other errors are more likely to occur. Sometimes another try at expressing the same idea may produce a better result.

**EXERCISE 2**

## Correcting Fragments by Adding the Missing Parts

**Make each of the following fragments into a complete sentence by adding the missing part or parts.**

1. returned to the sea (add a subject)

   _____

2. a bird on the oak branch (add a verb)

   _____

3. between the island and the mainland (add a subject and a verb)

   _____

4. the hawk in a soaring motion (add a verb)

   _____

5.   the fishing boats in the harbor (add a verb)

_____

6.   dropped like a stone into the water (add a subject)

_____

7.   the crescent moon (add a verb)

_____

8.   carried the fish to the tree (add a subject)

_____

9.   the fisherman put (complete the thought)

_____

10.   into the net (add a subject and a verb)

_____

**EXERCISE 3**

## Correcting Fragments That Belong to Other Sentences

Each of the following passages contains two or more fragments. First, read each passage carefully. Then place a check in front of each fragment you find.

**Finally, draw an arrow to indicate the sentence to which the fragment belongs. An example follows:**

Adelle assisted the dancers. She stood backstage during the performance. Between numbers. She helped the ballerinas change costumes.

1. Fishing is one of the oldest sports in the world. And can be one of the most relaxing. A person with a simple wooden pole and line can have as much fun as a sportsman. With expensive equipment. For busy executives, overworked teachers, and even presidents of nations. Fishing can be a good way to escape from the stress of demanding jobs.

2. The first electric car was built in 1887. It was sold commercially. Six years later. At the turn of the century, people had great faith in new technology. In fact, three hundred electric taxicabs were operating in New York City by 1900. However, electric cars soon lost their popularity. The new gasoline engine became more widely used. With our concern over pollution. Perhaps electric cars will become desirable once again.

3. Tiger Woods is famous for his success as a championship golfer. He is also known for his work with children. In Anaheim, California, Tiger has recently opened a learning center. For fourth to twelfth graders. Children can apply for a wide range of classes. Including robotics, creative writing, forensics, and photography. Eventually, the center will serve five thousand children. Tiger is planning the construction of other centers around the country. At a cost of five million dollars apiece. He is grateful for his loving and supportive family. And wants to help less fortunate children.

# WHAT IS A PHRASE AND HOW MANY KINDS OF PHRASES ARE THERE?

> A **phrase** is a group of words belonging together but lacking one or more of the three elements necessary for a sentence.

Fragments are usually made up of phrases. These phrases are often mistaken for sentences because they are words that go together as a group. However, they do not fit the definition of a sentence. *Do not confuse a phrase with a sentence.*

The English language has six kinds of phrases, and you should learn to recognize each one. You have already studied three of these kinds of phrases in Chapter 3.

## The Six Types of Phrases in English

**1. Noun phrase** — a noun with its modifiers:

**many large round stones**

**2. Prepositional phrase** — a preposition with its object and modifiers:

**among the large round stones**

**3. Verb phrase** — a main verb with its helping verbs and modifiers:

**were sweetly singing**

**has slowly vanished**

**4. Infinitive phrase** — the word *to* with the base form of the verb and any other words that complete the phrase:

**to move gracefully**

**5. Participial phrase** — a present or past participle and the other words that complete the phrase:

**moving gracefully**

**greatly encouraged**

The participial phrase functions as an **adjective:**

*Moving gracefully,* **the skater looked like a ballet dancer.**

*Greatly encouraged,* **the coach decided she was ready for competition.**

**6. Gerund phrase** — a present participle and the other words that complete the phrase:

**moving gracefully**

The gerund phrase functions as a **noun:**

*Moving gracefully* **was the skater's best quality.**

Like the verb phrase, the infinitive phrase, the participial phrase, and the gerund phrase are all formed from verbs. However, these phrases do not function as verbs in sentences.

## INFINITIVE PHRASE

An infinitive phrase usually functions as a noun.

### Infinitive phrase as subject

*To continue this argument* **would be useless.**

### Infinitive phrase as object

**She began *to move gracefully.***

**NOTE**: The word *to* can also be used as a preposition, as in *I wrote to my son.*

**Practice**   See whether you can distinguish between the infinitive phrases and the prepositional phrases. In each of the following sentences, label the italicized phrase as an infinitive phrase (INF) or prepositional phrase (PP).

_____   1.   I stopped by his office to *say goodbye.*

_____   2.   The trail of evidence led directly *to him.*

_____   3.   We were lucky *to have discovered* his fraudulent activities.

_____   4.   The manager had forced him *to tell the truth.*

_____   5.   His leaving will be a relief *to the staff.*

## PARTICIPIAL PHRASE

### How Is the Participle Formed?

The present and past participles are formed from the base verb:

**Present participle:**   base verb + *-ing*

**running, looking, trying**

**Past participle:**   base verb + the regular past tense ending *-d* or *-ed*

**disappointed, folded, turned**

or

base verb + irregular past tense form

**told, gone, given,**

Below are the same participles given above, this time with words that might complete their phrases.

Examples of **present participial phrases:**

**running home, looking very unhappy, trying hard**

Examples of **past participial phrases:**

**greatly disappointed, folded incorrectly, turned slightly**

**told tearfully, gone quickly, given gratefully**

### How Does a Participial Phrase Function?

A participial phrase functions as an **adjective** in a sentence. By studying the following sentences, you can observe how the above phrases can be used in complete sentences. These phrases function as adjectives for the noun or pronoun that follows them.

*Running home,* the worker lost her wallet.

*Looking very unhappy,* she retraced her steps.

*Greatly disappointed,* she could not find it.

*Told tearfully,* the story saddened her friends.

## GERUND PHRASE

The gerund is formed from the present participle. Along with any words that go with it, the gerund phrase functions as a **noun.** As such, it can be the subject or the object of a sentence.

**Gerund phrase as subject:**    *Long-distance running* is strenuous exercise.

**Gerund phrase as object:**    I like *long-distance running.*

**Practice**

See whether you can distinguish between participial phrases and gerund phrases. In each of the following sentences, label the italicized phrase as a participial phrase (P) or a gerund phrase (G). Remember, the participial phrase functions as an *adjective.* The gerund phrase functions as a *noun.*

_____  1.  *Standing totally still,* the child hoped the bee would fly away.

_____  2.  *Playing the violin* is not easy.

_____  3.  The athlete will try *deep-sea diving.*

_____  4.  *Waiting patiently,* we ordered something to drink.

_____  5.  *Edited slowly and carefully,* the essay was much improved.

**EXERCISE** ④

### Identifying Phrases

**Identify each of the underlined phrases.**

1.  <u>In the past</u>, play was usually unsupervised.                                        _____

2.  Parents <u>seldom made</u> "play dates" for their children.                              _____

3.  <u>Playing on the street or in a vacant lot</u> was the norm.                            _____

4.  <u>Expecting to be entertained</u>, children today often complain of being bored.       _____

5.  They depend on video games <u>to structure their time</u>.                              _____

6.  Parents <u>are spending</u> money on too many movies and video games.                   _____

7.  What is wrong <u>with boredom</u>?                                                       _____

8.  <u>Blessed with restless energy</u>, children could find more creative ways to play.    _____

9.  They need <u>to play outside</u> and get more exercise.  _____

10. <u>A community service project</u> could be a more beneficial outlet for their energy than watching television.  _____

**EXERCISE  5**

### Identifying Phrases

**The following sentences come from a paragraph by John Steinbeck. Identify each of the underlined phrases.**

1.  <u>At dawn</u> Cannery Row seems  _____

2.  <u>to hang suspended</u> out of time  _____

3.  <u>in a silvery light</u>.  _____

4.  The splashing <u>of the waves</u>  _____

5.  <u>can be heard</u>.  _____

6.  <u>Flapping their wings</u>, the seagulls  _____

7.  come <u>to sit</u> on the roof peaks shoulder to shoulder.  _____

8.  Cats drip <u>over the fences</u> and slither like syrup over the ground to look for fishheads.  _____

9.  <u>Silent early morning dogs</u> parade majestically.  _____

10. No automobiles <u>are running</u> then.  _____

**EXERCISE  6**

### Identifying Phrases

**Identify each of the underlined phrases.**

1.  <u>For years</u> scientists debated the existence of global warming.  _____

2.  In the last five years, <u>the serious debate</u> has ended.  _____

3.  <u>Pouring more and more greenhouse gases into the atmosphere</u>, humans are causing the earth to grow warmer.  _____

4.  Massive sections of ice <u>are melting</u> in the Arctic and Antarctic.  _____

5.  Sea levels are projected <u>to rise gradually</u>.  _____

6.  <u>Warming a full degree Fahrenheit since 1970</u>, the oceans are fueling more intense typhoons and hurricanes.  _____

7. <u>By the year 2050</u>, more than a million animal species worldwide may be extinct.

   _____

8. We <u>could be approaching</u> the point of no return.

   _____

9. <u>Curbing greenhouse gases</u> is now a worldwide emergency.

   _____

10. Congress needs <u>to regulate</u> greenhouse gases.

   _____

# THE THREE FUNCTIONS OF THE PRESENT PARTICIPLE

The present participle causes problems for students working with sentence fragments. Because the participle is used sometimes as a verb (in a verb phrase), sometimes as an adjective (in a participial phrase), and sometimes as a noun (in a gerund phrase), it causes a good deal of confusion for students.

The present participle can function in three different ways.

1. The participle functions as a *verb* in a **verb phrase.**

   **The student *was taking* an exam.**

2. The participle functions as an *adjective* in a **participial phrase.**

   ***Taking an exam*, the student felt stressed.**

3. The participle functions as a *noun* in a **gerund phrase.**

   ***Taking an exam* can be stressful.**

In each of these cases, the present participle is part of a phrase. Remember, a phrase is not a sentence.

**EXERCISE 7**

## Using the Present Participle in a Verb Phrase

Below are five present participles. Add a helping verb to each one and use this verb phrase to write a complete sentence of your own. An example follows:

**Present participle:**   sitting

**Verb phrase:**   is sitting

**Sentence:**   The couple is sitting on the balcony.

1. building _____

2. crying _____

3. traveling _____

4. writing _____

5. thinking _____

**EXERCISE 8**

## Using the Present Participle in a Participial Phrase

Each of the following phrases contains a present participle. Use each participial phrase to compose a sentence in which the phrase functions as an adjective. An example follows:

| | |
|---|---|
| **Present participle:** | sitting |
| **Participial phrase:** | sitting on the balcony |
| **Participial phrase used as an adjective in a sentence:** | Sitting on the balcony, the couple enjoyed the moonlight. |

1. building a house

_____

_____

2. crying over the broken vase

_____

_____

3. traveling in Mexico

_____

_____

4. hastily writing the letter

_____

_____

5. thinking about the problem

_____

_____

**EXERCISE 9**

## Using the Present Participle in a Gerund Phrase

Each of the following phrases contains a present participle. Use each gerund phrase to compose a sentence in which the phrase functions as a noun. An example follows:

| | |
|---|---|
| **Present participle:** | sitting |
| **Gerund phrase:** | sitting on the balcony |
| **Gerund phrase used as a noun in a sentence:** | Sitting on the balcony is relaxing. |

1. building a house

_____

_____

2. <u>crying</u> over the broken vase

_____

_____

3. <u>traveling</u> in Mexico

_____

_____

4. hastily <u>writing</u> the letter

_____

_____

5. <u>thinking</u> about the problem

_____

_____

# HOW DO YOU MAKE A COMPLETE SENTENCE FROM A FRAGMENT THAT CONTAINS A PARTICIPLE?

When a participle is used incorrectly, the result is often a fragment. Here are three ways to turn a fragment containing a participle into a sentence.

**Fragment: He _talking_ in his sleep.**

1.  Correct the main verb of the sentence.

    a.  Add a helping verb (such as _is_ or _was_) to the participle to form a verb phrase:

        **He _was talking_ in his sleep.**

    b.  Change the participle to a different form of the verb (such as the past tense).

        **He _talked_ in his sleep.**

2.  Use the participle as an adjective, being sure to provide a subject and verb for the sentence.

    **_Talking in his sleep_, he muttered something about his credit card bills.**

3.  Use the participle as a noun in a gerund phrase.

    **_Talking in his sleep_ revealed his innermost thoughts.**

**EXERCISE 10**

## Correcting the Fragment That Contains a Participle

**Make four complete sentences from each of the following fragments. Use the following model as your guide.**

**Fragment**: using the back stairway

    a.  He <u>is using</u> the back stairway. *(verb phrase)*

    b.  He <u>uses</u> the back stairway. *(simple present tense)*

    c.  <u>Using the back stairway,</u> he got away without being seen. *(participial phrase used as an adjective)*

    d.  <u>Using the back stairway</u> is not a good idea. *(gerund phrase used as a noun)*

1. moving out of the house

    a. _____

    b. _____

    c. _____

    d. _____

2. talking on the telephone

    a. _____

    b. _____

    c. _____

    d. _____

3. driving the car down Highway 60

    a. _____

    b. _____

    c. _____

    d. _____

**EXERCISE 11**

## Correcting the Fragment That Contains a Participle

**The following passage is made up of fragments containing participles. Rewrite the passage, creating complete sentences. Use any of the three correction methods discussed on page 90.**

    I walking through the deserted apartment building. Poking around in piles of junk. Broken furniture left behind. The brick walls crumbling. Water dripping from an overhead pipe. Two children playing in the dismal hallways. Waiting for someone to restore the building to its former glory.

_____

_____

_____

_____

**EXERCISE** ⑫

## Correcting the Fragment That Contains a Participle

The following passage has four fragments containing participles. Place a check in front of each fragment. Then rewrite the passage using complete sentences. Use any of the four correction methods discussed previously.

Finally at age 42 taking my driving test. I felt very nervous. My son was sitting in the back seat. All my papers sitting on the front seat. The inspector got into the car and sat on my insurance form. He looked rather sour and barely spoke to me. Trying not to hit the curb. I parallel parked surprisingly well. I managed to get through all the maneuvers. Now tensely waiting for the results.

_____

_____

_____

_____

_____

**EXERCISE** ⑬

## Correcting Fragments

**Rewrite each fragment so that it is a complete sentence.**

1. early morning a time of peace in my neighborhood

_____

2. the gray mist covering up all but the faint outlines of nearby houses

_____

3. the shapes of cars in the streets and driveways

_____

4. to sit and look out the window

_____

5. holding a steaming cup of coffee

_____

6. the only sound the rumbling of a truck

_____

7. passing by on the highway a quarter mile away

_____

8. children all in their beds

_____

9.   no barking dogs

_____

10.   in this soft, silent dreamworld

_____

**EXERCISE** **14**

## Correcting Fragments

**Each of the following groups of words is a phrase. First, name each phrase. Then, make each phrase into a complete sentence.**

1.   two champion boxers

   Name of phrase: _____

   Sentence: _____

   _____

2.   to watch the fight

   Name of phrase: _____

   Sentence: _____

   _____

3.   in the ring

   Name of phrase: _____

   Sentence: _____

   _____

4.   are punching each other

   Name of phrase: _____

   Sentence: _____

   _____

5.   at the sound of the bell

   Name of phrases: _____

   Sentence: _____

   _____

6.   gratefully supported

   Name of phrase: _____

   Sentence: _____

   _____

7.   to referee the fight

   Name of phrase: _____

   Sentence: _____

   _____

8.  the screaming fans

    Name of phrase: _____

    Sentence: _____

    _____

9.  by the second round

    Name of phrase: _____

    Sentence: _____

    _____

10. knocked unconscious

    Name of phrase: _____

    Sentence: _____

    _____

# MASTERY AND EDITING TESTS

**TEST 1**

## Recognizing and Correcting the Fragment

The following description of people on a dance floor at the Peppermint Lounge appeared in The *New Yorker* in the 1960s. The description is made up entirely of fragments. Rewrite the description, making each fragment into a sentence.

Place always jammed. Huge line outside. Portals closely guarded. Finally made it last night, after hour's wait. Exhilarating experience! Feel ten years younger. Hit Peppermint close to midnight, in blue mood. Inside, found pandemonium. Dance floor packed and popping. Was battered by wild swinging of hips and elbows. Some couples in evening dress, others in T shirts and blue jeans. Young. Old. Businessmen. Crew Cuts. Beatniks.

_____

_____

_____

_____

_____

_____

_____

_____

_____

_____

_____

_____

_____

_____

_____

_____

TEST **2**

## Recognizing and Correcting the Fragment

The following paragraph contains seven fragments. Read the paragraph and place a check in front of each fragment. Then rewrite the paragraph, being careful to use only complete sentences.

That afternoon the street was full of children. Taking a shower in the rain. Soaping themselves and rushing out into the storm. To wash off the suds. In a few minutes, it was all over. Including the rubdown. The younger children took their showers naked. Teetering on the tips of their toes and squealing to one another. The stately coconut palm in one corner of the patio. Thrashed its branches high over the dripping children bouncing on the cobblestones.

_____

_____

_____

_____

_____

_____

_____

_____

_____

_____

_____

TEST **3**

## Editing Student Writing: Recognizing and Correcting the Fragment

The following paragraph contains six fragments. Read the paragraph and place a check in front of each fragment. Then rewrite the paragraph, being careful to use only complete sentences.

We called it our house. It was only one room. With about as much space as a tent. Painted in a pastel color with a red-tiled roof. The front window reaching nearly from the sidewalk to the roof. We could look up and down the street.

Sitting indoors on the window seat. Our kitchen was a small narrow area. With the brick stove and two benches to serve as shelves. Three steel bars and a short piece of lead pipe from a scrap heap to make a grate.

_____

_____

_____

_____

_____

_____

_____

_____

_____

_____

_____

## TEST 4   Editing Student Writing Using Editing Symbols

As you learned in Test 4 of Chapter 4 (page 74), instructors often use editing symbols to mark errors in student writing. The editing symbol for a fragment is frag. In the paragraph below, find five fragments (frag) and five errors in subject-verb agreement (agr). Mark each error with the commonly used editing symbol, and then correct the errors on the lines provided following the paragraph.

[1]My younger brother is happy about his first job at McDonald's. [2] The most popular fast food restaurant. [3]His cousin and a friend also works here. [4]His uniform, a blue and white striped shirt with blue pants, are provided for free. [5]One of the employees show him the register. [6]Everyone learn all the different jobs. [7]Either the manager or the trainer tell him about the importance of patience. [8]Getting along with other people, too. [9]You start at the bottom. [10]Slowly working up the ladder. [11]After six months, a supervisor reviews your work. [12]Some workers in the group get a raise and become crew trainers. [13]One big disadvantage. [14]Low pay!

**Five corrected fragments**

1. _____

   _____

2. _____

3. _____

4. _____

5. _____

**Five subject-verb agreement corrections**

Subject                                           Correct form of the verb

6. _____        _____

7. _____        _____

8. _____        _____

9. _____        _____

10. _____        _____

## Exploring Online

Go to **www.cengage.com/devenglish/scarry/writersworkplace** to find the **Writer's Online Workplace**, a website designed for students using this book. You will find links to handouts, interactive quizzes, and other online resources as you explore the following topics:

- sentence fragments
- verbal phrases (infinitive, participial, and gerund phrases)

# Working Together

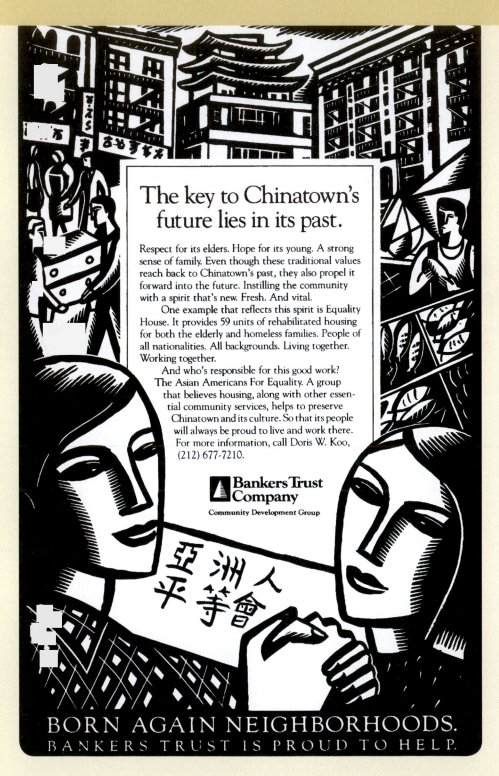

The key to Chinatown's future lies in its past.

Respect for its elders. Hope for its young. A strong sense of family. Even though these traditional values reach back to Chinatown's past, they also propel it forward into the future. Instilling the community with a spirit that's new. Fresh. And vital.

One example that reflects this spirit is Equality House. It provides 59 units of rehabilitated housing for both the elderly and homeless families. People of all nationalities. All backgrounds. Living together. Working together.

And who's responsible for this good work? The Asian Americans For Equality. A group that believes housing, along with other essential community services, helps to preserve Chinatown and its culture. So that its people will always be proud to live and work there. For more information, call Doris W. Koo, (212) 677-7210.

**Bankers Trust Company**
Community Development Group

BORN AGAIN NEIGHBORHOODS.
BANKERS TRUST IS PROUD TO HELP.

## EXAMINING AN ADVERTISEMENT FOR FRAGMENTS

1. Advertising companies devote a great deal of their time and attention to market research. This research helps the company target its message to the most likely audience for its product or service. Who is the advertiser in this newspaper ad? Who is the intended audience? What is the product or service being advertised?

2. Like many advertisements we see in magazines and newspapers, this Bankers Trust Company advertisement is made up of short, snappy constructions that are not always complete sentences. Advertisers write in this way because they want to attract our attention. However, when we write for school or for work, our compositions must be made up of only complete sentences. Review the advertisement at the left. Each of the three paragraphs contains mostly fragments. Underline each fragment you can find. With your classmates, rewrite the ad correcting all the fragments. Consider all the different answers and judge them for correctness. If needed, review the two ways to correct a fragment (page 81).

## PORTFOLIO SUGGESTION

Choose a product or a service that particularly appeals to you. Clip newspaper or magazine ads, or both, that deal with this product or service. Take notes on television ads or billboard ads. Review them at a later time for possible use in comparison or contrast essays.

# 6

# COMBINING SENTENCES USING THREE OPTIONS FOR COORDINATION

In this chapter, you will practice the three ways of creating a **compound sentence.** When you use any one of these three options to combine simple sentences into a single compound sentence, you are using **coordination.** You will learn these three options:

## WHAT IS COORDINATION?

So far you have worked with the simple sentence. If you review some of these sentences (such as the practice sentences on page 35), you will see that writing only simple sentences results in a choppy style and also makes it difficult to express complicated ideas. You will need to learn how to combine simple sentences correctly by using *coordination.* To understand coordination, be sure you know the meaning of the following three terms.

> A **clause** is a group of words that has a subject and a verb:
>
> **she spoke**
>
> **when she spoke**

**NOTE:** Of the two clauses above, only *she spoke* could be a sentence. The clause *when she spoke* could not stand alone as a sentence because it does not express a complete thought. (Chapter 7 will cover this second type of clause.)

> An ***independent clause*** is a clause that can stand alone as a simple sentence:
>
> **She spoke.**

> A ***compound sentence*** is a sentence that is created when two or more independent clauses are correctly joined, using the rules of coordination:
>
> **She spoke, and we listened.**

The three preceding terms are all part of the definition of coordination.

> ***Coordination*** is the combining of two or more related independent clauses (you may think of them as simple sentences) that contain ideas of equal importance. The result is a **compound sentence.**
>
> **Two independent clauses:**      **She spoke. We listened.**
>
> **Compound sentence:**            **She spoke, and we listened.**

# FIRST OPTION FOR COORDINATION: USING A COMMA PLUS A COORDINATING CONJUNCTION

The most common way to form a compound sentence is to combine independent clauses using a comma plus a coordinating conjunction.

## First Option for Coordination

| Independent clause | Comma and coordinating conjunction | Independent clause |
|---|---|---|
| I had worked hard | , so | I expected results. |

You will need to memorize the list of coordinating conjunctions given below. By doing this now, you will avoid confusion later on when you will be using a different set of conjunctions to combine clauses.

## Connectors: Coordinating Conjunctions

| | | | |
|---|---|---|---|
| and | but | for (meaning *because*) | so |
| nor | yet | or | |

**Practice**

In each of the following compound sentences, draw a single line under the subject and draw two lines under the verb for each independent clause. Then circle both the coordinating conjunction and the comma. An example follows:

The speaker rose to his feet, and the room became quiet.

1. The audience was packed  for this was a man with an international reputation.

2. He could have told about all his successes   but  instead he spoke about his disappointments.

3. His words were electric   so  the crowd was attentive.

4. I should have brought a tape recorder  or at least I should have taken notes.

Did you find a subject and verb for both independent clauses in each sentence? Now that you understand the structure of a compound sentence, be sure you understand the meanings of the different coordinating conjunctions. Keep in mind that these conjunctions are used to show the relationship between two ideas that have equal importance.

# Coordinating Conjunctions and Their Meanings

| CONJUNCTION | MEANING | EXAMPLE |
|---|---|---|
| **and** | to add an idea | He will call today, *and* he will call tomorrow. |
| **nor** | to add an idea when both clauses are in the negative | He will not call today, *nor* will he call tomorrow. |
| **but** | to contrast two opposing ideas | He will call today, *but* he might not call tomorrow. |
| **yet** | to emphasize the contrast between two opposing ideas (meaning: *and despite this fact*) | He promised to call today, *yet* he did not. |
| **for** | to introduce a reason | He will call today, *for* he wants a loan. |
| **or** | to show a choice | He will call today, *or* he will call tomorrow. |
| **so** | to introduce a result | He will call today, *so* I must stay home. |

**EXERCISE** **1**    Combining Sentences Using Coordinating Conjunctions

For each of the following compound sentences, choose the coordinating conjunction that best supports the meaning of the sentence. Circle the letter corresponding to your choice.

1. The two detectives carefully checked the scene for fingerprints, _____ they could not find one clear print. (contrast)

   a. so          b. but          c. nor          d. or

2. The safe was open, _____ a single bag of coins remained. (add)

   a. but          b. and          c. or          d. for

3. There was no sign of forced entry, _____ they believed it was probably an inside job. (result)

   a. so          b. nor          c. but          d. or

4. The restaurant owner could not be found, _____ could the two waiters be located. (add, both clauses are in the negative)

   a. and          b. for          c. so          d. nor

5. Suddenly they became interested in one of the tables, _____ the surface seemed splattered with blood. (reason)

   a. and          b. for          c. yet          d. so

6. The missing tablecloth could also be significant, _____ they took photographs of the other tablecloths. (result)

   a. nor          b. so          c. but          d. or

7. One detective looked in the closets, _____ he decided they contained nothing significant. (contrast)

   a. or          b. so          c. but          d. nor

8. They might find another clue, _____ the blood stains may be their only evidence. (choice)

   a. or          b. yet          c. nor          d. but

9. There were no witnesses, _____ maybe DNA would tell a story. (contrast)

   a. for          b. nor          c. or          d. but

10. Either they get a break in the case, _____ the mystery may never be solved. (choice)

    a. and          b. nor          c. so          d. or

**EXERCISE 2**

## Combining Sentences Using Coordinating Conjunctions

**Below are ten sentences. Some of them are compound sentences needing a comma and a coordinating conjunction. Some of them are simple sentences**

(with only compound subjects or compound verbs). These do not require a comma. Fill in each blank with a comma (if required) and a coordinating conjunction that best supports the meaning of the sentence.

1.  The San Francisco Earthquake of 1906 may have shaken down hundreds of buildings _____ the fire that followed destroyed nearly everything left standing.

2.  One hour after the earthquake smoke could be seen from one hundred miles away _____ for three days and nights the sky was filled with smoke.

3.  Outside the city not a flicker of wind stirred _____ the heated air of the fire produced an enormous gale within the city.

4.  This gale-force wind fed the flames _____ quickly spread the fire.

5.  Firefighters tried valiantly to save buildings _____ before long the flames would reappear on all sides and destroy the structures.

6.  The stories of many heroic deeds will never be told _____ will the number of dead ever be known.

7.  The flames could not be stopped _____ people had no choice but to flee.

8.  People pulling heavy trunks up and down the steep hills of the city eventually had to abandon them _____ their survival depended on moving more quickly.

9.  Tens of thousands of refugees camped around the city _____ fled to surrounding cities.

10. Nothing much remained of San Francisco following the fire except for memories _____ a few homes on the outskirts of the city.

**EXERCISE 3**

## Combining Sentences Using Coordinating Conjunctions

The simple sentences in each of the following pairs could be combined with a coordinating conjunction. Decide what relationship the second sentence has to the first, and then choose the conjunction that makes the most sense. Write your compound sentence on the line provided. Use the following model as your guide.

**Two simple sentences:**        **She broke her arm.**

                                 **She couldn't play in the finals.**

**Relationship of second sentence to first:**        result

**Conjunction that introduces this meaning:**        so

**Compound sentence:**        She broke her arm, SO she couldn't play in the finals.

1.   Mr. Watson is kind and patient.

     His brother is sharp and nagging.

     Relationship of second sentence to first:          _____

     Conjunction that introduces this meaning:       _____

     _____

     _____

2.   The two adults are having great difficulty.

     They are trying to raise a teenager.

     Relationship of second sentence to first:          _____

     Conjunction that introduces this meaning:       _____

     _____

3.   Young Michael has no family of his own.

     He feels angry and alone.

     Relationship of second sentence to first:          _____

     Conjunction that introduces this meaning:       _____

     _____

4.   Michael hasn't been doing well in school.

     He isn't involved in any activities outside school.

     Relationship of second sentence to first:          _____
                                                        _____

     Conjunction that introduces this meaning:       _____

     _____

     _____

5.   Mr. Watson encouraged Michael to do volunteer work at the hospital.

     This might give Michael the satisfaction of helping other people.

     Relationship of second sentence to first:          _____

     Conjunction that introduces this meaning:       _____

     _____

     _____

6.   Mr. Watson's brother wanted Michael to spend more time on his homework.

     He also wanted him to get a job after school to help with expenses.

     Relationship of second sentence to first:          _____

     Conjunction that introduces this meaning:       _____

_____

_____

7.  Michael liked going to the hospital.

He was doing something important.

Relationship of second sentence to first:    _____

Conjunction that introduces this meaning:    _____

_____

_____

8.  He didn't earn any money.

He liked helping people.

Relationship of second sentence to first:    _____

_____

Conjunction that introduces this meaning:    _____

_____

_____

9.  Michael has decided to have a career working in a hospital.

He now has a reason to work harder in school.

Relationship of second sentence to first:    _____

Conjunction that introduces this meaning:    _____

_____

_____

10.  Mr. Watson thinks the hospital volunteer work was a good idea.

His brother has to agree.

Relationship of second sentence to first:    _____

Conjunction that introduces this meaning:    _____

_____

_____

# SECOND OPTION FOR COORDINATION: USING A SEMICOLON, AN ADVERBIAL CONJUNCTION, AND A COMMA

The second way to form a compound sentence is to combine independent clauses by using a semicolon, an adverbial conjunction, and a comma.

<br>

> # Second Option for Coordination
>
> | Independent clause | Semicolon, adverbial conjunction, and comma | Independent clause |
> |---|---|---|
> | **I had worked hard** | **; therefore,** | **I expected results.** |

*Note: In some grammar books,* adverbial conjunctions *are called* conjunctive adverbs.

The conjunctions used for this option are called **adverbial conjunctions.** These conjunctions are similar in meaning to the common coordinating conjunctions, but they sound more formal than the shorter conjunctions such as *and* or *but*. Using these adverbial conjunctions gives more emphasis to the clause than using coordinating conjunctions.

**Less emphasis:**     He was late, and he had the wrong documents.

**More emphasis:**     He was late; furthermore, he had the wrong documents.

Just as you memorized the list of coordinating conjunctions on page 101, you should memorize the following list of adverbial conjunctions.

## Connectors: Frequently Used Adverbial Conjunctions

| Addition *(and)* | Contrast *(but)* | Alternative *(or)* | Result *(so)* | Likeness | Emphasis | To show time |
|---|---|---|---|---|---|---|
| in addition | however | instead | accordingly | likewise | indeed | meanwhile |
| also | nevertheless | on the other hand | hence | similarly | in fact | |
| besides | nonetheless | otherwise | therefore | | | |
| furthermore | | | thus | | | |
| moreover | | | | | | |

**Practice**

In each of the following compound sentences, draw a single line under the subject and draw two lines under the verb for both independent clauses. Then circle the semicolon, adverbial conjunction, and comma. An example follows:

The jet was the fastest way to get there (; moreover,) it was the most comfortable.

1. The restaurant is always too crowded on Saturdays ; nevertheless,  it serves the best food in town.

2. The land was not for sale ; however,  the house could be rented.

3. The lawsuit cost the company several million dollars ; consequently,  the company went out of business a short time later.

4. The doctor told him to lose weight ; furthermore,  she instructed him to stop smoking.

## EXERCISE ④   Combining Sentences Using Adverbial Conjunctions

The simple sentences in each of the following pairs could be combined by using an adverbial conjunction. Decide on the relationship between the two sentences, and circle the letter of the adverbial conjunction that makes the most sense.

1. Women are supposed to talk more than men.

   This may not always be true.

   a. thus                 b. moreover

   c. also                 d. however

2. The cell phone has become a part of everyday life.

   Researchers have become interested in this new area of study.

   a. furthermore          b. therefore

   c. on the other hand    d. nonetheless

3. Researchers began with a popular assumption about women and men.

   They found the results of the study led to an opposite conclusion.

   a. thus                 b. nonetheless

   c. also                 d. likewise

4. Women use their wireless phones 377 minutes a month.

   Men, on average, use their wireless phones a good deal more—438 minutes a month.

   a. on the other hand    b. therefore

   c. thus                 d. likewise

5. Men can be seen using their phones almost everywhere.

   Women use their phones mostly at home.

   a. similarly            b. in addition

   c. however              d. accordingly

6. Men use their phones in very public places.

   They prefer to conduct a great deal of their business in this way.

   a. however              b. meanwhile

   c. indeed               d. otherwise

7. Women still rule the traditional phones at home.

   Women talk 544 minutes a month at home compared with men's use of just 314 minutes.

   a. however              b. in fact

   c. besides              d. meanwhile

8.  Researchers counted the number of times men used their cell phones.

    They listened carefully to the male tone of voice.

    a.  otherwise          b.  therefore

    c.  in addition        d.  instead

9.  The use of cell phones in public is annoying to many.

    The use of cell phones while driving can be dangerous.

    a.  therefore          b.  furthermore

    c.  otherwise          d.  nevertheless

10. The cell phone is relatively new technology.

    Companies are hopeful about people's increased use of the cell phone.

    a.  likewise           b.  in addition

    c.  accordingly        d.  meanwhile

**EXERCISE 5**

### Combining Sentences Using Adverbial Conjunctions

The simple sentences in each of the following pairs could be combined by using an adverbial conjunction. Decide what relationship the second sentence has to the first, and then choose the adverbial conjunction that makes the most sense. Be careful to punctuate correctly. An example follows:

> Our family would like to purchase a computer, ; in addition, _____
>   ʷWe would like to buy a fax machine.

1.  In the past, people wrote with pen or pencil. _____

    The computer has now become the favorite writing tool.

2.  Computers provide a powerful way to create documents. _____

    They are essential for storing large amounts of information efficiently.

3.  At first, some feared the use of electronics for creating written work. _____

    Nearly all have now overcome their fears.

4.  Computers have already revolutionized today's offices. _____

    No modern business can afford to be without them.

5.  Most students are using computers in the classroom. _____

    Many students are e-mailing homework to their teachers from home computers.

6.  The prices of many computers are coming down these days. _____
    Owning a computer is a real possibility for more people.

7.  Some children know more about computers than many adults. _____
    Some children are teaching the adults.

8.  Professional writers have become enthusiastic about the use of computers. _____
    Some writers still use yellow pads.

9.  The electronic revolution is barreling ahead. _____
    The nation faces a great challenge to keep up with it.

10. We have many technological aids to writing. _____
    The source for all our ideas remains the human brain.

**EXERCISE  6**

### Combining Sentences Using Adverbial Conjunctions

Add an adverbial conjunction and an independent clause to each of the following sentences to form a compound sentence that makes sense. Choose from the following adverbial conjunctions: *consequently, furthermore, however, in fact, instead, meanwhile, moreover, nevertheless, otherwise, therefore.* Remember to punctuate correctly. An example follows:

Members of the congressional committee met every day.

Members of the congressional committee met every day **; nonetheless, they could not agree on the proposal.**

1.  The employees were told the good news.

    _____

2.  The novel was very well written.

    _____

3.  The snow kept falling.

    _____

4.  The employment rates have been rising.

    _____

5.  Several bridges need replacement.

    _____

6.    The job included health benefits.

_____

7.    The volunteer repainted the walls.

_____

8.    The reporter worked feverishly for days to research the story.

_____

9.    The inspector was suspicious.

_____

10.    The couple chose to refinance their home.

_____

# THIRD OPTION FOR COORDINATION: USING A SEMICOLON

A third and less commonly used way to form a compound sentence is to combine two independent clauses by using only a semicolon.

| Third Option for Coordination | | |
|---|---|---|
| Independent clause | Semicolon | Independent clause |
| I had worked hard | ; | I expected results. |

You might choose the semicolon if the grammatical structure of each independent clause is similar or if the ideas in each independent clause are very closely related.

In the following sentence, the grammatical structure of each independent clause is similar:

**The women pitched the tents; the men cooked the dinner.**

In the following sentence, the two independent clauses contain closely related ideas:

**The women pitched the tents; they were proud of their work.**

**EXERCISE  7**

## Combining Sentences Using the Semicolon

Read each of the following sentences. If the sentence is a compound sentence that requires a semicolon, insert the semicolon where needed. If the sentence requires no punctuation, leave it as is.

1.  The assistant wrote the speech  the manager delivered it at the national meeting.

2.  The man stood in front of me  the others stood to the side.

3.  The apartment was light and airy  the property was neat and clean.

4.  Shoppers were pushing grocery carts down the aisles workers were stocking the shelves.

5.  My sister plans to learn three foreign languages in the next four years.

6.  He worked in the stockroom counting inventory his coworkers handled the customers.

7.  He tried to explain  nobody gave him a chance.

8.  Many teenagers spend hours playing video games they neglect their studies.

9.  The forum was an annual gathering for poets and friends of poetry.

10. Ming-Na agreed to take the teaching position she turned down a job singing backup in a rock band.

**EXERCISE  8**

## Combining Sentences Using the Semicolon

Create a compound sentence by adding a semicolon and another independent clause to each of the following sentences. Both clauses in each compound sentence must have similar grammatical structures or have closely related ideas. Use the following example as your model.

**Simple sentence:**      Weight loss programs encourage proper nutrition.

**Compound sentence:**    Weight loss programs encourage proper nutrition; these programs also encourage consistent exercise.

1.  Some people live to eat.

    _____

    _____

2.  Children drink too much soda.

    _____

3.  White bread is not a healthy food choice.

_____

_____

4.  One very healthy exercise is jumping rope.

_____

_____

5.  Overweight children need healthy school lunch programs.

_____

_____

Before taking the mastery tests at the end of this chapter, review the information presented in the chapter by studying the following chart. (The same information can also be found on the inside front cover of this textbook.)

---

## Three Options for Coordination

### OPTION 1

Independent clause + **Comma and coordinating conjunction** *(and, nor, but, yet, for, or, so)* + Independent clause

I had worked hard, *so* I expected results.

### OPTION 2

Independent clause + **Semicolon, adverbial conjunction, and comma** + Independent clause

*(also, instead, nonetheless, likewise, besides, on the other hand, accordingly, similarly, in addition, otherwise, hence, indeed, furthermore, however, therefore, in fact, moreover, nevertheless, thus, meanwhile)*

I had worked hard; *therefore*, I expected results.

### OPTION 3

Independent clause + Semicolon + Independent clause

I had worked hard; I expected results.

" Your vital signs are all healthy... "

# MASTERY AND EDITING TESTS

TEST **1**

## Combining Sentences Using Coordination

**In the blank to the left of each group of four sentences, write the letter of the sentence that is the correct example of coordination.**

____ 1.  a.  Childhood obesity has doubled in the last twenty years in fact nine million children in this country are overweight.

   b.  Childhood obesity has doubled in the last twenty years, in fact nine million children in this country are overweight.

   c.  Childhood obesity has doubled in the last twenty years; in fact nine million children in this country are overweight.

   d.  Childhood obesity has doubled in the last twenty years; in fact, nine million children in this country are overweight.

____ 2.  a.  Childhood obesity leads to other health problems such as type 2 diabetes, high cholesterol, and hypertension so we must find ways to get this epidemic under control.

   b.  Childhood obesity leads to other health problems, such as type 2 diabetes, high cholesterol, and hypertension so we must find ways to get this epidemic under control.

   c.  Childhood obesity leads to other health problems such as type 2 diabetes and high cholesterol, so we must find ways to get this epidemic under control.

   d.  Childhood obesity leads to other health problems, such as type 2 diabetes and high cholesterol; so we must find ways to get this epidemic under control.

____ 3. a. Children should walk to school whenever possible they should walk the dog, do yard work, and play outside.

b. Children should walk to school whenever possible, they should walk the dog, do yard work, and play outside.

c. Children should walk to school whenever possible; they should walk the dog, do yard work, and play outside.

d. Children should walk to school whenever possible; they, should walk the dog, do yard work, and play outside.

____ 4. a. Sodas and other sugary beverages should be avoided instead pure water and milk should be encouraged.

b. Sodas and other sugary beverages should be avoided, instead pure water and milk should be encouraged.

c. Sodas and other sugary beverages should be avoided; instead pure water and milk should be encouraged.

d. Sodas and other sugary beverages should be avoided; instead, pure water and milk should be encouraged.

____ 5. a. It is important not to skip meals furthermore these meals should be eaten at regular times each day in order for the body to maintain energy.

b. It is important not to skip meals, furthermore these meals should be eaten at regular times each day in order for the body to maintain energy.

c. It is important not to skip meals, furthermore; these meals should be eaten at regular times each day in order for the body to maintain energy.

d. It is important not to skip meals; furthermore, these meals should be eaten at regular times each day in order for the body to maintain energy.

**TEST 2**

## Combining Sentences Using Coordination

**In the blank to the left of each group of four sentences, write the letter of the sentence that is a correct example of coordination.**

____ 1. a. The theater was crowded, consequently, not everyone could get a good seat.

b. The theater was crowded; consequently not everyone could get a good seat.

c. The theater was crowded, so not everyone could get a good seat.

d. The theater was crowded; so not everyone could get a good seat.

____ 2. a. The first apartment had no bedroom but it had a large beautiful living room.

b. The first apartment had no bedroom, however, it had a large beautiful living room.

    c.  The first apartment had no bedroom; nevertheless, it had a large beautiful living room.

    d.  The first apartment had no bedroom; yet it had a large beautiful living room.

_____ 3.  a.  January had been bitterly cold; therefore, few people had attended the festival.

    b.  January had been bitterly cold, however, few people had attended the festival.

    c.  January had been bitterly cold also few people had attended the festival.

    d.  January had been bitterly cold; in addition few people had attended the festival.

_____ 4.  a.  The community waited for the news, nonetheless the crew kept digging.

    b.  The community waited for the news; and the crew kept digging.

    c.  The community waited for the news; meanwhile, the crew kept digging.

    d.  The community waited for the news, yet, the crew kept digging.

_____ 5.  a.  The village should balance its budget, likewise the taxes will have to be raised.

    b.  The village should balance its budget; otherwise, the taxes will have to be raised.

    c.  The village should balance its budget, besides the taxes will have to be raised.

    d.  The village should balance its budget; or the taxes will have to be raised.

**TEST 3**

## Editing Student Writing: Combining Sentences Using Coordination

After reading the following paragraph, find three places where you could combine two simple sentences into a compound sentence using coordination. Use each of the three options learned in this chapter to form new compound sentences. Write your new sentences on the lines provided after the paragraph.

My children were still in college. My old job with an accounting firm had ended. I needed to earn some money. The thought of a new job made me nervous. What would it be like? Then I saw an ad for openings with Old Navy. I decided to apply. They offered a salary plus a good discount for employees. At the interview, I was the only person over twenty-five. They must have liked me. They hired me the next day! I was sent to their largest downtown location. The first day on the job was scary. I was assigned to a "buddy." The young woman could have been one of my daughters. She explained how to be in control of the stockroom. She showed me how to use a scanner to find out the current price of an item. She advised me on how to keep items on hold for customers. She gave me a feeling of confidence. I never thought I would feel that way. My spirit was willing. I learned a lot. My feet hurt by the end of the first day. I spent half of my first month's salary on Old Navy clothes. I had wanted new clothes for a long time. Some of the clothes were for myself. Some of the clothes were for my daughters.

Option 1:  _____

_____

_____

Option 2:  _____

_____

_____

Option 3:  _____

_____

_____

**TEST 4**

## Editing Student Writing Using Editing Symbols

The editing symbol for an error in coordination is coord. In the following paragraph, find five errors in coordination (coord), two fragments (frag), and three subject-verb agreement errors (agr). Mark the errors with the commonly used editing symbols, and then correct these errors on the lines provided after the paragraph.

¹Sometimes hardships make a person stronger. ²Even in childhood. ³My mother has always been sickly so I have learned to be independent. ⁴It has happened gradually. ⁵The phone would ring I would answer it. ⁶Here is some of my weekly duties. ⁷I help my brothers with their homework and go to their baseball games. ⁸I cook nightly dinners once a week I do the grocery shopping. ⁹Friends of our family feels sorry for us but we are not unhappy. ¹⁰Especially sitting around the fire at night in the family room. ¹¹During the last few years, my father and I have become very close. ¹²I have learned from adversity in fact I have found strength for the future. ¹³The knowledge of my father's love, kindness, and generosity remain my inspiration.

**Five coordination corrections**

1.  _____

_____

2. _____

3. _____

   _____

4. _____

   _____

5. _____

   _____

**Two corrected fragments**

6. _____

7. _____

   _____

**Three subject-verb agreement corrections**

|     | **Subject**                    | **Correct form of the verb**       |
| --- | ------------------------------ | ---------------------------------- |
| 8.  | _____ | _____ |
| 9.  | _____ | _____ |
| 10. | _____ | _____ |

## Exploring Online

Coordination and subordination are often studied together, and the skills needed for one are critical for the other. See the Exploring Online feature at the end of Chapter 7 for online work involving coordination and subordination.

# Working Together

## SUMMARIZING A CLASS DISCUSSION: WHAT IS A FAIR SALARY?

We often hear people expressing outrage at the salaries some people earn. For instance, sports figures and entertainers enjoy multimillion-dollar salaries, whereas daycare employees and postal workers, who have serious responsibilities in their jobs, earn a small fraction of that money in their lifetimes.

Discuss this topic in class, making sure that each person has the opportunity to express an opinion. Choose one person to record the important points made during the class discussion. These points should be written on the board even though everyone is responsible for keeping his or her own notes. While discussing this topic, keep the following questions in mind:

## Questions for Group Discussion

1. How are salaries set in our society? Give specific examples, based on your own experience and what you have learned from the media.

2. What is today's minimum wage? Is it possible for a person to live on a salary based on that minimum wage?

3. From time to time, there are discussions and disagreements among business and government leaders as to what the minimum wage should be—or even if there should be a minimum wage at all. What should be the minimum wage? In view of what entertainers and sports stars earn, should there be a *maximum* wage law?

4. How should society judge the value of some people's work over the work of others? In what kind of society could everyone receive the same salary, or is that not a desirable goal?

Following the class discussion, each student should use board notes and class notes to write a summary of the discussion. Remember that the summary must include all the important ideas that the discussion generated. If time permits, several students should read their summaries out loud. Did members of the class agree on the major points?

## PORTFOLIO SUGGESTION

Material such as the notes you have just taken on the class discussion can become part of the prewriting stage for an essay on this topic or a related topic. Save your notes and your summary in case you want to use the material for a future essay.

# 7

# COMBINING SENTENCES USING SUBORDINATION

In this chapter, you will learn how **subordination** is used to form **complex sentences.** This will involve the following skills:

**CHAPTER OBJECTIVES**

- Recognizing the difference between an independent clause and a dependent clause.
- Understanding the two options for combining an independent clause with a dependent clause that begins with a subordinating conjunction:

  > begin with the dependent clause and use a comma

  > begin with the independent clause and do not use a comma

- Understanding how to combine an independent clause with a dependent clause that begins with a relative pronoun:

  > use commas in a sentence with a relative clause that is non-essential to the main idea

  > do not use commas in a sentence with a relative clause that is essential to the main idea

  > place the relative pronoun and its clause immediately following the word to which it is related

## WHAT IS SUBORDINATION?

In Chapter 6, when you studied *coordination,* you learned that both clauses in a *compound sentence* are independent clauses. In *subordination,* only one clause can be an independent clause. Any other clause must be a dependent clause. Such a dependent clause is dependent on (that is, subordinate to) the independent clause, and together these clauses make up a *complex sentence.*

> **Subordination** is the method of combining two clauses that contain ideas not equally important. The more important idea is in the **independent clause,** and the less important idea is in the **dependent clause.** The result is a **complex sentence.**

**Independent clause:**       **We listened.**

**Dependent clause:**        **when she spoke**

**Complex sentences:**       **We listened when she spoke.**

                  **When she spoke, we listened.**

# THE DIFFERENCE BETWEEN AN INDEPENDENT CLAUSE AND A DEPENDENT CLAUSE

An *independent clause* stands alone as a complete thought; it could be a simple sentence.

**Independent clause:**   **I drank the water.**

A *dependent clause* begins with a connecting word, and even though the clause contains a subject and a verb, it does not stand alone as a complete thought. The idea is not complete.

**Dependent clause:**      **When I drank the water, . . .**

Before you write your own complex sentences, practice the following exercises to be sure you recognize the difference between an independent clause and a dependent clause.

**EXERCISE  1**

## Identifying Dependent and Independent Clauses

In the blank to the left of each group of words, write *IC* if the group of words is an independent clause (a complete thought) or *DC* if the group of words is a dependent clause (not a complete thought, even though it contains a subject and a verb).

____  1.  Americans adore pets

____  2.  although high-end pet food is very expensive

____  3.  when Fifi needs the right cut

____  4.  some pet stylists can earn one hundred dollars an hour

____  5.  many pet owners take their pets to daycare

____  6.  because pet play groups encourage socialization

____  7.  since veterinarians now treat animal obesity

____  8.  animals can be treated for skin disorders at an animal dermatologist

____ 9. pets have been shown to lower their owner's blood pressure

____ 10. even if some pets have been known to bite

**EXERCISE 2**

**Identifying Dependent and Independent Clauses**

In the blank to the left of each group of words, write *IC* if the group of words is an independent clause (a complete thought) or *DC* if the group of words is a dependent clause (not a complete thought, even though it contains a subject and a verb).

____ 1. William Faulkner was a regional writer

____ 2. he was born near Oxford, Mississippi

____ 3. where he lived and died

____ 4. even if he used the dialect of the area

____ 5. some of his books share the same characters and themes

____ 6. because Faulkner devoted many pages to greed, violence, and meanness

____ 7. until the year he died

____ 8. he won the Nobel Prize in 1950

____ 9. when he was recognized as one of America's greatest writers

____ 10. although Faulkner departed from the traditional style of prose

**EXERCISE 3**

**Identifying Dependent and Independent Clauses**

In the blank to the left of each group of words, write *IC* if the group of words is an independent clause (a complete thought) or *DC* if the group of words is a dependent clause (not a complete thought, even though it contains a subject and a verb).

____ 1. J.K. Rowling wrote her first book in a cafe

____ 2. while her infant daughter slept

____ 3. in one day, her first book sold seven million copies

____ 4. although the book was hundreds of pages long

____ 5. the success of the Harry Potter series has been astonishing

____ 6. Harry Potter Mania swept the country

____ 7. since the publication of the fourth book, *Harry Potter and the Goblet of Fire*

____ 8. bookstores have been holding midnight extravaganzas to release each new book in the series

___  9.  J.K. Rowling kept writing for seventeen years

___  10.  until she finished the last book in the series, *Harry Potter and the Deathly Hallows*

# USING SUBORDINATING CONJUNCTIONS

In *coordination,* you combined ideas by using connecting words called *coordinating conjunctions* and *adverbial conjunctions.* In *subordination,* you combine ideas by using two different sets of connecting words called *subordinating conjunctions* and *relative pronouns.* Begin this section by memorizing the list of subordinating conjunctions given in the chart below.

## Connectors: Frequently Used Subordinating Conjunctions

| | | |
|---|---|---|
| after | in order that | unless |
| although | once | until |
| as, as if | provided that | when, whenever |
| as long as, as though | rather than | where, wherever |
| because | since | whereas |
| before | so that | whether |
| even though | though | while |
| if, even if | | |

**We all went out for pizza *after the game was over.***

In the above sentence, the dependent clause *after the game was over* contains a subject *(game)* and a verb *(was).* The word *after* functions as a subordinating conjunction that joins the two clauses. The result is a *complex sentence* because the sentence contains an independent clause and a dependent clause.

However, many of the words in this chart may also function as prepositions.

**We all went out for pizza *after the game.***

In the above sentence, *after* functions as a preposition that introduces the prepositional phrase *after the game.* The sentence is a *simple sentence* because it contains only one independent clause.

In the next practice, see whether you can spot the difference between a word used as a preposition in a prepositional phrase and a word used as a subordinating conjunction at the beginning of a dependent clause.

**Practice**

Identify each of the following groups of words as a prepositional phrase (PP) or a dependent clause (DC).

___ 1. before the dance began

___ 2. before the dance contest

___ 3. since the first of the month

___ 4. since I started this journal

___ 5. after the Civil War

___ 6. after my dad visited

The following chart contains the subordinating conjunctions grouped according to their meanings. When you use one of these conjunctions, you must be sure that the connection made between the independent clause and the dependent clause has the meaning you intend.

---

# The Functions of Subordinating Conjunctions

**To introduce a condition:**    *if, even if, as long as, provided that, unless* (usually after a negative independent clause)

I will go *as long as* you go with me. I won't go *unless* you go with me.

**To introduce a contrast:**    *although, even though, though, whereas, while*

I will go *even though* you won't go with me.

**To introduce a cause:**    *as, because, since*

I will go *because* the meeting is very important.

**To show time:**    *after, before, since, when, whenever, while, until*

I will go *when* it is time.

I have voted every year *since* I was eighteen.

I won't go *until* it is time.

Note: *Until* usually follows a negative independent clause.

**To show place:**    *where, wherever*

I will go *wherever* you send me.

**To show purpose:**    *in order that, so that*

I will go *so that* I can hear the candidate for myself.

---

When you write a complex sentence, you can choose the order of the clauses. You can begin with the *independent clause,* or you can begin with the *dependent clause.*

---

## Two Options for Subordination Using Subordinating Conjunctions

**OPTION 1**

**Begin with the independent clause. Do not use a comma.**

**We can finish our homework if Tamika leaves.**

**OPTION 2**

**Begin with the dependent clause followed by a comma.**

**If Tamika leaves, we can finish our homework.**

---

Notice that you use a comma only when you choose option 2, beginning your sentence with the dependent clause. Your ear will remind you to use the correct punctuation. Read aloud the sample sentence given for option 2. Listen to the natural pause at the end of the dependent clause before continuing with the rest of the sentence. The place where you pause is the place where you put a comma.

**If Tamika leaves, we can finish our homework.**

**Practice**  **Use a subordinating conjunction to combine each of the following pairs of sentences.**

1. **Use the subordinating conjunction *after*:**

   Calvin went out to celebrate.

   He won the wrestling match.

   a. Begin with an independent clause:

   _____

   b. Begin with a dependent clause:

   _____

2. **Use the subordinating conjunction *when*:**

   Carla returned from Venezuela this spring.

   The family was excited.

   a. Begin with an independent clause:

   _____

   b. Begin with a dependent clause:

   _____

**EXERCISE** **4**

## Combining Sentences Using Subordination

Use subordination to combine each of the following pairs of sentences. Refer to the list of subordinating conjunctions if necessary.

1.　He was eating breakfast.

　　The results of the election came over the radio.

　　_____

　　_____

2.　The town council voted against the plan.

　　They believed the project was too expensive.

　　_____

　　_____

3.　I will see Maya Angelou tonight.

　　She is speaking at the university.

　　_____

　　_____

4.　The worker hoped for a promotion.

　　Not one person in the department had received a promotion last year.

　　_____

　　_____

5.　The worker hoped for a promotion.

　　All his work was done accurately and on time.

　　_____

　　_____

**EXERCISE** **5**

## Combining Sentences Using Subordination

Use each of the following subordinating conjunctions to compose a complex sentence. An example has been done for you.

**Subordinating conjunction:**　after

**Complex sentence:**　　　　**After the game was over, we all went out for pizza.**

1.　as if

　　_____

　　_____

2.   before

_____

_____

3.   until

_____

_____

4.   although

_____

_____

5.   because

_____

_____

**EXERCISE**  **6**

### Combining Sentences Using Subordination

**All the sentences in the following paragraph are simple sentences. Find three places in the paragraph where you could effectively combine two of the sentences to create a complex sentence (a sentence with one independent clause and at least one dependent clause). On the lines that follow the paragraph, write the three complex sentences you have created.**

At the present time, the United States recycles 10 percent of its trash. It burns another 10 percent. The remaining 80 percent goes to landfills. Over the next few years, many of our landfills will close. They are full. Some of them are leaking toxic wastes. Some parts of the Northeast already truck much of their trash to landfills in Pennsylvania, Ohio, Kentucky, and West Virginia. The garbage continues to pile up. The newspapers print stories about it every week. Trash is not a very glamorous subject. People in every town talk about the problem. One magazine, called *Garbage,* is printed on recycled paper. No town ever before gathered together information about garbage. The town of Lyndhurst, New Jersey, began what is the world's only garbage museum. One landfill now has a restaurant on its premises. Another landfill displays some of its unusual garbage. It displays these objects like trophies. We really want to solve the garbage problem. We must change our "buy more and throw everything old away" mentality.

1.   _____

_____

_____

2. _____

_____

_____

3. _____

_____

_____

## USING RELATIVE PRONOUNS

Begin this section by studying the relative pronouns in the following box.

---

### Relative Pronouns

| | | | |
|---|---|---|---|
| who (whose, whom) whoever (whomever) } | used if the pronoun refers to a person | what whatever which whicever } | used if the pronoun refers to a thing |
| that | used most often to refer to things, but is sometimes used to refer to people | where | used if the pronoun refers to a place |
| | | when | used if the pronoun refers to a time |

---

Sentences can often be combined with a relative pronoun. These two simple sentences sound short and choppy:

**The researcher had a breakthrough.**

**He was studying diabetes.**

To avoid this choppiness, a writer might want to join the two related ideas by using a relative pronoun.

---

A **relative clause** is a dependent clause that begins with a relative pronoun.

*whom* the journalist interviewed

*which* he incorporated into his article

*that* we read in the magazine

If the relative clause is put in the wrong place, the result will confuse the reader.

**Incorrectly combined:**   **The researcher had a breakthrough *who* was studying diabetes.**

The relative pronoun *who* refers to *researcher,* so the relative clause *who was studying diabetes* must be placed immediately after *researcher.*

**Correctly combined:**   **The researcher *who* was studying diabetes had a breakthrough.**

> **The relative pronoun and its clause must immediately follow the word to which it is related.**

A sentence may have more than one relative clause. Study the following sentence, which contains two relative clauses. Notice that each relative pronoun immediately follows the word to which it is related.

**The researcher *who* was studying diabetes had a breakthrough, *which* he reported to the press.**

**Practice**   **Combine each pair of sentences into one complex sentence by using a relative pronoun. Do not use commas. An example follows:**

**Simple sentence:**   **The florist created the flower arrangement.**

**Simple sentence:**   **She called us last weekend.**

**Complex sentence:**   **The florist *who* called us last weekend created the flower arrangement.**

1.  The chemistry lab is two hours long. I attend that chemistry lab.

    Combined: _____

    _____

2.  The student assistant is very knowledgeable. The student assistant is standing by the door.

    Combined: _____

    _____

3.  The equipment was purchased last year.

    The equipment will make possible some important new research.

    Combined: _____

    _____

## PUNCTUATING RELATIVE CLAUSES

In order to use correct punctuation in a sentence that contains a relative clause, the writer must understand the difference between two types of relative clauses.

1. The **restrictive clause** is a relative clause that is essential to the intended main idea of the sentence. Restrictive clauses often begin with the relative pronoun *that*. These clauses do not use any commas.

   **You should never eat fruit *that* you haven't washed first.**

   If we were to leave out the relative clause, what would remain is *You should never eat fruit.* Obviously, this is not the intended meaning. The dependent clause is essential.

2. The **nonrestrictive clause** is a relative clause that is not essential to the intended meaning of the main idea. Nonrestrictive clauses often begin with the pronoun *which.* They require commas to set off the relative clause.

   **Mother's fruit salad, *which* she prepares every Sunday, is delicious.**

   If we were to leave out the relative clause, what would remain is *Mother's fruit salad is delicious.* The main idea is clear without the relative clause. Because the relative clause is not essential to this main idea, it is set off by commas.

---

### Subordination: Distinguishing Between Two Types of Relative Pronoun Clauses

**RESTRICTIVE CLAUSE**

The relative clause is essential to the meaning of the sentence. No commas are used.

   **You should never eat fruit *that you haven't washed first.***

**NONRESTRICTIVE CLAUSE**

The relative clause in not essential to the meaning of the sentence. Commas must be used.

   **Mother's fruit salad, *which she prepares every Sunday*, is delicious.**

---

**PRACTICE**    **Punctuating Relative Clauses**

In the sentences that follow, insert commas wherever they are needed. The following examples should serve as your models.

   **The man *who is wearing the Hawaiian shirt* is the bridegroom.**

In the sentence above, the bridegroom can be identified only by his Hawaiian shirt. Therefore, the relative clause *who is wearing the Hawaiian shirt* is essential to the meaning. No commas are needed.

   **Al, *who was wearing a flannel shirt*, arrived late to the wedding.**

In the preceding sentence, the main idea is that Al was late. What he was wearing is not essential to that main idea. Therefore, commas are needed to set off this nonessential information.

1. The poem that my classmate read in class was very powerful.

2. The teacher who guided our class today is my favorite college professor.

3. Her biology course which met four times a week for two hours each session  was extremely demanding.

4. You seldom learn much in courses that are not demanding.

5. My own poetry  which has improved over the semester has brought me much satisfaction.

Now you are ready to practice combining your own sentences by using relative pronouns. The following exercises ask you to insert a variety of relative clauses into simple sentences. Pay careful attention to the punctuation.

**EXERCISE 7**

## Combining Sentences Using Relative Pronouns

Insert a relative clause into each of the following ten sentences. Use each of the possibilities *(who, whose, whom, which, that)* at least once. Be sure to punctuate correctly. An example has been done for you.

**Simple sentence**:     **The leader was barely five feet tall.**

**Complex sentence**:     **The leader, who was always self-conscious about his height, was barely five feet tall.**

1. The president _____ asked his advisors for help

2. His advisors _____ met with him in his office.

3. The situation _____ was at a critical point.

4. Even his vice president _____ appeared visibly alarmed.

5. Stacked on the table, the plans _____ looked impressive.

6. The meeting _____ began at two o'clock.

7. Every idea _____ was examined in great detail.

8. Several maps _____ showed the area in question.

9.  One advisor _____
    was vehemently opposed to the plan.

10. Finally, the group agreed on a plan of action _____

**EXERCISE  8**

### Combining Sentences Using Relative Pronouns

**Combine each of the following pairs of sentences by using a relative pronoun.**

1.  Stress can do a great deal of harm.
    We experience stress every day.

    _____

2.  People often use food to help them cope.
    Some people's jobs are demanding.

    _____

3.  The practice of eating to cope with stress is often automatic.
    The practice of eating to cope usually goes back to childhood.

    _____
    _____

4.  Some foods can actually increase tension.
    People turn to foods in times of stress.

    _____

5.  Sweet foods are actually not energy boosters.
    Sweet foods are popular with people who need a lift.

    _____
    _____

6.  Another substance is caffeine.
    People use other substances to get an energy boost.

    _____

7.  One of the biggest mistakes people make is to use alcohol as an aid to
    achieving calm.
    Alcohol is really a depressant.

    _____
    _____

8.  People should eat three light meals a day and two small snacks.
    People want to feel a sense of calm.

    _____
    _____

9.  Getting enough protein is also important in keeping an adequate energy level.

An adequate energy level will get you through the day.

_____

_____

10.  A person should eat regularly to avoid binges.

Binges put on pounds and drain one's energy.

_____

_____

**EXERCISE**  **9**     **Combining Sentences Using Relative Pronouns**

**Combine each of the following pairs of sentences by using a relative pronoun.**

1.  a.  Dr. Jose Abreo had an idea for social reform.

b.  He is a successful economist.

_____

_____

2.  a.  He believed classical music could save thousands of children.

b.  These children lived in crime-ridden neighborhoods throughout Venezuela.

_____

_____

_____

_____

3.  a.  In 1975 Dr. Abreo started a youth orchestra.

b.  This first orchestra had only eleven children.

_____

_____

4.  a.  Gradually, after-school centers were begun in many poor neighborhoods.

b.  In these neighborhoods, children were being lost to drugs and gang violence.

_____

_____

5.  a.  These centers offered free music lessons.

b.  These centers gave musical instruments to children as young as four.

_____

_____

6.   a.   The children seemed to love hard work.

      b.   Children practiced six days a week.

_____

7.   a.   Learning classical music instilled confidence and self-esteem.

      b.   Classical music transported them to another world.

_____

_____

8.   a.   In thirty years, 800,000 children have passed through the system.

      b.   The system has now grown to 220 youth orchestras.

_____

_____

9.   a.   Gustavo Dudamel is the first Venezuelan classical superstar.

      b.   He conducts The Simon Bolivar National Youth Orchestra.

_____

_____

10.   a.   Classical music has a spiritual richness.

       b.   Classical music can lift children's spirits from their physical poverty.

_____

_____

## Subordination

### I:   USE A SUBORDINATING CONJUNCTION

a. **Begin with the independent clause. Do not use a comma.**

   We can finish our homework *if* Tamika leaves.

b. **Begin with the dependent clause followed by a comma.**

   *If* Tamika leaves, we can finish our homework.

### II:   USE A RELATIVE PRONOUN

a. **If the relative clause is essential information, the clause is restrictive. Do not use commas.**

   You should never eat fruit *that you haven't washed first*.

b. **If the relative clause is not essential information, the clause is nonrestrictive. Use commas.**

   Mother's fruit salad, *which she prepares every Sunday*, is delicious.

# MASTERY AND EDITING TESTS

**TEST 1**   ## Combining Sentences with a Subordinating Conjunction

Combine each of the following pairs of sentences by using either a subordinating conjunction or a relative pronoun.

1.  Here is the apartment building.
    It will be torn down next year.

    _____

    _____

2.  The police stood by the door.
    They blocked our entrance.

    _____

    _____

3.  She wore high heels.
    They made marks in the wooden floor.

    _____

    _____

4.  My aunt is a tyrant.
    Her name is Lena.

    _____

    _____

5.  Her outfit was classy.
    Her hair was dirty and unattractive.

    _____

    _____

6.  The interviewer did not smile.
    He discovered we had a friend in common.

    _____

    _____

7.  I had a test the next day.
    I stayed up to watch a Bette Davis movie.

    _____

    _____

8.  The skater fell and broke his arm.
    He was trying to skate backward.

    _____

    _____

9. For a moment her face glowed with pleasure.
   Her face was usually serious.

   _____

   _____

10. I was thinking.
    The toast burned.

    _____

    _____

TEST 2    **Combining Sentences Using Coordination and Subordination**

**The following paragraph is composed of mostly simple sentences. The result is very choppy. Read the entire paragraph and then choose three places where sentences could be combined to create a compound or complex sentence that will improve the style. Do not be afraid to change the wording to accommodate the changes you want to make. You can combine clauses using coordination or subordination. Write your new compound or complex sentences on the lines provided after the paragraph.**

Our history is filled with stories of curious coincidences. One such example involves the two families of Lincoln and Booth. We all know the tragic story of the assassination of Abraham Lincoln in 1865. The president

was murdered by a member of America's most famous theatrical family, the Booth family. The murderer's name was John Wilkes Booth. He was a handsome actor. He was greatly admired in many popular roles. About a year before this terrible event, another member of Lincoln's family was in great danger. This was Robert Todd Lincoln. He was the president's son. The young man was waiting for a train in the Jersey City train station. It was late at night. Passengers were crowding against the passenger car. They pressed against Robert. Then the train began to move. Robert lost his footing. He fell into the open space between the train and the platform. Suddenly, someone seized his coat collar and pulled him up and onto the platform. The man saved the boy's life. He was none other than Edwin Booth, the most famous actor in America. He was the brother of John Wilkes Booth!

1. _____
   _____
   _____

2. _____
   _____
   _____

3. _____
   _____
   _____

**TEST 3**

### Editing Student Writing: Combining Sentences Using Coordination and Subordination

The following student paragraph is composed of mostly simple sentences. The result is very choppy. Read the entire paragraph and then choose three places where sentences could be combined to create compound or complex sentences that will improve the style. Do not be afraid to change the wording to accommodate the changes you want to make. You can combine clauses using coordination or subordination.

William Sidney Porter had a difficult start in life. He was born in Greensboro, North Carolina, in 1862. At three he lost his mother. His father was an alcoholic.

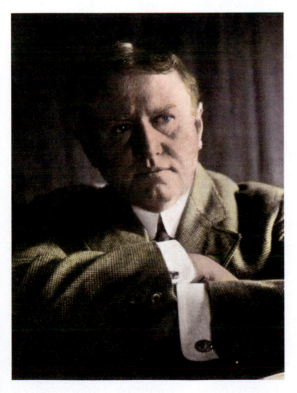

Before long, he was sent to live with family friends on a cattle ranch in Texas. That is where he grew up. In 1887, he met Athol Estes. He married her in 1887. Four years later Porter took a position as a bank clerk. It proved disastrous. He was charged with stealing bank funds. Before the trial, he fled to Honduras. He met other fugitives in Honduras. He traveled with them to Mexico and South America. He returned in 1897 to Texas to be with his dying wife. She was dying of tuberculosis. He was arrested. He was found guilty of embezzlement. He was sentenced to five years in prison. It was during his time in prison that William Sydney Porter began to write short stories. He published them in national publications under another name, O. Henry. Following his release from prison, he moved to New York City. In the next few years he produced nearly three hundred short stories! On his endless walks through the crowded streets of New York, O. Henry observed shop girls, millionaires, and homeless people. He included them in his many stories. These tales give us a portrait of New York at the beginning of the twentieth century. Some of O. Henry's best-known stories, such as "The Gift of the Magi," are set in New York. This famous writer also used the American Southwest as well as Central and South America as settings for several of his tales.

1. _____

   _____

   _____

2. _____

   _____

   _____

3. _____

   _____

   _____

## TEST 4  Editing Student Writing Using Editing Symbols

**In the following paragraph, editing symbols mark the sentences that need revision or correction. Make your corrections on the lines provided after the paragraph.**

[1]Fashion is always looking for a fresh idea. [2]Are you tired yet of the low-rise pants with the cropped shirts that *reveals* (agr) the bellybutton? [3]Have you seen too many young men, (subord) who walk along holding up their pants? [4]Are you glad to see lime green become last season's popular color? [5]And the wedding scene! (frag) [6]Every young female guest wears a black dress (coord) every bride wears a strapless gown. [7]One fact is for certain. [8]Another fad will replace a fading one. [9]Take, for example, shoe fashions. [10]After a generation of women enjoyed wearing comfortable shoes to work (subord) now young women are once again wearing pointed toes and spiked heels. [11]This new generation of women will ruin their feet, if (subord) they wear such shoes for very long. [12]While older people look for safety and (subord) comfort it seems younger people prefer being provocative and even dangerously shocking. [13]Another purpose of fads, of course, *are* (agr) to keep up our spirits. [14]After the tragedy of 9/11, several fashion ads were recalled, (subord) because they were in bad taste. [15]The patriotic look was in with a lot of red, white, and blue. [16]The fashion industry is likely to be responsive to our nation's sobering circumstances (coord)

however it is unlikely to come up with anything bordering on dowdy. [17]Too many teens want to express themselves by the clothes they wear.

**Corrections**

1.  agreement (sentence 2):     _____

2.  subordination (sentence 3):    _____
    _____

3.  fragment (sentence 5):     _____

4.  coordination (sentence 6):    _____
    _____

5.  subordination (sentence 9):    _____
    _____
    _____
    _____

6.  subordination (sentence 11):    _____
    _____
    _____

7.  subordination (sentence 12):    _____
    _____
    _____

8.  agreement (sentence 13):    _____

9.  subordination (sentence 14):    _____
    _____

10.  coordination (sentence 16):    _____
    _____
    _____
    _____

## Exploring Online

Go to **www.cengage.com/devenglish/scarry/writersworkplace** to find the **Writer's Online Workplace,** a website designed for students using this book. You will find links to handouts, interactive quizzes, and other online resources as you explore the following topics:

• coordination and subordination
• combining sentences with the comma and semicolon

# Working Together

## MY FIRST JOB

### ANITA SANTIAGO

# A Hard Lesson, Learned Door to Door

My first job seared me. I was 19 years old in Caracas, Venezuela, reading a local newspaper, when I saw a help-wanted ad for selling encyclopedias.

I loved books, so I thought the job would be perfect. I had all of these idealistic fantasies—picturing myself enlightening children, teaching them about flowering trees and Rome.

At first, I was absolutely lost. They just sent me out into the streets of Caracas to sell books. I planned to go to large apartment buildings. But people there wouldn't open their doors or talk to me. I felt humiliated, embarrassed.

We worked on commission. That was it. I did sell some, but I went through a lot.

I remember this huge gong in the center of the lobby at the office. Whenever you sold a set of books, the jolly little man in a black suit who hired us would hand you a hammer. The gong made a dull, hollow sound. You knew that when you heard the gong, somebody had just sold words.

Of course, I'm still selling words. And that first job taught me respect for how hard people have to work. It made me think analytically, to figure out who and what my target was. You have to walk through unpleasantness to get to success. No one is going to give you life direction; you have to create it for yourself.

The campaigns we create come quite easily to me, because I know this culture. Consider the "Got Milk?" campaign. If you translate the words literally into Spanish you get, "Are you lactating?" Instead, we focus our campaign on grandmothers, or abuelas, who are serving milk to their grandchildren.

I took all the lessons I learned in Caracas to heart. I didn't know it at the time, but I can trace my business success back to those six months.

I've always wanted be my own boss.

## NARROWING THE TOPIC THROUGH GROUP DISCUSSION: A PERSON'S FIRST JOB

When you get your first job, you are not only earning your first paychecks but also learning your first lessons about the world of work. In this newspaper article, Anita Santiago, the owner of a Los Angeles advertising agency, writes about her first job in her native city of Caracas, Venezuela. After you have read the article, discuss the questions that follow. As you exchange ideas suggested by the article, you will find yourself concentrating on those aspects of the subject that interest you the most. These particular areas of interest would make good topics for your own writing.

### Questions for Group Discussion

1.  At first, Anita Santiago thought the job of selling encyclopedias would be perfect because she loved books. What job experiences have members of the class had that turned out differently than expected?

2.  When the writer tells us that her company in Caracas "just sent me out into the streets . . . to sell books" without any preparation, she is reporting a common experience people have when they are hired for jobs but are not given any training. What experiences have students in the class had with jobs for which the employees were not properly trained? What were the results?

3.  Anita Santiago remembers that when someone sold a set of encyclopedias, a gong sounded in the company's office. In jobs that members of the class have had, how were accomplishments recognized? Were they ignored? What were the results of this attention or neglect?

5.  The writer admits that when she began her job she was very idealistic, but at some point she obviously became more realistic. When have you been idealistic about something in your life, but circumstances forced you to modify your thinking?

6.  Anita Santiago believes, "You have to walk through unpleasantness to get to success." Based on your experience, do you agree or disagree?

7.  Who is the hardest-working person you have ever known? Describe what this person did that makes you admire him or her so much.

8.  The writer tells us that her Spanish-language advertising campaigns "come quite easily" to her because she knows the culture so well. When has something come easily to you because of your background or some other source of special knowledge or expertise?

## PORTFOLIO SUGGESTION

Save your notes from this discussion of a person's first job. From this general topic, narrow down the issues to three or four specific aspects that would be of interest to you for future writing projects.

# CORRECTING FRAGMENTS AND RUN-ONS

As you work with the material in this chapter, you will understand the value of all your previous study on phrases and clauses. Here you will see more complicated fragments and several types of run-on sentences. You will learn how each one can be made into an acceptable sentence. Mastering the skills of this chapter will make editing your own work much easier.

**CHAPTER OBJECTIVES**

- Identify **three types of fragments:**
    - one or more phrases
    - one or more dependent clauses
    - a combination of phrases and dependent clauses
- Identify **three types of run-on sentences:**
    - the *and* run-on
    - the fused run-on
    - the comma splice

## WHAT IS A FRAGMENT?

> A *fragment* is a piece of a sentence.

## HOW MANY KINDS OF FRAGMENTS ARE THERE?

1.  A fragment could be a phrase:

    **I sat down. *In the school bus.* Howard, the school bully, came and sat down beside me.**

    **NOTE:** The prepositional phrase *in the school bus* is a fragment, not a sentence.

2.  A fragment could be a dependent clause:

> *As I sat down.* **Howard, the school bully, came and sat down beside me.**

**NOTE:** The dependent clause *as I sat down* is a fragment, not a sentence.

3.  A fragment could be a combination of phrases and dependent clauses:

> *As I sat down in the school bus that was filled with screaming kids.*

**NOTE:** *As I sat down* is a dependent clause; *in the school bus* is a prepositional phrase; *that was filled* is a dependent clause; and *with screaming kids* is a prepositional phrase. A combination of phrases and dependent clauses is not a sentence.

## HOW DO YOU MAKE A COMPLETE SENTENCE FROM A FRAGMENT?

| | |
|---|---|
| 1. **If the fragment is a phrase:** | **I sat down.** *In the school bus* |
| Revision Option 1: | Does it belong to the sentence that comes before it or after it? |
| | **I sat down** *in the school bus.* |
| Revision Option 2: | Could you add an independent clause to the phrase? |
| | **I sat down. Forty other screaming kids were already** *in the school bus.* |
| 2. **If the fragment is a dependent clause:** | **as I sat down** |
| Revision Option 1: | Does it belong to the sentence that comes before it or after it? In other words, can you add it to an already existing independent clause? |
| | *As I sat down,* **Howard, the school bully, came and sat down beside me.** |
| Revision Option 2: | Could you add an independent clause to the dependent clause? |
| | *As I sat down,* **my worst fears were realized. Howard, the school bully, came and sat down beside me.** |
| Revision Option 3: | Could you omit the subordinate conjunction so you are left with an independent clause? |
| | *I sat down.* **Howard, the school bully, came and sat down beside me.** |
| 3. **If the fragment is a combination of phrases and dependent clauses:** | **As I sat down in the school bus that was filled with screaming kids** |

| | |
|---|---|
| Revision Option 1: | You need an independent clause. Could you change a dependent clause to an independent clause by dropping the subordinate conjunction? |
| | **_I sat down_ in the school bus that was filled with screaming kids.** |
| Revision Option 2: | You need an independent clause. Could you add an independent clause? |
| | **As I sat down in the school bus that was filled with screaming kids, Howard, the school bully, came and sat down beside me.** |

**EXERCISE**  **Recognizing Fragments**

**Identify each of the examples below as one of the following:**

a.  sentence

b.  fragment—phrase

c.  fragment—dependent clause

d.  fragment—combination of phrases and dependent clauses

____  1.  At the bus stop.

____  2.  While I was not looking.

____  3.  Someone took my bookbag.

____  4.  Because so many people were watching.

____  5.  Although someone must have seen the theft when they were waiting for the bus around three o'clock.

____  6.  Even though I asked everyone.

____  7.  Nobody seemed to have noticed.

____  8.  After I reported the theft to the police because I knew I should because it's important to document these kinds of incidents.

____  9.  In the event of other similar thefts.

____ 10.  When I got home and called my husband who was really upset about the situation.

**EXERCISE**  **Recognizing and Correcting Fragments**

**Revise the ten examples from Exercise 1. Put your revised sentences into paragraph form, correcting all fragments.**

_____

_____

_____

_____

_____

_____

**EXERCISE  3**

## Student Writing: Recognizing and Correcting Fragments

**Read the following paragraph carefully. Find the five fragments and underline them. Then fix each fragment (using the options for correcting fragments, found on pages 143–144), and write the new sentences on the lines below.**

Howard Crane the shortest kid in my entire seventh grade. He was always getting into fights, and he used terrible language. If you've ever known a bully. Howard was a prime example. One Friday afternoon as we sat in the school bus on our way home. Howard began taunting my younger brother. Because our parents had told us to ignore Howard. So my brother just looked straight ahead. Saying nothing. I was growing angrier and angrier. I had to do something.

1. _____

   _____

2. _____

   _____

3. _____

   _____

4. _____

   _____

5. _____

   _____

## WHAT IS A RUN-ON?

In conversation, when we retell events that have occurred, we often link our thoughts together in one long narrative. Here is what one person involved in a car accident reported to a police officer at the scene:

I was driving along on Route 80 and my daughter asked my wife to change the radio station and my wife told my daughter to do it herself so my daughter unhooked her seatbelt and reached over from the back seat to change the station but then her brother tickled her and she lost her balance and fell on the gear shift and that moved the gear into neutral so the car instantly lost power and that's when we were hit by the van behind us.

The man relating the accident ran all the parts of this entire event together without any separations. As a result, the account appears as a **run-on.** In formal writing, a run-on is considered a serious error.

> **Run-ons** are independent clauses that have been combined incorrectly.

## HOW MANY KINDS OF RUN-ONS ARE THERE?

Run-ons may occur when the writer is unable to recognize where one complete thought ends and another thought begins. Run-ons also may occur if the writer is not sure of the standard ways of connecting ideas. Certain marks of punctuation are needed to show where two clauses join. Other punctuation signifies the end of a thought. Study the following three types of run-ons.

1. **The *and* run-on:** two or more relatively long independent clauses connected with a coordinating conjunction without any punctuation

    **Incorrect:**    I met Charlyce in a yoga class at the YWCA and we liked each other immediately and we soon became friends.

2. **The fused run-on:** two or more independent clauses run together without any punctuation

    **Incorrect:**    I met Charlyce in a yoga class at the YWCA we soon became friends.

3. **The comma splice:** two or more independent clauses run together with only a comma

    **Incorrect:**    I met Charlyce in a yoga class at the YWCA, we soon became friends.

## HOW DO YOU CORRECT A RUN-ON SENTENCE?

There are three basic ways to correct a run-on sentence.

1. Make two sentences with end punctuation.

    **Correct:**    I met Charlyce in a yoga class at the YWCA. We soon became friends.

2. Make a compound sentence using one of the three methods of coordination.

    **Correct:**    I met Charlyce in a yoga class at the YWCA, and we soon became friends.

    I met Charlyce in a yoga class at the YWCA; indeed, we soon became friends.

    I met Charlyce in a yoga class at the YWCA; we soon became friends.

3. Make a complex sentence using subordination.

    **Correct:**    Soon after I met Charlyce in a yoga class at the YWCA, we became friends.

    Charlyce and I became friends soon after we met in a yoga class at the YWCA.

**NOTE:** See the inside front cover for a quick review of coordination and subordination.

**Practice**

**Below are five run-on sentences. Correct them by using any of the three strategies given for correcting run-ons.**

1. In recent years several celebrities, including Michael J. Fox, Lance Armstrong, and Melissa Etheridge, have shared their health situations with the public, this has had a beneficial effect.

2. In 1995, Christopher Reeve became a quadriplegic after a horse riding accident, he and his wife worked tirelessly until their untimely deaths to draw attention to the need for better treatments and cures for spinal cord injuries.

3. Katie Couric, the American media personality, lost her husband to colon cancer in 1998 after his death, Katie became a spokeswoman for colon cancer awareness.

4. In fact, Katie had a colonoscopy on the air in March of 2000 and she inspired many to follow her example.

5. Katie Couric's efforts have become known as the "Couric effect," we now know a celebrity can draw significant attention and support to worthwhile causes.

**EXERCISE**  **4**

### Recognizing and Correcting Run-Ons

Here is the same run-on sentence that you read earlier in this chapter. Rewrite the police report correctly. Put a period at the end of each complete thought. You may have to omit some of the words that loosely connect the ideas, or you may want to use coordination and subordination. Remember to make each new sentence begin with a capital letter.

I was driving along on Route 80 and my daughter asked my wife to change the radio station and my wife told my daughter to do it herself so she unhooked her seatbelt and reached over from the back seat to change the station but then her brother tickled her and she lost her balance and fell on the gear shift and that moved the gear into neutral so the car instantly lost power and that's when we were hit by the van behind us.

_____

_____

_____

_____

_____

_____

**EXERCISE** **5**

## Recognizing and Correcting Run-Ons

The following story is written as one sentence. Rewrite the story correctly. Put a period at the end of each complete thought. You may have to omit some of the words that loosely connect the ideas, or you may want to use coordination and subordination. Remember to make each new sentence begin with a capital letter.

My best friend is accident-prone if you knew her you'd know that she's always limping, having to write with her left hand or wearing a bandage on her head or ankle, like last week for example she was walking down the street minding her own business when a shingle from someone's roof hit her on the head and she had to go to the emergency room for stitches, then this week one of her fingers is purple because someone slammed the car door on her hand sometimes I think it might be better if I didn't spend too much time with her you know her bad luck might be catching!

_____

_____

_____

_____

_____

_____

_____

**EXERCISE** **6**

## Student Writing: Recognizing and Correcting Run-Ons

The following story is written as one sentence. Rewrite the story correctly. Put a period at the end of each complete thought. You may have to omit some of the words that loosely connect the ideas, or you may want to use coordination and subordination. Remember to make each new sentence begin with a capital letter.

One morning, not too early, I will rise and slip downstairs to brew the coffee and no baby will wake me up and no alarm clock will rattle my nerves and the weather will be so warm that I will not have to put on my coat and hat to go out for the paper there will be no rush I will go to the refrigerator and take out eggs and sausage the bathroom will be free so I will be able to take a shower with no one knocking on the door and I will not have to run up and down the stairs first looking for someone's shoes and then for someone's car keys I will leisurely fix my hair and pick out a lovely suit to wear the phone might ring and it will be a friend who would like to have lunch and share the afternoon with me money will be no problem maybe we'll see a movie or drive to the nearby city to visit a museum and the countryside will be beautiful and unspoiled my life will seem fresh and promising.

_____

_____

_____

_____

_____

_____

_____

_____

# MASTERY AND EDITING TESTS

**TEST 1**

## Editing for Fragments and Run-Ons

**On the lines provided below the paragraph, identify each numbered group of words as a sentence (S), fragment (F), or run-on (R). Then rewrite the paragraph, correcting any fragments and run-ons.**

[1]In laboratory experiments, scientists have discovered a diet. [2]That extends the life of their animals up to 50 percent or more. [3]This diet prevents heart disease, diabetes, and kidney failure and it greatly retards all types of cancer. [4]Even slowing down the aging process of cataracts, gray hair, and feebleness. [5]Staying on this diet keeps the mind flexible and the body active to an almost biblical old age. [6]These rats, fish, and worms stay very slim, they are fed a diet of necessary vitamins and nutrients but only 65 percent of the calories of the animal's normal diet. [7]Every creature fed this restricted diet has had a greatly extended life span. [8]The results of caloric restriction are spectacular. [9]Says Richard Weindruch, a gerontologist at the National Institute on Aging

in Bethesda, Maryland. [10]Gerontologists have tried many things to extend life but this is the only experiment that works every time in the lab. [11]Animals that received enough protein, vitamins, and minerals to prevent malnutrition. [12]They survived to a grand old age and it does not seem to matter whether they ate a diet composed largely of fats or carbohydrates. [13]Researchers warn against people undertaking this diet too hastily, it is very easy to become malnourished. [14]Dr. Roy Walford is a pioneer in the field from the University of California he believes humans could live to an extraordinarily advanced age. [15]If they were to limit their caloric intake.

1. _____  5. _____  9. _____  13. _____

2. _____  6. _____  10. _____  14. _____

3. _____  7. _____  11. _____  15. _____

4. _____  8. _____  12. _____

**Your version:**

_____

_____

_____

_____

_____

_____

_____

_____

_____

_____

_____

_____

_____

_____

**TEST  2**

## Editing for Fragments and Run-Ons

On the lines provided below, identify each numbered group of words as a sentence (S), fragment (F), or run-on (R). Then rewrite the paragraph, correcting any fragments and run-ons.

¹Recently, I watched a daytime show on laser peels and viewers watched a procedure that took less than two minutes. ²In front of the television cameras and the live audience. ³A guest had the wrinkles zapped away from around her eyes. ⁴These high-energy laser beams which are said to be quick, painless, and safe. ⁵Adding this technology to face-lifts, dermabrasion, collagen injections, and chemical peels! ⁶Lasers were first used by dermatologists to remove port-wine stains in the 1970s. ⁷Now these laser peels have become quite common. ⁸For many people, this means they can now look as young as they feel but the healing process can be painful and messy. ⁹Most physicians believe this is a much more precise method of rejuvenating the skin. ¹⁰Because it's so much more accurate, so much more predictable, and so much safer than other methods. ¹¹One note of caution. ¹²Any physician with little or no training can buy the equipment therefore a person should always check out the doctor's experience. ¹³A practitioner without experience could zap too deeply and cause tissue damage. ¹⁴Following a laser zap, a person must scrupulously avoid the sun for several months, afterwards one must always wear sunscreen. ¹⁵One bad point. ¹⁶Laser technology is expensive full-face laser peels cost thousands of dollars. ¹⁷Sorry, no long-term scientific studies to prove their safety.

1. _____    6. _____    11. _____    16. _____

2. _____    7. _____    12. _____    17. _____

3. _____    8. _____    13. _____

4. _____    9. _____    14. _____

5. _____    10. _____   15. _____

**Your version:**

_____

_____

_____

_____

_____

_____

_____

_____

_____

_____

_____

_____

_____

_____

_____

_____

**TEST ③**

## Editing Student Writing: Correcting Fragments and Run-Ons

On the lines provided below, identify each numbered group of words as a sentence (S), fragment (F), or run-on (R). Then rewrite the paragraph, correcting any fragments and run-ons.

[1]Many parents worry that their children are not reading enough others worry about what the children are reading. [2]In fact, most children are not reading anything at all, houses are filled with the sounds from CD players, television sets, and video games. [3]If children never see their parents reading or going to the library. [4]They will most likely not develop good reading habits. [5]Children who see their parents reading magazines, books, and newspapers. [6]These children will grow up thinking that reading is a natural part of daily life. [7]Parents can do many things to encourage reading. [8]Like accompanying them to the library and helping them pick out books. [9]Parents can encourage children to memorize poetry and they can show them how to read maps when they travel. [10]Since most young people like children's magazines with pictures and short texts on current topics. [11]Parents could subscribe to these magazines for their children. [12]Reading stories out loud as a family, with everybody participating, after the workday is over.[13] That is the best idea of all.

1. _____     3. _____     5. _____

2. _____     4. _____     6. _____

7. _____     10. _____     13. _____

8. _____     11 _____     

9. _____     12. _____     

Your version:

_____

_____

_____

_____

_____

_____

_____

_____

_____

_____

_____

_____

**TEST 4**

## Editing Student Writing Using Editing Symbols

**The editing symbol for a run-on error is *ro*. In the paragraph below, ten errors are marked with editing symbols. Correct each error on the lines provided after the paragraph.**

*subord*
[1]If human development is to continue we will eventually have to develop forms of renewable energy. [2]In the 1980s and 1990s, the United States lagged behind Europe and Asia in the development of wind power *ro* in fact, many of our machines were inefficient, of poor design, and expensive to maintain. [3]Mostly only people living along coastal areas having high winds were attracted to investing in wind power. [4]Because the major technology to enable the commercial use of wind power improved dramatically starting

*subord*
in 1999 wind farms have begun springing up in much broader geographical
           *frag*                                              *frag*
areas. ⁵Not only along the coastal areas. ⁶Undoubtedly, many refinements and
                                                                    *ro*
improvements in the years to come. ⁷Wind power is extremely attractive, once
the equipment is set up, nobody has to buy the wind that blows across the land.
⁸Portland, Oregon, is planning a wind farm that will supply all of that city's energy
                 *frag*
needs. ⁹And this would be the equivalent of taking 12,000 cars off the road every
                                                         *ro*
year. ¹⁰One farmer in the Portland area has several windmills, he tells everyone
that he cultivates three crops: wheat, cattle, and wind. ¹¹He has power for his
         *ro*                                                      *agr*
own use and he sells the extra power to the region's power grid. ¹²Each of his
windmills bring in three to four thousand dollars a year in income.

## Corrections

1. subordination (sentence 1):    _____
   _____
   _____

2. run-on (sentence 2):    _____
   _____
   _____
   _____
   _____

3. subordination (sentence 4):    _____
   _____
   _____
   _____

4. fragment (sentence 5):    _____

5. fragment (sentence 6):    _____
   _____

6. run-on (sentence 7):    _____
   _____
   _____

7. fragment (sentence 9):    _____
   _____

8. run-on (sentence 10):    _____
   _____
   _____

9.   run-on (sentence 11):        _____

                                  _____

10.   agreement (sentence 12):    _____

## Exploring Online

Go to **www.cengage.com/devenglish/scarry/writersworkplace** to find the **Writer's Online Workplace,** a website designed for students using this book. You will find links to handouts, interactive quizzes, and other online resources as you explore the following topics:

- fragments and run-ons
- comma splice run-ons

# Working Together

## DISCUSSION AND FREEWRITING: FIRST IMPRESSIONS

Some modern approaches to dating are very different from those of years ago. When people date nowadays, they may use up-to-date technology to help ensure success in their personal lives. Some use chat rooms on the Internet, but others depend on services that match people according to their tastes and backgrounds. Still other people use a special face-to-face encounter. Following is an account of the phenomenon known as "speed dating."

Have you heard of the term speed dating? It's the latest trend for time-starved singles in major metropolitan areas. A host of new entrepreneurs have risen up to take advantage of the craze, forming companies with descriptive names such as 8 Minute Dating, Hurry Date, and PreDate. According to PreDate, speed dating "is a fun and efficient way for busy single professionals to meet. You'll meet other people in your age and interest group through a series of face-to-face, six-minute 'predates' in a private area at a local upscale restaurant/bar." Wow … twelve face-to-face dates or more in one night!

Wow indeed. Make a good impression in those first six minutes or the "relationship" is over. That's a lot of pressure. And even six minutes may be too many by a factor of two. According to communications professor Michael Sunnafrank, people tend to draw conclusions about someone within as little as three minutes of having met them. And researchers at Carleton University suggest that it takes as little as one-twentieth of a second for people to register likes and dislikes about another person. That's fast.

First impressions exist, and they are powerful. As a class, discuss the following questions. All students should take notes. Following the discussion, each student should choose one aspect of the subject that is of interest and freewrite on the topic for the time allotted by the instructor.

1. Is it a good thing to act on first impressions?
2. When did you have a first impression that proved correct (or incorrect?)
3. Do you know any people who made an impulsive decision based on "love at first sight" and then lived to regret it?

4. Do you consider yourself an impulsive person? Do you act on first impressions?

5. Would you participate in speed dating?

6. What characteristics would you be looking for in those first six minutes?

7. What are some of the techniques advertisers use to ensure a good first impression of their products?

8. What could you do to ensure a good first impression (for a job interview, for a date, for starting in a new school)?

## PORTFOLIO SUGGESTION

Keep the notes and freewriting you have done on this topic in your portfolio. Your instructor may want you to return to this topic to develop your freewriting into a complete college essay.

# 9 CHOOSING CORRECT PRONOUNS

In this chapter, you will work on choosing the correct pronoun forms in constructions that tend to cause confusion. You will learn to do the following:

**CHAPTER OBJECTIVES**

- Use the correct pronoun **case**
    - with **comparisons**
    - with **compound constructions**
    - with *who/whom* constructions
- Understand the relationship between a pronoun and its **antecedent** in order to
    - choose a pronoun that agrees **in number** with its antecedent
    - choose a pronoun that agrees **in person** with its antecedent
    - make certain that the antecedent of a pronoun is not **missing, ambiguous,** or **repetitious**

## PRONOUNS AND CASE

Most of us generally use the correct pronoun forms when we speak and write. However, the fact that pronouns have **case** (that is, they can change forms depending on their function in a particular sentence) causes confusion in three particular constructions: comparisons, compound constructions, and *who/whom* constructions.

> *Case* refers to the form a noun or pronoun takes, depending on how it is used in a sentence. Notice in the following examples how the pronoun *I* changes its form when it changes its function:
>
> **Subject:**      *I* needed a car.
> **Object:**       Dad bought a used Honda for *me.*
> **Possessive:**   *My* commute to work will now be easier.
>                    The title to the car is *mine.*
> **Reflexive:**    I've assumed all responsibility for the car *myself.*

The following chart provides a helpful listing of the different pronoun forms.

## Pronoun Case

| | Pronouns used as subjects | Pronouns used as objects | Pronouns used as possessives | Pronouns used as reflexives |
|---|---|---|---|---|
| **Singular** | I | me | my, mine | myself |
| | you | you | you, yours | yourself |
| | he | him | his | himself |
| | she | her | hers | herself |
| | it | it | its | itself |
| **Plural** | we | us | our, ours | ourselves |
| | you | you | your, yours | yourselves |
| | they | them | their, theirs | themselves |
| **Singular or plural** | who | whom | whose | |

- Study the chart and notice there are no such forms as *hisself, themself,* or *theirselves.*
- Be careful not to confuse *whose* with *who's* (who is, who has) or *its* with *it's* (it is).

## PRONOUN CASE WITH COMPARISONS

Choosing the correct pronoun for a comparison is easier if you complete the comparison in your own mind. For example, choose the correct pronoun in the following sentence:

**The swimmer is much stronger than (he, him, his).**

You might be tempted to choose the pronoun *him.* However, if you complete the comparison in your own mind, you will choose the correct pronoun:

**The swimmer is much stronger than (*he*, him, his) *is*.**

The second sentence shows that *he* is the correct answer because the pronoun *he* is used as the subject in the clause *he is.* Now you can clearly see that "The swimmer is much stronger than him is" would be the wrong choice.

**Practice**   **First complete the comparison in your mind. Then circle the correct pronoun in each of the sentences.**

1.  My brother did not enjoy the vacation as much as ( I, me, mine).

**HINT**   **Before you choose, try adding *did* to complete the comparison:**

**My brother did not enjoy the vacation as much as (*I, me, mine*) did.**

2.  The altitude in Quito affected my brother more than (I, me ).

HINT

**Before you choose, try adding *it affected* to complete the comparison:**

**The altitude in Quito affected my brother more than *it affected (I, me).***

3.  The tour guide directed his speech to the travel agents rather than to my brother and (I, me ).

HINT

**Before you choose, try adding *to* after the *and*.**

**The tour guide directed his speech to the travel agents rather than to my brother and *to* (I, me).**

**EXERCISE** **1**

### Choosing the Correct Pronoun with Comparisons

**Circle the correct pronoun in each of the sentences below. Remember to complete the comparison in your own mind.**

1.  I am as deeply involved in this proposal as (they , them).

2.  Farida's research has been less extensive than (we, us, our, ours).

3.  She did study the final proposal more than (I, me).

4.  The attractiveness of the competing proposal troubled my coworkers more than (I, me).

5.  Their company had acquired fewer clients than (we, us).

6.  Our policies are much better than (them, theirs).

7.  The contract was awarded to us rather than (they, them).

8.  The results will matter more to the client than (she, her).

9.  I will celebrate much longer tonight than (she, her).

10. An immediate vacation is more important for me than (he, him).

## PRONOUN CASE IN COMPOUND CONSTRUCTIONS

In a sentence that has a compound subject or a compound object, choosing the correct pronoun will be easier if you read the sentence and leave out one part of the compound construction.

**Today, Diane and (I, me) should buy the tickets.**

You might be tempted to choose the pronoun *me*. However, if you try reading this same sentence leaving out the first part of the compound subject (Diane), you will choose the correct pronoun.

**Today, (I, me) *should buy* the tickets.**

The second sentence shows that *I* is the correct answer because the pronoun *I* is used as the subject for the verb *should buy*. Now you can clearly see that "Today, me should buy the tickets" is the wrong choice.

**PRACTICE**   Circle the correct pronoun in each of the sentences below. Remember to leave out one part of the compound construction to test your answer.

1.  Developers and (he, him) hope to renovate that building.

HINT

> **Try the sentence without the words *developers and*.**
>
> **(He, Him) hopes to renovate that building.**

2.  They spoke to the construction company and (I, me).

HINT

> **Try the sentence without the words *the construction company and*.**
>
> **They spoke to (I, me).**

**EXERCISE**  **Choosing the Correct Pronoun in Compound Constructions**

In each of the following sentences, circle the correct pronoun. Remember to leave out one part of the compound construction to test your answer.

1.  The head nurse called from the hospital to speak to my husband or (I, me).

2.  The other nurses and (she, her) had been very supportive throughout Sasha's illness.

3.  We were relieved to get the test results from the lab and (she, her).

4.  Both my husband and (I, me) were encouraged by the news.

5.  Among Sasha, my husband Tyrone, and (I, me), Sasha was the calmest.

6.  Tyrone and (I, me) were thrilled that Sasha was in remission.

7. Because our children and (we, us) were so exhausted, we decided to take a weekend vacation.

8. My husband, Sasha, and (I, me) got out the map.

9. (He, Him) and Sasha decided to drive to the harbor in Baltimore.

10. The vacation would give Sasha and (we, us) a chance to unwind.

## PRONOUN CASE IN *WHO/WHOM* CONSTRUCTIONS

At times, most of us are confused by the use of the *who* and *whom* pronouns, partly because *whom* has become uncommon in spoken English. In written English, however, the difference in the ways these two words function in a sentence is still important.

> **Who is always used in the subject position in a sentence.**

**Who is going with you to the performance?**

*Who* is the subject of the verb phrase *is going*.

**Who did you say is going with you to the performance?**

*Who* is the subject of the verb phrase *is going* (even though a second clause, *did you say*, interrupts the first clause).

**He is the person who is going with me.**

*Who* is the subject of the verb phrase *is going* in the second clause, *who is going with me*.

> **Whom is always used in the object position in a sentence.**

**Whom did the director choose for the part?**

*Whom* is the direct object of the verb phrase *did choose*.

**To whom did the director give the part?**

*Whom* is the object of the preposition *to*.

When a sentence has more than one clause, it is helpful to cross out all the words except the relative clause beginning with the *who/whom* pronoun. Then you will better understand how *who/whom* functions within its own clause.

~~The scholarship will be given to~~ **(whoever, whomever) wins the poetry contest.**

In the clause (*whoever, whomever*) *wins the poetry contest*, the pronoun *whoever* is the correct choice. *Whoever* is the subject for the verb *wins*. (The entire clause is considered the object of the preposition *to*.)

**Practice**        In each of the sentences below, cross out all the words except the clause containing the *who/whom* pronoun. Then **decide** whether the *who/whom* functions as a subject or as an object within that clause and circle the correct choice.

1.  She is the friend (who, whom) I treasured.

    **Look at:   (who, whom) I treasured**

2.  She is the friend (who, whom) I knew could be trusted.

    **Look at:   (who, whom) could be trusted**

3.  They will award the prize to (whoever , whomever) is the best.

    **Look at:   (whoever, whomever) is the best.**

4.  I don't know (who, whom) should do the work.

5.  That is the girl (who, whom) I hope will win.

**EXERCISE**  **3**

## Choosing the Correct Pronoun Using *Who/Whom*

Circle the correct pronoun in each of the sentences below. Remember, to avoid confusion, cross out other clauses in the sentence so you can focus on the clause in question.

**I don't know (who, whom) you think is good at money management.**

**This is the man (who, whom) I was told would give us good advice.**

1.  In relationships, the issue of (who, whom) is best suited to run the family's finances is always critical.

2.  Everyone knows couples for (who, whom) money is the source of endless squabbles.

3.  Most couples quickly decide (who, whom) is the right person to balance the checkbook.

4.  (Who, Whom) should the couple trust for financial advice?

5.  Another question is (who's, whose) responsible for the final decisions about making large purchases?

6.  To (who, whom) do most people listen about long-range financial planning?

7.  Researchers (who, whom) have studied this area of human behavior have reached some surprising conclusions.

8.  Couples (who's, whose) weddings were costly like to remember those expenses.

9.  However, these same couples (who, whom) have children to educate seldom want to talk about college costs.

10. A couple for (who, whom) future goals are very different need to listen to expert advice.

**EXERCISE** **4**

### Choosing the Correct Pronoun Using *Who/Whom*

**Circle the correct pronoun in each of the sentences below.**

1.  (Who, Whom) has Wynton Marsalis chosen as the lead soloist at tonight's jazz concert?

2.  (Whoever, Whomever) sold us the tickets gave us the best seats in the house.

3.  From (who, whom) can we obtain a program?

4.  (Who, Whom) of these soloists has come from New Orleans?

5.  Wynton Marsalis gave the solo parts to (whoever, whomever) could improvise the best.

6.  Our attention was focused on (whoever, whomever) was playing the piano.

7.  (Who's, Whose) improvisation did you think was the most creative?

8.  We will enjoy the trumpet player (who, whom) the critics have praised.

9.  (Who's, Whose) version of "St. Louis Blues" did you like best?

10. Most of the musicians (who, whom) I heard at the concert were impressive.

**EXERCISE**

### Choosing Correct Pronoun Forms

**Practice pronoun case with all three constructions (comparisons, compound constructions, and *who/whom* constructions). Circle the correct pronoun in each of the sentences below.**

1.  Jamel and (she, her) presented the project today.

2.  Between you and (I, me), I think it was outstanding.

3.  Their visual materials will help (whoever, whomever) will study the project later.

4.  He is usually a better speaker than (she, her).

5.  (Whoever, Whomever) heard them agreed that it was an impressive presentation.

6.  (Who, Whom) do you think made the best points?

7.  I am not as deeply involved in my project as (they, them).

8.  Their research was much more detailed than (us, our, ours).

9.  The professor gave both Carolyn and (he, him) A's.

10.  My partner and (I, me) will have to work harder to reach this standard.

**EXERCISE** **6**

### Student Writing: Choosing Correct Pronoun Forms

**Practice pronoun case with all three constructions. In the following paragraph, circle the correct pronoun wherever you have a choice.**

When my mother and (I, me) decided to care for my very ill father at home, some of our friends objected. My sister and (they, them) said we would be exhausted and unable to handle the stress. The people (who, whom) we met at the hospital had the same opinion. To (who, whom) could we go for help in the middle of the night? My father, (who, whom) we believed would be happier at home, had been our first consideration. Of course, we would have benefited if either my mother or (I, me) had been a nurse. However, we did have a visiting nurse available at times. We were more confident than (they, them) that we could handle the situation. We were the only ones for (who, whom) this work would be a labor of love.

## PRONOUN-ANTECEDENT AGREEMENT

When you use a pronoun in your writing, that pronoun must refer to a word used previously in the text. This previously used word is called the *antecedent*.

> An **antecedent** is a word (or words) that is replaced by a pronoun later in a piece of writing.
>
> **The *pool* was crowded. It was a popular place on a hot summer day.**
>
> In this example, the pronoun *it* replaces the word *pool*. *Pool,* in this case, is referred to as the *antecedent* of the pronoun *it*.

The next three rules concerning pronouns are often troublesome to writers. Study each rule carefully, and complete the exercises that follow.

RULE **1**

> A pronoun must agree in *number* (singular or plural) with any other word to which it refers.

The following sentences illustrate a lack of pronoun-antecedent agreement in **number.**

**Lacks agreement**:   The *pool* was crowded. *They* were popular places on a hot summer day.

In this example, *pool* is the antecedent of the pronoun *they*. However, *pool* is singular and *they* is plural. The pronoun *it* must be used to agree in number with the antecedent *pool*.

Pronoun-antecedent agreement can be particularly complicated if the pronoun is an indefinite pronoun. Words like *everyone* or *nobody* are singular. They require a singular pronoun.

**Lacks agreement**:   *Everyone* worked on *their* final draft.

Even though you may hear people use the plural pronoun *their* to refer to a singular subject, this usage is not correct in formal writing. Here are two other approaches writers often take:

**Sexist construction**:   *Everyone* worked on *his* final draft.

**Awkward construction**:   *Everyone* worked on *his or her* final draft.

This last form is technically correct, but the continual use of the construction *his or her* will soon begin to sound awkward and repetitious. Often, the best solution to the problem is to revise the construction so that both the pronoun and the antecedent are plural:

**Pronouns agree**:   *All* the students worked on *their* final drafts.

Another way around the problem is to avoid the pronoun altogether or use the article:

**Avoids the pronoun**:   Everyone worked on final drafts.

Everyone worked on the final drafts.

Another problem with pronoun-antecedent agreement in **number** occurs when a demonstrative pronoun (*this, that, these, those*) is used with a noun. In such a case, the pronoun must agree with the noun it modifies:

| | |
|---|---|
| **Singular:** | **this kind, that kind; this type, that type** |
| **Incorrect:** | ***These kind** of shoes hurt my feet.* |
| **Correct:** | ***This kind** of shoe hurts my feet.* |

| | |
|---|---|
| **Plural:** | **these kinds, those kinds; these types, those types** |
| **Incorrect:** | ***Those type** of cars always need oil.* |
| **Correct:** | ***Those types** of cars always need oil.* |

**Practice**

Rewrite each of the following sentences so that the pronoun agrees with its antecedent in *number*. It may be helpful to draw an arrow from the pronoun to its antecedent.

1.  Everyone should bring their suggestions to the meeting.

    _____

2.  This sorts of clothes are popular now.

    _____

3.  No one knew what they were doing.

    _____

4.  If the bird watchers hope to see anything, one must get up early.

    _____

5.  These type of book appeals to me.

    _____

RULE

> A pronoun must agree with its antecedent in *person.*

The following sentences illustrate a lack of pronoun-antecedent agreement in **person.**

| | |
|---|---|
| **Lacks agreement:** | **When mountain climbing, *one* must maintain *your* concentration at all times.** |

When you construct a piece of writing, you choose a "person" as the voice in that piece of writing. Your instructor may advise you which personal pronoun to use for a particular writing assignment. Whatever guidelines you are given, the important point is to be consistent and use the same **person.** Below are some examples in which the pronouns agree:

> When mountain climbing, *you* must maintain *your* concentration at all times.

> When mountain climbing, *I* must maintain *my* concentration at all times.

> When mountain climbing, *we* must maintain *our* concentration at all times.

**Practice**

Correct each of the following sentences so that the pronoun agrees with its antecedent in *person.*

1. I enjoy math exams because you can show what you know.

2. When I took geometry, we discovered that frequent review of past assignments helped make the course seem easy.

3. People always need to practice your skills to not forget them.

4. Math games can be fun for a student if you have a spirit of curiosity.

5. When studying math, you must remember that we have to "use it or lose it."

**RULE 3**

The antecedent of a pronoun should not be *missing, ambiguous,* or *repetitious.*

• **Missing antecedent:**

> In Florida, *they* have beautifully developed retirement areas.

In this sentence, we do not know to whom *they* refers. If the text has not told us that *they* refers to the Florida government, real estate developers, or some other group, then we must say that the antecedent is *missing.* The sentence should be rewritten to avoid *they.*

> **Acceptable revision:** Many Florida communities have beautifully developed retirement areas.

• **Ambiguous antecedent:**

> Margaret told Lin that *she* needed to earn one thousand dollars during the summer.

In this sentence, *she* could refer to either Margaret or Lin. The sentence should be revised in a way that will avoid this confusion.

> **Acceptable revision:** Margaret said that Lin needed to earn one thousand dollars during the summer.

- **Repetitious pronoun and antecedent:**

  **The book, *it* describes the Great Depression.**

  The subject in this sentence should be either the noun *book* or, if there is already an antecedent, the pronoun *it*. Using both the noun and the pronoun results in needless repetition.

  **Acceptable revision:   The book describes the Great Depression.**

**Practice**

Rewrite the following sentences so that the antecedents are not *missing, ambiguous,* or *repetitious.*

1. The biologist asked the director to bring back his microscope.

   _____

   _____

2. The report, it says that the number of science and engineering students seeking doctoral degrees has fallen 50 percent since the mid-1960s.

   _____

   _____

3. At the laboratory, they said the research had run into serious difficulties.

   _____

4. The testing equipment was accidentally dropped onto the aquarium, and it was badly damaged.

   _____

5. I don't watch the 10 o'clock news anymore because they have become too slick.

   _____

   _____

**EXERCISE  7**

## Making Pronouns and Antecedents Agree

The following sentences contain errors with pronouns. Rewrite each sentence so that pronouns agree with their antecedents and so that antecedents are not missing, ambiguous, or repetitious.

1. His father mailed him his high school yearbook.

   _____

2. No one wants their income reduced.

   _____

3. When a company fails to update its equipment, they often pay a price in the long run.

   _____

4.   The woman today has many more options open to them than ever before.

_____

5.   Everybody knows their own strengths best.

_____

6.   Each of the workers anticipates their summer vacation.

_____

7.   If the campers want to eat quickly, each one should help themselves.

_____

8.   These sort of bathing suits look ridiculous on me.

_____

9.   On the application, it says you must pay a registration fee of thirty-five dollars.

_____

10.  The doctor said that those type of diseases are rare here.

_____

**EXERCISE  8**

## Making Pronouns and Antecedents Agree

**The following sentences may contain errors with pronouns. Rewrite the sentences so that pronouns agree with their antecedents and so that antecedents are not missing, ambiguous, or repetitious. If a sentence is correct, mark a *C* on the line provided.**

1.   The teacher told the parent he needed the test results.

_____

2.   The county submitted their proposal for the bridge repairs.

_____

3.   We all rushed to our cars because you had to wait for the thunderstorm to stop.

_____

4.   Anyone who fails the final will be unlikely to get his or her diploma.

_____

5.   A young person does not receive enough advice on how they should choose their career.

_____

6.   These type of watches are very popular.

_____

7.   People were rescued from our homes.

_____

8.  No one brought their books today.

_____

9.  The college it is holding homecoming weekend on October 5.

_____

10.  They call Indiana the Hoosier state.

_____

**EXERCISE**  **Making Pronouns and Antecedents Agree**

Each of the following sentences contains an error in pronoun-antecedent agreement. Edit each sentence so that pronouns agree with their antecedents and so that antecedents are not missing, ambiguous, or repetitious.

1.  Everyone should go to a live concert once in their life.

2.  Last month, Cynthia invited Vermell to a Mary J. Blige concert because she loves her music.

3.  They said the tickets would be sold out quickly.

4.  If you get up early enough, a person has a good chance to buy decent seats.

5.  These type of events are very expensive.

6.  The night of the concert, the arena it was jammed with young people.

7.  The security guards told the fans that they must be careful about pushing and shoving.

8.  People have been trampled in these sort of crowds.

9.  Finally, you could hear the music begin; our long wait for tickets had been worth the trouble.

10.  Her songs have positive lyrics; that's why I like it so much.

# MASTERY AND EDITING TESTS

**TEST**  **Using Pronouns Correctly**

Each of the following sentences contains at least one pronoun. Edit each sentence to correct errors in any of the following: pronoun case, pronouns that do not agree with their antecedents, and missing, ambiguous, or repetitious antecedents. If the sentence does not contain an error, mark it with a *C*.

1.  Whom do you think will be our next Supreme Court justice?

2.  Frank sent his cousin his favorite CD.

3.  One must understand anatomy if you want to go into a medical field.

4.  Doctor Mustafa does these math calculations much faster than I.

5.  In the newspaper, it said that Yo-Yo Ma would be giving a cello concert next month at the university.

6.  My professor and me have a plan to work together on the research this summer.

7.  They ought to give more grants for scientific research.

8.  The tailor and he agreed on the fitting.

9.  He decided to complete the group project by hisself.

10.  These type of projects demand serious commitment.

## TEST ● 2    Using Pronouns Correctly

**Each of the following sentences contains at least one pronoun. Edit each sentence to correct errors in any of the following: pronoun case, pronouns that do not agree with their antecedents, and missing, ambiguous, or repetitious antecedents. If the sentence does not contain an error, mark it with a *C*.**

1.  In the ad it said you should send a résumé.

2.  To who do you think we should send these bulletins?

3.  A pharmacist must triple check every order he fills.

4.  Just between you and I, the firm is in financial trouble.

5.  Those lessons helped Karen more than him.

6.  We always buy these type of coats.

7.  The bank warns people that you should always balance your checkbooks.

8.  Janelle's sister brought her plan to the council.

9.  The assignments they are going to require library research.

10.  Everyone did his part.

**TEST** **3**

## Editing Student Writing: Using Pronouns Correctly

The following paragraph contains ten errors in pronoun usage. Edit the paragraph to correct all the errors.

Nobody wants their taxes increased. Last Tuesday, the tax assessor sent my father his statement. The letter reported a huge tax increase, so it was a shock. In the letter, they said the tax must be paid within five days. If one is not wealthy, you can have trouble paying such a bill on time. My father, who is generally calm in these kind of situations, was upset. This hardworking man, he marched to the town hall. He complained to them. They had nothing to say. One of them shook their head sympathetically, but he still had to pay the bill.

**TEST** **4**

## Editing Student Writing Using Editing Symbols

In the following paragraph, editing symbols mark the sentences that need revision or correction. These editing symbols include the following: agr (agreement), frag (fragment), ro (run-on), subord (subordination), pron ca (pronoun case), and pron ref (pronoun reference). Make your corrections on the lines provided after the paragraph.

                        pron ca
¹John Dickens, whom was the father of the great novelist Charles Dickens,
                                pron ref
was never able to handle their money successfully. ²The family had to move to smaller and smaller houses as the finances of the family became worse.
                                pron ca
³Eventually, they found themself living in a small part of a
                                                                        frag
house. ⁴Young Charles was sent to a pawnbroker's shop. ⁵To sell the family's books, silver teapots and spoons, and other family possessions. ⁶Little by little, even the family furniture
                        pron ref
had to be sold, and he was placed in debtor's prison. ⁷In
                                        pron ref
those days, this is what they did to the head of the family
                                                subord
if he or she could not pay debts. ⁸When Charles was twelve he suffered another traumatic event because of his family's
                        ro
situation. ⁹He was taken out of school and his parents put him to work pasting labels on bottles of shoe polish. ¹⁰He never recovered from the psychological shock. ¹¹His formal
                pron ref
education, it was over. ¹²As a result of these childhood traumas, Charles Dickens's numerous novels, which are
                                                agr
filled with many a colorful character, portrays children trapped by circumstances they cannot control.

**Corrections**

1.  pronoun case (sentence 1):            _____

2.  pronoun reference (sentence 1):       _____

3.  pronoun case (sentence 3):            _____

4.  fragment (sentence 5):                _____

5.  pronoun reference (sentence 6):       _____

6.  pronoun reference (sentence 7):       _____

7.  subordination (sentence 8):           _____

8.  run on sentence (sentence 9):         _____

9.  pronoun reference (sentence 11):      _____

10. agreement (sentence 12):              _____

## Exploring Online

Go to **www.cengage.com/devenglish/scarry/writersworkplace** to find the **Writer's Online Workplace,** a website designed for students using this book. You will find links to handouts, interactive quizzes, and other online resources as you explore the following topics:

- choosing the correct pronoun
- pronoun-antecedent agreement

# Working Together

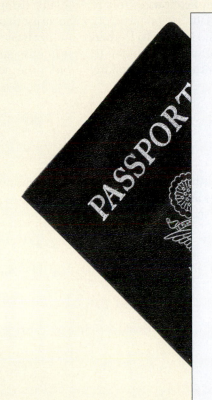

## Princess Must Face Immigration Charges

SAN DIEGO, July 17 (AP)—A princess who fled Bahrain with fake documents to marry an American marine must face charges of illegally entering the United States, an immigration judge said today.

The judge, Ignacio Fernandez, refused to dismiss the charges, a ruling that prevents the princess, Meriam Al Khalifa, from applying for permanent residency without seeking political asylum.

Ms. Al Khalifa, who is 19, plans to apply for asylum on the ground that she faces extreme persecution for marrying a non-Muslim if she returns to Bahrain, her lawyer said. She has up to a year to apply for political asylum.

A spokesman for the Bahraini Embassy in Washington said that the princess' family was eager for her to return and that she would not face persecution.

The hearing was closed to the public, but her lawyer provided an account of the ruling.

Ms. Al Khalifa lives with her husband, Lance Cpl. Jason Johnson, on Camp Pendleton, a Marine base 40 miles north of San Diego. They met last year in the Bahraini capital of Manama, where the 25-year-old marine was assigned to a security unit.

Ms. Al Khalifa's father is a cousin of Bahrain's head of state, Emir Hamad bin Isa Al Khalifa.

In July 2000, the news story of the princess from Bahrain who defied her parents and ran away with an American marine made international headlines. The story was of great interest to many readers and raised many complicated issues. For example, should the princess have obeyed her parents? Did she have the right to follow her heart, leave her country without the proper papers, and then enter the United States illegally? Readers wanted to know more about the princess and what eventually happened to her.

In addition to the conflict between romantic love and duty to one's parents, the story showed the clash between two cultures, each one with its distinct customs and values. In Bahrain, this nineteen-year-old Muslim princess had lived with servants and chauffeurs. In America, she would be adopting the modest lifestyle of her new husband and his family. She would no longer have the support of her mother and father. She would be among people who did not follow her customs or share her religious background.

## Group Discussion

Brainstorm with your classmates to make a list of the various issues this princess would have to face after she made her decision to elope with the American marine. Once the list is completed, briefly discuss each item, keeping in mind that each item could be a writing opportunity.

## Freewriting

Each student should respond to the facts and implications of this news event using the insights reached during the class discussion. Choose one aspect of the story that is of real interest and use the time given by your instructor to freewrite on this topic. Keep in mind that, as the work of the semester continues, some of these same issues are likely to resurface, and you will be able to continue your thinking about a theme that interests you as you approach other writing opportunities.

# PORTFOLIO SUGGESTION

You may want to pursue the topics of cross-cultural relationships or immigration raised here. Search the Internet for other articles and news stories relating to these topics. These issues are deeply relevant to most Americans today.

# WORKING WITH ADJECTIVES, ADVERBS, AND PARALLEL STRUCTURE

# 10

**Adjectives** and **adverbs** are used to describe, limit, or qualify other words. In this chapter, you will study the following:

- **adjectives and adverbs used in comparisons,** especially irregular forms

- the most commonly **confused adjectives and adverbs,** including *good* and *well*

- **misplaced modifiers** and **dangling modifiers**

- the adverb *not* and the avoidance of **double negatives**

Items listed in a series need to be presented in a similar form. In this chapter, you will also learn how to use **parallel structure:**

- making **words in a series** the same parts of speech

- making **phrases in a series** the same kinds of phrases

- making certain that **clauses in a series** are not combined with words or phrases

# WHAT IS THE DIFFERENCE BETWEEN AN ADJECTIVE AND AN ADVERB?

*Adjectives* modify nouns and pronouns.

Charlene is a *studious* person.

She is *studious.*

*Adverbs* modify verbs, adjectives, and other adverbs. They often end in *-ly.* They usually answer one of the following questions: *How? When? Where? Why?* or *To what extent?*

Charlene *happily* dreams about her vacation.

You cannot be *too* careful.

Charlene worked *very* quickly.

Because not all adverbs end in *-ly,* it is useful to learn some of the most common adverbs.

## List of Common Adverbs

| | | |
|---|---|---|
| always | much | seldom |
| even | never | sometimes |
| ever | not | surely |
| hardly | now | tomorrow |
| just | often | too |
| later | only | very |
| more | quite | yesterday |

**Practice**

In each of the following sentences, an adjective or an adverb has been underlined. Draw an arrow from the underlined word to the word that it modifies. Then identify the underlined word as an adjective (adj) or an adverb (adv). An example has been done for you.

<u>adj</u>       The <u>morning</u> sunlight felt good.

**NOTE:** In this case, *morning* modifies the noun *sunlight,* so it functions as an adjective.

____   1. Seasonal affective disorder (SAD) is a type of depression <u>also</u> known as the "winter blues."

____   2. An estimated 25 percent of the population suffers from a <u>mild</u> form of SAD.

____ 3. About 5 percent suffers from a <u>more</u> severe form of the disorder.

____ 4. Young people and women are at a <u>very</u> high risk for the disorder.

____ 5. The symptoms occur <u>regularly</u> during the fall or winter months.

____ 6. People with SAD may feel <u>anxious</u>.

____ 7. They may crave sugary or <u>starchy</u> foods.

____ 8. A brisk walk in the morning sunlight can be <u>helpful</u>.

# ADJECTIVES AND ADVERBS USED IN COMPARISONS

> **For most adjectives and adverbs of *one syllable*, add *-er* for the comparative form and *-est* for the superlative form.**

The following chart lists some one-syllable adjectives (adj) and adverbs (adv) along with their comparative and superlative forms.

## Comparative Forms of One-Syllable Adjectives and Adverbs

| ADJECTIVE OR ADVERB | COMPARATIVE FORM (COMPARES TWO THINGS OR GROUPS) | SUPERLATIVE FORM (COMPARES THREE OR MORE THINGS OR GROUPS) |
| --- | --- | --- |
| light (adj) | lighter | lightest |
| short (adj) | shorter | shortest |
| fast (adv) | faster | fastest |
| hard (adv) | harder | hardest |

> **Some adjectives and adverbs of *two syllables* take *-er* and *-est*, while others use *more (or less)* and *most (or least)*. When in doubt, consult a dictionary.**

The following chart lists some two-syllable adjectives and adverbs along with their comparative and superlative forms.

## Comparative Forms of Two-Syllable Adjectives and Adverbs

| ADJECTIVE OR ADVERB | COMPARATIVE FORM (COMPARES TWO THINGS OR GROUPS) | SUPERLATIVE FORM (COMPARES THREE OR MORE THINGS OR GROUPS) |
| --- | --- | --- |
| easy (adj) | easier | easiest |
| funny (adj) | funnier | funniest |
| happy (adj) | happier | happiest |
| lovely (adj) | lovelier | loveliest |
| helpful (adj) | more helpful | most helpful |
| famous (adj) | more famous | most famous |
| quickly (adv) | more quickly | most quickly |
| slowly (adv) | more slowly | most slowly |

For adjectives and adverbs of *three or more syllables*, use *more* (or *less*) for the comparative form and *most* (or *least*) for the superlative form.

The following chart lists some three-syllable adjectives and adverbs along with their comparative and superlative forms.

## Comparative Forms of Three-Syllable Adjectives and Adverbs

| ADJECTIVE OR ADVERB | COMPARATIVE FORM (COMPARES TWO THINGS OR GROUPS) | SUPERLATIVE FORM (COMPARES THREE OR MORE THINGS OR GROUPS) |
| --- | --- | --- |
| successful (adj) | more successful | most successful |
| delicious (adj) | more delicious | most delicious |
| easily (adv) | more easily | most easily |
| carefully (adv) | more carefully | most carefully |

Some commonly used adjectives and adverbs have irregular forms. Study the following chart of commonly used adjectives and adverbs that have irregular comparative and superlative forms.

## Irregular Comparative Forms

| ADJECTIVE OR ADVERB | COMPARATIVE FORM (COMPARES TWO THINGS OR GROUPS) | SUPERLATIVE FORM (COMPARES THREE OR MORE THINGS OR GROUPS) |
| --- | --- | --- |
| bad (adj) | worse | worst |
| badly (adv) | worse | worst |
| good (adj) | better | best |
| well (adv or adj) | better | best |
| many (adj) | more | most |
| much (adj or adv) | more | most |
| more (adj or adv) | more | most |
| far (adj or adv) | farther or further | farthest or furthest |
| little (adj or adv) | less | least |

### farther/further

Use *farther* or *farthest* to indicate physical distance.

**She could not walk any *farther*.**

Use *further* or *furthest* to indicate mental distance.

**The lawyer made a *further* argument.**

### little/few

Do not confuse *little* with *few*. Use *little* when you cannot easily count the item modified.

**They had *little grain* for the cattle.**

Use *fewer* when you can count the item modified.

**They had *fewer cattle* this year than last year.**

**EXERCISE 1**

### Adjectives and Adverbs Used in Comparisons

**In each of the following sentences, fill in the blank with the correct form of the adjective or adverb given in parentheses.**

1.  This chapter is _____ than the last one.
    (easy)

2.  She is the _____ woman in the police department.
    (tall)

3.  That machine is _____ operated than the one in the other room.
    (easily)

4.  He feels _____ today than he did yesterday.
    (good)

5.  That woman is the _____ chef in San Francisco.
    (famous)

6.  This paralegal is the _____ person in the office.
    (helpful)

7.  Would you please drive _____ than your father?
    (slowly)

8.  Unfortunately, this is the _____ business trip I have ever made.
    (bad)

9.  His illness became _____.
    (bad)

10. This lasagna is the _____ lasagna I have ever tasted.
    (delicious)

**EXERCISE  2**

## Adjectives and Adverbs Used in Comparisons

**In each of the following sentences, fill in the blank with the correct form of the adjective or adverb given in parentheses.**

1.  *Star Wars: Episode II* was _____ than *Star Wars: Episode I.*
    (exciting)

2.  She was _____ than she had been in a long time.
    (healthy)

3.  The _____ hamburger I ever ate was at a restaurant in Denver.
    (good)

4.  The cheetah is the _____ animal in the world.
    (fast)

5.  It is _____ to drive at night than during the day.
    (dangerous)

6.  That new law seems _____ written than the previous one.
    (carefully)

7.  My cat is the _____ pet I've ever had.
    (lazy)

8.   Quitting her job was the _____ thing from her mind.
                                            (far)

9.   Her second job was _____ than her first one.
                                      (bad)

10.  She is the _____ worker in the entire company.
                      (honest)

## THE MOST COMMONLY CONFUSED ADJECTIVES AND ADVERBS

To strengthen your understanding of modifiers, study the list of adjectives and adverbs given below along with example sentences showing how each modifier is used.

**awful/awfully**

**awful (adj):**   She looks *awful.* (*Awful* is a predicate adjective after the linking verb *looks.*)

**awfully (adv):**   She looks *awfully* tired. (*Awfully* is an adverb modifying the adjective *tired.*)

**bad/badly**

**bad (adj):**   The play was *bad.* (meaning *not good*)

He feels bad, even though the fever is down. (meaning *sick*)

He feels bad about losing the money. (meaning *sorry* or *upset*)

**badly (adv):**   He painted badly. (meaning *not well*)

The team *badly* needs a win. (meaning *very much*, with verbs such as *want* or *need*)

**good/well**

**good (adj):**   Alice Walker is a *good* writer.

The food tastes *good.*

He feels *good* about his work.

(Remember that *good* is always an adjective.)

**well (adv):**   He dances *well.* (meaning *skillfully*)

He behaved *well.* (meaning *in a proper manner*)

The praise for his book was *well* deserved. (meaning *fully*)

He gets along *well* with people. (meaning *successfully*)

**well (adj):**   He feels *well.* (*Well* is an adjective only when referring to *health.*)

| poor/poorly | *poor (adj):* | The *poor* man was now homeless. (meaning *pitiful* or *penniless*) |
| | *poorly (adv):* | She scored *poorly* on the exam. |
| quick/quickly | *quick (adj):* | She is *quick* at word games. |
| | *quickly (adv):* | She works *quickly*. |
| quiet/quietly | *quiet (adj):* | After ten at night, the dorm has *quiet* hours. |
| | *quietly (adv):* | Talk *quietly* after ten o'clock. |
| real/really | *real (adj):* | The medics responded to a *real emergency*. (meaning *genuine, not imaginary*) |
| | *really (adv):* | The student is *really* determined to do well. (meaning *genuinely, truly*) |
| sure/surely | *sure (adj):* | I am *sure* she was the person driving the car. (meaning *certain, confident, firm*) |
| | *surely (adv):* | She was *surely* speeding. (meaning *certainly, truly*) |

**NOTE:** *Real* and *sure* are often used informally in everyday conversation as adverbs to mean *very* or *certainly*, as in "I'm real sorry about your illness," or "I'm sure sorry about your illness." However, this usage is not acceptable in formal writing.

**Practice**    Choose the correct adjective or adverb in each of the following sentences. You may find it helpful to draw an arrow to the word that the adjective or adverb is modifying.

1.  The child was (awful, awfully) sick.

2.  The nurse felt (bad, badly) about the child.

3.  The child didn't do (good, well) in class.

4.  Let's act (quick, quickly) and try to help her.

5.  The mother was (real, really) upset.

# MISPLACED AND DANGLING MODIFIERS

Study the following five sentences. Notice how the meaning of each sentence is changed, depending on where in the sentence the modifier *only* is placed.

*Only* Charlene telephoned my brother yesterday. (Nobody else telephoned.)

Charlene *only* telephoned my brother yesterday. (She did not e-mail or visit.)

Charlene telephoned *only* my brother yesterday. (She called no one else.)

Charlene telephoned my *only* brother yesterday. (The writer has only one brother.)

Charlene telephoned my brother *only* yesterday. (She didn't telephone until yesterday.)

> *A **modifier*** is a word, phrase, or clause that functions as an adjective or an adverb.
>
> **my only brother**
>
> *Only* modifies the noun *brother*; therefore, *only* functions as an adjective.
>
> **the marine *who is my brother***
>
> *Who is my brother* is a clause that modifies the noun *marine*; therefore, *who is my brother* functions as an adjective clause.
>
> **just yesterday**
>
> *Just* modifies the adverb *yesterday*; therefore, *just* functions as an adverb.

## MISPLACED MODIFIERS

> A ***misplaced modifier*** is a modifier whose placement in a sentence makes the meaning of that sentence confusing, awkward, or ambiguous.

Below is a list of modifiers that are often misplaced. When you use one of these words, be sure it immediately precedes the word or word group it modifies.

### Modifiers Often Misplaced

| | | | | |
|---|---|---|---|---|
| almost | exactly | just | nearly | scarcely |
| even | hardly | merely | only | simply |

1.  The modifier is in a **confusing** position because it does not immediately precede the word it modifies.

    **Confusing placement of a *word* modifier:**

    > *Nearly* the salesperson sold the used car to the customer.

    *Nearly,* an adverb, cannot modify the noun *salesperson.*

    **Revised:**    The salesperson *nearly* sold the used car to the customer.

    *Nearly* correctly modifies the verb *sold.*

    **Confusing placement of a *phrase* modifier:**

    > *With all the rusty spots*, the salesperson could not sell the car.

    Is it the salesperson who has rusty spots or the car?

    **Revised:**    The salesperson could not sell the car *with all the rusty spots.*

    **Confusing placement of a *clause* modifier:**

    > The salesperson could not sell the used car to the customer *that needed extensive body work.*

    Is it the customer or the car that needs extensive body work?

    **Revised:**    The salesperson could not sell the used car *that needed extensive body work* to the customer.

2.  The modifier is in an **awkward** position, interrupting the flow of the sentence.

    **Awkward placement:**

    > We want *to* after the lunch hour *study* in the library.

    **Revised:**    After the lunch hour, we want *to study* in the library.

    Although the use of the infinitive that is interrupted (called a "split infinitive") has now become more accepted in standard English, the result is frequently awkward and often interrupts the flow of the sentence.

3.  The modifier is in an **ambiguous** position (sometimes called a "squinting modifier").

    **Ambiguous placement:**

    > The used-car salesperson when questioned *seriously* doubted he could sell the rusty car.

    Was the salesperson seriously questioned or did he seriously doubt? From the placement of *seriously,* it is impossible to know.

    **Revised:**    When *seriously questioned*, the used-car salesperson doubted he could sell the rusty car.

    > or, depending on the intended meaning,

    When questioned, the used-car salesperson *seriously doubted* he could sell the rusty car.

**EXERCISE  3**        **Revising Misplaced Modifiers**

**Revise each of the following sentences to avoid misplaced modifiers.**

1. I gave the puppy to my sister with the white paws.

   _____

2. I am looking for the keys to the filing cabinets that are missing.

   _____

3. We decided to before the camping trip buy better sleeping bags.

   _____

4. As a pilot, passenger safety had always come first.

   _____

5. They need to immediately after the party go directly home.

   _____

6. The dance contestants waited eagerly watching the faces of the judges.

   _____

7. The jeweler wanted to for his new customer design a special charm bracelet.

   _____

8. I took my daughter to my office who loved a day off from school.

   _____

9. The accountant forgot almost to tell his client about the change in the law.

   _____

10. There are five tablets in this medicine bottle exactly.

   _____

## DANGLING MODIFIERS

> A **dangling modifier** is a modifier without a logical or identifiable word, phrase, or clause to modify in the sentence.

**Sentence with a dangling modifier:**   **Working on the car's engine, the dog barked all afternoon.**

Who was working on the engine? According to the sentence, it is the dog who was working on the engine. *Working on the car's engine* is a participial phrase that modifies the subject *dog*. As it stands, the sentence makes no sense.

> ## Two Options for Revising a Dangling Modifier
>
> ### Option 1: Create a new subject for the independent clause.
>
> **Working on the car's engine, *I* heard the dog barking all afternoon.**
>
> Now the modifying phrase *working on the car's engine* modifies the pronoun subject *I*.
>
> ### Option 2: Create a dependent clause (a dependent clause begins with a subordinating conjunction or relative pronoun and has a subject and a verb).
>
> **While I was working on the car's engine, the dog barked all afternoon.**
>
> Now the modifying phrase *working on the car's engine* has been changed into a dependent clause.

**EXERCISE  4**

## Revising Dangling Modifiers

**Revise each of the following sentences to avoid misplaced or dangling modifiers.**

1. Victor fed the dog wearing his tuxedo.

   _____

2. Visiting Yellowstone National Park, Old Faithful entertained us by performing on schedule.

   _____
   _____

3. Hoping to see the news, the television set was turned on at seven o'clock.

   _____

4. Running up the stairs, the train had already left for Philadelphia.

   _____

5. After running over the hill, the farm was visible in the valley below.

   _____

6. Dressed in a Dracula costume, I thought my son looked perfect for Halloween.

   _____

7. Hanging from the ceiling in her bedroom, she saw three spiders.

   _____

8. After wiping my glasses, the redbird flew away.

   _____

9. Howling without a stop, we listened to the neighbor's dog all evening.

   _____

10. After painting my room all afternoon, my cat demanded her dinner.

_____

**EXERCISE 5**

### Revising Misplaced or Dangling Modifiers

Revise each of the following sentences to avoid misplaced or dangling modifiers.

1. Leaping upstream, we fished most of the day for salmon.

_____

2. At the age of ten, my family took a trip to Washington, D.C.

_____

3. Skimming every chapter, my biology textbook made more sense.

_____

4. A woodpecker was found in Cuba that had been considered extinct.

_____

5. Working extra hours last week, my salary dramatically increased.

_____

6. We watched a movie in the theater that had won an Academy Award for best picture.

_____

7. The truck caused a traffic jam, which was broken down on the highway, for miles.

_____

8. Last week while shopping, my friend's purse was stolen.

_____

9. While eating lunch outdoors, our picnic table collapsed.

_____

10. Our car is in the parking lot with two bags of groceries unlocked.

_____

## AVOIDING THE DOUBLE NEGATIVE WITH THE ADVERB *NOT* AND OTHER NEGATIVE WORDS

The adverb *not* is one of several words that carry a negative meaning. In standard English, having two negative words in the same sentence is not acceptable.

## Words That Carry a Negative Meaning

| | | | |
|---|---|---|---|
| no | no one | neither | barely |
| not | none | never | hardly |
| nobody | nothing | nowhere | scarcely |

You can correct a sentence that contains a double negative by removing either one of the two negative words.

**Incorrect:**              I *don't* have *no* food in my house.

**Possible corrections:**   I *don't* have food in my house.

                            I have *no* food in my house.

**Practice**    Revise each of the following sentences to correct the double negative.

1.  A person shouldn't never go out with something cooking on the stove.

2.  You haven't neither a bike nor a car.

3.  I don't want nothing.

4.  I won't never break my promise.

5.  I can't hardly wait until summer.

# PARALLEL STRUCTURE: MAKING A SERIES OF WORDS, PHRASES, OR CLAUSES BALANCED WITHIN THE SENTENCE

Which one of the following sentences has the more balanced structure?

**His favorite hobbies are playing the trumpet, listening to jazz, and to go to concerts.**

**His favorite hobbies are playing the trumpet, listening to jazz, and going to concerts.**

If you selected the second sentence, you made the better choice. The second sentence uses parallel structure to balance the three phrases in the series (*playing the trumpet, listening to jazz, going to concerts*). Matching each of the items in the series with the same -*ing* structure makes the sentence easier to understand and more pleasant to read. Words, phrases, and even sentences in a series can be made parallel.

RULE   **Words in a series should be the same parts of speech.**

**Not parallel:**  **The town was small, friendly, and the atmosphere was peaceful.**

The series is composed of two adjectives and one clause.

**Parallel:**  **The town was small, friendly, and peaceful.**

The series is composed of three adjectives: *small, friendly,* and *peaceful.*

RULE **2**  **Phrases in a series should be the same kind of phrases** *(infinitive phrase, prepositional phrase, verb phrase, noun phrase, or participial phrase).*

**Not parallel:**  **Her lost assignment is in her closet, on the floor, and a pile of clothes is hiding it.**

The series is composed of two prepositional phrases and one clause.

**Parallel:**  **Her lost assignment is in her closet, on the floor, and under a pile of clothes.**

The series is composed of three prepositional phrases beginning with *in, on,* and *under.*

RULE **3**  **Clauses in a series should not  be mixed with phrases.**

**Not parallel:**  **The street was narrow, the shops were charming, and crowds in the cafe.**

The series is composed of two clauses and one phrase.

**Parallel:**  **The street was narrow, the shops were charming, and the cafe was crowded.**

The series is composed of three clauses.

**Practice**  Each of the following sentences lacks parallel structure. In each sentence, revise the underlined section to make the series parallel.

1. My favorite armchair is lumpy, worn out, and <u>has dirt spots everywhere</u>.

2. She enjoys reading novels, studying the flute, and <u>sews her own clothes.</u>

3. He admires teachers who make the classroom an exciting place and

   <u>willingly explaining the lesson more than once.</u>

**EXERCISE**

## Revising Sentences for Parallel Structure

Each of the following sentences lacks parallel structure. Underline the word, phrase, or clause that is not parallel and revise it so that its structure balances with the other items in the pair or series. An example has been done for you.

> **Not parallel:**     The best leather comes from Italy, from Spain, and <u>is imported from Brazil</u>.
>
> **Parallel:**          The best leather comes from Italy, Spain, and Brazil.

1. Winter in Chicago is very windy, extremely snowy, and has many bitterly cold days.

2. I would prefer to fix an old car rather than watching television.

3. Mr. Lee is a helpful neighbor, a loyal friend, and dedicated to his children.

4. The apartment is crowded and without light.

5. The dancer is slender, tall, and moves gracefully.

6. The nursery was cheerful, large, and had a lot of sun.

7. My friend loves to play chess, to read science fiction, and working out at the gym.

8. For homework today I must read a chapter in history, do five exercises for Spanish class, and working on my term paper for political science.

9. The painting reveals the artist's talent and his imagination is revealed.

10. The cars race down the track, turn the corner at great speed, and then they are heading for the homestretch.

**EXERCISE**

## Revising Sentences for Parallel Structure

Each of the following sentences lacks parallel structure. Underline the word, phrase, or clause that is not parallel and revise it so that its structure balances with the other items in the pair or series.

1. The dog had to choose between jumping over the fence or he could have dug a hole underneath it.

2. She disliked going to the beach, hiking in the woods, and she didn't care for picnics, either.

3. As I looked down the city street, I could see the soft lights from restaurant windows, I could hear the mellow sounds of a nightclub band, and carefree moods of people walking by.

4. The singers have been on several road tours, have recorded for two record companies, and they would like to make a movie someday.

5. They would rather order a pizza than eating their sister's cooking.

6. I explained to the teacher that my car had broken down, my books had been stolen, and no assignment pad.

7. That night, the prisoner was sick, discouraged, and she was filled with loneliness.

8. As the truck rumbled down the street, it suddenly lurched out of control, smashed into a parked car, and then the truck hit the storefront of my uncle's hardware store.

9. The teacher is patient, intelligent, and demands a lot.

10. He was determined to pass the math course, not only to get his three credits but also for a sense of achievement.

**EXERCISE** **8**  **Revising Sentences for Parallel Structure**

**Each of the following sentences lacks parallel structure. Underline the word, phrase, or clause that is not parallel and revise it so that its structure balances with the other items in the pair or series.**

1. The first-grade teacher told us that our child was unruly, mischievous, and talked too much.

2. The dog's size, its coloring, and whenever it barked reminded me of a wolf.

3. Shabna is not only very talented but she is also acting kindly to everyone.

4. He dried the dishes; putting them away was the job of his wife.

5. Jordan would rather travel and see the world than staying home and reading about other places.

6. For weeks he tried to decide whether he should major in chemistry, continue with accounting, or to take a year off.

7.  Her depression was a result of the loss of her job, the breakdown of her marriage, and a teenage daughter who was a problem.

8.  She must either cut back on her expenses or selling her car.

9.  His office is down a dark hallway, on the fourth floor, and having no windows.

10. He went through four years of college, one year of graduate school, and then doing one year teaching seventh-grade science.

## MASTERY AND EDITING TESTS

**TEST 1**

### Revising Sentences for Correct Use of Modifiers and Parallel Structure

**Each sentence has an error in the use of a modifier or in parallel structure. Rewrite each sentence to correct the error you find.**

1.  The puppy devoured the bone, tore up his new bed, and jumping up on the new sofa.

    _____

2.  The student almost received enough money from his aunt to pay for his semester's tuition.

    _____
    _____

3.  She returned from vacation rested, with a great deal of energy, and happy.

    _____

4.  Joseph managed to find time to coach the team with two other day jobs.

    _____
    _____

5.  I'm the most happy man alive.

    _____

6.  Discovered by accident, the football fan took the diamond ring to the lost and found.

    _____
    _____

7.  Books were piled on the reading tables, magazines were tossed on chairs, and scraps of paper everywhere.

    _____
    _____

8.   Being nearly deaf, the whistle of the train did not warn him of the danger.

_____

9.   The audience was bored because he talked slow.

_____

10.   The bus, judging the fog was too thick, stopped by the side of the road.

_____

_____

**TEST 2**

## Revising Sentences for Correct Use of Modifiers and Parallel Structure

**Each sentence has an error in the use of a modifier or in parallel structure. Rewrite each sentence to correct the error you find.**

1.   The job demands computer skills, math ability, and with accounting background.

_____

2.   My sister is not only a talented musician, but she is also teaching with great success.

_____

3.   Raking the leaves this morning, more than one hundred geese flew overhead.

_____

_____

4.   Follow the directions for writing the essay carefully.

_____

5.   The astronomer completed the calculation at the observatory that he had been working on for nearly a decade.

_____

_____

6.   He's the baddest speaker I've ever heard.

_____

7.   My older brother is guilty of lecturing me instead of a good example.

_____

8.   The new highway follows the river, bypasses the small towns, and you can save a lot of time.

_____

_____

9.   He only ordered an appetizer.

_____

10.  I don't want nothing to eat.

_____


**TEST** **3**    ## Revising Sentences for Correct Use of Modifiers and Parallel Structure

**Each sentence has an error in the use of a modifier or parallel structure. Rewrite each sentence to correct the error you find.**

1.   The car stopped quick to avoid the child.

_____

2.   My friend is generous, hardworking, and a talker.

_____

3.   The members of Congress would rather stonewall the proposal than to pass the new law.

_____

_____

4.   When covered with thin ice, you should not skate on the lake.

_____

5.   Last year, the citizen just paid half of his taxes.

_____

6.   From the airport, I will either take the bus or the shuttle to the hotel.

_____

7.   For the holidays, we plan to do some cooking, see a few good movies, and listening to jazz.

_____

_____

8.   Working late into the night, the page numbering on my report kept printing out incorrectly.

_____

_____

9.   I haven't seen nobody today.

_____

10.  The child behaved real good during the performance.

_____

**TEST 4**

## Editing Student Writing Using Editing Symbols

The commonly used editing symbols for errors in modifiers are *adj* (adjective), *adv* (adverb), and *dm* (dangling modifier). The editing symbol for an error in parallel structure is *//*. In the paragraph below, ten errors are marked with editing symbols. Correct each error on the lines provided after the paragraph.

¹The criminal justice system in the United States has changed dramatically in recent years. ²We have come a long way since the nineteenth century, when the use of fingerprint evidence was all that an investigator had to help *them*. [*pron ref*] ³The use of DNA has led to this *real* [*adv*] important change. ⁴DNA testing is a scientific method of determining whether two samples of organic material *comes* [*agr*] from the same source. ⁵Testing for DNA, *an individual* [*dm*] may be placed at a particular crime scene. ⁶These scientific tests may contradict criminal convictions from the past. ⁷In such cases, this evidence becomes more *strong* [*adj*] than any jury finding. ⁸Just a few years ago, the discoveries made through the use of DNA testing in Illinois were so dramatic that the governor ordered all executions in that state canceled. ⁹Also, it appears that people elsewhere have been wrongfully convicted and jailed for many kinds of offenses, including first-degree murder, sexual assault, and people who [*//*] were dealing drugs. ¹⁰People who have been in prison for years, in New York, in Ohio, and the state [*//*] of California, have been found innocent and have been released. ¹¹One of the few problems with DNA evidence *are* [*agr*] the expense of running the tests. ¹²However, the *most best* [*adj*] news for the future is that problems of wrongful convictions by juries will occur a lot less often. ¹³Because [*frag*] DNA evidence will be presented whenever possible as part of courtroom evidence.

### Corrections

1. pronoun reference (sentence 2): _____

    _____

2. adverb (sentence 3): _____

    _____

3. agreement (sentence 4): _____

4. dangling modifier (sentence 5): _____

    _____

5. adjective (sentence 7): _____

6.  parallel structure (sentence 9):   _____

    _____

7.  parallel structure (sentence 10):   _____

    _____

8.  agreement (sentence 11):   _____

9.  adjective (sentence 12):   _____

10.  fragment (sentence 13):   _____

    _____

    _____

    _____

    _____

    _____

## Exploring Online

Go to **www.cengage.com/devenglish/scarry/writersworkplace** to find the **Writer's Online Workplace,** a website designed for students using this book. You will find links to handouts, interactive quizzes, and other online resources as you explore the following topics:

- misplaced and dangling modifiers
- humorous misplaced modifiers
- parallel structure

# Working Together

## PREPARING AND EDITING A RÉSUMÉ

Below is a draft of a résumé written by a college student who is looking for a summer job. This draft already has many of the elements needed for an effective résumé, but it also contains at least twenty errors (such as misspelling, typographical errors, faulty punctuation, or inconsistent design). Before it can be submitted to a potential employer, it will need to be edited and revised. Study each item on the résumé and then answer the questions that follow.

Gary Sommers
645 Franklin AVe.
Norman, Oklahoma
Home Telephone: 662-1919

| | |
|---|---|
| <u>Present Job Objective</u> | A summer position as an assistant in ~~teh~~ the mayor's office |
| <u>Education</u> | High School Diploma, Kennedy High School, Norman, Oklahoma |
| | B.A., Business Administration, University of Oklahoma |
| | Expected date of graduation: june 2012 |
| | Courses in Business and Computers: Principles of Accounting, Microeconomic Theory, Problem solving and Structured Programming, Computer Systems and Assembly |

### WORK EXPERIENCE

| | |
|---|---|
| 9/08 to present 2007–2008 | Tutor, Math Lab, University of Oklahoma Summer Volunteer at Camp Sunshine, a day camp for disabled children |
| <u>Special skills:</u> | fluent in spanish |
| <u>Computer Skills:</u> | familiar with Microsoft Word, EXCEL, |
| <u>Interests:</u> | soccer, guitar |
| <u>REFERENCES:</u> | Available on request |

## Questions for Résumé Editing

1. Can you find any typos, misspelled words, or errors in capitalization or punctuation?
2. Can you find anything inconsistent in the design or layout? (Look for places where parallel structures are needed.)

3. If Gary Sommers corrected even a single error by using an ink pen instead of printing out a corrected version of the entire résumé, what do you think a potential employer might conclude?

4. Is there any missing information in this résumé?

5. Why has Mr. Sommers not included such facts as date of birth and marital status?

6. When a person looks for a job, how many references should be listed? How does the person obtain these references?

7. How could Mr. Sommers highlight his interest in the particular job for which he is applying?

8. It is appropriate when sending a résumé to attach a covering letter. What should be included in a covering letter?

## PORTFOLIO SUGGESTION

Using the same headings found in this sample résumé, draft a résumé for yourself. Copy it onto a disk or CD that you will keep. Remember to update the résumé regularly. You may want to highlight a particular skill or emphasize different parts of your background by creating two or more versions of your resume.

# MASTERING IRREGULAR VERB FORMS

# 11

In this chapter, you will learn the principal parts of **fifty irregular verbs.** These verbs are divided into the following groups:

**CHAPTER OBJECTIVES**

- eight verbs that do not change their forms
- two verbs with the same simple and past participle forms
- twenty verbs with the same past tense and past participle forms
- twenty verbs that differ in all three forms

## WHAT ARE THE PRINCIPAL PARTS OF IRREGULAR VERBS?

The English language has more than one hundred verbs that do not form the past tense or past participle with the usual *-ed* ending. Their forms are irregular. When you listen to children aged four or five, you often hear them use *-ed* to form the past tense of every verb, as in "Yesterday, I *goed* to my aunt's house." Later on, they will learn that the verb *to go* is unusual, and they will change to the irregular form, "Yesterday, I *went*. . . ." The best way to learn these verbs is to listen to how they sound. In Appendix C of this book, you will find an extensive list of the three principal parts of these verbs: the simple form (also called dictionary form, infinitive form, or basic form), the past tense, and the past participle (used with perfect tenses, after *has, have, had,* or *will have,* or with the passive voice, after the verb *to be).*

## PRACTICING FIFTY IRREGULAR VERBS

Learn the three principal parts of all fifty irregular verbs given in this chapter. Pronounce them out loud until you have learned them. If you don't know the meaning of a particular verb or you cannot pronounce a verb and its forms, ask your instructor for help. Most irregular verbs are very common words that you will be using often in your writing and speaking. You will want to know them well.

## Eight Verbs That Do Not Change Their Forms

(notice that all the verb forms end in *-t* or *-d*)

| SIMPLE FORM | PAST TENSE | PAST PARTICIPLE | SIMPLE FORM | PAST TENSE | PAST PARTICIPLE |
|---|---|---|---|---|---|
| bet | bet | bet | hurt | hurt | hurt |
| cost | cost | cost | put | put | put |
| cut | cut | cut | quit | quit | quit |
| hit | hit | hit | spread | spread | spread |

## Two Verbs with the Same Simple and Past Participle Forms

| SIMPLE FORM | PAST TENSE | PAST PARTICIPLE |
|---|---|---|
| come | came | come |
| become | became | become |

**Practice**

Using the verb given in parentheses, fill in the correct form in each of the following sentences.

1. Last year, the tuition for my education _____ 7 percent more than it did the year before.
   (cost)

2. I have _____ trying to guess my expenses for next year.
   (quit)

3. The message has _____ that college costs continue to spiral.
   (spread)

4. Most parents have been _____ with large tax increases.
   (hit)

5. Financing a child's higher education has _____ a difficult task.
   (become)

# Twenty Verbs with the Same Past Tense and Past Participle Forms

| SIMPLE FORM | PAST TENSE | PAST PARTICIPLE | SIMPLE FORM | PAST TENSE | PAST PARTICIPLE |
|---|---|---|---|---|---|
| bend | bent | bent | creep | crept | crept |
| lend | lent | lent | keep | kept | kept |
| send | sent | sent | sleep | slept | slept |
| spend | spent | spent | sweep | swept | swept |
|  |  |  | weep | wept | wept |
| catch | caught | caught |  |  |  |
| teach | taught | taught | bring | brought | brought |
|  |  |  | buy | bought | bought |
| bleed | bled | bled | fight | fought | fought |
| feed | fed | fed | seek | sought | sought |
| lead | led | led | think | thought | thought |
| speed | sped | sped |  |  |  |

**Practice**

Using the verb given in parentheses, fill in the correct form in each of the following sentences.

1. Last year, the school district _____ new chemistry texts.
   (buy)

2. Some citizens felt the district had _____ too much money on these new books.    (spend)

3. They claimed the taxpayers were being _____ dry.
   (bleed)

4. These citizens argued that the school should have _____ the old books.                                      (keep)

5. The teachers _____ the old books were worn out.
   (think)

6. Parents, on the other hand, _____ to hire two new teachers.
   (seek)

7. They _____ for a smaller class size.
   (fight)

8.  Most teachers _____ classes that were too large.
    (teach)

9.  One father _____ a campaign to educate the community.
    (lead)

10. He _____ every citizen a letter to explain the problem.
    (send)

## Twenty Verbs That Differ in All Three Forms

| SIMPLE TENSE | PAST TENSE | PAST PARTICIPLE | SIMPLE TENSE | PAST TENSE | PAST PARTICIPLE |
|---|---|---|---|---|---|
| blow | blew | blown | begin | began | begun |
| fly | flew | flown | drink | drank | drunk |
| grow | grew | grown | ring | rang | rung |
| know | knew | known | shrink | shrank | shrunk |
| throw | threw | thrown | sing | sang | sung |
|  |  |  | sink | sank | sunk |
| bite | bit | bitten (or bit) | spring | sprang | sprung |
| drive | drove | driven | swim | swam | swum |
| hide | hid | hidden (or hid) |  |  |  |
| ride | rode | ridden |  |  |  |
| rise | rose | risen |  |  |  |
| stride | strode | stridden |  |  |  |
| write | wrote | written |  |  |  |

**Practice**     **Using the verb given in parentheses, fill in the correct form in each of the following sentences.**

1.  We have _____ many country and western singers over the years, but
    (know)
    Patsy Cline remains a special figure.

2.  She _____ her career near her small hometown in Virginia.
    (begin)

3.  She _____ wherever she could find people to listen.
    (sing)

4.  People immediately recognized the exceptional quality of

her voice, and her audiences _____.
                                (grow)

5.  At sixteen, Patsy Cline auditioned for a local radio station

and _____ from town to town, singing in clubs and
        (drive)
taverns.

6.  During the early 1960s, her records _____ on
                                          (rise)
popularity charts throughout the country.

7.  After the worldwide success of "Walkin' after Midnight,"

Patsy Cline _____ her way to stardom.
            (ride)

8.  In 1963, on her way back from Kansas City, the singer had _____ as
                                                               (fly)
far as Tennessee when her plane crashed, and she was killed.

9.  Other stars have _____ up in the last forty years, but Patsy Cline will
                     (spring)
remain one of the great legends of country music.

10.  Much has been _____ about Patsy Cline, and a feature-length film
                   (write)
titled *Sweet Dreams* has been made about her life.

**EXERCISE** ❶     **Practicing Irregular Verb Forms**

**For each verb given in parentheses, supply the past tense or the past participle.**

Ever since people _____ to write, they have _____ about the great
                  (begin)                        (write)
mysteries in nature. For instance, why did the dinosaurs disappear? In the

past, no one _____ why. Scientists now have _____ on one strong possi-
             (know)                             (bet)
bility. That possibility is that sixty-five million years ago, a six-mile-wide

chunk of rock _____ the earth and _____ up a thick cloud of dust. The dust
                (hit)                (throw)

_____ the sunlight from the earth; therefore, certain life forms disap-
  (keep)

peared. Some scientists have _____ to the conclusion that this could have
                            (come)

_____ the earth's animal population by as much as 70 percent. Other
  (shrink)

scientists are not so sure that this is true. They believe time has _____
                                          (hide)

the real reason for the disappearance of the dinosaurs.

**EXERCISE 2**

## Practicing Irregular Verb Forms

**For each verb given in parentheses, supply the past tense or the past participle.**

Nearly everyone has _____ a cold at some time or another. Medical
                     (catch)

researchers have long _____ a cure for the common cold, but so far they
                (seek)

have had no success. The cold virus has _____ throughout the world,
                          (spread)

and the number of its victims has _____ every year. Past experience has
                      (rise)

_____ us that people who have _____ plenty of liquids and taken
  (taught)                  (drink)

aspirin have gotten over colds more quickly than those who have not, but this

is not a good enough remedy. People once believed that you _____ a fever
                                (feed)

and starved a cold, but recent research has _____ to a disclaimer of this
                        (lead)

belief. Other research, including the search for a vaccine, has _____ a lot
                                (cost)

of time and effort. So far, the new knowledge has not _____ a cure.
                      (bring)

**EXERCISE 3**

## Practicing Irregular Verb Forms

**The following paragraph is written in the present tense. Rewrite the paragraph using the past tense.**

The jockey drives his pickup truck to the race track. He strides into the stalls
where the horses are kept. His head swims with thoughts of the coming race.

He springs into the saddle and rides to the starting gate. The bell rings, and the horses fly out of the gate. They speed around the first turn. The crowd grows tense, and excitement spreads as the horses sweep across the finish line.

_____

_____

_____

_____

_____

# MORE IRREGULAR VERBS

Appendix C gives an alphabetical listing of nearly every irregular verb. Use that list to supply the correct form for each verb in the following exercises.

**EXERCISE 4**

## Practicing More Irregular Verb Forms

**For each verb given in parentheses, supply the past tense or the past participle.**

1. The photographer _____ several rolls of film.
   (shoot)

2. The contractor _____ two houses in the neighborhood.
   (build)

3. The audience _____ when the singer attempted the high notes.
   (flee)

4. The pipe _____ yesterday; we are waiting for a plumber.
   (burst)

5. He _____ the dog for a wolf.
   (mistake)

6. The firefighters _____ down the ladder.
   (slide)

7. Life _____ the family a cruel blow.
   (deal)

8. The artist had _____ two portraits of his wife.
   (draw)

9. The pond was _____ enough for ice skating.
   (freeze)

10. He had washed and _____ out all his clothes in the sink.
    (wring)

**EXERCISE 5**

## Practicing More Irregular Verb Forms

**Read the following paragraph. Find and circle the ten irregular verbs that are written incorrectly. In the spaces provided, write the correct forms of the ten irregular verbs.**

Mr. Weeks, an alumnus of our university, had gave a large sum of money to the school just before he died. A committee was choosen to study how the money should be used. Each member thunk about the possibilities for several weeks before the meeting. Finally, the meeting begun in late November. Each member brung his or her ideas. One gentleman fealt the school should improve the graduate program by hiring two new teachers. Another committee member layed out a proposal for remodeling the oldest dormitory on campus. Janice Spaulding had writen a plan for increasing scholarships for deserving students. A citizen unexpectedly swang open the door and strode into the room. She pleaded with the school to provide more programs for the community. After everyone had spoke, the committee was asked to make a more thorough study of each project.

1. _____        6. _____

2. _____        7 _____

3. _____        8. _____

4. _____        9. _____

5. _____        10. _____

**EXERCISE 6**

## Practicing More Irregular Verb Forms

**For each verb given in parentheses, supply the past tense or the past participle.**

1. We _____ in the sand for clams.
   (dig)

2. The director _____ the script on the table.
   (fling)

3. The family had _____ the child's birthday.
   (forget)

4. The antique dealer _____ the old clock.
   (wind)

5.  The door seemed to be _____.
    (stick)

6.  The dog _____ itself as it came out of the water.
    (shake)

7.  The youth _____ he was telling the truth.
    (swear)

8.  Yesterday, the food had _____ on the table all day without being
    (lie)
    touched.

9.  The bill has been _____.
    (pay)

10. The hosts _____ their guests to drink in their home.
    (forbid)

# MASTERY AND EDITING TESTS

**TEST 1**

## Using Correct Irregular Verb Forms

**In each of the following sentences, underline the irregular verb. If the verb form is wrong, correct it. If the form is correct, mark it with a *C*.**

1.  He lended his son the money.

2.  The fan blowed the smoke across the room.

3.  The stuffing was shook out of the teddy bear.

4.  She has rode on many spirited horses.

5.  The members of the team had swum in the pool for two hours.

6.  The children had fed the cat.

7.  The famous soprano sung for the president when he was inaugurated.

8.  The soldiers creeped up on the enemy position.

9.  The novel was writen in just two years.

10. The galleon sunk shortly after it had left Puerto Rico for Spain.

**TEST 2**

## Using Correct Irregular Verb Forms

**For each irregular verb given in parentheses, supply the past tense or past participle.**

1. Barack Obama _____ up in Hawaii and Indonesia before he came
   (grow)

   to Occidental College in Los Angeles.

2. Obama tells how, on his first trip to New York as a young man, he _____
   (sleep)

   in an alley the first night.

3. He has _____ hard times.
   (know)

4. After college and law school, he _____ working as a community
   (think)

   organizer would be a job where he could make a difference in people's lives.

5. He _____ a Ford Escape hybrid.
   (drive)

6. On his desk in Chicago, he _____ a carving of a wooden hand holding
   (keep)

   an egg, symbolic of the fragility of life.

7. Before long, his charm, intelligence, and speaking ability _____ the
   (catch)

   attention of the public.

8. A man of his generation, Barack _____ his BlackBerry® to the White
   (bring)

   House when he became president.

9. The presidential plane _____ him to Canada for his first international
   (fly)

   trip as president.

10. President Obama has not _____ from tackling the huge economic
    (shrink)

    problems facing the country.

**TEST 3**

## Using Correct Irregular Verb Forms

**In each of the following sentences, underline the irregular verb. If the verb form is wrong, correct it. If the form is correct, mark it with a C.**

1. The salesperson strided into the room with the utmost confidence.

2. The fork was bended out of shape.

3.    My mom sweeped the kitchen floor every night.

4.    She was hurt by the unkind comments.

5.    The patient drunk the quart of pink liquid.

6.    She weeped when she heard the news.

7.    The sisters seeked out their family's history.

8.    Stan throwed the first pitch in the game.

9.    My name was put on the list.

10.    The pipe sprung a leak.

## TEST 4    Editing Student Writing Using Editing Symbols

**The correction symbol for an error in verb form is vb. In the paragraph below, ten errors are marked with editing symbols. Correct each error on the lines provided after the paragraph.**

¹In 1903, Horatio Nelson Jackson made a bet of fifty dollars that he could drive across the country in less than three months. ²No one at that time had ever drove [vb] an automobile from California to New York. ³When he begun [vb] his trip, he had no worries about traffic problems. ⁴Because there were hardly any cars. [frag] ⁵However, there were other concerns. ⁶One major problem a hundred years ago were [agr] the absence of service stations along the way. ⁷When his car broke down, Horatio slept [vb] in whistle-stop towns, waiting for parts to be delivered by train. ⁸The roads were trails of mud or dust. ⁹If they existed at all. [frag] ¹⁰Furthermore, the cars at that time had no shock absorbers, power steering, air conditioning, seatbelts, and they [//] had no radios either. ¹¹Despite these difficulties, Horatio won his bet. ¹²He rumbled down Fifth Avenue in New York with his mechanic and his bulldog named Bud. ¹³He become [vb] the first person to drive an automobile across the country. ¹⁴Recently, an Indiana dentist and his wife reenacted that trip of a century ago in a 1904 Winton, a car that is no longer produced. ¹⁵The century-old car speeded [vb] along at twenty-five or thirty miles an hour. ¹⁶The couple faced problems when a wheel fell off, the brakes catched [vb] fire, and a tire went flat. ¹⁷After the trip, the dentist commented, "By comparison, driving in a modern car is like riding on a magic carpet."

**Corrections**

1.  verb form (sentence 2):           _____

2.  verb form (sentence 3):           _____

3.  fragment (sentence 4):            _____
                                      _____
                                      _____


4.  agreement (sentence 6):           _____

5.  verb form (sentence 7):           _____

6.  fragment (sentence 9):            _____
                                      _____


7.  parallel structure (sentence 10): _____
                                      _____
                                      _____


8.  verb form (sentence 13):          _____

9.  verb form (sentence 15):          _____

10. verb form (sentence 16):          _____

## Exploring Online

Go to **www.cengage.com/devenglish/scarry/writersworkplace** to find the **Writer's Online Workplace,** a website designed for students using this book. You will find links to handouts, interactive quizzes, and other online resources as you explore the following topic:

• irregular verbs

# Working Together

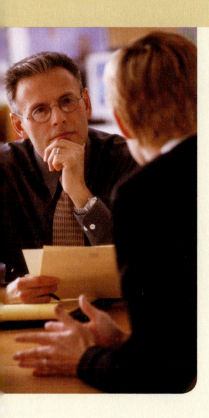

## PREPARING FOR A JOB INTERVIEW

Among the most important moments in our working lives are those times when we are searching for a first job or when we find ourselves moving from one job to another. Because a critical part of any job search is a successful interview, it is essential to be prepared to answer direct questions from the person who may hire you. Personnel officers of companies, along with counselors who help people get jobs in those companies, all agree that a job applicant should expect certain questions in an interview.

Here are five questions considered to be the most important:

1. What is your notion of the ideal job?

2. What image do you have in mind of the supervisor or manager you would like to work for?

3. What qualifications separate you from any other candidate for this job?

4. What is the most balanced portrait you can give of yourself?

5. What are your greatest strengths? What weaknesses about yourself have you recognized?

Experts say that the last two questions are especially tricky because they call for very personal answers. Also, when people respond to these questions, they tend either to talk too much about themselves or to give answers that are too brief.

The president of one counseling service suggests that an effective way to answer the question about a self-portrait is to ask another question, such as "Can you tell me about some problems you have had in your company, so I can focus my response?" In this way, you will have some good examples to use as part of your answer. Another counselor says that, when you are interviewed, you should "be honest, be yourself, and do your homework."

## Working in Groups

Divide into five groups. Each group should take one of the five questions from the above list. Each student should devote ten minutes of freewriting to respond to his or her group's question. Following the freewriting, the group should then spend another ten minutes discussing the responses generated by its members. Sometimes groups like to exchange their freewriting so others can read their responses aloud or silently. One member of the group will then present a summary of the group's response to the rest of the class.

## PORTFOLIO SUGGESTION

Use this opportunity to work on your own answers to these job-interview questions. Write out your answers and save them for future reference. You may find them useful when you are preparing for an actual job interview.

# USING VERB TENSES CORRECTLY

# 12

Using verb tenses correctly is at the heart of understanding a language. In this chapter, you will learn to do the following:

**CHAPTER OBJECTIVES**

- Use the **present perfect** and **past perfect tenses** correctly.
- Understand the **sequence of tenses.**
- Avoid unnecessary **shifts in verb tense.**
- Understand when to choose the **active voice** and when to choose the **passive voice.**
- Recognize constructions that require the **subjunctive mood.**
- Know how to use *should/would, used to/supposed to, can/could,* and *will/would.*

## HOW MANY VERB TENSES ARE THERE IN ENGLISH?

Not all languages express time by using exactly the same verb tenses. Students for whom English is a second language know that one of their major tasks in learning English is to understand how to use each of the tenses. Because the next sections of this chapter concern common problems with tense, a chart of the English verb tenses is provided on the next page. You may want to refer to this list from time to time. Notice that the chart gives example sentences for each tense and continuous form.

## The Six English Verb Tenses and Their Continuous Forms

| THREE SIMPLE TENSES | SIMPLE CONTINUOUS FORMS | THREE PERFECT TENSES | PERFECT CONTINUOUS FORMS |
|---|---|---|---|
| **1. Present** | **Present continuous** | **4. Present perfect** | **Present perfect continuous** |
| you walk | you are walking | you have walked | you have been walking |
| I run | I am running | I have run | I have been running |
| **2. Past** | **Past continuous** | **5. Past perfect** | **Past perfect continuous** |
| you walked | you were walking | you had walked | you had been walking |
| I ran | I was running | I had run | I had been running |
| **3. Future** | **Future continuous** | **6. Future perfect** | **Future perfect continuous** |
| you will walk | you will be walking | you will have walked | you will have been walking |
| I will run | I will be running | I will have run | I will have been running |

# HOW DO YOU USE THE PRESENT PERFECT AND THE PAST PERFECT TENSES?

The perfect tenses need special attention because they are generally not well understood or consistently used in the accepted way.

## HOW DO YOU FORM THE PERFECT TENSES?

The **present perfect tense** consists of *has* or *have* plus the past participle of the main verb:

**has worked**

**have worked**

The **past perfect tense** consists of *had* plus the past participle of the main verb:

**had worked**

## WHAT DO THESE TENSES MEAN?

> The **present perfect tense** can be used to describe an action that started in the past and continues to the present time.

**Jennifer *has worked* at the hospital for ten years.**

This sentence indicates that Jennifer began to work at the hospital ten years ago and is still working there now. The following time line shows that the action began ten years ago and continues up to the present time.

Study these other examples of sentences using the present perfect tense: In each case, the action started in the past and continues up to the present time.

**She *has studied* violin since 1990.**

**I *have* always *appreciated* his generosity.**

> The ***present perfect tense*** can also be used to describe an action that has just taken place or an action that took place at an indefinite time in the past.

An action that has just taken place:

***Has* Jennifer *found* a job yet?**

**Jennifer *has* (just) *found* a new job in Kansas City.**

An action that took place at an indefinite time:

***Have* you ever *been* to San Diego?**

**Yes, I *have been* there three times.**

**NOTE:** If the time were definite, you would use the simple past:

**Jennifer *found* a new job yesterday.**

**Yes, I *was* in San Diego last week.**

**Practice**

Complete the following sentences by filling in the blanks with either the simple past tense or the present perfect tense.

1.  I _____ to Mexico in 2002.
    (go)

2.  I _____ deep-sea diving a few times.
    (go)

3.  The drummer in the band _____ percussion since he was five.
    (study)

4.  It _____ the jury two hours to reach their verdict yesterday.
    (take)

5.  Washington, D.C., _____ the capital of our country for many years.
    (be)

> The **past perfect tense** describes an action completed in the past before another past action or a specific time.

**Jennifer *had worked* at the hospital for ten years before she *moved* away.**

In this sentence, there are two past actions: Jennifer *worked* and Jennifer *moved*. The action that took place first is in the past perfect *(had worked)*. The action that took place later, but was also completed in the past, is in the simple past *(moved)*. The following time line shows that one past action *(had worked)* was completed before another past action *(moved)*.

| first action in the past | second action in the past | moment of speaking | |
| --- | --- | --- | --- |
| x | x | | |
| **PAST** | | **PRESENT** | **FUTURE** |
| had worked | moved | | |

Study these other examples of sentences using the past perfect tense:

**I *had* just *finished* when the bell *rang.***

**He *said* that Randall *had told* the class about the experiment.**

**We *had provided* the information long before last week's meeting.**

**He *had left* for work by 8 a.m.**

**NOTE:** In informal speech and writing, the simple past tense is often used to express the past perfect tense.

| **Informal writing or speech:** | **The child *witnessed* the accident before he ran away.** |
| --- | --- |
| **Formal writing:** | **The child *had witnessed* the accident before he ran away.** |

**Practice**

Complete the following sentences by filling in the blanks with either the present perfect tense or the past perfect tense of the verb given.

1. Mexico City _____ visitors for many years.
   (fascinate)

2. This city _____ the third-largest city in the world, and people
   (become)

   _____ it grow larger every year.
   (watch)

3. The suburbs of the city _____ old villages that _____
   (replace)                                                      (exist)

   peacefully since the days of the Aztecs.

4.  Yolanda told us that she _____ in Fort Worth before she moved to
                                  (live)

    Mexico City.

5.  Today, Mexico City _____ a computer-controlled subway system to
                             (build)

    deal with its huge transportation problem.

# WHAT IS THE SEQUENCE OF TENSES?

> The term **sequence of tenses** refers to the logical relationship of verb tenses in sentences that have more than one clause.

If the tense of the independent clause is in the **present** (he *knows*), here are the possibilities for the dependent clause:

| Independent clause (IC) | Dependent clause (DC) | Time of the DC in relation to the IC |
|---|---|---|
| | that she studies. | same time |
| He knows | that she studied. | earlier |
| | that she *will* study. | later |

If the tense of the independent clause is in the **past** (he *knew*), here are the possibilities for the dependent clause:

| Independent clause (IC) | Dependent clause (DC) | Time of the DC in relation to the IC |
|---|---|---|
| | that she studied. | same time |
| He knew | that she *had* studied. | earlier |
| | that she *would* study. | later |

If the independent clause is in the **future** (he *will know*), here are the possibilities for the dependent clause:

| Independent clause (IC) | Dependent clause (DC) | Time of the DC in relation to the IC |
|---|---|---|
| | if she studies. | same time |
| He will know | if she *has* studied. | earlier |
| | if she *will* study. | Later |

**EXERCISE** ●1

## Practicing with Sequence of Tenses

In each of the following sentences, the verb in the independent clause has been underlined. Choose the correct verb tense for the verb in the dependent clause. Use the preceding examples if you need help.

1. The program <u>will continue</u> only after the coughing and fidgeting
   _____.
      (stop)

2. Because he was poor and unappreciated by the music world when he died in 1791, Mozart <u>did not realize</u> the importance that his music
   _____ in the future.
      (have)

3. Dad <u>will tell</u> us tonight if he _____ a new car next month.
                                          (buy)

4. Albert Einstein <u>failed</u> the entrance exam at the Swiss Federal Institute of Technology because he _____ a very disciplined student.
                                    (be + never)

5. Einstein <u>studied</u> only subjects that he _____.
                                                  (like)

6. Cancer researchers <u>think</u> it's likely that a cure for most cancers
   _____ found.
      (be + soon)

7. We <u>know</u> that scientists _____ now close to finding a cure for
                                    (be)
   leukemia.

8. The interviewer <u>felt</u> that the young woman _____ more than she
                                                     (know)
   was telling him.

9. The doctor went into the operating room. She <u>hoped</u> that the operation
   _____ as planned.
      (go)

10. The doctor came out of the operating room. She <u>said</u> that the operation was over and _____ well.
                              (go)

**EXERCISE** **2**      **Practicing with Sequences of Tenses**

**Complete each of the following sentences by choosing the verb tense that makes the meaning clear. Circle the letter of the correct answer.**

1.  In 1896, the Olympic games consisted of 41 events with 13 nations competing; since then, the number of events and the number of nations participating _____.

    a.  is increasing          c.  has increased
    b.  increased              d.  had increased

2.  In 1936, the Olympic games _____ place in Berlin, Germany.

    a.  take                   c.  took
    b.  had taken              d.  has taken

3.  Adolf Hitler, the Nazi dictator, _____ only blond, blue-eyed athletes to win all the gold medals in track.

    a.  is expecting           c.  has been expecting
    b.  was expecting          d.  will expect

4.  One year earlier, Jesse Owens, a student at Ohio State University, _____ three world records in track.

    a.  breaks                 c.  had been breaking
    b.  was breaking           d.  had broken

5.  As a result, young Owens _____ in Berlin in 1936 to represent the United States in track.

    a.  is arriving            c.  arrived
    b.  will arrive            d.  has arrived

6.  To Hitler's dismay, Jesse Owens stunned the crowds when he _____ the world records in the 100 meter, the 200 meter, and the broad jump events.

    a.  set                    c.  was setting
    b.  had set                d.  has set

7.  After he _____ these events, he then helped his team win the 400 meter relay race as well.

    a.  wins                   c.  had won
    b.  has won                d.  had been winning

8.  At the time, Adolph Hitler was furious at the victories a black athlete
    _____ ; he refused to acknowledge him.

    a.  has achieved          c.  achieves

    b.  had achieved          d.  will achieve

9.  Today, everyone _____ that Jesse Owens was the outstanding
    athlete at the Olympic games that year.

    a.  will realize          c.  realized

    b.  realizes              d.  had realized

10. His achievements _____ young athletes of color ever since that
    historic day.

    a.  have been inspiring   c.  inspire

    b.  had been inspiring    d.  will inspire

# AVOIDING UNNECESSARY SHIFTS IN VERB TENSE

Unless there is some reason to change tenses, inconsistent shifting from one tense to another should be avoided. Study the following examples:

| | |
|---|---|
| **Shifted tenses:** | **The customer demanded** (past tense) **to see the manager. He** *was* (past tense) **angry because every jacket he** *tries* **on** (Why present tense?) *has* (Why present tense?) **something wrong with it. A button** *was* (past tense) **missing on the first, the lining** *did* **not** *hang* (past tense) **properly on the second, and the collar** *had* (past tense) **a stain on the third.** |

**Revised:**   **The customer demanded** (past tense) **to see the manager. He *was*** (past tense) **angry because every jacket he *tried* on** (past tense) ***had*** (past tense) **something wrong with it. A button *was*** (past tense) **missing on the first, the lining *did* not *hang*** (past tense) **properly on the second, and the collar *had*** (past tense) **a stain on the third.**

**NOTE:** When the subject is a created work, such as a book, play, poem, or piece of music, be especially careful about the verb tense. Although the work was created in the past, it is still enjoyed in the present. In this case, the present tense is used.

**Shakespeare's *Hamlet* <u>is</u> a great play. It <u>was</u> written four centuries ago.**

EXERCISE **3**

## Correcting Unnecessary Shifts in Verb Tense

**Each sentence has an unnecessary shift in verb tense. Revise each sentence so that the tenses remain consistent.**

1.  After I complete that writing course, I took the required history course.

2.  In the beginning of the movie, the action was slow; by the end, I am sitting on the edge of my seat.

3.  The textbook gives the rules for writing a bibliography, but it didn't explain how to do footnotes.

4.  While working on her report in the library, my best friend lost her note cards and comes to me for help.

5.  The encyclopedia gave several pages of information about astronomy, but it doesn't give any information about black holes.

6.  "Salvation" was written by Langston Hughes; it continued to be widely read today.

7.  This is an exciting book, but it had too many characters.

8.  The senator was doing just fine until along comes a younger and more energetic politician.

9.  At the end of *Gulliver's Travels,* the main character rejects the company of people; he preferred the company of horses.

10. My sister arrives late, as usual, and complained that her dinner was cold.

EXERCISE

## Correcting Unnecessary Shifts in Verb Tense

The following paragraph contains unnecessary shifts in verb tense. Change each incorrect verb to its proper form.

Charles Dickens was a nineteenth-century author whose work is well known today. One of the reasons Dickens remained so popular is that so many of his stories are available not only as books but also as movies, plays, and television productions. We all knew from our childhood the famous story of Uncle Scrooge and Tiny Tim. Often we saw a television version of *A Christmas Carol* at holiday time. If you have never read the story of Oliver Twist in book form, you might have seen the musical *Oliver!* Also, there was a movie version of *Great Expectations.* Many students still studied *A Tale of Two Cities* in high school. No matter how many adaptations of Dickens's books they see, people seem to agree that there was no substitute for the books themselves. At first, the vocabulary seemed difficult, but if you concentrate on the story and read a chapter or two every day, you will find yourself not only comprehending these wonderful stories but also loving the richness of Dickens's use of language.

EXERCISE 5

## Editing Student Writing: Correcting Unnecessary Shifts in Verb Tense

The following paragraph was part of an essay written by a first-year college student. It contains unnecessary shifts in verb tense. Revise the paragraph so that verb tenses are consistent.

I remember last year when I was trying to choose the right school and worrying about it a lot. One day, a friend says that, instead of talking about it all the time, I should visit a few places and actually see them. One afternoon, I decide to do just that. I take the bus, get off in the center of town, and from there walked to the campus. It's very clean, with no graffiti on any of the walls. Behind the visitor's desk stood two students passing out brochures on programs and majors. The student union looks inviting, so I went in to get a soda and check it out. I sit down and started listening to the students at the other tables. I was curious to hear bits of their conversations. Students seemed to be treating each other with respect. I did not hear one sarcastic remark, and no one is rude to anyone else. I went to the library and had the same experience. Everyone seems so helpful and friendly. I knew this was the kind of atmosphere I would like. On my way out, I pick up an application from the visitor's desk. Both of the students behind the desk are smiling at me as I leave.

# WHAT IS THE DIFFERENCE BETWEEN THE PASSIVE VOICE AND THE ACTIVE VOICE?

In the **active voice,** the subject is doing something.

**The committee made the decision.**

> In general, choose the active voice to achieve direct, economical, and forceful writing. Most writing should be in the active voice.

In the **passive voice,** something is done to the subject.

**The decision was made by the committee.**

or

**The decision was made.**

The first passive sentence de-emphasizes the actor *(the committee)* by moving it out of the subject place. The second passive sentence omits the actor entirely.

> Choose the passive voice to de-emphasize the actor or to avoid naming the actor altogether.

Study the three sentences that follow. All three deal with President Kennedy's assassination. The first is in the active voice, and the other two are in the passive voice. Discuss with your classmates and instructor what would cause a writer to choose each of the following sentences to express the same basic fact.

1. Lee Harvey Oswald shot President John F. Kennedy in 1963.
2. President John F. Kennedy was shot by Lee Harvey Oswald in 1963.
3. President John F. Kennedy was shot in 1963.

## HOW DO YOU FORM THE PASSIVE VOICE?

A sentence in the passive voice consists of the subject acted upon, followed by a form of the verb *to be* and the past participle. The actor may appear in a *by* phrase at the end.

## Forming the Passive Voice

| SUBJECT ACTED UPON + | VERB *TO BE* + | PAST PARTICIPLE + | *BY* PHRASE (OPTIONAL) |
|---|---|---|---|
| The race | was | won | (by the runner) |
| The meals | have been | cooked | (by the chef) |
| The books | are | illustrated | (by the artists) |

EXERCISE

### Forming Active Voice and Passive Voice

Complete each of the following examples by supplying either the active or the passive voice. Then discuss with the rest of the class the reasons a writer would choose either the active or the passive voice to express each idea.

**Active Voice**

1. _____
   _____

2. _____
   _____

3. The tornado struck Cherry Creek last spring.

4. The wind blew the leaves across the yard.

5. _____
   _____
   _____

**Passive Voice**

1. The wrong number was dialed (by the child).

2. The sweater was crocheted very carefully (by my grandmother).

3. _____
   _____

4. _____
   _____

5. In the seventies, platform shoes were worn (by many fashionable young men and women).

EXERCISE

### Forming Active Voice and Passive Voice

Complete each of the following examples by supplying either the active or the passive voice. Then discuss with the rest of the class the reasons a writer would choose either the active or the passive voice to express each idea.

**Active Voice**

1. The jury announced the verdict after five hours of deliberation.

2. _____
   _____

**Passive Voice**

1. _____
   _____

2. "Blue Suede Shoes" was sung by Elvis Presley.

3.  The sleet turned the old municipal        3.  _____
    building into an ice castle.                   _____

4.  _____          4.  The priceless vase was smuggled
    _____              (by someone) out of the country.

5.  _____          5.  More concern was shown (by
    _____              television viewers) over the Super
    _____              Bowl than over the outbreak of
    _____              an international conflict.

# WHAT IS THE SUBJUNCTIVE MOOD?

Verbs in the English language have three possible moods.

1.  The **indicative mood** expresses statements of fact:

    **He *drives* home every Sunday.**

    Most sentences call for the indicative mood.

2.  The **imperative mood** expresses commands:

    ***Drive* home on Sunday!**

3.  The **subjunctive mood** expresses conditions contrary to fact:

    ***If I were you*, I would drive home on Sunday.**

    or follows certain verbs of demand or urgency:

    **I insist *that he drive* home on Sunday.**

Of the three moods possible for verbs in English, the subjunctive mood has the most
limited use.

> The ***subjunctive mood,*** the most limited of the three moods for English
> verbs, uses special verb forms to express statements contrary to fact
> or to express demand or urgency after certain verbs.

Three instances follow that call for the subjunctive. In each of these three instances,
notice that the *-s* is *not* added in the third person singular present tense.

1.  **For unreal conditions introduced with *if* or *wish*, use *were* if the verb is *be*.**

    If (he were) my teacher, I would be pleased.

    I wish (he were) my teacher.

2.  **For clauses starting with *that* after verbs such as *ask, request, demand,
    suggest, order, insist,* or *command*, use the infinitive form of the verb.**

    I demand that (she be) on time.

    Sullivan insisted that (Jones report) on Tuesday.

3.  **For clauses starting with *that* after adjectives expressing urgency, as in it is *necessary, it is imperative, it is urgent, it is important,* and *it is essential,* use the infinitive form of the verb.**

It is necessary that (she wear) a net covering her hair.

She insisted that (Robert be) ready by five a.m.

**Practice**

In the following sentences, underline the word or phrase that determines the subjunctive and circle the subjunctive. An example has been done for you.

Truman *suggested that* the (country adopt) the Marshall Plan in 1947.

1.  When President Roosevelt died in 1945, the law required that Vice President Truman take over immediately.

2.  It was essential that President Truman act quickly and decisively.

3.  Truman must have wished that he were able to avoid using the atomic bomb to bring an end to World War II.

4.  He felt it was necessary that the United States help Europe recover from the destruction of World War II.

5.  President Truman always insisted that other countries be economically strong.

# KNOWING HOW TO USE *SHOULD/WOULD; CAN/COULD; WILL/WOULD;* AND *USED TO/ SUPPOSED TO*

## *should/would*

> Do not use more than one modal auxiliary *(can, may, might, must, should, ought)* with the main verb.

**Incorrect:**     Joel *shouldn't ought* to sell his car.
**Correct:**        Joel *ought not* sell his car.

or

Joel *shouldn't* sell his car.

Do not use *should of, would of,* or *could of* to mean *should have, would have,* or *could have.*

Incorrect:     Elana *would of* helped you if she *could of.*
Correct:       Elana *would have* helped you if she *could have.*

## can/could; will/would

Use *could* as the past tense of *can.*

I *see* that he *can do* the job.

I *saw* that he *could do* the job.

Use *would* as the past tense of *will.*

I *see* that he *will do* a good job.

I *saw* that he *would do* a good job.

## used to/supposed to

Do not omit the final *-d* in the phrases *used to* and *supposed to.*

Incorrect:     I am *use to* walking to school.
Correct:       I am *used to* walking to school.
Incorrect:     We are *suppose to* meet him for dinner.
Correct:       We are *supposed to* meet him for dinner.

# MASTERY AND EDITING TESTS

 **TEST 1**

### Using Correct Verb Forms

Revise each of the following sentences to avoid problems with verbs.

1.  He hadn't ought to drive so fast.

_____

2.   The officer said that the motorist drove through a red light.

_____

HINT: Here two actions took place in the past, one of them preceding the other.

3.   I wish I was a senior.

_____

4.   "Araby" was written by James Joyce; it told the story of a young boy's first love.

_____

5.   She is working on the project since 1997.

_____

6.   The map was studied by the motorist. *(Use active voice.)*

_____

7.   My father ask me last night to help him build a deck.

_____

8.   I should of kept the promise I made.

_____

9.   I insist that she keeps her clothes on her side of the room.

_____

10.  Someone washes the floor every Monday. *(Use passive voice.)*

_____

**TEST 2**

## Editing Student Writing: Using Correct Verb Forms

**In the following paragraph, change ten verb forms to the correct forms.**

[1]When the day arrived, my mother was jubilant. [2]We drive to the synagogue. [3]My aunt Sophie and her daughters come with us. [4]Once in the temple, the women were separated from the men. [5]They sat upstairs in their assigned places. [6]I was ask to keep my hat on and was given a shawl to wear that I seen before. [7]I was suppose to wait for the rabbi to call me. [8]My turn finally comes. [9]I walked up to a table in the front. [10]There I read from the sacred scriptures in Hebrew. [11]My mother had told me that if I was to read the scriptures fluently, she would be very proud. [12]I knew I could of read louder, but

I was nervous. [13]Afterward, I was taken by my family to a fine kosher restaurant for a celebration. *(Change to the active voice.)* [14]There I receive a beautiful gold charm bracelet.

---

**TEST 3**

### Editing Student Writing: Using Correct Verb Forms

**In the following paragraph, change ten verb forms to the correct forms.**

[1]My semester of chemistry seemed ill-fated from the very start. [2]When I lost my textbook the first week of classes, I should of known I was in for trouble. [3]The second week, I had the flu and miss two classes. [4]On the following Monday, when I finally start off for class again, the bus was so delayed that I walked into the classroom half an hour late. [5]The teacher scowls at me and ask to speak to me after class. [6]I always use to sit in the front row so I could see the board and hear the lectures. [7]Because I am late, I will have to take a seat in the last row. [8]I wish I was able to start this class over again the right way. [9]No one had ought to have such an unlucky start in any class.

---

**TEST 4**

### Editing Student Writing Using Correction Symbols

**In the paragraph below, ten errors are marked with editing symbols. Correct each error on the lines provided after the paragraph.**

[1]Our college professor was amazed last year when a man comes *(vb)* to our English class to deliver a pizza to a student. [2]The student later explained that he missed *(vb)* lunch. [3]The professor was surprised that the student seen *(vb)* no problem with this incident. [4]The pizza was confiscated. [5]Across America today, cell phones and other electronic gadgets in the classrooms are a cause for concern among teachers, administrators, and sometimes even students *(//)* are getting upset. [6]Going *(dm)* off in class, the lessons are disturbed by cell phones. [7]Some students leave classes, *(ro)* they go out into the hallways to make calls. [8]Others play video games or watch movies, *(subord)* that they have downloaded onto their laptops. [9]Cheating with handheld organizers and cell phone messaging *(agr)* are also problematic for teachers. [10]At the college I attend, many professors have made policies regarding electronic devices in their classrooms. [11]Banning these devices is suppose *(vb)* to result in a more controlled classroom. [12]I am not convinced this is a good idea. [13]Because *(frag)* a student may urgently need to communicate with someone.

**Corrections**

1.  verb form (sentence 1): _____

2.  verb, form (sentence 2): _____

3.  verb, form (sentence 3): _____

4.  parallel structure (sentence 5): _____
    _____
    _____
    _____

5.  dangling modifier (sentence 6): _____

6.  run-on (sentence 7): _____
    _____

7.  subordination (sentence 8): _____
    _____

8.  Agreement (sentence 9): _____

9.  verb (sentence 11): _____

10. fragment (sentence 13): _____
    _____
    _____

## Exploring Online

Go to **www.cengage.com/devenglish/scarry/writersworkplace** to find the **Writer's Online Workplace,** a website designed for students using this book. You will find links to handouts, interactive quizzes, and other online resources as you explore the following topics:

- verb tense consistency
- active and passive voice
- subjunctive mood

# Working Together

## PROBLEM SOLVING: INTEGRITY IN THE WORKPLACE

Recently, a young office worker went to his superior and reported that a fellow worker was incorrectly reporting the company's profits. It was clear that the intention was to give the impression the company was doing better than it really was. His superior told the young worker not to worry about the situation, and that he himself would take care of it. Before long, this same worker was let go. He believed he was fired because of his honesty, and he began to suspect a conspiracy of dishonesty among the others in his company. The worker may have paid a high price for being a whistle-blower: he lost his job.

The lack of integrity in today's workplace has reached the level of a national disgrace. Consider the following list of scandals that have reached the public's awareness in recent years.

- The lobbyist Jack Abramoff defrauds Indian tribes by promising them favors he cannot or will not act upon.
- Red Cross workers steal money donated for the victims of Hurricane Katrina.
- Government officials attempt to silence a NASA scientist when he tries to publish his findings on global warming.
- Bernard Madoff, Wall Street money manager, defrauds investors (including many charities) of $50 billion.

### Working in Groups

Divide into groups. Each group should develop a presentation in which an account of dishonesty in the workplace is given. It may be an actual situation a member of the group has personally observed, or it may be a current scandal that has just made the news. Part of each group's presentation should include a list of the steps the employee should take. Do not forget to consider what precautions the employee should take to protect himself or herself.

Each member of the class should take notes during the presentations and jot down questions, along with any points of disagreement. After all the presentations have been given, determine if the class agrees or disagrees on the process that an employee should follow if he or she uncovers dishonesty in the workplace.

## PORTFOLIO SUGGESTION

All groups (charitable organizations, educational institutions, political institutions, and social institutions) are affected by dishonesty. Depending on your interests and job goals, you might want to study how a scandal or case of corruption has affected one of these institutions. A fascinating research paper could develop from the notes you save from the class presentations.

# 13 LEARNING THE RULES FOR CAPITALIZATION AND PUNCTUATION

In this chapter, you will learn the basic rules of capitalization and punctuation that govern English. Many of these rules you undoubtedly know already.

**CHAPTER OBJECTIVES**

- ten basic rules for **capitalization**
- ten basic uses of the **comma**
- three uses for the **apostrophe**
- four uses for **quotation marks**
- three uses for the **semicolon**
- four uses for the **colon**
- use of the **dash** and **parentheses**

In college and at work, you will have to be in control of capitalization and punctuation. When is a word important enough to need a capital letter? Where are commas needed in a sentence? These and other questions will be answered when you know the fundamental rules and how to apply them. Carefully study the examples that are given under each rule. Notice that you will often learn how to capitalize and punctuate by learning what *not* to do.

## TEN BASIC RULES OF CAPITALIZATION

RULE **1** | Capitalize the first word of every sentence.

Every building was old. Our house was the oldest.

RULE **2** | Capitalize the names of specific things and places.

Specific buildings:

**I went to the Jamestown Post Office.**

but

**I went to the post office.**

Specific streets, cities, states, and countries:

**She lives on Elam Avenue.**

but

**She lives on the same street as my mom and dad.**

Specific organizations:

**He collected money for the March of Dimes.**

but

**He collected money for his favorite charity.**

Specific institutions:

**The loan is from the First National Bank.**

but

**The loan is from one of the banks in town.**

Specific bodies of water:

**My uncle fishes every summer on Lake Michigan.**

but

**My uncle spends every summer at the lake.**

RULE **3**

**Capitalize days of the week, months of the year, and holidays. Do not capitalize the names of seasons.**

**The last Thursday in November is Thanksgiving Day.**

but

**I cannot wait until spring.**

RULE **4**

**Capitalize the names of all languages, nationalities, races, religions, deities, and sacred terms.**

**My friend who is Ethiopian speaks very little English.**

**The Koran is the sacred book of Islam.**

**RULE 5**

Capitalize the first word and every important word in a title. Do not capitalize articles, prepositions, or short connecting words unless they begin the title.

*For Whom the Bell Tolls* is a famous novel by Ernest Hemingway.

Her favorite short story is "A Rose for Emily."

**RULE 6**

Capitalize the first word of a direct quotation.

The teacher said, "You have been chosen for the part."

But

"You have been chosen," she said, "for the part."

NOTE: In the second sentence, *for* is not capitalized because it is a continuation of the sentence in quotation marks.

**RULE 7**

Capitalize historical events, periods, and documents.

The American Revolution

The Colonial Period

The Bill of Rights

**RULE 8**

Capitalize the words *north*, *south*, *east*, and *west* when they are used as places rather than as geographical directions.

He comes from the Midwest.

but

The farm is about twenty miles west of Omaha.

**RULE 9**

Capitalize people's names.

Proper names:

**Charles Wong**

Professional titles when they are used with the person's proper name:

| | | |
|---|---|---|
| **Judge Lowry** | but | **the judge** |
| **Professor Shapiro** | but | **the professor** |

Terms for relatives (mother, sister, nephew, uncle) when they are used in the place of proper names:

**I told Grandfather I would meet him later.**

but

**I told my grandfather I would meet him later.**

**NOTE:** Terms for relatives are not capitalized if a pronoun, article, or adjective is used with the name.

RULE  **10**        **Capitalize brand names.**

**Lipton's Noodle Soup**        but        **noodle soup**

**Velveeta Cheese**        but        **cheese**

EXERCISE  **1**        ## Capitalization

**In each of the following sentences correct any word that requires capitalization.**

1.  The artist replied, "we are hoping for space in the newly renovated commercial center."

2.  All of the villagers celebrated the winter solstice with a festival in the town square.

3.  The head of general motors came to Washington, D.C. looking for a loan.

4.  The movie was based on a story from the old testament.

5.  In 1803, we negotiated the louisiana purchase from france.

6.  Many senior citizens go to the southwest in the winter.

7.  The members of the automobile workers union appealed to president Obama.

8.  Many dominican students are in one of the health-related programs in this university.

9.  My favorite television programs are *lost* and *law and order.*

10.  The law professor wrote a letter to judge Johnson.

**EXERCISE**      ## Capitalization

**In each of the following sentences correct any word that requires capitalization.**

1.  Every tuesday, the general visits the hospital.

2.  On one level, the book *the lord of the rings* can be read as a fairy tale; on another level, the book can be read as a christian allegory.

3.  The golden gate bridge in san francisco may be the most beautiful bridge in the world.

4.  She is the sister of my french teacher.

5.  I've always wanted to take a trip to the far east in spring.

6.  The kremlin, located in moscow, once housed the soviet government.

7.  I needed to see dr. Ghavami, but the nurse told me the doctor would not be in until next week.

8.  He shouted angrily, "why don't you ever arrive at your history class on time?"

9.  The scholastic aptitude test will be given on january 18.

10. While yet a teenager growing up in harlem, james Baldwin became a baptist preacher.

**EXERCISE** **3**     ## Capitalization

**In each of the following sentences correct any word that requires capitalization.**

1.  The lawyer's office is located on south pleasant street.

2.  My uncle lives farther south than grandmother.

3.  I'd like to move to the south if I could find a job there.

4.  The well-known anthropologist Margaret Mead was for many years director of the museum of natural history in new york city.

5.  The constitution of the united states was signed in constitution hall on september 17, 1787.

6.   Sculptor John Wilson was commissioned to create a bust of rev. Martin Luther King jr.

7.   The project will be funded partly with money from the national endowment for the arts.

8.   I read the magazine article in *newsweek* while I was waiting in the dentist's office yesterday.

9.   The tour took the retired teachers above the arctic circle.

10.  Many gerber baby foods no longer have sugar and salt.

# TEN BASIC USES OF THE COMMA

You may feel uncertain about when to use commas. One of the best ways to become more confident with using commas is to concentrate on a few basic rules. These rules will cover most of your needs.

The tendency now in English is to use fewer commas than in the past. There is no one complete set of rules on which everyone agrees. However, if you learn these ten basic uses, your common sense will help you figure out what to do in other cases. Remember that a comma usually signifies a pause in a sentence. As you read a sentence out loud, listen to where you pause within the sentence. This pause is often a clue that a comma is needed. Notice that in each of the examples for the following ten uses, you can pause where the comma should be placed.

RULE **1**

> Use a comma to separate three or more items in a series. These items can be composed of words, phrases, or clauses.

Three **words** (in this case, adjectives) in a series:

He was *silent, lonely,* and *afraid.*

Three **phrases** (in this case, verb phrases) in a series:

He *ran in the race, finished among the top ten,* and *collapsed happily on the ground.*

Three **clauses** in a series:

Alex Rodriguez, *who joined the Yankees in 2004, who is the highest paid player in baseball,* and *who is widely viewed as the most talented player today,* tested positive for performance-enhancing drugs.

NOTE: Although some grammar authorities omit the comma between the last item of a series and the coordinating conjunction, check with your instructor to determine the preferred style. Be mindful that omitting the final comma may change the meaning, as in the following examples.

**The cell phones come in red, green, pink, and black.**

**The cell phones come in red, green, pink and black.**

**NOTE:** No comma is used for only two items:

**He was *silent and lonely.***

RULE **2**

> Use a comma to set off parts of dates, addresses, and geographical names.

**I was born on August 18, 1965, in the middle of a hurricane.**

**I lived at 428 North Monroe Street, Madison, Wisconsin, for many years.**

**I dreamed of spending a semester in Quito, Ecuador, to study art.**

RULE **3**

> Use a comma to set off a number of adjectives that modify a noun.

**I carried my *favorite, old, green* coat.**

Sometimes two adjectives in front of a noun go together to give a distinct meaning. In this case, they would not be separated by commas:

**I carried my favorite, *dark green* coat.**

The words *dark* and *green* belong together to give the meaning of a single color: *dark* modifies the color *green,* and the two words together describe the color of the coat.

**Practice**

**In each of the following sentences, insert commas wherever they are needed.**

1.  On November 14 1977 officials discovered a major body of polluted water in Oswego New York.

2.  Problems with the water supply of the United States Europe Canada and other parts of the world are growing.

3.  Water is colorless tasteless odorless and free of calories.

4.  You will use on an average day twenty-four gallons of water for flushing thirty-two gallons for bathing and washing clothes and twenty-five gallons for other uses.

5.  It took 120 gallons of water to create the eggs you ate for breakfast 3,500 gallons for the steak you might eat for dinner and more than 60,000 gallons to produce the steel used to make your car.

**RULE** **4**

Use a comma along with a coordinating conjunction to combine two simple sentences (also called independent clauses) into a single compound sentence. (See Chapter 6 on coordination.)

**The house was on fire, but I was determined not to leave my place of safety.**

Be careful to use the comma with the conjunction only when you are combining sentences. When you are combining words or phrases, no comma is used.

**My sister was safe but not happy.**

**My mother and father were searching for her.**

**She was neither in class nor at work.**

**Practice**    In each of the following sentences, insert commas wherever they are needed.

1. The most overused bodies of water are our rivers but they continue to serve us daily.

2. American cities often developed next to rivers and industries followed soon after in the same locations.

3. The people of the Industrial Age can try to clean the water they have used or they can watch pollution take over.

4. The Great Lakes are showing signs of renewal yet the struggle against pollution there must continue.

5. Many people have not yet been educated about the dangers to our water supply nor are all our legislators fully aware of the problem.

**RULE** **5**

Use a comma to follow introductory words, expressions, phrases, or clauses.

- introductory words (such as *yes, no, oh, well):*

    ***Oh,*** **I never thought he would do it.**

- introductory expressions (transitions such as *as a matter of fact, finally, secondly, furthermore, therefore):*

    ***As a matter of fact,*** **I will give you a second chance.**

- introductory phrases:

    | **Long prepositional phrase:** | *In the beginning of the course,* **I thought I would never be able to do the work.** |
    | --- | --- |
    | **Participial phrase:**  | *Walking on tiptoe,* **the young mother quietly peeked into the nursery.** |
    | **Infinitive phrase:** | *To be quite honest,* **I don't believe he's feeling well.** |

- introductory dependent clauses beginning with a subordinating conjunction:

  **When the food arrived, we all grabbed for it.**

(For more examples, see Chapter 7 on subordination.)

**Practice**

**In each of the following sentences, insert commas wherever they are needed.**

1. To many people from the East the plans to supply more water to the western states seem unnecessary.

2. However people in the West know that they have no future without a good water supply.

3. When they entered Salt Lake Valley in 1847 the Mormons found dry soil that needed water before crops could be grown.

4. Confidently the new settlers dug ditches that brought the needed water.

5. Learning from the past modern farmers are trying to cooperate with nature.

RULE  **6**

**Use a commas to set off a word, phrase, or clause when the word, phrase or clause interrupts the main idea.**

- interrupting word:

  **We will, *however,* take an X-ray.**

- interrupting phrase:

  **Prepositional phrase:**     **I wanted, *of course,* to stay.**

  **Appositive phrase:**     **Mariella, *the girl with the braids,* has a wicked sense of humor.**

- interrupting clause:

  **He won't, *I think,* try that again.**

  **Mariella, *who wears braids,* has a wicked sense of humor.**

**NOTE:** Keep in mind that the same word, phrase, or clause may function in more than one way. The way the word functions determines the rule for punctuation. Consider again the word *however.* Although we have seen that commas set off the word when it interrupts in the middle of a clause, we use a semicolon and a comma if the word connects two independent clauses:

**We will, *however,* take an X-ray.**

**We will take an X-ray; *however,* the doctor cannot read it today.**

Another example of how function determines punctuation is in the case of a relative clause. *Commas are used* if the relative clause interrupts and is not essential to the main idea:

**My sister, *who wears braids,* has a wicked sense of humor.**

*Commas are not used* if the clause is part of the identity, necessary to the main idea:

**The girl *who wears braids* is my sister.**

The clause *who wears braids* is necessary for identifying which girl is the sister.

(For more examples of the use of the comma with relative clauses, see Chapter 7.)

**Practice**     **In each of the following sentences, insert commas wherever they are needed.**

1. Some parts of our country I believe do not have ample supplies of water.

2. The rocky soil of Virginia for example cannot absorb much rainwater.

3. Johnstown, Pennsylvania an industrial city of forty-eight thousand is situated in one of the most flood-prone valleys of America.

4. It is not therefore a very safe place to live.

5. The Colorado which is one of our longest rivers gives up most of its water to farmers and cities before it reaches the sea.

RULE

> **Use commas around nouns in direct address. (A noun in *direct address* is the name or title used in speaking to someone.)**

**I thought, *Rosa,* that I saw your picture in the paper.**

**Practice**     **In each of the following sentences, insert commas wherever they are needed.**

1. Dear your tea is ready now.

2. I wonder Jason if the game has been canceled.

3. Dad could I borrow five dollars?

4. I insist sir on speaking with the manager.

5. Kim is that you?

RULE

> **Use commas in numbers of one thousand or larger.**

**1,999**

**1,999,999,999**

**Practice**          In each of the following numbers, insert commas wherever they are needed.

1.  4 8 7 6 4 5 4

2.  8 7 6 0 2

3.  1 5 6 4 3 9 6 0 0

4.  1 8 7 0 0 0

5.  1 0 0 0 0 0 0 0 0 0 0 0 0 0

RULE

> **Use a comma to set off exact words spoken in dialogue.**

**"Let them," she said, "eat cake."**

**NOTE:** Commas (as well as periods) are placed inside the quotation marks.

**Practice**          In each of the following sentences, insert commas wherever they are needed.

1.  "I won't" he insisted "be a part of your scheme."

2.  He mumbled  "I plead the Fifth Amendment."

3.  "I was told" the defendant explained "to answer every question."

4.  "This court case" the judge announced "will be televised."

5.  "The jury" said Al Tarvin of the press "was handpicked."

RULE

> **Use a  comma wherever it is necessary to prevent a misunderstanding.**

**Before eating, the cat prowled through the barn.**

**Practice**          In each of the following sentences, insert commas wherever they are needed.

1.  Kicking the child was carried off to bed.

2.  To John Russell Baker is the best columnist.

3.  When you can come and visit us.

4.  We surveyed the students in the class; out of the twenty seven were married.

5.  Some types of skin cancers can kill doctors say.

**EXERCISE 4**

## Using the Comma Correctly

**In each of the following sentences, insert commas wherever they are needed.**

1.  In Weaverville California the local high school administrators made an interesting discovery.

2.  At a cost of four hundred dollars a year per student a private company was offering college-level advanced placement courses on the web.

3.  Because some students need these courses to get into more competitive colleges everyone thought this would be a perfect way to take advantage of the new technology.

4.  The problems however soon became apparent when two students signed up for a government course.

5.  Brian Jones a senior who wants to be a record producer and Jeremy Forbes a classmate who dreams of being a cartoonist found these problems very frustrating.

6.  Their worst problems were long delays getting online many technical glitches and the absence of a teacher to encourage persistence.

7.  Out of six hundred students who enrolled in one of the company's online courses last year two-thirds did not complete enough course work to take the final exam.

8.  Government officials have praised the use of this electronic support for schools but others say online courses are a poor replacement for the 1 8 0 0 0 0 new teachers the country really needs.

9.  Still others worry that too many cyberspace offerings provide only supplemental services such as SAT training college counseling and virtual field trips.

10. Francisco J. Hernandez an educator at the University of California at Santa Cruz says "Our intent is not to be an alternative to a high-quality teacher and classroom but to be an alternative to nothing because that's what students are getting right now."

**EXERCISE 5**

### Using the Comma Correctly

**In each of the following sentences, insert commas wherever they are needed.**

1.  Abraham Lincoln was born on February 12 1809 in Kentucky.

2.  In 1816 after selling most of their possessions the Lincoln family moved to Indiana.

3.  During their first weeks in Indiana the family hunted for food drank melted snow and huddled together for warmth.

4.  After a little formal education Lincoln worked on a ferryboat on the Ohio River.

5.  The first large city that Lincoln visited was New Orleans an important center of trade in 1828.

6.  Among the 4 0 0 0 0 people living in New Orleans at the time of Lincoln's visit there were people from every state and several foreign countries.

7.  New Orleans also showed Lincoln such city luxuries as fancy clothes gleaming silverware expensive furniture and imported china and glassware.

8.  As a result of this visit Lincoln must have compared the log cabin of his childhood with the wealthy houses of the big city.

9.  A few years later Lincoln became a merchant but his failure in business left him in debt for more than ten years.

10. We should be grateful that Lincoln who started off in a business career turned his attention to politics.

**EXERCISE 6**

### Using the Comma Correctly

**In each of the following examples, insert commas wherever they are needed.**

1.  The Hope Diamond is one of the most famous if not *the* most famous gems in the world.

2.  Mined in India the diamond reached Europe in 1668 along with the story that there was a curse on the stone.

3.  The curse or so the legend goes is that bad fortune followed the diamond because it had been stolen from a temple in India.

4. Nearly all of its owners including Queen Marie Antoinette of France a French actress who was shot to death and an American woman whose children were killed in accidents have met with tragedy.

5. Well if we cannot share in the history of the Hope Diamond we can see it in the Smithsonian Institution in our nation's capital.

6. Other gems not as famous have served people throughout history as payments for ransom as bribes and as lavish wedding presents.

7. One of the most famous mines in South America is an emerald mine started in 1537 in Colombia.

8. As the earth's crust erodes rough stones may find their way into streams rivers and other bodies of water.

9. The greatest quantity of diamonds emeralds amethysts topazes and other precious and semiprecious stones is to be found in Africa and South America.

10. We could travel to these places if we had the time the money and the interest.

# THREE USES FOR THE APOSTROPHE

RULE **1**

**Use an apostrophe to form the possessive.**

- For most singular nouns, add 's:

  | | |
  |---|---|
  | **the pen of the teacher** | **= the teacher's pen** |
  | **the strategy of the boss** | **= the boss's strategy** |
  | **the wheel of the car** | **= the car's wheel** |

Be careful to choose the right noun when you form the possessive. Always ask yourself *who* or *what* possesses something. In the previous examples, the teacher possesses the pen, the boss possesses the strategy, and the wheel belongs to the car. Note the following unusual possessives:

| | |
|---|---|
| **Hyphenated words:** | **mother-in-law's advice** |
| **Joint possession:** | **Lucy and Desi's children** |
| **Individual possession:** | **John's and Steve's ideas** |

- For most indefinite pronouns, add 's:

  **everyone's responsibility**

  **somebody's wallet**

  **another's problem**

**NOTE:** A **possessive pronoun** (*his, hers, its, ours, yours, theirs, whose*) never takes an apostrophe.

> **Whose key is this?**
>
> **The key is *his.***
>
> **The car is *theirs.***

- For nouns that form their plurals in a regular way (by adding *–s* or *–es*), add only an apostrophe:

> **the coats of the ladies    = the ladies' coats**
>
> **the store of the brothers = the brothers' store**

- For nouns that form their plural in an irregular way (they do not end in *–s*), add 's:

> **the hats of the children = the children's hats**
>
> **the harness of the oxen = the oxen's harness**

**NOTE:** A few singular nouns ending in the *s* or *z* sound are awkward to pronounce if another *s* sound is added. In those cases, the final *-s* is optional. Let your ear help you make the decision.

> **Jesus's robe** or **Jesus' robe**
>
> **Moses's law** or **Moses' law**

---

RULE **2**    **Use 'S to form certain plurals to prevent confusion.**

---

- letters of the alphabet:

> **When he writes, all his *a*'s look like *o*'s.**

- abbreviations with periods:

> **My sisters both have Ph.D.'s from the University of Buffalo.**

- words referred to in a text:

> **He uses too many *you know*'s when he speaks.**

**NOTE:** Never use an apostrophe to form any other plurals.

---

RULE **3**    **Use an apostrophe to show where one or more letters have been omitted in a contraction.**

---

> **cannot       = can't**
>
> **should not = shouldn't**
>
> **will not      = won't** (This is the only commonly used contraction that changes its spelling.)

I am          = I'm

she will      = she'll

**EXERCISE 7**

## Using the Apostrophe

**Fill in each of the blanks below with the correct form of the word, following the rules for using the apostrophe.**

1.  rays of the sun                          the _____ rays

2.  the reputation of the press              the _____ reputation.

3.  length of the room                       the _____ length

4.  the house of Anthony and Maria           _____ house
    (*joint possession*)

5.  the idea of nobody                       _____ idea

6.  The book belongs to him.                 The book is _____.

7.  in the reign of Queen Elizabeth          in _____

8.  That is her opinion. (*form a contraction*)   _____ her opinion.

9.  shirts for boys                          _____ shirts

10. the cover of the book                    the _____ cover

**EXERCISE 8**

## Using the Apostrophe

**Fill in each of the blanks below with the correct form of the word, following the rules for using the apostrophe.**

1.  the value of the property               the _____ value

2.  the plans of the developers             the _____ plans

3.  the ideas of anybody                    _____ ideas

4.  Visitors cannot park on this block.     Visitors _____ park on
    (form a contraction)                    this block.

5.  the rights of the owners                  the _____ rights

6.  the claims of the father-in-law           the _____ claims

7.  the inventions of Westinghouse            _____
    and Edison (individual                    inventions
    possession)

8.  The money belongs to him.                 The money is _____.

9.  The windshield of the bus                 the _____ windshield

10. The enamel of the teeth                   the _____ enamel

**EXERCISE** ❾        **Using the Apostrophe**

**Fill in each of the blanks below with the correct form of the word, following the rules for using the apostrophe.**

1.  the engine of the train                   the _____ engine

2.  the spirit of the class                   the _____spirit

3.  the center for women                      the _____center

4.  the wish of everybody                     _____ wish

5.  The toys belong to them.                  The toys are _____.

6.  The child mixes up *b* and *d*.           The child mixes up _____.
    (*use the plural*)

7.  I will not leave this house.              I _____ leave this house.
    (*form a contraction*)

8.  the grain of the wood                     the _____grain

9.  the verdict of the jurors                 the _____ verdict

10. the policies of Ridge School              _____
    and Orchard School                        policies
    (*individual possession*)

# FOUR USES FOR QUOTATION MARKS

**RULE 1** — Use quotation marks for a direct quotation (a speaker's exact words).

**"Please," I begged, "go away."**

Do not use quotation marks for an indirect quotation (reporting a speaker's words).

**I begged her to go away.**

**RULE 2**  — Use quotation marks for material copied word for word from a source.

**According to the *New York Times*, "The average adult body contains 40 to 50 quarts of water. Blood is 83 percent water; muscles are 75 percent water; the brain is 74 percent water; and even bone is 22 percent water."**

**RULE 3** — Use quotation marks for titles of shorter works such as short stories, poems, articles in magazines and newspapers, songs, essays, and chapters of books.

**"A Modest Proposal," an essay by Jonathan Swift, is a masterpiece of satire.**

**"The Lottery," a short story by Shirley Jackson, created a sensation when it first appeared in the *New Yorker.***

**NOTE:** The title of a full-length work (such as a book, a play, a magazine, or a newspaper) is italicized in print and underlined when handwritten.

**In print:**     **Many famous short stories have first appeared in the *New Yorker.***

**Handwritten form:**     Many famous short stories have first appeared in the <u>New Yorker.</u>

**RULE 4**  — Use quotation marks for terms referred to in a special way.

**"Duckie" is a term of affection used by the British, in the same way we would use the word "honey."**

**Practice**

In each of the following sentences, insert quotation marks wherever they are needed.

1.  The Gift of the Magi is one of the short stories in O. Henry's book *The Four Million*.

2.  Franklin Delano Roosevelt said, We have nothing to fear but fear itself.

3.  The president told his cabinet that they would have to settle the problem in the next few days.

4.  The term reggae refers to a popular musical style originating in Jamaica.

5.  She read the article Can Empathy Be Taught? in a recent issue of *Academe*.

If these five sentences had been handwritten, which words would have been underlined?

# THREE USES FOR THE SEMICOLON

RULE **1**
> Use a semicolon to join two independent clauses whose ideas or sentence structures are related.

He decided to consult the map  she decided to ask a pedestrian.

RULE **2**
> Use a semicolon in front of an adverbial conjunction used to combine two sentences.

He decided to consult the map  however, she decided to ask a pedestrian.

RULE **3**
> Use a semicolon to separate items in a series when the items themselves contain commas.

I had lunch with Linda, my best friend  Mrs. Armstrong, my English teacher  and Jan, my sister-in-law.

**NOTE:** If the writer had used only commas to separate the items in this example, the reader might think five or six people had gone to lunch together.

**Practice**

In each of the following sentences, insert a semicolon wherever needed.

1.  One of the best ways to remember a vacation is to take numerous photos one of the best ways to recall the contents of a book is to take notes.

2. The problem of street crime must be solved otherwise, the number of vigilantes will increase.

3. The committee was made up of Kevin Corey, a writer Anita Poindexter, a professor and Jorge Rodriguez, a politician.

4. The bank president was very cordial however, he would not approve the loan.

5. The retailer wants higher profits the customer wants lower cost.

# FOUR USES FOR THE COLON

RULE **1**

> Use a colon after an independent clause when the material that follows is a series of items, an illustration, or an explanation.

- **a series of items:**

   **Please order the following items: five dozen pencils, twenty rulers, and five rolls of tape.**

Notice that in the sentence below, no colon is used because there is not a complete sentence (or independent clause) before the list.

   **The courses I am taking this semester are Freshman Composition, Introduction to Psychology, Art Appreciation, and Survey of American Literature.**

Do not use a colon directly after a verb; after the preposition *except* or *regarding;* or after the expression *such as, for example, especially,* or *including.*

   **The merchant ordered the following items: belts, handbags, and shoes.**

   **The merchant *ordered* belts, handbags, and shoes.**

   **The merchant ordered everything in the catalog: belts, handbags, and shoes.**

   **The merchant ordered everything in the catalog *except* belts, handbags, and shoes.**

   **The merchant ordered many items: belts, handbags, and shoes.**

   **The merchant ordered many items *including* belts, handbags, and shoes.**

- **an explanation or illustration:**

   **She was an exceptional child: at seven she was performing on the concert stage.**

**RULE ② Use a colon for the salutation of a business letter.**

**Dear Sales Office Manager:**

**Dear President Gonzalas:**

**RULE ③ Use a colon when using numerals to indicate time.**

**We will eat at 5:15.**

**RULE ④ Use a colon between the title and the subtitle of a book.**

*Plain English Please: A Rhetoric*

**Practice**   In each of the following sentences, insert colons wherever they are needed.

1. Three vocalists performed in Los Angeles recently Natalie Cole, Bruce Springsteen, and Sheryl Crow.

2. The official has one major flaw in his personality greed.

3. The restaurant has lovely homemade desserts such as German chocolate layer cake and baked Alaska.

4. The college offers four courses in English literature Romantic Poetry, Shakespeare's Plays, The British Short Story, and The Modern Novel.

5. Arriving at 6 1 5 in the morning, Marlene brought me a sausage and cheese pizza, soda, and a gallon of ice cream.

# USE OF DASHES AND PARENTHESES

Commas, dashes, and parentheses can all be used to show an interruption of the main idea. The particular form of punctuation you choose depends on the degree of interruption.

**RULE ① Use dashes for a less formal and more emphatic interruption of the main idea. Dashes are seldom used in formal writing.**

**He came—I thought—by car.**

**She arrived—and I know this for a fact—in a pink Cadillac.**

RULE

> Use parentheses to insert extra information that some of your readers might want to know but that is not at all essential for the main idea. Such information is not emphasized.

**Johann Sebastian Bach (1685–1750) composed the six Brandenburg Concertos.**

**Plea bargaining (see Section 4.3) was developed to speed court verdicts.**

## Practice

Insert dashes or parentheses wherever needed.

1. Herbert Simon is and I don't think this is an exaggeration a genius.

2. George Eliot her real name was Many Ann Evans wrote *Silas Marner*.

3. You should in fact, I insist see a doctor.

4. Unemployment brings with it a number of other problems see the study by Brody, 2010.

5. Mass media television, radio, movies, magazines, and newspapers are able to transmit information over a wide range and to a large number of people.

## EXERCISE 10    Other Marks of Punctuation

In each of the following sentences, insert marks of punctuation wherever they are needed. Choose from quotation marks, semicolon, colon, dashes, and parentheses.

1. To measure crime, sociologists have used three different techniques official statistics, victimization surveys, and self-report studies.

2. The Bells is one of the best-loved poems of Edgar Allan Poe.

3. The lake has one major disadvantage to swimmers this summer weeds.

4. E. B. White wrote numerous essays for adults however, he also wrote some very popular books for children.

5. Tuberculosis also known as consumption has once again become a serious health issue.

6. The Victorian Period 1837–1901 saw a rapid expansion of industry.

7. He promised me I know he promised that he would come to my graduation.

8. Do you know what the French expression déjà vu means?

9.   She wanted to go to the movies he wanted to stay home and watch a movie on the DVD player.

10.  She has the qualifications needed for the job a teaching degree, a pleasant personality, two years' experience, and a love of children.

**EXERCISE**  **11**    ## Other Marks of Punctuation

**In each of the following sentences, insert marks of punctuation wherever they are needed. Choose from quotation marks, semicolon, colon, dashes, and parentheses.**

1.   Many young people have two feelings about science and technology awe and fear.

2.   The three people who helped work out the real estate transaction were Mr. Doyle, the realtor Mrs. White, the bank officer and Scott Castle, the lawyer.

3.   The book was titled *English Literature The Victorian Age.*

4.   I decided to walk to school, she said, because the bus fare has been raised again.

5.   She brought the following items to the beach a bathing suit, towel, sunglasses, and several books.

6.   The conference I believe it is scheduled for sometime in January will focus on the development of a new curriculum.

7.   The song Memories comes from the Broadway show *Cats.*

8.   The complex lab experiment has these two major problems too many difficult calculations and too many variables.

9.   The mutt that is to say, my dog is smarter than he looks.

10.  Violent crime cannot be reduced unless the society supports efforts such as strengthening the family structure, educating the young, and recruiting top-notch police.

**EXERCISE** **12**    ## Other Marks of Punctuation

**In each of the following sentences, insert marks of punctuation wherever they are needed. Choose from quotation marks, semicolon, colon, dashes, and parentheses.**

1.   Star Wars is the popular term for the development of atomic weapons for use in space.

2.  My father enjoyed spending money my mother was frugal.

3.  The student's short story Ten Steps to Nowhere appeared in a collection titled *The Best of Student Writing.*

4.  The report stated specifically that the company must if it wants to grow sell off at least 10 percent of its property.

5.  The foreign countries she visited were Mexico, Israel, and Morocco.

6.  Remember, the doctor told the patient, the next time I see you, I want to see an improvement in your condition.

7.  These students made the high honor roll Luis Sanchez, Julie Carlson, and Tenesha Moore.

8.  The scientist showed the students a glass of $H_2O$ water and asked them to identify the liquid.

9.  He said that he would give us an extension on our term papers.

10. The work was tedious nevertheless, the goal of finding the solution kept him motivated.

# MASTERY AND EDITING TESTS

**TEST 1**

## Editing for Correct Capitalization and Punctuation

**In the following sentences, each underlined portion may contain an error. If an error exists, circle the letter of the proper correction. If there is no error, circle the letter for "No change is necessary."**

1.  An article titled "The Biker Question: To Roar or Not to Roar" appeared in the *New York Times* on Friday July 25, 2003.

    a.  Article

    b.  "The biker question: To roar or not to roar"

    c.  Friday, July 25, 2003.

    d.  No change is necessary.

2.  Motorcycle enthusiasts have a choice, they can have their engines run quietly, or they can replace the exhaust systems and assault people with the loud noise.

    a.  enthusiasts have a choice: they can

    b.  quietly or they can

    c.  exhaust systems, and assault people

    d.  No change is necessary.

3. <u>Wayne Doenges, a seventy-five-year-old retired engineer,</u> rides the roads of Indiana on his quietly running, chromed-out, six-cylinder <u>Honda Valkyrie.</u>

   a.  Wayne Doenges, a seventy-five-year-old retired Engineer,

   b.  Wayne Doenges a seventy-five-year-old retired engineer

   c.  honda valkyrie

   d.  No change is necessary.

4. <u>My bike attracts attention he boasts in a positive way.</u>

   a.  "My bike attracts attention" He boasts "In a positive way."

   b.  "My bike attracts attention," he boasts, "in a positive way."

   c.  "My bike attracts attention, he boasts, in a positive way."

   d.  No change is necessary.

5. <u>Other bikers however prefer</u> the thunderous noise from special exhaust systems that have no noise dampening system.

   a.  Other bikers, however, prefer

   b.  Other bikers; however, prefer

   c.  Other Bikers however prefer

   d.  No change is necessary.

6. Sometimes these two groups meet at the <u>American Motorcycle Rally</u> that is held <u>every Summer in June at Lake George, New York.</u>

   a.  american motorcycle rally

   b.  every Summer in june at Lake George, New York.

   c.  every summer in June at Lake George, New York.

   d.  No change is necessary.

7. For Rick <u>Gray, a lawyer from Lancaster, Pennsylvania,</u> riding a quiet motorcycle is like a form of <u>Buddhist meditation.</u>

   a.  Gray, a Lawyer from Lancaster, Pennsylvania,

   b.  Gray a lawyer from Lancaster Pennsylvania

   c.  buddhist meditation

   d.  No change is necessary.

8. <u>Mr. Gray, who is the Chairman of the American Motorcycle Association,</u> owns thirteen <u>motorcycles and rides 20,000 to 35,000 miles each year.</u>

   a.  Mr. Gray, who is the chairman of the American Motorcycle Association,

   b.  Mr. Gray, who is the Chairman of the American Motorcycle association,

   c.  motorcycles, and rides 20000 to 35000 miles each year.

   d.  No change is necessary.

9. <u>Vice President Pamela Amette</u> of the <u>Motorcycle Industry Council</u> says, <u>"it's illegal to install</u> an exhaust system that does not meet federal requirements."

   a.  Vice president Pamela Amette

   b.  motorcycle industry council

   c.  "It's illegal to install

   d.  No change is necessary.

10. Although some bikers think a loud level of noise will warn cars and trucks of their <u>presence, a study</u> done by <u>the university of California at Los Angeles</u> shows that the level of noise does not decrease the chance of accidents.

   a.  presence; a study

   b.  presence—a study

   c.  the University of California at Los Angeles

   d.  No change is necessary.

**TEST 2**

## Editing for Correct Capitalization and Punctuation

**Read the following paragraph and insert the correct capitalization and marks of punctuation wherever they are needed.**

[1]The expression  your name is mud has its origin in a person from history. [2]Samuel Mudd was a doctor in Maryland during the civil war. [3]About 4 a.m. on april 15 1865 at his home in charles county Maryland  dr. Mudd was awakened by men who needed medical attention. [4]One was john wilkes booth who had just shot president Abraham Lincoln at ford's theatre in Washington, d.c. [5]Mudd set and bandaged booths broken leg before the assassin went on his way. [6]A few days later the doctor was arrested and charged with being part of the conspiracy to kill the president. [7]He was convicted by a military court and sentenced to life in prison but in 1869 president Andrew Johnson commuted his sentence. [8]Since that time dr. Mudds descendants have tried without success to overturn that original conviction. [9]One politician  united states representative Steny Hoyer introduced a bill the Samuel Mudd relief act that would have cleared the doctor s name but it failed to pass. [10]Last march after another setback Richard Mudd the grandson of Samuel Mudd said to reporters as long as the United States lasts the story of my 31-year-old grandfather being put in prison for life for setting a broken leg is never going to end.

**TEST 3**    ## Editing for Correct Capitalization and Punctuation

Read the following paragraph and insert the correct capitalization and marks of punctuation wherever they are needed.

Valentines day is celebrated on february 14 as a romantic festival. People send their sweethearts greeting cards that say wont you be my valentine? Children like to make their own cards from paper doilies red construction paper bright foils and samples of wallpaper. All of these customs probably have their origin in the ancient roman festival of lupercalia which took place every winter. The festival honored juno the goddess of women and marriage and pan the god of nature. According to the book *popular antiquities,* which was written in 1877 England began observing this holiday as early as 1446. In the united states the holiday became popular after the civil war. Admirers continue to send their sweethearts cards, chocolates, and flowers.

**TEST 4**    ## Editing Student Writing Using Editing Symbols

**In the following paragraph, ten errors are marked with editing symbols. Correct each error on the lines provided after the paragraph.**

[1]When I was growing up in Honduras, my *cap* Grandmother made me a delicious cup of hot chocolate every morning. [2]I've only recently learned about its interesting history. [3]Chocolate is made from the seeds of the fruit of the cacao tree *punc* which is an unusual plant that produces flowers and fruits on its trunk, not on its branches. [4]The story of chocolate goes back to its origins in *cap* central America more than 1,500 years ago. [5]Recently, they *pro ref* found a piece of chocolate in a tomb that dates back to 600 BC. [6]The ancient *cap* maya made the cacao into a drink *punc* but it was the foam, not the liquid, that they most enjoyed. [7]Scientists had always *vb* believe that the common people had not been allowed access to cacao plants, but this idea was proved wrong. [8]Cacao plants were

found in the ashes of the ancient Salvadoran village of Ceren. *frag* ⁹A village that had been buried by a volcano in 590. ¹⁰The people of Ceren made beautiful ceramics into which they mixed cacao *punc* paste vanilla chiles and other spices to concoct a delicious drink. ¹¹In some marketplaces in southern Mexico, it is still possible to buy a similar drink, referred to by the locals as *punc* popo. ¹²You are lucky if you have the opportunity to sample a cup.

## Corrections

1.  capitalization (sentence 1):    _____

2.  punctuation (sentence 3)    _____
    subordination:    _____
    _____

3.  capitalization (sentence 4):    _____

4.  pronoun reference (sentence 5):    _____
    no antecedent

5.  capitalization (sentence 6):    _____

6.  punctuation (sentence 6):    _____
    coordination    _____
    _____

7.  verb form (sentence 7):    _____

8.  fragment (sentence 9) :    _____
    _____
    _____

9.  punctuation (sentence 10):    _____
    items in a series    _____
    _____
    _____

10. punctuation (sentence 11)    _____
    special term:

## Exploring Online

Go to **www.cengage.com/devenglish/scarry/writersworkplace** to find the **Writer's Online Workplace**, a website designed for students using this book. You will find links to handouts, interactive quizzes, and other online resources as you explore the following topics:

- capitalization
- punctuation, including
    apostrophes
    commas
    colons
    periods
    question marks
    semicolons

# Working Together

## WRITING A REVIEW: EATING OUT

Newspapers and magazines hire writers to review movies and plays, restaurants, concerts, art gallery openings, and other events. You might think that being paid to eat out would be the perfect way to earn a living!

Read the following newspaper review of a typical neighborhood restaurant. The review contains important information that a customer would need to know, such as location, days and hours of operation, menu, atmosphere, price, and other special features.

### Eating Out

If you appreciate authentic Chinese food, you should go for lunch or dinner to the Golden Fortune Restaurant, located at 99 Elm Avenue in Ellington. It is just above the South Side Plaza, walking distance from the center of town. The Golden Fortune Restaurant is the kind of restaurant you will want to visit more than once. The food is expertly prepared, the prices are very moderate, and the service is always friendly. We particularly liked the warm and relaxed atmosphere, partly the result of soft classical music playing in the background.

Many of the lunch and dinner selections at the Golden Fortune are traditional, with a few surprises. All of the vegetables used are fresh, and a special section of the menu is devoted to dieters. The appetizers are large enough to serve two people. On our first visit, we were delighted with the combination platter. It is the most popular appetizer on the menu because it allows diners to sample a half dozen of the house specialties.

One unique touch at this restaurant is the choice of 24 different teas. Instead of having an ordinary pot of green tea placed in front of you, as in most Chinese restaurants, at the Golden Fortune you can choose from a wide variety. These include green tea with passion fruit, peach tea, and even milk tea with oatmeal. Customers enjoy trying new combinations each time they visit. Our favorite is the black tea with plum. If you like, you may bring your own wine or beer, and the waiters will be happy to serve it.

Some of the most popular main courses are beef with garlic sauce, crispy honey chicken on a bed of rice and vegetables, and a variety of delicious stir-fry dishes. If you choose a stir-fry at the Golden Fortune, you may select a favorite sauce and type of noodle along with a meat or fish, and the kitchen will make up the dish you want.

The Golden Fortune is open for lunch from noon to 4 p.m. and for dinner from 5 p.m. until 11 p.m. every day of the week. No reservations are needed. For take-out orders, call 548-4407 after 11 a.m.

Divide into groups of five. Each group should decide on a restaurant or event to review and list the basic subjects that will be covered in that review. Each person in the group should then select one subject and write a paragraph of at least five sentences about it. Return to the group to listen to each other's paragraphs as they are read. Decide on the best order for the paragraphs, and together compose an introduction and conclusion for the piece. Then put these paragraphs together to construct a complete review.

## PORTFOLIO SUGGESTION

Keep this review in your portfolio. Whenever you go to a restaurant, musical event, or movie, keep in mind that these are all places where reviewers go and write down their reactions. You can too!

# Understanding the Power of Words

When some writers start work on a project, they first brainstorm or cluster their ideas. Other writers feel more comfortable freewriting to produce their first drafts. No matter which approach a writer takes, making thoughtful word choices is one of the most important parts of the writing process. When writer and social activist Malcolm X set out to educate himself in prison, he copied a complete dictionary by hand—certainly a systematic approach to the study of words! You too should concentrate on individual words. This unit focuses on aspects of the writing process that relate to words: word choice, word meanings, wordiness, appropriate words, and words often confused.

# 14 CHOOSING WORDS THAT WORK

The right choice of words is always of critical importance for a writer's finished product. In this chapter, you will explore ways to improve your word choices by learning about the following:

**CHAPTER OBJECTIVES**

- words rich in meaning
- denotations and connotations of words
- wordiness:

  redundant expressions

  wordy phrases

  overuse of the verb *to be*

  unnecessary repetition of the same word

  unnecessary use of *there is* or *there are*

  flowery or pretentious language

  apologetic, tentative expressions

- language inappropriate for formal writing:

  slang

  clipped language

  sexist language

  trite expressions (clichés)

## USING WORDS RICH IN MEANING

Writing involves a constant search to find the right words to express thoughts and feelings as accurately as possible. When a writer wants to be precise or wants to give a flavor to a piece of writing, the creative possibilities for word choice and sentence construction are almost endless. The creative writer looks for words that have rich and appropriate meanings and associations.

For instance, if you were describing a person under five years of age, you might choose one of these words:

| imp | brat | preschooler | child |
|-----|------|-------------|-------|
| toddler | tot | youngster | |

Some words have no associations beyond their strict dictionary meaning; these words are said to be neutral. Which word in the list is the most neutral, communicating the least negative or positive emotional associations?* A person writing a brochure for a nursery school would probably choose the word *preschooler* because it identifies the age of the child. A person talking about a child who has just learned to walk might use the word *toddler* because it carries the association of a small child who is toddling along a bit unsteadily. What informal and unkind word might an angry older sibling shout when a younger brother or sister has just colored all over a favorite book?**

**EXERCISE  1**

## Using Words Rich in Meaning

The five words in Column A all have the basic meaning of *thin.* However, an additional meaning makes each word richer and more specific. Match each word in Column A with the letter of the definition from Column B that best fits the word.

| Column A | Column B |
|---|---|
| ____ 1. slender | a. unattractively thin |
| ____ 2. emaciated | b. thin and bony with a haggard appearance |
| ____ 3. lean | c. gracefully long and slim |
| ____ 4. skinny | d. containing little fat, in shape, fit |
| ____ 5. gaunt | e. extremely thin, undernourished, and sickly |

Most languages are rich with words that describe *eating.* Column A contains a few English words about eating. Match each word in Column A with the letter of the definition from Column B that best fits the word.

| Column A | Column B |
|---|---|
| ____ 1. taste | a. to eat with small quick bites |
| ____ 2. devour | b. to bite or chew on something persistently |
| ____ 3. nibble | c. to eat between meals |
| ____ 4. gorge | d. to test the flavor of a food |
| ____ 5. gnaw | e. to stuff oneself with food |
| ____ 6. snack | f. to eat up greedily |

**EXERCISE  2**

## Using Words Rich in Meaning

The words *eat, drink, song,* and *walk* are neutral words (having no positive or negative associations). Each neutral term is followed by four words, each one with its own precise meaning. In each case, give a definition for the word. Use your dictionary.

> **Example:  crunch: to eat with a noisy crackling sound**

*Your answer should be *child.*
**Your answer should be *brat.*

**to eat**

1. gobble: _____

2. savor: _____

3. munch: _____

4. chomp: _____

**to drink**

1. sip: _____

2. gulp: _____

3. slurp: _____

4. lap: _____

**a song**

1. aria: _____

2. lullaby: _____

3. ballad: _____

4. hymn: _____

**to walk**

1. lumber: _____

2. amble: _____

3. stride: _____

4. roam: _____

# UNDERSTANDING LOADED WORDS: DENOTATION/CONNOTATION

The careful writer considers more than the dictionary meaning of a word. Some words have different meanings for different people.

The **denotation** of a word is its strict dictionary meaning. The **connotation** of a word is the meaning (apart from the dictionary meaning) that a person attaches to a word because of that individual's personal experience with the word.

| | |
|---|---|
| **Word:** | liberal (adj) |
| **Denotation (political):** | favoring nonrevolutionary progress or reform |
| **Possible connotations:** | socially active, freethinking, too generous, far left, favoring many costly government programs |

Politicians are usually experts in understanding the connotations of a word. They know, for instance, that if they want to get votes in a conservative area, they should not refer to their own views as liberal. The strict dictionary meaning of *liberal* is "favoring nonrevolutionary progress or reform," certainly an idea that most people would support. However, when most people hear the words *liberal* and *conservative,* they bring to the words many political biases and experiences from their past: their parents' attitudes, the political and social history of the area in which they live, and other factors that may correctly or incorrectly influence their understanding of the words.

Choosing words that are not neutral but that have more exact or appropriate meanings is a powerful skill for a writer, one that will help your reader better understand the ideas you want to communicate. As your vocabulary grows, your writing will become richer and deeper. Your work will reflect your understanding of the many shades of meaning that words can have.

**EXERCISE  3**

## Denotation/Connotation

In this exercise, you have the opportunity to think of words that are richer in associations than the neutral words underlined in the sentences below. Write your own word choice in the space to the right of each sentence. Discuss with others in your class the associations you make with the words you have chosen.

1.  I live in a <u>house</u> at the edge of town.          _____

2.  I <u>walk</u> home from work every night.          _____

3.  Usually the same <u>person</u> is always walking behind me.          _____

4.  She is always carrying a lot of <u>stuff</u>.          _____

5.  She looks as if she is <u>old</u>.          _____

6.  She has <u>marks</u> all over her face.          _____

7.  Sometimes I try to <u>talk</u> with her.          _____

8.  She has such <u>awful</u> clothing.                    _____

9.  Sometimes I can hear her <u>talking</u> to herself.     _____

10. At night when I am <u>sitting</u> in my favorite
    armchair, I often think of her and wish she
    could tell me the story of her life.                   _____

**EXERCISE  4**

### Denotation/Connotation

The following sentences contain words that have positive or negative asso-ciations for most people. Read each sentence and study the underlined word or phrase. Below each sentence, write the emotional meaning the underlined word or phrase has for you. Discuss your answers with your classmates. An example follows.

**Sentence:**     Her <u>brother</u> went with her so that she would not have to drive alone.

**Explanation:**  The word *brother* usually has a positive connotation. We expect a brother to be someone who is helpful and protective.

1.  The <u>dog</u> stood at the door; his size was quite astounding.

    _____

    _____

2.  The <u>foreigner</u> approached the ranch slowly.

    _____

    _____

3.  His <u>pickup truck</u> was parked in front.

    _____

    _____

4.  A woman and child were peering out from behind the <u>fence</u>.

    _____

    _____

5.  The <u>stranger</u> carried a long object of some kind.

    _____

    _____

**EXERCISE  5**

### Denotation/Connotation

When you write, you create a tone by the words you choose. Review the sentences you worked with in Exercise 4. For each sentence, create a more positive tone, either by changing the underlined word or phrase to a different word or phrase or by adding adjectives to modify the underlined word or phrase.

1. _____

   _____

2. _____

   _____

3. _____

   _____

4. _____

   _____

5. _____

   _____

# WORDINESS: IN WRITING, LESS CAN BE MORE!

In his book *The Elements of Style*, the famous writer E. B. White quotes his old teacher William Strunk Jr., who said that a sentence "should contain no unnecessary words" and a paragraph "no unnecessary sentences." Strunk's philosophy of writing also includes the commandment he gave many times in his classes at Cornell University: "Omit needless words!" It was a lesson that E. B. White took to heart, with the wonderful results that we see in his own writing.

Following is a summary of some important ways you can cut the number of your words to strengthen the power of your ideas. Read each example of wordiness, and notice how the revision makes the idea more concise.

| 1. **Redundant expressions** | **Revisions** |
|---|---|
| circle around | circle |
| blue in color | blue |
| past history | history |
| connect together | connect |
| true fact | fact |
| surrounded on all sides | surrounded |
| very unique | unique |

| 2. **Wordy phrases** | **Revisions** |
|---|---|
| in the event that | if |
| due to the fact that | because |
| for the stated reason that | because |
| in this day and age | today |
| at this point in time | now |
| in the neighborhood of | about |

**3. Overuse of the verb *to be***

The man is in need of help.

They are of the opinion that a lawyer should be called.

**Revisions**

The man needs help.

They believe a lawyer should be called.

**4. Unnecessary repetition of the same word**

The book is on the table. The book is my favorite. I have read the book five times.

**Revision**

The book on the table is my favorite. I have read it five times

**5. Unnecessary use of *there is* or *there are***

There are two major disadvantages to the new proposal.

There is no doubt but that the sun will rise tomorrow.

**Revisions**

The new proposal has two major disadvantages.

No doubt the sun will rise tomorrow.

**6. Flowery or pretentious language**

It is delightful to contemplate the culinary experience we will enjoy after the termination of this cinematic event.

**Revision**

I can't wait until we have pizza after the movie.

**7. Apologetic, tentative expressions**

In my opinion, the grading policy for this course should be changed.

Right now, it seems to me that finding a job in my field is very difficult.

In this paper, I will try to explain my views on censorship of the campus newspaper.

**Revisions**

The grading policy for this course should be changed.

Right now, finding a job in my field is very difficult.

Censoring the campus newspaper is a mistake.

**EXERCISE 6**

## Revising Wordy Sentences

**In each of the following sentences, underline the wordy phrase. Then revise each sentence to avoid wordiness. (If needed, refer to the list on pages 271–272.)**

1. The date for the final completion of your project is May 18.

2. The thought of the exam is causing her to be in a constant state of tension.

   _____

3. There is no better place to study than in our library.

   _____

4. Some people have the belief that astrology is a science.

   _____

5. We are all in need of better organizational skills.

   _____

6.    As far as mechanical ability is concerned, Mike is very handy.

_____

7.    She is in the process of cooking dinner.

_____

8.    Due to the fact of the rain, the game will be canceled.

_____

9.    In my opinion, it would seem to me that the reasons for unemployment are complex.

_____

10.    The box had an oblong shape.

_____


**EXERCISE**     ### Revising Wordy Sentences

**In each of the following sentences, underline the wordy phrase. Then revise each sentence to avoid wordiness. (If needed, refer to the list on pages 271–272.)**

1.    The gentleman is of a kindly nature.

_____

2.    I was told he is a male actor.

_____

3.    The price was in the neighborhood of fifty dollars.

_____

4.    In regard to the letter, it was sent to the wrong address.

_____

5.    It is everyone's duty to be in attendance at the meeting today. (Avoid the verb *to be*.)

_____

6.    My best friend is above me in height.

_____

7.    I tiptoed down the stairs on my toes in order to surprise everyone.

_____

8.    They made the discovery that I was not upstairs.

_____

9.  A member of the teaching staff at this institution of higher learning failed to submit in a timely fashion the fruits of my endeavors for the course during this entire period from September to December.

_____

10. Even though I am not an expert, I think that more neighborhood health clinics are needed.

_____

# RECOGNIZING LANGUAGE APPROPRIATE FOR FORMAL WRITING

When we have conversations with family and friends, or when we write to them, we use informal language. This relaxed use of language may include slang and other informal words and phrases familiar to our particular group or region. When we write or speak in public, however, we need to use more formal language. In this case, slang is not appropriate, nor is any type of sexist language or disrespectful use of words.

> **Slang** is a term that refers to special words or expressions used by a particular group of people, often with the intention of keeping that meaning private. One characteristic of a slang word or expression is that it is often used only for a limited time and then forgotten.
> For example:
>
> **The party was *swell*. (1940s)**
> **The party was *groovy*. (1960s)**
> **The party was *awesome*. (1980s)**
> **The party was *phat*. (1990s)**
> **The party was *hot*. (2000s)**

| Slang or informal words | Acceptable words |
|---|---|
| bucks | dollars |
| kids | children |
| cops | police |
| a bummer | a bad experience |
| off the wall | crazy |
| yummy | delicious |
| chow | food |

> **Clipped language** refers to the use of shortened words to make communication more relaxed and informal. Clipped language is not appropriate in more formal writing, which requires standard English.

| Clipped language | Acceptable words |
|---|---|
| doc | doctor |
| fridge | refrigerator |
| pro | professional |
| TV | television |

> **Sexist language** refers to the use of single-gender nouns or pronouns to apply to both men and women. This was standard usage in the past, but writers and publishers today avoid such language.
>
> **Sexist language:   Everyone must bring *his* project on Tuesday.**

**Options for revising sexist language:**

1.  Use plural pronouns and plural antecedents.

    *All students* **must bring *their* projects on Tuesday.**

2.  Change the pronoun to an article.

    **Everyone must bring *a* project on Tuesday.**

3.  Replace a single-gender term with an inclusive term.

    **Everyone must bring *his or her* project on Tuesday.**

4.  Use the passive voice, thus avoiding the need for a pronoun.

    **Projects must be brought to class on Tuesday.**

5.  Use a gender neutral term.

    **Sexist language:**      **The teacher is an important *man*. *He* can influence the lives of many children in a community.**

    **Nonsexist language:**   **The teacher is an important person who can influence the lives of many children in the community.**

The following partial list of sexist terms is accompanied by present-day acceptable forms.

| Sexist terms | Acceptable terms |
|---|---|
| authoress | author |
| businessman | business executive, businessperson |
| chairman | chairperson |
| common man | average person |
| congressman | member of congress, legislator |
| fireman | firefighter |
| forefathers | ancestors |
| mailman | mail carrier, postal worker |
| mankind | humanity, people |
| salesman | sales associate, salesperson, sales representative |
| stewardess | flight attendant |

> **Trite expressions (or clichés)** are expressions that may have been fresh at one time but now have become stale from overuse.

| Trite expressions | Acceptable expressions |
|---|---|
| cool as a cucumber | calm |
| mad as a hornet | angry |
| a golden opportunity | an exceptional opportunity |
| light as a feather | light |
| busy as a bee | busy |
| dead as a doornail | dead |
| slowly but surely | gradually |
| without rhyme or reason | senseless |

**EXERCISE** **8**

## Recognizing Language Inappropriate for Formal Writing

The following sentences contain words that are informal, slang, sexist, or trite. Circle the word or phrase in each sentence that is inappropriate for formal writing, and on the line to the right of each sentence, provide a more formal word or expression to replace the inappropriate one.

1. I wish you would stop beating around the bush. _____

2. She told her friends to chill out. _____

3. The entire evening turned out to be a bummer. _____

4. The businessmen in the community support the science project. _____

5. It is time to come clean with the director. _____

6. The first experiment turned out to be a downer. _____

7. The scientist has guts to continue the research. _____

8. The entire lab is a dump. _____

9. The guys often spend the night there. _____

10. They work until two or three in the morning and then crash. _____

**EXERCISE 9**

## Recognizing Language Inappropriate for Formal Writing

The following sentences contain words that are informal, slang, sexist, or trite. Circle the word or phrase in each sentence that is inappropriate for formal writing, and on the line to the right of each sentence, provide a more formal word or expression to replace the inappropriate one.

1. Don't bug me about studying.                                  _____

2. I aced the last French test.                                  _____

3. Bring me some grub tonight.                                   _____

4. He's my buddy.                                                _____

5. How lousy is the weather outside?                             _____

6. The bodybuilder is as strong as an ox.                        _____

7. He was well-known in the hood.                                _____

8. The medical doctor is a well-respected
   person in most communities; he is
   considered a role model for our
   children.                                                     _____

9. I think it's gonna be nice tomorrow.                          _____

10. I ain't seen the new neighbors yet.                          _____

# STUDYING A STUDENT ESSAY FOR WORD CHOICES

**ACTIVITY 1**

## Making Better Word Choices

When Sandra Russell wrote an essay on the experience of living through a tornado, she composed more than one draft. Below are six sentences that she could have written when she worked on the first draft of her essay. Rewrite each sentence, focusing particularly on revising the underlined words. Your revisions could include different word choices or additional words, phrases, and clauses that make the sentences more descriptive and interesting.

1. All afternoon, <u>clouds were getting dark</u>. *(Add more descriptive detail.)*

   _____

   _____

2. I could <u>see lightning</u> and <u>hear thunder</u>. *(Add more descriptive detail.)*

   _____

   _____

3.  She <u>took</u> my hand and <u>took</u> me to the storm cellar. *(Choose more descriptive verbs.)*

_____

_____

4.  We <u>sat</u> in the <u>cellar</u>. *(Choose more descriptive words.)*

_____

_____

5.  <u>Stuff</u> lay around our yard. *(Be more specific.)*

_____

_____

6.  <u>The storm</u> came through my neighborhood, <u>destroying lots of property</u>. *(Be more specific.)*

_____

_____

**ACTIVITY 2**

### Sharing Sentence Revisions

Share your revised sentences with other members of your class. For each of the six sentences, choose three revised examples to write on the board for the class to review.

**ACTIVITY 3**

### Working with a Student Essay

Read the complete student essay out loud. Following the reading, search the essay to discover how Sandra Russell expressed the six ideas you revised in Activity 1. Underline the six sentences as you find them. Discuss with class members how these ideas were successfully expressed by the student writer.

### Bad Weather

I was born in Booneville, Arkansas, and grew up on a small farm about five miles south of Paris. Naturally, I grew up in an area where tornados are feared each spring. I didn't really understand this until one humid, still night in April of 1985.

All afternoon, dark threatening clouds had been building up in the west, blocking out the sun. I could see the lightning dance about the sky as the thunder responded by shaking the ground beneath my feet. The wind softly stirred the tree tops but then quickly died as it got darker and darker.

I walked outside and listened to the silence ringing in my ears. In the distance, I could hear a rumble, soft at first but slowly and steadily intensifying. My mom came outside and stood at my side and listened to the rumbling noise. Everything was still; nothing dared to move. Even my dog

continued on next page

Moose lay quietly, as if punished, in his doghouse. It was almost as if he knew what was about to happen.

"Mama, what's that noise?" I asked her, but she didn't answer. She grabbed my hand and dragged me to the storm cellar. I didn't have time to argue with her before I heard the rumble nearly upon us. We huddled in the musty-smelling cellar. The roar was so loud it hurt my ears. I could hear the whistling of the wind above us. I cried and screamed for the awful noise of the whistle to stop, but no one could hear me above the ferocious noise. The rumble barreled on us, and it seemed as if it would never end. The air was still in the dark cellar, but I could hear it as it moved violently above our heads. I didn't think the thundering noise would ever end.

I hadn't realized that I had quit breathing until it finally stopped. I drew a quick breath and thanked God it was over and my mother and I were safe. We crawled out of the cellar and took the first real look at our home. Trees were uprooted. Glass and boards and even a stop sign lay scattered around our yard. The roof on our house was damaged and a few windows were broken out, but that was all. Even most of our animals had survived that day, including Moose.

That night is one that I'll never forget. A moderately sized tornado (about an F3 on the Fujita scale) ripped through my neighborhood, destroying ten houses and damaging fifty others. No tornado warnings were issued for that area until ten minutes after it was already over, but still no one was seriously injured. The local television station didn't even bother to comment on its mistake. Until that night I had never realized how an event could change the way you feel about something for the rest of your life. I look at the television and see tornado, hurricane, and even flood victims with new eyes. They are real, just like me.

by Sandra Russell

## MASTERY AND EDITING TESTS

**TEST** **1**

### Student Writing: Editing for Wordiness

Below is an introductory paragraph of six sentences, taken from a student essay. On the lines that follow, revise the paragraph so that wordiness in each sentence is eliminated.

In the paragraph that follows, I am going to make an attempt to name at least some of the earliest Spanish explorations in the New World. To take just the first example, it was in 1513 that an extraordinary event of considerable magnitude took place in what is now Florida when the Spanish explorer Ponce de Leon landed there. It was in the same area, and little more than a quarter of a century later, that the explorer Hernando de Soto, who later discovered the

Mississippi River, also landed in Florida in 1539. Among historians and among those who are interested in cultural history, Florida has reached noteworthy status for another reason. In 1565, Pedro Menendez de Aviles landed in Florida and began building the city of St. Augustine, the oldest permanent settlement in the United States. We all know that explorers in every age and in every part of the world have to be of a courageous nature and personality, but in those days Spanish explorers were perhaps the bravest of their time because they dared to be among the very first to set foot in what was then known as the New World.

_____

_____

_____

_____

_____

_____

_____

_____

_____

_____

_____

_____

**TEST 2**

## Student Writing: Editing for Inappropriate Language

Each sentence in the following paragraph contains at least one example of inappropriate language. Underline the inappropriate words, and then rewrite the paragraph, revising any language that is not appropriate in formal writing.

When my sis was hired by a major electronics company last summer, we were a little worried about her. She had flunked math in school, so we wondered if she had chosen the right kind of company. The person who had the job before her was let go because he had an attitude. Imagine our surprise when she soon announced that she had been selected chairman of an important committee at work. She said that she really didn't want to be in a leadership position, but we all knew she was nuts about it.

_____

_____

_____

_____

_____

_____

_____

_____

_____

_____

_____

**TEST 3**

## Editing for Wordiness and Inappropriate Language

The following paragraph contains examples of wordiness as well as inappropriate language (slang, clipped words, and sexist terms). Underline each problem as you find it, and then revise the paragraph. (Hint: Fifteen words or phrases need revision. Find and revise at least ten.)

One of the most outstanding scientists in the U.S. today came from China in 1936. She is Chien-Hsiung Wu, and her story is the story of the development of physics in our century. When Miss Wu came to America in 1936, she intended to do grad work and hightail it back to China. However, World War II broke out, and she remained to teach at Smith College, where she enjoyed working with the Smithies. Very soon after that, she was employed by Princeton U. At that time, she was the only girl physicist hired by a top research university. Later, she became an important workman on Columbia University's Manhattan Project, the project that developed the A bomb. She hunkered down at Columbia for more than thirty years, her many scientific discoveries bringing her world recognition. In 1990, Chien-Hsiung Wu became the first living scientist to have an asteroid named in her honor. This celestial object whirling in the darkest corners of outer space is now carrying her name.

_____

_____

_____

_____

_____

_____

_____

_____

_____

_____

_____

_____

_____

_____

## Exploring Online

Go to **www.cengage.com/devenglish/scarry/writersworkplace** to find the **Writer's Online Workplace,** a website designed for students using this book. You will find links to handouts, interactive quizzes, and other online resources as you explore the following topics:

- tone
- reducing wordiness
- avoiding sexist language

# Working Together

## BEING TACTFUL IN THE WORKPLACE

Words are charged with meanings that can be either encouraging and supportive or hurtful and wounding. Although workers in government offices and other public places are there to help the public, they often are so overworked that they do not always respond in positive ways. Below are several comments or questions that might be heard in an office where a person has gone to get help. In each case, revise the language so that the comment or question is more encouraging.

1. I don't have any idea what you're talking about.

   _____

   _____

2. Why don't you learn to write so people can read it?

   _____

   _____

3. We don't accept sloppy applications.

   _____

   _____

4. How old are you anyway?

   _____

   _____

5. Can't you read directions?

   _____

   _____

6. What's the matter with you? Why can't you understand this simple procedure?

   _____

   _____

7. I don't have time today for people like you!

   _____

   _____

Share your revisions with each other. Then, as a class, discuss some individual experiences in which the use of language made you or someone you know feel hurt or upset. These experiences may have occurred at a campus office, a local bank, or a local shop. How could a change of language have improved each situation?

## PORTFOLIO SUGGESTION

Using the "Working Together" activity and class discussion, write on one of the following:

- Discuss the importance of using polite language in the workplace. (You can use the examples given during classroom discussion.)

- Give advice to employers on how to train employees to speak in an encouraging and supportive way while on the job.

- Describe the difficulty workers have when customers or clients are rude. (If you have had a job, you may have experienced such a situation. How did you deal with the situation?)

- Over the course of the semester, keep a record of actual incidents that happen to you in which the language used was less than respectful. At some future time, you could write an essay analyzing each situation and suggesting how the experiences could have been more positive.

# PAYING ATTENTION TO LOOK-ALIKES AND SOUND-ALIKES

# 15

In this chapter, you will focus on forty-eight sets of words that are frequently confused.

**CHAPTER OBJECTIVES**

- Group I: ten sets of words that sound alike
- Group II: ten additional sets of words that sound alike
- Group III: five sets of words including contractions that sound like other words
- Group IV: ten sets of words that sound or look almost alike
- Group V: ten additional sets of words that sound or look almost alike
- Group VI: three sets of verbs that are often confused: *lie/lay*, *rise/raise*, and *sit/set*

Many words in English are confusing because they either sound alike or look alike but are spelled differently and have completely different meanings. Every student needs to watch out for these troublesome words, often called "look-alikes" and "sound-alikes." Students whose first language is not English will find this chapter especially helpful.

In this chapter, words that are often confused have been grouped into six manageable sections so that you can study each section in one sitting. Within each set of confused words, each word is defined and used in a sentence. After you have studied the spellings and definitions, fill in the blanks with the correct words. Master each group before you proceed to the next.

## GROUP I: WORDS THAT SOUND ALIKE

aural/oral

**aural (adj):** related to hearing

**oral (adj):** related to the mouth

> The ear specialist gave the child an *aural* exam.

> The dentist urged him to improve his *oral* hygiene.

The student dreaded giving _____ reports in class because a high fever had caused _____ nerve damage and affected his hearing.

**buy/by**

**buy (verb):**     to purchase
**by (prep):**      [1]near; [2]past; [3]not later than

**He hopes to *buy* a car.**
**Let's meet *by* the clock.**
**They drive *by* my house every morning.**
**Please arrive *by* six o'clock.**

_____ the time they are ready to _____ a house, the market will have passed them _____ .

**capital/capitol**

**capital (adj):**      [1]adding financial value; [2]fatal
**capital (noun):**     [1]leading city; [2]money
**capitol (noun):**     a legislative building

**The new addition is a *capital* improvement on their home.**
**The governor opposes *capital* punishment.**
**The *capital* [leading city] of Wyoming is Cheyenne.**
**The retailer has *capital* to invest in remodeling.**
**The dome of the state *capitol* [legislative building] is gold.**

She needed _____ to rebuild her home, but she first went to the _____ [legislative building] to obtain needed permits.

**close/clothes**

**close (verb):**      to shut
**close (noun):**      end or conclusion
**clothes (noun):**    garments

**Please *close* the door.**
**Finally, the war came to a *close*.**
**The *clothes* were from the local women's store.**
**NOTE: Cloth** is a piece of fabric, not to be confused with the word *clothes*, which as a noun is always plural.
**The *cloth* for the table was my mother's.**

Because she wanted to buy new _____, she shopped all day until the of _____ business.

coarse/course    **coarse (adj):**    rough; common or of inferior quality
                 **course (noun):**   [1]direction; [2]part of a meal; [3]unit of study

> **The coat was made from a *coarse* fabric.**
> **He told a *coarse* joke.**
> **What is the *course* of the spaceship?**
> **The main *course* of the meal was served.**
> **English is a required *course* at my school.**

A few students in that _____ made _____ comments during every class meeting.

complement/
compliment     **complement (noun):**   [1]what is required to make a thing complete; [2]something that completes
               **complement (verb):**   to complete
               **compliment (noun):**   an expression of praise
               **compliment (verb):**   to praise

> **The kitchen has a full *complement* of pots and pans.**
> **Her shoes *complement* the outfit.**
> **The chef received a *compliment* on his dessert.**
> **The food critic *complimented* the chef.**

The library had such a full _____ of books in my field, I felt I had to _____ the librarian.

forward/foreword    **forward (verb):**    to send a letter or a package to another address
                    **forward (adj):**     [1]bold or pushy; [2]going toward the front or the future
                    **forward (adv):**     toward the front or the future
                    **foreword (noun):**   introduction to a book, usually written by someone other than the author of the book

> **Please *forward* my mail.**
> **She was so *forward*; she pushed her way in.**
> **He took one step *forward*.**
> **Read the *foreword* first.**

Please excuse me for being so _____ as to offer advice to a stranger, but be sure to read the book's _____ before you begin.

passed/past    **passed (verb):**   (past tense of *to pass*) to move ahead or by
               **past (noun):**     the time before the present

**past (prep):**    beyond
**past (adj):**     no longer current

> She *passed* the library.
> Don't live in the *past*.
> He walked *past* the house.
> Her *past* failures have been forgotten.

When he walked _____ the professor's office, he found out that he had

_____ both tests he had taken during the _____ week.

**plain/plane**

**plain (adj):**    [1]ordinary; [2]clear
**plain (noun):**   flat land without trees
**plane (noun):**   [1]aircraft; [2]carpenter's tool for shaving wood; [3]level of development

> We ate a *plain* meal of soup and bread.
> The directions were given in *plain* English.
> They crossed the *plain* by covered wagon.
> The passengers were seated on the *plane*.
> A carpenter's *plane* and drill are needed for the job.
> Scientists think on a different *plane* from most people.

He wanted _____ directions on how to operate the jet _____.

**presence/presents**

**presence (noun):**    [1]the state of being present; [2]a person's manner
**presents (noun):**    gifts
**presents (verb):**    (third person singular of *to present*) to introduce or offer

> Your *presence* is needed in the dean's office.
> She has a wonderful *presence*.
> The child had many birthday *presents*.
> The senator *presents* the award each year.

The singer showed great _____ as she accepted the _____ from

her fans.

**EXERCISE** ❶    ### Group I Words

**Circle the words that correctly complete each of the following sentences.**

1. When I telephoned the doctor, he warned me that the (aural, oral) medicine was to be used only in my child's ear; this medicine was not an (aural, oral) medicine.

2. (Buy, By) the time I arrived at the store, the sale was over and I could not (buy, by) what I needed.

3. The senators met in Athens, the (capital, capitol) of Greece, to discuss the question of (capital, capitol) punishment.

4. I hurried to take several yards of wool (close, clothes, cloth) to the tailor, who had agreed to make some new winter (close, clothes, cloth) for my family; I knew he would (close, clothes, cloth) at five o'clock.

5. Every (coarse, course) in the meal was delicious, but the bread was rather (coarse, course).

6. She always wears clothes that (complement, compliment) each other, but she never expects a (complement, compliment).

7. I so much looked (forward, foreword) to reading the new book that I read the (forward, foreword) the very first day.

8. I have spent the (passed, past) few days wondering if I (passed, past) the exam.

9. The storm had been raging over the (plain, plane) for hours when the (plain, plane) suddenly went down.

10. Each year, the mayor (presence, presents) an award as well as several lovely (presence, presents) to outstanding members of the community.

**EXERCISE 2**

### Group I Words

**In the following paragraph, find ten often confused words that you have just studied in Group I. Circle each of the words, and then on the lines below the paragraph correct those words that are incorrect. If a word has been used correctly, write *correct as is.***

Wolfgang Mozart was a child star of the eighteenth century. At three years old, he could pick out chords and tunes on the piano. Buy age four, he was composing at the piano. As a musical genius, Mozart had an extremely well-developed oral sense. When Mozart was only six, he and his sister played before the emperor in Vienna, the capitol of Austria. The emperor paid Mozart a complement by having his portrait painted. Among other presence was an embroidered suit of cloths. In the course of his life, Mozart wrote church music, sonatas, operas, and chamber music. Like many great artists of the passed, he was ahead of his time and created on such a different plain from other composers of his day that his own era never fully appreciated him. Today, Mozart is recognized as one of music's greatest composers. You might be interested in reading a book of Mozart's letters. Be sure to read the forward.

_____      _____

_____      _____

_____      _____

_____      _____

# GROUP II: WORDS THAT SOUND ALIKE

**principal/principle**

| | |
|---|---|
| **principal (adj):** | [1]most important; [2]main |
| **principal (noun):** | [1]head of a school; [2]sum of money invested or borrowed |
| **principle (noun):** | rule or standard |

> The *principal* dancer was superb.
>
> What is the *principal* reason for your decision?
>
> The *principal* of the school arrived late.
>
> The *principal* and interest on the loan were due.
>
> He is a man of *principle*.

The _____ reason the _____ resigned was a matter of _____ .

**rain/reign/rein**

| | |
|---|---|
| **rain (noun):** | water falling to earth in drops |
| **reign (noun):** | period of a king or queen's rule |
| **rein (noun):** | strap attached to a bridle, used to control a horse |

> I'm singing in the *rain*.
>
> When was the *reign* of Henry the Eighth?
>
> I grabbed the pony's frayed *rein*.

The queen's _____ began on a day of heavy _____ .

**sight/site/cite**

| | |
|---|---|
| **sight (noun):** | [1]ability to see; [2]something seen |
| **site (noun):** | [1]plot of land where something is, was, or will be located; [2]place for an event |
| **cite (verb):** | to quote as an authority or example |

His *sight* was limited.

The Grand Canyon is an awesome *sight*.

Here is the *site* for the new courthouse.

Please *cite* the correct law.

The ancient burial _____ was a very impressive _____. The archaeologists _____ the old inscriptions when they published their findings.

**stationary/ stationery**

**stationary (adj):**    standing still

**stationery (noun):**    writing paper, usually with matching envelopes

He hit a *stationary* object.

She wrote the letter on her *stationery*.

She remained _____ as she read the letter written on the blue _____ .

**to/too/two**

**to (prep):**    in a direction toward

**too (adv):**    [1]also; [2]excessively

**two (noun, adj):**    the number 2

We walked *to* the movies.

We walked home *too*.

The tickets were *too* expensive.

She has *two* children.

Billy and Maria are _____ movie fans who go _____ a show every week; their daughter always goes_____ .

**vain/vane/vein**

**vain (adj):**    [1]conceited; [2]unsuccessful

**vane (noun):**    ornament, often in the shape of a rooster, that turns in the wind (seen on tops of barns)

**vein (noun):**    [1]blood vessel; [2]branching framework of a leaf; [3]area in the earth where minerals such as gold or silver are found; [4]passing attitude

He was attractive but *vain*.

We made a *vain* attempt to contact his brother.

The weather *vane* pointed southwest.

The *veins* carry blood to the heart.

The miner found a *vein* of silver.

She spoke in a humorous *vein.*

Carla is so _____ ; she wears makeup to conceal every splotch and
_____ on her cheeks.

**waist/waste**

| **waist (noun):** | middle portion of the body |
| **waste (verb):** | to use carelessly |
| **waste (noun):** | discarded objects |

His *waist* is thirty-six inches around.

He *wasted* too much time watching television.

The *waste* was put into the garbage pail.

Jewel is concerned about the size of her _____ , but she will not
_____ her money on diet pills.

**weather/whether**

| **weather (noun):** | atmospheric conditions |
| **whether (conj):** | if it is the case that |

The *weather* in Hawaii is gorgeous.

I'll go *whether* I'm ready or not.

I will go to the islands on vacation, _____ the _____ is good or not.

**whole/hole**

| **whole (adj):** | complete |
| **hole (noun):** | opening |

He ate the *whole* pie.

I found a *hole* in the sock.

Despite the _____ in the apple, he ate the _____ apple.

**write/right/rite**

| **write (verb):** | [1]to form letters and words; [2]to compose |
| **right (adj):** | [1]correct; [2]conforming to justice, law, or morality |
| **right (noun):** | [1]power or privilege to which one is entitled; [2]direction opposite to left |
| **rite (noun):** | traditional, often religious, ceremony |

I will *write* a poem for your birthday.

What is the *right* answer?

**Trial by jury is a _right_ under the law.**

**The senator's position is to the _right._**

**A bridal shower is a _rite_ of passage.**

Each of the speakers wanted to _____ the _____ kind of speech for the ceremony, a _____ that happens only once a year.

**EXERCISE  3**

## Group II Words

**Circle the words that correctly complete each of the following sentences.**

1.  The (principal, principle) was respected because he would not compromise his one fundamental (principal, principle).

2.  The museum had on display a horse's (rain, reign, rein) that dated from the (rain, reign, rein) of Queen Isabella.

3.  You do not have to (sight, site, cite) statistics to convince me of the importance of caring for my (sight, site, cite).

4.  He bought the (stationary, stationery) from a clerk who said nothing and remained (stationary, stationery) behind the counter the entire time.

5.  I want (to, too, two) go (to, too, two) the movies, and I hope you do (to, too, two).

6.  I could tell the actor was (vain, vane, vein) when she kept hiding a long blue (vain, vane, vein) on her leg.

7.  It is a (waist, waste) of time to try to get him to admit the size of his (waist, waste).

8.  We always listen to the (weather, whether) report, (weather, whether) it's right or wrong.

9.  I am telling you the (whole, hole) story about the (whole, hole) in our new carpet.

10.  Every American has the (write, right, rite) to participate in any religious (write, right, rite) of his or her own choosing.

**EXERCISE  4**

## Group II Words

**In the following paragraph, find ten often confused words that you have just studied in Group II. Circle each of the words, and then on the lines below the paragraph correct those words that are incorrect. If a word has been used correctly, write _correct as is._**

The company officials searched for years until they found the proper sight for their gem mine. First, they investigated legal records to make sure they had the rite to drill in the area. Then they drilled several wholes to see if there were any vanes worth exploring. They were surprised to learn they were in the area that had been the principal mining area for Spanish colonizers in the sixteenth century. No exploration had been done since the rein of King Philip IV. They even found stationary in the archives that had been sent from Spain. The modern explorers eventually determined that they were to late to find any more emeralds, but they did have a good chance of discovering semiprecious stones. They did not want to waist any more time. They began work right away. In all kinds of whether, the work progressed. The results were worth their efforts.

_____        _____

_____        _____

_____        _____

_____        _____

_____        _____

# GROUP III: CONTRACTIONS THAT SOUND LIKE OTHER WORDS

**it's/its**    **it's:**    contraction of *it is*
                **its:**    possessive pronoun of *it*

> *It's* **early.**

> *Its* **tail is short.**

_____ too late now to put the space vehicle into _____ orbit.

**they're/their/there**    **they're:**    contraction of *they are*
                           **their:**    possessive pronoun of *they*
                           **there:**    at that place

> *They're* **happy.**

> *Their* **children are healthy.**

> **Look over** *there.*

_____ excited about the new apartment; _____ is more light, and

_____ son will have his own room.

**we're/were/where**

| | |
|---|---|
| **we're:** | contraction of *we are* |
| **were:** | past tense of *are* |
| **where:** | at or in what place |

**We're happy.**

**The days *were* too short.**

**Where are we?**

We need to know _____ you were last night. _____ you safe?

After all, _____ your parents.

**who's/whose**

| | |
|---|---|
| **who's:** | contraction of *who is* |
| **whose:** | possessive pronoun |

**Who's the author of this book?**

**Whose clothes are these?**

_____ beach chair is this, and _____ to blame for breaking it?

**you're/your**

| | |
|---|---|
| **you're:** | contraction of *you are* |
| **your:** | possessive pronoun of *you* |

**You're the boss.**

**Your team has won.**

When _____ diploma is in hand, _____ a happy graduate.

**EXERCISE**  **5**

## Group III Words

**Circle the words that correctly complete each of the following sentences.**

1.   (It's, Its) obvious that the car has lost (it's, its) muffler.

2.   The pearl has lost (it's, its) luster, and (it's, its) impossible to restore it.

3.   When (they're, their, there) in school, (they're, their, there) parents work in the restaurant (they're, their, there) on the corner.

4.   Now that (they're, their, there) living in the country, (they're, their, there) expenses are not so great, so they might stay (they're, their, there).

5.   (We're, Were, Where) hoping our friends (we're, were, where) not hurt at the place (we're, were, where) the accident occurred.

6.   (We're, Were, Where) did the coupons go that (we're, were, where) saving?

7. (Who's, Whose) car is double-parked outside, and (who's, whose) going to move it?

8. (Who's, Whose) the pitcher at the game today, and (who's, whose) glove will he use?

9. When (you're, your) a father, (you're, your) free time is never guaranteed.

10. Please give me (you're, your) paper when (you're, your) finished writing.

**EXERCISE**  **6**

### Group III Words

**In the following paragraph, find ten often confused words that you have just studied in Group III. Circle each of the words, and then on the lines below the paragraph correct those words that are incorrect. If a word has been used correctly, write *correct as is*.**

Psychologists tell us that laughter is found only among human beings. Of all creatures, where the only ones who laugh. Psychologists are interested in what makes people laugh, but so far there best explanations are only theories. From a physical point of view, your healthier if you laugh often. Laughter is good for you're lungs, and it's an outlet for extra energy. Among it's other effects are the release of anxieties and anger. The comedian, who's job depends on figuring out what makes people laugh, often pokes fun at the behavior of other people. However, a joke about a local town might not be funny in front of an audience of people who like living their. Were all familiar with jokes that are in bad taste. Its a good idea to recognize who your audience is.

_____    _____

_____    _____

_____    _____

_____    _____

_____    _____

## GROUP IV: WORDS THAT SOUND OR LOOK ALMOST ALIKE

**accept/except**

**accept (verb):**   [1]to receive with consent; [2]to admit; [3]to regard as true or right
**except (prep):**   other than, but

I *accept* the invitation with pleasure.

I *accept* responsibility.

I *accept* your explanation.

Everyone *except* me was ready.

I _____ all the applications _____ the late one.

advice/advise   **advice (noun):**   opinion as to what should be done
                **advise (verb):**   [1]to suggest; [2]to counsel

I need good *advice.*

He *advised* me to take a different course.

I _____ you to get the best _____ possible.

affect/effect   **affect (verb):**   [1]to influence; [2]to change
                **effect (noun):**   result
                **effect (verb):**   to bring about

Smoking will *affect* your health.

The *effects* of the hurricane were evident.

The hurricane *effected* devastating changes in the county.

The low grade will _____ his chances of getting into law school; this could have a terrible _____ on his future.

breath/breathe   **breath (noun):**   [1]air that is inhaled or exhaled; [2]the act of inhaling or exhaling
                 **breathe (verb):**   to inhale or exhale

You seem out of *breath.*

Don't *breathe* in these fumes.

When they went mountain climbing, every _____ was difficult. By the time they reached the top, they could hardly _____ .

choose/chose   **choose (verb):**   to select
               **chose (verb):**   past tense of *choose*

I *choose* a bagel for breakfast every day.

Yesterday I *chose* to sleep late.

This year I will try to _____ my clothes more carefully because last year I _____ several items that didn't suit me.

| conscience/<br>conscious/<br>conscientious | **conscience (noun):** | a person's recognition of right and wrong |
|---|---|---|
| | **conscious (adj):** | [1]awake; [2]aware of one's own existence |
| | **conscientious (adj):** | [1]careful; [2]thorough |

His *conscience* bothered him.

The patient was *conscious* and able to talk.

The student was *conscientious* about doing her homework.

In the story of Pinocchio, Jiminy Cricket acts as the puppet's _____ because Pinocchio is not _____ of right and wrong. The cricket does a very _____ job.

| costume/custom | **costume (noun):** | special style of dress for a particular occasion |
|---|---|---|
| | **custom (noun):** | common tradition |

The child wore a clown *costume* for Halloween.

One *custom* at Thanksgiving is to serve turkey.

My cousin in New Orleans follows the _____ of wearing a special _____ for Mardi Gras.

| council/counsel/<br>consul | **council (noun):** | group that governs |
|---|---|---|
| | **counsel (verb):** | to give advice |
| | **counsel (noun):** | [1]advice; [2]a lawyer |
| | **consul (noun):** | government official in the foreign service |

The student *council* meets every Tuesday.

Please *counsel* the elderly couple.

The patient needs legal *counsel*.

The prisoner has requested *counsel*.

He was appointed a *consul* by the president.

When I appeared before the _____, they gave me good _____, advising me to meet with El Salvador's own _____.

| desert/dessert | **desert (verb):** | to abandon |
|---|---|---|
| | **desert (noun):** | barren land |
| | **dessert (noun):** | last part of a meal, often sweet |

**Don't *desert* me now.**

**The cactus flowers in the *desert* are beautiful.**

**We had apple pie for *dessert.***

When the caravan became lost in the _____ , they did not think about a

full meal with _____ . All they wanted was some water.

**diner/dinner**     **diner (noun):**     ¹person eating a meal; ²restaurant with a long counter and booths
**dinner (noun):**     main meal of the day

**The *diner* waited for her check.**

**I prefer a booth at the *diner.***

**What is for *dinner?***

That _____ is a good place for _____ . You can tell by the number

of satisfied _____ there.

**EXERCISE**  **7**     **Group IV Words**

**Circle the words that correctly complete each of the following sentences.**

1.  The judge refused to (accept, except) most of the evidence (accept, except)
    for the testimony of one witness.

2.  I need some good (advice, advise); is there anyone here who could (advice,
    advise) me?

3.  How does the allergy medicine (affect, effect) you? Some medicine may have
    more than one adverse side (affect, effect).

4.  The injured skier was told to (breath, breathe) deeply and exhale slowly; the
    doctor could see her (breath, breathe) in the chilly winter air.

5.  Now we (choose, chose) fruit for a snack; in the past we usually (choose,
    chose) junk food.

6.  The thief, when he became (conscience, conscientious, conscious), gave
    himself up to the police because his (conscience, conscientious, conscious)
    was bothering him.

7.  Before you visit China, you should read about its (costumes, customs),
    including its New Year celebration at which colorful (costumes, customs)
    are worn.

8.  The town (council, counsel, consul) needs its own legal (council, counsel,
    consul) to help interpret the law.

9.  The chef made a chocolate layer cake for (desert, dessert); don't (desert, dessert) me before we eat it all.

10. All I want for (diner, dinner) is a salad; do you think I can get a good one at this local (diner, dinner)?

**EXERCISE ⑧**

**Group IV Words**

In the following paragraph, find ten often confused words that you have just studied in Group IV. Circle each of the words, and then on the lines below the paragraph correct those words that are incorrect. If a word has been used correctly, write *correct as is*.

For thousands of years, it has been a costume to enjoy wine. Today, some people chose to drink wine with diner, while others wait until desert. There are wine clubs where people look for advise as to what they should drink; these people are very conscience about making the correct choice. Others look for council in magazines that tell them how to chose the correct wine for a food. They except the words of the experts on some wines whose prices would take your breath away.

_____     _____

_____     _____

_____     _____

_____     _____

_____     _____

# GROUP V: WORDS THAT SOUND OR LOOK ALMOST ALIKE

emigrate/
immigrate
emigrant/
immigrant

**emigrate (verb):**   to leave (a country or region)
**immigrate (verb):**   to come (into a country or region)
**emigrant (noun):**   person who leaves one country to settle in another country
**immigrant (noun):**   person who comes into a country to settle there

They *emigrated* from Europe.

Many people have *immigrated* to the United States.

Each *emigrant* left home with childhood memories.

Nearly every *immigrant* landed first at Ellis Island.

People who _____ from Eastern Europe often _____ to the United States. In the old country, the _____ are missed by their relatives; in the new country, they become valued _____.

**farther/further**

| | |
|---|---|
| **farther (adj, adv):** | a greater distance (physically) |
| **further (adj, adv):** | a greater distance (mentally); additional |
| **further (verb):** | to help advance (a person or a cause) |

**They had to walk *farther* down the road.**

**The speaker made a *further* point.**

**The tutor will *further* my chances on the exam.**

The judge made a _____ argument when he said the building should be _____ from the creek.

**loose/lose**

| | |
|---|---|
| **loose (adj):** | not tightly fitted |
| **lose (verb):** | ¹to be unable to keep or find; ²to fail to win |

**The dog's collar is *loose*.**

**Don't *lose* your keys.**

**Don't *lose* the game.**

She warned him that his watch was _____ and he might _____ it.

**personal/ personnel**

| | |
|---|---|
| **personal (adj):** | ¹relating to an individual; ²private |
| **personnel (noun):** | people employed by an organization |

**Is this your *personal* account or your corporate account?**

**He asked for his *personal* mail.**

**All *personnel* in the company were interviewed.**

The manager took a _____ interest in the _____ in his department.

**quiet/quit/quite**

| | |
|---|---|
| **quiet (adj):** | ¹free from noise; ²calm |
| **quit (verb):** | ¹to give up; ²to stop |
| **quite (adv):** | ¹completely; ²rather |

**They loved the *quiet* village.**

**He *quit* smoking.**

**She is not *quite* alone.**

**She is coming *quite* soon.**

Christina was _____ determined to find a _____ spot to study before she _____ for the day.

**receipt/recipe**

**receipt (noun):**     paper showing that a bill has been paid
**recipe (noun):**     formula for preparing a mixture, especially in cooking

**No exchanges can be made without a *receipt*.**

**I found my *recipe* for caramel flan.**

Here is your sales _____ for the cookbook; I hope you enjoy each _____ in it.

**special/especially**

**special (adj):**     not ordinary
**especially (adv):**     particularly

**We're planning a *special* weekend.**

**She is *especially* talented in art.**

A sixteenth birthday party is a _____ event for a girl, _____ when all of her friends can attend.

**than/then**

**than (conj or prep):**     used to make a comparison
**then (adv):**     [1]at that time; [2]next

**This cake is sweeter *than* that one.**

**I was at work *then*.**

**First he blamed his parents; *then* he blamed me.**

Billy and Janice cook at home rather _____ eat out; _____ they usually go to a movie.

**thorough/though/
thought/through/
threw**

**thorough (adj):**     accurate and complete
**though (adv or conj):**     despite the fact that
**thought (verb):**     past tense of *think*
**through (prep):**     from one end to the other (Note: *thru* is not standard
                         spelling.)
**threw (verb):**     past tense of *throw*

**She always does a *thorough* job.**

**I worked even *though* I was exhausted.**

**I *thought* about my goals.**

**We drove *through* the tunnel.**

**He *threw* the ball to me.**

We _____ she did a _____ job of cleaning the apartment, even

_____ she _____ out some papers that she should have looked

_____ more carefully.

**use/used to**

| | |
|---|---|
| **use (verb):** | to employ for a purpose (past tense is *used*) |
| **used to:** | [1]an expression indicating that an activity is no longer done in the present; [2]accustomed to or familiar with |

**Yesterday, I *used* my father's car.**

**I *used to* take the bus to school, but now I ride my bike.**

**I am *used to* walking to school.**

I _____ enjoy fixing my own car, but then I _____ my local garage

for the first time, and now I _____ that garage all the time.

**EXERCISE 9**

## Group V Words

**Circle the word that correctly completes each of the following sentences.**

1. My parents (emigrated, immigrated) from Greece.

2. Let's not travel any (farther, further) tonight.

3. Your belt is too (loose, lose).

4. Most of the (personal, personnel) at this company are well trained.

5. Please be (quiet, quit, quite) while she is performing.

6. Keep this (receipt, recipe) for tax purposes.

7. He made a (special, especially) trip to visit his daughter.

8. I would rather read a good book (than, then) watch television.

9. When she walked (thorough, though, thought, through, threw) the door, he didn't recognize her even (thorough, though, thought, through, threw) he had known her all his life.

10. I am not (use, used) to staying up so late.

**EXERCISE 10**

## Group V Words

**In the following paragraph, find ten often confused words that you have just studied in Group V. Circle each of the words, and then on the lines below the**

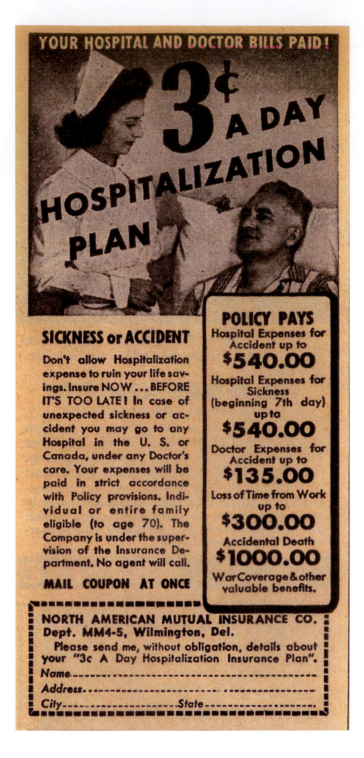

paragraph correct those words that are incorrect. If a word has been used correctly, write *correct as is*.

Advertising is very old: some advertisements on paper go back further than three thousand years. In ancient Greece, it was quiet common to see signs advertising different kinds of services, but it was not until printing was invented that modern advertising was born. In Europe in the seventeenth century, people use to place ads in newspapers; some of these ads were personnel messages, but most were for business. When emigrants came to the United States, they used advertisements to find jobs; we can imagine them going thorough each newspaper very carefully. Today, advertising is all around us, special on television. If we are not careful, we can loose our focus when we watch advertising. For example, when a commercial interrupts a chef who is giving us a receipt for a complicated new dish, we are likely to remember the flashy commercial better then the chef's directions.

_____     _____

_____     _____

_____     _____

_____     _____

_____     _____

## GROUP VI: *LAY/LIE, RAISE/RISE,* AND *SET/SIT*

These six verbs (*lay/lie, raise/rise,* and *set/sit*) are perhaps the most troublesome verbs in the English language. Not only are their principal parts irregular and easily confused with each other, but in addition, one set must always take a direct object whereas the other set is reflexive and never takes an object. First learn the principal parts of the set that always takes a direct object.

## VERBS ALWAYS TAKING A DIRECT OBJECT: *LAY*, *RAISE*, AND *SET*

The three verbs *lay*, *raise*, and *set* always require a direct object.

I *lay* the book down.

I *raise* a flag.

I *set* the table.

### Principal Parts of Verbs *lay*, *raise*, and *set*

| Verb meaning | Present | Present participle | Past | Past participle |
|---|---|---|---|---|
| **lay:** to put something down | lay | laying | laid | has laid or have laid |
| **raise:** to move something up | raise | raising | raised | has raised or have raised |
| **set:** to place something | set | setting | set | has set or have set |

Here are some additional examples of these verbs. Notice that each verb takes a direct object.

**The cat *laid her ball* on the rug.**

**The sunshine *raised our spirits*.**

**The woman *set her hat* on the sofa.**

**PRACTICE** Fill in the first blank in each of the following sentences with the correct form of the verb. Then choose a direct object for each verb and put it in the second blank.

1. The postal worker said he had _____ the _____ on the back porch.
   (lay)

2. The father _____ his _____ to be a caring person. (*Use past tense.*)
   (raise)

3. We always _____ the _____ on the counter.
   (set)

4. They are _____ down the new _____ today.
   (lay)

5. Every night, I _____ out my _____ for the following day.
   (lay)

6.  The citizen _____ many _____ whenever the board meets.
    (raise)

7.  She has _____ the _____ to record tonight's program.
    (set)

8.  Last week, the coach _____ the _____ for the game.
    (lay)

9.  We were _____ the _____ for dinner.
    (set)

10. He has _____ a substantial amount of _____ for the charity.
    (raise)

## VERBS NEVER TAKING A DIRECT OBJECT: *LIE, RISE,* AND *SIT*

The reflexive verbs *lie, rise,* and *sit* are used when the subject is doing the action without any help. No other person or object is needed to accomplish the action.

> **The verbs *lie, rise,* and *sit* do not require an object.**

I *lie* down.

I *rise* up.

I *sit* down.

## Principal Parts of *lie, rise,* and *sit*

| Verb meaning | Present | Present participle | Past | Past participle |
|---|---|---|---|---|
| **lie:** to recline | lie | lying | lay | has lain or have lain |
| **rise:** to stand up or move upward | rise | rising | rose | has risen or have risen |
| **sit:** to take a sitting position | sit | sitting | sat | has sat or have sat |

Here are some additional sentences with reflexive verbs:

The *cat is lying* on the rug.

The *sun rose* in the east.

The *woman sat* on the sofa.

**PRACTICE**    Fill in the blank in each of the following sentences with the correct form of the reflexive verb.

1.  As I write this postcard, the sun is _____.
        (rise)

2.  The new tools _____ on the workbench. (*Use present tense.*)
        (lie)

3.  He was _____ at the breakfast table when the phone rang.
        (sit)

4.  Last night, we _____ in bed watching a television show.
        (lie)

5.  Last year, the workers _____ at five o'clock every morning.
        (rise)

6.  The cat is always _____ on my favorite chair.
        (lie)

7.  It was very late when they _____ down to dinner.
        (sit)

8.  The price of cigarettes has _____ dramatically.
        (rise)

9.  The newspapers have _____ in the driveway for days.
        (lie)

10. The child has _____ a long time in front of the camera.
        (sit)

**EXERCISE 11**    ## Group VI Words

Fill in the blank in each of the following sentences with the correct form of the correct verb.

1.  I have _____ the suitcases in your room.
        (lie, lay)

2.  I am _____ in my favorite rocking chair.
        (sit, set)

3.  She likes me to _____ by her bed and read to her in the evening.
        (sit, set)

4.  Last spring, the manufacturers _____ the prices.
    (rise, raise)

5.  Yesterday, the price of the magazine _____ by a dime.
    (rise, raise)

6.  When I entered the room, the woman _____ to greet me.
    (rise, raise)

7.  The woman _____ her head when I entered the room.
    (rise, raise)

8.  I usually _____ down in the afternoon.
    (lie, lay)

9.  The auto mechanic is _____ under the car.
    (lie, lay)

10. I can't remember where I _____ my keys.
    (lie, lay)

**EXERCISE 12**

## Group VI Words

**Fill in the blank in each of the following sentences with the correct form of the correct verb.**

1.  The cat has _____ in the sun all day.
    (lie, lay)

2.  If you feel sick, _____ down on that bed.
    (lie, lay)

3.  The elevator always _____ quickly to the tenth floor.
    (rise, raise)

4.  The boss _____ her salary twice this year.
    (rise, raise)

5.  His parents _____ down the law when he came home late.
    (lie, lay)

6.  The carpenters _____ the roof when they remodeled the house.
    (rise, raise)

7.  The dog _____ up every night and begs for food.
    (sit, set)

8.  Last week, I _____ in front of my television set nearly every night.
    (sit, set)

9.  I always watch the waiter _____ on a stool after his shift is done.
    (sit, set)

10. We have _____ out cookies and milk for Santa Claus every year
    (sit, set)
    since the children were born.

## MASTERY AND EDITING TESTS

**TEST** 1

### Choosing Correct Words

**Circle the words that correctly complete the sentences.**

In the (past, passed), the major way to identify people was (thorough, though, thought, through, threw) the use of fingerprints. That technique was developed during the (rain, reign, rein) of Queen Victoria in England. With modern technology has come iris recognition, a method of identification that uses the information stored in the iris, the colored section of the eye that surrounds the pupil. The iris contains more information (than, then) any other part of the body; (it's, its) 266 features can be measured fully. In contrast, fingerprints contain only 30 features. Iris recognition was developed in 1994 by a computer scientist at Cambridge University in England, and now (it's, its) used to identify people at airport security checkpoints and in some banks. To scan a person's iris, a machine directs a beam of infrared light on the person from fourteen inches away. The (whole, hole) procedure takes about one minute. For thirty-five thousand dollars, a bank could (buy, by) a machine that would measure an iris, but (they're, their, there) is a problem: the bank's customers would not be able to use a different bank's ATM. So far, the questions about this new technology have concerned accuracy and cost, but (who's, whose) to judge the importance of safeguarding an individual's privacy?

**TEST 2**

## Choosing Correct Words

**Circle the words that correctly complete the sentences.**

Coffee has a long history and an interesting one. Long before it was brewed, coffee was enjoyed (plain, plane) or mixed with vegetables and eaten as food. The (sight, site, cite) of the first cultivated coffee was most likely Kaffa, a part of Ethiopia not far from the (capital, capitol) of that country. That is (we're, were, where) coffee most likely got (it's, its) name. (Than, Then) in the fourteenth century, merchants came across the (desert, dessert) from Arabia to Kaffa, obtained coffee seeds, and began to grow coffee in their own countries. The people of Arabia were (quiet, quite, quit) happy to enjoy coffee, (special, especially) because it took the place of alcohol, which they were not allowed to drink. The first (loose, lose) coffee beans came to Europe in 1615, and the drink has remained popular ever since.

**TEST 3**

## Choosing Correct Words

**Circle the words that correctly complete the sentences.**

People have pierced their ears (thorough, though, thought, through, threw) every period of recorded history. Ancient Egyptians, Persians, Hebrews, and others would (sit, set) jewels, pearls, and other precious stones into gold and silver to make earrings. They even (use, used) to hang earrings from the statues of their gods and goddesses. When the Egyptians put mummies in their tombs, they would (lie, lay) earrings in the coffins as decorations for the people to wear in the afterlife. Centuries ago, both men and women wore earrings, but one Roman emperor thought his people were becoming (to, too, two) (vain, vane, vein). After speaking out against the use of earrings, he (farther, further) stated that men could not wear them. We do not know how people reacted to that announcement, but there would be an uproar today because people see wearing (they're, their, there) jewelry as a (right, write, rite). Hardly anyone would (accept, except) such a regulation today.

## Exploring Online

Go to **www.cengage.com/devenglish/scarry/writersworkplace** to find the **Writer's Online Workplace,** a website designed for students using this book. You will find links to handouts, interactive quizzes, and other online resources as you explore the following topic:

• look-alikes and sound-alikes

# Working Together

## EXAMINING THE ISSUE OF PLAGIARISM

Plagiarism is the unlawful use of another writer's words or ideas as if they were your own. When you use material from the work of another writer, you must give credit to that author, or you will be accused of plagiarism. All writers are expected to acknowledge the sources they use for their own work, and college students should be especially careful in this regard. Students are often under pressure to submit assignments on time; they may be tempted to use already published work and copy too much from that work. If a student writer is found to have turned in plagiarized material, the consequences can be serious indeed.

A professional writer who should have been fully aware of plagiarism and its implications is Alexander Theroux. Theroux, who has taught at Harvard and Yale, published a collection of essays under the title *The Primary Colors*. A reader happened to be examining Theroux's book, and was reminded of passages in another work, a volume titled *Song of the Sky*, by an aviator named Guy Murchie. Murchie's book had been published in 1954 and was not well known. In fact, it had been out of print for some time.

The reader noticed remarkable similarities between some passages from the two books. Compare the following passages from the Theroux book and *Song of the Sky*.

| *Song of the Sky*, page 29 | *The Primary Colors*, page 16 |
|---|---|
| "Blue water is salty, warm, and deep and speaks of the tropics where evaporation is great and dilution small—the Sulu Sea, the Indian Ocean, the Gulf Stream. Green water is cool, pale with particles, thin with river and rain, often shallow." | "Incidentally, blue water is invariably salty, warm, and deep and speaks of the tropics, where evaporation is great and dilution minimal—the Sulu Sea, the Indian Ocean, the Gulf Stream. Green water, on the other hand, is cool, pale with particles, thin with river and rain, often shallow." |

## QUESTIONS FOR SMALL-GROUP DISCUSSION

1. Discuss the extent to which the two passages differ.
2. When asked about the striking similarities between his book and *Song of the Sky*, Alexander Theroux stated, "I just thought it was my own work. I can't always remember the source of where I found something." Discuss the writer's explanation. Is it satisfactory? Do you think there is a more likely explanation?
3. When this example of plagiarism was discovered, the publisher of the Theroux book announced that future editions would either leave out the plagiarized passages or give direct credit to *Song of the Sky*. Was this a good solution? In your opinion, is there anything else the publisher should do in such a case?
4. If a college student is found guilty of plagiarism, what should the penalty be?
5. It has been said that when students plagiarize material in school those students really cheat themselves because any benefit from learning is lost. Discuss.
6. What is the policy on plagiarism given in the catalogue of the educational institution you attend?

## PORTFOLIO SUGGESTION

A democracy depends on the integrity of its institutions and its individual citizens to function. Make a list of the ways college students you have observed reveal a lack of integrity. Have you observed cheating on tests, buying papers on the Internet, or copying of other students' assignments? You may want to write an essay in which you predict the effects this behavior will have when these same students graduate and assume leadership positions in their communities.

# Part 4

# Creating Effective Paragraphs

In many ways, Part 4 is the heart of your work in this course. After you have carefully focused on the importance of the topic sentence, you will study the different methods used to develop ideas, with particular emphasis on achieving coherence. You will then have several opportunities to write paragraphs of your own, using more than one approach: following a guided step-by-step

(continued on next page)

approach or a more creative approach that first presents carefully chosen professional model paragraphs and then lists a number of related topics for writing assignments.

# WORKING WITH PARAGRAPHS: TOPIC SENTENCES AND CONTROLLING IDEAS

The well-developed paragraph almost always has a topic sentence. In this chapter, you will learn how to recognize and generate your own strong topic sentences. The following skills are covered:

**CHAPTER OBJECTIVES**

- identifying the characteristics of an acceptable paragraph
- finding the topic sentence of a paragraph
- distinguishing between a topic sentence and a title
- finding the topic in a topic sentence
- finding the controlling idea of a topic sentence
- choosing controlling ideas
- writing topic sentences

## WHAT IS A PARAGRAPH?

> A **paragraph** is a group of sentences that develops one main idea. A paragraph may stand by itself as a complete piece of writing, or it may be a section of a longer piece of writing, such as an essay.

No single rule can prescribe how long a paragraph should be, but a paragraph that is too short can make a reader think that some basic information is missing. On the other hand, a paragraph that is too long will likely make a reader lose interest. An effective paragraph must be long enough to develop the main idea the writer is expressing, usually six or seven sentences in length, but no more than ten or twelve sentences. While it is true that newspapers or magazines take liberties with the paragraph form and often have paragraphs as short as a single sentence, a well-developed piece of writing will seldom present a single sentence as a paragraph (unless the sentence is a piece of dialogue).

Before you begin writing and printing out your own paragraphs, your instructor may want you to demonstrate your ability to work with the computer. You may need to show your ability to set margins, to double space the text, and to paginate. Your instructor will also explain other specific information needed for turning in written assignments (such as your name, the class, and the date of submission). This information may be placed on a separate title page. Standard paragraph form will require consistent margins, an indented first sentence, a capitalized word at the beginning of each sentence, and correct punctuation to end each complete sentence. These are the basic requirements that all students must be able to meet in order to do college-level work.

While you are studying in college, you will need to become comfortable using a computer, so take this opportunity to learn new word processing skills. For example, if you have never paginated a paper before or you have never used the spell-check option, explore these features. Find something new to learn. Because jobs for your generation will demand computer literacy, you will need to have an enthusiastic attitude about learning new skills on the computer.

**EXERCISE 1**

### Standard Paragraph Form

**Type the following sentences into a standard paragraph. Follow your instructor's requirements for margins and spacing. Then print out your work, being sure to check the page for typos and other errors.**

1.  The local high school became a haven for disaster victims.

2.  In the large basement, thirty families huddled in little groups of four or five.

3.  Volunteer workers were busy carrying in boxes of clothing and blankets.

4.  Two Red Cross women stood at a long table sorting through boxes to find sweaters and blankets for the shivering flood victims.

5.  One heavyset man in a red woolen hunting jacket stirred a huge pot of soup.

6.  Men and women with tired faces sipped their steaming coffee and wondered if they would ever see their homes again.

7.  Outside, the downpour continued.

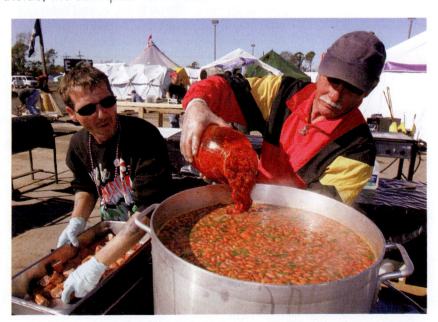

# WHAT IS A TOPIC SENTENCE?

> A *topic sentence* states the main idea of a paragraph. It is the most general sentence of the paragraph. All the other sentences serve to explain, describe, extend, or support this main-idea sentence.

Most paragraphs you read will begin with the topic sentence. However, some topic sentences come in the middle of the paragraph; others come at the end. Some paragraphs have no stated topic sentence at all; in those cases, the main idea is implied. Students are usually advised to use topic sentences in all their work to be certain that the writing has a focus and develops a single idea at a time. Whether the task is an essay exam in a history course, a research paper for a sociology course, or an essay in a composition course, thoughtful use of topic sentences will always bring better results. Good topic sentences help both the writer and the reader think clearly about the main points.

Below are two paragraphs. Each paragraph makes a separate point, which is stated in its topic sentence. In both of these paragraphs, the topic sentence happens to be first. Read the paragraphs and notice how the topic sentence is the most general sentence; it states the main idea of each paragraph. The other sentences explain, describe, extend, or support the topic sentence.

> *I went through a difficult period after my father died.* I was moody and sullen at home. I spent most of the time in my bedroom listening to music on the radio, which made me feel even worse. I stopped playing soccer after school with my friends. My grades in school went down. I lost my appetite and seemed to get into arguments with everybody. My mom began to look worried, but I couldn't bring myself to participate in an activity with any spirit. It seemed life had lost its joy for me.
>
> *Fortunately, something happened that spring that brought me out of my depression.* My uncle, who had been disabled while serving in the army, came to live with us. I learned many years later that my mother had asked him to come and live with us in the hope that he could bring me out of myself. I, on the other hand, was told that it was my responsibility to help my uncle feel at home. My mother's plan worked. My uncle and I were both lonely people. A friendship began that was to change both our lives for the better.

**EXERCISE** ② **Finding the Topic Sentence of a Paragraph**

**Each of the following five paragraphs contains a topic sentence that states the main idea of the paragraph. Find the sentence that best states the main idea and underline it. Keep in mind that the topic sentence will not always be the first sentence of the paragraph.**

1.    Mountains of disposable diapers are thrown into garbage cans every day. Tons of yogurt containers, soda cans, and other plastic items are discarded without so much as a stomp to flatten them out. If the old Chevy is not worth fixing, tow it off to sit with thousands of others on acres of fenced-in

junkyards. Radios, televisions, and toasters get the same treatment because it is easier and often less expensive to buy a new product than to fix the old one. Who wants a comfortable old sweater if a new one can be bought on sale? No thought is given to the fact that the new one will look like the old one after two or three washings. We are the great "Let's junk it" society!

2.      Anyone who has been in the hospital with a serious illness can tell you that the sight of a good nurse is the most beautiful sight in the world. Today, the hospital nurse has one of the hardest jobs of all. Although a doctor may direct the care and treatment of a patient, it is the nurse who must see to it that the care and treatment are carried out. A nurse must pay attention to everything, from the condition of the hospital bed to the scheduling of medication throughout the day and night. In addition to following a doctor's orders for the day, the nurse must respond to whatever the patient might need at any given moment. A sudden emergency requires the nurse to make an immediate judgment: can the situation be handled with or without the doctor being called in? More recently, nurses have become increasingly burdened by paperwork and other administrative duties. Many people worry that the increasing demands on nurses will take them away from what they do best—namely, taking care of people on a one-to-one basis.

3.      Anything can happen at a county agricultural fair. It is the perfect human occasion, the harvest of the fields and of the emotions. To the fair come the man and his cow, the boy and his girl, the wife and her green tomato pickles, each anticipating victory and the excitement of being separated from his or her money by familiar devices. It is at a fair that a man can be drunk forever on liquor, love, or fights; at a fair that your front pocket can be picked by a trotting horse looking for sugar, and your hind pocket by a thief looking for his fortune.

4.      This was one of the worst situations I had ever been in. There was a tube in my nose that went all the way to the pit of my stomach. I was being fed intravenously, and there was a drain in my side. Everybody came to visit me, mainly out of curiosity. The girls were all anxious to know where I had gotten shot. They had heard all kinds of tales about where the bullet struck. The bolder ones wouldn't even bother to ask: they just snatched the cover off me and looked for themselves. In a few days, the word got around that I was in one piece.

5.     Many people go to the grocery store without much thought. Once there, they become victims to clever product placement. In order to shop wisely, several basic rules should be kept in mind. First, the wise shopper should make a list. This will keep a focus on the person's needs, not wants. Grocery stores purposely place tempting items such as candy and magazines near the checkout counters; these are things that are not basic needs on anyone's list. A person who sticks to the list will save a substantial amount of money within a few months. Secondly, the shopper should avoid delis and convenience stores where the markups tend to be higher than in the large grocery chains. Next, buying store brands can result in big savings. In many cases, these store brands are of the same quality as the higher priced brands. Of course, we all know we should clip coupons, but be careful not to buy items that are not really necessary. Sometimes a store brand is still cheaper than the more expensive item even after the coupon amount has been deducted. Some people claim they can save by buying in bulk. They might buy a bushel of apples or 40 pounds of potatoes. However, if the food spoils before you can eat it, this may be a big mistake. It is true that a bargain is not always a bargain.

**EXERCISE 3**

### Finding the Topic Sentence of a Paragraph

**Each of the following five paragraphs contains a topic sentence that states the main idea of the paragraph. Find the sentence that best states the main idea and underline it. Keep in mind that the topic sentence will not always be the first sentence of the paragraph.**

1.     Last evening at a party, a complete stranger asked me, "Are you a Libra?" Astrology is enjoying increasing popularity all across the United States. My wife hurries every morning to read her horoscope in the paper. At the local stores, cards, books, T-shirts, and other useless astrological products bring fat profits to those who have manufactured them. Even some public officials, like the British royal family, are known to consider the "science" of astrology before scheduling an important event.

2.     Participating in fundraising walks and runs can raise needed research money for good causes, such as cures for multiple sclerosis or breast cancer. Donating used clothing to organizations like the Salvation Army is better than having closets full of clothes you never wear. It only takes an hour to donate blood, and this one hour of your time may save someone's life. Volunteers are badly needed at animal shelters and food pantries. What

about volunteering to tutor a child or take an elderly person to medical appointments? Anyone with a caring heart can find some time in the week to make a difference in another person's life.

3.      When we remember something, our brain uses more than one method to store the information. Short-term memory helps recall recent events; long-term memory brings back items that are further in the past; and deep retrieval gives access to long-buried information that is sometimes difficult to recall. Whether these processes are chemical or electrical, we do not yet know, and much research remains to be done before we can say with any certainty. The brain is one of the most remarkable organs, a part of the body that we have only begun to investigate. It will be years before we even begin to understand all its complex processes.

4.      ~ Some of the homes were small with whitewashed walls and thatched roofs. We were eager to see how they were furnished. The living rooms were simple, often with only a plain wooden table and some chairs. The tiny bedrooms usually had room for only a single bed and a small table. Occasionally, a bedroom would be large enough to have a stove made of richly decorated tiles. Visiting these houses was an experience that would always stay in our memory. All of the windows held boxes for flowers so that even in the dark of winter there was the promise of a blaze of colors in the spring.

5.      Advertisements that claim you can lose five pounds overnight are not to be trusted. Nor are claims that your luck will change if you send money to a certain post office box in a distant state. You should also avoid chain letters you receive in the mail that promise you large amounts of money if you will cooperate and keep the chain going. Many people are suspicious of the well-publicized million-dollar giveaway promotions that seem to offer enormous cash prizes, even if you do not try the company's product. We should always be suspicious of offers that promise us something for little or no effort or money.

**EXERCISE** 4   **Finding the Topic Sentence of a Paragraph**

**The topic sentence is missing in each of the following four paragraphs. Read each paragraph carefully and circle the letter of the best topic sentence for that paragraph.**

1.      I would probably have lived my entire existence within a one-mile radius of where I was born. I would undoubtedly have married a woman of

my identical religious, socioeconomic, and cultural background. I would almost certainly have become a medical doctor, an engineer, or a software programmer. I would have socialized within my ethnic community and had cordial relations, but few friends, outside that group. I would have a whole set of opinions that could be predicted in advance; indeed, they would not be very different from what my father believed, or his father before him.

   a. If I had remained in India, my destiny would to a large degree have been predictable.

   b. If I had remained in India, I would have been very happy living in the neighborhood where I grew up.

   c. If I had remained in India, I would have married someone very like my own mother.

   d. If I had remained in India, I would have had an excellent education.

2.     It is not that poor people in the Third World don't work hard. On the contrary, they labor incessantly and endure hardships that are almost unimaginable to people in the West. In the villages of Asia and Africa, for example, a common sight is a farmer beating a pickax into the ground, women wobbling under heavy loads, children carrying stones. These people are performing very hard labor, but they are getting nowhere. The best they can hope for is to survive for another day. Their clothes are tattered, their teeth are rotted, and disease and death constantly loom over their horizon.

   a. Poor people from the Third World live in small villages in Asia and Africa.

   b. The lives of many poor people in the Third World are defined by an ongoing struggle to exist.

   c. Disease is a constant threat to poor people in the Third World.

   d. Poor people in the Third World work constantly.

3.     The roads are not properly paved. The water is not safe to drink. Pollution in the cities has reached hazardous levels. Public transportation is overcrowded and unreliable. There is a two-year waiting period to get a telephone. Government officials, who are very poorly paid, are inevitably corrupt, which means that you must pay bribes on a regular basis to get things done. Most important, there are limited prospects for the children's future.

   a. It is difficult to live in a Third World country where corruption is so widespread.

   b. Everyday life in the Third World is filled with hardships for everyone.

   c. Only the very poor in the Third World suffer; the Upper and Middle Classes live an easy life.

   d. Governments in the Third World do not care about the common people.

4.      Let me illustrate with the example of my sister, who got married several years ago. My parents began the process by conducting a comprehensive survey of all the eligible families in our neighborhood. First they examined primary criteria such as religion, socioeconomic position, and educational background. Then my parents investigated subtler issues: the social reputation of the family, reports of a lunatic uncle, the character of the son, and so on. Finally my parents were down to a dozen or so eligible families, and they were invited to our house for dinner with suspicious regularity. My sister was "free to choose." My sister knew about, and accepted, the arrangement; she is now happily married with two children. I am not quarreling with the outcome.

   a.  Children in India are free to choose the person they want to marry.

   b.  In India, the reputation of the family into which you are married is very important.

   c.  A person's future in India is largely determined by the parents.

   d.  In all cultures, parents want their children to marry for love.

## DISTINGUISHING A TOPIC SENTENCE FROM A TITLE

The topic sentence works like a title by announcing to the reader what the paragraph is about. However, keep in mind that the title of an essay or book is usually a single word or short phrase, whereas the topic sentence of a paragraph must *always* be a complete sentence.

| | |
|---|---|
| **Title:** | **Backpacking in the mountains** |
| **Topic sentence:** | **Backpacking in the mountains last year was an exhausting experience.** |
| **Title:** | **The stress of college registration** |
| **Topic sentence:** | **College registration can be stressful.** |

**EXERCISE 5**

### Distinguishing a Topic Sentence from a Title

**Indicate whether each of the following examples is a title (T) or a topic sentence (TS) by writing *T* or *TS* in the space provided.**

____  1.  The benefits of a college education

____  2.  The outstanding achievements of aviator Charles Lindbergh

____  3.  The president's cabinet faced two major problems

____  4.  The basis of the Arab-Israeli conflict

____  5.  The Mediterranean diet is perhaps the healthiest diet in the world

____  6.  The astounding beauty of the Rocky Mountains at dusk

____  7.  The finest sports car on the market

_____ 8.  Fast-food restaurants are popular with families having small children

_____ 9.  The expense of maintaining a car

_____ 10. Maintaining a car is expensive

**EXERCISE 6**

### Distinguishing a Topic Sentence from a Title

Indicate whether each of the following examples is a title (T) or a topic sentence (TS) by writing *T* or *TS* in the space provided.

_____ 1.  Dreams can be frightening

_____ 2.  The advantages of term limits for people in public offices

_____ 3.  *Frida* tells the tragic story of a famous Mexican artist

_____ 4.  The home of my dreams

_____ 5.  Taking a walk can be calming

_____ 6.  Sewing requires great patience as well as skill

_____ 7.  Selecting the right camera for an amateur

_____ 8.  A regular routine is healthy for children

_____ 9.  The worst bargain of my life

_____ 10. My last used car was a bargain

**EXERCISE 7**

### Distinguishing a Topic Sentence from a Title

Indicate whether each of the following examples is a title (T) or a topic sentence (TS) by writing *T* or *TS* in the space provided.

_____ 1.  How to make friends at college and still have time to study

_____ 2.  With the widespread use of computers, word-processing skills are needed for many jobs

_____ 3.  The disadvantages of living alone

_____ 4.  The fight to keep our neighborhood park

_____ 5.  The peacefulness of a solitary weekend at the beach

_____ 6.  Our investigation into the mysterious death of Walter D.

_____ 7.  The flea market looked promising

_____ 8.  The two main reasons divorce is common

_____ 9.  The single life did not turn out to be as glamorous as I had hoped

_____ 10. The increasing popularity of board games

## FINDING THE TOPIC IN A TOPIC SENTENCE

To find the topic in a topic sentence, ask yourself what subject the writer is going to discuss. In the first sentence that follows, the topic is underlined. Underline the topic in the second example.

**<u>Backpacking in the mountains last year</u> was an exhausting experience.**

**College registration can be stressful.**

Note that a topic sentence may have a two-part topic:

**The differences between <u>softball and baseball</u> may not be readily apparent to the person who is unfamiliar with the games.**

**EXERCISE 8**

### Finding the Topic in a Topic Sentence

Find the topic in each of the following topic sentences. For each sentence, ask yourself this question: What topic is the writer going to discuss? Then underline the topic.

1. Remodeling an old house can be frustrating.

2. College work demands more independence than high school work.

3. A well-made suit has three easily identified characteristics.

4. Growing up near a museum had a profound influence on my life.

5. My favorite room in the house would seem ugly to most people.

6. The huge trade imbalance of the United States has several sobering consequences.

7. One of the disadvantages of skiing is the expense.

8. Spanking is the least successful way to discipline a child.

9. An attractive wardrobe does not have to be expensive.

10. Of all the years in college, the first year is usually the most demanding.

**EXERCISE 9**

### Finding the Topic in a Topic Sentence

Find the topic in each of the following topic sentences. For each sentence, ask yourself this question: What topic is the writer going to discuss? Then underline the topic.

1. Taking care of a house can easily be a full-time job.

2. Many television news programs are more interested in entertaining than providing newsworthy information.

3.  One of the undisputed goals in teaching is to be able to offer individualized instruction.

4.  Whether it's a car, a house, or a college, bigger isn't always better.

5.  Violence on television is disturbing to most child psychologists.

6.  In today's economy, carrying at least one credit card is probably advisable.

7.  Much highway advertising is not only ugly but also distracting for the driver.

8.  Figuring out a semester course schedule can be a complicated process.

9.  In recent years, we have seen a dramatic revival of interest in quilting.

10. Working for a small company can be more rewarding than working for a large corporation.

**EXERCISE 10**

### Finding the Topic in the Topic Sentence

**Find the topic in each of the following topic sentences. For each sentence, ask yourself this question: What topic is the writer going to discuss? Then underline the topic.**

1.  To my surprise, the basement had been converted into a small studio apartment.

2.  Of all the presidents, Abraham Lincoln probably enjoys the greatest popularity.

3.  Nature versus nurture is a controversial issue in child psychology.

4.  Many people find dependence on public transportation frustrating.

5.  When we met for dinner that night, I was shocked at the change that had come over my friend.

6.  According to the report, current tax laws greatly benefit those who own real estate.

7.  Marian Anderson, the famous singer, began her career in a church choir.

8.  As we rode into town, the streets seemed unusually empty.

9.  The United Parcel Service offers its employees many long-term benefits.

10. Many people claim that clipping coupons can save them as much as 30 percent on their food bills.

# WHAT IS A CONTROLLING IDEA?

A topic sentence should contain not only the topic but also a controlling idea.

> The **controlling idea** of a topic sentence is the point the writer makes about the topic.
>
> **Backpacking trips are *exhausting*.**

A particular topic could have any number of possible controlling ideas, depending on the writer's focus. On the same topic of *backpacking*, three writers might make different points:

> **A family backpacking trip can be much more *satisfying* than a trip to an amusement park.**
>
> or
>
> **Our recent backpacking trip was a *disaster*.**
>
> or
>
> **A backpacking trip *should be a part of every teenager's experience*.**

## FINDING THE CONTROLLING IDEA OF A TOPIC SENTENCE

When you look for the controlling idea of a topic sentence, ask yourself this question: What is the point the writer is making about the topic?

In each of the following examples, underline the topic and circle the controlling idea.

> **Sealfon's Department Store is my favorite store in town.**

The writer of this topic sentence announces that the focus will be on what makes the store a favorite.

> **Sealfon's Department Store is too expensive for my budget.**

The writer of this topic sentence announces that the focus will be on the store's high prices.

**EXERCISE 11**

## Finding the Controlling Idea

**Below are ten topic sentences. For each sentence, underline the topic and circle the controlling idea.**

1. Vigorous exercise is a good way to reduce the effects of stress on the body.

2. Buffalo and Toronto differ in four major ways.

3. Television violence causes aggressive behavior in children.

4.   Athletic scholarships available to women are increasing.

5.   Caffeine has several adverse effects on the body.

6.   Serena Williams and her sister Venus have dominated the world of women's tennis.

7.   Training a parakeet to talk takes great patience.

8.   Babysitting for a family with four preschool children was the most difficult job I've ever had.

9.   The hours between five and seven in the morning are my most productive.

10.   The foggy night was spooky.

**EXERCISE 12**

## Finding the Controlling Idea

**Below are ten topic sentences. For each sentence, underline the topic and circle the controlling idea.**

1.   Piano lessons turned out to be an unexpected delight.

2.   The training of Japanese policemen is quite different from American police training.

3.   An Olympic champion has five distinctive characteristics.

4.   The candidate's unethical financial dealings will have a negative impact on this campaign.

5.   A bicycle ride along the coast is a breathtaking trip.

6.   The grocery store is another place where people waste a significant amount of money every week.

7.   Being an only child is not as bad as people think.

8.   Rewarding children with candy or desserts is an unfortunate habit of many parents.

9.   A childhood hobby often develops into a promising career.

10.   The writing of a dictionary is an incredibly detailed process.

**EXERCISE 13**

## Finding the Controlling Idea

Below are ten topic sentences. For each sentence, underline the topic and circle the controlling idea.

1.  Learning to type takes more practice than talent.

2.  Shakespeare's plays are difficult for today's students.

3.  Atlanta, Georgia, is one of the cities in the Sunbelt that is experiencing significant population growth.

4.  Half a dozen new health magazines are enjoying popularity.

5.  The importance of good preschool programs for children has been sadly underestimated.

6.  The disposal of toxic wastes has caused problems for many manufacturers.

7.  Censorship of school textbooks is a controversial issue in some towns.

8.  Finding an inexpensive method to make saltwater drinkable has been a difficult problem for decades.

9.  Developing color film is more complicated than developing black and white.

10. The cloudberry is one of the rare berries of the world.

## CHOOSING CONTROLLING IDEAS

Teachers often assign one general topic on which all students must write. Likewise, when writing contests are announced, the topic is often the same for all contestants. Because very few people have exactly the same view or attitude toward a topic, it is likely that no two papers will have the same controlling idea. In fact, there could be any number of controlling ideas. The secret to writing a successful topic sentence is to find the controlling idea that is right for you.

**EXERCISE 14**

## Choosing Controlling Ideas for Topic Sentences

Below are two topics. For each topic, think of three possible controlling ideas, and then write a topic sentence for each of these controlling ideas. An example is done for you.

**Topic:** My mother

**Three possible controlling ideas:**

1.  Unusual childhood

2.    Silent woman

3.    Definite ideas about alcohol

**Three different topic sentences:**

1.    My mother had a most unusual childhood.

2.    My mother is a very silent woman.

3.    My mother has definite ideas about alcohol.

1.    **Topic:** My grandmother

First controlling idea: _____

First topic sentence: _____

_____

Second controlling idea: _____

Second topic sentence: _____

_____

Third controlling idea: _____

Third topic sentence: _____

_____

2.    **Topic:** California (or another state)

First controlling idea: _____

First topic sentence: _____

_____

Second controlling idea: _____

Second topic sentence: _____

_____

Third controlling idea: _____

Third topic sentence: _____

_____

**EXERCISE 15**

## Choosing Controlling Ideas for Topic Sentences

Below are two topics. For each topic, think of three possible controlling ideas, and then write a topic sentence for each of these controlling ideas. An example is done for you.

**Topic:** The movie *Gran Torino*

**Three possible controlling ideas:**

1. Explores the clash of cultures in a Detroit neighborhood

2. Shows Clint Eastwood's acting and directing talent

3. Reveals how a close-minded character can be transformed

**Three different topic sentences:**

1. *Gran Torino* explores the clash of cultures in a Detroit neighborhood.

2. *Gran Torino* shows Clint Eastwood's great talent for both acting and directing.

3. *Gran Torino* is a movie whose main character, played by Clint Eastwood, is transformed from a close-minded individual to someone who is open to change.

1. **Topic:** Late night talk shows

First controlling idea: _____

First topic sentence: _____

_____

Second controlling idea: _____

Second topic sentence: _____

_____

Third controlling idea: _____

Third topic sentence: _____

_____

2. **Topic:** Working in a nursing home

First controlling idea: _____

First topic sentence: _____

_____

Second controlling idea: _____

Second topic sentence: _____

_____

Third controlling idea: _____

Third topic sentence: _____

_____

**EXERCISE**  **16**    **Choosing Controlling Ideas for Topic Sentences**

Below are two topics. For each topic, think of three possible controlling ideas, and then write a topic sentence for each of these controlling ideas. An example is done for you.

**Topic:** Fitness and health

**Three possible controlling ideas:**

1.  The growth of new lines of products

2.  Increased popularity of health clubs

3.  Use of exercise DVDs and equipment at home

**Three different topic sentences:**

1.  Recent years have seen the creation of entire lines of products devoted to fitness and health.

2.  The high level of interest in physical fitness and health has resulted in a widespread growth of health clubs across the country.

3.  A person can improve his or her health by exercising at home with a professional on DVD or working out on one of the many pieces of equipment available for private use.

1.  **Topic:** Rap music

    First controlling idea: _____

    First topic sentence: _____

    _____

    Second controlling idea: _____

    Second topic sentence: _____

    _____

    Third controlling idea: _____

    Third topic sentence: _____

    _____

2.  **Topic:** Junk food

    First controlling idea: _____

    First topic sentence: _____

    _____

    Second controlling idea: _____

    Second topic sentence: _____

    _____

    Third controlling idea: _____

Third topic sentence: _____

_____

# MASTERY AND EDITING TESTS

**TEST 1**

## Further Practice Writing Topic Sentences

Develop each of the following topics into a topic sentence. In each case, the controlling idea is missing. Decide on the point you wish to make about the topic. Then include this controlling idea as part of your topic sentence. When you are finished, underline the topic and circle your controlling idea. Be sure your topic sentence is a complete sentence and not a fragment. An example has been done for you.

**Topic:**            My brother's car accident

**Controlling idea:**    Tragic results

**Topic sentence:**    My brother's car accident had (tragic results) for the entire family.

1. **Topic:** Teaching a child good manners

   Controlling idea: _____

   Topic sentence: _____

   _____

2. **Topic:** Two years in the military

   Controlling idea: _____

   Topic sentence: _____

   _____

3. **Topic:** Living with in-laws

   Controlling idea: _____

   Topic sentence: _____

   _____

4. **Topic:** Moving to a new location

   Controlling idea: _____

   Topic sentence: _____

   _____

5. **Topic:** Cheating

   Controlling idea: _____

   Topic sentence: _____

   _____

**TEST 2**

## Further Practice Writing Topic Sentences

Develop each of the following topics into a topic sentence. In each case, the controlling idea is missing. Decide on the point you wish to make about the topic. Then include this controlling idea as part of your topic sentence. When you are finished, underline the topic and circle your controlling idea. Be sure your topic sentence is a complete sentence and not a fragment.

1. **Topic:** Camping

   Controlling idea: _____

   Topic sentence: _____

   _____

2. **Topic:** Vegetarians

   Controlling idea: _____

   Topic sentence: _____

   _____

3. **Topic:** Noisy neighbors

   Controlling idea: _____

   Topic sentence: _____

   _____

4. **Topic:** Driving lessons

   Controlling idea: _____

   Topic sentence: _____

   _____

5. **Topic:** Subways

   Controlling idea: _____

   Topic sentence: _____

   _____

**TEST 3**

## Further Practice Writing Topic Sentences

Develop each of the following topics into a topic sentence. In each case, the controlling idea is missing. Decide on the point you wish to make about the topic. Then include this controlling idea as part of your topic sentence. When you are finished, underline the topic and circle your controlling idea. Be sure your topic sentence is a complete sentence and not a fragment.

1. **Topic:** Computer programming

   Controlling idea: _____

   Topic sentence: _____

   _____

2.  **Topic:** Body piercing

    Controlling idea: _____

    Topic sentence: _____

    _____

3.  **Topic:** Allergies

    Controlling idea: _____

    Topic sentence: _____

    _____

4.  **Topic:** The Red Cross

    Controlling idea: _____

    Topic sentence: _____

    _____

5.  **Topic:** Text messaging

    Controlling idea: _____

    Topic sentence: _____

    _____

## Exploring Online

Go to **www.cengage.com/devenglish/scarry/writersworkplace** to find
the **Writer's Online Workplace,** a website designed for students using
this book. You will find links to handouts, interactive quizzes, and other
online resources as you explore the following topics:

- paragraphs and topic sentences
- paragraph development
- finding the topic sentence

# Working Together

## EXPLORING CONTROLLING IDEAS: A PERSON'S LIFESTYLE

In developing a topic into a paragraph, a writer can choose from an endless number of controlling ideas. Student writers are often surprised by another writer's approach to a given topic. We will explore some of these approaches as we brainstorm for different controlling ideas on the following topic: a person's lifestyle.

The controlling idea in the following topic sentence uses *comparison or contrast* as a method of development. It contrasts the writer's lifestyle with his or her parents' lifestyle.

**My parents' lifestyle is *a completely different arrangement* from my own.**

Divide into groups. Each group should prepare a list of possible controlling ideas for a paragraph or essay on the topic of *a person's lifestyle*. Each person in the group should contribute two controlling ideas. Then come together as a class and share the controlling ideas with each other. (If possible, write them on a board for all to see.) When all the groups have shared their lists, the following questions should be answered:

1. How many different controlling ideas have emerged from the work of all the groups?

2. How many methods of development *(description, example, narration, process, classification, cause and effect, definition, comparison and contrast, or argument)* are represented in the several controlling ideas generated by the groups in the class?

## PORTFOLIO SUGGESTION

Each student in the class should copy a complete list of controlling ideas developed by the class. Organize the ideas into groups according to the most obvious method of development. Save this list in your portfolio as a reminder of the ways you could develop your own thinking on a given topic. Put a check mark beside the controlling ideas that you would consider for your own writing. Your instructor may ask you to write a paragraph or essay using the controlling idea that is most interesting to you.

# WORKING WITH PARAGRAPHS: SUPPORTING DETAILS

# 17

To develop a paragraph successfully, you must use appropriate details to support the main idea of that paragraph. In this chapter, you will learn several skills related to the use of supporting details:

**CHAPTER OBJECTIVES**

- identifying supporting details
- choosing supporting details based on the method of paragraph development
- avoiding restatement of the topic sentence
- making supporting details specific

## WHAT IS A SUPPORTING DETAIL?

Once you have constructed a topic sentence made up of the topic and its controlling idea, you are ready to support your statement with details. The quality and number of these details will largely determine the effectiveness of the writing. You can hold your readers' attention with your choice of details, or you can lose your readers' interest because your details are not compelling.

> A *supporting detail* is a piece of evidence used by a writer to make the controlling idea of the topic sentence convincing and interesting to the reader. A piece of evidence might be a descriptive image, an example taken from history or personal experience, a reason, a fact (such as a statistic), a quotation from an expert, or an anecdote used to illustrate a point.
>
> **Poor supporting details:**     **Many people died of the flu in the 1960s.**
>
> **Effective supporting details:**     **In 1968 in the United States, seventy thousand people died of the Hong Kong flu.**

## HOW DO YOU CHOOSE SUPPORTING DETAILS?

For a paragraph to be well developed, the main idea must be supported with several details. As you work through the chapters in this section, you will have opportunities to use many types of supporting details. The chart on this page lists the various methods of paragraph development. A writer chooses supporting details according to what best fits the method of development. For instance, if the writer is describing someone's appearance, the details are made up of sensory images (for example, *a raspy voice, olive skin,* and *the scent of Old Spice cologne*).

### Methods of Paragraph Development

| | |
|---|---|
| **Narration:** | telling a story using a sequence of events |
| **Description:** | using sensory images to create a picture with words |
| **Process:** | using steps explaining how to do something or explaining how something works |
| **Illustration or example:** | giving instances of the main idea |
| **Comparison/contrast:** | showing similarities or differences |
| **Cause and effect:** | examining reasons or outcomes |
| **Extended definition:** | analyzing at some length the meaning of a word or concept |
| **Classification:** | dividing a subject into groups or parts |

As you choose your supporting details, keep in mind that the readers do not necessarily have to agree with your point of view. However, your supporting details must be good enough to make your readers at least respect your attitude. Your goal should be to educate your readers. Try to give them some understanding of your subject. Don't assume they know about your topic or are interested in it. If you provide enough specific details, your readers will feel they have learned something new about the subject, and this alone is a satisfying experience for most people. Effective supporting details will encourage readers to keep on reading. Such details will make your points more memorable, and they will give pleasure to those who are learning new material or picturing the images you have created.

Read the following paragraph and observe how it provides effective details that support the controlling idea of the topic sentence.

*Topic sentence*

Everyone has heard of surefire formulas to prevent getting a cold. Popular home methods include a cold shower, regular exercise, and a hot rum toddy. Some people swear by cod-liver oil, tea with honey, citrus fruit juices, or keeping one's feet dry. Americans spent billions last year for cold and cough remedies. Advertisers have claimed preventive and curative virtues for vitamins, alkalizers, lemon drinks, antihistamines, decongestants, timed-release capsules, antibiotics, antiseptic gargles, bioflavonoids, nose drops and sprays, and a variety of other products. There are at least three hundred over-the-counter products, most of which are a combination of ingredients sold for the treatment of symptoms of the common cold. Many of these drugs neither benefit nor harm the cold victim, but there is no doubt that they benefit the drug manufacturers! Now—just as fifty years ago—Americans on average will suffer two to three colds a year, with the infectious stages lasting about a week, regardless of any physical measure, diet, or drug used. U.S. Public Health Service studies show that, during the winter quarter of the year, 50 percent of the population experiences a common cold; during the summer quarter, the figure drops to 20 percent. The increased incidence of colds in winter reflects the fact that people spend more time indoors, thereby allowing the viruses to travel from person to person. In fact, one is less likely to catch a cold after exposure to the elements than after mixing with a convivial group of snifflers and sneezers at a fireside gathering.

**Practice**

Using the lines provided, copy the topic sentence from the previous paragraph. Then answer the questions about the details that support the topic sentence.

Topic sentence: _____

_____

What are some examples of home remedies?

_____

_____

What are some examples of over-the-counter remedies?

_____

_____

_____

What fact is given?

_____

_____

What expert is named? What is the statistic given by that source?

_____

_____

_____

**EXERCISE** **1**

### Finding the Topic Sentence and Supporting Details

**Read each paragraph below. On the lines that follow, write the topic sentence and identify the supporting details.**

1.    Heroes in American movies usually fall into types. One kind of hero is the tight-lipped loner, men like Clint Eastwood and Humphrey Bogart. Another movie hero is the quiet, shy, or fumbling type who has appeared in movies since the beginning. The main characteristic of this hero is lovableness, as seen in actors like Jimmy Stewart. Perhaps the most one-dimensional and predictable hero is the superman who battles tough odds. This kind of hero is best illustrated by Sylvester Stallone as Rocky and Rambo.

Topic sentence: _____

First type: _____

Second type: _____

Third type: _____

2.    Blue jeans have become a tradition, and along the way have acquired a history of their own. There was, for example, the turn-of-the-century trainman who replaced a faulty coupling with a pair of jeans; the Wyoming man who used his jeans as a towrope to haul his car out of a ditch; and the Californian who found several pairs in an abandoned mine, wore them, then discovered they were sixty-three years old and still as good as new and turned them over to the Smithsonian as a tribute to their toughness. And then there is the particularly terrifying story of the careless construction worker who dangled fifty-two stories above the street until rescued, his sole support the Levi's belt loop through which his rope was hooked.

Topic sentence: _____

_____

First historical example: _____

_____

Second historical example: _____

_____

Third historical example: _____

_____

Fourth historical example: _____

_____

**EXERCISE** **2**

### Finding the Topic Sentence and Supporting Details

**Read each paragraph. On the lines that follow, write the topic sentence and identify the supporting details.**

1.      Hilda takes an enormous amount of space, though so little time, in my adolescence. Even today, her memory stirs me; I long to see her again. She was three years older than I, and for a short while all I wanted was to look like, sound like, and dress like her. She was the only girl I knew who told me I wrote excellent letters. She made a plaster cast of my face. She had opinions on everything. She took a picture of me, at sixteen, which I have still. She and I were nearly killed, falling off a hillside road in her small car. Hilda was so full of life, I cannot believe her dead.

FROM HAN SUYIN,
*A Mortal Flower*

Topic sentence: _____

_____

First detail: _____

_____

Second detail: _____

Third detail: _____

Fourth detail: _____

Fifth detail: _____

Sixth example: _____

2.      A steadily accumulating body of evidence supports the view that cancers are caused by things that we eat, drink, breathe, or are otherwise exposed to. That evidence is of three kinds. First, the incidence of many types of cancers differs greatly from one geographic region of the world to another. Second, when groups of people permanently move from one country to another, the incidence of some types of cancer changes in their offspring. For example, when Japanese move to this country, the relatively high rate of occurrence of stomach cancer they experience in Japan falls so that their children experience such cancer only a fifth as frequently, the same incidence as other Americans. Asians have low incidence of breast cancer, but when they come to the United States, it increases sixfold. Third, we are becoming aware of an increasing number of chemical pollutants in air and water and food that have proven to be cancer-producing.

FROM MAHLON B. HOAGLAND,
*The Roots of Life*

Topic sentence: _____

_____

First piece of evidence: _____

_____

Second piece of evidence (and example): _____

_____

_____

_____

Third piece of evidence: _____

_____

**EXERCISE** **3**

## Finding the Topic Sentence and Supporting Details

**Read each paragraph below. On the lines that follow, write the topic sentence and identify the supporting details.**

1.    Transportation was simple then. Two good horses and a sturdy wagon met most needs of a villager. Only five or six individuals possessed an automobile in the Pueblo of 300. A flatbed truck fixed with wooden rails and a canvas top made a regular Saturday trip to Santa Fe. It was always loaded beyond capacity with Cochitis taking their wares to town for a few staples. With an escort of a dozen barking dogs, the straining truck made a noisy exit, northbound from the village.

FROM JOSEPH H. SUINA,
*And Then I Went to School*

Topic sentence: _____

First example: _____

Second example: _____

_____

Third example: _____

_____

_____

2.    Fairness is the ability to see more than one side in a situation, and sometimes it even means having the ability to decide against your own interests. For example, in San Antonio, Texas, a woman was locked in a bitter custody dispute that involved her thirteen-year-old son. The mother loved her son and wanted custody of him, even though she had a major health problem. She listened patiently while her ex-husband argued for full custody of the child. The woman felt that she had presented a good case before the judge, but when the boy was asked for his feelings in the matter, the mother found herself faced with a difficult situation: her son wanted to live with his father.

Topic sentence: _____

_____

Anecdote: _____

_____

_____

_____

_____

_____

# AVOIDING RESTATEMENT OF THE TOPIC SENTENCE

Writers need to recognize the difference between a genuine supporting detail and a simple restatement of the topic sentence. The following is a poor paragraph because all its sentences merely restate the topic sentence.

> The wedding day was the highest point in a girl's life—a day to which she looked forward all her unmarried days and to which she looked back for the rest of her life. All the events of the day were unlike those of any other day in her life before or after. Everyone would remember this day. Each event was unforgettable. The memories would last a lifetime. A wedding was the beginning of living "happily ever after."

By contrast, this paragraph, from Margaret Mead's "From Popping the Question to Popping the Pill," has excellent supporting details:

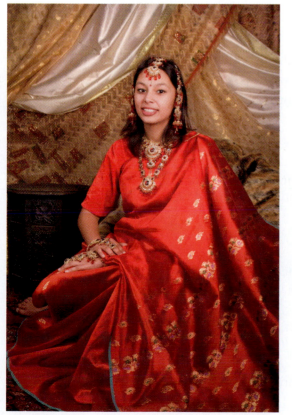

> The wedding day was the highest point in a girl's life—a day to which she looked forward all her unmarried days and to which she looked back for the rest of her life. The splendor of her wedding, the elegance of dress and veil, the cutting of the cake, the departure amid a shower of rice and confetti, gave her an accolade of which no subsequent event could completely rob her. Today people over fifty years of age still treat their daughter's wedding this way, prominently displaying the photographs of the occasion. Until very recently, all brides' books prescribed exactly the same ritual they had prescribed fifty years before. The etiquette governing wedding presents—gifts that were or were not appropriate, the bride's maiden initials on her linen—was also specified. For the bridegroom the wedding represented the end of his free, bachelor days, and the bachelor dinner the night before the wedding symbolized this loss of freedom. A woman who did not marry—even if she had the alibi of a fiancé who had been killed in war or had abilities and charm and money of her own—was always at a social disadvantage, while an eligible bachelor was sought after by hostess after hostess.

**EXERCISE** 4

### Distinguishing a Supporting Detail from a Restatement of the Main Idea

Each topic sentence below is followed by four additional sentences. Three of these additional sentences contain acceptable supporting details, but one of the sentences is simply a restatement of the topic sentence. In each of the spaces provided, identify each sentence as *SD,* for supporting detail, or *R,* for restatement.

1.  I am surprised when I think how neat I used to be before school started.

    _____ a.   In my closet, I had my clothes arranged in matching outfits with shoes, hats, and even jewelry to go with them.

    _____ b.   I have always taken great pride in having all my things in order.

    _____ c.   If I opened my desk drawer, compartments of paper clips, erasers, staples, pens, pencils, stamps, and rulers greeted me, without a penny or safety pin out of place.

    _____ d.   On top of my chest of drawers sat a comb and brush and two oval frames with pictures of my best friends; that was all.

2.  Iceland has a very barren landscape.

    _____ a.   One-tenth of the island is covered by ice.

    _____ b.   There is not a single forest on the entire island.

    _____ c.   Nearly everywhere you look in Iceland, you see vast desolate areas.

    _____ d.   Three-fourths of the island is uninhabitable.

3.  Until recently, books have been the most important method of preserving knowledge.

    _____ a.   Without books, much of the knowledge of past centuries would have been lost.

    _____ b.   Leonardo da Vinci kept notebooks of his amazing inventions and discoveries.

    _____ c.   During the Middle Ages, monks spent their entire lives copying books by hand.

    _____ d.   The Library of Congress in Washington, D.C., is given a copy of every book published in the United States.

4.  Most adults no longer wonder whether cigarette smoking is bad for their health.

    _____ a.   Based on the evidence from more than thirty thousand studies, a federal law requires that cigarette manufacturers place a health warning on their packages.

    _____ b.   Studies have shown that smoking causes nearly 80 percent of lung cancer deaths in this country.

    _____ c.   Few people today have any doubts about the connection between cigarette smoking and poor health.

    _____ d.   We know that 30 percent of the deaths from coronary heart disease can be attributed to smoking.

5.  When the Mexican earthquake struck in 1985, scientists and city planners learned a great deal about the kinds of buildings that can survive an earthquake.

_____ a.  Buildings that had foundations resting on giant rollers suffered very little damage.

_____ b.  Buildings that were made only of adobe material simply fell apart when the earthquake struck.

_____ c.  Many modern buildings were designed to vibrate in an earthquake, and these received the least amount of shock.

_____ d.  After the 1985 Mexican earthquake was over, officials realized why some buildings were destroyed and others suffered hardly any damage at all.

**EXERCISE 5**

## Distinguishing a Supporting Detail from a Restatement of the Main Idea

Each topic sentence below is followed by four additional sentences. Three of these additional sentences contain acceptable supporting details, but one of the sentences is simply a restatement of the topic sentence. In each of the spaces provided, identify each sentence as *SD*, for supporting detail, or *R*, for restatement.

1.  In the last thirty years, the number of people living alone in the United States has increased by 400 percent.

_____ a.  People are living alone because the number of divorces has dramatically increased.

_____ b.  Many young people are putting off marriage until they are financially more secure or emotionally ready.

_____ c.  More and more Americans are finding themselves living alone.

_____ d.  An increasing percentage of our population is in the age group over sixty-five, among whom are many widows and widowers.

2.  Today, people are realizing the disadvantages of using credit cards too often.

_____ a.  People should think twice before borrowing money on credit.

_____ b.  Interest rates on credit cards can reach alarming rates.

_____ c.  Credit cards encourage buying on impulse, rather than planning a budget carefully.

_____ d.  Many credit card companies charge an annual fee for the privilege of using their cards.

3.  In medicine, prevention is just as important as treatment.

_____ a.  A good way for a person to keep in touch with his or her health is to have an annual physical.

_____ b.  To stay healthy, people should watch their weight.

_____ c.  Some researchers claim that taking an aspirin every day thins the blood, which prevents clotting.

_____ d.  Where health is concerned, warding off a disease is as critical as curing it.

4. Since World War II, the status of women in Japan has changed.

_____ a. In 1947, women won the right to vote.

_____ b. Women's position in Japanese society has altered over the past forty-five years.

_____ c. Many Japanese women now go on to get a higher education.

_____ d. A woman can now own property in her own name and seek divorce.

5. Certain factors that cannot be changed have been shown to contribute to heart attacks and stroke.

_____ a. Three out of four heart attacks and six out of seven strokes occur after the age of sixty-five, so age is definitely a factor.

_____ b. Heart attacks and strokes have many causes, some of which we can do nothing about.

_____ c. African Americans have nearly a 45 percent greater risk of having high blood pressure, a major cause of heart attacks and strokes.

_____ d. Men are at greater risk than women in their chance of suffering from cardiovascular disease.

## HOW DO YOU MAKE SUPPORTING DETAILS SPECIFIC?

Students often write paragraphs that are made up of too many general statements. With such paragraphs, the writer's knowledge is in doubt, and the reader may suspect that the point being made has no basis in fact. Here is one such paragraph that never rises beyond generalities.

> Doctors are terrible. They cause more problems than they solve. I don't believe most of their treatments are necessary. History is full of the mistakes doctors have made. We don't need all those operations. We should never ingest all those drugs doctors prescribe. We shouldn't allow them to give us all those unnecessary tests. I've heard plenty of stories that prove my point. Doctors' ideas can kill you.

Here is another paragraph on the same topic. It is much more interesting and convincing because the writer has made use of supporting details rather than relying on general statements.

> Evidence shows that "medical progress" has been the cause of tragic consequences and even death for thousands of people. X-ray therapy was thought to help patients with tonsillitis. Now many of these people are found to have developed cancer from these X-rays. Not so long ago, women were kept in bed for several weeks following childbirth. Unfortunately, this cost

many women their lives because they developed fatal blood clots from being kept in bed day after day. One recent poll estimates that thirty thousand people each year die from the side effects of drugs that were prescribed by doctors. Recently, the Centers for Disease Control and Prevention reported that 25 percent of the tests done by clinical laboratories were done poorly. All this is not to belittle the good done by the medical profession, but to impress on readers that it would be foolish to rely totally on the medical profession to solve all our health problems.

This paragraph is much more likely to be of real interest. Even if the reader wanted to disprove the author's point, it would be very hard to dismiss these supporting details, which are based on facts and information that can be verified. Because the writer sounds reasonable, the reader has respect for the presentation of specific facts, even if he or she has a different position on the topic.

In writing effectively, the ability to go beyond the general statement and get to the accurate pieces of information is what counts. A good writer tries to make his or her reader an expert on the subject. Readers should go away excited to share the surprising information they have just learned. A writer who has a statistic, a quotation, an anecdote, a historical example, or a descriptive detail has the advantage over all other writers, no matter how impressive these writers' styles may be.

Good writing, therefore, is filled with supporting details that are specific, accurate, and appropriate for the subject. Poor writing is filled with generalizations, stereotypes, vagueness, untruths, and sometimes even sarcasm and insults.

**EXERCISE 6**

## Creating Supporting Details

**Five topic sentences follow. Supply three supporting details for each one (inventing, when necessary). Be sure each detail is specific, not general or vague, and use complete sentences for your answers.**

1. Parenting is not an easy job.

   a. _____

   b. _____

   c. _____

2. At certain times in life, a person needs the support of family and friends.

   a. _____

   b. _____

   c. _____

3. There is more than one kind of intelligence.

   a. _____

   b. _____

   c. _____

4.  The snacks we love are often not the healthiest.

a. _____

b. _____

c. _____

5.  My father is the most self-sacrificing person I know.

a. _____

b. _____

c. _____

**EXERCISE  7**

## Creating Supporting Details

**Below are five topic sentences. Supply three supporting details for each one (inventing, when necessary). Be sure each detail is specific, not general or vague, and use complete sentences for your answers.**

1.  The recent financial crisis has had far-reaching consequences for many American families.

a. _____

b. _____

c. _____

2.  On a college campus today, current trends in fashion are noticeable.

a. _____

b. _____

c. _____

3.  Owning a pet can be expensive.

a. _____

b. _____

c. _____

4.  My manager at work often exhibits very odd behavior.

a. _____

b. _____

c. _____

5.  There are several reasons why people today do not get enough exercise.

a. _____

b. _____

c. _____

**EXERCISE  8**

### Creating Supporting Details

Below are five topic sentences. Supply three supporting details for each one (inventing, when necessary). Be sure each detail is specific, not general or vague, and use complete sentences for your answers.

1. Maintaining a car is a continual drain on one's budget.

   a. _____

   b. _____

   c. _____

2. Each sport has its own peculiar injuries associated with it.

   a. _____

   b. _____

   c. _____

3. Last year, I redecorated my bedroom.

   a. _____

   b. _____

   c. _____

4. Washington, D.C., is the best city for a family vacation.

   a. _____

   b. _____

   c. _____

5. The amateur photographer needs to consider several points when selecting a camera.

   a. _____

   b. _____

   c. _____

## Exploring Online

Go to **www.cengage.com/devenglish/scarry/writersworkplace** to find the **Writer's Online Workplace,** a website designed for students using this book. You will find links to handouts, interactive quizzes, and other online resources as you explore the following topics:

- supporting details
- using specific and concrete details

# Working Together

## PEER EDITING: RECORDING FAMILY, COMMUNITY, OR NATIONAL TRADITIONS

Rituals and celebrations are important milestones for individuals, groups, and even entire nations. These milestones affirm people's lives and help them feel connected. They also support a nation's need to preserve its history.

Divide into groups. Make a list of all the celebrations and traditions (from an individual's birthday to national holidays) your group is able to generate. Then note what makes each celebration special. Discuss what supporting details you could use when writing about a particular celebration. For example, if you chose Thanksgiving, the details would most likely center around the meal that would be served. How many of these celebrations have this same emphasis on food?

Each person should then write a paragraph describing a particular celebration. Remember that the paragraph must have a topic sentence and seven or eight additional sentences to support that topic sentence. Be sure that these sentences provide specific details that will help the reader imagine the event.

Exchange papers. After you have read the paper you have been given, mark it in the following ways:

1.  Underline the topic sentence.
2.  Make a ✔ in front of the sentence you believe contains the most effective supporting detail.
3.  Make an **X** in front of the sentence you believe has the weakest supporting detail.
4.  Using the editing symbols from the inside back cover of your book, mark any errors that you find.
5.  The following sentences could have been found in student essays on the subject of *Thanksgiving*. Each of the sentences has been rated on a scale from one to four (one being the best). Use the rating guide to judge the paper you are reading. In the upper right-hand corner of the paper, rate the overall quality of the details by giving the essay a score of one to four.

Rating 1:   The details are usually very specific. For example, most of the details are as specific as those in the following sentence:

**Mamma always ordered her fresh Thanksgiving turkey three weeks in advance from Ike at Goldfinger's Meat Market on Fourth Street.**

Rating 2:   The details are somewhat specific. For example, many of the details are as specific as those in the following sentence:

**Mamma ordered our Thanksgiving turkey from the local meat market.**

Rating 3:   The details are often too general. For example, many of the details are as general as those in the following sentence:

**Mamma fixed a turkey every Thanksgiving.**

Rating 4:   The details are almost always too general. For example, most of the sentences lack specific details just like the following sentence:

**Thanksgiving dinner was always great.**

6.  From the paper you are reviewing, select one sentence to revise. Rewrite it with more specific details that you think would make the sentence more interesting. Write your new version at the bottom of the student's paper.

## PORTFOLIO SUGGESTION

When your paragraph has been returned to you, identify it as your first draft. Write a second version in which you add more details or make the existing details more specific. Label this version as your second draft. Be sure to show both versions to someone who can comment on your changes. Are you happier with the second version? Save both versions in your portfolio.

# 18

# DEVELOPING PARAGRAPHS: ILLUSTRATION

Among the many methods of developing a paragraph (see the list on page 338), **illustration** or **example** is chosen when a writer wants to give clarity to a general idea or an abstract notion. Using illustration or example is the focus of this chapter. The following topics are presented:

**CHAPTER OBJECTIVES**

- three ways to illustrate a point
- four sources of examples
- transitions to introduce examples
- analyzing paragraphs with examples
- taking a step-by-step approach to create paragraphs that use illustration
- studying models to create paragraphs that use illustration

## WHAT IS ILLUSTRATION?

A main idea must be supported by details. Using an illustration is one of the best ways to do this.

> *Illustration* (often called **example** or **exemplification**) is a method of developing an idea by providing one or more instances of that idea. Illustrations or examples serve to clarify the idea, make the idea more convincing, or make an abstract idea more concrete.
>
> **One example of American craftsmanship is the Tiffany lamp.**

Writers use illustration in three basic ways.

1. To provide a list of brief examples, given without any particular grouping:

*Topic sentence*

> <u>As a child, I had pen pals from all over the world</u>. These included my cousin Britt-Marie from Sweden, Ying from Hong Kong, Simone from France, Etsuko from Japan, and several children from Kenya.

2. To provide a list of brief examples arranged into groups:

*Topic sentence*

> <u>As a child, I had pen pals from all over the world</u>. From Europe were my Swedish cousin Britt-Marie and a pretty French girl named Simone. From the Pacific came the beautiful monthly letters of Etsuko and an occasional postcard from Ying in Hong Kong. Finally, from Africa came a number of charming letters from several school-children in Kenya.

3. To select one item from a possible list and develop it more fully into a longer and more developed example, called an **extended example** (possibly consisting of an **anecdote** based on the principles of narration):

*Topic sentence*

> <u>As a child, I had pen pals from all over the world</u>. It all started when my cousin Britt-Marie in Sweden sent me a funny little letter in crazy English. Sitting on our front porch swatting flies one morning in August, I was considering walking the two miles uptown to the library when the mailman handed me an envelope with colorful stamps on it. It was probably the first piece of mail I had ever received. I barely knew I had a cousin Britt-Marie. But there she was—a young girl writing just to me from across the Atlantic Ocean. I was hooked from that very day. Although I eventually had pen pals from many other countries, Britt-Marie remained my favorite. In fact, we still communicate, now by e-mail, at least once every few weeks.

Always remember that the anecdote must support the larger point contained in the topic sentence—namely, the writer had pen pals from all over the world.

# WHERE DOES THE WRITER FIND EXAMPLES?

Writers draw on four main sources for examples.

1. **Personal experience and knowledge of the world.** Writers find supporting examples for their work everywhere, beginning with their own experience. What you have observed and what has happened to you are two excellent sources of examples for your writing. You have gained a great deal of knowledge either formally or informally, and you can call upon that knowledge when you look for examples to illustrate your points.

2. **Imagination.** When writers need examples for their work, they often find it useful to create imaginary examples or situations that provide specific details. Humorous writers do this all the time when they tell jokes. You, too, can use your

imagination to generate examples when your writing does not require strictly factual information. A hypothetical example is particularly useful to illustrate a point, and it often begins with a phrase such as "Imagine the following situation" or "Consider this hypothetical case" or "Ask yourself what would happen if. . . ."

3. **Interviews and surveys.** Obtaining examples through interviews and informal surveys can enrich your writing by allowing you to present very specific information and facts about your main idea. We see and hear interviews on television and radio every day, as people from all walks of life tell their stories on every topic imaginable. We are accustomed to seeing professional interviewers ask questions, but you can also gain examples in this way by talking to your friends and classmates and learning from them.

4. **Outside research.** Printed or electronic material from outside sources can provide specific examples for your work. This research usually involves the resources of a library, using the online databases as well as other online resources. This kind of research is necessary for term papers and many other kinds of college work, and it always requires a careful listing of the sources used.

**EXERCISE**  **1**   ## The Sources for Illustrations

**Each of the following three paragraphs develops an idea by using illustration. Read each paragraph and decide what source the writer used to obtain the illustration. Choose from the following list:**

- example from personal experience or knowledge

- imaginary or hypothetical example

- information from an interview or survey conducted by the writer

- outside research (material found in books, in articles, or on the Internet)

*Topic sentence*   1.     <u>Most students today believe they must learn how to use a computer if they are to be competitive in the job market</u>. A case in point is my first-year writing class. Out of the twenty-three students surveyed, all but two felt they must be computer literate before they leave college or they might not be able to get the jobs they want. Fifteen of the students currently own their own computers and claim they are able to get their college work done more easily. Two of these fifteen students actually have part-time jobs, one in the library and one in the history department, where they both enter data on computers. This seems to show that these students already are at an advantage over the rest of the students who are still learning to use a computer.

**Type of illustration:** _____

*Topic sentence*   2.     <u>Most students today believe they must learn how to use a computer if they are to be competitive in the job market</u>. Just to illustrate, if a person wants a career in auto mechanics and thinks he or she has no need to learn how to use a computer, that person is likely to be surprised. What if the auto mechanic needs to operate a sophisticated computer to determine malfunctions in cars? What if the staff expects the mechanic to understand how to enter data on the office computer and also expects the person to know how to read the computer printouts? What if he or she must go to school to learn the newest technology, and instead of working with actual cars, everyone works on computer simulations?

**Type of illustration:** _____

*Topic sentence*    3.    <u>Most students today realize they must learn how to use computers to compete in the job market</u>. Last semester, I took my first computer course. To my great pleasure, I found that my new skills helped me not only write compositions but also practice my math. I also discovered that I could go online and talk with people all over the world who have interests similar to my own. In addition, I was able to use the computer to access information from the school library. I plan to become a teacher, and I will be able to use my computer skills to make tests and worksheets, research information for class, and help students make discoveries for themselves.

**Type of illustration:** _____

**EXERCISE** 2    ## The Sources for Illustrations

Below is a topic sentence. Write a paragraph in which you support the idea of the topic sentence by using an example from your personal experience or knowledge.

**Topic sentence:** *Many advertising claims are deceptive.*

**Your paragraph:**

_____

_____

_____

_____

_____

_____

_____

**EXERCISE** 3    ## The Sources for Illustrations

Below is a topic sentence. Write a paragraph in which you support the idea by using information from a survey of several of your classmates.

**Topic sentence:** *Taste in music is very personal.*

**Your paragraph:**

_____

_____

_____

_____

_____

_____

_____

_____

## ACHIEVING COHERENCE

### CHOOSING AN ORDER DEPENDING ON THE TYPE OF ILLUSTRATION USED

1. If the illustration is a *story* or an *anecdote,* the writer usually uses *time order.*
2. If the illustration is made up of *several descriptive examples,* the writer might use *spatial order* (top to bottom, right to left, etc.).
3. If the illustration calls for a *logical order,* this logic will determine the sequence.
4. If no special order seems necessary, the writer often places the *strongest or most important example last,* because this is what the reader is likely to remember best.

### USING TRANSITIONS

Writers often signal the beginning of an illustration by using a key phrase. Below is a list of phrases commonly used to signal the beginning of an illustration.

---

**Transitions Commonly Used in Illustration**

| | |
|---|---|
| For example, . . . | Consider the case of . . . |
| Another example is . . . | For instance, . . . |
| To illustrate, . . . | A personal anecdote that |
| An illustration of this is . . . |    illustrates this point is . . . |
| One such case is . . . | To be specific . . . |

---

**EXERCISE  4**

### Analyzing Paragraphs That Use Examples

**Read the following paragraph by Suzanne Britt, and then answer the questions about it.**

*Topic sentence*

   <u>Being a connoisseur of junk has wonderfully mucked up my entire life</u>. You know the song about favorite things like raindrops on roses and whiskers on kittens? Well, I've got my own list of favorite things: I like the insides of filthy bus stations, unsavory characters, a Dr Pepper can floating on the sun-flecked water, Jujubes, the greasy tug and tang of beef jerky wrapped in cellophane, the kitchen drawer beside the phone, the Sunday clutter around the house, the noble whiff of manure, the sweaty odor of a person I love, the smoke-filled room in which I get to inhale the equivalent of eleven cigarettes without breaking my promise to quit, the pigeon droppings in the square, the grease under the fingernails of a gas station attendant (if I can still find one), the rusty Brillo on the sink, the bathroom glass placidly growing bacteria for the whole family, *People* magazine, a dog-eared paperback, a cold pork chop eaten at the refrigerator door.

1. State the topic sentence in your own words. _____

   _____

2. How many examples are given in the paragraph? _____

3. Underline the examples in the paragraph.

4. Does the author use any words or phrases to signal any of the examples? If so, circle each one. _____

5. If there is more than one example, can you suggest any order for them?

   _____

**EXERCISE 5**

### Analyzing Paragraphs That Use Examples

**Read the following paragraph and then answer the questions about it.**

Dr. George Gallup and his American Institute of Public Opinion conducted surveys for two years on the reading habits of Americans in all walks of life and different sections of the land; one of the striking facts "that is scored and under-scored in these studies is the tremendous influence of Hollywood on reading *Topic sentence* tastes." Gallup points out that Hollywood boosts the classics of literature into new and extraordinary popularity. When the movie *David Copperfield* was being publicized, the Cleveland library system ordered more than 125 extra copies of the book to meet the probable rise in demand; and although the system of libraries had 500 copies of the book, library shelves were bare of *David Copperfield* and other Dickens novels for weeks. The film *Wuthering Heights* served as a remarkable boomerang to that book's popularity. Four publishing houses sold out all their editions of the work in a short time, and bookstores and public libraries could not cope with demand after the rediscovery of the Brontë masterpiece.

1. State the topic sentence in your own words. _____

   _____

2. How many examples are given in the paragraph? _____

3. Underline the examples in the paragraph.

4. Does the author use any words or phrases to signal any of the examples? If so, circle each one. _____

5. If there is more than one example, can you suggest any order for the examples?

   _____

   _____

   _____

   _____

   _____

**EXERCISE**  **6**

### Analyzing Paragraphs That Use Examples
**Read the following paragraph and then answer the questions about it.**

*Topic sentence*

One of the most wonderful aspects of Sabatini's teaching was his desire to give encouragement. Even if the student did not have a great voice or did not show true promise, Sabatini would find something to praise, some little ray of hope that might help the student continue in the right direction. Let me relate an anecdote that will demonstrate this man's positive approach. One day, I was called in to Sabatini's studio to play the piano for a new pupil. This young man had come many miles to study with Sabatini, and I could see at once that he was very nervous. That he knew just a few words of Italian only made him more apprehensive. I started to play the music for the test aria. As usual, Sabatini sat in his chair with his eyes closed, listening. The young man's voice floated through the room, small and shaky at first, but growing a little more confident as he went on. Finally, after it was over, we all waited for the great man's judgment. Sabatini looked up and spoke through me. "I cannot do much for this young man," he said slowly, "because God has already done so much for him." When I translated this for the student, his face gained a new color and he smiled for the first time. That day started his period of study with Sabatini, and three years later he made his first appearance in the opera house. I have always known that his great career really began with those first words of encouragement from his teacher.

1.  State the topic sentence in your own words. _____
    _____

2.  How many examples are given in the paragraph? _____

3.  Mark the example (or examples) in the paragraph.

4.  Does the author use any words or phrases to signal the use of an illustration? If so, circle each one. _____

## WRITING A PARAGRAPH USING A STEP-BY-STEP APPROACH TO ILLUSTRATION

Mastering any skill, including writing, requires a disciplined attitude. One way to master the skill of creating a piece of writing is to take a step-by-step approach, focusing on one issue at a time. This approach results in a minimum of stress. Another advantage is that the writer does not miss important points or misunderstand any part of the process. Of course, there are other ways to build effective paragraphs through illustration, but here is one logical method you can use that will always achieve good results.

## Step-by-Step Approach to Writing a Paragraph Using Illustration

1. Compose your topic sentence, being sure to consider carefully your choice of controlling idea.

2. When using examples, consider the options: personal experience, hypothetical examples, interviews or surveys, and research. What type of example will fit your idea best? At this stage, brainstorming with a group of classmates is usually helpful.

3. Decide how many examples you will provide to develop your paragraph. Will there be one extended example with several sentences or several brief examples of one sentence each?

4. If you have more than one example, decide on the order to present them. Many writers start with the least important example and end with the most important.

5. Use complete sentences when you write down your examples. Each example must support the main idea, or the paragraph will lack unity.

6. Write a final sentence that concludes what you want to say about this idea.

7. Copy your sentences into standard paragraph form. Indent five spaces to begin the paragraph and be sure to double-space.

8. Always make a final check for spelling errors and other mistakes such as omitted words.

**NOTE:** When you use a computer spell-check feature, keep in mind that this feature will alert you only to spellings that do not match words in its dictionary. If you type *there* when you mean *their*, the spell-checker will see an acceptable word. When it comes to a final editing, there is no substitute for your own careful reading.

**EXERCISE  7**

### Writing a Paragraph Using a Step-by-Step Approach to Illustration

This exercise will guide you through the construction of a paragraph using illustration. Start with the topic suggested below. Use the eight steps to help you work through the stages of the writing process.

**Topic:**   Animals that make good pets

People have many reasons for enjoying pets, ranging from the desire for simple companionship to a need for protection. In recent years, the list of animals has expanded beyond the traditional animals we all know—dogs,

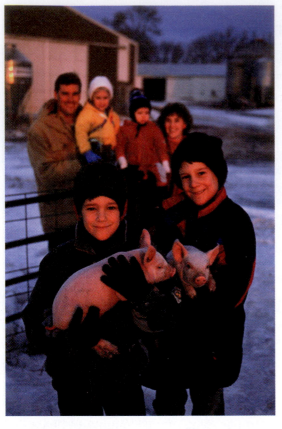

cats, fish, and birds—as people have chosen some very exotic animals to keep as pets. People have been known to keep deadly snakes in their homes, and in New York City a man was discovered to have a dangerous Bengal tiger in his small apartment. Keeping in mind the subject of traditional and nontraditional pets, choose a controlling idea about keeping a pet, an idea that will give you the opportunity to use several specific examples of pets people like to have. For instance, you might write about whether society should outlaw certain pets as inappropriate or even dangerous or, if you could choose two or three pets for yourself, which ones you would choose and why.

1.  Topic sentence:

    _____

    _____

2.  Which type of example (or types of examples) will you use?

    _____

    _____

3.  How many examples will you give? _____

    _____

4.  List your examples in order. (One good example may be enough. Probably no more than three or four brief examples would fit in one paragraph.)

    a.  _____

    b.  _____

    c.  _____

    d.  _____

5.  Write down each example.

    _____

    _____

    _____

    _____

    _____

    _____

    _____

    _____

    _____

    _____

6.  Write the sentence that will conclude your paragraph.

_____

_____

7.  On a separate piece of paper or on the computer, copy your sentences into standard paragraph form.

8.  Do a final reading to check for errors and omissions.

**EXERCISE** **8**   **Writing a Paragraph Using a Step-by-Step Approach to Illustration**

This exercise will guide you through the construction of a paragraph using illustration. Start with the topic suggested below. Use the eight steps to help you work through the stages of the writing process.

**Topic:**   Examples of art in our daily lives

We often think of *art* as something far removed from our lives, intended only for galleries and museums. However, if we think about the items we use every day (our dishes, our clothes, the colors we choose to paint our walls), we realize that our choices of these items represent our individual attempts to make our lives more beautiful and more satisfying. What examples can you give that show your own artistic taste or style? In what ways have you tried to make your own world include things of beauty or artistic value?

1.  Topic sentence:

_____

_____

2.  Which type of example (or types of examples) will you use?

_____

_____

3.  How many examples will you give? _____

4.  List your examples in order. (One good example may be enough. Probably no more than three or four brief examples would fit in one paragraph.)

a.  _____

b.  _____

c.  _____

d.  _____

5.  Write down each example.

_____

_____

_____

_____

_____

_____

_____

_____

_____

_____

6. Write the sentence that will conclude your paragraph.

_____

_____

7. On a separate piece of paper or on the computer, copy your sentences into standard paragraph form.

8. Do a final reading to check for errors and omissions.

# STUDYING MODEL PARAGRAPHS TO CREATE PARAGRAPHS USING ILLUSTRATION

## ASSIGNMENT 1: A PERSON'S PASSION

Many people are passionate about something in their lives. Perhaps it is a sport or perhaps it is an interest in music or collecting. Study the paragraph below. Use it as a model to write your own paragraph giving examples that show how a person's passion occupies an important place in his or her life. The following paragraph is taken from "The Joy of Reading and Writing: Superman and Me," by Sherman Alexie.

### Model Paragraph: A Passion for Reading

*Topic sentence*

My father, who is one of the few Indians who went to Catholic school on purpose, was an avid reader of westerns, spy thrillers, murder mysteries, gangster epics, basketball player biographies, and anything else he could find. He bought his books by the pound at Dutch's Pawn Shop, Goodwill, Salvation Army, and Value Village. When he had extra money, he bought new novels at supermarkets, convenience stores, and hospital gift shops. Our house was filled with books. They were stacked in crazy piles in the bathroom, bedrooms, and living room. In a fit of unemployment-inspired creative energy, my father built a set of bookshelves and soon filled them with a random assortment of books about the Kennedy assassination, Watergate, the Vietnam War, and the entire 23-book series of the Apache westerns. <u>My father loved books.</u> Since I loved my father with an aching devotion, I decided to love books as well.

*Ten suggested topics*

Things people might be passionate about:

1. Video games

2. News

3. Movies

4. Music

5. Cooking

6. New technology

7. A new pet

8. A sport

9. Fashion

10. Celebrity watching

## ASSIGNMENT 2: SHOPPING

Most people have very strong feelings about having to do certain shopping tasks. Write a paragraph that gives one or more examples of your worst or favorite shopping tasks. The following paragraph is taken from Phyllis Rose's essay "Shopping and Other Spiritual Adventures in America Today."

*Model Paragraph: Shopping for Blue Jeans*

*Topic sentence*

Try to think of a kind of shopping in which the object is all important and the pleasure of shopping is at a minimum. For example, consider the purchase of blue jeans. I buy new blue jeans as seldom as possible because the experience is so humiliating. For every pair that looks good on me, fifteen look grotesque. But even shopping for blue jeans at Bob's Surplus on Main Street—no frills, bare-bones shopping—is an event in the life of the spirit. Once again I have to come to terms with the fact that I will never look good in Levi's. Much as I want to be mainstream, I never will be.

*Ten suggested topics*    Shopping

1.  For weekly groceries

2.  For a bathing suit

3.  For an outfit to wear to a party

4.  For a gift for a very fussy relative

5.  By catalogue

6.  On the Home Shopping Network

7.  For a used car

8.  For bargains

9.  For a gift for a child

10. For shoes

## ASSIGNMENT 3: OUR EXPECTATIONS OF OTHERS

We enter into relationships believing that people will behave in an expected way. Often we are sadly disappointed. Write a paragraph in which you give one or more examples of how you expect people to act when they are in certain relationships. The following paragraph is from a piece of advice written by the famous columnist Ann Landers.

## Model Paragraph: Advice to Parents

*Topic sentence*

<u>Parents have the right to expect their children to pick up after themselves and perform simple household chores</u>. For example, every member of the family over six years of age should clean the bathtub and the sink so they will be in respectable condition for the next person. He or she should also run errands and help in the kitchen if asked—in other words, carry a share of the load without feeling persecuted. The days of "hired help" are, for the most part, gone. And this is good. Boys as well as girls should be taught to cook and clean, do laundry, and sew on buttons. This is not "sissy stuff." It makes for independence and self-reliance.

*Ten suggested topics*    Expectations of

1. Domestic partners

2. Grandparents

3. Teachers

4. Students

5. Waiters

6. Customers

7. Patients

8. Employers

9. Coworkers

10. Friends

## ASSIGNMENT 4: REMEDIES TO CURE WHAT AILS US

Health-food stores are enjoying great popularity, partly because so many people believe that natural products can alleviate a wide range of complaints. Write a paragraph in which you give examples of popular trends for solving an everyday problem. In the following paragraph, the author provides several examples of currently available remedies that people are using in place of traditional medicine.

### Model Paragraph: The Popularity of Natural Remedies

*Topic sentence*

    Many stores today are selling newly accepted natural remedies for all types of human ailments. For instance, people with AIDS use the herb astragalus as a natural way to boost their immune systems. Other people concerned about their immune systems but only worried about colds or flu use echinacea, a plant extract, to help them resist sickness. People who want to lose weight also are seeking out help from natural remedies. One of the most popular examples of remedies for overweight people is the Chinese herb ma huang. This is a powerful substance and can be dangerous for some because it can cause heart attacks or strokes, especially if it is used with caffeine. One of the cures most sought after is the cure for cancer, and again natural substances hold out some promise of relief. For example, shark cartilage is believed by many to stop the growth of cancerous tumors or even eliminate them altogether. Many users of herbs and other natural healing substances take these supplements to improve their general health. For instance, ginseng is used throughout the world as a revitalizing tonic, and garlic has been said to combat infections, prevent blood clots, and lower blood pressure. Although many claims are made for natural remedies, we do not always have proof that they work as well as some people say they do.

*Ten suggested topics*

Remedies for

1. Stress
2. The common cold
3. The "blues"
4. The hiccups
5. Thumbsucking
6. Smoking
7. Shyness
8. Writer's block
9. Insomnia
10. Boredom

## Exploring Online

Go to **www.cengage.com/devenglish/scarry/writersworkplace** to find the **Writer's Online Workplace,** a website designed for students using this book. You will find links to handouts, interactive quizzes, and other online resources as you explore the following topic:

• using examples in paragraphs

# Working Together

## RESEARCHING EXAMPLES: PHOBIAS

> Roberto Gomez has a serious problem. His job involves a significant amount of travel, but he has an abnormal fear of flying. He may have to change jobs if he can't find a way to deal with his fear.

A phobia is deep fear of an object or situation. All of us fear one thing or another, but when a fear is abnormally deep and does not have any logical basis, we call it a phobia. People who suffer from phobias often realize that their emotional reactions are unreasonable, but they cannot control them. They also suffer from real physical reactions, including a pounding of the blood, a sinking feeling in the stomach, trembling, and a feeling of faintness. Very often, phobias are the result of traumatic experiences in childhood.

### Working in Groups

Working in groups of three or so, locate information on at least three phobias. Common ones include *claustrophobia, agoraphobia, acrophobia,* and *xenophobia.* Find enough information about these phobias so that you would be able to write a well-developed paragraph on each one. This could be the basis for an essay on the topic. You will want to define each phobia, and you will also want to explain how the phobia complicates the life of the person who has to deal with it.

## PORTFOLIO SUGGESTION

When your group finds an article or some other source of information on one of the selected phobias, print out or make copies of the material. Each group member will then have information. Add your paragraphs on phobias in your portfolio. You are building material for possible essays and research papers.

# DEVELOPING PARAGRAPHS: NARRATION

# 19

If you are an effective storyteller or if you like to have a good story told to you, you will enjoy this chapter on narration. You will improve your writing skills by focusing on these narrative elements:

**CHAPTER OBJECTIVES**

- **making a point**
- ordering details according to **time sequence**
- using **transitions** to show a shift in time
- taking a step-by-step approach to create narrative paragraphs
- studying model paragraphs to create narrative paragraphs

## WHAT IS NARRATION?

> **Narration** is the oldest and best-known form of verbal communication. It is, quite simply, the telling of a story.

Every culture in the world, past and present, has used narration to provide entertainment as well as information for the people of that culture. Because everyone likes a good story, the many forms of narration, such as novels, short stories, soap operas, and full-length movies, are always popular.

The following narrative paragraph, taken from Helen Keller's autobiography, tells the story of her realization that every object has a name. The paragraph shows the enormous difficulties faced by a seven-year-old girl who was unable to see, hear, or speak.

> The morning after my teacher came, she led me into her room and gave me a doll. The little blind children at the Perkins Institution had sent it and Laura Bridgman had dressed it; but I did not know this until afterward. When

(continued on next page)

*Topic sentence*

I had played with it a little while, Miss Sullivan slowly spelled into my hand the word "d-o-l-l." I was at once interested in this finger play and tried to imitate it. When I finally succeeded in making the letters correctly, I was flushed with childish pleasure and pride. Running downstairs to my mother I held up my hand and made the letters for doll. I did not know that I was spelling a word or even that words existed; I was simply making my fingers go in monkey-like imitation. In the days that followed I learned to spell in this uncomprehending way a great many words, among them *pin*, *hat*, *cup* and a few verbs like *sit, stand,* and *walk*. But my teacher had been with me several weeks before I understood that everything has a name.

# USING NARRATION TO MAKE A POINT

At one time or another, you have probably met a person who loves to talk on and on without making any real point. This person is likely to tell you everything that happened during the day, including every sight and every sound. Your reaction to the unnecessary and seemingly endless supply of details is probably one of fatigue and hope for a quick getaway. This is not narration at its best! A good story is almost always told to make a point: it can make us laugh, it can make us understand, or it can change our attitudes.

When Helen Keller tells the story of her early experiences with her teacher, she is careful to use only those details that are relevant to her story. For example, the doll her teacher gave her is an important part of the story. This doll reveals not only something about Helen Keller's teacher but also the astounding fact that Helen did not know that objects have names. With this story, we see the beginning of Helen's long struggle to communicate with other people.

**EXERCISE  1**

## Using Narration to Make a Point

**Each of the following is the beginning of a topic sentence for a narrative paragraph. Complete each sentence by providing a controlling idea that could serve as the point for the story.**

1. When the four-year-old boy flushed the puppy down the toilet by mistake, the fire department _____

   _____

2. After all my father's efforts to find a job were unsuccessful, he realized

   _____

   _____

3. After claiming for many years to believe in family values, the governor revealed _____

   _____

4. When the child arrived at the emergency room, the doctors thought

_____

_____

5. Following the death of Michael Jackson, interest in his life

_____

_____

**EXERCISE  2**

## Using Narration to Make a Point

**Each of the following is the beginning of a topic sentence for a narrative paragraph. Complete each sentence by providing a controlling idea that could serve as the point for the story.**

1. When I looked more closely at the man, I realized _____

_____

2. When the president finished his speech, commentators criticized _____

_____

_____

3. By the end of the campaign, the advisors of the candidate decided

_____

4. After the college changed the requirements for a degree, students believed

_____

_____

5. When nobody could get past the office secretary, we concluded that _____

_____

**EXERCISE  3**

## Using Narration to Make a Point

**Each of the following is the beginning of a topic sentence for a narrative paragraph. Complete each sentence by providing a controlling idea that could serve as the point for the story.**

1. When the photographer finished showing his slides, the audience thought

_____

_____

2. When there were so many responses to the ad, the homeowner concluded

_____

_____

3. After two days of trying to sell magazine subscriptions, I knew _____

_____

4. After the team of scientists had actually performed the crucial experiment in the lab, they understood _____

_____

5. The first time I tried to cook dinner for a large group of people, I found out

_____

_____

# ACHIEVING COHERENCE

## PLACING DETAILS IN ORDER OF TIME SEQUENCE

When you write a narrative paragraph, the details given are usually ordered according to time sequence. That is, you tell what happened first, then what happened next, and next, until finally you get to the end of the story. In your narrative, you could be describing events that took place in a matter of minutes or over a period of many years.

In the following paragraph, the story takes place in a single day. The six events that made the day a disaster are given in the order they happened. Although some stories flash back to the past or forward to the future, most use the chronological order of the events.

*Topic sentence*

<u>My day was a disaster.</u> First, it had snowed during the night, which meant I had to shovel before I could leave for work. I was mad that I hadn't gotten up earlier. Then I had trouble starting my car, and to make matters worse, my daughter wasn't feeling well and said she didn't think she should go to school. When I eventually did arrive at work, I was twenty minutes late. Soon I found out my assistant had forgotten to make copies of a report I needed at nine o'clock. I quickly had to make another plan. By five o'clock, I was looking forward to getting my paycheck. Foolish woman! When I went to pick it up, the office assistant told me that something had gone wrong with the computers. I would not be able to get my check until Tuesday. Disappointed, I walked down the hill to the parking lot. There I met my final defeat. In my hurry to park the car in the morning, I had left my parking lights on. Now my battery was dead. Even an optimist like me had the right to be discouraged!

**EXERCISE**  **4**

### Placing Details in Order of Time Sequence

The topic given is followed by supporting details. These supporting details are not in any particular order. Put the events in order according to time sequence by placing the appropriate number in the space provided.

An emergency in an apartment building

___3___ He ran to the corner and pulled the fire alarm.

___1___ The fire began around six o'clock.

___4___ When the firefighters came, they found flames leaping out of the third-floor windows.

___2___ A man walking his dog spotted smoke coming from the building.

___5___ Official orders were given to evacuate the building.

**EXERCISE 5**

### Placing Details in Order of Time Sequence

The topic below is followed by supporting details. These supporting details are not in any particular order. Put the events in order according to time sequence by placing the appropriate number in the space provided.

The story of Flight 1549

___6___ Another possibility was to try to get to an airport in New Jersey, but again there was not enough power.

___7___ A flock of birds had hit the engines without warning.

___8___ Amazingly everybody survived this crash, which has become known as "Miracle on the Hudson."

___1___ The flight began at La Guardia Airport without incident.

___4___ The pilot spoke to the air traffic controllers and discussed their options.

___5___ One possibility was to return to the original airport, but the airplane did not have enough power.

___6___ Everyone was shocked when the pilot announced he would have to ditch the plane in the frigid Hudson River.

___3___ Suddenly, the pilot and co-pilot experienced a loss of power in both engines.

**EXERCISE 6**

### Placing Details in Order of Time Sequence

The topic given is followed by supporting details. These supporting details are not in any particular order. Put the events in order according to time sequence by placing the appropriate number in the space provided.

From the life of Sojourner Truth, crusader, preacher, and the first African American woman to speak out against slavery

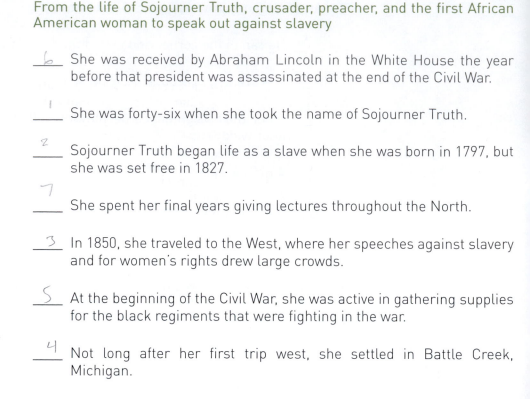

__6__ She was received by Abraham Lincoln in the White House the year before that president was assassinated at the end of the Civil War.

__1__ She was forty-six when she took the name of Sojourner Truth.

__2__ Sojourner Truth began life as a slave when she was born in 1797, but she was set free in 1827.

__7__ She spent her final years giving lectures throughout the North.

__3__ In 1850, she traveled to the West, where her speeches against slavery and for women's rights drew large crowds.

__5__ At the beginning of the Civil War, she was active in gathering supplies for the black regiments that were fighting in the war.

__4__ Not long after her first trip west, she settled in Battle Creek, Michigan.

## USING TRANSITIONS THAT SHOW A SHIFT IN TIME

> *Transitions* are words and phrases that help a reader move smoothly from one idea to another and make the proper connection between those ideas.

Although transitions must not be overused, they are important tools for every writer. Here is the Helen Keller paragraph you studied previously, this time with each of the transitional words and phrases printed in boldface.

**The morning after** my teacher came, she led me into her room and gave me a doll. The little blind children at the Perkins Institution had sent it and Laura Bridgman had dressed it; but I did not know this **until afterward.** When I had played with it **a little while,** Miss Sullivan slowly spelled into my hand the word "d-o-l-l." I was **at once** interested in this finger play and tried to imitate it. When I **finally** succeeded in making the letters correctly, I was flushed with childish pleasure and pride. Running downstairs to my mother I held up my hand and made the letters for doll. I did not know that I was spelling a word or even that words existed; I was simply making my fingers go in monkey-like imitation. **In the days that followed** I learned to spell in this uncomprehending way a great many words, among them *pin, hat, cup* and a few verbs like *sit, stand,* and *walk.* But my teacher had been with me **several weeks** before I understood that everything has a name.

Notice how the time transitions used in this paragraph make the order of events clear. *"The morning after my teacher came"* gives the reader the sense that the action of the story is being told day by day. In the second sentence, Helen Keller gives information she learned *afterward.* The writer then tells us that when she had played with the doll *a little while,* she *at once* became interested in the connection between an object and the word for that object. This realization was one of the central lessons in young Helen Keller's education, and it became the starting point for all of her later learning. She uses two more transitional phrases to tell us about the beginning of this education: *In the days that followed,* we learn, she mastered a great many words, although it took her *several weeks* before she learned the even more important concept that everything has a name. In addition to the fact that these transitions make the sequence of events clear, they further emphasize the intended meaning of the sentence, that it was the gradual dawning on Helen Keller's part that led to her realization that every object has a name. We need transitions in narration to establish the passage of time.

As you write your own narrative paragraphs, you will find yourself using your own transitional words and expressions. However, as a reminder and a guide, the following chart will serve as a helpful reference.

## Transitions Commonly Used in Narration to Show a Shift in Time

| Expresses the past | Expresses the present | Expresses time close to the present | Expresses a long passage of time |
| --- | --- | --- | --- |
| recently | now; by now | within a few minutes | several weeks later |
| previously | at once | soon; soon afterward | the following month |
| earlier | suddenly | later; later on | finally |
| in the past | immediately | after a little while | eventually |
| a few days ago | meanwhile | then | in the end |
| a hundred years ago | at the same time | next; the next day | |

**EXERCISE**  **7**    ### Working with Transitions

**Below is a paragraph taken from an essay by John McMurtry on the topic of the violent nature of football. Fill in each of the blanks with a transition of time that might have been the author's choice.**

[1]_____ my neck got a hard crick in it. I couldn't turn my head; to look left or right I'd have to turn my whole body. [2]But I'd had cricks in my neck since I started playing grade-school football and hockey, so I just ignored it. [3]_____ I began to notice that when I reached for any sort of large book (which I do pretty often as a philosophy teacher at the University of Guelph) I had trouble lifting it with one hand. [4]I was losing the strength in my left arm, and I had

such a steady pain in my back I often had to stretch out on the floor of the room I was in to relieve the pressure. **5**_____ I mentioned to my brother, an orthopedic surgeon, that I'd lost the power in my arm since my neck began to hurt. **6**_____ I was in a Toronto hospital not sure whether I might end up with a wasted upper limb. **7**Apparently the steady pounding I had received playing college and professional football in the late 1950s and early 1960s had driven my head into my backbone so that the discs had crumpled together at the neck—"acute herniation"—and had cut the nerves to my left arm like a pinched telephone wire (without nerve stimulation, of course, the muscles atrophy, leaving the arm crippled). **8**So I spent my Christmas holidays in the hospital in heavy traction and for much of_____ my neck was in a brace. **9**_____ most of the pain has gone, and I've recovered most of the strength in my arm. **10**But _____ I still have to don the brace, and surgery remains a possibility.

**EXERCISE 8**

## Working with Transitions

**Below is a narrative paragraph. On the lines provided, list all the transitions of time that give order to the paragraph.**

> By now, Jason was skating along feeling in the best of moods. He was aware every moment that he was wearing his new pair of roller blades, and several times he even smiled from so much inner pleasure. He hardly noticed when suddenly he found himself skating down his own street. Immediately, neighborhood children spotted him and ran up to him, calling to him by name, "Jason, Jason, where did you get those skates?" In a short time, Jason found himself surrounded by nine or ten children who were running alongside him. Finally, with a flair, he turned, stopped dead, and blurted out happily, "It's my birthday today!"

_____    _____

_____    _____

_____    _____

_____

**EXERCISE 9**

## Working with Transitions

**A narrative paragraph from a story by the Russian writer Ivan Turgenev follows. Note all the transitions of time that give order to the paragraph and list them on the lines provided.**

> I went to the right through the bushes. Meantime the night had crept close and grown up like a storm cloud; it seemed as though, with the mists of evening, darkness was rising up on all sides and flowing down from overhead. I had come upon some sort of little, untrodden, overgrown path; I walked along it, gazing intently before me. Soon all was blackness and

silence around—only the quail's cry was heard from time to time. Some small nightbird, flitting noiselessly near the ground on its soft wings, almost flapped against me and scurried away in alarm. I came out on the farther side of the bushes, and made my way along a field by the hedge. By now I could hardly make out distant objects; the field showed dimly white around; beyond it rose up a sullen darkness, which seemed to be moving up closer in huge masses every instant. My steps gave a muffled sound in the air that grew colder and colder. The pale sky began again to grow blue—but it was the blue of night. The tiny stars glimmered and twinkled in it.

_____        _____

_____        _____

_____        _____

## WRITING A NARRATIVE PARAGRAPH USING A STEP-BY-STEP APPROACH

Mastering any skill, including writing, requires a disciplined attitude. One way to master the skill of creating a piece of writing is to take a step-by-step approach, focusing on one issue at a time. This approach results in a minimum of stress. Another advantage is that the writer does not miss important points or misunderstand any part of the process. Of course, there are other ways to build effective narrative paragraphs, but here is one logical method you can use that will always achieve good results.

### Step-by-Step Approach to Writing a Narrative Paragraph

1. Study the given topic, and then plan your topic sentence with its controlling idea.

2. List all the events that come to your mind when you think about the story you have chosen.

3. Choose the important events, dropping any that do not directly relate to your controlling idea.

4. Put your list in the correct time sequence.

5. Write one complete sentence for each of the events you have chosen from your list, adding any significant details.

6. Write a concluding statement that gives some point to the events of the story.

7. Copy your sentences into standard paragraph form.

8. Always make a final check for spelling errors and other mistakes, such as omitted words.

**NOTE:** When you use a computer spell-check feature, keep in mind that this feature will alert you only to spellings that do not match words in its dictionary. If you type *there* when you mean *their,* the spell-checker will see an acceptable word. When it comes to a final editing, there is no substitute for your own careful reading.

**EXERCISE 10**

## Writing a Narrative Paragraph Using a Step-by-Step Approach

This exercise will guide you through the construction of a complete narrative paragraph. Start with the suggested topic. Use the eight steps to help you work through the stages of the writing process.

**Topic:** Nearly every family has a favorite story they like to tell about one of their members, often a humorous incident that happened to one of them. There are also crises and tragic moments in the life of every family. Choose a story, funny or tragic, from the life of a family member you have known.

1.    Topic sentence: _____

       _____

       _____

2.    Make a list of the events that took place.

   a. _____

   b. _____

   c. _____

   d. _____

   e. _____

   f. _____

   g. _____

   h. _____

   i. _____

   j. _____

3.    Circle the five or six events you believe are the most important for the point of the story.

4.    Put your final choices in order by numbering each of them.

5.    Using your final list, write at least one sentence for each event you have chosen.

   a. _____

       _____

b. _____

_____

c. _____

_____

d. _____

_____

e. _____

_____

f. _____

_____

6.  Write a concluding statement. _____

_____

_____

7.  On a separate piece of paper or on the computer, copy your sentences into standard paragraph form.

8.  Do a final reading to check for errors and omissions.

**EXERCISE  11**     ### Writing a Narrative Paragraph Using a Step-by-Step Approach

**This exercise will guide you through the construction of a complete narrative paragraph. Start with the suggested topic. Use the eight steps to help you work through the stages of the writing process.**

**Topic:** Tell the story of an incident you witnessed that revealed an unfortunate lack of sensitivity (or even cruelty) on someone's part. What did you observe the person doing? How did other people react? What did you do or what do you wish you had done in response to this incident?

1.  Topic sentence: _____

_____

2.  Make a list of the events that took place.

a. _____

b. _____

c. _____

d. _____

e. _____

f. _____

g. _____

h. _____

i. _____

j. _____

3. Circle the five or six events you believe are the most important for the point of the story.

4. Put your final choices in order by numbering each of them.

5. Using your final list, write at least one sentence for each event you have chosen.

a. _____

_____

b. _____

_____

c. _____

_____

d. _____

_____

e. _____

_____

f. _____

_____

6. Write a concluding statement. _____

_____

_____

7. On a separate piece of paper or on the computer, copy your sentences into standard paragraph form.

8. Do a final reading to check for errors and omissions.

## STUDYING MODEL PARAGRAPHS TO CREATE PARAGRAPHS USING NARRATION

### ASSIGNMENT 1: THE STORY OF HOW YOU FACED A NEW CHALLENGE

Write a paragraph telling the story of a day when you faced an important challenge of some kind. It could have been a challenge in school, at home, or on the job. The following paragraph was written by the journalist Betty Rollin who began her career in the days when typewriters, not computers, were the instruments used by writers.

**Model Paragraph: *Deadline***

*Topic sentence*

 When I awoke that morning I hit the floor running. I washed my face, brushed my teeth, got a pot of coffee going, tightened the sash on my bathrobe, snapped my typewriter out of its case, placed it on the kitchen table, retrieved my notes from the floor where they were stacked in manila folders, unwrapped a pack of bond paper, put the top sheet in the typewriter, looked at it, put my head on the keys, wrapped my arms around its base and cried.

*Ten suggested topics*

1. The day I started a new job

2. My first day in a difficult course

3. The day I began my first research paper

4. The day I organized my room

5. The day of an important job interview

6. The day I faced a large debt

7. The day I had to end a relationship

8. The day I started driving lessons

9. The day I was faced with a death in the family

10. The day I met a deadline

## ASSIGNMENT 2: THE STORY OF A FIGHT OR ARGUMENT

Write a paragraph in which you tell the story of a fight or confrontation you were involved in or witnessed. Include the important details that will hold your reader's attention. The following paragraph, from Albert Halper's short story "Prelude," tells the story of a street fight.

### Model Paragraph: The Fight

*Topic sentence*

But the people just stood there afraid to do a thing. Then while a few guys held me, Gooley and about four others went for the stand, turning it over and mussing and stamping on all the newspapers they could find. Syl started to scratch them, so they hit her. Then I broke away to help her, and then they started socking me too. My father tried to reach me, but three guys kept him away. Four guys got me down and started kicking me and all the time my father was begging them to let me up and Syl was screaming at the people to help. And while I was down, my face was squeezed against some papers on the sidewalk telling about Austria and I guess I went nuts while they kept hitting me, and I kept seeing the headlines against my nose.

*Ten suggested topics*

A confrontation between

1. Two friends

2. Two neighbors

3. An angry customer and a store employee

4. A frustrated parent and a child

5. A manager and an unhappy employee

6. A judge and an unwilling witness

7. A museum guard and a careless tourist

8. A politician and an angry citizen

9. Two siblings

10. Two roommates

## ASSIGNMENT 3: THE BEGINNING OF A SPECIAL RELATIONSHIP

Write a paragraph that tells the story of how you became close to another person. Select one particular moment when the relationship changed from casual friendliness to something deeper and more lasting. Perhaps you shared an experience that brought you together. The following paragraph, taken from Morley Callaghan's short story "One Spring Night," tells of a young man who is falling in love.

## Model Paragraph: Falling in Love

*Topic sentence*

<u>Bob had taken her out a few times when he had felt like having some girl to talk to who knew him and liked him</u>. And tonight he was leaning back good-humoredly, telling her one thing and then another with the wise self-assurance he usually had when with her; but gradually, as he watched her, he found himself talking more slowly, his voice grew serious and much softer, and then finally he leaned across the table toward her as though he had just discovered that her neck was full and soft with her spring coat thrown open, and that her face under her little black straw hat tilted back on her head had a new, eager beauty. Her warm, smiling softness was so close to him that he smiled a bit shyly.

*Ten suggested topics*

1.  A moment when my relationship with a parent changed

2.  The day my relationship with a fellow student changed

3.  A moment when I understood my child in a new way

4.  The day I learned something new about a neighborhood merchant

5.  The day I shared an experience with a fellow worker

6.  The day I made friends with someone older or younger than myself

7.  The moment my relationship with a classmate changed

8.  The moment when my attitude about a parent or grandparent changed

9.  The time when a stranger became a friend

10. The time when a relationship deepened

## ASSIGNMENT 4: YOU WON'T BELIEVE WHAT HAPPENED TO ME TODAY!

Tell the story of a day you found yourself facing a difficult or frustrating situation. The following paragraph, from Berton Roueche's short story "Phone Call," describes a day in the life of a young man, a day when nothing seemed to go right.

### Model Paragraph: The Truck Breaks Down

I got out of the truck and got down on my knees and twisted my neck and looked underneath. Everything looked O.K. There wasn't anything hanging down or anything. I got up and opened the hood and looked at the engine. I don't know too much about engines—only what I picked up working around Lindy's Service Station the summer before last. But the engine looked O.K., too. I slammed down the hood and lighted a cigarette. It really had me beat. A school bus from that convent over in Sag Harbor came piling around the bend, and all the girls leaned out the windows and yelled. I just waved. They didn't mean anything by it—just a bunch of kids going home. The bus went on up the road and into the woods and out of sight. I got back in the truck and started it up again. It sounded fine. I put it in gear and let out the clutch and gave it the gas, and nothing happened. The bastard just sat there. So it was probably the transmission. I shut it off and got out. There was nothing to do but call the store. I still had three or four deliveries that had to be made and it was getting kind of late. I knew what Mr. Lester would say, but this was one time when he couldn't blame me. *It wasn't my fault*. It was him himself that told me to take this truck.

*Topic sentence* (margin note)

*Ten suggested topics* (margin note)

1.  The day I discovered I had been deceived

2.  The day I was falsely accused

3.  The day I lost an important game

4.  The day I was confronted by the police (or by some other authority)

5.  The day I was shocked by . . .

6.  The day nothing went right

7.  The day I failed to . . .

8.  The day I lost my keys (or some other important item)

9.  The day I could have used a cell phone.

10. The day I was fired

## Exploring Online

Go to **www.cengage.com/devenglish/scarry/writersworkplace** to find the **Writer's Online Workplace,** a website designed for students using this book. You will find links to handouts, interactive quizzes, and other online resources as you explore the following topic:

- writing a narrative composition
- the importance of sentence order

# Working Together

## TELLING STORIES THAT MAKE A POINT

It is believed that Aesop was a Greek slave who lived about 2,500 years ago. He is credited with over two hundred fables, short tales that point to an instructive moral at the end. Aesop's fables have become part of our international literary heritage. The following fable is a classic example of a tale from Aesop, one with a timeless moral at the end.

A farmer realized he was dying. He did not want to leave this world without being sure that all of his sons knew how to be good farmers. He called them to his bedside and said, "My sons, I am about to depart from this world. After I go, however, I want you to search for what I have hidden in the vineyard. When you find it, you will possess all that I am able to leave you."

The young men were convinced their father had buried some great treasure on the property. After he died, they all took their shovels and dug up every part of the vineyard. They found no treasure at all, but their digging helped the grapevines so much that the next year's harvest saw the best crop of grapes in many years.

**Moral:** Our greatest treasure is what comes from our own hard work.

### Group Discussion

Nearly all of us would like to get something for nothing? Have you ever heard of someone who reminds you of the farmer's sons in the fable? Do you know people who gamble? Have you heard of people who expect their family to support them instead of taking responsibility for their actions? Have you read about people who have inherited money or have won a lottery but who did not know how to handle the money? Share these stories with your classmates.

On the other hand, what is a story you could share about someone who has worked very hard. To what extent is Aesop's moral true, that our greatest treasure is what we achieve by our own hard work?

## PORTFOLIO SUGGESTION

Write one of the following narratives to keep in your portfolio:

1. A fable with a one sentence moral at the end.

2. A narrative paragraph that tells the story of someone you know who either tried to get something for nothing or worked very hard to achieve a goal. Be sure your story has a point at the end.

# DEVELOPING PARAGRAPHS: DESCRIPTION

# 20

To create effective paragraphs of description, a writer must call upon the five senses. This chapter focuses on several skills important to descriptive writing:

**CHAPTER OBJECTIVES**

- creating a topic sentence containing a **dominant impression**
- avoiding vague dominant impressions
- supporting the topic sentence with details that evoke **sensory images**
- putting the details in a logical order, usually a **spatial order** of some kind
- taking a step-by-step approach to create descriptive paragraphs
- studying model paragraphs to create descriptive paragraphs

## WHAT IS DESCRIPTION?

One method of developing a paragraph is to use descriptive details. For example, when you read the opening pages of almost any novel, you notice that the author has begun the story with one or more paragraphs of description that set the stage for that story.

> **Description** uses sensory images to create a picture with words.

The following example comes from a personal essay written by Joseph H. Suina. In this paragraph, he describes his childhood home. As you study this description, look for the details that make this paragraph effective.

*Topic sentence*

> <u>During those years, Grandmother and I lived beside the plaza in a humble one-room house</u>. It consisted of a traditional fireplace, a makeshift cabinet for our few tin cups and dishes, and a wooden crate that held our two buckets of all-purpose water. At the far end of the room were two rolls of bedding we used as comfortable sitting "couches." Consisting of thick quilts, sheepskin, and assorted blankets, these bed rolls were undone each night. A wooden pole the length of one side of the room was suspended about 10 inches from the ceiling beams. A modest collection of colorful shawls, blankets, and sashes draped over the pole making this part of the room most interesting. In one corner was a bulky metal trunk for our ceremonial wear and few valuables. A dresser, which was traded for some of my grandmother's well-known pottery, held the few articles of clothing we owned and the "goody bag." Grandmother always had a flour sack filled with candy, store bought cookies, and Fig Newtons. These were saturated with a sharp odor of moth balls. Nevertheless, they made a fine snack with coffee before we turned in for the night. Tucked securely in my blankets, I listened to one of her stories or accounts of how it was when she was a little girl. These accounts seemed so old fashioned compared to the way we lived. Sometimes she softly sang a song from a ceremony. In this way I fell asleep each night.

When you use effective sensory images in your writing, the descriptive details that result will be memorable and convincing to your reader. Such details will make a tremendous difference in how well your reader is able to imagine what you are describing. You can demonstrate this to yourself by answering the following questions about the descriptive paragraph above on Suina's childhood home.

1. What do you see? _____

    _____

2. What do you hear? _____

3. What suggests how something would feel to the touch? _____

    _____

4. What can you smell? _____

5. What can you taste? _____

# WORKING WITH DESCRIPTION

## SELECTING THE DOMINANT IMPRESSION

It is not enough to give random pieces of information about the particular person, object, or place you are describing. The overall effect of a paragraph of descriptive writing should be the sense of a *dominant impression*. Each individual sentence that you write should be part of a picture that becomes clear when the reader finishes the paragraph.

> The **dominant impression** is the overall impression created by a descriptive piece of writing. This impression is often summed up by one word or phrase in the topic sentence.
>
> **Topic sentence:** My childhood home was *humble*.

When you write a descriptive paragraph, you should know what impression you are trying to achieve with your supporting details. For example, when you describe a place, the dominant impression you want to create could be one of *comfort* or it could be one of *elegance*. When you write a description of a person, you might want to present the impression of an outgoing, gregarious person or perhaps the very opposite, that of a *shy, withdrawing* sort of person. Often it is useful to incorporate the dominant impression into the topic sentence. This will help you focus as you write and will leave no doubt in the reader's mind as to the direction of your thinking. All the other sentences should support this impression you are working to create.

The following charts contain two short lists of possible dominant impressions. Use them as a guide while you work through this chapter.

---

## Dominant Impressions for Descriptions of Place

| | | | | |
|---|---|---|---|---|
| crowded | cozy | inviting | cheerful | dazzling |
| romantic | restful | dreary | drab | uncomfortable |
| cluttered | ugly | tasteless | unfriendly | gaudy |
| stuffy | eerie | depressing | spacious | sunny |

---

## Dominant Impressions for Descriptions of People

| | | | | |
|---|---|---|---|---|
| creative | angry | independent | proud | dependable |
| tense | shy | aggressive | generous | sullen |
| silent | witty | pessimistic | responsible | efficient |
| snobbish | placid | bumbling | bitter | easygoing |

---

EXERCISE  1

### Selecting the Dominant Impression

Each of the following places could be the topic for a descriptive paragraph. Fill in the blank to the right of each topic with an appropriate dominant impression. Use the list in the box if you need help. Remember that there is no single right answer; the word you choose should represent the impression you want to create.

| Topic | Dominant impression |
|---|---|
| A hotel lobby | spacious |
| 1.  A high school gym on prom night | _____ |
| 2.  Your barber or hairdresser's shop | _____ |

3. The room where you are now sitting    _____

4. The grocery store nearest you    _____

5. A hardware store    _____

6. The post office on Saturday morning    _____

7. A waiting room    _____

8. A sports stadium    _____

9. The home of your best friend    _____

10. The kitchen in the morning    _____

**EXERCISE 2**

### Selecting the Dominant Impression

Each of the following people could be the topic for a descriptive paragraph. Fill in the blank to the right of each topic with an appropriate dominant impression. Use the list in the box if you need help. Remember that there is no single right answer; the word you choose should represent the impression you want to create.

| Topic | Dominant impression |
|---|---|
| 1. An actor being interviewed on television | _____ |
| 2. An old woman in a nursing home | _____ |
| 3. A librarian | _____ |
| 4. A bank clerk on a busy day | _____ |
| 5. A farmer | _____ |
| 6. A politician running for office | _____ |
| 7. A cab driver | _____ |
| 8. A shoe salesperson | _____ |
| 9. A bride | _____ |
| 10. A soldier returning home | _____ |

## REVISING VAGUE DOMINANT IMPRESSIONS

Certain words have become so overused that they no longer have any specific meaning for a reader. Careful writers avoid these words because they are almost useless in descriptive writing. Here is a list of the most commonly overused words:

### Vague and Overused Words

| | | |
|---|---|---|
| good | fine | typical |
| bad | okay | interesting |
| nice | normal | beautiful |

The following paragraph is an example of the kind of writing that suffers from the continued use of vague words:

> I had a typical day. The weather was nice and my job was interesting. The food for lunch was okay; supper was good. After supper I saw my girlfriend, who is beautiful. That's when my day really became fun.

Notice that all the details in the paragraph are vague. The writer has told us what happened, but we cannot visualize any of the details that are mentioned. The writer has made the mistake of using words that have lost much of their meaning.

The next group of exercises will give you practice in recognizing and eliminating overused words.

**EXERCISE 3**

### Revising Vague Dominant Impressions

In each of the spaces provided, write a word or phrase that creates a more specific dominant impression than the underlined word. An example has been done for you. You might want to work in groups to think of words and phrases that are more specific.

**Vague:** The tablecloth was <u>beautiful</u>.

**Revised:** The tablecloth was <u>of white linen with delicate blue embroidery</u>.

1.  The sky was <u>beautiful</u>.                          _____

2.  The water felt <u>nice</u>.                            _____

3.  Walking along the beach was <u>fun</u>.               _____

4.  The storm was <u>bad</u>.                              _____

5.  The diner was <u>typical</u>.                          _____

6.  The main street is <u>interesting</u>.                _____

7.  The dessert tasted <u>good</u>.                        _____

8.  My brother seems <u>normal</u>.                        _____

9.  Our house is <u>fine</u>.                              _____

10. My job is <u>okay</u>.                                 _____

**EXERCISE 4**

### Revising Vague Dominant Impressions

In each of the spaces provided, write a word or phrase that creates a more specific dominant impression than the underlined word. Working in groups may be helpful.

1.  The reunion turned out to be a <u>nice</u> event.     _____

2.  The window display was <u>beautiful</u>.              _____

3.  The boat ride was <u>fine</u>.                         _____

4.  The circus was <u>fun</u>.                             _____

5.  The lemonade tasted <u>awful</u>.    _____

6.  The play was <u>bad</u>.    _____

7.  His new suit looked <u>okay</u>.    _____

8.  The dance class was <u>fine</u>.    _____

9.  Her new watch was <u>nice</u>.    _____

10.  It was a <u>good</u> lecture.    _____

**EXERCISE 5**

### Revising Vague Words

**Below is the paragraph from page 391 that is filled with vague words. Rewrite the paragraph, replacing the vague words with more specific details.**

I had a typical day. The weather was nice and my job was interesting. The food for lunch was okay; supper was good. After supper I saw my girlfriend, who is beautiful. That's when my day really became fun.

_____

_____

_____

_____

_____

_____

## RECOGNIZING AND CREATING SENSORY IMAGES

One of the basic ways all good writers communicate experiences to their readers is by using sensory images. We respond to writing that makes us *see* an object, *hear* a sound, *touch* a surface, *smell* an odor, or *taste* a flavor. When a writer uses one or more sensory images in a piece of writing, we tend to pay more attention to what the writer is saying, and we tend to remember the details of what we have read.

For example, if you came across the word *door* in a sentence, you might or might not pay attention to it. However, if the writer told you it was a *heavy wooden door, rough to the touch and creaking loudly when it opened,* you would not be as likely to forget it. The door would stay in your mind because the writer used sensory images.

> *Sensory images* are those details that relate to our senses: sight, sound, touch, smell, and taste.
>
> **Effective description:**
>
> The floors were of black and white tile, the walls cream-colored with huge casement windows that opened onto a long veranda where the strains of violin music, soft voices, and the clink of glasses could be heard.
>
> **Less effective description:**
>
> The room had tiled floors, painted walls and big windows. We could hear music and voices coming from outside.

**Practice**

The following sentences describe a delicatessen. Each sentence contains at least one sensory image. For each or the sentences, identify which of the physical senses (sight, sound, touch, smell, taste) the writer has appealed to.

1.  A large refrigerator case against one wall was always humming loudly from the effort of keeping milk, cream, and several cases of soda and beer cool at all times.

    Physical senses: _____

    _____

2.  Stacked on top of the counter were baskets of fresh rolls and breads that gave off an aroma containing a mixture of onion, caraway seed, and pumpernickel.

    Physical senses: _____

3.  Mr. Rubino was always ready with a sample piece of cheese or smoked meat as a friendly gesture.

    Physical senses: _____

When you use sensory images, you will stimulate readers' interest, and these images will stay in their minds.

**EXERCISE 6**

### Recognizing Sensory Images

The following paragraph contains examples of sensory images. Find the images and list them in the spaces provided.

*Topic sentence*
<u>I knew how a newspaper office should look and sound and smell—I worked in one for thirteen years.</u> The paper was the *New York Herald Tribune,* and its city room, wide as a city block, was dirty and disheveled. Reporters wrote on ancient typewriters that filled the air with clatter; copy editors labored on coffee-stained desks over what the reporters had written. Crumpled balls of paper littered the floor and filled the wastebaskets—failed efforts to write a good lead or a decent sentence. The walls were grimy—every few years they were painted over in a less restful shade of eye-rest green—and the atmosphere was hazy with the smoke of cigarettes and cigars. At the very center the city editor, a giant named L. L. Engelking, bellowed his displeasure with the day's work, his voice a rumbling volcano in our lives. I thought it was the most beautiful place in the world.

FROM WILLIAM ZINSSER,
*Writing with a Word Processor*

**Sensory images**

Sight: _____

_____

Sound: _____

Smell: _____

EXERCISE **7**

## Recognizing Sensory Images

**The following paragraph contains examples of sensory images. Find the images and list them in the spaces provided.**

The lake ice split with a sound like the crack of a rifle. Thick slabs of ice broke apart, moving ponderously, edge grinding against edge, up-thrusting in jagged peaks, the green-gray water swirling over half-submerged floes. In an agony of rebirth, the splitting and booming of the ice reverberated across the thawing land. Streams raced toward the lake, their swift currents carrying fallen branches and undermining overhanging banks of earth and softened snow. Roads became mires of muck and slush, and the meadows of dried, matted grass oozed mud.

FROM NAN SALERNO,
*Shaman's Daughter*

**Sensory images**

Sight: _____

_____

Sound: _____

Touch: _____

EXERCISE **8**

## Recognizing Sensory Images

**The following paragraph contains examples of sensory images. Find the images and list them in the spaces provided.**

*Topic sentence*

In the waiting room there were several kerosene stoves, placed about to warm the shivering crowd. The stoves were small black chimneys with nickel handles. We stood around them rubbing hands and watching our clothes steam. An American lady, in a slicker, like the men, and rubber boots up to her knees, kept bringing bowls of soup and shiny tin cups with hot coffee. Whatever she said to us and whatever we said to her neither understood, but she was talking the language of hot soup and coffee and kindness and there was perfect communication.

FROM ERNESTO GALARZA,
*Barrio Boy*

**Sensory images**

Sight: _____

_____

Sound: _____

Touch: _____

Taste: _____

Smell: _____

EXERCISE  **9**

### Creating Sensory Images

Each of the following topic sentences contains an underlined word that identifies a physical sense. For each topic sentence, write three sentences that give examples of sensory images. For example, in a sentence describing *sounds* near a hospital, a writer could use ambulance sirens, loudspeakers calling doctors, and the voices of patients and staff.

1.   As the baseball fans entered the stadium, they recognized the usual <u>sounds</u>.

   Write three sentences with sensory images:

   a.   _____

   _____

   b.   _____

   _____

   c.   _____

   _____

2.   I can't help stopping in the bakery every Sunday morning because the <u>smells</u> are so tempting.

   Write three sentences with sensory images:

   a.   _____

   _____

   b.   _____

   _____

   c.   _____

   _____

3.   I wasn't prepared for the <u>sight</u> that greeted me when I walked off the plane.

   Write three sentences with sensory images:

   a.   _____

   _____

   b.   _____

   _____

   c.   _____

   _____

EXERCISE  **10**

### Creating Sensory Images

Each of the following topic sentences contains an underlined word that identifies a physical sense. For each topic sentence, write three sentences that give examples of sensory images.

1.  In the dark hallway, I <u>felt</u> in my purse for the keys.

    Write three sentences with sensory images:

    a.  _____

        _____

    b.  _____

        _____

    c.  _____

        _____

2.  They knew the garbage strike had gone on for a long time when they had to <u>hold their noses</u> walking down some streets.

    Write three sentences with sensory images:

    a.  _____

        _____

    b.  _____

        _____

    c.  _____

        _____

3.  Sitting on the cabin porch early in the morning, I hear the <u>sounds</u> of a world waking up.

    Write three sentences with sensory images:

    a.  _____

        _____

    b.  _____

        _____

    c.  _____

        _____

**EXERCISE 11**

## Creating Sensory Images

**Each of the following topic sentences contains an underlined word that identifies a physical sense. For each topic sentence, write three sentences that give examples of sensory images.**

1.  Going to a dance club can be an overwhelming experience because of the many different <u>sounds</u> you hear there.

    Write three sentences with sensory images:

    a.  _____

        _____

    b. _____

    _____

    c. _____

    _____

2. My friend Bill says he loves the <u>taste and texture</u> of the chocolate, the nuts, and the coconut when he eats that candy bar.

   Write three sentences with sensory images:

    a. _____

    _____

    b. _____

    _____

    c. _____

    _____

3. I could <u>see</u> that the tourist standing on the corner was confused.

   Write three sentences with sensory images:

    a. _____

    _____

    b. _____

    _____

    c. _____

    _____

# ACHIEVING COHERENCE: PUTTING DETAILS IN SPATIAL ORDER

In descriptive writing, supporting details are usually arranged according to **spatial order.** The writer describes items in much the same way as a camera might move across a scene. Items could be ordered from top to bottom, from left to right, from outside to inside, from nearby to farther away, or even around in a circle. Sometimes the most important image is saved for last to give the greatest impact to that image.

Here is a description of a hotel room in Bogota, Colombia, written by Virginia Paxton:

> The room was about the size of New York's Grand Central Station. It had been painted a fiendish dark green. A single light bulb hung from the thirteen-foot-high ceiling. The bed was oversized. The desk was gigantic, and the leather-covered chairs engulfed us. Although hot water ran from the cold faucet and cold from the hot, we were delighted.

Notice how the writer begins with a general description of the room, including its size and color, the height of the ceiling, and the source of light. Then the writer moves on to give details about the furniture. The final detail is one that is meant to be humorous (the mix-up with the hot and cold water); the writer wants to amuse us and convince us that she enjoyed the adventure of staying in an unusual hotel room. You might also say the order of details here goes from the outer edges of the room to the center. When writing a descriptive paragraph, no matter which method of spatial order you choose, the details should be in a sequence that will allow your reader to visualize the scene in a logical order. Can you explain why the dominant impression is the last word of the paragraph?

**EXERCISE** ⑫　　## Using Spatial Order

**Each of the following topic sentences is followed by four or more descriptive sentences that are not in any particular order. Put these descriptive sentences in order by placing the appropriate number in the space provided.**

1. The Statue of Liberty, now completely restored, is a marvel to visitors from all over the world.

   *(Order the material from bottom to top.)*

   _____　With current restoration finished, the crown continues to be used as a place where visitors can get a good view of New York Harbor.

   _____　The granite for the base of the statue was quarried and cut many miles from New York City and then taken by boat to Bedloe's Island, where the statue was built.

   _____　The torch has been repaired and will now be illuminated by outside lights, not lights from inside the torch itself.

   _____　The seven spikes that rise above the crown represent the seven seas of the world.

   _____　The body was covered with copper that was originally mined on an island off the coast of Norway.

2. The runway models in the designer's winter fashion show presented a classic look.

   *(Order the material from top to bottom.)*

   _____　The skirts were beautifully designed and made of quality fabrics.

   _____　The shoes were all high-heeled basic black pumps.

   _____　Exquisite silk scarves flowed as the models walked past the audience.

   _____　Meticulous attention was paid to hairstyles and makeup.

   _____　The sweaters were all made of cashmere in vibrant colors.

3. My aunt's kitchen is an orderly place.

   *(Order the material from near to far.)*

   _____　As usual, in the center of the table sits a vase with a fresh yellow daffodil.

   _____　Nearby on the refrigerator, a magnet holds the week's menu.

_____   Sitting at the kitchen table, I am struck by the freshly pressed linen tablecloth.

_____   Looking across the room through the stained glass doors of her kitchen cupboards, I can see neat rows of dishes, exactly eight each, matching the colors of the tablecloth and wallpaper.

**EXERCISE 13**

### Using Spatial Order

Each of the following topic sentences could be expanded into a fully developed paragraph. In the spaces provided, give four appropriate sensory images for the topic sentence. Be sure to give your images in a particular order. That is, the images should go from top to bottom, from outside to inside, from close to far, or around the area you are describing.

1.  The airport terminal was as busy inside as it was outside.

    a. _____

    _____

    b. _____

    _____

    c. _____

    _____

    d. _____

    _____

2.  The student lounge is a quiet and relaxing place in our school.

    a. _____

    _____

    b. _____

    _____

    c. _____

    _____

    d. _____

    _____

3.  The motel lobby had once been elegant, but now it was beginning to look shabby.

    a. _____

    _____

    b. _____

    _____

    c. _____

    _____

    d. _____

    _____

**EXERCISE** **14**

## Using Spatial Order

Each of the following topic sentences could be expanded into a fully developed paragraph. In the spaces provided, give four appropriate sensory images for the topic sentence. Be sure to give your images in a particular order. That is, the images should go from top to bottom, from outside to inside, from close to far, or around the area you are describing.

1.  The shopping mall was supposed to be enjoyable, but the experience gave me a headache.

    a. _____

    _____

    b. _____

    _____

    c. _____

    _____

    d. _____

    _____

2.  The pizza shop is so tiny that people are not likely to stay and eat.

    a. _____

    _____

    b. _____

    _____

    c. _____

    _____

    d. _____

    _____

3.  The bus was filled with a strange assortment of people.

    a. _____

    _____

    b. _____

    _____

    c. _____

    _____

    d. _____

    _____

# WRITING A DESCRIPTIVE PARAGRAPH USING A STEP-BY-STEP APPROACH

Mastering any skill, including writing, requires a disciplined attitude. One way to master the skill of creating a piece of writing is to take a step-by-step approach, focusing on one issue at a time. This approach results in a minimum of stress. Another advantage is that the writer does not miss important points or misunderstand any part of the process. Of course, there are other ways to build effective descriptive paragraphs, but here is one logical method you can use that will always achieve good results.

## Step-by-Step Approach to Writing a Descriptive Paragraph

1. Study the given topic, and then plan your topic sentence, especially the dominant impression.

2. List at least ten sensory images that come to your mind when you think about the topic you have chosen.

3. Choose the five or six most important images from your list. Be sure these details support the dominant impression.

4. Put your list in a spatial order.

5. Write at least one complete sentence for each of the images you have chosen from your list.

6. Write a concluding statement that offers some reason for describing this topic.

7. Copy your sentences into standard paragraph form.

8. Always make a final check for spelling errors and other mistakes, such as omitted words.

**NOTE:** When you use a computer spell-check feature, keep in mind that this feature will only alert you to spellings that do not match words in its dictionary. If you type *there* when you mean *their*, the spell-checker will see an acceptable word. When it comes to a final editing, there is no substitute for your own careful reading.

**EXERCISE 15**

### Writing a Descriptive Paragraph Using a Step-by-Step Approach

The following exercise will guide you through the construction of a descriptive paragraph. Start with the suggested topic. Use the eight steps to help you work through the stages of the writing process.

**Topic:**     A place you have lived

1. Topic sentence (including a dominant impression): _____

_____

2.  Make a list of possible sensory images.

    a. _____

    b. _____

    c. _____

    d. _____

    e. _____

    f. _____

    g. _____

    h. _____

    i. _____

    j. _____

3.  Check the five or six images you believe are the most important for the description.

4.  Put your selected details in a spatial order by numbering them.

5.  Using your final list, write at least one sentence for each image you have chosen.

a. _____

_____

b. _____

_____

c. _____

_____

d. _____

_____

e. _____

_____

f. _____

_____

6.  Write a concluding statement._____

_____

7.  On a separate piece of paper or on the computer, copy your sentences into standard paragraph form.

8.  Do a final reading to check for errors and omissions.

**EXERCISE** **16**    ### Writing a Descriptive Paragraph Using a Step-by-Step Approach

The following exercise will guide you through the construction of a descriptive paragraph. Start with the suggested topic. Use the eight steps to help you work through the stages of the writing process.

**Topic:**    The junk drawer in your kitchen

1. Topic sentence (including a dominant impression): _____

    _____

2. Make a list of possible sensory images.

    a. _____

    b. _____

    c. _____

    d. _____

    e. _____

    f. _____

    g. _____

    h. _____

    i. _____

    j. _____

3. Check the five or six images you believe are the most important for the description.

4. Put your selected details in order by numbering them.

5. Using your final list, write at least one sentence for each image you have chosen.

    a. _____

    _____

    b. _____

    _____

    c. _____

    _____

    d. _____

    _____

    e. _____

    _____

    f. _____

    _____

6.   Write a concluding statement. _____

_____

7.   On a separate piece of paper or on the computer, copy your sentences into standard paragraph form.

8.   Do a final reading to check for errors and omissions.

# STUDYING MODEL PARAGRAPHS TO CREATE DESCRIPTIVE PARAGRAPHS

## ASSIGNMENT 1: A DESCRIPTION OF A HOME

Write a paragraph in which you describe a house or room that you remember clearly. Choose your dominant impression carefully and then select your sensory images to support that impression. In your description you may want to include the person who lives in the house or room. In the following model paragraph from Charles Chaplin's *My Autobiography,* notice the importance of the last sentence, in which the writer gives added impact to his paragraph by identifying the person who lives in the house he has described.

## Model Paragraph: The Bungalow

It was dark when we entered his bungalow, and when we switched on the light I was shocked. The place was empty and drab. In his room was an old iron bed with a light bulb hanging over the head of it. A rickety old table and one chair were the other furnishings. Near the bed was a wooden box upon which was a brass ashtray filled with cigarette butts. The room allotted to me was almost the same, only it was minus a grocery box. Nothing worked. The bathroom was unspeakable. One had to take a jug and fill it from the bath tap and empty it down the flush to make the toilet work. <u>This was the home of G. M. Anderson, the multimillionaire cowboy.</u>

*Topic sentence*

*Ten suggested topics*

1. A student's apartment

2. A vacation cottage

3. A dormitory

4. The house of your dreams

5. Your bedroom

6. A kitchen

7. The messiest room you have ever seen

8. The strangest room you have ever seen

9. A house you will never forget

10. A house that did not fit the character of the person living there

## ASSIGNMENT 2: A DESCRIPTION OF A PERSON

Write a paragraph in which you describe a person whose appearance made a deep impression on you. You might recall someone you have personally known, or you might choose a familiar public figure. Brainstorm by making a list of the images you remember when you think of this person, images that will create a vivid picture for your readers. What dominant impression do you want to leave with the reader? Is there one single word that would convey this impression? Remember that your supporting details should all support your choice of dominant impression. In the model paragraph that follows, Colin Powell, the first African American Chairman of the Joint Chiefs of Staff, gives us a picture in words of the most memorable person he recalls from his youth. Notice how the description reveals personality traits.

## Model Paragraph: The Dominant Figure of My Youth

*Topic sentence*

The dominant figure of my youth was a small man, five feet two inches tall. In my mind's eye, I am leaning out the window of our apartment, and I spot him coming down the street from the subway station. He wears a coat and tie, and a small fedora is perched on his head. He has a newspaper tucked under his arm. His overcoat is unbuttoned, and it flaps at his sides as he approaches with a brisk, toes-out stride. He is whistling and stops to greet the druggist, the baker, our building super, almost everybody he passes. To some kids on the block he is a faintly comical figure. Not to me. This jaunty, confident little man is Luther Powell, my father.

*Ten suggested topics*

1.  An elderly relative

2.  Your favorite television personality

3.  An outstanding athlete

4.  A loyal friend

5.  An overworked waitress

6.  A cab driver

7.  A fashion model

8.  A gossipy neighbor

9.  A street vendor

10. A rude salesperson

## ASSIGNMENT 3: A DESCRIPTION OF A TIME OF DAY

Write a paragraph in which you describe the sights, sounds, and events of a time of day in a place that you know well. For instance, it could be a Sunday morning at your house or Friday night at the movies. In the model paragraph that follows, Neil Degrasse Tyson, astrophysicist and Director of the Hayden Planetarium in New York City, describes a life-changing night when he was nine years old.

### Model Paragraph: A Dark and Starry Night

**Topic sentence**

It was a dark and starry night. I felt as though I could see forever. Too numerous to count, the stars of the autumn sky, and the constellations they track were rising slowly in the east while the waxing crescent moon was descending into the western horizon. Aloft in the northern sky were the Big and Little Dippers just where they were described to appear. The planets Jupiter and Saturn were high in the sky. One of the stars seemed to fall toward the horizon. It was a meteor streaking through the atmosphere. I was told there would be no clouds that night, but I saw one. It was long and skinny and stretched across the sky from horizon to horizon. No, I was mistaken. It wasn't a cloud. It was the Milky Way. I had never seen the sky of the Milky Way with such clarity and majesty as that night. Forty-five minutes swiftly passed when the house lights came back on in the planetarium sky theater. <u>That was the night—the night the universe poured down from the sky and flowed into my body.</u> I had been called. The study of the universe would be my career, and no force on Earth would stop me.

**Ten suggested topics**

1. A Saturday afternoon filled with errands

2. The dinner hour at my house

3. Lunchtime in a cafeteria

4. A midnight raid on the refrigerator

5. New Year's Eve

6. TGIF (thank God it's Friday)

7. Getting ready to go out on a Friday night

8. My Sunday morning routine

9. Coming home from school or work

10. Watching late-night movies

## ASSIGNMENT 4: A DESCRIPTION OF A TIME OF YEAR

Write a paragraph in which you describe a particular time of year. Make sure that all of the details you choose relate specifically to that time of year. In the model paragraph that follows, from "Boyhood in Jamaica" by Claude McKay, the writer remembers springtime on his native island.

### Model Paragraph: Seasons in Jamaica

*Topic sentence*

Most of the time there was hardly any way of telling the seasons. To us in Jamaica, as elsewhere in the tropics, there were only two seasons—the rainy season and the dry season. We had no idea of spring, summer, autumn, and winter like the peoples of northern lands. Springtime, however, we did know by the new and lush burgeoning of grasses and the blossoming of trees, although we had blooms all the year round. The mango tree was especially significant of spring, because it was one of the few trees that used to shed its leaves. Then, in springtime, the new leaves sprouted—very tender, a kind of sulphur brown, as if they had been singed by fire. Soon afterwards the white blossoms came out and we knew that we would be eating juicy mangoes by August.

*Ten suggested topics*

1. A winter storm

2. A summer picnic

3. Summer in the city

4. A winter walk

5. Jogging in the spring rain

6. Sunbathing on a beach

7. Signs of spring in my neighborhood

8. The woods in autumn

9. Ice skating in winter

10. Halloween night

## Exploring Online

Go to **www.cengage.com/devenglish/scarry/writersworkplace** to find the **Writer's Online Workplace,** a website designed for students using this book. You will find links to handouts, interactive quizzes, and other online resources as you explore the following topics:

- learning new strategies of writing description
- generating sensory details

# Working Together

## WRITING A CHARACTER SKETCH

The following personal ad appeared on the bulletin board of a college campus center:

> Young man seeks neat, responsible roommate to share off-campus apartment for next academic year. Person must be a nonsmoker and respect a vegetarian who cooks at home. Furniture not needed, but microwave and computer would be welcome!

Different personal habits often have a way of causing friction between people who share the same living space. This is the reason it can be very difficult to find the right roommate in a college dormitory, the right person to share an apartment, or the right long-term companion to share a lifestyle.

Divide into groups. The members of each group should develop a list of habits that can become problems when people share a living space. Then, working together, group the items on your list into categories with general headings. For example, one general heading might be *food issues*. You could find it of value to group items in order of increasing importance.

Finally, each student should choose from one of the topics below and write a serious or amusing character description.

1.  Write a paragraph or two in which you provide a character description of yourself for an agency that will match you up with a roommate. As you write, be sure to include information about your interests, habits, attitudes, and other personal characteristics that could make a difference in the kind of person the agency will select for you.

2.  Write a paragraph or two in which you provide a character sketch of the roommate you would like the agency to find for you.

3.  Write a description of what you imagine would be the "roommate from hell."

## PORTFOLIO SUGGESTIONS

Keep your character sketch in your portfolio. You may want to collect other examples of paragraphs of description that you find effective. These models may suggest ways you would want to revise your own character sketch, or they may inspire you to write other character sketches of people you observe or know well.

# DEVELOPING PARAGRAPHS: PROCESS ANALYSIS

# 21

Giving instructions or explaining how something is done involves careful reconstruction of a sequence of steps. With a careless omission, an entire process can be misunderstood. In this chapter, you will learn the elements of writing good process paragraphs:

**CHAPTER OBJECTIVES**

- distinguishing between **directional** and **informational** process writing
- understanding the importance of **completeness**
- achieving coherence through **logical sequence** and the use of **transitions**
- taking a step-by-step approach to create process paragraphs
- studying model paragraphs to create process paragraphs

## WHAT IS PROCESS ANALYSIS?

> *Process analysis* is a method of development that provides a step-by-step explanation of how something is done or how something works.

A paragraph using process analysis may be **directional;** that is, the paragraph may be intended for a reader who needs to follow the directions to perform a task. Read the following example of a **directional** process paragraph:

*Directional process paragraph*

### TICK BITES

Remove the tick with a pair of tweezers. Never try to remove a tick by burning it or applying kerosene or other substances. Gently grasp the tick with the tweezers as close to the skin as possible. Slowly pull the insect

(continued on next page)

**Topic sentence**

straight out. Do not twist as you pull, or the tick's body will separate from its head, leaving the head buried under your skin. As you pull, do not squeeze the body of the tick. Squeezing can inject infectious fluids from the tick to you. After removing the tick, thoroughly clean the bite area and your hands, preferably with an antiseptic such as rubbing alcohol. If the tick came from an area with a high incidence of Lyme disease, save the tick and consult a doctor. Otherwise, monitor the bite area. If small raised bumps appear at the bite site or if you develop a rash around the bite or flu-like symptoms, see your doctor. <u>In the case of a tick bite, time is critical because the longer the tick is attached to a person's body, the greater the risk of contracting Lyme disease.</u>

You can find examples of directional process writing everywhere you look—in newspapers, magazines, and books, as well as on the containers and packages of products you use every day. Your daily life is filled with activities that involve the need for directional process. Instructions on a test, directions on how to get to a wedding reception, and your favorite spaghetti recipe are a few examples of the kinds of process writing you see and use regularly.

The other type of process writing is **informational.** In this case, you explain how something works or how something worked in the past. There is no expectation or even possibility that the reader will or could act upon it. The purpose of describing the process is purely to provide information. History books are filled with such writing. For instance, if you described how a Civil War general planned his battle strategy, this would be informational process writing. The following example tells how the writer and social activist Malcolm X accomplished his self-education. In the paragraph, the transitional words that signal the steps or stages of the process have been italicized.

**Topic sentence**

**Informational process paragraph**

<u>When Malcolm X was in prison, he became very frustrated because he could not express his thoughts in letters written to his family and friends.</u> Nor could he read well enough to get the meaning from a book. He decided to change this situation. *First,* he got hold of a dictionary along with some paper and pencils. He was astounded at how many words there were. Not knowing what else to do, he turned to the first page and *began* by copying words from the page. It took him the entire day. *Next,* he read what he had written aloud, over and over again. He was excited to be learning words he never knew existed. *The next morning,* he reviewed what he had forgotten and *then* copied the next page. He found he was learning about people, places, and events from history. This process *continued until* he had filled a tablet with all the A's and *then* all the B's. *Eventually,* Malcolm X copied the entire dictionary!

## MAKING SURE ALL THE STEPS ARE INCLUDED

All of us have been given directions that seemed very clear at first but that did not produce the result we expected. Perhaps we misunderstood one of the steps in the process, or perhaps a step was missing. Maybe the person giving the information assumed that we already knew certain parts of the process or didn't think through the process carefully enough to identify all the steps. Directions must always be accurate and complete, even down to any special equipment needed to carry out the process.

The writer who presents a process is almost always more of an authority on the subject than the reader. In providing information or giving directions on how to do something, it is easy to leave out steps because they may seem too obvious to be worth mentioning. A writer should never assume that the reader will be able to fill in any missing steps. An important part of process writing is always being aware of the audience.

**EXERCISE**  **1**

### Is the Process Complete?

Read the steps in the following recipe. Imagine yourself baking the cake using only the information provided. Has any information been left out, or have any needed steps been omitted? (Although recipes are generally not presented in paragraph or essay form, they are good examples of process writing in which the order and completeness of the step-by-step procedure are of critical importance.)

**How to make a Swedish spice cake**

1. Butter an 8-inch tube pan and sprinkle with 2 tbsp. of fine dry bread crumbs.

2. Cream ½ cup of butter; add 1 cup firmly packed brown sugar and cream until light and fluffy.

3. In a small bowl, beat 2 egg yolks until light and add to the creamed mixture.

4. Sift together 1 ½ cups all-purpose flour, 1 tsp. baking power, 2 tsp. ground cardamom, and 2 tsp. ground cinnamon.

5. Add the dry ingredients to the creamed ingredients, mixing alternately with ½ cup light cream.

6. Beat egg whites until stiff and fold into batter.

7. Turn into prepared pan, bake, and serve unfrosted.

Missing step or steps: _____

_____

_____

_____

**EXERCISE** **2**

### Is the Process Complete?

Imagine that at long last, a family is ready to remodel a bathroom or a kitchen in their home. Read the following steps that should be followed for a successful completion of the job. Can you think of any steps that might be missing?

**Steps to remodeling a room in your home**

1. Have a good idea of what you want before contacting a carpenter or contractor.

2. Be realistic about what you can afford to spend.

3. Get at least two estimates for the job.

4. Plan to be present when the work is being done.

5. Do not pay the final payment until everything is finished and you are satisfied with the job.

Possible missing step or steps: _____

_____

_____

_____

_____

_____

**EXERCISE  3**

## Is the Process Complete?

**In the following process, decide whether any important steps have been omitted. Imagine yourself going through the process using only the information provided.**

**How to prepare for an essay exam**

1. All of the assigned reading should be read well in advance of the date of the test.

2. Throughout the semester, notes should be taken in class from the instructor's lessons.

3. Several days before the exam, the instructor usually explains what material will be covered on the exam. Students should ask whether the exam will be made up of one main essay question or several shorter essay questions.

4. A good night's sleep before the day of the test will ensure clear thinking.

5. At least two pens should be brought to the test, to avoid the problem of having a pen break or run out of ink.

6. To maintain a sense of calm, students should arrive at the test site a few minutes early so they have plenty of time to relax and get settled.

Missing step or steps: _____

_____

_____

_____

## ACHIEVING COHERENCE

### ORDERING IN LOGICAL SEQUENCE

When you are working with a process, it is important not only to make sure that the steps in the process are complete but also to present the steps in the right sequence. For example, if you are describing the process of cleaning an electric mixer, it is important to point out that you must first unplug the appliance before you remove the blades. A person could lose a finger if this part of the process were missing. Improperly written instructions have caused serious injuries and even death.

**EXERCISE 4**

### Ordering in Logical Sequence

**The following steps describe the process of refinishing hardwood floors. Put the steps into their proper sequence.**

_____ Sanding with coarse sandpaper continues until the hardwood is exposed.

_____ A coat of polyurethane finish is applied.

_____ When the sanding is done, the floor is thoroughly cleaned with a vacuum sweeper to remove all the sawdust.

_____ The finish must then dry for three days before waxing and buffing.

_____ All furnishings are removed from the room.

_____ The initial sanding is done with a coarse sandpaper on the sanding machine.

_____ The edger and hand sander are used after the machine sanding to get to hard-to-reach places.

_____ A second coat of polyurethane finish is applied on the following day, using a brush or a roller.

_____ The coarse sandpaper on the machine is changed to a fine sandpaper for the final sanding.

_____ Nails sticking out from the floor should be either pulled out or set below the surface of the boards before starting the sanding.

**EXERCISE 5**

### Ordering in Logical Sequence

**The following steps describe the process of devising a filing system. Put the steps into their proper sequence.**

_____ Filing of additional items should stop when mental fatigue sets in.

_____ Now the file folder is labeled, and the piece of paper is slipped in.

_____ All the pages to be filed should be gathered in one area, perhaps in the room where the filing cabinet is located.

_____ The file folders are alphabetized and put away in the file drawer. Your session for that time is finished.

_____ In addition, a wastebasket, file folders, labels, and a pen will be needed.

_____ The same procedure should be repeated with the next piece of paper, keeping in mind that this piece of paper might have a place in an existing file rather than a new one.

_____ Any page can be picked up at random to be studied. Does the item need to be saved? If the item has no value, it should be thrown away. If the item has value, the process moves to the next step.

_____ Once the filing system has been established, it is easy to maintain if, every time a particular file is consulted, the complete file is scanned quickly to identify any items that are no longer useful and need to be discarded.

_____ When the item seems worth saving, the question should be asked: What is this item about? That subject will be the title for the label on the file folder.

## USING TRANSITIONS

Like writers of narration, writers who analyze a process usually order their material by time sequence. Although it would be tiresome to use the words *and then* for each new step, some transitions are necessary for the process to read smoothly and coherently. Here is a list of transitions frequently used in a process paragraph.

### Transitions Commonly Used in Process Analysis

| | | |
|---|---|---|
| the first step | while you are . . . | the last step |
| in the beginning | as you are . . . | the final step |
| to start with | next | finally |
| to begin with | then | at last |
| first of all | the second step | eventually |
| | after you have . . . | |

**EXERCISE  6**

## Using Transitions to Go from a List to a Paragraph

Select one of the three processes presented on pages 413–414. Use the list of steps, including missing steps that you supplied, to write a process paragraph. Be sure to include transitional devices to make the paragraph read smoothly and coherently.

_____

_____

_____

_____

_____

_____

_____

_____

_____

_____

_____

_____

_____

_____

_____

_____

_____

# WRITING A PROCESS PARAGRAPH USING A STEP-BY-STEP APPROACH

Mastering any skill, including writing, requires a disciplined attitude. One way to master the skill of creating a piece of writing is to take a step-by-step approach, focusing on one issue at a time. This approach results in a minimum of stress. Another advantage is that the writer does not miss important points or misunderstand any part of the process. Of course, there are other ways to build effective process paragraphs, but here is one logical method you can use that will always achieve good results.

## Step-by-Step Approach to Writing a Process Paragraph

1. After you have chosen your topic and controlling idea, plan your topic sentence.

2. List as many steps or stages in the process as you can.

3. Eliminate irrelevant steps, add any equipment or materials needed, and explain any special circumstances of the process.

4. Put the steps in order.

5. Write at least one complete sentence for each of the steps you have chosen from your list.

6. Write a concluding statement that says something about the results of completing the process.

7. Copy your sentences into standard paragraph form.

8. Make a final check for spelling errors and other mistakes, such as omitted words.

**NOTE:** When you use a computer spell-check feature, keep in mind that this feature will alert you only to spellings that do not match words in its dictionary. If you type *there* when you mean *their*, the spell-checker will see an acceptable word. When it comes to a final editing, there is no substitute for your own careful reading.

**EXERCISE**  **7**    **Writing a Process Paragraph Using a Step-by-Step Approach**

This exercise will guide you through the construction of a complete process paragraph. Start with the topic suggested below. Use the eight steps to take you through the stages of the writing process.

    **Topic:** How to lose weight

Perhaps no topic has filled more book and magazine pages than the "lose five pounds in one week" promise. The wide variety of diet plans boggles the mind. Here is your chance to add your own version.

1. Topic sentence: _____

    _____

    _____

    _____

    _____

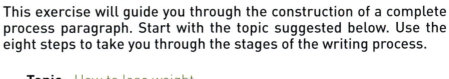

2.   Make a list of all necessary steps.

   a. _____

   b. _____

   c. _____

   d. _____

   e. _____

   f. _____

   g. _____

   h. _____

   i. _____

   j. _____

3.   Eliminate irrelevant steps, add any equipment or materials needed, and explain any special circumstances.

4.   Put your steps in order by numbering them.

5.   Using your final list, write at least one sentence for each step you have chosen.

   a. _____

      _____

   b. _____

      _____

   c. _____

      _____

   d. _____

      _____

   e. _____

      _____

   f. _____

      _____

   g. _____

      _____

6.   Write a concluding statement. _____

_____

_____

7.  On a separate piece of paper or on the computer, copy your sentences into standard paragraph form.

8.  Do a final reading to check for errors and omissions.

**EXERCISE  8**

### Writing a Process Paragraph Using a Step-by-Step Approach

**This exercise will guide you through the construction of a complete process paragraph. Start with the topic suggested below. Use the eight steps to take you through the stages of the writing process.**

**Topic:** How to set up a budget

Imagine you are the expert who has been hired by a couple to help them sort out their money problems. Together they bring in a reasonable salary, but despite this, they are always spending more than they earn.

1.  Topic sentence: _____

_____

2.  Make a list of all necessary steps.

a. _____

b. _____

c. _____

d. _____

e. _____

f. _____

g. _____

h. _____

i. _____

j. _____

3.  Eliminate irrelevant steps, add any equipment or materials needed, and explain any special circumstances.

4.  Put your steps in order by numbering them.

5.  Using your final list, write at least one sentence for each step you have chosen.

a. _____

_____

b. _____

_____

c. _____

_____

d. _____

_____

e. _____

_____

f. _____

_____

g. _____

_____

6.  Write a concluding statement. _____

_____

_____

7.  On a separate piece of paper or on the computer, copy your sentences into standard paragraph form.

8.  Do a final reading to check for errors and omissions.

## STUDYING MODEL PARAGRAPHS TO CREATE PROCESS PARAGRAPHS

### ASSIGNMENT 1 (DIRECTIONAL): HOW TO ACCOMPLISH A DAILY TASK

Write a paragraph in which you describe the process of carrying out a task. For example, you might write about how to learn to drive a car, how to play a musical instrument, or how to set up a new computer. The following paragraph describes a process for making a common beverage used by millions of people every day: an ordinary cup of tea.

### Model Paragraph: How to Make a Good Cup of Tea

*Topic sentence*

Making a good cup of tea is exquisitely simple. First, the teapot is heated by filling it with water that has just come to a boil. This water is then discarded, and one teaspoon of loose tea per cup is placed in the teapot (the exact amount may vary according to taste). Fresh water that has just come to a boil is poured into the pot. A good calculation is six ounces of water for each cup of tea. The tea must now steep for three to five minutes; then it is poured through a strainer into a cup or mug. A pound of loose tea will yield about two hundred cups of brewed tea. Using a tea bag eliminates the strainer, but it is still best to make the tea in a teapot so that the water stays sufficiently hot. The typical restaurant service—a cup of hot water with the tea bag on the side—will not produce the best cup of tea because the water is never hot enough when it reaches the table and because the tea should not be dunked in the water; the water should be poured over the tea. Although tea in a pot often becomes too strong, that problem can be dealt with very easily by adding more boiling water.

*Ten suggested topics*

1. How to plan a move from one home to another
2. How to program a new cell phone
3. How to make time for some fun
4. How to change the oil in your car
5. How to make the best . . . (choose your favorite dish)
6. How to prepare a package for mailing
7. How to pack a suitcase
8. How to inexpensively furnish an apartment
9. How to wallpaper or paint a room
10. How to plan a barbeque

## ASSIGNMENT 2 (DIRECTIONAL): HOW TO CARE FOR YOUR HEALTH

Awareness of the importance of health and physical fitness has increased, bringing in big profits to health-related magazines, health clubs, health-food producers, and sports equipment manufacturers. Write a paragraph in which you show steps you could take for your mental or physical health. The following paragraph tells how to get a good night's sleep.

### Model Paragraph: How to Get a Good Night's Sleep

*Topic sentence*

   Getting a good night's sleep depends on following several important steps. First, the conditions in the bedroom must be correct. The temperature should be around sixty-five degrees, and the room should be as quiet as possible. Next, an important consideration is the bed itself. A good-quality mattress goes a long way toward preventing aches, which often wake people up when they turn over during the night. Using natural fabrics such as cotton and wool is a much better choice than using sheets and blankets made of synthetic materials that do not breathe. In addition, pillows that are either too soft or too hard can cause stiffness of the neck and lead to a poor night's sleep. Once the room is prepared, sleep is still not ensured. The next requirement is that the person going to bed feel relaxed and tired enough to sleep. This will not happen if the person has been lying around all day napping and, in general, leading a very inactive life. People who have trouble sleeping should try to keep an active schedule. Then, as bedtime nears, activities should become less stimulating and more relaxing. Finally, people often forget the importance of what they eat in the hours preceding bedtime. People should not go to bed hungry, nor should they overeat. Foods such as candy bars or cookies are full of sugar and act as stimulants. Such foods should be avoided, along with all caffeinated beverages. When these steps are followed, nearly everyone can look forward to a good night's sleep.

*Ten suggested topics*

1.  How to plan a healthful diet

2.  How to care for someone who is ill

3.  How to plan a daily exercise program

4.  How to choose a sport that is suitable for you

5.  How to live to be one hundred

6.  How to pick a doctor

7.  How to deal with anger

8.  How to stop eating junk food

9.  How to deal with depression

10. How to find a spiritual side to life

## ASSIGNMENT 3 (INFORMATIONAL): HOW TEAMWORK ACCOMPLISHES A TASK

Write a paragraph in which you describe the process used by an agency or group of people to achieve some important goal. The following paragraph, describing how wildfires are presently fought, is an example of informational process writing.

**Model Paragraph: Fighting Wildfires**

*Topic sentence*

When a wildfire starts, a process to protect lives and property is set in motion. At first, the fire is watched. Many fires do not go beyond the initial burn. If the fire appears to be spreading, the next step is to call on weather forecasters to study the weather patterns to predict where the fire will spread next. Firefighters called "hot shots" may hike into the area to begin their work of scraping, cutting, and clearing the brush that gives fuel to the fire. The first goal of the hot shots is to cut a containment perimeter around the fire rather than put it out. If it is too far to hike into an area, parachutists called "smoke jumpers" will go in to do the work. If the fire is moving too fast or in extremely rugged terrain, helicopter pilots drop chemicals or water on the fire to retard it. Although some fires are set by Mother Nature during lightning storms, the sad fact is that most fires are set by humans who carelessly toss away cigarette butts that have not been completely extinguished.

*Ten suggested topics*

1. How a charity accomplishes its goal

2. How lab experiments use teamwork

3. How a band requires teamwork

4. How a community garden or beautification project is organized

5. How a neighborhood crime-watch group functions

6. How an ambulance crew works together

7. How a town council operates

8. How an office should be run

9. How a school yearbook depends on team effort

10. How a student newspaper demands a dedicated team

## Exploring Online

Go to **www.cengage.com/devenglish/scarry/writersworkplace** to find the **Writer's Online Workplace,** a website designed for students using this book. You will find links to handouts, interactive quizzes, and other online resources as you explore the following topics:

- writing a process composition
- questions to consider when writing a process essay
- reading a sample process essay

# Working Together

## BUILDING A TEAM

Either in school or in business, being able to work well with a group is of vital importance. If a team member does not understand or respect how groups should function, the experience may be frustrating at best and a failure at worst. Below are several questions for a discussion on teamwork. Select one student in the class to direct the discussion, while another student writes the main points of the discussion on the board.

### Class Discussion

1. When a group meets to work, what procedure should be followed?
2. How important is it that everybody first understand the task?
3. How can a group avoid the situation where only one person seems to be doing all the work?
4. What should be done about a person who tends to dominate all the discussions?
5. What can be done for a person who is very shy?
6. What can be done about a person who has an "attitude"?
7. How can the group be sure that the meeting does not end up with people chatting instead of focusing on the task?
8. How can personality conflicts be avoided?
9. How should disagreements be handled?

Use the material from the classroom discussion to write a process essay. In your essay, describe the procedure that should be followed when a group of people meets to work on a project. It might be helpful to use as an example a group of workers doing a particular job: teachers getting together to design a series of courses; magazine editors meeting to decide on a theme for their next issue; or a school's coaches planning their strategies for the upcoming season.

## PORTFOLIO SUGGESTION

Record some of the comments that you heard during the group discussion, making special note of two or three points you found especially interesting. Write at least one or two sentences for each of these special points, concentrating on some aspect about which you feel strongly. Place these completed sentences in your portfolio for possible use in future writing assignments. As you record the general comments and as you generate your own sentences, keep in mind that your notes may apply directly to your work in other college courses. The idea of building team spirit or learning to work with others has many direct applications, including the fields of sports, science, psychology, and sociology.

# DEVELOPING PARAGRAPHS: COMPARISON/CONTRAST

# 22

Writing a paragraph using comparison or contrast requires the development of two topics at the same time. In this chapter, you will concentrate on the special needs of this challenging rhetorical form.

**CHAPTER OBJECTIVES**

- choosing a **two-part topic**
- ordering material using the **point-by-point method** or the **block method**
- improving coherence by using **transitional phrases** common to comparison/contrast writing
- taking a step-by-step approach to create comparison/contrast paragraphs
- studying model paragraphs to create comparison/contrast paragraphs

## WHAT IS COMPARISON/CONTRAST?

We use comparison and contrast every day. In the grocery store, we judge similar products before we decide to buy one of them; we listen to two politicians on television and think about the differences between their positions before we vote for one of them; and we read college catalogues and talk to our friends before we make a final choice as to which school we should attend.

When we compare or contrast two items, we need to consider exactly which points should be compared. We usually have a purpose or a need for making our decision as to which item is better or worse. For instance, if we are making an expensive purchase, a person who has not analyzed the situation might be tempted to rely on a clever salesperson, who may want to make an easy sale. A person might also be swayed by the price alone or make the decision based on impulse. We have all experienced the sad consequences of making such a decision without thinking it through. Comparison or contrast uses a logical process that will help us think through the critical similarities or differences.

Consider the common experience of finding the best apartment to rent. The search for an appropriate place to live directly affects one's budget and has many implications for a person's daily life. Does the monthly rent include utilities, and, if not, how high could those costs go? Can you rent month-to-month, or are you held to a lease? How much of a security deposit will you have to put down? Are pets allowed? Is the apartment available now? Is it furnished or unfurnished? What condition is it in?

Aside from the apartment itself, some basic questions about the building and the neighborhood come to mind. What floor is the apartment on, and if it is on one of the upper floors, is there an elevator? Is the building well maintained? Does it have good security? Is the building close to public transportation? Is there shopping nearby?

If your piece of writing were concerned with this subject of choosing the right apartment, the points listed above would make your writing fall into the category of *comparison/contrast*. In this case, because the search for the right apartment is such an important one, you can see that comparison or contrast is not only a useful tool—it is an absolutely essential one.

> **Comparison or contrast,** as a method of development, examines similarities or differences between people, objects, or ideas in order to arrive at a judgment or conclusion.

**NOTE:** Although the term *comparison* is sometimes used in a general sense to include both comparisons and contrasts, here we use the term *comparison* when we focus on similarities, and we use the term *contrast* when we focus on differences.

## CHOOSING A TWO-PART TOPIC

Much of the difficulty in writing a paragraph of comparison or contrast is caused by having a two-part topic. Careful thought, therefore, must be given to creating the topic sentence of that paragraph. You must choose a two-part topic that has a sufficient number of points to compare or contrast, but you must avoid selecting two-part topics that would have so many points to compare or contrast that you would not be able to discuss all the material in one paragraph. For example, a student trying to compare the Spanish word *río* with the English word *river* might be able to come up with only two sentences of material. With only a dictionary to consult, it is unlikely that the student would find enough material for several points of comparison. On the other hand, contrasting the United States with Europe would present such an endless supply of points that the tendency would be to give only general facts that the reader would already know. When the subject is too broad, the writing is often too general. A better two-part topic might be to compare traveling by train in Europe with traveling by train in the United States.

Once you have chosen a two-part topic that you feel is not too limiting and not too broad, you must remember that a good comparison/contrast paragraph devotes an equal or nearly equal amount of space to each of the two parts. If the writer is interested in only one of the topics, the danger is that the paragraph will end up being one-sided.

Here is an example of a one-sided contrast:

**American trains go to only a few towns, are infrequent, and are often shabby and uncomfortable. In contrast, European trains are much nicer.**

The following example is a better-written contrast, which gives attention to both topics:

**American trains go to only a few large cities, run infrequently, and are often shabby and uncomfortable. In contrast, European trains go to virtually every small town, are always dependable, and are clean and attractive.**

EXERCISE **1**

## Evaluating the Two-Part Topic

Study the following topics. Decide whether each topic is *too broad* or could be *suitable* for a paragraph of comparison or contrast. Mark your choice in the appropriate space to the right of each topic given. Be prepared to explain your choices.

| Topic | Too broad | Suitable |
|---|---|---|
| 1.  Australia and England | _____ | _____ |
| 2.  Indian elephants and African elephants | _____ | _____ |
| 3.  California champagne and French champagne | _____ | _____ |
| 4.  Wooden furniture and plastic furniture | _____ | _____ |
| 5.  Wood and plastic | _____ | _____ |
| 6.  Paperback books and hardcover books | _____ | _____ |
| 7.  Mothers and fathers | _____ | _____ |
| 8.  Taking photographs with a flash and taking photographs using available light | _____ | _____ |
| 9.  Doctors and lawyers | _____ | _____ |
| 10.  Trains and airplanes | _____ | _____ |

EXERCISE **2**

## Working with Comparison or Contrast

For each comparison or contrast, supply your own two parts of the topic. Each two-part topic should be one that you could develop as an example of comparison or contrast.

1.  Compare/contrast two friends:

    My friend _____ with my friend _____

2.  Compare/contrast two kinds of coats:

    _____ coats with _____ coats

3. Compare/contrast two kinds of diets:

   The _____ diet and the _____ diet

4. Compare/contrast two kinds of floors:

   _____ floors with _____ floors

5. Compare/contrast two kinds of entertainment:

   Watching _____ with looking at _____

6. Compare/contrast two kinds of rice:

   _____ rice with _____ rice

7. Compare/contrast two places where you can study:

   Studying in the _____ with studying in the _____

8. Compare/contrast the wedding customs of two groups:

   What _____ do at a wedding with what _____ do at a wedding

9. Compare/contrast two textbooks:

   A textbook that has _____ with a textbook that contains _____

10. Compare/contrast two political philosophies:

   One political philosophy that believes _____ with another political philosophy that believes _____

**EXERCISE** ❸   ## Working with Comparison or Contrast

For each comparison or contrast, supply your own two parts of the topic. Each two-part topic should be one that you could develop as an example of comparison or contrast.

1. Compare/contrast two kinds of popular board games people play:

   Playing _____ with playing _____

2. Compare/contrast two ways of looking at movies:

   Watching movies on _____ with going to _____

3. Compare/contrast two careers:

   A career in _____ with a career as a _____

4. Compare/contrast two ways of paying for a purchase:

   Using _____ to buy something with using _____ to buy something

5. Compare/contrast two different lifestyles:

   Living the life of a _____ with living as a _____

6.   Compare/contrast two places to go swimming:

Swimming in a _____ with swimming in a _____

7.   Compare/contrast a no-frills product with the same product sold under a standard brand name (such as no-frills corn flakes with Kellogg's corn flakes):

A no-frills _____ with _____

8.   Compare/contrast two popular magazines:

_____ with _____

9.   Compare/contrast two leisure activities:

Collecting _____ with _____

10.   Compare/contrast two kinds of tests given in school:

The _____ kind of test with the _____ kind of test

# ACHIEVING COHERENCE: TWO APPROACHES TO ORDERING MATERIAL

## POINT-BY-POINT METHOD

One method for ordering material in a paragraph of comparison or contrast is known as the **point-by-point method.** When you use this method, you compare/contrast point 1 of topic 1 and then point 1 of topic 2. Then you go on to your second points for each of the two topics. You continue until you have covered all the points. For example, here is a paragraph from Julius Lester's *All Is Well*. In the paragraph, the writer uses the point-by-point method to compare the difficulties of being a boy in our society a generation ago with the difficulties of being a girl at that same time.

*Topic sentence*

> <u>Now, of course, I know that it was as difficult being a girl as it was a boy, if not more so.</u> While I stood paralyzed at one end of a dance floor trying to find the courage to ask a girl for a dance, most of the girls waited in terror at the other, afraid that no one, not even I, would ask them. And while I resented having to ask a girl for a date, wasn't it also horrible to be the one who waited for the phone to ring? And how many of those girls who laughed at me making a fool of myself on the baseball diamond would have gladly given up their places on the sidelines for mine on the field?

Notice how, after the opening topic sentence, the writer uses half of each sentence to describe a boy's situation growing up and the other half to describe a girl's experience. This technique is often used in longer pieces of writing in which many points of comparison are made. This method helps the reader keep the comparison or contrast carefully in mind at each point.

If the paragraph is broken down into its parts, this is how the **point-by-point method** might look in chart form:

**Topic Sentence:**   **Now, of course, I know that it was as difficult being a girl as it was a boy, if not more so.**

| Point-by-Point Method | | | |
|---|---|---|---|
| **Points to Compare or Contrast** | **First Topic: Boys** | | **Second Topic: Girls** |
| Point 1 ⟶ | While I stood paralyzed at one end of the dance floor trying to find the courage to ask a girl for a dance, . . . | ⟶ | . . . most of the girls waited in terror at the other, afraid that no one, not even I, would ask them. |
| Point 2 ⟶ | And while I resented having to ask a girl for a date, . . . | ⟶ | . . . wasn't it also horrible to be the one who waited for the phone to ring? |
| Point 3 ⟶ | And how many of those girls who laughed at me making a fool of myself on the baseball diamond . . . | ⟶ | . . . would have gladly given up their places on the sidelines for mine on the field? |

## BLOCK METHOD

The other method for ordering material in a paragraph of comparison or contrast is known as the **block method.** When you use this approach, you present all of the facts and supporting details about one part of your topic, and then you give all of the facts and supporting details about the other part. Here, for example, is another version of the paragraph by Julius Lester, this time written according to the block method:

*Topic sentence*

> <u>Now, of course, I know that it was as difficult being a girl as it was being a boy, if not more so</u>. I stood paralyzed at one end of the dance floor trying to find the courage to ask a girl for a dance. I also resented having to ask a girl for a date. Furthermore, I often felt foolish on the baseball diamond. On the other hand, most of the girls waited in terror at the other end of the dance floor, afraid that no one, not even I, would ask them to dance. In addition, it was a horrible situation for the girls who had to wait for the phone to ring, hoping for a date. And how many of those girls who stood on the sidelines would have gladly traded places with me on the baseball diamond?

Notice how the first half of this version presents all of the details about the boy, and the second part of the paragraph presents all of the information about girls. This method is often used in shorter pieces because the reader will easily remember three or four short points and thus not need each comparison/contrast side by side.

If the paragraph is broken down into its parts, this is how the **block method** might look in chart form:

**Topic Sentence:**   Now, of course, I know that it was as difficult being a girl as it was a boy, if not more so.

| Block Method | | | | | | | |
|---|---|---|---|---|---|---|---|
| **Topics** | | **Point 1** | | **Point 2** | | **Point 3** | |
| **First Topic** | → | I stood paralyzed at one end of the dance floor trying to find the courage to ask a girl for a dance. | → | I resented having to ask a girl for a date,... | → | ...just as I often felt foolish on the baseball diamond. | |
| **Second Topic** | → | On the other hand, most of the girls waited in terror at the other end of the dance floor, afraid that no one, not even I, would ask them to dance. | → | In addition, it was a horrible situation for the girl who had to wait for the phone to ring to be asked out on a date. | → | And how many of those girls who stood on the sideline at a baseball game would have gladly traded places with me on the baseball diamond? | |

You will want to choose one of these methods before you write a comparison or contrast assignment. Keep in mind that although the block method is most often used in shorter writing assignments, such as a paragraph, you can often effectively employ the point-by-point method as well.

**EXERCISE**  **4**

### Recognizing the Two Approaches to Ordering Material

Each of the following passages is an example of comparison or contrast. Read each paragraph carefully and decide whether the writer has used the point-by-point method or the block method. Also decide whether the piece emphasizes similarities or differences. Indicate your choices in the spaces provided after each passage.

*Topic sentence*

1.    <u>Female infants speak sooner, have larger vocabularies, and rarely demonstrate speech defects</u>. (Stuttering, for instance, occurs almost exclusively among boys.) Girls exceed boys in language abilities, and this early linguistic bias often prevails throughout life. Girls read sooner, learn foreign languages more easily, and, as a result, are more likely to enter occupations involving language mastery. Boys, in contrast, show an early visual superiority. They are also clumsier, performing poorly at something like arranging a row of beads, but excel at other activities calling on total body coordination. Their attentional mechanisms are also different. A boy will react to an inanimate object as quickly as he will to a person. A male baby will often ignore the mother and babble to a blinking light, fixate on a geometric figure, and at a later point, manipulate it and attempt to take it apart.

_____ Point-by-point          _____ Block

_____ Similarities            _____ Differences

2.    The streets are littered with cigarette and cigar butts, paper wrappings, particles of food, and dog droppings. How long before they become indistinguishable from the gutters of medieval towns when slop pails were emptied from the second-story windows? Thousands of New York women no longer attend evening services in their churches. They fear assault as they walk the few steps from bus or subway station to their apartment houses.

**Topic sentence**

**°footpad (obsolete)**
a mugger

The era of the medieval footpad° has returned, and, as in the Dark Ages, the cry for help brings no assistance, for even grown men know they would be cut down before the police could arrive.

_____ Point-by-point          _____ Block

_____ Similarities          _____ Differences

**Topic sentence**

3.     I first realized that the act of writing was about to enter a new era five years ago when I went to see an editor at the *New York Times.* As I was ushered through the vast city room I felt that I had strayed into the wrong office. The place was clean and carpeted and quiet. As I passed long rows of desks, I saw that almost every desk had its own computer terminal and its own solemn occupant—a man or a woman typing at the computer keyboard or reading what was on the terminal screen. I saw no typewriters, no paper, no mess. It was a cool and sterile environment; the drones at their machines could have been processing insurance claims or tracking a spacecraft in orbit. What they didn't look like were newspaper people, and what the place didn't look like was a newspaper office. I knew how a newspaper office should look and sound and smell—I worked in one for thirteen years. The paper was the *New York Herald Tribune,* and its city room, wide as a city block, was dirty and disheveled. Reporters wrote on ancient typewriters that filled the air with clatter; copy editors labored on coffee-stained desks over what the reporters had written. Crumpled balls of paper littered the floor and filled the wastebaskets—failed efforts to write a good lead or a decent sentence. The walls were grimy—every few years they were painted over in a less restful shade of eye-rest green—and the atmosphere was hazy with the smoke of cigarettes and cigars. At the very center the city editor, a giant named L. L. Engelking, bellowed his displeasure with the day's work, his voice a rumbling volcano in our lives. I thought it was the most beautiful place in the world.

_____ Point-by-point          _____ Block

_____ Similarities          _____ Differences

4.     We went fishing the first morning. I felt the same damp moss covering the worms in the bait can, and saw the dragonfly alight on the tip of my rod as it hovered a few inches from the surface of the water. It was the arrival of this fly that convinced me beyond any doubt that everything was as it always had been, that the years were a mirage and there had been no years. The small waves were the same, chucking the rowboat under the chin as we fished at anchor, and the boat was the same boat, the same color green and the ribs broken in the same places, and under the floorboards the same freshwater leavings and debris—the dead hellgrammite°, the wisps of moss, the rusty discarded fishhook, the dried blood from yesterday's catch. We stared silently at the tips of our rods, at the dragonflies that came and went. I lowered the tip of mine into the water, tentatively, pensively dislodging the fly, which darted two feet away, poised, darted two feet back, and came to rest again a little farther up the rod. There had been no years between the ducking of this dragonfly and the other one—the one that was part of memory. I looked at the boy, who was silently watching his fly, and it was my hands that held his rod, my eyes watching. I felt dizzy and didn't know which rod I was at the end of.

**Topic sentence**

**hellgrammite°**
the larva of the dobsonfly, often used as bait for fishing

_____ Point-by-point          _____ Block

_____ Similarities          _____ Differences

**EXERCISE  5**

### Using the Point-by-Point Method for Contrast

Passage 3 on page 434 uses the block method to make its points of contrast. Rewrite the passage using the point-by-point approach.

_____

_____

_____

_____

_____

_____

_____

_____

_____

_____

_____

**EXERCISE  6**

### Using the Point-by-Point and Block Methods for Comparison or Contrast

Use the lists below to write a paragraph comparing or contrasting life in the city with life in a suburban area. First review the lists provided, adding your own ideas and omitting any you do not wish to use. Then, selecting either the block method or the point-by-point method, write a comparison or contrast paragraph.

> **Topic sentence:**  **If I could move back to the city from the suburbs, I know I would be happy.**

Below is one student's list contrasting living in the city with living in the suburbs.

| Points to compare or contrast | Topic 1: Living in the city | | Topic 2: Living in the suburbs |
|---|---|---|---|
| Point 1 → | A quick ride on the bus or subway gets you to work. | → | Commuting to work from the suburbs to the city is often time-consuming, exhausting, and expensive. |
| Point 2 → | Men are as visible as women in the neighborhood. | → | Because most men in the suburbs work in the city, few of them are active in the suburban community. |
| Point 3 → | The architecture and diversity of people are stimulating. | → | The sameness of streets and people is monotonous. |
| Point 4 → | Shopping for nearly everything can be done on foot. | → | Most shopping requires a car. |
| Point 5 → | People walk in their neighborhoods. | → | People go everywhere by car. |

Notice that the writer who created this list emphasized the disadvantages of the suburbs, in contrast to the advantages of the city. No mention was made, for example, of overcrowding or high crime rates in the city. Another list could be created from the point of view of a person who prefers the suburbs.

## ACHIEVING COHERENCE: USING TRANSITIONS

In addition to ordering your material using either the block method or the point-by-point method, the careful use of transitions will also help to achieve coherence. The transitions in the following chart are useful to keep in mind when writing a comparison or contrast paragraph. Some of them are used in phrases, some in clauses. For example, notice the difference between *like* and *as*. *Like* is used as a preposition in a prepositional phrase:

**My sister is just *like* me.**

*As* is used as a subordinating conjunction to begin a clause:

**Every evening my sister reads in bed, *as* does her older daughter.**

### Transitions Commonly Used in Comparison/Contrast

| | | | |
|---|---|---|---|
| again | like | although | instead |
| also | likewise | and yet | nevertheless |
| as well as | moreover | but | on the contrary |
| both | the same as | despite | on the other hand |
| equally | similar to | different from | otherwise |
| furthermore | similarly | even though | still |
| just as | so | except for | though |
| just like | too | however | unlike |
| | | in contrast with | whereas |

EXERCISE  7

### Using Transitions in Comparisons and Contrasts

Read each of the following pairs of sentences and decide whether the idea being expressed is a comparison or a contrast. Next, combine the two sentences by using a transition you have chosen from the list above. Then write your new sentence on the lines provided. If needed, you may reword your new sentence to make it grammatically correct. An example has been done for you.

**Mr. Costello is a teacher.**

**His wife is a teacher.**

First you decide that the two sentences show a comparison. Then you combine the two by using an appropriate transition:

**Mr. Costello is a teacher, and so is his wife.**

or

**Mr. Costello is a teacher; his wife is too.**

Do not use the same transition more than once.

1.  Dr. Rappole has an excellent bedside manner.

    Dr. Connolly is very withdrawn.

    Your combined sentence: _____

    _____

2.  The first apartment had almost no furniture, was badly in need of painting, and felt dark and cheerless.

    The second apartment was bare, felt totally neglected, and looked out onto a brick wall.

    Your combined sentence: _____

    _____

    _____

3.  In the United States, interest in soccer has become apparent only in recent years.

    Soccer has always been immensely popular in Brazil.

    Your combined sentence: _____

    _____

4.  The French Revolution was directed by the common people.

    The Russian Revolution was directed by an elite group of thinkers.

    Your combined sentence: _____

    _____

5.  Amy is carefree and fun loving, with little interest in school.

    Noreen, Amy's sister, is so studious and hardworking that she is always on the honor roll.

    Your combined sentence: _____

    _____

    _____

**EXERCISE 8**

## Using Transitions in Comparisons and Contrasts

First, identify each of the following pairs of sentences as a comparison or a contrast. Then combine the two sentences by using a transition from the list on page 436. Do not use the same transition more than once. Finally, write your new sentence on the lines provided.

1.  Oprah Winfrey's daytime talk show deals with current controversial issues that are of importance to society.

    David Letterman's program gives people light entertainment in the evening.

    Your combined sentence: _____

    _____

    _____

2.  Shakespeare's *Romeo and Juliet* is a famous love story that takes place in Italy.

    *West Side Story* is a modern-day version of Shakespeare's love story that takes place in New York City.

    Your combined sentence: _____

    _____

    _____

3.  Hemingway's *Death in the Afternoon* deals with the theme of man against nature.

    Hemingway's *The Old Man and the Sea* deals with the theme of man against nature.

    Your combined sentence: _____

    _____

4.  Some scientists believe that dinosaurs became extinct because they ran out of food.

    Some scientists think that dinosaurs were victims of a climate change induced by dust clouds thrown up by a meteor hitting earth.

    Your combined sentence: _____

    _____

    _____

5.  The Museum of Modern Art in New York City shows paintings, photographs, movies, and many other forms of twentieth-century art.

    The Metropolitan Museum of Art in New York City contains sculptures, paintings, and other forms of art that date from the beginning of recorded history.

    Your combined sentence: _____

    _____

    _____

    _____

## WRITING A COMPARISON/CONTRAST PARAGRAPH USING A STEP-BY-STEP APPROACH

Mastering any skill, including writing, requires a disciplined attitude. One way to master the skill of creating a piece of writing is to take a step-by-step approach, focusing on one issue at a time. This approach results in a minimum of stress. Another advantage is that the writer does not miss important points or misunderstand any part of the process. Of course, there are other ways to build effective comparison or contrast paragraphs, but here is one logical method you can use that will always achieve good results.

### Step-by-Step Approach to Writing a Comparison/Contrast Paragraph

1.  After you have chosen your two-part topic, plan your topic sentence.

2.  List each point that could be compared or contrasted.

3.  Choose the three or four most important points from your list.

4.  Decide whether you want to use the point-by-point method or the block method of organizing your paragraph.

5.  Write at least one complete sentence for each of the points you have chosen from your list.

6.  Write a concluding statement that summarizes the main points, makes a judgment, or emphasizes what you believe is the most important point.

7.  Copy your sentences into standard paragraph form.

8.  Always make a final check for spelling errors and other mistakes, such as omitted words.

**NOTE:** When you use a computer spell-check feature, keep in mind that this feature will alert you only to spellings that do not match words in its dictionary. If you type *there* when you mean *their,* the spell-checker will see an acceptable word. When it comes to a final editing, there is no substitute for your own careful reading.

**EXERCISE 9**

### Writing a Comparison or Contrast Paragraph Using a Step-by-Step Approach

This exercise will guide you through the construction of a comparison or contrast paragraph. Start with the suggested topic. Use the eight steps as a guide.

> **Topic:**  **Compare or contrast how you spend your leisure time with how your parents or friends spend their leisure time.**

1.  Topic sentence: _____

_____

_____

2. Make a list of possible comparisons or contrasts.

a. _____

b. _____

c. _____

d. _____

e. _____

f. _____

g. _____

h. _____

i. _____

j. _____

3. Circle the three or four comparisons or contrasts that you believe are most important and put them in order.

4. Choose either the point-by-point method or the block method.

5. Using your final list, write at least one sentence for each comparison or contrast you have chosen.

a. _____

_____

b. _____

_____

c. _____

_____

d. _____

_____

6. Write a concluding statement. _____

_____

_____

7. On a separate piece of paper or on the computer, copy your sentences into standard paragraph form.

8. Do a final reading to check for errors and omissions.

**EXERCISE  10**

## Writing a Comparison or Contrast Paragraph Using a Step-by-Step Approach

This exercise will guide you through the construction of a comparison or contrast paragraph. Start with the suggested topic. Use the eight steps as a guide.

> **Topic:** **Compare or contrast the styles of two television personalities (or two other public figures often in the news).**

1.  Topic sentence: _____

    _____

    _____

2.  Make a list of possible comparisons or contrasts.

    a. _____

    b. _____

    c. _____

    d. _____

    e. _____

    f. _____

    g. _____

    h. _____

    i. _____

    j. _____

3.  Circle the three or four comparisons or contrasts that you believe are most important and put them in order.

4.  Choose either the point-by-point method or the block method.

5.  Using your final list, write at least one sentence for each comparison or contrast you have chosen.

    a. _____

    _____

    b. _____

    _____

    c. _____

    _____

    d. _____

    _____

6.   Write a concluding statement. _____

_____

_____

7.   On a separate piece of paper or on the computer, copy your sentences into standard paragraph form.

8.   Do a final reading to check for errors and omissions.

## STUDYING MODEL PARAGRAPHS TO CREATE COMPARISON OR CONTRAST PARAGRAPHS

### ASSIGNMENT 1: CONTRASTING A PLACE THEN AND NOW

Write a paragraph in which you compare or contrast the appearance of a place when you were growing up with the appearance of that same place now. The following paragraph contrasts the way a small city appeared some years ago with how it appeared to the writer on a recent visit.

*Topic sentence*

### Model Paragraph: Thirty Years Later

As I drove up Swede Hill, I realized that the picture I had in my mind all these years was largely a romantic one. It was here that my father had boarded, as a young man of eighteen, with a widow who rented rooms in her house. Now the large old wooden frame houses were mostly two-family homes; no single family could afford to heat them in the winter. The porches, which had once been beautiful and where people had passed their summer evenings, had peeling paint and were in need of repair. No one now stopped to talk; the only sounds to be heard were those of cars whizzing past. The immigrants who had come to this country and worked hard to put their children through school were now elderly and mostly alone. Their more educated children had long ago left the small upstate city for better opportunities elsewhere. From the top of the hill, I looked down fondly on the town built on the hills and noticed that a new and wider highway now went through the town. My father would have liked that; he would not have had to complain about Sunday drivers on Foote Avenue. In the distance I could see the large shopping mall, which now had most of the business in the surrounding area and which had forced most in-town businesses to close. Now the center of town no longer hummed with activity, as it once had. My town was not the same place I had known. I could see that the years had not been kind to my hometown.

*Ten suggested topics for contrast*

**Contrast the way a place appears now with how it appeared some years ago:**

1. A city, town, or village
2. Your childhood home
3. A barber shop or beauty salon
4. A friend's home
5. A local "corner store"
6. Your elementary school
7. A downtown shopping area
8. A restaurant or diner
9. An undeveloped place such as an open field or wooded area
10. A favorite local gathering place

## ASSIGNMENT 2: COMPARING TWO INDIVIDUALS WHO SHARE SIMILAR QUALITIES

Write a paragraph in which you compare two individuals you know or you have observed. The following paragraph is a classic comparison by the historian Bruce Catton. Using the point-by-point method, he compares two legendary generals from the American Civil War, Ulysses S. Grant, head of the Union Army, and Robert E. Lee, leader of the Confederate forces of the South.

*Topic sentence*

### Model Paragraph: Grant and Lee

Different as they were—in background, in personality, in underlying aspiration—these two great soldiers had much in common. Each man had, to begin with, the great virtue of utter tenacity and fidelity. Grant fought his way down the Mississippi Valley despite acute personal discouragement and profound military handicaps. Lee hung on in the trenches at Petersburg after hope itself had died. In each man there was an indomitable quality ...the born fighter's refusal to give up as long as he can still remain on his feet and lift his two fists. Daring and resourcefulness they had, too; the ability to think faster and move faster than the enemy. These were the qualities that gave Lee the dazzling campaigns of Second Manassas and Chancellorsville and won Vicksburg for Grant.

*Ten suggested topics for comparison*

**Compare:**

1. Two friends who have similar qualities
2. Two singers who have similar musical styles
3. Two jobs that call for similar qualifications
4. Two religious leaders who have similar goals or who perform similar duties
5. Two talk show hosts
6. A plumber and a doctor
7. Two brothers or two sisters who share certain personality traits
8. A baby and an elderly person
9. A child's art with modern art
10. A ballet dancer with a football player

## ASSIGNMENT 3: COMPARING TWO APPROACHES TO A SUBJECT

Write a paragraph in which you compare or contrast two ways of considering a particular topic. The following paragraph contrasts two approaches to the art of healing—the traditional medical approach and the approach that involves less dependence on chemicals and more reliance on the body's natural defense system.

**Model Paragraph: The Medical Profession and Natural Healing**

**Topic sentence**

    <u>Natural healing is basically a much more conservative approach to health care than traditional medical practice</u>. Traditional medical practice aims for the quick cure by means of introducing substances or instruments into the body that are highly antagonistic to whatever is causing the disease. A doctor wants to see results, and he or she wants you to appreciate that traditional medicine is what is delivering those results to you. Because of this desire for swift, decisive victories over disease, traditional medicine tends to be dramatic, risky, and expensive. Natural healing takes a slower, more organic approach to the problem of disease. It first recognizes that the human body is superbly equipped to resist disease and heal injuries. But when disease takes hold or an injury occurs, the first instinct in natural healing is to see what might be done to strengthen that natural resistance and those natural healing agents so that they can act against the disease more effectively. Results are not expected to occur overnight, but neither are they expected to occur at the expense of the body, which may experience side effects or dangerous complications.

**Ten suggested topics**

**Compare or contrast:**

1. Retiring and working after age sixty-five
2. Owning your own business and working for someone else
3. Two views on abortion
4. Two attitudes toward divorce
5. Two political viewpoints
6. Your lifestyle today and five years ago
7. Mothers who work at home and those who work away from home
8. Buying U.S.-made products and buying foreign-made goods
9. Two attitudes on the "right to die" issue
10. Two attitudes toward religion

## ASSIGNMENT 4: CONTRASTING CULTURAL APPROACHES

Write a paragraph in which you compare or contrast two cultures or an aspect of culture that may be observed in two societies. The following paragraph was written by Brenda David, an American teacher who worked with schoolchildren in Milan, Italy, for several years.

**Topic sentence**

> ## Model Paragraph: Children of Two Nations
>
>
> All young children, whatever their culture, are alike in their charm and innocence—in being a clean slate on which the wonders and ways of the world are yet to be written. <u>But during the three years I worked in a school in Milan, I learned that American and Italian children are different in several ways</u>. First, young American children tend to be active, enthusiastic, and inquisitive. Italian children, on the other hand, tend to be passive, quiet, and not particularly inquisitive. Second, American children show their independence while their Italian counterparts are still looking to their parents and grandparents to tell them what to do or not do. Third, and most important to those who question the influence of environment on a child, the American children generally surpass their Italian schoolmates in math, mechanical, and scientific abilities. But American children are overshadowed by their Italian counterparts in their language, literature, art, and music courses. Perhaps the differences, which those of us at the school confirmed in an informal study, were to be expected. After all, what priority do Americans give to the technological skills? And what value do Italians—with the literature of poets and authors like Boccaccio, the works of Michelangelo, and the music of the world-famous La Scala opera at Milan—place on the cultural arts?

**Ten suggested topics**

### Contrast:

1.  Two different cuisines
2.  Courtship in two cultures
3.  Attitudes toward women's roles in two societies
4.  Two musical traditions
5.  Raising children in two different cultures
6.  Urban people with small-town people
7.  Care for the elderly in two cultures
8.  The culture of your neighborhood with the general culture of our society
9.  The culture you live in now with the culture in which your parents were raised
10. Medical care in our society with the medical care of another society

## ASSIGNMENT 5: CONTRASTING TWO VERSIONS OF REALITY

Write a paragraph in which you contrast two versions of a topic. The following paragraph contrasts the Disney film depiction of the Pocahontas story with what we know to be more historically correct about the real Pocahontas.

### Model Paragraph: Two Versions of the Pocahontas Story

*Topic sentence*

The Disney version of the Pocahontas story is not an accurate portrayal of what we know to be true. A seventeenth-century portrait of Pocahontas reveals her to be buxom, full-faced, and strong, not the Barbie-like glamour girl of Disney. John Smith, too, is portrayed inaccurately in the film. Far from the young blond heroic figure shown in the movie, John Smith was in actuality a bearded and weathered-looking man of thirty when he met Pocahontas. The dramatic version of romance and rescue is another historical inaccuracy of the Disney film. Most historians contend that the supposed "rescue" of John Smith was in fact a farce. The Powhatans, historians claim, may have been adopting Smith into their tribe through a ritual that required a little playacting. So, although Pocahontas may have rescued Smith, the circumstances of that rescue may have been very different from the film's depiction. Furthermore, there is no historical evidence to support a romance between Pocahontas and John Smith as the movie shows. The unfortunate reality was that Pocahontas was taken captive by the English and forced to marry an English tobacco planter named John Rolfe. The ending of the film is certainly the final blow to what we know to be fact. Pocahontas did not, as Disney suggests, stay in North America while John Smith sailed into the distance toward his native England. Instead, she traveled to England with Rolfe, her new husband. On the return trip to her native North America, at the young age of twenty-two, Pocahontas fell ill, probably with smallpox, and died.

*Ten suggested topics*

**Choose one of the topics suggested below or a topic you think of yourself, and compare or contrast the two versions of reality.**

1. A sports figure's public image with details of his or her private life exposed by the media

2. Traditional portrayals of women's roles with today's portrayals

3. A "friend" before and after a major disagreement

4. Today's attitudes toward smoking contrasted to attitudes of your parents' generation

5. A politician's reputation in the past with his or her reputation today

6. A person who sees life as a glass that is half empty with a person who sees the same glass as half full

7.  The present level of commercialization of sports with the degree of commercialization years ago

8.  Attitudes toward AIDS when the virus was first discovered with attitudes toward the disease today

9.  The initial idealized version of a loved one contrasted to a more realistic version

10. How a member of your family acts at home with how that same person acts in public

## Exploring Online

Go to **www.cengage.com/devenglish/scarry/writersworkplace** to find the **Writer's Online Workplace,** a website designed for students using this book. You will find links to handouts, interactive quizzes, and other online resources as you explore the following topics:

• paragraph development using comparison/contrast

• an interactive quiz about comparison/contrast

• examples of comparison/contrast paragraphs

# Working Together

## A BEFORE AND AFTER STORY

Below is an account of a radical change in one man's life. When you have read this before and after report (which uses the block method), share with your classmates some stories of changes in the lives of people you have known. Then write a before and after story of your own. Use the chart provided on the next page to help you plan your approach to the two-part topic.

### Before

Since I was fifteen, I've saved all kinds of stuff: bureau handles, small bottles, marbles, mirrors, nuts, screws, wire, cord, bathtub stoppers, mothballs, empty cigarette packs, frying pans, pencils that say different things on them, trusses, parking tickets. In 1997, my brother Harry, with whom I lived, slipped on some of my papers and got brought to a nursing home. The social worker wouldn't let him come back unless I got rid of my collections. So I bought a bus pass and visited him once a week. He died last year at eighty-five. If he'd had a hobby like me, he might have lived longer. I liked living in my junk, and I always knew where everything was. In the living room, the junk came up to about my chest. In the bedroom, it wasn't too bad; it just came up to my knees. I made paths to get around. It made me feel important. But I guess I overdid it. The landlord wanted me to get rid of my junk. A third of my neighbors wouldn't talk to me. I suspected I might get evicted. So this summer I had to let my junk go.

### After

My nephew cleaned it out with some friends of his. It took ten days. I wasn't there. When I came back, I was disappointed. I thought more stuff would be saved. I had an empty feeling, like I was robbed. I lost memories of my four brothers and my mother. But things happen—what can you do? I'm too old to worry anymore. All that's left is my necktie collection and my cat, Wagging. The emptiness is a little hard to get used to. For one thing, the traffic noise is very loud now. And I feel hollow. My junk was sort of a freedom. I put so much work into saving—years and years—and it's suddenly gone. It's like somebody had died, a fire or an earthquake. It's like the change from hot to cold water. I may start saving certain things, like books, but I don't go out as much as I used to, so I can't collect as much. From now on, I'll have fewer hobbies.

Preparing to write a comparison or contrast paragraph involves noting points of comparison or contrast. Use the chart provided below.

| POINTS TO COMPARE OR CONTRAST | BEFORE | AFTER |
|---|---|---|
| Point 1 | | |
| Point 2 | | |
| Point 3 | | |
| Point 4 | | |
| Point 5 | | |

## PORTFOLIO SUGGESTION

You might find it interesting to do some research on a personality type known as the "pack rat." This is a person who fills an apartment or house with useless stuff that is never thrown away. Go online and find information on the Collyer brothers, two "pack rats" who died in New York City shortly after World War II. Use the information you find on Homer and Langley Collyer to write an essay about people who cannot bring themselves to throw anything away.

# DEVELOPING PARAGRAPHS: CAUSE AND EFFECT

# 23

In our daily lives, we often look for connections between two actions or events. We wonder if these events are accidental, coincidental, or connected in some more causal way. When writers examine causal relationships, they are using a cause and effect method of development. This chapter focuses on important considerations for developing this rhetorical form.

**CHAPTER OBJECTIVES**

- recognizing **terms** that signal causal relationships
- avoiding errors in **logic**
- identifying **immediate causes, underlying causes, immediate effects,** and **long-term effects**
- improving coherence by using **transitional phrases** common to cause and effect
- taking a step-by-step approach to create cause and effect paragraphs
- studying model paragraphs to create cause and effect paragraphs

## WHAT IS CAUSE AND EFFECT?

> *Cause and effect,* as a method of development, is the search for the relationship between two actions or two events, one of which we conclude is the reason for the other action or event.

People have always looked at the world and asked, "Why did this happen?" or "What will be the result?" Ancient societies created beautiful myths and legends to explain the mysteries of the universe. Modern civilization has emphasized the use of scientific methods of observation to find answers to such mysteries as the cause of a particular disease or the reason why the planet Mars appears to be covered by canals. When we examine the spiritual or physical mysteries of our world, we are trying to discover the connections or links between events. In this chapter, we will refer to such connections between events as **causal relationships.**

Not everything that happens to us is due to luck or chance. For instance, a magic trick may appear to have no logical explanation to the child who watches, but the person performing that trick knows the secret of the connection between the rabbit and the hat. The search for causes or effects is a bit like detective work. A person looks for clues that will explain what might at first seem unexplainable. Learning to recognize causal relationships can help us better understand some of the events that happen to us over the course of our lives. This search for connections can be complex. Often the logical analysis of a problem reveals more than one possible explanation. Sometimes the best one can do is find **possible causes** or **probable effects.**

# RECOGNIZING TERMS THAT SIGNAL CAUSE AND EFFECT

Writers who examine the causal relationship between two events are likely to use one or more of the terms in the following chart. Study the chart to become familiar with these terms associated most often with cause and effect.

---

## Terms That Signal Causal Relationships

**Causes:**    explaining **why**

giving **reasons**

understanding **problems**

determining **immediate causes** and **underlying causes**

**Effects:**    predicting **results**

understanding **consequences**

providing **solutions**

determining **immediate effects** and **long-term effects**

---

Following are some examples of how a writer could signal causal relationships.

1. *If . . . , then . . .*

   **If** the school budget is defeated, **then** several teachers will have to be dismissed.

2. *The cause/reason/result/consequence/effect . . . was that . . .*

   **The reason** several teachers were dismissed **was that** the school budget was defeated.

   **The result** of the school budget defeat **was that** several teachers were dismissed.

3.  *The problem…could be solved…*

> **The problem** of funding the school's wrestling team **could be solved** if enough people in the community would get together to raise the needed money.

**Practice**

Use the preceding patterns to create sentences of your own on the following topic: Writing a research paper.

1.  If _____

    then _____

2.  The reason _____

    was that _____

3.  The cause for _____

    was that _____

4.  The consequence of _____

    was that _____

5.  The problem of _____

    could be solved _____

**EXERCISE  1**

### Finding Causes and Effects in Paragraphs

Two paragraphs follow about a single topic: headaches. One paragraph examines the causes of a headache while the other describes the effects of recurring headaches.

**Cause: explaining why, giving reasons, understanding problems**

*Topic sentence*

> Headaches can have several causes. Many people think that the major cause of headache is nervous tension, but strong evidence suggests diet and environment as possible factors. Some people get headaches because they are dependent on caffeine. Other people may be allergic to salt, or they may have low blood sugar. Still other people are allergic to household chemicals, including polishes, waxes, bug killers, and paint. If they can manage to avoid these substances, their headaches tend to go away. When a person has recurring headaches, it is important to look for the underlying cause, especially if the result of that search is freedom from pain.

According to the above paragraph, what causes a headache?

1.  _____

2.  _____

    a.  _____

    b.  _____

    c.  _____

3. _____

   a. _____

   b. _____

   c. _____

   d. _____

**Effect: predicting results, understanding consequences, suggesting solutions**

*Topic sentence*

> <u>Recurring headaches can have several disruptive effects on a person's life.</u> Severe headaches are more than temporary inconveniences. In many cases, these headaches make a person nauseated to the point that he or she must go to bed. Sleep is often interrupted because of the pain. This worsens the physical and emotional state of the sufferer. Those who try to maintain a normal lifestyle often rely on drugs to get through the day. Such drugs, of course, can have negative side effects. Productivity on a job can certainly be reduced, even to the point of regular absences. Finally, perhaps the most distressing aspect of all this is the seemingly unpredictable occurrence of these headaches. The interruption to a person's family life is enormous: plans canceled at the last minute and relationships with friends and family strained. It is no wonder that many of these people feel discouraged and even depressed.

According to the preceding paragraph, what are some of the effects of recurring headaches?

1. _____

2. _____

3. _____

4. _____

5. _____

**EXERCISE 2**

### Separating the Cause from the Effect

**In each sentence, separate the *cause* (reasons or problems) from the *effect* (results, consequences, or solutions). Remember that the cause is not necessarily given first.**

1. More than half of the mothers with children under one year of age work outside the home, which has resulted in the unprecedented need for daycare in this country.

   Cause: _____

   _____

   Effect: _____

2. Today, more than two-thirds of all preschool children have mothers who work, and four out of five school-age children have working mothers, which has led to increased strains on the daycare system.

Cause: _____

_____

Effect: _____

3. In one national survey, more than half the working mothers reported that they had either changed jobs or cut back on their hours to be more available for their children.

Problem: _____

Solution: _____

4. Because they feel their children need the supervision of a parent, many mothers who work do so only when their children are in school, and other mothers work only occasionally during the school year.

Cause: _____

Effect: _____

_____

5. Many mothers experience deep emotional crises as a result of the conflict between the financial obligations of their home and their own emotional needs as parents.

Problem: _____

Result: _____

# AVOIDING ERRORS IN LOGIC

Here is an example of a possible error in logic:

**Every time I try to write an essay in the evening, I have trouble getting to sleep. Therefore, writing must prevent me from sleeping.**

In this case, the act of writing may indeed stimulate the person and prevent that person from getting to sleep. However, if the person is serious about finding the cause of the insomnia, he or she must find out whether other *factors* are to blame. For instance, if the person is drinking several cups of coffee while writing each evening, this could cause the person's sleep problems.

## Avoid These Common Errors in Logic

1. Do not confuse coincidence or chronological sequence with evidence of a causal relationship.

2. Look for underlying causes beneath the obvious ones and for far-reaching effects beyond the ones that first come to mind. Often what appears to be a single cause or a single effect is part of a much more complex relationship.

**EXERCISE** 3

## Looking for the Causal Relationship

Study each of the following situations. If the sequence of events is merely coincidental or the conclusion is unfounded, write *U* (unfounded) in the space provided. If the relationship is most likely causal, write *C*. Be prepared to explain your answers in class.

_____ 1. Every time I carry my umbrella, it doesn't rain. I am carrying my umbrella today; therefore, it won't rain.

_____ 2. We put fertilizer on the grass. A week later, the grass had grown two inches and turned a deeper green.

_____ 3. On Tuesday morning, I walked under a ladder. On Wednesday morning, I walked into my office and was told I had lost my job.

_____ 4. The child grew up helping her mother cook. In adulthood, she became a famous chef.

_____ 5. Tar and nicotine from cigarettes damage the lungs. People who smoke cigarettes increase their chances of dying from lung cancer.

_____ 6. A political scandal was exposed in the city on Friday. On Saturday night, only twenty-four hours later, a power blackout occurred in the city.

_____ 7. Increasing numbers of tourists came to the island last year. The economy of the island reached new heights.

_____ 8. Many natural disasters have occurred this year. The world must be coming to an end.

_____ 9. The biggest factory in a nearby town decided to relocate to another country. The town officials invited different industries to consider moving to the town.

_____ 10. That woman sings beautifully. She must have an equally beautiful personality.

**EXERCISE** 4

## Underlying Causes

Five topics follow. For each topic, give a possible immediate or direct cause and then give a possible underlying cause. Discuss your answers in class. An example has been done for you.

Causes of a particular disease, such as tuberculosis

Immediate cause:     contact with a carrier of the disease

Underlying cause:     immune system weakened by poor nutrition

1. Causes for being selected out of several candidates for a position

   Immediate cause _____

   Underlying cause _____

2. Causes for immigration to the United States

   Immediate cause _____

   Underlying cause _____

3. Causes for spanking a child

Immediate cause _____

Underlying cause _____

4. Causes of an unreasonable fear you have

Immediate cause _____

Underlying cause _____

5. Causes of a bad habit you have

Immediate cause _____

Underlying cause _____

**EXERCISE 5**

## Immediate or Long-Term Effects

**Below are five topics. For each topic, give an immediate effect and then give a possible long-term effect. Discuss your answers in class. An example has been done for you.**

Effects of using credit cards

Immediate effect:    money available on the spot for purchases

Long-term effect:    greater cost because of interest payments

1. Effects of horror movies on young children

Immediate effect _____

Long-term effect _____

2. Effects of tuition increases at four-year colleges

Immediate effect _____

Long-term effect _____

3. Effects on family life when both parents work outside the home

Immediate effect _____

Long-term effect _____

4. Effects of an after-school tutoring program

Immediate effect _____

Long-term effect _____

5. Effects of having a family member with special needs

Immediate effect _____

Long-term effect _____

# ACHIEVING COHERENCE: USING TRANSITIONS

Several transitional words and expressions are particularly useful in writing about causes or effects. You will need to feel comfortable using these words and expressions, and you will need to know what punctuation is required.

## Transitions Commonly Used in Cause and Effect Writing

**Common transitions for cause**

| | |
|---|---|
| because | He missed the opportunity because he was ill. |
| caused by | The missed opportunity was caused by illness. |
| the reason…is that | The reason he missed the opportunity is that he became ill. |
| results from | The missed opportunity resulted from his illness. |

**Common transitions for effect**

| | |
|---|---|
| accordingly | He was ill; accordingly, he missed the opportunity. |
| as a result | He was ill; as a result, he missed the opportunity. |
| resulted in | His illness resulted in his missing the opportunity. |
| consequently | He was ill; consequently, he missed the opportunity. |
| for this reason | He was ill. For this reason he missed the opportunity. |
| so | He was ill, so he missed the opportunity. |
| therefore | He was ill; therefore, he missed the opportunity. |
| thus | He was ill; thus, he missed the opportunity. |

**EXERCISE**  **Using Transitional Words and Expressions for Cause**

Use each of the following words or phrases in a complete sentence that demonstrates you understand how to use the given term to express a causal relationship.

1. caused by

   _____

   _____

2. because

   _____

   _____

3. results from

   _____

   _____

4. the reason for . . . is that

   _____

   _____

**EXERCISE**  **Using Transitional Words and Expressions for Effect**

Use each of the following words or phrases in a complete sentence that demonstrates you understand how to use the given term to point to an effect.

1. accordingly

   _____

   _____

2. as a result

   _____

   _____

3. results in

   _____

   _____

4. consequently

   _____

   _____

5. for this reason

   _____

   _____

6. so

   _____

   _____

7. therefore

   _____

   _____

## WRITING A CAUSE AND EFFECT PARAGRAPH USING A STEP-BY-STEP APPROACH

Mastering any skill, including writing, requires a disciplined attitude. One way to master the skill of creating a piece of writing is to take a step-by-step approach, focusing on one issue at a time. This approach results in a minimum of stress. Another advantage is that the writer does not miss important points or misunderstand any part of the process. Of course, other ways build effective cause and effect paragraphs, but here is one logical method you can use that will always achieve good results.

### Step-by-Step Approach to Writing a Cause and Effect Paragraph

**1.** After you have chosen your topic, plan your topic sentence.

**2.** Brainstorm by jotting down all possible causes or effects. Ask others for their thoughts. Do research if necessary. Consider long-range effects or underlying causes.

(continued on next page)

**3.** Choose the three or four best points from your list.

**4.** Decide on the best order for these points. (One way to organize them is from least important to most important.)

**5.** Write at least one complete sentence for each of the causes or effects you have chosen from your list.

**6.** Write a concluding statement.

**7.** On a separate piece of paper or on the computer, copy your sentences into standard paragraph form.

**8.** Always make a final check for spelling errors and other mistakes, such as omitted words.

**NOTE:** When you use a computer spell-check feature, keep in mind that this feature will alert you only to spellings that do not match words in its dictionary. If you type *there* when you mean *their*, the spell-checker will see an acceptable word. When it comes to a final editing, there is no substitute for your own careful reading.

**EXERCISE 8**

## Writing a Causal Paragraph Using a Step-by-Step Approach

This exercise will guide you through writing a paragraph using *cause* as the method of development. Start with the suggested topic. Use the eight steps to help you work through the stages of the writing process.

**Topic:  Why do so few Americans learn a second language?**

1.  Topic sentence: _____

_____

_____

2.  Make a list of possible causes. *(Consider underlying causes.)*

a.  _____

b.  _____

c.  _____

d.  _____

e.  _____

3.  Cross out any points that may be illogical or merely coincidental.

4.  Put your list in order.

5.  Using your final list, write at least one sentence for each of the causes you have found.

a. _____

_____

b. _____

_____

c. _____

_____

d. _____

_____

e. _____

_____

6.  Write a concluding statement. _____

_____

_____

7.  On a separate piece of paper or on the computer, copy your sentences into standard paragraph form.

8.  Do a final reading to check for errors and omissions.

**EXERCISE 9**

### Writing an Effect Paragraph Using a Step-by-Step Approach

This exercise will guide you through writing a paragraph using *effect* as the method of development. Start with the suggested topic. Use the eight steps to help you work through the stages of the writing process.

> **Topic:** **People today do not read as much as those of previous generations. What are the effects (both immediate and long term) for our society?**

1.  Topic sentence: _____

_____

_____

2.  Make a list of possible effects. *(Consider long range effects.)*

a. _____

_____

b. _____

_____

c. _____

_____

d. _____

_____

e. _____

_____

3. Cross out any points that may be illogical or merely coincidental.

4. Put your list in order.

5. Using your final list, write at least one sentence for each of the effects you have found.

a. _____

_____

b. _____

_____

c. _____

_____

d. _____

_____

e. _____

_____

6. Write a concluding statement. _____

_____

_____

7. On a separate piece of paper or on the computer, copy your sentences into standard paragraph form.

8. Do a final reading to check for errors and omissions.

# STUDYING MODEL PARAGRAPHS TO CREATE CAUSE AND EFFECT PARAGRAPHS

## ASSIGNMENT 1: THE CAUSES OF A SOCIAL PROBLEM

Write a paragraph about the causes of a social problem that is of concern to you. The following paragraph by Lillian Neilson looks at possible causes for placing an elderly relative in a nursing home.

### Model Paragraph: Old Age in Modern Society

*Topic sentence*

Industrialized societies have developed homes for elderly who are unable to care for themselves. Despite much criticism, these homes care for a growing percentage of our nation's elderly. Why do some people feel forced into placing parents in a nursing home? The most immediate cause is that, following serious illness, there is often no place for the elderly person to go where he or she can be cared for. In the family of today, it is often the case that both partners work outside the home, so no one is home during the day to care for the person. Hiring a full-time nurse is beyond the budget of nearly every family. Even when a family member can be home to care for the elderly person, the problems can be overwhelming. The older person can be too heavy for one or even two caretakers to manage. Giving a bath can be especially dangerous in these circumstances. In addition, many elderly people have to be watched very carefully because of their medical condition. Many families do not have the proper training to meet these needs. Finally, elderly people who are suffering from senility and are often unpredictable can make it impossible for a caregiver to leave the house or get a proper night's rest. Perhaps improving the system of home health care could help families keep their loved ones in their homes longer.

*Ten suggested topics*

1. The causes of homelessness

2. The causes of prostitution

3. The causes of teenage runaways

4. The causes of high school dropout rates

5. The causes of divorce

6. The causes of child abuse

7. The causes of white-collar crime

8. The causes of high stress among college students

9. The causes of road rage

10. The causes of the increase in childless couples

## ASSIGNMENT 2: THE CAUSES THAT LED TO A PARTICULAR HISTORICAL EVENT

Write a paragraph about the causes that led to a particular event in history. This assignment will require some research. The following model paragraph looks at the causes for the loss of life when a supposedly unsinkable ship sank on its maiden voyage nearly one hundred years ago.

### Model Paragraph: The Sinking of the Titanic

*Topic sentence*

After the British ship *Titanic sank* in the Atlantic Ocean on April 15, 1912, with the loss of more than 1,500 lives, investigators began an exhaustive search for the causes of the tragedy. The immediate cause of this terrible loss of life was a large iceberg that tore a three-hundred-foot gash in the side of the ship, flooding five of its watertight compartments. Some believe that the tragedy took place because the crew members did not see the iceberg in time, but others see a chain of different events that contributed to the tragedy. First was the fact that the ship was not carrying enough lifeboats for all of its passengers: It had enough boats for only about half of the people onboard. Furthermore, the ship's crew showed a clear lack of caring about the third-class, or "steerage," passengers, who were left in their cramped quarters below decks with little or no help as the ship went down. It has often been said that this social attitude of helping the wealthy and neglecting the poor was one of the real causes of the loss of life that night. Indeed, some of the lifeboats were not filled to capacity when the rescue ships eventually found them. Finally, the tragedy of the *Titanic* was magnified by the fact that some ships nearby did not have a radio crew on duty and therefore missed the distress signals sent by the *Titanic*. Out of all this, the need to reform safety regulations on passenger ships became obvious.

*Ten suggested topics*

1. Causes for an economic recession or depression
2. Causes for the growth of the Civil Rights Movement in the 1960s in the United States
3. Causes for the war in Iraq or Afghanistan
4. Causes for the decreasing number of fish in the ocean
5. Causes for the victory (or loss) of a particular political candidate in a recent election
6. Causes for the loss of life and property after Hurricane Katrina
7. Causes for the unemployment rate in the United States
8. Causes for the failure of so many banking institutions in 2008 and 2009
9. Causes for the rise to power of Adolf Hitler in Germany
10. Causes for the repeal of Prohibition in 1932

## ASSIGNMENT 3: THE EFFECTS OF A SUBSTANCE OR ACTIVITY ON THE HUMAN BODY

**Write a paragraph about what happens to the human body when it uses a substance or engages in some activity. The following model paragraph is adapted from Norman Taylor's *Plant Drugs That Changed the World.***

*Topic sentence*

### Model Paragraph: Effects of Caffeine

How much caffeine is too much? The ordinary cup of coffee, of the usual breakfast strength, contains about 1½ grains of caffeine (100 mg). That "second cup of coffee" hence means just about three grains of caffeine at one sitting. Its effects upon the nervous system, the increased capacity for thinking, its stimulating effects on circulation and muscular activity, not to speak of its sparking greater fluency—these are attributes of the beverage that few will give up. If it has any dangers, most of us are inclined to ignore them. But there is no doubt that excessive intake of caffeine at one time, say up to seven or eight grains (that is, 5 or 6 cups), has harmful effects such as restlessness, nervous irritability, insomnia, and muscular tremor. The lethal dose in humans is unknown, for there are no records of it. Experimental animals die in convulsions after overdoses, and from such studies it is assumed that a fatal dose of caffeine in humans may be about 150 grains (that is, ½ ounce). That would mean about one hundred cups of coffee!

*Ten suggested topics*

1.  The effects of alcohol on the body

2.  The effects of regular exercise

3.  The effects of overeating

4.  The effects of a strict diet

5.  The effects of fasting

6.  The effects of drug abuse

7.  The effects of smoking

8.  The effects of allergies

9.  The effects of a sedentary lifestyle

10.  The effects of vitamins

## ASSIGNMENT 4: THE EFFECTS OF A COMMUNITY EMERGENCY OR DISASTER

Think of an emergency or disaster that took place in or around your community. This could be an event that you witnessed or that you heard about in the media. Describe the effects this disaster had on you or the people who were involved. The following model paragraph describes the effects that a large power outage had on the communities of the Northeast.

## Model Paragraph: *The Blackout of 2003*

*Topic sentence*

On Thursday, August 14, 2003, a large area of the northeastern United States was plunged into darkness because of a power failure, resulting in what has become known as the Blackout of 2003. This unprecedented power failure, which affected several states and parts of Canada, struck in an instant and without warning. The result was a near paralysis of normal activity. Most seriously affected, of course, were those individuals, businesses, and institutions caught in a variety of dangerous situations. For example, many people were stuck in elevators; others were underground in dark, hot, crowded subways. In hospitals, patients requiring life support depended on emergency equipment to work properly. Apart from these dangerous aspects of the blackout, the financial loss to certain businesses was considerable. Restaurants and other food-related industries were forced to throw away much of their food. In such states as Michigan and Ohio, the National Guard had to distribute water. Sewage treatment plants that could not operate had to release raw sewage into their waterways. Transportation became another major problem. People who needed gasoline for their cars found that most gasoline pumps depended on electricity. The absence of working traffic lights made for huge traffic nightmares, and many airline flights were canceled. Even farmers needed generators rushed to them so they could operate their milking machines. Sadly, one effect of the emergency was that a few greedy individuals took advantage of the situation and overcharged people for items or services they needed. Reports surfaced of people paying forty dollars for simple nine-dollar flashlights. Luckily the power returned for most people within twenty-four hours and ended their discomfort. A more lasting effect, however, was the emerging realization that our electrical infrastructure is much more vulnerable than the general public had ever realized. In fact, the first thought on everyone's mind when the blackout occurred was that terrorists might have caused it. Some experts fear that even if terrorists did not initiate the blackout, the event will become a model or case study for future terrorist plans and activities. As soon as the emergency had passed, blame was placed on power company officials for not paying attention to the longstanding needs of the electrical system. People now must face the truth that creating a better system is going to involve huge amounts of money. Without any question, we can expect an increase in the cost of electricity. Surprisingly, not all of the long-term effects may be negative: officials may now be forced to plan and execute improvements that will lead to improved monitoring and maintenance of our power supply.

*Ten suggested topics*

1. The effects of a hurricane

2. The effects of an unexpected outbreak of a disease

3. The effects of a flood or other extensive water damage on a home or community

4. The effects of a prolonged heat wave

5. The effects of a bus, train, or taxi strike on a community

6. The effects of a major fire in a downtown block

7. The effects of the loss of small businesses in a community

8. The effects of the loss of an important community leader

9. The effects of decreased (or increased) services in communities

10. The effects of civil unrest in a city neighborhood

## Exploring Online

Go to **www.cengage.com/devenglish/scarry/writersworkplace** to find the **Writer's Online Workplace,** a website designed for students using this book. You will find links to handouts, interactive quizzes, and other online resources as you explore the following topic:

• writing a cause and effect composition

# Working Together

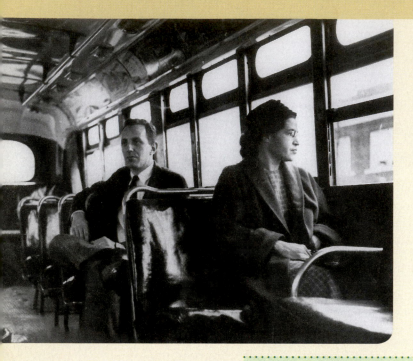

## LOOKING AT IMMEDIATE AND LONG-TERM EFFECTS: THE STORY OF ROSA PARKS

Rosa Parks (1913–2005), who refused to give up her seat on an Alabama bus, set off a spark that inflamed the civil rights movement of that era. Her action is the subject of the following article by Ruth Edmonds Hill. The instructor or a member of the class should read the excerpt aloud while the rest of the class listens, noting immediate or long-term effects and marking the text where each effect is given.

1   The incident that changed Parks's life occurred on Thursday, December 1, 1955, as she was riding home on the Cleveland Avenue bus from her job at Montgomery Fair, a downtown department store where she worked as an assistant tailor. The first ten seats on the city buses, which were always reserved for whites, soon filled up. She sat down next to a man in the front of the section designated for blacks, when a white male got on and looked for a seat. In such situations, the black section was made smaller. The driver, who was white, requested that the four blacks move. The others complied, but Parks refused to surrender her seat, so the driver called the police. Parks had been evicted from a bus twelve years earlier by the same driver, but this time it was different. In a *Black Women Oral History Project* interview, she said, "I didn't consider myself breaking any segregation laws...because he was extending what we considered our section of the bus." And in *Black Women* she explained, "I felt just resigned to give what I could to protest against the way I was being treated."

2   At this time there had been fruitless meetings with the bus company about the rudeness of the drivers and other issues—including trying to get the bus line extended farther into the black community, because three-quarters of the bus riders were from there. In the previous year three black women, two of them teenagers, had been arrested for defying the seating laws on the Montgomery buses. The community had talked many times about a citywide demonstration, such as boycotting the bus line, but it never developed. The Women's Political Council already had a network of volunteers in place and had preprinted flyers; they needed only a time and place for a meeting.

(continued on next page)

3   About six o'clock that evening, Parks was arrested and sent to jail. She was later released on a one-hundred-dollar bond, and her trial was scheduled for December 5. Parks agreed to allow her case to become the focus for a struggle against the system of segregation. On December 2, the Women's Political Council distributed more than fifty-two thousand flyers throughout Montgomery calling for a one-day bus boycott on the day of Parks's trial. There was a mass meeting of more than seven thousand blacks at the Holt Street Baptist Church. The black community formed the Montgomery Improvement Association and elected Martin Luther King Jr. president. The success of the bus boycott on December 5 led to its continuation. In the second month it was almost 100 percent effective, involving thirty thousand black riders. When Parks was tried, she was found guilty and fined ten dollars plus court costs of four dollars. She refused to pay and appealed the case to the Montgomery Circuit Court.

4   Following her release from jail, Parks went back to work but later lost her job, as did her husband. At home, the couple had to deal with threatening telephone calls. Rosa Parks devoted her time to arranging rides in support of the boycott. Blacks were harassed and intimidated by the authorities in Montgomery, and there was an attempt to break up their car-pools. Parks served for a time on the board of directors of the Montgomery Improvement Association and often was invited elsewhere to speak about the boycott.

5   On February 1, 1956, in an attempt to have the Alabama segregation laws declared unconstitutional, the Montgomery Improvement Association filed a suit in the United States District Court in the names of four women and on behalf of all who had suffered indignities on the buses. On June 2 the lower court declared segregated seating on the buses unconstitutional. The Supreme Court upheld the lower court order that Montgomery buses must be integrated, and on December 20, 1956, the order was served on Montgomery officials. After 381 days of boycotting, resulting in extreme financial loss to the bus company, segregation and other discriminatory practices were outlawed on the city buses. Parks's refusal to give up her seat on a bus was the beginning of the civil rights movement of the 1950s and 1960s. Her action marked the beginning of a time of struggle by black Americans and their supporters as they sought to become an integral part of America.

6   With the notoriety surrounding her name, Parks was unable to find employment in Montgomery. Her husband became ill and could not work, so Parks, her husband, and her mother moved to Detroit in 1957 to join Parks's brother. Although her husband did not have a Michigan barber's license, he found work in a training school for barbers. In 1958 Parks accepted a position at Hampton Institute in Virginia for one year, after which she returned to Detroit and worked as a seamstress. She continued her efforts to improve life for the black community, working with the Southern Christian Leadership Conference in Detroit. In 1965 Parks became a staff assistant in the Detroit office of United States Representative John Conyers; she retired in 1988.

## Working in Groups

After the excerpt has been read, the class should divide into groups. Each group should work up two lists: the immediate effects and the long-term effects of Rosa Parks's decision, as presented in the article. Come together again as a class and compare the lists. Has each group agreed on which effects were immediate and which effects were long-term?

Since the day in 1955 when Rosa Parks took her historic stand, many changes have taken place in civil rights in our society. Your instructor may want you to choose another area of civil rights (such as one of those listed below) to study the causes of that particular group's discontent or to study the effects of that group's struggle to obtain legal rights.

- rights of the dying
- rights of the unborn
- gay rights
- rights of immigrants

## PORTFOLIO SUGGESTION

Because civil rights is constantly evolving in our society, and because many different groups are continuing to press for their rights, we need to understand the underlying causes and the long-term effects of those struggles. Investigate newspapers, magazines, and the Internet for material on current civil rights struggles. You may have a particular struggle that you are deeply interested in. Keep the results in your portfolio. The material you collect could well be useful later when you might be asked to write about some aspect of this important topic.

# DEVELOPING PARAGRAPHS: DEFINITION AND ANALYSIS

# 24

Definition and analysis is another method used to develop ideas. To avoid misunderstandings and confusion, definitions are needed for any terms that may be unfamiliar to the reader or that are open to different interpretations. In fact, defining terms is a part of most nonfiction writing.

**CHAPTER OBJECTIVES**

- placing the term into a larger **class**
- identifying the term's **characteristics**
- using **negation**
- providing **examples**
- using **extended definition** or **analysis**
- taking a step-by-step approach to create definition paragraphs
- studying model paragraphs to create definition paragraphs

## WHAT IS DEFINITION?

> **Definition,** as a method of development, explores the meaning or significance of a term.

### PLACING A TERM IN ITS LARGER CLASS

The starting point for any good definition is to place the word into a larger **category** or **class.** For example, a *trout* is a kind of fish; a *doll* is a kind of toy; a *shirt* is an article of clothing. Here are the first four meanings of a dictionary entry for the word *family.*

**family** (fam´e -le, fam´le) *n., pl.* **-lies.** *Abbr.* **fam.** 1. The most instinctive fundamental social or mating group, traditionally consisting of two parents rearing their children. 2. One's spouse and children. 3. A group of persons sharing a common ancestry: relatives, kinfolk, clan. 4. All the members of a household; those who share one's domestic home.

According to this dictionary entry, the *family* is the most basic of social groups. Therefore, the larger category that the term *family* can be placed into is a *social group*.

**EXERCISE** **1**

### Defining by Class

Define each of the following terms by placing it in a larger class. Keep in mind that when you define something by *class*, you are placing it in a larger category so that the reader can see where it belongs. Use the dictionary if you need help. An example has been done for you.

Chemistry is *one of the branches of science.*_____

1. Mythology is _____

2. Nylon is _____

3. An amoeba is _____

4. A tricycle is _____

5. Cabbage is _____

6. Democracy is _____

7. Asbestos is _____

8. A piccolo is _____

9. Poetry is _____

10. A university is _____

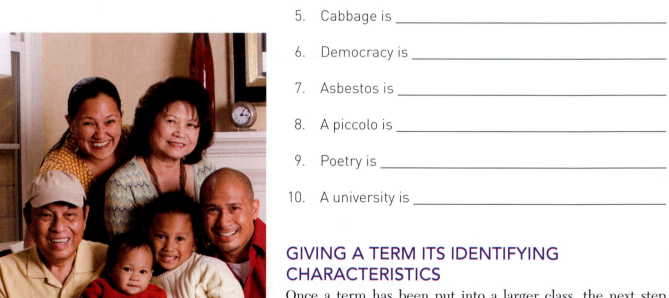

## GIVING A TERM ITS IDENTIFYING CHARACTERISTICS

Once a term has been put into a larger class, the next step is to provide the **identifying characteristics** that make the term different from other members in that class. What makes a *trout* different from a *bass*, a *doll* different from a *puppet*, a *shirt* different from a *sweater*? Here a definition can give examples. Look back again at the dictionary definition of *family*. Notice that the first meaning gives an example of a family: "traditionally two parents rearing their children." The three additional meanings provide suggestions for some other variations.

**EXERCISE   2**   **Identifying Characteristics**

Using the same terms as in Exercise 1, give one or two identifying character-istics that differentiate your term from other terms in the same class. Use a dictionary. An example is done for you.

Chemistry is *the study of the structure, properties, and reactions of matter.*

1.  Mythology _____

    _____

2.  Nylon _____

    _____

3.  An amoeba _____

    _____

4.  A tricycle _____

    _____

5.  Cabbage _____

    _____

6.  Democracy _____

    _____

7.  Asbestos _____

    _____

8.  A piccolo _____

    _____

9.  Poetry _____

    _____

10. A university _____

    _____

# DEFINING BY NEGATION

The writer could also have defined *family* by **negation.** That is, the writer could have described what a family is *not:*

**A family is not a corporation.**

**A family is not a formal school.**

**A family is not a religion.**

When a writer defines a concept using negation, the definition should be completed by stating what the subject actually *is*:

**A family is not a corporation, but it is an economic unit of production and consumption.**

**A family is not a formal school, but it is a major center for learning.**

**A family is not a religion, but it is where children learn their moral values.**

**EXERCISE** **3**

## Defining by Negation

**Define each of the following terms, using negation to construct your definition. Keep in mind that such a definition is not complete until you have also included a positive statement about the topic that you are defining. You may want to work in groups to arrive at your answers.**

1.  A *disability* does not mean _____

    but it may mean _____

2.  The *perfect car* need not be _____

    but it should be _____

3.  *Drugs* are not _____

    but they are _____

4.  *Freedom* is not _____

    but it is _____

5.  A *good job* does not have to _____

    but it should _____

6.  *Exercise* should not _____

    but it should _____

7.  A *university* is not _____

    it is _____

8.  A *legislator* should not _____

    but he or she should _____

9.  The *ideal pet* is not _____

    it _____

10. A *boring person* is not _____

    but he or she is _____

# DEFINING WITH EXAMPLES

Examples make a concept more concrete. For each of the following terms, provide one good example that would help make a stronger definition. You may need to consult an encyclopedia. An example has been done for you.

**Term:**     Chemistry

**Example:** Chemistry teaches us that hydrogen has the simplest structure of all the elements, with only one electron and one proton. It is colorless, highly flammable, the lightest of all gases, and the most abundant element in the universe.

**EXERCISE  4**

## Providing Examples

1.  Mythology _____

    _____

2.  Friendship _____

    _____

3.  Philanthropist _____

    _____

4.  Planet _____

    _____

5.  Gland _____

    _____

6.  Greed _____

    _____

7.  Volcano _____

    _____

8.  Patriotism _____

    _____

9.  Terrorism _____

    _____

10. Equality _____

    _____

# DEFINING WITH ANALYSIS OR EXTENDED DEFINITION

When you write a paragraph or an essay that uses definition, the dictionary entry is only the beginning. It is not the function of a dictionary to go into great depth. A dictionary can provide only basic meanings and synonyms. To help your reader understand a difficult term or idea, you will need to expand this definition into what is called an **extended definition.** With an *extended definition,* you seek to analyze a concept so that the reader will have a more complete understanding of it. For instance, you might include a historical perspective. When or how did the concept begin? How did the term change or evolve over the years, or how do different cultures understand the term? When you ask these questions, you become involved in the term's *connotations.* An extended definition, or *analysis* as it is also called, draws on more than one method to arrive at an understanding of a term.

> An **extended definition** is an expanded definition or **analysis** of a concept or term, giving additional information that conveys a fuller meaning.

The following paragraph, taken from *Sociology: An Introduction* by John E. Conklin, is the beginning of a chapter on the family. The author's starting point is very similar to the dictionary entry seen above.

*Topic sentence*

> In every society, social norms define a variety of relationships among people, and some of these relationships are socially recognized as family or kinship ties. A *family* is a socially defined set of relationships between at least two people who are related by birth, marriage, or adoption. We can think of a family as including several possible relationships, the most common being between husband and wife, between parents and children, and between people who are related to each other by birth (siblings, for example) or by marriage (a woman and her mother-in-law, perhaps). Family relationships are often defined by custom, such as the relationship between an infant and godparents, or by law, such as the adoption of a child.

The author begins this definition by putting the term into a larger class. *Family* is one type of social relationship among people. The writer then identifies the people who are members of this group. Family relationships can be formed by marriage, birth, adoption, or custom. The author does not stop here. In the pages that follow this paragraph the writer explores the functions of the family, conflicts in the family, the structure of the family, and the special characteristics of the family.

## Terms Commonly Used for Definition

| | | |
|---|---|---|
| connotes | includes | signifies |
| characteristics | indicates | suggests |
| consists of | is/is not | symptoms |

(continued on next page)

| constitutes | is more than | is thought to be |
| denotes | is not only | traits |
| defined as | means | is understood to be |

## Transitions Commonly Used for Definition

| For multiple meanings: | first; second; third; in one case; in another case |
| For identifying characteristics: | one trait; another trait |
| For examples: | for example; for instance; like; such as |
| To show change over time: | at one time; now |
| To specify: | in particular; specifically; in fact |
| To add: | also; in addition; furthermore |

## WRITING A DEFINITION PARAGRAPH USING A STEP-BY-STEP APPROACH

Mastering any skill, including writing, requires a disciplined attitude. One way to master the skill of creating a piece of writing is to take a step-by-step approach, focusing on one issue at a time. This approach results in a minimum of stress. Another advantage is that the writer does not miss important points or misunderstand any part of the process. Of course, there are other ways to build effective paragraphs using definition as the method of development, but here is one logical method you can use that will always achieve good results.

### Step-by-Step Approach to Writing a Definition Paragraph

1. After you have selected a term, put that term into its larger class.

2. Give the term its identifying characteristics.

3. Construct your topic sentence. You may want to provide a framework around the term you are defining by putting it into a context of a specific time and place.

4. If helpful, use *negation* to tell what your term does not mean.

5. Provide examples. Write at least one or two sentences for each example.

(continued on next page)

**6.** Provide any additional analysis necessary for an understanding of the term.

**7.** Write a concluding statement.

**8.** On a separate piece of paper or on the computer, copy your sentences into standard paragraph form. Redraft as necessary.

**9.** Do a final reading to check for errors and omissions.

**EXERCISE  5**

## Writing a Definition Paragraph Using a Step-by-Step Approach

This exercise will guide you through the construction of a paragraph using definition as the method of development. Start with the suggested term. Use the seven steps to help you work through the stages of the writing process.

**Term: Cyberbullying**

1.  Put the term into a larger class _____

2.  What are the identifying characteristics of the term?

    _____

    _____

    _____

3.  Define the term using negation.

    _____

4.  Give examples of the term. Write at least one or two complete sentences for each example.

    _____

    _____

    _____

    _____

    _____

    _____

5.  Provide further analysis, historical or cultural, that would help the reader understand the term.

    _____

    _____

    _____

_____

_____

_____

6.  Copy your sentences into standard paragraph form. Redraft as necessary.

7.  Final editing: Do a final reading to check for errors and omissions.

# STUDYING MODEL PARAGRAPHS TO CREATE DEFINITION PARAGRAPHS

## ASSIGNMENT 1: DEFINITION OF A MEDICAL CONDITION

Write a paragraph that will define a current medical concern, one that is gaining a good deal of national attention. The following paragraph attempts to define the phenomenon of *autism* and includes some of the symptoms that are used to help diagnose the condition.

### Model Paragraph: What Is Autism?

*Topic sentence*

Autism is a developmental disability that until the 1940s was unrecognized. In 1988, the film *Rain Man* starring Dustin Hoffman brought the condition to greater public awareness. Now some researchers claim that one in every 91 American children has some form of autism. This is because the definition has broadened to include a wide range of identifying symptoms. The three most distinctive symptoms that lead to a diagnosis of autism are (1) a difficulty with social interaction, (2) a problem with verbal and nonverbal communication, and (3) repetitive actions or obsessive interests. For instance, a parent may slowly realize that a child is not making eye contact or smiling. Sometimes a child is developing normally and then suddenly loses language and social skill. Experts point out that autism is not to be confused with mental retardation. Autistic children are often gifted in one or more areas. While there is still much to learn about the syndrome, doctors all agree that the earlier parents start intervention therapies, the better the outcome.

*Ten suggested topics*

1. ADD (Attention Deficit Disorder)

2. Childhood Obesity

3. Alzheimer's Disease

4. Asthma

5. Munchausen Syndrome

6. Borderline Personality Disorder

7. Dyslexia

8. Anorexia Nervosa

9. Postpartum Depression

10. Asperger Syndrome

## ASSIGNMENT 2: DEFINITION OF A CONTROVERSIAL TERM

Write a paragraph that will define a controversial term. The following extended definition is how Lawrence M. Friedman, Professor of Law at Stanford University, defines the term *crime.*

### *Model Paragraph: What Is Crime?*

*Topic sentence*

There is no real answer to the question, What is crime? There are popular ideas about crime: crime is bad behavior, antisocial behavior, blameworthy acts, and the like. But in a very basic sense crime is a *legal* concept; what makes some conduct criminal, and other conduct not, is the fact that some, but not others, are "against the law." Before some act can be isolated and labeled as a crime, there must be a special, solemn, social and political decision. In our society, Congress, a state legislature, or a city government has to pass a law or enact an ordinance adding the behavior to the list of crimes. Then this behavior, like a bottle of poison, carries the proper label and can be turned over to the heavy artillery of law for possible enforcement.

*Ten suggested topics*

1. Pornography

2. Child abuse

3. Torture

4. Freedom

5. Intelligence

6. Patriotism

7. Marriage

8. Masculinity

9. Justice

10. Conservatism

## ASSIGNMENT 3: YOUR DEFINITION OF A TYPE OF PERSON

Write a paragraph that defines a type of person according to your own opinion. In the following paragraph, semantics expert S. I. Hayakawa defines his idea of the creative person.

### Model Paragraph: The Creative Person

*Topic sentence*

A creative person, first, is not limited in his thinking to "what everyone knows." "Everyone knows" that trees are green. The creative artist is able to see that in certain lights some trees look blue or purple or yellow. The creative person looks at the world with his or her own eyes, not with the eyes of others. The creative individual also knows his or her own feelings better than the average person. Most people don't know the answer to the question, "How are you? How do you feel?" The reason they don't know is that they are so busy feeling what they are supposed to feel, thinking what they are supposed to think, that they never get down to examining their own deepest feelings.

*Ten suggested topics*  Your definition of a type of person

1.  The couch potato

2.  The worry bird

3.  The drama queen

4.  The abusive person

5.  The hypochondriac

6.  The gang member

7.  The taker (or, the giver)

8.  The artist

9.  The egotist

10.  The dependent person

### Exploring Online

Go to **www.cengage.com/devenglish/scarry/writersworkplace** to find the **Writer's Online Workplace,** a website designed for students using this book. You will find links to handouts, interactive quizzes, and other online resources as you explore the following topics:

• writing definitions

• looking at examples of definition paragraphs

# Working Together

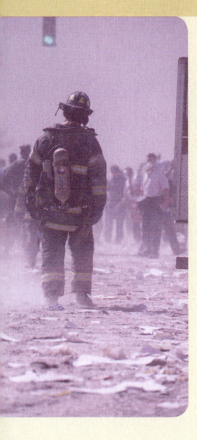

## WHO IS A HERO?

Some words or ideas are hard to define, either because they are complicated or because they are controversial. One such idea is the concept of *heroism*. The following paragraph, from Nicholas Thompson's essay "Hero Inflation," gives us a useful review of the changing definition of *heroism* in our society today.

Roughly speaking, American heroes first needed bravery. But bravery is not sufficient because evil people can be brave, too. So, the second trait in American historical lore is nobility. Heroes must work toward goals that we approve of. Heroes must show ingenuity. Lastly, they should be successful. Rosa Parks wouldn't have been nearly as much of a hero if she hadn't sparked a boycott that then sparked a movement. Charles Lindbergh wouldn't have been nearly as heroized if the *Spirit of St. Louis* had crashed into the Atlantic, or if scores of people had made the flight before. Recently, though, a fourth trait—victimhood—seems to have become as important as anything else in determining heroic status. Today, heroes don't have to do anything: they just need to be noble victims.

## Working in Groups

Working together as a class, discuss the following Americans. Would you consider each one of them a hero? Why or why not?

- Pilot Chesley Sullenberger, who guided a disabled US Airways jetliner to safely land in the Hudson River in the winter of 2009
- Roberto Clemente, famous Puerto Rican baseball player, who was killed in an airplane crash trying to deliver relief supplies to earthquake victims in Nicaragua
- Hollywood celebrity Angelina Jolie, who has adopted several children from other lands
- Bill Gates, a wealthy businessman who gives away millions of dollars
- A bone marrow donor
- A firefighter killed in the World Trade Center attacks
- The boxer Muhammad Ali, also known for his political courage in the Civil Rights era
- An American in the Armed Services who has been killed in battle

Work together to create a definition of *heroism* in a single sentence. Then look up the dictionary definition. How close are the two definitions?

## PORTFOLIO SUGGESTIONS

Using the list from the group exercise, look up some of the more famous of these figures, either in an encyclopedia or on the Internet. Examine these people's lives and then make judgments about them. Do you think these people are true heroes? Keep a list of heroic individuals and their deeds for possible use in a future essay.

# DEVELOPING PARAGRAPHS: CLASSIFICATION

# 25

Classification as a method of development is very useful when the topic involves a large body of information. This chapter will explain the thinking behind the use of classification in your writing and will give you opportunities to explore this method of development.

**CHAPTER OBJECTIVES**

- finding a **basis for classification**
- making **distinct categories**
- making the classification **complete**
- making sure the classification has a **useful purpose**
- using a step-by-step approach to create classification paragraphs
- studying model paragraphs to create classification paragraphs

## WHAT IS CLASSIFICATION?

Every day we are helped by systems that take large amounts of information and organize that information into groups or categories so that we can better manage the information. Libraries classify books and periodicals according to a specific system; in biology, plants and animals are classified into groups and subgroups (*kingdom, phylum, class, genus, species,* for example). In our jobs, office documents must be organized into some logical filing system both in physical files and on computer files. Classification is also a method for developing a piece of writing. This chapter will guide you through the thinking process needed to create paragraphs of classification.

> **Classification** is a logical way of thinking that enables us to separate a large number of items into categories. The result is a more manageable way to understand or analyze the material.

(continued on next page)

- A marketing analyst might write a brochure to classify the types of products a company offers.
- A historian might classify a century of history into its time periods, decades, or eras.

# FINDING THE BASIS FOR CLASSIFICATION

Not all topics are suitable for classification. To break something down into its parts you must find an important basis for those divisions. For instance, if you were a travel agent, a customer who wanted to go on a vacation might ask you to provide a list of vacation spots ranging from least expensive to most expensive. Another customer might ask for vacation possibilities that would be near a beach. Still another might want to know about vacations that would involve renting a cabin in a fishing area. In other words, there could be many ways to approach the classification of vacations.

**Topic:** Vacation spots

Three possible bases for classifying vacations:

1. By price (first class, second class, economy)
2. By special attractions (the beach, the mountains, the desert)
3. By accommodations (motel, cabin, trailer)

**EXERCISE 1**

## Finding the Basis for Classification

**For each of the following topics, pick three different ways the topic could be classified.**

1. Topic: Movies

Ways to divide the topic: _____

_____

2. Topic: Cars

Ways to divide the topic: _____

_____

3. Topic: Houses

Ways to divide the topic: _____

_____

4. Topic: Religions

Ways to divide the topic: _____

_____

5. Topic: Soft drinks

Ways to divide the topic: _____

_____

# MAKING DISTINCT CATEGORIES

To classify items properly, we must find *distinct categories* into which these items will fit. Each item must belong to only one category. For example, classifying motorcycles into three categories—imported motorcycles, U.S.-made motorcycles, and used motorcycles—would not be an effective use of classification because an *imported* motorcycle or a U.S.-made motorcycle could also be a *used* motorcycle. These categories would, therefore, not be distinct.

**EXERCISE 2**

### Making Distinct Categories

For each of the following topics, first choose a basis for classification. Then divide the topic into as many distinct categories as you think the classification requires. Write your answers on the lines provided.

Keep in mind that, when you divide your topic, each item must belong to only one category. For example, if you were to classify cars by type, you would not want to make *sports cars* and *imported cars* two of your categories because several kinds of sports cars are also imported cars.

1.  Dogs

Basis of Classification: _____

Distinct categories:

_____    _____    _____

_____    _____    _____

2.  Television commercials

Basis of Classification: _____

Distinct categories:

_____    _____    _____

_____    _____    _____

3.  College sports

Basis of Classification: _____

Distinct categories:

_____    _____    _____

_____    _____    _____

4.  Doctors

Basis of Classification: _____

Distinct categories:

_____    _____    _____

_____    _____    _____

5.   The courses offered in one of your college's departments

Basis of Classification: _____

Distinct categories:

_____    _____    _____

_____    _____    _____

## MAKING THE CLASSIFICATION COMPLETE

A classification must also be *complete.* For example, if you classified motorcycles into the two categories of *new* and *used,* your classification would be complete because all motorcycles have to be either *new* or *used.* If this is your choice for classifying motorcycles, your classification is complete. There is no other possible category. Depending on your purpose, however, there could be other possible bases for classifications that would also have distinct and complete categories.

The following paragraph, taken from Judith Viorst's essay "Friends, Good Friends—and Such Good Friends," shows the writer classifying different kinds of friends.

*Topic sentence*

> There are medium friends, and pretty good friends, and very good friends indeed, and these friendships are defined by their level of intimacy. And what we'll reveal at each of these levels of intimacy is calibrated with care. We might tell a medium friend, for example, that yesterday we had a fight with our husband. And we might tell a pretty good friend that this fight with our husband made us so mad that we slept on the couch. And we might tell a very good friend that the reason we got so mad in that fight that we slept on the couch had something to do with that girl who works in his office. But it's only to our very best friends that we're willing to tell all, to tell what's going on with that girl in his office.

In this paragraph, the writer not only gives us the basis of classification (levels of intimacy) but she names the levels: *medium friends, pretty good friends, very good friends*, and *very best friends.* Her classification is complete because it covers a full range of friendships.

## MAKING SURE THE CLASSIFICATION HAS A USEFUL PURPOSE

Finally, a classification should serve some *useful purpose.* For a person thinking about buying a motorcycle, classifying motorcycles into the categories of *new* or *used* may be a helpful way to make a wise decision.

**EXERCISE 3**

### Making Sure the Classification Has a Useful Purpose

**In each example, suggest a reason why a writer might want to classify the following topics:**

1.   Chairs _____

2.   Divorces _____

3. Lunches _____

4. Music _____

5. Mail _____

## ACHIEVING COHERENCE

In a paragraph or essay that uses classification to develop the ideas, certain terms are almost always to be found. These terms are used to signal that the writer is transitioning from one category to the next. Often an actual number will come before the term, such as *the first group*, *the second group*, and *the third group*.

---

### Terms That Signal Classification

| | | |
|---|---|---|
| aspects | groups | qualities |
| areas | kinds | sorts |
| brands | levels | systems |
| categories | parts | traits |
| forms | principles          • | types |
| features | | |

---

## WRITING A CLASSIFICATION PARAGRAPH USING A STEP-BY-STEP APPROACH

Mastering any skill, including writing, requires a disciplined attitude. One way to master the skill of creating a piece of writing is to take a step-by-step approach, focusing on one issue at a time. This approach results in a minimum of stress. Another advantage is that the writer does not miss important points or misunderstand any part of the process. Of course, there are other ways to build effective classification paragraphs, but here is one logical method you can use that will always achieve good results.

---

### Step-by-Step Approach to Writing a Classification Paragraph

1. After you have selected a topic, decide on the basis for your classification.

2. Determine the categories for your classification. Give each category an identifying title or name. Be as creative as possible. You may want to take a humorous tone. Remember, no item should belong in more than one group, and your classification should be complete.

---

(continued on next page)

3. Write your topic sentence. Use one of the terms (such as *group* or *type)* that signal a classification.

4. Write at least one or two sentences for each group, remembering that each group should be given approximately equal space and importance.

5. Write a concluding statement. If you have not already indicated a useful purpose for the classification, do so in the conclusion.

6. On a separate piece of paper or on the computer, copy your sentences into standard paragraph form. Before printing, read the paragraph again to check for any changes that may be needed.

7. Do a final reading once you have printed the paragraph to check for any errors or omissions.

**EXERCISE** **4**

## Writing a Classification Paragraph Using a Step-by-Step Approach

**The following exercise will guide you through the construction of a classification paragraph. Start with the suggested topic. Use the seven steps to help you work through the stages of the writing process.**

Topic: Games I have played

1. What is the basis for your classification?_____

   _____

2. What are the categories for your classification? Give each category a name.

   a. _____

   b. _____

   c. _____

   d. _____

3. Write your topic sentence. (Use one of the classification terms given on page 489.)

   _____

   _____

4. Write at least one or two sentences about each category.

   a. _____

   _____

   b. _____

   _____

c. _____

_____

d. _____

_____

5. Write a concluding sentence. Suggest a useful purpose for the classification.

_____

_____

_____

6. On a separate piece of paper or on the computer, copy your sentences into standard paragraph form.

7. Do a final reading to check for errors and omissions.

# STUDYING MODEL PARAGRAPHS TO CREATE CLASSIFICATION PARAGRAPHS

## ASSIGNMENT 1: CLASSIFYING EVERYDAY ITEMS

Write a paragraph that classifies items we use every day. The following paragraph classifies types of automobiles now being developed.

## Model Paragraph: *The Future Car*

**Topic sentence**

Everyone knows that this country must develop cars that are more efficient and less polluting. Today's internal combustion engine uses only 13% of its fuel to move the vehicle. The race is on to find the car of the future. At present, five basic types of cars are in different stages of development. The first type is the *hypercar.* This automobile continues to use gasoline or alternative fuels like ethanol to power the car but the car itself as well as the engine has dramatic new designs that improve its efficiency. The second type of car is the *electric car.* This car uses hybrid electric batteries to store energy, but its main disadvantage is its dependence on frequent recharging. The third type is the *hybrid car.* While this car continues to use gasoline, it also uses batteries that can improve the efficiency. The fourth type is a car run by *hydrogen fuel cells.* Its advantage is that the only emission it produces is water, but many other problems remain. The fifth type is the *solar powered car.* Unfortunately, whenever there is no sunlight for a number of days, there is no power. No single type of car has yet emerged as the perfect solution although some, like the hybrid, are available for purchase now. We will have to wait and see if any alternative energy-saving car will be a clear winner in the race for a better and more environmentally friendly car.

**Ten suggested topics**    Every day items that could be classified:

1.  Work clothes
2.  Cell phones
3.  Hairstyles
4.  Desserts
5.  Shoes
6.  Television sets
7.  Magazines
8.  Tools
9.  Makeup
10. Computers

## ASSIGNMENT 2: CLASSIFYING PLACES

Write a paragraph that classifies places with which you are familiar. The following paragraph is a famous example of classification, written in the late 1940s by the master American essayist E.B. White.

*Topic sentence*

### Model Paragraph: *The Three New Yorks*

There are roughly three New Yorks. There is, first, the New York of the man or woman who was born here, who takes the city for granted and accepts its size and its turbulence as natural and inevitable. Second, there is the New York of the commuter—the city that is devoured by locusts each day and spat out each night. Third, there is the New York of the person who was born somewhere else and came to New York in quest of something. Of these three trembling cities the greatest is the last—the city of final destination, the city that is a goal. It is this third city that accounts for New York's high strung disposition, its poetical deportment, its dedication to the arts, and its incomparable achievements. Commuters give the city its tidal restlessness; natives give it solidity and continuity; but the settlers give it passion. And whether it is a farmer arriving from Italy to set up a small grocery store, or a young girl arriving from a small town in Mississippi to escape the indignity of being observed by her neighbors, or a boy arriving from the Corn Belt with a manuscript in his suitcase and a pain in his heart, it makes no difference: each embraces New York with the intense excitement of first love, each absorbs New York with the fresh eyes of an adventurer, each generates heat and light to dwarf the Consolidated Edison Company.

*Ten suggested topics*

Places that could be classified:

1. Colleges
2. Parks
3. Clubs
4. Restaurants
5. Places to study
6. Party locations
7. Clothing stores
8. Neighborhoods
9. Places to play sports
10. Popular honeymoon locations

## ASSIGNMENT 3: CLASSIFYING TYPES OF PEOPLE

Write a paragraph that classifies a group of people. The following paragraph divides movie heroes into three distinct groups.

### Model Paragraph: Movie Heroes

*Topic sentence*

Heroes in American movies usually fall into types. One kind of hero is the tight-lipped loner, men like Clint Eastwood and Humphrey Bogart. Another movie hero is the quiet, shy, or fumbling type who has appeared in movies since the beginning. The main characteristic of this hero is lovableness, as seen in actors like Jimmy Stewart. Perhaps the most one-dimensional and predictable hero is the superman who battles tough odds. This kind of hero is best illustrated by Sylvester Stallone as Rocky and Rambo.

*Ten suggested topics*

People to Classify:

1. Politicians
2. Neurotics
3. Annoying people
4. Celebrities
5. Supervisors
6. Babysitters
7. Cheaters
8. Coworkers
9. People in the neighborhood
10. Relatives

## Exploring Online

Go to **www.cengage.com/devenglish/scarry/writersworkplace** to find the **Writer's Online Workplace,** a website designed for students using this book. You will find links to handouts, interactive quizzes, and other online resources as you explore the following topic:

• classification techniques

# Working Together

## CLASSIFICATION: PERSONALITIES IN THE CLASSROOM

How could you categorize students in the classrooms you have known? Here are a few popular stereotypes that could be used when exploring this topic:

the class clown

the overachiever

the teacher's pet

the quiet student

the inattentive student

### Brainstorming

Brainstorm with the class for the names of other student types found in the classroom. Put all the possibilities on the board. Then decide which combinations would work well together for a classification paragraph or essay, remembering that the categories should be distinct and complete. (Of course, there could be some flexibility with the completeness of the categories if your intention is humorous.) How many different groupings can the members of the class arrange?

### Writing

Each student should then write a classification paragraph using one of the groupings in the class brainstorming session.

### Peer Editing

After fifteen minutes or so, pass the paragraphs around so that all students can read each other's work. On a separate sheet of paper that travels with each paragraph, each student should make one positive criticism and one constructive criticism. Finally return the paragraph with its separate page of comments to the owner.

## PORTFOLIO SUGGESTION

The paragraph you have written in class would make a good introductory paragraph for a full-length essay, in which you might devote an entire paragraph to each student type. Keep your paragraph as well as the brainstorming list developed in the class. You might find this material useful when writing an essay in your current class or in another writing class in the future.

# Part 5

# Structuring the College Essay

In previous parts of this book, you focused on sentence mechanics and the construction of strong, well-developed paragraphs. As you worked on those paragraphs, you were also sharpening many of the same skills you will need to develop full-length college essays. Part 5 will take you through the additional requirements for expanding a single developed paragraph into a multi-paragraph essay. This expansion includes careful construction of an inviting introductory paragraph with its important thesis statement, along with the construction of a concluding paragraph that is needed for a logical and satisfying ending. You will continue to practice the different methods for the development of body paragraphs. You will be organizing a greater amount of material than before, and you will be giving even greater attention to the careful use of transitions, so important in longer pieces of writing. Finally, in the last two chapters of Part 5, you will focus on three very challenging skills: writing an

(continued on next page)

essay of persuasion or argument, writing a college research paper, and preparing for an essay examination. These final skills are intended to prepare you for the demands of additional college course work and for the needs of the workplace beyond.

# 26

# MOVING FROM THE PARAGRAPH TO THE ESSAY

To prepare you for writing fully developed college essays, your work in this chapter will focus on the essential parts of the essay form:

**CHAPTER OBJECTIVES**

- recognizing and writing a **thesis statement**
- writing an effective **introductory paragraph**
- using **transitions** between body paragraphs to achieve coherence
- writing an effective **concluding paragraph**
- composing **titles**

## WHAT IS A COLEGE ESSAY?

No matter what major a student declares in college, developing writing skills is a critical part of that student's growth and progress. Nearly every course will require at least some writing. This writing most often takes the form of the college essay (also called *composition, theme,* or simply *paper).*

When we constructed paragraphs in Part 4, with topic sentences and supporting details, we were aiming for an organized result, with unity and coherence. The full-length essay must have this same objective. Making all the parts of an essay work together is, of course, a greater challenge than writing a paragraph because in an essay, a topic is developed at greater length and in greater depth.

> A *college essay* is a piece of writing that develops a topic in five or more paragraphs, including an introductory paragraph that states the thesis, three or more supporting paragraphs that develop the topic, and a concluding paragraph.

## KINDS OF PARAGRAPHS IN THE COMPLETE COLLEGE ESSAY

1. The **introductory paragraph** is the first paragraph of the essay. Its purpose is to lead the reader to the **thesis statement** in an inviting and interesting way that will encourage the reader to continue reading.

2. **Support paragraphs** (sometimes called **body paragraphs**) provide evidence that the thesis is valid. An acceptable college essay must have at least three well-developed support paragraphs. (You have studied these types of support paragraphs in Part 4 of this book.) Each support paragraph should flow logically to the next support paragraph. This is often accomplished by the careful use of **transitional expressions.**

3. The **concluding paragraph** is the final paragraph of the essay. Its purpose is to give the reader a sense that the essay has come to a satisfying conclusion. By this point, the reader should have the feeling that everything the essay needed to say has been said.

# WHAT IS A THESIS STATEMENT?

> A *thesis statement* gives the main idea of an essay.

The thesis statement of an essay tells what the writer intends to prove, defend, or explain about the topic. It may show the writer's viewpoint toward the topic or show how the writer intends to treat the topic. We say that the thesis has a *controlling idea*. This most important sentence is usually placed at the end of the introductory paragraph.

**Sample thesis statement:**   All-day kindergarten programs benefit children in several important ways.

Do not confuse a thesis statement with a title or a simple fact. A **title** is usually a phrase, not a complete sentence.

**Sample title:**   The Advantages of All-Day Kindergarten

A **fact** is something known for certain. It can be verified. A fact does not suggest a personal viewpoint.

**Sample fact:**   Very few kindergartens in the United States offer a full day of instruction.

**Practice**

Read each of the following statements. If the statement is a thesis, mark *TH* on the blank line. If the statement is a title, mark *T.* If the statement is a fact, mark *F.*

_____   1.   In the United States, kindergarten is not compulsory.

_____   2.   Children should begin learning to read in kindergarten.

_____   3.   Putting a child into kindergarten before he or she is ready can have several unfortunate effects on that child.

_____   4.   Learning to read in kindergarten

_____   5.   In some European countries, children do not begin formal schooling until the age of seven.

**EXERCISE  1**

## Recognizing a Thesis Statement

Identify each of the following as a *title* (T), a *thesis* (TH), or a *fact* (F).

_____  1. It is estimated that two hundred grizzly bears live in Yellowstone National Park.

_____  2. The survival of grizzly bears in our country should be a top priority.

_____  3. When bears are young cubs, there are twice as many males as females.

_____  4. Only about 60 percent of bear cubs survive the first few years of life.

_____  5. Bears, a precious natural resource

_____  6. The average life span of a bear today is only five or six years.

_____  7. The sad plight of the American grizzly bear

_____  8. Five actions need to be taken to save the grizzly bear from extinction.

_____  9. To save the grizzly bear, we need laws from Congress, the cooperation of hunters and campers, and an educated general public.

_____  10. A decision to save the grizzly bear

**EXERCISE  2**

## Recognizing a Thesis Statement

Identify each of the following as a *title* (T), a *thesis* (TH), or a *fact* (F).

_____  1. The merchandising madness of pharmaceutical companies

_____  2. Americans are spending approximately 10.4 billion dollars a year on the four leading antidepressants, namely, Zoloft, Paxil, Wellbutrin, and Celexa.

_____  3. The American love affair with pills

_____  4. Washing your blues away with Prozac

_____  5. Consumers need to be better educated about the questionable promises made by the marketers of antidepressants.

_____  6. After the attacks of September 11, national sales for the top-selling antidepressants rose 20 percent.

_____ 7. Advertisements for antidepressants after September 11 featured American flags, candles, and firefighters.

_____ 8. A culture seeking self-stimulation and self-sedation

_____ 9. In recent years we have seen an unfortunate blurring between real and imagined medical need.

_____ 10. Americans should understand the difference between normal anxiety and pathological anxiety.

**EXERCISE ③**

### Recognizing a Thesis Statement

**Identify each of the following as a _title_ (T), a _thesis_ (TH), or a _fact_ (F).**

_____ 1. The personal interview is the most important step in the employment process.

_____ 2. Looking for a job

_____ 3. Sixty percent of all jobs are obtained through newspaper advertisements.

_____ 4. The best time to begin a foreign language is in grade school.

_____ 5. The importance of learning a foreign language

_____ 6. In the 1970s, the number of students studying foreign languages declined dramatically.

_____ 7. Most Americans doing business with Japan do not know a word of Japanese.

_____ 8. Working and studying at the same time

_____ 9. Many students in community colleges have part-time jobs while they are going to school.

_____ 10. Working a part-time job while going to school puts an enormous strain on a person.

## CREATING AN EFFECTIVE THESIS STATEMENT

### NARROWING THE SCOPE OF THE TOPIC

Student writing suffers when the chosen topic is too general. A good writer must recognize when the topic needs to be narrowed or qualified so that the material will fit the length of an essay (which is often only a few paragraphs long) and also fit the writer's knowledge and experience. Consider the following example:

**General topic:**    Swimming

A writer decides to write something about swimming, but the topic *swimming* seems too general for an interesting essay, so the writer thinks about how to limit or qualify that topic.

To *limit the topic*, the writer chooses a different term that covers a smaller part of the topic and thus narrows the scope.

| | |
|---|---|
| **Limited topic:** | Floating |

To *qualify the topic*, the writer adds a descriptive word or phrase to the general topic. This change will also result in narrowing the scope of the topic.

| | |
|---|---|
| **Qualified topic:** | Swimming two hours a week |

**EXERCISE** **4**

## Building the Thesis Statement: Limiting or Qualifying a Topic

Below are four topics. For each one, show how a writer could narrow the scope by either limiting the topic or qualifying the topic. An example is done for you.

| | |
|---|---|
| **General topic:** | Dentistry |
| **Limited topic:** | Orthodontics<br>(changes the general term to a more narrowed focus) |
| **Qualified topic:** | Preventive dentistry<br>(adds a descriptive word that narrows the focus) |

1. Language

   limited topic        _____

   qualified topic      _____

2. Illness

   limited topic        _____

   qualified topic      _____

3. Games

   limited topic        _____

   qualified topic      _____

4. Vacations

   limited topic        _____

   qualified topic      _____

## CHOOSING A CONTROLLING IDEA THAT CAN BE SUPPORTED

The controlling idea is what you want to show or prove about your topic. It is your point of view. A controlling idea must be something you can defend. Often this controlling idea is expressed by an adjective such as *beneficial, difficult,* or *unfair.* The writer who narrowed the scope of the topic *swimming* to either *floating* or *swimming two hours a week* may have chosen the following italicized words as the **controlling ideas** for an essay.

| | |
|---|---|
| Topic: | Swimming |
| Narrowed topic: | Floating |
| Possible thesis statement: | Learning to float at the age of twenty was a *terrifying* experience. |
| Qualified topic: | Swimming two hours a week |
| Possible thesis statement: | Swimming two hours a week can *dramatically change a person's health.* |

**EXERCISE 5**

### Building the Thesis Statement: Adding the Controlling Idea

Each of the following topics has been limited or qualified. In each case, provide a possible controlling idea.

1. Dancing

   limited topic:      tango _____

   controlling idea:   _____

2. School

   qualified topic:    after-school programs _____

   controlling idea:   _____

3. Transportation

   limited topic:      electric cars _____

   controlling idea:   _____

4. Personality

   qualified topic:    common personality flaws _____

   controlling idea:   _____

5. Clubs

   qualified topic:    our local clubs _____

   controlling idea:   _____

## PLANNING FOR THE STRATEGY OF DEVELOPMENT

Sometimes the strategy of development is included in the thesis statement. The reader recognizes the strategy by the use of specific words that signal the strategy:

| | |
|---|---|
| description (sight, sound, taste, smell,touch) | advantages, disadvantages |
| example, anecdote | causes, effects, reasons, why |
| classify, groups, types, kinds | definition, meaning, analysis |
| comparison, contrast | persuasion, argument |
| | process, steps, stages, how to |

Study the following thesis statement:

**Studying in a group can sometimes be more helpful than studying alone.**

Now look at the thesis sentence again and analyze its parts.

| | |
|---|---|
| **General topic:** | studying |
| **Qualified topic:** | studying in a group (contrasted to studying alone) |
| **Controlling idea:** | more helpful |
| **Strategy of development:** | contrast |

Here the writer has not used the word *contrast* in the thesis, but it is clear that a contrast will be made between *studying alone* and *studying in a group*. A writer should always have in mind what major strategy will be used to defend the viewpoint of the essay. While it is true that professional writers often use more than one strategy within an essay, student writers would do well to develop essays using one strategy at a time. By working in this way, a writer can concentrate on understanding and developing the skills needed for each specific strategy.

**EXERCISE 6**

### The Thesis Statement: Adding the Strategy of Development

**In each of the following thesis statements, underline the topic, circle the controlling idea, and indicate on the line provided what you believe will be the strategy of development.**

1.  The effects of gambling are disastrous.

    Strategy of Development:  _____

2.  Learning how to do your own tax return can be frustrating.

    Strategy of Development:  _____

3.  The sight of our neighborhood park is dismaying.

    Strategy of Development:  _____

4.  The meaning of the term *patriotism* is often controversial.

    Strategy of Development:  _____

5.  Which type of loan a person takes out is very consequential.

    Strategy of Development:  _____

**EXERCISE 7**

## Composing the Thesis Statement

For each of the three general topics given, compose a thesis sentence by (a) limiting or qualifying the general topic, (b) choosing a controlling idea that could be supported, (c) indicating a strategy of development. An example is done for you.

| | |
|---|---|
| General Topic: | Community Services |
| Qualified topic: | Community Services for Senior Citizens in Ann Arbor, Michigan |
| Controlling idea: | Explain the different types of services available. |
| Strategy of development: | Classification |
| Thesis Statement: | The community services available to senior citizens in Ann Arbor, Michigan, can be classified into three major groups: services to deal with health, housing, and leisure. |

1. **General topic:** Female vocalist

   a. Limited or qualified topic:

   _____

   b. Controlling idea:

   _____

   c. Strategy for development (see list on page 504):

   _____

   Thesis statement:

   _____

   _____

   _____

2. **General topic:** Credit cards

   a. Limited or qualified topic:

   _____

   b. Controlling idea:

   _____

   c. Strategy for development (see list on page 504):

   _____

   Thesis statement:

   _____

   _____

   _____

3.  **General topic:** Medical technology

    a.  Limited or qualified topic:

    _____

    b.  Controlling idea:

    _____

    c.  Strategy for development (see list on page 504):

    _____

Thesis statement:

_____

_____

_____

**EXERCISE 8**

## Creating Thesis Statements

**Three topics follow. For each one, develop a thesis statement by (a) limiting or qualifying the general topic, (b) choosing a controlling idea (what you want to explain or prove about the topic), and (c) selecting a strategy that you could use to develop that topic. Review the example in Exercise 7.**

1.  **General topic:** Books

    a.  Limited or qualified topic:

    _____

    b.  Controlling idea:

    _____

    c.  Strategy for development (see list on page 504):

    _____

Thesis statement:

_____

_____

_____

2.  **General topic:** Math

    a.  Limited or qualified topic:

    _____

    b.  Controlling idea:

    _____

    c.  Strategy for development (see list on page 504):

    _____

Thesis statement:

_____

_____

_____

3.  **General topic:** Snacks

    a.  Limited or qualified topic:

        _____

    b.  Controlling idea:

        _____

    c.  Strategy for development (see list on page 504):

        _____

Thesis statement:

_____

_____

_____

# WRITING AN EFFECTIVE INTRODUCTORY PARAGRAPH

> An *introductory paragraph* is the first paragraph of an essay. It has one main purpose, and that is to make its readers eager to read more. In most essays, this introductory paragraph contains a thesis sentence.

Although there is no single way to write an introductory paragraph, many effective introductions follow predictable patterns. A list of the most commonly found patterns follows. When you are ready to create your own introductions, you can consider trying out some of these patterns.

## Common Introductory Patterns

1. Begin with a general subject that can be narrowed down into the specific topic of your essay.

2. Begin with specifics (a brief anecdote, a specific example or fact) that will broaden into the more general topic of your essay.

3. Give a definition of the concept that will be discussed.

4. Make a startling statement.

(continued on next page)

5. Start with an idea or statement that is a widely held point of view, and then surprise the reader by stating that this idea is false or that you hold a different point of view.

6. Start with a familiar quotation from a famous book or a famous person.

7. Give a number of descriptive images that will lead to the thesis of your essay.

8. Ask a question that you intend to answer.

9. Use classification to indicate how your topic fits into the larger class to which it belongs or how your topic can be divided into categories that you are going to discuss.

**EXERCISE**  **Identifying Common Introductory Patterns**

**The introductions to three essays follow. Each one is an example of a common introductory pattern used to begin an essay. Using the chart on pages 507–508 identify each paragraph by its pattern.**

1. Here is the introduction to the essay "Some American Drugs Familiar to Everybody," by Adam Smith:

> Our attitude toward the word "drug" depends on whether we are talking about penicillin or heroin or something in between. The unabridged three-volume Webster's says a drug is "a chemical substance administered to prevent or cure disease or enhance physical and mental welfare" or "a substance affecting the structure or function of the body." Webster's should have added "mind," but they probably thought that was part of the body. Some substances that aren't drugs, like placebos, affect "the structure or function of the body," but they work because we *think* they're drugs.

Introductory Pattern _____

2. Here is the opening of the lengthy essay "Obsessed with Sport: On the Interpretation of a Fan's Dreams" by Joseph Epstein:

> I cannot remember when I was not surrounded by sports, when talk of sports was not in the air, when I did not care passionately about sports. As a boy in Chicago in the late Forties, I lived in the same building as the sister and brother-in-law of Barney Ross, the welter-weight champion. Half a block away, down near the lake, the Sullivan High School football team worked out in the spring and autumn. Summers the same field was given over to baseball and men's softball on Sundays.

(continued on next page)

A few blocks to the north was the Touhy Avenue Field House, where basketball was played, and lifeguards trained, and behind which, in a softball field frozen over in winter, crack-the-whip, hockey, and speed skating took over. To the west, a block or so up Morse Avenue, was the Morse Avenue "L" Recreations, a combined pool hall and bowling alley. Life, in short, was games.

Introductory Pattern _____

3.  Here is an introduction to an essay about a family making cider on their farm. It is titled "Falling for Apples," by Noel Perrin.

The number of children who eagerly help around a farm is rather small. Willing helpers do exist, but many more of them are five years old than fifteen. In fact, there seems to be a general law that says as long as a kid is too little to help effectively, he or she is dying to. Then, just as they reach the age when they really could drive a fence post or empty a sap bucket without spilling half of it, they lose interest. Now it's cars they want to drive, or else they want to stay in the house and listen for four straight hours to The Who. There is one exception to this rule. Almost no kid that I have ever met outgrows an interest in cidering.

Introductory Pattern _____

_____

**EXERCISE 10**

### Identifying Common Introductory Patterns

**The introductions to four essays follow. Each one is an example of a common introductory pattern used to begin an essay. Using the chart on pages 507–508 identify each paragraph by its pattern.**

1.  Below is the introduction to the essay "Getting Dizzy by the Numbers," by Frank Trippett.

*"The very hairs of your head,"* says Matthew 10:30, *"are all numbered."* There is little reason to doubt it. Increasingly, everything tends to get numbered one way or another, everything that can be counted, measured, averaged, estimated or quantified. Intelligence is gauged by a quotient, the humidity by a ratio, pollen by its count, and the trends of birth, death, marriage, and divorce by rates. In this epoch of runaway demographics, society is as often described and analyzed with statistics as with words. Politics seems more and more a game played with percentages turned up by pollsters, and economics a learned babble of ciphers and indexes that few people can translate and apparently nobody can control. Modern civilization, in sum, has begun to resemble an interminable arithmetic class in which, as Carl Sandburg put it, "numbers fly like pigeons in and out of your head."

Introductory Pattern _____

2.  This is how Stanley Millgram begins his essay "Confessions of a News Addict."

> Let me begin with a confession. I am a news addict. Upon awakening I flip on the *Today* show to learn what events transpired during the night. On the commuter train which takes me to work, I scour the *New York Times*, and find myself absorbed in tales of earthquakes, diplomacy and economics. I read the newspaper as religiously as my grandparents read their prayerbooks. The sacramental character of the news extends into the evening. The length of my workday is determined precisely by my need to get home in time for Walter Cronkite. My children understand that my communion with Cronkite is something serious and cannot be interrupted for light and transient causes. What is news, and why does it occupy a place of special significance for so many people?

Introductory Pattern _____

_____

3.  Here is how the American composer Aaron Copland began an essay on listening to music:

> We all listen to music according to our separate capacities. But, for the sake of analysis, the whole listening process may become clearer if we break it up into its component parts, so to speak. In a certain sense we all listen to music on three separate planes. For lack of a better terminology, one might name these: the sensuous plane, the expressive plane, the sheerly musical plane. The only advantage to be gained from mechanically splitting up the listening process into these hypothetical planes is the clearer view to be had of the way in which we listen.

Introductory Pattern _____

4.  Marya Mannes wrote this introduction for her essay "How Do You Know It's Good?"

> Suppose there were no critics to tell us how to react to a picture, a play, or a new composition of music. Suppose we wandered innocent as the dawn into an art exhibition of unsigned paintings. By what standards, by what values would we decide whether they were good or bad, talented or untalented, successes or failures? How can we ever know that what we think is right?

Introductory Pattern _____

## WHAT *NOT* TO SAY IN YOUR INTRODUCTION

1.  Avoid telling your reader that you are beginning your essay:

    **In this essay I will discuss . . .**

    **I will talk about . . .**

    **I am going to prove . . .**

2.  Do not apologize:

   **Although I am not an expert ...**

   **In my humble opinion ...**

3.  Do not refer to later parts of your essay:

   **By the end of this essay you will agree ...**

   **In the next paragraph you will see ...**

4.  Do not use trite expressions. Because these expressions have been overused, they have lost all interest and effectiveness. Using such expressions shows that you have not taken the time to come up with your own words to express your ideas. The following are some examples of trite expressions:

   **busy as a bee**

   **you can't tell a book by its cover**

   **haste makes waste**

**EXERCISE  11**

### Composing an Introductory Paragraph

Compose your own introductory paragraph using one of the nine patterns that you have just studied. You may want to use one of the topics that were provided in Exercises 4 and 5 and for which you have already written a thesis statement. On the line below, write the number from the list of given patterns you have chosen to use. When you have finished, underline your thesis statement.

Pattern number _____

_____

_____

_____

_____

_____

_____

_____

_____

_____

# ACHIEVING COHERENCE BY USING TRANSITIONS

Successful essays use transitional expressions to help the reader understand the logic of the writer's thinking. Usually they occur when the writer is moving from one point to the next. They can also occur whenever an idea is complicated. The writer may need to summarize the points so far, emphasize a point already made, or repeat an important point. The transition may be a word, a phrase, a sentence, or even a paragraph.

Here are some transitional expressions that might be used to help the reader make the right connections.

1. To make your points stand out clearly:

| | | |
|---|---|---|
| the first reason | second, secondly | finally |
| first of all | another example | most important |
| in the first place | even more important | all in all |
| | also, next | in conclusion |
| | then | to summarize |

2. To provide an example of what has just been said:

   for example

   for instance

3. To show the consequence of what has just been said:

   therefore

   as a result

   then

4. To make a contrasting point clear:

   on the other hand

   but

   contrary to current thinking

   however

5. To admit a point:

   of course

   granted

6. To resume your argument after admitting a point:

   nevertheless

   even though

   nonetheless

   still

7. To call the reader's attention to your organization:

   Before attempting to answer these questions, let me . . .

   In our discussions so far, we have seen that . . .

   At this point, it is necessary to . . .

   It is beyond the scope of this paper to . . .

A more subtle way to link one idea to another in an essay is to repeat a word or phrase from the preceding sentence. Sometimes a pronoun can take the place of the actual word.

**Repeating a word from a preceding sentence:**

> I have many memories of my childhood in Cuba. These *memories* include the aunts, uncles, grandparents, and friends I had to leave behind.

**Using a pronoun to refer to a phrase from a preceding sentence:**

> My family and I have had to build a new life from almost nothing. *It* was often difficult, but I believe the struggle made us strong.

**EXERCISE**  **12**

### Finding Transitional Expressions

Following are four paragraphs from a selection titled "Politics and the World," written by Kathryn and Ross Petras. Find the words that give this selection its coherence. Circle all the transitional expressions, underline pronouns that refer to antecedents, and box key terms that are repeated.

Some world problems have a way of lingering and festering. They appear, disappear, then reappear again in the daily newspapers of the world. Ususaly they're based on land: who controls it, who gets to live on it.

In the past the U.S. and the Soviet Union usually took opposing sides in these conflicts. Sometimes there were very real moral reasons for backing one side or another, but many times the reasons were said to be "geopolitical," which really meant if the Soviets were on one side, we decided to join the other—and vice versa.

All this could get pretty cynical. For one thing, almost every obscure corner of the world was declared "geopolitically strategic" at one point or another. For another, the morality could get very dicey. For example, during the 1970s we supported Ethiopia and the Soviets supported Somalia in their dispute over the Ogaden, a dry and remote desert region populated by Somali nomads but controlled by Ethiopia. Naturally, we set up military posts in our ally Ethiopia and the Soviets put in military bases in their ally Somalia, and each superpower talked of its love of and historic ties to its ally. Then local Marxists seized control in Ethiopia—and after a short while the U.S. and the Soviets calmly switched client states. The U.S. moved into the former Soviet bases in Somalia, the Soviets moved into Ethiopia, and both sides started talking about their *real* ties to their new ally.

Of course, once the Cold War was over, no one cared about either nation anymore, and they both degenerated into anarchy, aided by mounds of heavy weapons and automatic rifles helpfully supplied by both sides. Finally we moved in to save Somalia from itself and our legacy of arms sales—and congratulated ourselves on our humanity.

# WRITING AN EFFECTIVE CONCLUDING PARAGRAPH

A concluding paragraph has one main purpose: to give the reader the sense of having reached a satisfying ending to the topic discussed. Students often feel they have nothing to say at the end. A look at how professional writers frequently end their essays may ease your anxiety about writing an effective conclusion. You have more than one possibility. Here are some of the most frequently used patterns for ending an essay:

1.  **Come full circle—that is, return to the material in your introduction.** Finish what you started there. Remind the reader of the thesis. Be sure to restate the main idea using different wording. Here is the conclusion to the essay "Confessions of a News Addict." (The introductory paragraph appears on page 510)

    Living in the modern world, I cannot help but be shaped by it, suckered by the influence and impact of our great institutions. The *New York Times*, CBS, and *Newsweek* have made me into a news addict. In daily life I have come to accept the supposition that if the *New York Times* places a story on the front page, it deserves my attention. I feel obligated to know what is going on. But sometimes, in quieter moments, another voice asks: If the news went away, would the world be any worse for it?

2.  **Summarize by repeating the main points.** This example is the concluding paragraph to an essay on African art.

    In summary, African art explains the past, describes values and a way of life, helps man relate to supernatural forces, mediates his social relations, expresses emotions, and enhances man's present life as an embellishment denoting pride or status as well as providing entertainment such as with dance and music.

3.  **Show the significance of your thesis by making predictions, giving a warning, giving advice, offering a solution, suggesting an alternative, or telling the results.** This example is the concluding paragraph to "Falling for Apples." (The introductory paragraph appears on page 509.)

    This pleasure goes on and on. In an average year we start making cider the second week of September, and we continue until early November. We make all we can drink ourselves, and quite a lot to give away. We have supplied whole church suppers. One year the girls sold about ten gallons to the village store, which made them some pocket money they were prouder of than any they ever earned from babysitting. Best of all, there are two months each year when all of us are running the farm together, just like a pioneer family.

4. **End with an anecdote that illustrates your thesis.** This example is the concluding paragraph to the essay "Obsessed with Sport." (The introductory paragraph appears on page 508.)

> When I was a boy I had a neighbor, a man who, after retirement, had a number of strokes. An old man and a young boy, we had in common a love of sports, which, when we met on the street, was our only topic of conversation. He once inspected a new glove of mine, and instructed me to rub it down with neat's-foot-oil, place a ball firmly in the pocket, wrap string tightly around the glove, and leave it like that for the winter. I did, and it worked. After his last stroke but one, he seldom left his house. Afternoons he spent in a chair in his bedroom, a blanket over his lap, listening to Cub games over the radio. It was while listening to a ball game that he quietly died. I cannot imagine a better way.

## WHAT *NOT* TO SAY IN YOUR CONCLUSION

1. Do not introduce a new point.
2. Do not apologize.
3. Do not end up in the air, leaving the reader feeling unsatisfied. This sometimes happens if the very last sentence is not strong enough.

# A NOTE ABOUT TITLES

Be sure to follow the standard procedure for writing your title.

1. Capitalize the first and last words and all other principal words. This excludes articles (*the, a, an*), coordinating conjunctions (*and, but, or, nor, for, yet, so*), prepositions, and the *to* in infinitives.
2. Do not underline the title or put quotation marks around it.
3. Think of a short and catchy phrase (three to six words). Often writers wait until they have written a first draft before working on a title. A phrase taken from the essay might be perfect. If you still cannot think of a clever title after you have written a draft, choose some key words from your thesis statement.
4. Center the title at the top of the page, and remember to leave about an inch of space between the title and the beginning of the first paragraph.

## Exploring Online

Go to **www.cengage.com/devenglish/scarry/writersworkplace** to find the **Writer's Online Workplace,** a website designed for students using this book. You will find links to handouts, interactive quizzes, and other online resources as you explore the following topics:

- parts of the essay
- the thesis statement
- how to write an introduction
- how *not* to write an introduction
- body of the essay
- transitions
- writing a conclusion

# Working Together

## PLANNING THE PARTS OF AN ESSAY

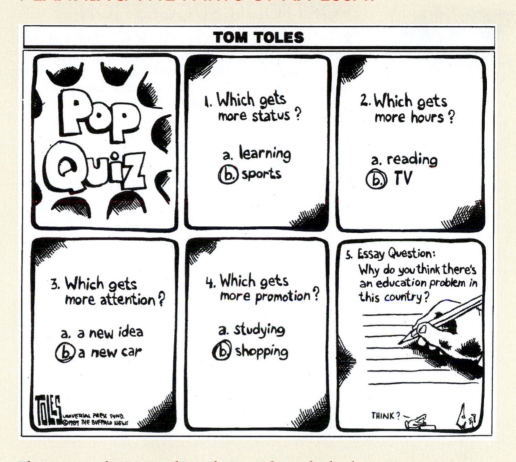

The cartoon above uses the technique of a multiple-choice quiz to suggest some possible reasons education in America is in trouble. As a class, discuss each of the four areas of concern raised by the cartoonist. What do you think is the *thesis* for this cartoon?

Break into groups of five or six. Work together to produce a five- or six-paragraph essay using the organization and content suggested by Tom Toles. Include ideas that were presented in the class discussion or in your group. Assign each person in your group to one of the following paragraphs:

Introductory paragraph

Four paragraphs of support:

1. Learning versus sports
2. Reading versus television
3. A new idea versus a new car
4. Studying versus shopping

Concluding paragraph

Before you write, review the basic content for each paragraph so that each group member understands what should be in his or her paragraph.

## PORTFOLIO SUGGESTION

Keep this group essay in your portfolio. How well did the members of your group succeed in helping each other build one unified essay? Many people in their jobs are expected to work with colleagues to produce annual reports, write-ups of experiments, or brochures that advertise their products or services. Seek to improve your ability to work with others in school and on the job.

# FOLLOWING THE PROGRESS OF A STUDENT ESSAY

# 27

In this chapter, you will develop an essay of your own as you follow the progress of a student essay written by Raluca, a woman who was raised in another culture and whose second language is English. Learning from Raluca's work, students will accomplish the following:

**CHAPTER OBJECTIVES**

- use the **prewriting techniques** of freewriting, brainstorming (to create a list), and clustering
- find a **controlling idea** for the thesis statement
- write an **introductory paragraph**
- decide on **the topic sentences** for three or more body paragraphs
- study the student essay for the **development of the body paragraphs**
- put the paragraphs into essay form, with a **concluding paragraph**
- **revise the draft** using peer evaluation
- **proofread** the final essay for errors and omissions

## THE ASSIGNMENT: DESCRIPTION OF A SCHOOL EXPERIENCE

In many college courses, you will have an opportunity to pick your own topic for a writing project. In other courses, topics will be assigned. For the greatest benefit in the work of this chapter, all students will be developing the same general assignment: the description of a school experience. Notice that *description* is the method of development.

**Your Assignment:**    **Write an essay describing your experience in a school you have attended.**

**Raluca's narrowed topic:**    The school I attended as a child in Romania

Notice that the topic has been narrowed from *a school* to the very specific school the writer attended. By narrowing the focus, the writer will hopefully avoid generalities and be able to produce a unique and interesting piece of writing.

Now narrow your topic to a specific school experience. You are free to select any educational institution that you have attended. Your topic could be based on your experience in a grade school, middle school, high school, driving school, summer school, institute, or the college you are now attending.

**Your narrowed topic:** _____

_____

# STEP 1: USING PREWRITING TECHNIQUES TO EXPLORE WHAT YOU KNOW ABOUT THE TOPIC

As you already know, writers may choose from a number of prewriting techniques to help gather their first thoughts on a topic. We will consider *freewriting, brainstorming (to create a list),* and *clustering.* You will have the chance to experiment with these three techniques and decide which of them works best for you.

## FOCUSED FREEWRITING: LETTING YOUR MIND MAKE FREE ASSOCIATIONS

The purpose of freewriting is to put on paper whatever ideas come to mind when the topic is explored. Without any concerns about form or content, this "free" writing can often create a flow of thoughts that surprises even the writer. New and different ideas, some of which the writer is not consciously aware of, may emerge.

Raluca chose freewriting as her prewriting technique. She expressed her first thoughts on the topic without any concern for grammar or organization. Below is her piece of freewriting.

### Raluca's Freewriting

Its hard to explain what life in an communist country was like. Besides the fears, the unfulfilled needs and the constant untrust, life continued to be lived. School in Romania was mandatory and free. We had uniforms, this was a way of making all of us equal, we wore red scarfs, white socks and blue jumpers. The classrooms were very austere, with 15 double-desks, a blackboard and a map on the wall.

(continued on next page)

> The framed portrait of our president was present in the middle of the wall, above the blackboard, in every classroom. One teacher was teaching all subjects, and the day was divided in hours, with a 10 minutes break between hours. We didn't have to switch classrooms and we didn't spent a lot of time in school. Every day we had 4 or 5 hours, every hour with another subject. In literature, a lot of emphasis was placed on memorization, poems of the important Romanian authors, and during the vacations, mandatory lecture. We had to bring every day a soap and a towel, to wash our hands before eating. Food was brought from home and eaten in the classroom. The teachers were tough. Communist education is based on humiliation, it was a shame if you didn't give the right answer to a question or if you got bad grades. Sometimes the teachers enjoyed their power. It was like a sort of social stratification, based on how good your grades were. The results of the tests and the grades were communicated in front of the class. The grades were from 1–10. There were no multiple-choice tests. You had to memorize and give the answers, written, on the paper.

In this piece of freewriting, Raluca has recalled several memories from her school days. When she wrote this, she did not worry about mistakes or the order of her details. Since English is her second language, she has several phrases that are not idiomatic. She has some errors with spelling and punctuation. She also has a run-on sentence. However, these kinds of mistakes should not be her concerns at this stage in the process.

Freewriting is very different from a more finished piece of writing. Freewriting usually has no title, lacks an introduction and conclusion, and contains no carefully planned paragraphs that include topic sentences. A piece of freewriting may also be repetitious and hard to follow. For all of these reasons freewriting would never be confused with a finished essay. Student writers must always be aware that freewriting is a first response to a topic, not a carefully constructed college-level essay.

**ACTIVITY 1A**

## Your Freewriting

**Your freewriting may be shorter or longer than Raluca's, but at this point, length is not important. Do not allow the fear of making mistakes to slow you down.**

Name of your school: _____

_____

_____

_____

_____

_____

_____

_____

_____

## MAKING A BRAINSTORMING LIST

Making a list of words or phrases that come to mind is another helpful method of gathering information on any topic. When asked to provide a brainstorming list, Raluca produced the following items (notice there is no particular order):

### Raluca's Brainstorming List

| | |
|---|---|
| communism | testing and grading |
| president's portrait | humiliation and shame |
| uniforms: red scarves, blue jumpers | one teacher for all subjects |
| soap and towel | atmosphere of fear |
| bring your own lunch | teachers enjoyed power |
| blackboard | no place for joy |
| map | dreary room |
| memorization of poems | |

**ACTIVITY 1B**

## Constructing Your Brainstorming List

Make a list of words or phrases that come to mind when you think about a specific school you attended. Put the name of your school at the top of your brainstorming list to identify your topic.

Name of your school: _____

_____      _____

_____      _____

_____      _____

_____      _____

_____      _____

Different prewriting techniques may bring different ideas to the surface. For instance, a brainstorming list might very well include different details from those details produced in the freewriting. Is there any item included in your brainstorming list that was not part of your freewriting?

## CLUSTERING

A third prewriting technique writers use to explore their ideas is called *clustering*. This technique demands more organizational skill than freewriting or listing because when a writer uses clustering, words or phrases are put into groupings that have specific headings. We can think of the cluster as an outline in visual form. Some

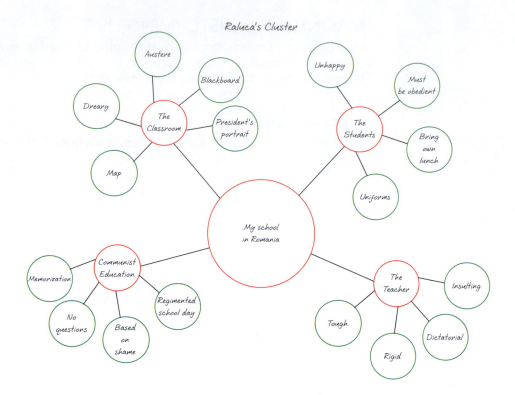

Raluca's Cluster

writers find that the act of drawing a circle and inserting an idea, resulting in a kind of diagram, is a helpful way to express their thinking on a topic.

**ACTIVITY 1C**

## Your Cluster

Now explore how you could arrange your thoughts as a visual cluster, placing your topic in the middle of your cluster and grouping related ideas around that central topic.

# STEP 2: FINDING THE CONTROLLING IDEA FOR THE THESIS STATEMENT

Once a writer has explored the topic with the use of prewriting techniques and has generated ideas and details important for the essay, it is time to find the controlling idea for the thesis statement. The freewriting, listing, or clustering that a writer produces during the prewriting stage will not necessarily result in an obvious controlling idea. The writer must search for the word or phrase that best states the overriding attitude or viewpoint of the essay.

## Raluca Works on Her Controlling Idea for the Thesis Statement

The material in Raluca's prewriting activities produced many ideas and details that Raluca will use in her essay. However, she must still compose her thesis statement. To do this, Raluca needs to decide on a controlling idea that will unify all the details about her childhood school. Here are some of the possible thesis statements that Raluca could have considered. In each example, the controlling idea has been circled.

1.  Life for a schoolchild in Romania was (regimented).

2.  The Romanian schoolroom was (austere).

3.  Life under communism was (filled with fear).

4.  The experience of schoolchildren in Romania in the 1970s was (harsh).

5.  Most teachers in Romanian schools during the 1970s were (dictatorial).

**Practice**      **Review Raluca's possible thesis statements and answer the following questions:**

1.  Which thesis statement is too general and off the topic of the assignment? ___

2.  Which thesis statements seem too narrow and might provide only enough material for one or two paragraphs? _____

The success of an entire essay often depends on taking the time to determine what word or phrase would best express your controlling idea. Without a clear controlling idea in mind, the essay is much less likely to develop into a unified piece.

In writing about the school you have attended, here are some possible controlling ideas you might consider for your thesis sentence.

### Possible Controlling Ideas

| | |
|---|---|
| supportive | unsupportive |
| well run | not well run |
| a happy place | an unhappy place |
| carefully maintained | run-down |
| safe | dangerous |
| challenging | unchallenging |
| technologically up-to-date | not well equipped |
| academically solid | academically weak |
| disciplined | undisciplined |

Remember, it is your *controlling idea* that will unify the essay. All the body paragraphs will have to serve and support the controlling idea.

**ACTIVITY 2**

## Choosing Controlling Ideas for Possible Thesis Statements

Keep in mind your prewriting activities as well as the suggested list of controlling ideas given previously. Now, think of three words or phrases that could be possible controlling ideas for your essay. Then compose a thesis statement for each one. Make a check beside the thesis statement you intend to use.

Controlling idea _____

Thesis statement _____

_____

Controlling idea _____

Thesis statement _____

_____

Controlling idea _____

Thesis statement _____

_____

# STEP 3: DECIDING ON THE TOPIC SENTENCES FOR THREE OR MORE BODY PARAGRAPHS

## Raluca Plans the Main Divisions of Her Essay and Writes a Topic Sentence for Each of These Divisions

When Raluca did her freewriting, she was not thinking about how to divide her material into body paragraphs. Now she must invest her time doing a better job of organizing that material. Thinking about all the details she has generated, she decides on possible major divisions. Each of these main divisions could become a developed paragraph, each one beginning with a topic sentence. Here is the list she initially considered:

> What the classroom looked like
> How teachers treated students
> How students were dressed
> What a day was like
> What subjects were studied
> The communist approach to education
> How students felt about school

Notice how this list differs from her brainstorming list. Here, Raluca is working on the major divisions that will form the different sections of her essay. The details she uses will all have to fall within one of these divisions. Here are the four main divisions Raluca chose for her essay and the topic sentence she composed for each one.

1.  How the classroom looked:          The classroom was *stark*.
2.  How the students were treated:     Students were expected to be *obedient*.
3.  What a class day was like:         The school day was very *rigid*.
4.  The communist approach             Communist education was *based on*
    to education:                      *humiliation*.

Notice that each topic sentence has the topic and a controlling idea (in italics). Now she realizes exactly which details to place in each of these paragraphs. She will use only details that will support the controlling idea of each topic sentence.

**ACTIVITY  3**

### Composing the Topic Sentences for Your Body Paragraphs

**Think about your material. What three or four main divisions could you make? Each one of these will be developed into a paragraph. Write a topic sentence for each one of these. Circle the controlling idea in each sentence.**

1. _____

2. _____

3. _____

4. _____

# STEP 4: WRITING THE INTRODUCTORY PARAGRAPH

## Raluca Composes the Introductory Paragraph, Ending with the Thesis Statement

Raluca's freewriting lacks an introductory paragraph with its thesis statement that will unify the entire piece of writing. She needs to compose her introduction, perhaps starting with the same general remarks she made in her freewriting. These general remarks can lead to the more narrowed focus of her thesis statement.

Below is the introductory paragraph that Raluca used in her final draft. The thesis statement is in boldface. Compare this introduction to the first two sentences of Raluca's freewriting. How do they differ? Circle her controlling idea.

> Thirty-five years ago, life in a Communist country such as Romania was filled with fears, unfulfilled needs, and the constant distrust of others who might be spying on their neighbors. To a person born in the West, on this side of the Iron Curtain, it is hard to imagine what schoolchildren faced. Nevertheless, life had to be lived, and children went off to school every day. Remembering my childhood school days does not bring back many happy memories. **The experience of a schoolchild in Romania in the 1970s was harsh.**

**ACTIVITY** **4**

## Composing Your Introductory Paragraph

Write a possible introductory paragraph for your own essay. You might do as Raluca did by starting with general remarks that will lead to your more specific thesis statement with its controlling idea. Aim for at least four to five sentences, ending with the thesis statement. Underline the thesis statement.

(For more ideas of common patterns used to write introductory paragraphs, review pages 507–508.)

_____

_____

_____

_____

_____

_____

_____

# STEP 5: STUDYING THE STUDENT ESSAY FOR PARAGRAPH DEVELOPMENT

Before you work on developing your body paragraphs, read Raluca's essay and discuss her body paragraphs. What are the strengths and weaknesses of each paragraph? Are there any additional details you would like to have known?

## Raluca's Final Draft

### Going to School Behind the Iron Curtain

Life in a Communist country such as Romania in the 1970s was filled with fears, unfulfilled needs, and the constant distrust of others who might be spying on their neighbors. To a person born in the West, on this side of the Iron Curtain, it is hard to imagine what schoolchildren faced. Nevertheless, life had to be lived, and children went off to school every day. Remembering my childhood school days does not bring back many happy memories. **The experience of a schoolchild in Romania in the 1970s was harsh.**

**The classroom was stark.** The only furniture in the room were the fifteen double desks for students and the teacher's desk at the front. A blackboard was on the front wall. The room was often quite cold and only on very dark days were the old ceiling lights turned on. When you entered the room, the only object to look at was the framed portrait of the country's president dominating the

(continued on next page)

front wall above the blackboard. His unsmiling face and somber eyes looked down on everything we did. All across the country his face was at the head of every classroom. We were never allowed to forget who controlled our lives.

**Students were expected to be obedient.** We all wore uniforms: blue jumpers or blue pants, white blouses or shirts, red scarves or ties and white socks. This dress code kept us all looking the same. No one should look different or special in any way. I cannot remember that anyone complained. Each child brought his or her own lunch and soap. We ate our lunch in the classroom. We accepted our situation and did not expect anyone to provide us with any food or supplies. We understood our teachers would not have tolerated any complaints or unwillingness to follow orders.

**The school day was very rigid.** One teacher taught us all the subjects. The school day was divided into four or five hour-long classes, each one with a different subject. There was a ten-minute break between hours. We did not have to change rooms, and we were finished by early afternoon, sent home with lessons to do. Subjects were taught largely by memorization of facts. The individual teacher had no say in what material to cover. The curriculum was set by the authorities and rigidly adhered to. For instance, in literature classes, most of the emphasis was placed on memorizing poems by important Romanian authors. Children were not encouraged to ask questions, and discussions were most uncommon. When it was test time, we were given blank sheets of paper. There was no such thing as multiple-choice tests. Answers were right or wrong. Grading was from one to ten, with ten being the best.

**Communist education was based on humiliation.** It was shameful if we did not give the right answer to a question or if we got bad grades. Sometimes we could see that the teachers enjoyed their power. When test results were returned, our grades were shared in front of the entire class. Everyone knew that the only way to get ahead was to do well on the tests. There was no misbehaving. Bad behavior was not tolerated. Corporal punishment was allowed.

My memory of school in Romania is of days of dutiful work. There was little room for the joy of learning or the freedom of expression. If I were to pick a color to describe my school time, it would be gray. Education was memorizing and repeating what we were told—that was all.

## ACTIVITY 5

### Developing Your Body Paragraphs

On the computer or on the lines provided below, develop each of your body paragraphs using only details that support the controlling idea in each topic sentence you have created. Underline your topic sentences.

Body Paragraph 1

_____

_____

_____

_____

_____

_____

_____

Body Paragraph 2

_____

_____

_____

_____

_____

_____

Body Paragraph 3

_____

_____

_____

_____

_____

_____

_____

# STEP 6: PUTTING THE DRAFT INTO ESSAY FORM WITH A CONCLUDING PARAGRAPH

Here is Raluca's conclusion again. Do any key words from her introduction appear again in the conclusion? Notice how Raluca has summed up the points of her essay in a creative way. Review Raluca's conclusion as a possible model for the ending of your own essay.

My memory of school in Romania is of days of dutiful work. There was little room for the joy of learning or the freedom of expression. If I were to pick a color to describe my school time, it would be gray. Education was memorizing and repeating what we were told—that was all.

**ACTIVITY**

### Putting Your Paragraphs into Essay Form and Adding a Conclusion

On the computer, follow your instructor's specifications for typing your introduction and body paragraphs. Add a concluding paragraph that will bring the essay to a satisfying end.

(Review pages 514–515 for other examples of common patterns used for conclusions.)

## STEP 7: REVISING THE DRAFT USING PEER EVALUATION

In the revision process you must think, rethink, and think again about all the parts that will make up the whole. One of the most helpful ways to begin thinking about your revision is to have others read your work and make suggestions. The peer evaluation form that follows will help others analyze your work.

**ACTIVITY** 7

### Using a Peer Evaluation Form

Ask an individual or a group of individuals to use the following form to evaluate your work. With the feedback you receive, you will be ready to revise your draft.

---

## Peer Evaluation Form

1. Introductory paragraph
   a. Is the introduction interesting? Could you make any suggestions for improvement?
   b. Underline the thesis. Circle the controlling idea.

2. Body paragraphs
   a. Has the writer used description as the method of development?
   b. Does each body paragraph have a topic sentence? Draw a wavy line under each topic sentence.
   c. Has each body paragraph been adequately developed with at least six to eight sentences?
   d. Do the topic sentences all support the controlling idea of the thesis?
   e. Does the material in each body paragraph relate to its topic sentence? Put a check next to any sentence that should be dropped.

3. Details
   a. What is the overall quality of the details? Are they specific enough? Does the writer give names, dates, titles, places, colors, shapes, etc.? In the margin, suggest better details wherever they occur to you.
   b. You might be able to count the number of details in each paragraph. Do you believe there are enough details? Indicate in the margin where you believe additional details would improve the essay.

---

(continued on next page)

4. Coherence

   a. Does the essay follow a logical progression? If not, place a question mark where you begin to feel confused.

   b. Has the writer used transitional words or phrases at any point to move from one idea to another? If so, put a box around these expressions. Can you suggest a spot where a transitional word or phrase would be an improvement?

   c. Has the writer used synonyms, substitutions, or pronouns to replace key words? If so, put a box around these words. If the writer repeats certain words too often, can you suggest in the margin any other synonyms, substitutions, or pronouns that would be an improvement?

5. What detail or idea did you like best about this essay?

6. Does the essay come to a satisfying conclusion?

# STEP 8: PROOFREADING THE FINAL ESSAY FOR ERRORS AND OMISSIONS

Below are four sentences taken from Raluca's freewriting. Can you find any errors that need to be corrected?

1. Its hard to explain what life in an communist country was like.
2. Besides the fears, the unfulfilled needs and the constant untrust, life continued to be lived.
3. We didn't spent a lot of time in school.
4. Communist education is based on humiliation, it was a shame if you didn't give the right answer to a question or if you got bad grades.

**ACTIVITY  8**

## Proofread Your Essay

After your revisions are complete, you will need to proofread your essay. In a dictionary, look up any word that you suspect might have been misspelled. Run the spell-check program on your computer. Read each sentence aloud to check for omitted words, typos, or other corrections that might have to be made. Sometimes hearing a sentence read out loud helps a writer hear that place where a better word choice or a punctuation mark is needed. In fact, don't be embarrassed to ask someone else to proofread your essay.

## Exploring Online

Go to **www.cengage.com/devenglish/scarry/writersworkplace** to find the **Writer's Online Workplace,** a website designed for students using this book. You will find links to handouts, interactive quizzes, and other online resources as you explore the following topics:

• sample student essays

# Working Together

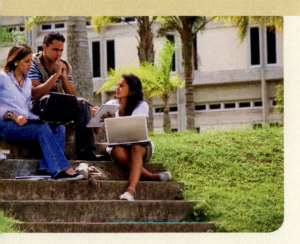

## PEER EDITING: THE REVISION STAGE

Below are four paragraphs taken from a student essay titled "How Students Are Managing the High Costs of a College Education."

### Paragraph 1

¹Going to college is now a big investment for many students and their families. ²Total costs average thirty-two thousand dollars at private schools and roughly half that amount at state universities. ³To make matters worse, the interest rates on educational loans have increased another 1.5 percentage points.

### Paragraph 2

¹In fact, 74 percent of full-time students now must combine school with work. ²This is much higher than in the past. ³And nearly half of those students work more than twenty-five hours a week. ⁴It is hard to believe. ⁵Of those who work more than twenty-five hours a week, 20 percent work full time and go to school full time. ⁶Students who work twenty-five hours or more a week are more likely to earn lower grades and often have to drop out of courses.

### Paragraph 3

¹Perhaps the best jobs are the ones that are right on campus. ²Work-study programs are popular at most schools, and some jobs such as designing websites or maintaining websites can be well paid. ³If a school offers a cooperative education program, it is usually a good thing. ⁴Real-world work experience can give a student the experience they need to qualify for good paying jobs as soon as they graduate and they are also building up their résumés for future job hunting. Some professional services charge a lot of money to help students polish their résumés

### Paragraph 4

¹There are some ways to afford an education even when your family cannot help you. ²There are some young people who go to work for companies like UPS, who help their workers go to college by providing two thousand to three thousand dollars for their school costs. ³There are others who join the military so they can receive a free education. ⁴Some people feel that a soldier's free education comes with another sort of high price. ⁵More students are going to community colleges and living at home, cutting down on costs. ⁶And you can always work during the summer saving money for the next semester's courses.

## Working in Groups

Each of the paragraphs has at least one major need for revision.

Paragraph 1: Add a thesis statement at the end of the paragraph.

Paragraph 2: Compose a topic sentence.

Paragraph 3: Revise any sentences with pronoun problems. To maintain unity, find a sentence that does not belong. Correct the run-on sentence.

Paragraph 4: Revise the first three sentences so that they avoid the repetitious and wordy "There are" expression. Is the meaning of sentence 4 clear? What is your understanding about beginning a sentence with "and," as in sentence 6?

Each group should decide on what revisions are needed for the four paragraphs and be prepared to present these revisions to the class.

## PORTFOLIO SUGGESTION

Remember that when you are preparing a manuscript on a computer, you must frequently save your file, giving each draft a different name. Keep your earlier drafts until you have made a final review of your last draft, and you feel certain you will have no further need to consult your old drafts again. Be sure to keep a disk as well as a hard copy of papers submitted to your instructors. These safety measures help avoid lost or misplaced submissions.

# WRITING AN ESSAY USING EXAMPLES, ILLUSTRATIONS, OR ANECDOTES

# 28

This chapter will take you through the process of writing an essay using examples:

**CHAPTER OBJECTIVES**

- exploring the topic: Living with a Disability
- reading and analyzing a model essay: "Darkness at Noon," by Harold Krents
- following the writing process to develop your own essay using examples

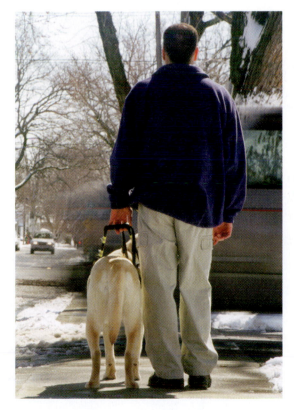

## EXPLORING THE TOPIC: LIVING WITH A DISABILITY

Most of us have to cope with a variety of disadvantages in our lives. For some people, however, these disadvantages can be serious disabilities that threaten the quality of their lives. Society's view of people with disabilities has changed a great deal over the years. In the past, people with serious disabilities tended to avoid being in public and often did not try to join the rest of society in seeking an education or job advancement. Today, the situation is very different, as laws have been passed to protect the rights of people who have limitations. Being disabled should no longer mean being deprived of a productive life.

1. What in your judgment are the most serious disabilities some people have to endure? What disabilities are less obvious than others?

   _____

   _____

   _____

   _____

   _____

2. Despite the more open and supportive atmosphere in our society today, many people are unsure how to interact with disabled people. What are some misconceptions people have about those with disabilities? What mistakes do people often make when they encounter a disabled person?

_____

_____

_____

_____

3. Recently, an American man who had lost the use of both legs reached the top of Japan's Mount Fuji by riding a bicycle with a central hand crank. Do you know of any other remarkable accomplishments of people with serious disabilities?

_____

_____

_____

_____

4. What are some special considerations provided by schools or employers to help people with disabilities? In your opinion, what more could be done?

_____

_____

_____

_____

# READING A MODEL ESSAY WITH EXAMPLES, ILLUSTRATIONS, OR ANECDOTES

## DARKNESS AT NOON

### Harold Krents

In the following essay, which appeared in the *New York Times*, the lawyer Harold Krents gives us a frank picture of his daily life as a sightless person, trying to retain his dignity in a world that is not always supportive.

°**narcissistic**
characterized by excessive admiration of oneself

°**enunciating**
clearly pronouncing

1    Blind from birth, I have never had the opportunity to see myself and have been completely dependent on the image I create in the eye of the observer. To date, it has not been narcissistic.°

2    There are those who assume that since I can't see, I obviously cannot hear. Very often people will converse with me at the top of their lungs, enunciating° each word very carefully. Conversely,° people will also often whisper, assuming that since my eyes don't work, my ears don't either.

**°conversely**
in the opposite
or reverse way

3    For example, when I go to the airport and ask the ticket agent for assistance to the plane, he or she will invariably pick up the phone, call a ground hostess and whisper: "Hi, Jane, we've got a 76 here." I have concluded that the word "blind" is not used for one of two reasons: Either they fear that if the dread word is spoken, the ticket agent's retina will immediately detach, or they are reluctant to inform me of my condition of which I may not have been previously aware.

4    On the other hand, others know that of course I can hear, but believe that I can't talk. Often, therefore, when my wife and I go out to dinner, a waiter or waitress will ask Kit if *"he* would like a drink" to which I respond that "indeed *he* would."

**°graphically**
in sharp and vivid
detail

5    This point was graphically° driven home to me while we were in England. I had been given a year's leave of absence from my Washington law firm to study for a diploma-in-law degree at Oxford University. During the year I became ill and was hospitalized. Immediately after admission, I was wheeled down to the X-ray room. Just at the door sat an elderly woman—elderly I would judge from the sound of her voice. "What is his name?" the woman asked the orderly who had been wheeling me.

6    "What's your name?" the orderly repeated to me.

7    "Harold Krents," I replied.

8    "Harold Krents," he repeated.

9    "When was he born?"

10    "When were you born?"

11    "November 5, 1944," I responded.

**°intoned**
said in a monotone

12    "November 5, 1944," the orderly intoned.°

13    This procedure continued for approximately five minutes, at which point even my saint-like disposition deserted me. "Look," I finally blurted out, "this is absolutely ridiculous. Okay, granted I can't see, but it's got to have become pretty clear to both of you that I don't need an interpreter."

14    "He says he doesn't need an interpreter," the orderly reported to the woman.

15    The toughest misconception of all is the view that because I can't see, I can't work. I was turned down by over forty law firms because of my blindness, even though my qualifications included a cum laude° degree from Harvard College and a good ranking in my Harvard Law School class.

**°cum laude**
"with honors," a
distinction bestowed
at graduation from a
college or university

16    The attempt to find employment, the continuous frustration of being told that it was impossible for a blind person to practice law, the rejection letters, not based on my lack of ability but rather on my disability, will always remain one of the most disillusioning experiences of my life.

17    I therefore look forward to the day, with the expectation that it is certain to come, when employers will view their handicapped workers as a little child did me years ago when my family still lived in Scarsdale.

18    I was playing basketball with my father in our backyard according to procedures we had developed. My father would stand beneath the hoop, shout, and I would shoot over his head at the basket attached to our garage. Our

next-door neighbor, aged five, wandered over into our yard with a playmate. "He's blind," our neighbor whispered to her friend in a voice that could be heard distinctly by Dad and me. Dad shot and missed; I did the same. Dad hit the rim; I missed entirely; Dad shot and missed the garage entirely. "Which one is blind?" whispered back the little friend.

19    I would hope that in the near future when a plant manager is touring the factory with the foreman and comes upon a handicapped and nonhandicapped person working together, his comment after watching them work will be, "Which one is disabled?"

## Analyzing the Writer's Strategies

1. In the opening paragraph, the writer establishes the situation that his blindness has placed him in, namely, that to form an image of himself, he must depend on others who can see him. Explain what the writer means when he tells us that, up until now, this image "has not been narcissistic."

2. Harold Krents points out three misconceptions people have about blind people. Find where in the essay the writer states each of these misconceptions and mark them.

3. Each of the misconceptions is followed by one or two anecdotes that illustrate the misconception. Mark each anecdote and notice which ones use a quotation or a piece of dialogue. Why do you think Harold Krents has included these quotations or conversations?

4. Despite the essentially serious nature of the subject, Harold Krents is able to maintain his sense of humor. Where in the essay do you see him demonstrating this sense of humor?

## WRITING AN ESSAY USING EXAMPLES, ILLUSTRATIONS, OR ANECDOTES

Of the many ways writers choose to support their ideas, none is more useful or appreciated than the example. All of us have ideas in our minds, but these ideas will not become real for our readers until we use examples to make our concepts clear, concrete, and convincing. Writers who use good examples will be able to hold the attention of their readers.

> *Illustration* or *example* is a method of developing ideas by providing one or more instances of the idea in order to make what is abstract more concrete, give more clarity to the idea, or make that idea more convincing.

### Closely Related Terms Used in Example Essays

**Example:** a specific instance of something being discussed

**Extended example:** an example that is developed at some length, often taking up one or more complete paragraphs

**Illustration:** an example used to clarify or explain

**Anecdote:** a brief story used to illustrate a point

## CHOOSING A TOPIC AND CONTROLLING IDEA FOR THE THESIS STATEMENT

Here is a list of possible topics that could lead to an essay in which *example* is used as the main method of development. The rest of this chapter will help you work through the various stages of the writing process.

1. Three challenges I have overcome
2. The three greatest inventions of all time
3. Crises children face
4. Three things I cannot live without
5. Three ways to enjoy music
6. The world's worst habits
7. The three biggest needs in our community
8. Superstitions
9. Poor role models
10. The three best recording artists today

Using this list or drawing upon ideas of your own, jot down two or three topics that you could develop by providing examples.

_____

_____

_____

From these topics, select the one that seems most promising. Which one is most likely to interest your readers? Which one appeals to you the most?

**Selected topic:** _____

Your next step is to decide what your controlling idea will be. What is the point you want to make about the topic you have chosen? For instance, if you chose to write about "The World's Worst Habits" your controlling idea might be "unhealthy" or "dangerous."

**Controlling idea:** _____

Now put your topic and controlling idea together to form your thesis statement.

**Thesis statement:** _____

_____

## GATHERING INFORMATION USING BRAINSTORMING TECHNIQUES

Take at least fifteen minutes to jot down every example you can think of that you could use in your essay. If your topic is not of a personal nature, you might form a group to help each other think of examples, anecdotes, and illustrations. Later, if you feel your examples need to be improved, you may want to refer to material from magazines or newspapers. If you do use outside sources, be sure to take notes, checking the correct spelling of names and the accuracy of dates and facts.

_____

_____

_____

_____

_____

_____

_____

_____

_____

_____

_____

## SELECTING AND ORGANIZING THE MATERIAL

Review your list of examples, crossing out any ideas that are not useful. Do you have enough material to develop three body paragraphs? This might mean using three extended examples, some anecdotes, or several smaller examples that could be organized into three different groups. Decide on the order in which you want to present your examples. Do you have any ideas as to how you might want to write the introduction? On the lines that follow, show your plan for organizing your essay. You may want to make an outline that shows your major points, putting supporting details under each major point.

_____

_____

_____

_____

_____

_____

_____

_____

_____

## WRITING THE ROUGH DRAFT

Now you are ready to write your rough draft. Approach the writing with the attitude that you are going to write down all your thoughts on the subject without worrying about mistakes of any kind. It is important that your mind be relaxed enough to allow your thoughts to flow freely. You do not need to follow your plan exactly. Just get your thoughts on paper. You are free to add ideas, drop others, or rearrange the order of your details at any point. Sometimes a period of freewriting leads to new ideas that are better than the ones you had in your brainstorming session. Once a writer has something on paper, he or she usually feels a great sense of relief, even though it is obvious that revisions lie ahead.

Keep in mind that, in a paragraph with several examples, you will achieve coherence when the order of these examples follows some logical progression. You could start with the less serious and then move to the more serious, or you might start with the simpler one and move to the more complicated. If your examples consist of events, you might begin with examples from the more distant past and move forward to examples from the present day. Whatever logical progression you choose, you will find it helpful to signal your examples by using some of the transitional expressions that follow.

## Transitions Commonly Used in Examples

| | | | |
|---|---|---|---|
| an example of this is | for example | a typical case | the following illustration |
| to illustrate this | for instance | such as | To illustrate my point, let me tell you a story. |
| as an illustration | specifically | one such case | Let me clarify my point with an anecdote. |

### REVISING THE ROUGH DRAFT

You may revise your rough draft alone, with a group, with a peer tutor, or directly with your instructor. Here are some of the basic questions you should consider at this most important stage of your work.

## Guidelines for Revising an Essay Developed by Example

1.  Does the rough draft satisfy the conditions for the essay form? Is there an introductory paragraph? Are there at least three well-developed paragraphs in the body of the essay? Does each of these paragraphs have at least one example? Is there a concluding paragraph? Remember, a single sentence is not considered an acceptable paragraph in standard essay writing unless it is a piece of dialogue with quotation marks.

2.  Have you used *example* as your major method of development? Could you make your examples even better by being more specific or by looking up statistics or facts that would lend more authority to your point of view? Could you quote an expert on the subject?

3.  What is the basis for the ordering of your examples? Whenever appropriate, did you use transitions to signal the beginning of an example?

(continued on next page)

4. Is any important part missing? Are there any parts that seem irrelevant or out of place?

5. Are there words or expressions that could have been better chosen? Are any sentences or paragraphs repetitious?

6. Find at least two verbs (usually some form of the verb *to be*) that could be replaced with more descriptive verbs. Add at least two adjectives that will provide better sensory images for the reader.

7. Find at least one place in your draft where an additional sentence or two would make an example better.

8. Can you think of a more effective or creative way to begin or end?

9. Show your draft to two other readers and ask each one to give you at least one suggestion for improvement.

## PREPARING THE FINAL COPY, PRINTING, AND PROOFREADING

The typing of the final version should follow the traditional rules for an acceptable submission.

## Checklist for the Final Copy

Use only 8½-by-11-inch paper (never paper torn out of a spiral-bound notebook).

Type on only one side of the paper.

Double-space.

Leave approximately a 1½-inch margin on each side of the paper.

Put your name, the date, the title of your paper, and any other relevant information either on a separate title page or at the top of the first page. (Ask your instructor for specific advice on what information to include.)

Center the title. Do not put quotation marks around the title and do not underline it.

Do not hyphenate a word at the end of a line unless you are willing to consult a dictionary to check on the acceptable division of the word into syllables.

Indent each paragraph five spaces.

If your paper is more than one page, number the pages and staple the pages together so they will not get lost.

Do not forget to make a copy before you submit the paper.

**NOTE:** In most cases, college instructors will not accept handwritten work. However, if you are submitting handwritten work, be sure to write on every other line and have legible handwriting. Begin today to learn to type on a computer. You will be at a disadvantage if you cannot use the current technology.

Once you have typed your final version and printed it out, an important step still remains. This step can often mean the difference of an entire letter grade. You must *proofread* your paper. Even if you have used a spell-check feature available on your word-processing program, errors could remain in your paper. The spell-check feature finds only groupings of letters that are not words. For example, if you typed the word *form* when you meant to type *from,* the spell-checker would not catch this error. The secret of good proofreading is to look at each word and sentence construction by itself without thinking about the paper's content.

## Checklist for Proofreading

**Study each sentence:** One way to proofread is to read backwards, starting with the last sentence and examining every sentence, one at a time. First, check that the sentence is really complete and not a fragment or a run-on. Then check the punctuation. Go on to the next sentence and do the same. In this way, you will develop a critical eye for spotting any problems with sentence-level errors.

**Study each word:** Read the paper again, this time studying each word in every sentence. Look at the letters of the word. Have you transposed any letters, or have you left off an ending such as *-ed* or *-s*? If there are any words you are not sure how to spell, do not forget to check the correct spelling. Are there any words you have omitted?

## Exploring Online

Go to **www.cengage.com/devenglish/scarry/writersworkplace** to find the **Writer's Online Workplace,** a website designed for students using this book. You will find links to handouts, interactive quizzes, and other online resources as you explore the following topics:

- how to write an effective illustration essay
- things to watch for when writing the illustration essay

# Working Together

## BRAINSTORMING FOR EXAMPLES: JOB ADVANCEMENT

Many people think that to keep a good job they need to demonstrate that they are especially clever or smart, that they are a favorite of their employer, or that they are special in some other way. However, when employers have been surveyed, their responses show that the first item on their list of priorities is a surprisingly simple one: they just want their workers to show up!

Assume that a worker is dependable and does show up every day. How does that worker obtain good performance evaluations that will lead to a more permanent position, a salary increase, or, eventually, a job promotion?

### Working in Groups

Sometimes, without being aware of it, people act in ways at work that harm their chances for job advancement. Bad evaluations can even result in a person being fired. Develop a list of examples of actions or attitudes that keep workers from moving ahead in their careers. Then come together as a class and make a composite list of examples on the board. Do any class members recall an actual incident they observed that would illustrate one of the examples?

## PORTFOLIO SUGGESTION

Keep your list of examples in your portfolio for a possible essay on the topic of job advancement. Following are a few other work-related topics that you might want to consider for longer research papers:

What is the place of labor unions in the workforce?

Explain the problems with health insurance in this country.

Argue for or against tenure for teachers.

Compare working for a big company versus working for a small company.

Tell the stories of some famous "whistleblowers" (John Dean, Erin Brockovich, Mary McCarthy, Harry Markopolos).

What are some of the best-rated companies to work for and why? (For instance, see Google.)

# WRITING AN ESSAY USING NARRATION

**29**

This chapter will take you through the process of writing an essay using narration:

**CHAPTER OBJECTIVES**

- exploring the topic: A Lasting Childhood Memory
- reading and analyzing a childhood memory by Langston Hughes titled "Salvation"
- following the writing process to develop your own essay using narration

## EXPLORING THE TOPIC: A LASTING CHILDHOOD MEMORY

For most of us, childhood holds a mixture of happy and painful memories. Some memories are so lasting that they become part of our permanent consciousness. The recollection that the writer Langston Hughes shares with us in the following selection is one of these lasting memories, in which a child finds his perceptions to be in conflict with those of the adults around him. The essay you will write in this chapter will be a narrative based on a childhood experience that made a lasting impression on you. As you answer the following questions, think about what childhood experience you might want to recall.

1.  What different roles should adults play in the various stages of a child's life?

    _____

    _____

    _____

    _____

2.  What are some of the demands often made by adults that children typically resist?

    _____

    _____

    _____

    _____

3.  What are some of the experiences common to most childhoods?

    _____

    _____

    _____

    _____

4.  What are some examples of painful experiences that occur in some childhoods?

    _____

    _____

    _____

    _____

# READING A MODEL ESSAY WITH NARRATIVE ELEMENTS

## SALVATION

### Langston Hughes

Langston Hughes (1902–1967) was one of the most important writers of the twentieth century, bringing to his poetry, fiction, and essays profound commentary on the black experience in America. He was a leader of the Harlem Renaissance, a movement that took place during the 1920s when African American arts flourished in New York. Although Langston Hughes is perhaps best known for his poetry, the following selection, from his 1940 autobiography *The Big Sea,* has become famous. In it, he looks back on a central event of his youth, an event he realizes changed his vision of himself and his world.

- - - - - - - - - - - - - - - - - - - - - - - - - - - - - - - - - - - - - - - - - - - - - - - - - - - - - - - - - - - - - - - - - - - -

**°revival**

meeting for the purpose of bringing people into the faith

**°mourners' bench**

first pew in a church, where those who have not been saved await conversion

**°dire**

terrible

**°fold**

fenced enclosure for animals

**°work-gnarled**

misshapen from hard work

**°rounder**

someone who makes rounds, such as a security guard or a policeman

**°deacons**

members of the church chosen to help the minister

**°serenely**

calmly

1    I was saved from sin when I was going on thirteen. But not really saved. It happened like this. There was a big revival° at my Auntie Reed's church. Every night for weeks there had been much preaching, singing, praying, and shouting, and some very hardened sinners had been brought to Christ, and the membership of the church had grown by leaps and bounds. Then just before the revival ended, they held a special meeting for children, "to bring the young lambs to the fold." My aunt spoke of it for days ahead. That night I was escorted to the front row and placed on the mourners' bench° with all the other young sinners, who had not yet been brought to Jesus.

2    My aunt told me that when you were saved you saw a light, and something happened to you inside! And Jesus came into your life! And God was with you from then on! She said you could see and hear and feel Jesus in your soul. I believed her. I had heard a great many old people say the same thing and it seemed to me they ought to know. So I sat there calmly in the hot, crowded church, waiting for Jesus to come to me.

3    The preacher preached a wonderful rhythmical sermon, all moans and shouts and lonely cries and dire° pictures of hell, and then he sang a song about the ninety and nine safe in the fold,° but one little lamb was left out in the cold. Then he said: "Won't you come? Won't you come to Jesus? Young lambs, won't you come?" And he held out his arms to all us young sinners there on the mourners' bench. And the little girls cried. And some of them jumped up and went to Jesus right away. But most of us just sat there.

4    A great many old people came and knelt around us and prayed, old women with jet black faces and braided hair, old men with work-gnarled° hands. And the church sang a song about the lower lights are burning, some poor sinners to be saved. And the whole building rocked with prayer and song.

5    Still I kept waiting to see Jesus.

6    Finally all the young people had gone to the altar and were saved, but one boy and me. He was a rounder's° son named Westley. Westley and I were surrounded by sisters and deacons° praying. It was very hot in the church, and getting late now. Finally Westley said to me in a whisper: "God damn! I'm tired o' sitting here. Let's get up and be saved." So he got up and was saved.

7    Then I was left all alone on the mourners' bench. My aunt came and knelt at my knees and cried, while prayers and songs swirled all around me in the little church. The whole congregation prayed for me alone, in a mighty wail of moans and voices. And I kept waiting serenely° for Jesus, waiting, waiting—but he didn't come. I wanted to see him, but nothing happened to me. Nothing! I wanted something to happen to me but nothing happened.

8    I heard the songs and the minister saying: "Why don't you come? My dear child, why don't you come to Jesus? Jesus is waiting for you. He wants you. Why don't you come? Sister Reed, what is this child's name?"

9    "Langston," my aunt sobbed.

10      "Langston, why don't you come? Why don't you come and be saved? Oh, Lamb of God! Why don't you come?"

11      Now it was really getting late. I began to be ashamed of myself, holding everything up so long. I began to wonder what God thought about Westley, who certainly hadn't seen Jesus either, but who was now sitting proudly on the platform, swinging his knickerbockered° legs and grinning down at me, surrounded by deacons and old women on their knees praying. God had not struck Westley dead for taking his name in vain or for lying in the temple. So I decided that maybe to save further trouble, I'd better lie, too, and say that Jesus had come, and get up and be saved.

12      So I got up.

13      Suddenly the whole room broke into a sea of shouting, as they saw me rise. Waves of rejoicing swept the place. Women leaped in the air. My aunt threw her arms around me. The minister took me by the hand and led me to the platform.

14      When things quieted down, in a hushed silence, punctuated by a few ecstatic "Amens," all the new young lambs were blessed in the name of God. Then joyous singing filled the room.

15      That night, for the last time in my life but one—for I was a big boy of twelve years old—I cried. I cried, in bed alone, and couldn't stop. I buried my head under the quilts, but my aunt heard me. She woke up and told my uncle I was crying because the Holy Ghost had come into my life, and because I had seen Jesus. But I was really crying because I couldn't bear to tell her that I had lied, that I had deceived everybody in the church, that I hadn't seen Jesus, and that now I didn't believe there was a Jesus any more, since he didn't come to help me.

**°knickerbockered**
dressed in short pants gathered below the knees

## Analyzing the Writer's Strategies

1.  A narration is a story, usually set in a particular time, place, and culture. Several details in "Salvation" refer to religious ideas and rituals that may be unfamiliar to some readers. Review the story and make a list of any religious references that are unfamiliar to you. Learn their meanings through the Internet, library resources, or discussion with your classmates.

2.  A narration achieves coherence when details are placed in order of time sequence. Review the essay and underline the transitional words and expressions that indicate time, starting with "every night for weeks" in paragraph 1.

3.  What do you believe is Hughes's purpose in telling this story? (See Chapter 2 for a review of the three purposes for writing.)

4.  Many of the sentences in this story provide descriptive details that capture the sights or sounds of a particular moment. Choose the five sentences that you found to be the most effective. Mark them in the text so you can discuss them with your classmates.

5.  Three individuals are heard speaking in the story, but the narrator himself is never heard directly. As we read the story, what effect is created by being able to hear other people, but not the storyteller himself?

6.  In life and in literature, the gap between what we expect and what actually takes place is called *irony*. Study the ending of this story. Why is the ending *ironic*?

# WRITING AN ESSAY USING NARRATION

> **Narration** is the oldest and best-known form of verbal communication. It is, quite simply, the telling of a story.

## CHOOSING A STORY AND THE POINT YOU WISH TO MAKE WITH THAT STORY

Here is a list of possible topics that could lead to an essay in which *narration* is the main method of development.

1.  The experience (positive or negative) of moving to a new neighborhood
2.  Surviving a parent's separation or divorce
3.  A lesson learned from the mistake (or success) of an older brother or sister (or other relative)
4.  A spiritual experience
5.  When I stood alone against others
6.  An experience that made me feel alone
7.  An experience that made me more confident in myself
8.  A memorable classroom experience
9.  An accident that affected my childhood
10. The story of someone in my childhood whose change in values or beliefs led that person to reject a culture or group

Using the above list of suggested topics to start you thinking, jot down two or three powerful memories you have from your own childhood. These will be possible topics for your writing.

_____

_____

_____

From these topics, select the one that seems the most promising. Which one do you feel strongest about? Which one is most likely to interest your readers? Which topic is most suitable for a college essay?

**Selected topic:** _____

Good narration makes a point. A writer may not always come right out and state the point, but the reader should understand the point by the time he or she reaches the end of the story. Think about your story. What is the point you would like to make?

**Point of your story:** _____

The introductory paragraph for a story usually sets the scene. What time (for example, the time of year or the time of day), place, and mood will you establish in your introductory paragraph?

**Time:** _____

**Place:** _____

**Mood:** _____

## GATHERING INFORMATION USING BRAINSTORMING TECHNIQUES

Take at least fifteen minutes to jot down the sequence of events for your story as you remember it. Try to remember the way things looked at the time, how people reacted (what they did, what they said), and what you thought as the events were happening. If you can go to the actual spot where the events took place, you might go there and take notes on the details of the place. Later on, you can sort through the material and pick out what you want to use.

_____

_____

_____

_____

_____

## SELECTING AND ORGANIZING THE MATERIAL

Review your brainstorming list, crossing out any details that are not appropriate. Prepare to build on the ideas that you like. Put these remaining ideas into an order, such as an outline. This will serve as your temporary guide.

_____

_____

_____

_____

_____

_____

## WRITING THE ROUGH DRAFT

Find a quiet place where you will not be interrupted for at least one hour. With the plan for your essay in front of you, sit down and write the story that is in your mind. Do not try to judge what you are putting down as right or wrong. What is important is that you let your mind relax and allow the words to flow freely. Do not worry if you find yourself not following your plan exactly. Keep in mind that you are free to add parts, drop sections of the story, or rearrange details at any point. Sometimes, if you allow your thoughts to take you wherever they lead, new ideas may emerge. You may like these inspirations better than your original plan. Writing a rough draft is a little like setting out on an expedition; there are limitless possibilities, so it is important to be flexible. Keep in mind that in a narrative essay you will achieve coherence when the details are ordered according to a time sequence. One way to make the time sequence clear is to use transitional words that signal a time change. Here are some examples of transitional words that will help the reader move smoothly from one part of a story to the next.

---

## Transitions Commonly Used in Narration

| | | | |
|---|---|---|---|
| in December of 2009... | suddenly | after a little while | several weeks passed |
| the following month | now; by now | then | later; later on |
| soon afterward | immediately | meanwhile | at the same time |
| at once | in the next month | next; the next day | finally |

---

### REVISING THE ROUGH DRAFT

You may revise your rough draft alone, with a group, with a peer tutor, or directly with your instructor. If you are working on a computer, making changes is so easy that you will feel encouraged to explore alternatives. Unlike making changes using traditional pen and paper, inserting or deleting material on a computer is a simple matter. Here are some of the basic questions you should consider when the time comes to revise your narration.

---

## Guidelines for Revising an Essay Developed by Narration

1. Does the rough draft satisfy the conditions for the essay form? Is there an introductory paragraph? Are there at least three well-developed paragraphs in the body of the essay? Is there a concluding paragraph? Remember, a single sentence is not considered an acceptable paragraph in standard essay writing unless it is a piece of direct dialogue using quotation marks. (In the case of dialogue, a new paragraph is begun each time a different person speaks.)

2. Is your essay a narration? Does it tell the story of one particular incident that takes place at a specific time and location? A writer who talks about incidents in a general way in order to comment on the meaning of these incidents is not using narration. You must be a storyteller. Where does the action take place? Can the reader visualize it? What time of day, week, or year is it? What is the main character in the story doing?

3. Have you put the events of the story in a time order? Find the expressions you have used to show the time sequence.

4. Can you think of any part of the story that is missing and should be added? Is there any material that is irrelevant and should be omitted?

---

(continued on next page)

5.  Are any sentences or paragraphs repetitious?

6.  Find several places where you can substitute stronger verbs or nouns. Add adjectives to give the reader better sensory images.

7.  Find at least three places in your draft where you could add details. Perhaps you might add an entire paragraph that will more fully describe the person or place that is central to your story.

8.  Can you think of a more effective or creative way to begin or end?

9.  Does your story have a point? If a person told you every little thing that happened in the day, this would not make an interesting story. A good story should have a point.

10. Show your rough draft to at least two other readers and ask for suggestions.

## PREPARING THE FINAL COPY, PRINTING, AND PROOFREADING

The typing of the final version should follow the traditional rules for an acceptable submission.

## Checklist for the Final Copy

Use only 8½-by-11–inch paper (never paper torn out of a spiral-bound notebook).

Type on only one side of the paper.

Double-space.

Leave approximately a 1½-inch margin on each side of the paper.

Put your name, the date, the title of your paper, and any other relevant information either on a separate title page or at the top of the first page. (Ask your instructor for specific advice on what information to include.)

Center the title. Do not put quotation marks around the title and do not underline it.

Do not hyphenate a word at the end of a line unless you are willing to consult a dictionary to check on the acceptable division of the word into syllables.

Indent each paragraph five spaces.

If your paper is more than one page, number the pages and staple the pages together so they will not get lost.

Do not forget to make a copy before you submit the paper.

**NOTE:** In most cases, college instructors will not accept handwritten work. However, if you are submitting handwritten work, be sure to write on every other line and have legible handwriting. Begin today to learn to type on a computer. You will be at a disadvantage if you cannot use the current technology.

Once you have typed your final version and printed it out, an important step still remains. This step can often mean the difference of an entire letter grade. You must *proofread* your paper. Even if you have used a spell-check feature available on your word-processing program, errors could remain in your paper. The spell-check feature finds only groupings of letters that are not words. For example, if you typed the word *there* when you meant to type *their,* the spell-checker would not catch this error. The secret of good proofreading is to look at each word and sentence construction by itself without thinking about the paper's content.

## Checklist for Proofreading

**Study each sentence:** One way to proofread is to read backwards, starting with the last sentence and examining every sentence, one at a time. First, check that the sentence is really complete and not a fragment or a run-on. Then check the punctuation. Go on to the next sentence and do the same. In this way, you will develop a critical eye for spotting any problems with sentence-level errors.

**Study each word:** Read the paper again, this time studying each word in every sentence. Look at the letters of the word. Have you transposed any letters, or have you left off an ending such as *-ed* or *-s?* If there are any words you are not sure how to spell, do not forget to check the correct spelling. Are there any words you have omitted?

## Exploring Online

Go to **www.cengage.com/devenglish/scarry/writersworkplace** to find the **Writer's Online Workplace,** a website designed for students using this book. You will find links to handouts, interactive quizzes, and other online resources as you explore the following topics:

- writing the narrative essay
- principles and conventions of the narrative essay

# Working Together

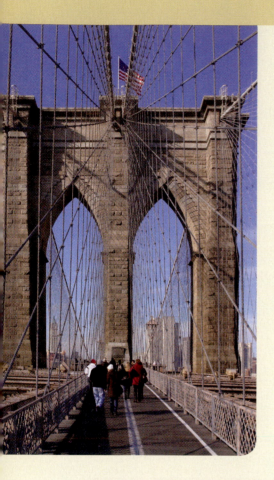

## SHARING OUR NARRATIVES

In the early part of the twentieth century, a Jewish girl from Poland, in the United States only weeks, went to a dinner party in Brooklyn. As she entered the house, a young man was putting on his coat to leave. When he saw the young woman coming through the door, he promptly removed his coat. Before the end of the night, he asked her to take a walk on the Brooklyn Bridge, and she accepted. As they stood together, overlooking the wide expanse of Manhattan and Brooklyn and the East River, he proposed marriage. She accepted that too.

Everyone loves a good story. We especially value those stories about our parents and grandparents: what their childhoods were like, how they met, and what were their struggles when they were young adults.

1. The paragraph above is taken from the essay "Bridges" by Joanna Hershon. Using the paragraph as your model, write a narrative telling how two people in your life met and started their relationship. These people could have been your parents, grandparents, two friends, or even yourself and your significant other.

2. After each person has drafted a narrative, exchange papers and enjoy reading the stories your classmates have produced. Your instructor may ask if some students would be willing to read their stories aloud.

3. If time permits, discuss what would be some of the reasons why recording these stories could be important.

## PORTFOLIO SUGGESTION

Keep all the narratives you have worked on in this chapter in your portfolio. These narratives could be the beginning of a series of stories written to capture the memories of your own family members. These stories may become the basis for a wonderful gift to your own children some day.

# WRITING AN ESSAY USING PROCESS ANALYSIS

# 30

This chapter will take you through the process of writing an essay using process analysis:

**CHAPTER OBJECTIVES**

- exploring the topic: Preparing for a Job Interview
- reading and analyzing a model essay: "How to Ace a Job Interview," by Richard Koonce
- following the writing process to develop your own essay explaining to your readers how to do something

## EXPLORING THE TOPIC: PREPARING FOR A JOB INTERVIEW

You are in the market for a job. You have searched the Internet and read the newspaper ads, asked your friends for suggestions, made phone calls, and sent out résumés. Now you have a very promising interview coming up next week. What can you do to prepare for this important interview?

Everyone who works or who is looking for work has been in this situation. Whether preparing for an interview or having gone through the experience, everyone is interested in the all-important process of obtaining a satisfying work situation.

1.  If you have ever gone through a job interview, share your experience with the class. (What was the best or worst aspect of the interview? What questions were you asked? Were you prepared? Did you get the job?)

    _____

    _____

    _____


2.  Imagine you are the person conducting a job interview. What would you be looking for in a prospective employee?

    _____

    _____

    _____

3.  From what you have heard, what are some successful actions or remarks people have made during their interviews?

_____

_____

_____

4.  What should a person *never* do in a job interview?

_____

_____

_____

# READING A MODEL ESSAY WITH STEPS IN A PROCESS

## HOW TO ACE A JOB INTERVIEW

### Richard Koonce

In the following essay, Richard Koonce takes us through the stages of the interview process, giving valuable pointers to job seekers. Whether we are heading toward an interview ourselves or advising a friend who is looking for a job, the following essay is filled with practical wisdom about what it takes to have a successful job interview.

1   Next to public speaking, most people think that enduring a job interview is one of the most stressful human experiences.

2   I wouldn't quibble with that. However, a lot of people not only manage to master the art of effective interviewing as they go about job searches, but actually grow to enjoy the interview experience.

3   Good thing! Job interviews are something we all have to deal with from time to time in our careers. So, it pays to know how to handle yourself effectively when you're sitting across the desk from a prospective employer. Indeed, knowing how to navigate the terrain° of job interviews can pay off big time for your career, land you a better job than the one you initially interview for, and position you for the job success and satisfaction you deserve.

4   How do you ace a job interview? Here are some tips.

5   Recognize that when you interview for a job, employers are looking for evidence of four things: your ability to do the job, your motivation, your compatibility with the rest of the organization, and your self-confidence. If you

°**navigate the terrain**
find the way

understand how all those things play into an interviewer's questions (and an employer's hiring decisions), you'll have a better chance of getting hired.

6    Often the first thing an employer wants to know is, "Will you fit in?" Presuming a company has seen your résumé ahead of time and invited you for an interview, it may assume you have certain skills. Now they want to know, "Will you be compatible with everyone else who works here?"

7    Fitting in is a real hot button for employers. That's because it's expensive to go through the rehiring process if someone doesn't work out.

8    Along with determining compatibility, employers want to know that you're motivated to do a job. And, they want to know why you want to work for their organization. So be ready with career highlights that illustrate why hiring you would be a good decision for the organization. Showcase your talents as an instructional designer for example, or tell the interviewer about the process improvement efforts you've put in place in your current job that ensure continuous refinement of training courses. Concise oral vignettes° like these can make a great impression on interviewers.

°**vignettes**
short descriptive accounts

9    Throughout the interview, breathe deeply, speak slowly, and focus on projecting yourself confidently. This is important. Employers want to see self-confidence in job seekers. A lot of job seekers are too modest. They downplay their accomplishments. Don't embellish or exaggerate, but don't be a shrinking violet either. Rehearse ahead of time the answers to key questions that you expect to be asked, especially that all-time favorite: "Tell me about yourself."

10   Some other points to keep in mind:

11   Before the interview, do some research on the company you're interviewing with. That will enable you to demonstrate knowledge of the company when you meet the interviewer. It may also prompt questions that you'll want to get answers to, even as questions are being asked of you.

12   There are lots of research options. You can tap into the Internet and pull down everything from company profiles to *Dun and Bradstreet* financial reports. You can talk to friends or coworkers that may know something about the organization. And don't forget to watch the paper for late-breaking developments about the company. (If you read in the paper the day of your interview that your prospective employer is about to file Chapter 11,° you may want to think twice about working there!)

°**file Chapter 11**
apply for bankruptcy

13   Arrive for the interview early enough to go to the restroom to check yourself out. The last thing you want is to arrive for your interview beaded with sweat, having just sprinted there from the subway stop two blocks away.

14   Once in the interview, concentrate on making a pleasant and strong first impression. Eighty percent of the first impression an interviewer gets of you is visual—and it's formed in the first two minutes of the meeting! So, men, wear a well-made suit, crisply starched white or blue shirt, and polished shoes. Women, you can get away with more color than men, but dress conservatively in dresses, or jacket and skirt combinations. Wearing a colorful scarf is a good way to weave in color, but keep jewelry to a minimum.

15   As you answer questions, be sure to emphasize as often as you can the reasons why your skills, background, and experience make you a good fit for the job that you're interviewing for.

16      After the interview, immediately send a thank-you note to the interviewer. This is a critical point of interview etiquette. Many job candidates eliminate themselves from competition for a job because they don't do this.

17      Finally, learn from every job interview you have. Don't be hard on yourself if things don't go your way. Even job interviews that don't go well can be great learning experiences. And in my own life, I can look back on interviews where I'm glad I didn't get the job!

## Analyzing the Writer's Strategies

1.  How many paragraphs comprise the introduction?

2.  According to the author, what are the four pieces of information employers want to know about a prospective employee?

3.  According to Richard Koonce, the stages in the interview process consist of the following: (a) what you should know before the interview, (b) how you should prepare for the interview, (c) what you should do upon arrival at the interview, (d) how you should conduct yourself during the interview, and (e) what you should do after the interview. Mark each of these stages in your text. What is the author's advice at each of these stages?

4.  From your own experience, can you think of any other advice that should have been included?

5.  How does the writer's last paragraph provide a useful conclusion to the essay?

# WRITING AN ESSAY USING PROCESS ANALYSIS (HOW TO...)

> **Process analysis,** as a method of developing ideas, involves giving a step-by-step explanation of how to do something (called *directional process*) or how something works (called *informational process*).

The "how to" section of a library or bookstore is usually a busy area. People come to find books that will help them perform thousands of different tasks—from plumbing to flower arranging. If you want to learn how to cook Chinese dishes, assemble a child's bicycle, start your own business, or remodel your bathroom, you can find a book that will tell you how to do it. Thousands of books and articles have been written that promise to help people accomplish their goals in life. What do you think are the best-selling "how to" books in America? Perhaps you have guessed the answer: books on how to lose weight! For the essay that you write, be sure to choose a process with which you are already familiar.

## CHOOSING A TOPIC AND CONTROLLING IDEA FOR THE THESIS STATEMENT

Here is a list of possible topics for an essay in which process analysis is the main method of development.

1.  How to get good grades in college
2.  How to prepare for a driver's test

3.   How to plan a budget
4.   How to buy a used car
5.   How to study for a test
6.   How to change a tire
7.   How to redecorate a room
8.   How to buy clothes on a limited budget
9.   How to find the right place to live
10.   How to make new friends

Using the above list of topics or ideas of your own, jot down two or three processes with which you are familiar.

_____

_____

_____

_____

_____

From all these topics, which one will give you the best opportunity for writing? Which one is most likely to interest your readers? For which topic do you have the most first-hand experience?

**Selected topic:** _____

Your next step is to decide on your purpose in writing. Which of the two types of process writing will you be doing? Do you want to give directions on how to carry out each step in a process so that your readers can do this process themselves? For instance, will you provide directions on how to change a tire, perhaps suggesting that your readers keep these directions in the glove compartments of their cars? Or do you want to provide information on how a process works because you think your readers might find it interesting? For instance, you might explain the process involved in getting an airplane off the ground. Not many of us understand how this works, and very few of us will ever pilot a plane. Perhaps you know a lot about an unusual process that might interest or amuse readers. Check below which one of the two types of process you will use.

**Your choice or process:** Directional _____       Informational _____

**What will be your controlling idea?** _____

Now put your topic and controlling idea together into a thesis statement.

**Thesis statement:** _____

_____

## GATHERING INFORMATION USING BRAINSTORMING TECHNIQUES

Take at least fifteen minutes to list as many steps or stages in the process as you can. If the process is one that others in your class or at home already know, consult with them about additional steps that you may have overlooked. You may also need to think of the precise vocabulary words associated with the process (such as the names of tools used for building or repairing something). The more specific you are, the more helpful and interesting the process analysis will be for your readers. List below the steps or stages in the process you have chosen:

_____

_____

_____

_____

_____

## SELECTING AND ORGANIZING THE MATERIAL

In a process essay, the most essential elements are the **completeness,** the **accuracy,** and the **order** of all the steps.

### Completeness and Accuracy

Review your brainstorming list, asking yourself whether or not the list is complete. For someone who is unfamiliar with this process, is there any step he or she might need to know? (The step may seem obvious to you, but for someone else it may be a necessary step to mention.) Is there any additional piece of information that, while not essential, would be helpful or encouraging? Perhaps you have a special warning about something that the reader should be careful *not* to do? Finally, you might consider telling your readers exactly where in the process most problems are likely to occur.

### Order

Now make an outline dividing the process into its major steps or stages. Underneath each major stage, list all of the details, including any vocabulary words that are particular to the process, and the name of any special tool or piece of equipment that is needed at any stage of the process. If your process involves a sequence that must be followed in a definite order, be careful that the order is correct.

_____

_____

_____

_____

_____

_____

_____

## WRITING THE ROUGH DRAFT

Write your rough draft, keeping in mind that your outline is only a guide. As you write, you will find yourself reevaluating the logic of your ideas, a perfectly natural step that may involve making some changes to your outline. You may think of some special advice that would help the reader; if you do, feel free to add the details. Your main goal is to get the process down on paper as completely and accurately as possible.

When you buy a product, the instructions that go with it usually take the form of a list of numbered items, each telling you what to do. In an essay, you do not usually number the steps. Instead, you signal the movement from one step to another by changing to a new paragraph, by using a transitional expression, or both. Like other methods for developing ideas, *process analysis* has its own special words and expressions that can be used to signal movement from one step to the next.

---

## Transitions Commonly Used in Process Analysis

| | | | |
|---|---|---|---|
| the first step | first of all | then | the last step |
| in the beginning | while you are | the second step | the final step |
| to start with | as you are | after you have | finally |
| to begin with | next | at last | eventually |

---

## REVISING THE ROUGH DRAFT

If you can set aside your rough draft and return to it at a later time, you will be able to view your work with more objectivity and thus revise your writing more effectively.

You may revise alone, with a group, with a peer tutor, or directly with your instructor. The following guidelines contain basic questions you should consider when you approach this most important stage of your work.

---

## Guidelines for Revising an Essay Developed by Process Analysis

1.  Does the rough draft satisfy all the conditions for the essay form? Is there an introductory paragraph? Are there at least three well-developed paragraphs in the body of the essay? Have you written a concluding paragraph? Remember, a single sentence is not considered an acceptable paragraph in standard essay writing unless it is a piece of direct dialogue using quotation marks.

2.  Does the essay describe the process, in either a directional or an informational way?

3.  Are the steps in the process in the correct order? In a process essay, the sequence of the steps is crucial. Placing a step out of order could result in a disaster of major proportions.

(continued on next page)

4. Are the directions accurate and complete? Check more than once that no important piece of information has been left out. Have you considered the points where some special advice might be helpful? Are there any special tools that would be useful?

5. Is any of the material not relevant?

6. Are any sentences or words repetitious?

7. Find several places where more specific verbs, nouns, or adjectives can be substituted. Always try to use vocabulary that is appropriate for the process being described.

8. Can you think of a more effective way to begin or end?

9. Does the essay flow logically from one idea to the next? Could you improve this flow with better use of transitional expressions?

10. Show your draft to at least two other readers and ask for suggestions.

## PREPARING THE FINAL COPY, PRINTING, AND PROOFREADING

The typing of the final version should follow the traditional rules for an acceptable submission.

## Checklist for the Final Copy

Use only 8½-by-11–inch paper (never paper torn out of a spiral-bound notebook).

Type on only one side of the paper.

Double-space.

Leave approximately a 1½-inch margin on each side of the paper.

Put your name, the date, the title of your paper, and any other relevant information either on a separate title page or at the top of the first page. (Ask your instructor for specific advice on what information to include.)

Center the title. Do not put quotation marks around the title and do not underline it.

Do not hyphenate a word at the end of a line unless you are willing to consult a dictionary to check on the acceptable division of the word into syllables.

Indent each paragraph five spaces.

If your paper is more than one page, number the pages and staple the pages together so they will not get lost.

Do not forget to make a copy before you submit the paper.

**NOTE:** In most cases, college instructors will not accept handwritten work. However, if you are submitting handwritten work, you must be sure to write on every other line and have legible handwriting. Begin today to learn to type on a computer. You will be at a disadvantage if you cannot use the current technology.

Once you have typed your final version and printed it out, an important step still remains. This step can often mean the difference of an entire letter grade. You must *proofread* your paper. Even if you have used a spell-check feature available on your word-processing program, errors could remain in your paper. The spell-check feature finds only groupings of letters that are not words. For example, if you typed the word *then* when you meant to type *than*, the spell-checker would not catch this error. The secret of good proofreading is to look at each word and sentence construction by itself without thinking about the paper's content.

## Checklist for Proofreading

**Study each sentence:** One way to proofread is to read backwards, starting with the last sentence and examining every sentence, one at a time. First, check that the sentence is really complete and not a fragment or a run-on. Then check the punctuation. Go on to the next sentence and do the same. In this way, you will develop a critical eye for spotting any problems with sentence-level errors.

**Study each word:** Read the paper again, this time studying each word in every sentence. Look at the letters of the word. Have you transposed any letters, or have you left off an ending such as *-ed* or *-s*? If there are any words you are not sure how to spell, do not forget to check the correct spelling. Are there any words you have omitted?

## Exploring Online

Go to **www.cengage.com/devenglish/scarry/writersworkplace** to find the **Writer's Online Workplace,** a website designed for students using this book. You will find links to handouts, interactive quizzes, and other online resources as you explore the following topics:

- writing the process essay
- issues to consider when writing a process essay

# Working Together

## DECIDING ON A LOGICAL ORDER: SEXUAL HARASSMENT IN THE WORKPLACE

The following letter was sent to the advice column of a local newspaper:

> Dear Dr. Karen: I have been with a bank for more than five years now, and at meetings every month or so I find myself working with one of the regional managers. He has always been polite at these meetings, but a few weeks ago, he started sending me e-mail that is very suggestive. He has even left inappropriate messages on my home telephone.
>
> I live alone, and these messages have upset me and have even frightened me. What should I do? Should I report this to my supervisor, who will probably think I am just overreacting? Everybody likes this man.
>
> Running Scared

Being harassed at work can create very complicated issues on the job. In many cases, the situation comes down to one person's word against that of another. Often, the person in the less powerful position is afraid to report a more powerful person to outside authorities. Fear of losing one's job is a strong incentive to remain silent. However, a person should not have to endure unacceptable behavior.

Consider the specific example described in the letter to Dr. Karen. Divide into groups and discuss the following questions concerning the woman who wrote the letter. Decide on the most logical order for the steps this person should take.

1. Should she confront the man who is harassing her?
2. Should she go to her supervisor? Should she tell her coworkers about the problem?
3. Should she share her problem with her friends or her boyfriend?
4. Should she avoid the problem by quitting her job?
5. How important is evidence for a person in this situation? How and when should she gather documentation for a possible formal action?
6. Does she need a lawyer? Does she need to consider the consequences of a formal action?

## PORTFOLIO SUGGESTION

Write a process essay in which you outline the steps a person should take if he or she is being harassed on the job.

Discussion of this issue may remind you of other problems that arise in the workplace. If so, you may want to start gathering ideas on some of these other problems that are of interest to you. Your examination of these issues could relate directly to other subject areas you might study, such as psychology, sociology, business ethics, or business management.

# 31

# WRITING AN ESSAY USING COMPARISON/ CONTRAST

This chapter will take you through the process of writing an essay using comparison/contrast:

## EXPLORING THE TOPIC: MEN AND WOMEN LOOK AT BEAUTY

Standards of beauty may change, but the search for beauty is a continual one in our lives. Whether we accept society's definition of beauty or have our own ideas on the subject, the question of how we see ourselves in the context of our culture is of genuine interest to most people.

1. When you look at another person, what is the first thing you notice about that person? Is this the feature or quality you always find most attractive about someone else?

   _____

   _____

   _____

   _____

2. To what extent do you judge someone by his or her appearance? Are you critical of people who do not pay a great deal of attention to how they look?

   _____

   _____

_____

_____

_____

_____

3.  All of us have met people who are very attractive, and our first tendency is to admire such people. However, are there some possible disadvantages to being very handsome or very beautiful?

_____

_____

_____

_____

_____

_____

4.  What are some of the more extreme measures people take to make themselves more attractive? Do you think these attempts are the result of pressures from society, the media, and the fashion and makeup industries, or do they result from inborn desires that people have?

_____

_____

_____

_____

_____

5.  What public figure (entertainer, politician, sports figure, and so on) do you consider to be especially handsome or beautiful? Why?

_____

_____

_____

_____

6.  Is there too much of an emphasis in the media today on impossible standards of beauty? At what point does this affect people's health?

_____

_____

_____

_____

# READING A MODEL ESSAY THAT USES COMPARISON/CONTRAST

## THE UGLY TRUTH ABOUT BEAUTY

## Dave Barry

The writer Dave Barry has been called "the funniest man in America." His career has been largely devoted to pointing out the lighter side of life. After graduating from college, he worked as a newspaper reporter before discovering his true talent as a writer of humorous essays. The wry observations about modern life that filled his columns earned Barry a Pulitzer Prize in 1988. In the following essay, which first appeared in the *Philadelphia Inquirer* in 1998, the writer gives us an amusing look at how both sexes view the questions of what is beauty and who is beautiful.

1       If you're a man, at some point a woman will ask you how she looks.

2       "How do I look?" she'll ask.

3       You must be careful how you answer this question. The best technique is to form an honest yet sensitive opinion, then collapse on the floor with some kind of fatal seizure. Trust me, this is the easiest way out. Because you will never come up with the right answer.

4       The problem is that women generally do not think of their looks in the same way that men do. Most men form an opinion of how they look in seventh grade, and they stick to it for the rest of their lives. Some men form the opinion that they are irresistible stud muffins, and they do not change this opinion even when their faces sag or their noses bloat to the size of eggplants and their eyebrows grow together to form what appears to be a giant forehead-dwelling tropical caterpillar.

5       Most men, I believe, think of themselves as average-looking. Men will think this even if their faces cause heart failure in cattle at a range of 300 yards. Being average does not bother them; average is fine, for men. This is why men never ask anybody how they look. Their primary form of beauty care is to shave themselves, which is essentially the same form of beauty care that they give to their lawns. If, at the end of his four-minute daily beauty regimen, a man has managed to wipe most of the shaving cream out of his hair and is not bleeding too badly, he feels that he has done all he can, so he stops thinking about his appearance and devotes his mind to more critical issues, such as the Super Bowl.

6       Women do not look at themselves this way. If I had to express, in three words, what I believe most women think about their appearance, those words would be: "not good enough." No matter how attractive a woman may appear to be to others, when she looks at herself in the mirror, she thinks: woof. She thinks that at any moment a municipal animal-control officer is going to throw a net over her and haul her off to the shelter.

7       Why do women have such low self-esteem? There are many complex psychological and societal reasons, by which I mean Barbie. Girls grow up playing with a doll proportioned such that, if it were a human, it would be seven feet tall and weigh

81 pounds, of which 53 pounds would be bosoms. This is a difficult appearance standard to live up to, especially when you contrast it with the standard set for little boys by their dolls . . . excuse me, by their action figures. Most of the action figures that my son played with when he was little were hideous-looking. For example, he was very fond of an action figure (part of the He-Man series) called "Buzz-Off," who was part human, part flying insect. Buzz-Off was not a looker. But he was extremely self-confident. You could not imagine Buzz-Off saying to the other action figures: "Do you think these wings make my hips look big?"

8          But women grow up thinking they need to look like Barbie, which for most women is impossible, although there is a multibillion-dollar beauty industry devoted to convincing women that they must try. I once saw an Oprah show wherein supermodel Cindy Crawford dispensed makeup tips to the studio audience. Cindy had all these middle-aged women applying beauty products to their faces; she stressed how important it was to apply them in a certain way, using the tips of their fingers. All the women dutifully did this, even though it was obvious to any sane observer that, no matter how carefully they applied these products, they would never look remotely like Cindy Crawford, who is some kind of genetic mutation.

9          I'm not saying that men are superior. I'm just saying that you're not going to get a group of middle-aged men to sit in a room and apply cosmetics to themselves under the instruction of Brad Pitt, in hopes of looking more like him. Men would realize that this task was pointless and demeaning.° They would find some way to bolster° their self-esteem that did not require looking like Brad Pitt. They would say to Brad: "Oh YEAH? Well what do you know about LAWN CARE, pretty boy?"

**°demeaning**
degrading

**°bolster**
support or buoy up

10         Of course many women will argue that the reason they become obsessed with trying to look like Cindy Crawford is that men, being as shallow as a drop of spit, WANT women to look that way. To which I have two responses:

11         1. Hey, just because WE'RE idiots, that does not mean YOU have to be; and

12         2. Men don't even notice 97 percent of the beauty efforts you make anyway. Take fingernails. The average woman spends 5,000 hours per year worrying about her fingernails; I have never once, in more than 40 years of listening to men talk about women, heard a man say, "She has a nice set of fingernails!" Many men would not notice if a woman had upward of four hands.

13         Anyway, to get back to my original point: If you're a man, and a woman asks you how she looks, you're in big trouble. Obviously, you can't say she looks bad. But you also can't say that she looks great, because she'll think you're lying, because she has spent countless hours, with the help of the multibillion-dollar beauty industry, obsessing about the differences between herself and Cindy Crawford. Also, she suspects that you're not qualified to judge anybody's appearance. This is because you have shaving cream in your hair.

## Analyzing the Writer's Strategies

1.   Underline the thesis of Barry's essay.

2.   Read the introduction (paragraphs 1–3) and the conclusion (paragraph 13) of the essay and explain how Barry's conclusion echoes what he wrote in the introduction.

3.  Find three sentences in the essay that you find humorous and explain what makes these sentences funny for you.

4.  Dave Barry uses informal language. Find five examples of informal language or slang.

5.  Find an example of Barry's use of simile (a comparison using *like* or *as).*

6.  Summarize how Barry contrasts each of the following:

    a.  a man's daily regimen and a woman's daily regimen
    b.  a man's attitude about himself and a woman's attitude about herself
    c.  a Barbie doll and an action figure called Buzz-Off
    d.  a woman's attitude toward Cindy Crawford and a man's attitude toward Brad Pitt

# WRITING AN ESSAY USING COMPARISON/ CONTRAST

> ***Comparison/contrast,*** as a method for developing ideas, involves the careful examination of similarities and differences between people, objects, or ideas to arrive at a judgment or conclusion.

## CHOOSING A TOPIC AND CONTROLLING IDEA FOR THE THESIS STATEMENT

Here is a list of possible topics for an essay in which comparison/contrast is the main method of development.

1.  High school classes and college classes
2.  Studying with a friend and studying alone
3.  Male and female stereotypes
4.  Your best friend in childhood and your best friend now
5.  Using public transportation and driving your own car
6.  Our current president and any previous chief executive
7.  Two items you have compared when shopping
8.  Two apartments or houses where you have lived
9.  Cooking dinner at home and eating out
10. Watching television and reading a book

Using the above list of topics or ideas of your own, jot down a few two-part topics that appeal to you.

_____

_____

_____

_____

From your list of two-part topics, which one will give you the best opportunity for writing? Which one is most likely to interest your readers? For which topic do you have the most first-hand experience?

**Selected topic:** _____

Your next step is to decide what your controlling idea should be. What is your main purpose in comparing or contrasting these two topics? Do you want to show that although people think the two topics are similar, they actually differ in important ways? Do you want to show that one topic is better in some ways than the other? Do you want to analyze how something has changed over the years (a "then and now" essay)?

**Controlling idea:** _____

At this point, combine your two-part topic and controlling idea into one thesis statement.

**Thesis statement:** _____

_____

## GATHERING INFORMATION USING BRAINSTORMING TECHNIQUES

Take at least fifteen minutes to brainstorm (using listing or clustering) as many points of comparison or contrast as you can on your chosen topic. You will probably want to think of at least three or four points. Under each point, brainstorm as many details as come to mind. For instance, if you are comparing two friends and the first point concerns the interests you have in common, recall as much as you can about the activities you share together. If you are brainstorming on a topic that other classmates or family members might know something about, ask them to help you think of additional points to compare. If special vocabulary comes to mind, jot that down as well. The more specific you are, the more helpful and interesting your comparison or contrast will be for your readers.

### Points to Compare or Contrast

| | Topic One _____ | Topic Two _____ |
|---|---|---|
| Point 1 | | |
| Point 2 | | |
| Point 3 | | |
| Point 4 | | |
| Point 5 | | |

## SELECTING AND ORGANIZING THE MATERIAL

Comparison/contrast always involves a two-part topic. For instance, you might compare the school you attend now with a school you attended in the past. Often we need to make choices or judgments, and we can make better decisions if we compare or contrast the two items in front of us. Because of the two-part topic, you have a choice in organizing the essay:

1. **The block method.** With this method, you write everything you have to say about one topic or idea, and then in a later paragraph or paragraphs you write entirely about the other topic. If you choose this method, when you discuss the second topic, you must be sure to bring up the same points and keep the same order as when you discussed the first topic.

2. **The point-by-point method.** With this method, you discuss one point and show in one paragraph how both topics relate to this point. Then, in a new paragraph, you discuss the second point and relate it to both topics, and so forth.

Which method will be better for the topic you have selected—the block method or the point-by-point method?

At this stage, review your brainstorming list, asking yourself if you have a complete list. Have you left out any point that might need to be considered? Do you have at least three points, and do you have enough material to develop both parts of the topic? You do not want the comparison or contrast to end up one-sided, with most of the content focused on only one part of the topic.

Depending on your choice of block method or point-by-point method, outline your topic based on one of the two formats below. The example contrasts high school classes with college classes.

### Outline for Block Method

**I. Topic 1**                          **High school classes**

  A. First Point                     meet five days a week
    (how often classes meet)

  B. Second Point                   daily homework
    (homework)

  C. Third Point                    seldom require research papers
    (research papers)

  D. Fourth Point                   discipline problems
    (discipline)

**II. Topic 2**                         **College classes**

  A. First Point                     meet only two or three days a week
    (how often classes meet)

  B. Second Point                   long-term assignments
    (homework)

  C. Third Point                    often require research papers
    (research papers)

  D. Fourth Point                   few discipline problems
    (discipline)

**Outline for Point-by-Point Method**

**I. First Point**             **How often classes meet**

A. Topic 1          high school classes:    meet five days a week

B. Topic 2          college classes:        meet only two or three days a week

**II. Second Point**           **Homework**

A. Topic 1          high school classes:    have daily homework

B. Topic 2          college classes:        have long-term assignments

**III. Third Point**           **Research papers**

A. Topic 1          high school classes:    seldom require research papers

B. Topic 2          college classes:        often require research papers

**IV. Fourth Point**           **Discipline**

A. Topic 1          high school classes:    often have discipline problems

B. Topic 2          college classes:        seldom have discipline problems

**Your Outline**

_____

_____

_____

_____

_____

_____

_____

_____

_____

_____

_____

## WRITING THE ROUGH DRAFT

Write your rough draft. Remember that your outline is a guide. Most writers find that additional details occur to them as they write. If you have new thoughts, you should feel free to explore them. Of course, you must then reevaluate the logic of your ideas.

As is true with other methods of developing ideas, comparison/contrast has its particular words and expressions to indicate movement from one point to the next.

## Transitions Commonly Used in Comparison/Contrast

| Transitions for comparison | | Transitions for contrast | |
| --- | --- | --- | --- |
| again | like | although | instead |
| also | likewise | and yet | nevertheless |
| as well as | moreover | but | on the contrary |
| both | the same as | despite | on the other hand |
| equally | similar to | different from | otherwise |
| furthermore | similarly | even though | still |
| just as | so | except for | though |
| just like | too | however | unlike |
| | | in contrast with | whereas |
| | | in spite of | while |

## REVISING THE ROUGH DRAFT

If you are able to leave your rough draft and return to it later for revision, you will view your work with greater objectivity. In the best circumstances, you might be able to leave your first draft aside for a day or two before you revise.

When you revise, you may work alone, with a group, with a peer tutor, or directly with your instructor. Here are some of the basic questions you should consider during this most important stage of your work.

## Guidelines for Revising an Essay Developed by Comparison/Contrast

1. Does the rough draft satisfy the conditions for the essay form? Is there an introductory paragraph? Are there at least three well-developed paragraphs in the body of the essay? Is there a concluding paragraph? Remember, a single sentence is not considered an acceptable paragraph in standard essay writing unless it is a piece of dialogue using quotation marks.

2. Does the essay compare or contrast a two-part topic and come to some conclusion about the comparison or contrast?

3. Has the essay been organized by the point-by-point method or the block method?

(continued on next page)

4.   Have important points been omitted? Is any of the material irrelevant?

5.   Are there repetitious sentences or paragraphs?

6.   Find several places where more specific verbs, nouns, or adjectives can be substituted. Use vocabulary that is appropriate for the topic being discussed.

7.   Can you think of a more effective or creative way to begin or end?

8.   Does the essay flow logically from one idea to the next? Would using any transitional expressions improve this flow?

9.   Show your draft to at least two other readers and ask for suggestions.

## PREPARING THE FINAL COPY, PRINTING, AND PROOFREADING

The typing of the final version should follow the traditional rules for an acceptable submission.

---

# Checklist for the Final Copy

Use only 8½-by-11–inch paper (never paper torn out of a spiral-bound notebook).

Type on only one side of the paper.

Double-space.

Leave approximately a 1½-inch margin on each side of the paper.

Put your name, the date, the title of your paper, and any other relevant information either on a separate title page or at the top of the first page. (Ask your instructor for specific advice on what information to include.)

Center the title. Do not put quotation marks around the title and do not underline it.

Do not hyphenate a word at the end of a line unless you are willing to consult a dictionary to check on the acceptable division of the word into syllables.

Indent each paragraph five spaces.

If your paper is more than one page, number the pages and staple the pages together so they will not get lost.

Do not forget to make a copy before you submit the paper.

---

**NOTE:** In most cases, college instructors will not accept handwritten work. However, if you are submitting handwritten work, you must be sure to write on every other line and have legible handwriting. Begin today to learn to type on a computer. You will be at a disadvantage if you cannot use the current technology.

Once you have typed your final version and printed it out, an important step still remains. This step can often mean the difference of an entire letter grade. You must *proofread* your paper. Even if you have used a spell-check feature available on your word-processing program, errors could remain in your paper. The spell-check feature finds only groupings of letters that are not words. For example, if you typed the word *van* when you meant to type *ban*, the spell-checker would not catch this error. The secret of good proofreading is to look at each word and sentence construction by itself without thinking about the paper's content.

## Checklist for Proofreading

**Study each sentence:** One way to proofread is to read backwards, starting with the last sentence and examining every sentence, one at a time. First, check that the sentence is really complete and not a fragment or a run-on. Then check the punctuation. Go on to the next sentence and do the same. In this way, you will develop a critical eye for spotting any problems with sentence-level errors.

**Study each word:** Read the paper again, this time studying each word in every sentence. Look at the letters of the word. Have you transposed any letters, or have you left off an ending such as *-ed* or *-s*? If there are any words you are not sure how to spell, do not forget to check the correct spelling. Are there any words you have omitted?

## Exploring Online

Go to **www.cengage.com/devenglish/scarry/writersworkplace** to find the **Writer's Online Workplace,** a website designed for students using this book. You will find links to handouts, interactive quizzes, and other online resources as you explore the following topics:

• writing the comparison/contrast essay
• block method versus point-by-point method

# Working Together

## CONTRASTING MEN AND WOMEN

The essay previously in this chapter is a humorous look by Dave Barry as he examines one of the major differences between men and women. Below is a more serious assessment of another difference between the sexes. The following paragraphs are taken from an essay by Deborah Tannen, a professor at Georgetown University and a widely published author who writes on the subject of gender. As you read the paragraphs, see if you agree with her ideas.

For women, as for girls, intimacy is the fabric of relationships, and talk is the thread from which it is woven. Little girls create and maintain friendships by exchanging secrets; similarly, women regard conversation as the cornerstone of friendship. So a woman expects her husband to be a new and improved version of a best friend. What is important is not the individual subjects that are discussed but the sense of closeness, of a life shared, that emerges when people tell their thoughts, feelings and impressions.

Bonds between boys can be as intense as bonds between girls, but they are based less on talking, more on doing things together. Since they don't assume talk is the cement that binds a relationship, men don't know what kind of talk women want, and they don't miss it when it isn't there.

Is it true that one can predict the behavior of most women and most men? Deborah Tannen believes that when it comes to close relationships, women want conversation while men are more interested in actually doing things together. Divide into groups and discuss what you think would be the predictable way a man would act and a woman would act in each of the following situations.

    A. meeting for a family gathering

    B. handling a disobedient teenager

    C. dealing with a problem in a child's school

    D. breaking up with a girlfriend or boyfriend

    E. being stopped by the police

    F. getting poor service in a restaurant

1. Does your group agree that women and men are, in general, predictable in their behavior?

2. Do you think culture plays a role?

3. To what extent does education play a role?

4. Can your group think of some other areas where behavior between men and women generally differ?

## PORTFOLIO SUGGESTION

Keep a list of ideas generated by the class discussion. If you are required to write an essay contrasting typical male behavior with typical female behavior, you might consider the values, actions, goals, or priorities of the sexes. Since this topic has intrigued writers from many disciplines, you would also find this a rich subject for research. It is always interesting to find out if the research you uncover changes any of your current beliefs.

# WRITING AN ESSAY USING PERSUASION

## 32

In this chapter, you will build an understanding of the different elements that make up the persuasive essay.

**CHAPTER OBJECTIVES**

- analyze a basic persuasive essay
- study a list of guidelines for writing an effective persuasive essay
- compare and discuss two arguments with opposing viewpoints
- review a list of common transitions to help achieve coherence
- write a persuasive essay on the topic: Laptops in the Classroom
- consider additional topics for writing persuasive essays

## WHAT IS PERSUASION?

From one point of view, all writing is persuasion because the main goal of any writer is to convince a reader to see, think, or believe in a certain way. There is, however, a more formal definition of persuasive writing. Anyone who has ever been a member of a high school debate team knows there are techniques that the effective speaker or writer uses to present a case successfully. Learning how to recognize these techniques of persuasion and how to use them in your own writing is the subject of this chapter.

> An essay of **persuasion** presents evidence intended to convince the reader that the writer's position is valid. Evidence can include facts, statistics, testimony, and the support of recognized authorities. The writer may appeal to logic, emotion, and worthiness.

579

# ANALYSIS OF A BASIC PERSUASIVE ESSAY

Study the following persuasive essay to focus on the different elements present in an effective argument.

### Don't Call, Don't Text, Just Drive!

We live in a country where our freedoms are a point of pride. However, one person's exercise of a freedom should not be allowed to endanger the safety of others. This is particularly true in the case of people who talk and text-message while they are driving a vehicle. States should enact strict laws, accompanied by penalties, forbidding talking or text-messaging with a handheld cell phone while operating a vehicle.

In the past twenty years or so, the use of cell phones in the United States has exploded. In 1985, we had nearly 350,000 cell phone subscribers, but by 2004, more than 182 million people had cell phones. In 2005, the National Highway Traffic Safety Administration conducted a study that found ten percent of all drivers were using cell phones while on the road during the day. Such widespread use of cell phones while driving has lawmakers worried. What should they do about the growing national problem of distracted drivers?

According to Peter D. Loeb, Professor at Rutgers University, cell phones are contributing to numerous vehicle fatalities. For example, in 2008, five teenagers were in a head-on collision in upstate New York. At first, it was rumored that the driver must have been drinking, but it was soon determined that the driver was distracted while text-messaging. Everyone in the car was killed. In another horrendous accident, a train operator in California was text-messaging a young friend and failed to observe a red light. Twenty-five people were killed and many others were seriously

(continued on next page)

injured. Although not every accident results in fatalities, this risky behavior while driving is causing needless property damage and injury. Common sense tells us that state laws are needed to discourage cell phone usage while driving.

Opponents will say that banning the use of cell phones while driving is an invasion of privacy. They ask, "Will the authorities also regulate eating a sandwich or even talking to a passenger while driving?" They claim every driver does things while driving that could be considered distracting: turning on the radio, playing a CD, or looking at a map, just to name a few. Is the state going to ban all these activities, too? These opponents believe citizens must be educated to use good judgment instead of proposing more regulations. While we could wish that people would regulate themselves, we know this is not going to happen. Most drivers are already in the habit of using their cell phones while driving. They are not going to change their habits unless they would face some kind of penalty.

Other critics of regulation argue that people should be able to make and receive calls because people often find themselves in serious situations that can be solved by using the cell phone. This sounds reasonable; however, in most cases, a driver can pull over to the side of the road to make or take a call. And if a driver is in an accident, it is more likely a nearby witness, not the driver, who makes the call. We all know that the majority of calls are simply for friendly conversation, and many of the people making these calls are teenagers who do not have the maturity to recognize the implications of being distracted at the wheel.

We can all agree that any activity that causes a person to take his or her eyes off the road is a serious risk for an accident. The state has a responsibility to protect the lives of all drivers on the road. Ideally, drivers themselves should accept responsibility for the safety of their fellow citizens, but the fact is most people are now using their cell phones while driving. Perhaps we cannot regulate against shaving or putting on makeup behind the wheel, but at least society should do what it can to save lives and property. State governments must therefore make regulations that carry stiff fines for those who disregard the law in order to enforce standards of safety.

ACTIVITY 1

## Analyzing The Writer's Argument

1.  In your own words, what is the issue being argued?

    _____

2.  Underline the thesis statement.

3.  Mark each sentence that presents a fact.

4.  What are the sources for the writer's facts?

    _____

    _____

5. In your own words, why are these facts included?

_____

_____

6. How many examples in the form of anecdotes are given? _____

7. According to the writer, what is the opposition's point of view?

_____

_____

8. What are the reasons given by the writer for the necessity of a law regulating cell phone use?

_____

_____

9. Does the author provide a reasonable solution to the problem? Explain.

_____

10. Can you think of any other ways to strengthen the argument?

_____

_____

# GUIDELINES FOR WRITING A PERSUASIVE ESSAY

Following are some basic guidelines for writing an effective persuasive essay.

1. **State a clear thesis.** Use words such as *must*, *ought*, or *should*. Study the following three sample thesis statements:

   **The United States must reform its prison system.**

   **All states ought to have the same legal drinking age.**

   **We should not ban all handguns.**

2. **Give evidence or reasons for your beliefs.** Your evidence is the heart of the essay. You must show the wisdom of your logic by providing the best evidence available. Your evidence may include personal observation, facts, statistics, expert opinion, and examples. You might even appeal to common sense.

3. **Use examples.** Well-chosen examples are among the best evidence for an argument. People can identify with a specific example from real life in a way that they cannot with an abstract idea. Without examples, essays of persuasion would be flat, lifeless, and unconvincing.

4. **Use opinions from recognized authorities to support your points.** One of the oldest methods of supporting an argument is to use one or more persons of authority to support your position. People will usually believe what well-known experts claim. However, be sure that your expert is someone who is respected in the area you are discussing. For example, if you are arguing that we must address the problem of global warming, your argument will be stronger if you quote a respected scientist who has studied the serious implications of global warming. A famous movie star giving the same information might be more glamorous and get more attention, but he or she would not be as great an authority as the scientist.

5. **Be careful to avoid faulty logic.**

   a.  Do not appeal to fear or pity.

   > **Example:**  **If we don't double the police force, innocent children will die.**

   b.  Do not make sweeping or false generalizations.

   > **Example:**  **All women belong in the kitchen.**

   c.  Do not oversimplify with an either-or presentation.

   > **Example:**  **A woman should either stay home and take care of her children or go to work and remain childless.**

   d.  Do not give misleading or irrelevant support to your argument.

   > **Example:**  **Don't hire that man; he has six children.**

6. **Answer your critics in advance.** When you point out, beforehand, what your opposition is likely to say in answer to your argument, you are writing from a position of strength. You are letting your reader know that there is another side to the argument you are making. By pointing out this other side and then answering its objections in advance, you strengthen your own position.

7. **In your conclusion, point out the results, make predictions, or suggest a solution.** Here, you help your reader see what will happen if your argument is (or is not) believed or acted upon as you think it should be. You should be very specific and very rational when you point out results, making sure that you avoid exaggeration. For example, if you were arguing against the possession of handguns, it would be an exaggeration to say that if we don't ban handguns, "everyone will be murdered."

# OPPOSING VIEWPOINTS: SHOULD THE DRINKING AGE BE LOWERED?

You will now study two opposing arguments on a subject that has led to an intense national debate. Recently, a group of college presidents proposed that the nation lower the drinking age from 21 to 18. Two faculty members, Professor Nancy Lynne Hogan from Michigan and Eva Erskine from Illinois have taken opposite sides of the issue. Study their arguments and answer each of the questions that follow.

## A Debate: Should the Drinking Age Be Lowered?

### PRO

The drinking age debate has been a hot topic for years. Should 18-year-olds be allowed to drink or should the age of alcohol consumption be 21 years old? What is the difference?

Some believe 21-year-olds are more mature and more responsible while critics argue that at 18, men and women already are mature in that they can marry, serve in the armed forces, and make their own legal decisions.

The real issue is often ignored. The laws are supposed to reflect society's boundaries of acceptable behavior. Thus, the majority of citizens should agree with these boundaries and abide by them. No one would argue that murder is an acceptable behavior except in defending oneself. The problem with alcohol usage laws is that the majority of 18-year-olds drink. This pattern of behavior has not changed for 30 years.

Thus, the law has not shaped the boundaries of behavior; it has actually contributed to a more dangerous environment of binge drinking, alcohol poisoning, and criminal records that can affect students' careers. In Michigan, the laws has gone overboard by making a "Minor in Possession" a misdemeanor. Thus, a large percentage of Michigan students leave college with a degree and a criminal record.

The bottom line is that the law cannot shape morality. Our culture promotes alcohol usage for entertainment and relaxation. The media promotes this in commercials, television shows, and movies. Criminalizing a behavior for legal adults that is culturally acceptable is wrong. Focusing on responsible drinking is a much more important goal than chalking up citations!

—Professor Nancy Lynn Hogan

### CON

If it were possible to guarantee that 18 - to 21-year-olds would drink responsibly and under-stand the consequences of alcohol consumption, I would favor lowering the drinking age. I have not seen evidence that this is true. Therefore, I must oppose lowering the drinking age.

I suggest to the college presidents in favor of lowering the drinking age that they research the number of teenage alcohol-related deaths. The numbers are staggering. In addition, some research on alcohol-related healthcare costs, both medical and psychological, may sway their opinion. I am thinking particularly of Korsakoff's syndrome and fetal alcohol syndrome. Alcoholism is an addictive, serious medical condition that also affects family members of the alcoholic.

Some may argue that I may be jumping the gun; just because someone drinks at 18 doesn't mean that they will become an alcoholic. That may be true. But, that doesn't mean we have to encourage young adult drinking

I challenge this group of college presidents to give me some sound economic reasons for lowering the drinking age, other than profits from liquor sales. Much more importantly, I would like to know how their position is socially responsibly. How does society benefit if the drinking age is lowered?

What is a college president's motive in lowering the drinking age? I am wondering if it makes a college president's job a little easier if the drinking age is lowered. Discipline in any organization is time-consuming and disrup-tive. Is the discipline issue for illegal drinking too much to handle?

When Ivory Tower academics can back up and substantiate their position with scientific research, maybe I will listen to them.

—Eva Erskine

ACTIVITY **2**   **Discussion Questions For Pro And Con Essays On Lowering The Drinking Age**

Following the Guidelines for Writing a Persuasive Essay on pages 582–583, discuss the effectiveness of the two arguments.

1.  Is each thesis clearly stated?

2.  Evaluate the evidence given by each writer. Is the evidence convincing?

3.  Have both writers provided examples? Mark them in the text.

4.  Does either writer support the argument by giving expert opinions from authorities?

5.  Discuss the logic of each argument. Can you find any weaknesses?

6.  Does either writer pay attention to the opposing point of view?

7.  Does each argument conclude with some type of suggestion, prediction, or solution?

## ACHIEVING COHERENCE

Like other methods of developing an essay, persuasion has its own special words that signal parts of the argument. The following chart can help you find transitional expressions that will move you from one part of your argument to the next.

### Transitions Commonly Used to Signal the Parts of a Persuasive Essay

**To signal the thesis of an argument**

I agree (disagree) that . . .

I support (do not support) the idea that . . .

I am in favor (not in favor) of . . .

I propose . . .

. . . must (must not) be changed

. . . should (should not) be adopted

**To signal a reason**

| | |
|---|---|
| The first reason is . . . | because |
| An additional reason is . . . | can be shown |
| Another reason is . . . | for (meaning *because*) |
| The most convincing piece of evidence is . . . | in the first place |
| | in view of |
| | just because |

(continued on next page)

**To admit an opponent's point of view**

Most people assume that . . .

One would think that . . .

We have been told that . . .

Popular thought is that . . .

Some may claim . . .

The opposition would have you believe . . .

**To signal a conclusion**

| | |
|---|---|
| We can conclude that . . . | as a result |
| This proves that . . . | consequently |
| This shows that . . . | so |
| This demonstrates that . . . | therefore |
| This suggests that . . . | thus |
| This leads to the conclusion that . . . | |
| It follows that . . . | |

# OPPOSING VIEWPOINTS: SHOULD LAPTOPS BE ALLOWED IN THE CLASSROOMS?

Below is an essay by Professor Thom Curtis of the University of Hawaii arguing against the use of laptops in the classroom. Read the essay carefully and then discuss the essay with your classmates. Use the Guidelines for Writing a Persuasive Essay on pages 582–583 to analyze the argument.

### No, to Laptops in the Classrooms

Last fall, I was called upon to teach a large section of our introductory sociology class for the first time in years. Almost immediately, I was struck by the walls of laptop screens stretching across the risers of the lecture hall. About half of the students were busily typing away.

My assumption that the students were using their machines to take notes was shattered a couple weeks later when during a break I walked to the top of the classroom and looked across the hall from the rear. On most of the students' screens were games, chats, e-mail, and videos. I even sat down in any empty seat in the back now next to a student playing a video game. He was oblivious of my presence until other students sitting around us began to laugh.

Later. I talked with the class about my observations. I was regaled with stories about their abilities to multitask. Interestingly, none of the computerless students spoke up during the discussion. After class was a different story. Student after student approached me to report

(continued on next page)

how distracting it was to have classmates all around them "multitasking" on games, chats and music videos. They were having similar experiences in every class they were taking and their levels of frustration were rising because teachers didn't seem to care.

My eyes were opened that day by what I saw from the rear of the lecture hall and the stories that I heard from frustrated students. I established a row in the front of the class for students who needed or desired to use laptops for talking notes and banned computers from the rest of the lecture hall. There were a few groans from students initially, but no substantive complaints after the first day. However, there are few things that I have done in class over the years that have earned more positive comments.

—Professor Thom Curtis

**ACTIVITY 3**

## Writing A Persuasive Essay To Answer The Opposition

Now using all you have learned about writing a persuasive essay in this chapter, compose your own essay arguing in favor of laptops in the classroom.

### Yes, to Laptops in the Classroom

_____

_____

_____

_____

_____

_____

_____

_____

_____

_____

_____

_____

_____

_____

_____

_____

_____

_____

_____

_____

_____

_____

_____

_____

_____

_____

_____

_____

_____

_____

# SUGGESTED TOPICS FOR WRITING A PERSUASIVE ESSAY

*Essay topics*

Argue for or against:

1.  Legalized prostitution

2.  Gambling casinos

3.  Stricter immigration laws

4.  Prayer in the public schools

5.  Abortion

6.  Tax exemption for religious organizations

7.  Capital punishment

8.  Single-parent adoption

9.   The right to same-sex marriage

10.   Offensive song lyrics

11.   Required courses in college

12.   Stricter gun laws

13.   School uniforms

14.   Suspending a driver's license for drunk driving

15.   Random drug testing in the workplace

## Exploring Online

Go to **www.cengage.com/devenglish/scarry/writersworkplace** to find the **Writer's Online Workplace,** a website designed for students using this book. You will find links to handouts, interactive quizzes, and other online resources as you explore the following topics:

• how to plan a persuasive essay and determine its effectiveness

• writing the persuasive essay

# Working Together

## ANALYZING A NEWSPAPER EDITORIAL

The following editorial appeared in the *Chicago Tribune* on Father's Day, June 18, 1995. Instead of the expected tribute to fathers, this editorial is highly critical of a growing number of men who have not faced up to their obligations to support their children. The problem discussed is as timely today as the day it was written. Read the piece out loud. Then divide into groups and discuss the questions that follow.

### Where Have All the Fathers Gone?

1   Today is Father's Day, so let's talk about dads. Not the ones who cheer their sons and daughters at baseball and soccer games or the ones who fix dinner for the family every night or the ones who come home dead tired after a day at the Merc° or McDonald's but still have time for a little family conversation.

2   No, let's talk about the invisible dads, the ones who don't marry mom, don't support their kids and don't hang around for hugs, kisses and helping with homework. There are millions of them in the United States, and their numbers are growing.

3   In 1950, 14 of every 1,000 unmarried women had babies. By 1992, 45 of every 1,000 did. In fact, almost one-third of the children born in the United States in 1992 were born to unwed parents, a 54 percent increase over 1980, according to figures released this month by the National Center for Health Statistics.

4   And though the figures generally are compiled° in terms of unmarried women and the resulting hand-wringing is done in the name of unwed mothers, the facts of life are that for every one of those unmarried mothers there is an unmarried father.

5   The moms are a lot more visible though, because in the over-whelming number of cases, they are the ones raising the kids. So who's the real problem here? And why should we care?

6   We must care because the social and financial cost of children growing up in households without fathers is immense. Many of the country's most troublesome social problems—poverty, poor performance in schools, gang activity, juvenile crime, mounting welfare costs—have their roots in families where a father has abdicated° responsibility for his children.

°**Merc**
Chicago Mercantile Exchange

°**compiled**
put together or organized

°**abdicated**
given up

(continued on next page)

**°disapprobation**
moral disapproval

**°squandered**
wasted

7    Women who do not marry before having their first child are three times more likely to wind up on welfare for 10 years or more than those who do marry. And census figures indicate that an intact mother-father household has a far better chance for financial security than a single-parent family.

8    Moreover, children who have little or no contact with their fathers are robbed of a crucial role model for fashioning their own lives.

9    What's to be done? For starters, parents, grandparents, churches and schools must hammer home the lesson that a man who conceives a child without marrying and being prepared to support the child for 18 years unfairly burdens his family and his community. He must understand that his action will be met by community disapprobation,° not the respect and awe of his peers.

10   And while government can't legislate morality, it can encourage responsibility. Legislators should make that a priority by providing tax incentives for couples to marry and by requiring every woman to name her child's father on the birth certificate. Law enforcement officers can (and are beginning to) go after the fathers for child support.

11   Fatherhood, like motherhood, is its own reward—as most dads have found. Sadly, for the others, the invisible ones, it is a gift foolishly squandered.°

## Questions for Group Discussion

1.  What is the thesis of the editorial?
2.  What supporting evidence for the thesis is given in the editorial?
3.  Were any outside sources used to support the thesis? If so, mark these in the text?
4.  Does the editorial say what will happen if nothing is done about the problem?
5.  Does the editorial propose any solution to the problem?
6.  Does the editorial seem reasonable to you?
7.  Are you persuaded by the position the editorial takes? Why or why not?

Following the group discussion, your instructor may require each student to write his or her own analysis of the editorial using the above discussion as the basis for the analysis.

## PORTFOLIO SUGGESTION

For many readers, the editorial page is the best part of the newspaper. It is on this page that writers argue, passionately at times, about issues that are of great importance to society. Go to http://www.refdesk.com/paper3.html for a list of newspapers and their editorial pages. Pick a newspaper in your state and make a habit of reading the daily editorials. Print out editorials that interest you. If you subscribe to a newspaper, clip editorials that are about subjects that interest you. Reading newspaper editorials is a very effective way of developing a sense for argumentative or persuasive writing. You can learn from editorials that are outrageous in their points of view, as well as from those that are logical and convincing.

# 33

# OTHER COLLEGE WRITING: THE RESEARCH PAPER AND THE ESSAY EXAM

In this chapter you will learn two critical skills needed for success in college:

## HOW TO WRITE A RESEARCH PAPER

Of all the skills you must learn during your time in college, mastering the research and writing skills necessary to do the term paper is certainly among the most important. Writing a well-researched and fully documented term paper has been called the single most useful skill a student can acquire in college. Writing a successful term paper calls for a number of closely related skills; therefore, it is not an easy task. These integrated skills are explained in the pages that follow.

## SETTING UP A TIMETABLE

In school or work situations, effective use of time is critical to success. The writer of a college research paper is working under very real time pressures. The paper is due by a certain date, and the grade may well suffer if that deadline is not met. Given that the student is also taking several other courses and must also pay attention to the requirements of these courses, the demands of producing a research paper may easily overwhelm a student. Therefore, as soon as a research paper assignment is given, a student should begin to plan a work schedule. Keeping on target during each stage is a key element in completing a research paper on time. The following schedule is intended as a general guide for a student who has been given a typical five-week period to produce a finished paper. The breakdown that follows is not a rigid week-by-week prescription but a series of pointers that may be adapted to individual circumstances and specific needs.

**Week 1.** Make sure that you understand the instructor's requirements and that the topic you have chosen is one you will be able to control. Make any modifications needed to the topic, obtaining approval for any individual changes to the assignment. Start gathering relevant information.

**Week 2.** Gather materials that are immediately available, including standard books and articles and information that can be downloaded. Highlight the important sections in these sources, write summaries of material, and take notes.

**Week 3.** Continue to look for additional sources of material. Write an outline containing your thesis and main points. If you are in doubt regarding these points, talk to your instructor immediately. Changing direction after this point could be disastrous. Write a first draft to give yourself an overview of your entire paper.

**Week 4.** Continue to review your collected materials, revising summaries and refining your choices of quotes. Review the first draft of your paper, adding sections as needed and inserting quoted material.

**Week 5.** Place a halt on looking for new sources. Work on the final draft and make a complete bibliography of sources (works cited). Edit all of the written parts and do a final review of the bibliography. Check quotations for accuracy. Do a final editing.

## CHOOSING A TOPIC

If your English instructor does not assign a specific topic, and you are free to choose your own, you may wish to use subject matter from another course you are taking—sociology, history, or psychology, for example. Your work on the term paper for your English class would then be based on material you are already covering in another course. It is an advantage to be dealing with subject matter that is already somewhat familiar.

Whether you are free to choose your own topic or the topic is assigned, ask yourself what you hope to gain from researching and writing on a particular topic. Will your paper deepen your understanding of an area of study? Could your research help you explore some aspect of your own life that you have not examined before? The work you do needs to feel meaningful if you are to do your best work!

No matter what topic you choose, be sure you have your instructor's clear approval before you proceed. As soon as the topics are being decided, pay immediate attention to your choice of topic. If for any reason you find that your topic is inappropriate, or you sense that the material on the subject is too narrow (you cannot find enough information), too broad (too much information), or overwhelming (the information is too technical and hard to understand), be sure to change your focus—and change it early in the course. If you lose time by not making a needed change, you could easily lessen the quality of your work and damage your final grade.

## LOOKING FOR SOURCES

Once your topic has been decided, you will want to begin gathering information for the writing of your paper. For this you will need to become familiar with the available research tools. The best way to begin is to visit your library. If you haven't already done so, ask for a tour of the library to become familiar with the general system. Then do not hesitate to find a librarian to direct you to the best places to look for information on your particular topic. Advice from a librarian can save you from wasting countless hours looking in the wrong places.

### Catalog of Library Holdings

This catalog will tell you all the information that is readily available on the open library shelves. It will include encyclopedias and other reference works, books, magazines, journals, and newspapers. In the past, libraries depended on printed (and even handwritten) card catalogs to document their holdings, but today we have all the advantages of the computer. Libraries now use the resources of the electronic age and have their catalog online. The Catalog of Library Holdings will allow you to search for information by subject, author, or key words. What once took researchers weeks and even months can now be accomplished in only minutes!

If you are somewhat unfamiliar with your topic, it may be good to begin with general background information that can be found in reference books. These reference books may even help sharpen your focus on the topic you have already chosen. Other books and articles will contain more in-depth and specialized information, which will require your judgment as to their usefulness.

### Selected Databases

College and local libraries subscribe to various databases. With these services, users will more easily find bibliographic sources, abstracts, full texts of articles, and other published materials. These databases change from one library to the next, so always consult with the librarian where you are working to determine what databases your library carries and, most importantly, which databases would be most useful for finding information on your topic. One very useful database is InfoTrac College Edition. You may want to ask your instructor how to access it. This database contains information in more than 6,000 newspapers, magazines, and scholarly journals.

### Gateways to the Resources of Other Libraries

If your own library does not have a book you need, ask your librarian how to find the book or material at another library. Most libraries have a system of cooperative lending, and a librarian can show you how to access that system to search for what you need.

## Accessing the Library Resources from Home

Most students today have home computers with access to the Internet. This makes it possible to do much of your research at home. Once you have the right connections, find out which library systems you will be able to access from outside the library.

## The Internet and Search Engines

With the help of powerful search engines, (such as Google, Google Scholar, and Yahoo), you can supplement your library research. For instance, Google Scholar will search academic sources. By typing in a key word or phrase, a search engine will explore its databases to find all the matches to your word or phrase. If you find too many hits, try to refine or add a detail to your key word or phrase. If there are not enough hits, try a more general term or phrase.

A word of caution: Not everything on the Internet is to be thought of as having equal value for the researcher. Many articles and other pieces of writing have not been carefully edited or even reviewed. Remember, anybody can put a page on the Internet. Often material is biased or inaccurate. For example, Wikipedia is widely considered to be unreliable. Students are advised not to rely on information from Wikipedia for their research.

Most instructors will want you to use a variety of sources. Some will specify the number of books and articles that must be used; others will allow you to choose your own combination of sources. No matter how many sources are called for, it is always a good idea to seek out a variety of research materials. A term paper containing material from an array of sources always gains strength and authority from the rich combination of information, and such a paper will almost certainly obtain a higher grade for you.

Now you need to gather all your sources for review. You will want to download articles from Internet-related sources and have those articles in printed form. For this material, you should underline or highlight paragraphs and larger sections of material that contain information that may be useful to you. For materials that are difficult or impossible to duplicate (such as entire books, reference works, other full-length sources, or interviews), you will have to rely completely on careful note-taking.

Writers of research papers today should know how seriously the academic community considers plagiarism. In the past, proving a charge of plagiarism was a long and tedious process, one that involved reviewing many books and articles to match original sources with the suspected material. Today software programs such as Turnitin, with their databases of millions of items, make these matches a much simpler matter, with technology providing the kind of support that could not have been imagined years ago.

## AVOIDING PLAGIARISM BY CAREFUL NOTE-TAKING

In doing research, whether conducting an interview, listening to a lecture, reading an article in a library periodical, or searching on the Internet, a student needs to be good at taking notes. Taking notes is not always a simple task because it involves making a judgment about what will be needed later on (for a research paper or for a test). Some people try to write down everything; others do not write down enough. Still others have trouble distinguishing between major points and minor details. Learning to take good notes is one of the most important skills a college student can master. Depending on how the information is going to be used, note-taking can be done by quoting (directly or indirectly), summarizing, paraphrasing, or any combination of these. Paying careful attention when note-taking will avoid the problem of unintentional *plagiarism*. Whenever exact words, ideas, facts, or opinions from the works of other writers are used in a research paper and the sources are not specifically identified, the writer of the research paper is guilty of inappropriate use, known as *plagiarism*. When you are researching and writing reports and term papers, you must be constantly aware of the dangers of plagiarism. As long as you quote sources correctly and cite your sources properly, the integrity of your own work will be assured.

> *Plagiarism* is the use of another person's work without acknowledging the source.

**Some plagiarism is deliberate.** This happens when a writer copies another person's work and presents it as his or her own with no intention of acknowledging the real source. The public is rightly shocked when such dishonesty is exposed. Over the years, a number of news reports have revealed people in important positions who have plagiarized. At the university, plagiarism is considered a very serious academic offense, one that often results in receiving a failing grade for a course and, in some cases, results in expulsion from a school.

For those students who are tempted to deliberately plagiarize an assignment, not because they are lazy or unwilling to do the work, but because they feel inadequate to the task, we would encourage them to go to their instructors right from the start and ask for special help. Most colleges have writing labs that can lead students through the process of writing research papers.

**Most plagiarism in unintentional.** Unintentional plagiarism is most often the result of carelessness during the research stage. The student's notes fail to report the exact source of the information used, or those notes do not indicate whether the words or sentences have been copied word for word, are paraphrased, or are summarized. Not keeping accurate notes at the research stage can lead to serious (and avoidable) problems at the writing stage. Careful note-taking is one of the keys to conducting a successful piece of research.

## INCORPORATING SOURCES INTO THE RESEARCH PAPER

The following paragraphs appear in the book *Fatherless America: Confronting Our Most Urgent Social Problem*, by David Blankenhorn. These paragraphs will be used to demonstrate how a student can incorporate sources into a research paper.

> The United States is becoming an increasingly fatherless society. A generation ago, a child could reasonably expect to grow up with his or her father. Today, a child can reasonably expect not to. Fatherlessness is approaching a rough parity with fatherhood as a defining feature of childhood.
>
> This astonishing fact is reflected in many statistics, but here are the two most important: Tonight, about 40 percent of U.S. children will go to sleep in homes in which their fathers do not live. More than half of our children are likely to spend a significant portion of childhood living apart

(continued on next page)

°**demographic**
characteristic
of a certain
population

from their fathers. Never before in this country have so many children been voluntarily abandoned by their fathers. Never before have so many children grown up without knowing what it means to have a father.

Fatherlessness is the most harmful demographic° trend of this generation. It is the leading cause of the decline in the well-being of children. It is also the engine driving our most urgent social problems, from crime to adolescent pregnancy to domestic violence. Yet, despite its scale and social consequences, fatherlessness is frequently ignored or denied.

## Avoiding Plagiarism: Using Direct and Indirect Quotation

A large part of writing a research paper is knowing how to incorporate the ideas of others into your text. This involves using a combination of carefully chosen direct and indirect quotations that will appear throughout the research paper. These quotations will lend authority to the points you are making. You must, however, be selective in using quotations. Students are sometimes tempted to include too many quotations or use quotations that are too long. Another common problem is the use of quotations that are not justified in the context of the material being presented. Unless every part of the quotation relates directly to the content of your paper, the quotation will seem out of place. Also, don't assume that your reader will see the relevance of a quotation. Always use the quotation in such a way that your reader will understand how the quotation relates to the point you are making.

> **Direct quotation** reproduces the exact words of another writer, using quotation marks.

The example below shows how a student could incorporate a **direct quotation** from the second paragraph of the Blankenhorn excerpt into a research paper.

> According to David Blankenhorn, "Tonight, about 40 percent of U.S. children will go to sleep in homes in which their fathers do not live."

> **Indirect quotation** uses one's own words to report on what another person has spoken or written.

The example below shows how the direct quotation above can be changed into an **indirect quotation.** Notice that the information is the same, but in the case of the indirect quotation, the writer uses his or her own words to express the ideas. No quotation marks are used.

> David Blankenhorn claims that approximately 40 percent of American children live without fathers in their homes.

**NOTE:** If a direct quotation is four or more lines long, it is usually set off by indenting the quotation and not using quotation marks.

## Terms Used to Introduce a Quote

| | |
|---|---|
| The author **claims** | As the author **says** |
| The author **states** | As the author **points out** |
| The author **explains** | As the author **reported** |
| **According to** the author | As the author **notes** |
| The author **added** | |

## Avoiding Plagiarism: Paraphrasing

A second method of using the words or ideas of another writer is called *paraphrasing*. You use paraphrasing when you want to retain all the information a source offers, from a paragraph to a full page of material. When you paraphrase, you are required to pay close attention to your source because you must restate every idea contained in that source. Your paraphrase will be almost the same length as the original material. When you paraphrase, you cannot leave out any part of the original piece of writing, nor can you add any ideas of your own as you incorporate the material into your research paper. Paraphrasing demands a great deal of skill because a writer has to have extensive control of language to be able to restate ideas using different words and different sentence structures.

> **Paraphrasing** uses one's own words to restate each and every idea of a passage from another's work and results in a new passage that is virtually the same length as the original.

Here is how the first paragraph in the original text by David Blankenhorn might have been incorporated into a research paper using **paraphrase.**

> Our country is turning into a society without fathers. Twenty-five years ago, children could look forward to being raised by their fathers, but that is no longer true. We are reaching the point when childhood is just as accurately described as growing up without a father as growing up with a father.

Note that the paraphrase has fifty-two words and the original has only forty-seven words. It is difficult to be as succinct as an experienced writer. Your own paraphrases may well be slightly longer than the originals.

## Avoiding Plagiarism: Summarizing

A final method of incorporating the ideas of another writer into your research paper is *summarizing*. A summary includes only the main ideas of a published source; it is therefore a reduced version of the original. To write a summary, you will probably need to review the original material more than once to separate the main ideas from the details and specific examples. Although a summary should be significantly shorter than the text you are working from, you must not leave out any of that text's main ideas. Also, you may not add any ideas of your own. Writing successful summaries is a skill that is often used by writers as they research material for their own work. Extracting the main ideas from the works of others is at the heart of education itself.

> **Summarizing** uses one's own words to provide a condensed restatement of the main ideas of another person's work.

Below is a writer's **summary** of the first paragraph of the David Blankenhorn excerpt. Compare it to the paraphrase of the same material given on p. 598.

> American children today are as likely to grow up without a father as those of a generation ago were likely to be raised with one.

**EXERCISE  1**

## Using Note-Taking Techniques

**The third paragraph from the David Blankenhorn excerpt is reproduced below.**

> Fatherlessness is the most harmful demographic trend of this generation. It is the leading cause of the decline in the well-being of children. It is also the engine driving our most urgent social problems, from crime to adolescent pregnancy to domestic violence. Yet, despite its scale and social consequences, fatherlessness is frequently ignored or denied.

**Demonstrate your skill with note-taking techniques by using material from the paragraph to write direct and indirect quotations, a paraphrase, and a summary.**

1. Show how you could incorporate a *direct quotation* of the first sentence into a research paper.

   _____

   _____

2. Show how you could incorporate an *indirect quotation* of the first sentence into a research paper.

   _____

   _____

3. Write a *paraphrase* of the paragraph.

   _____

   _____

   _____

   _____

   _____

4. Write a *summary* of the paragraph.

   _____

   _____

   _____

   _____

## DOCUMENTING SOURCES USING MLA GUIDELINES

Whether you use direct quotation, indirect quotation, paraphrase, or summary, you must acknowledge your sources in a consistent format. This format can vary, depending on the style your instructor wants you to use. The most commonly accepted authorities are the Modern Language Association (MLA style) and the American Psychological Association (APA style). MLA style is often used in the humanities, and APA style is recommended for use in scientific writing. Because so many different combinations of sources and authorship are possible, you will need some guidelines for the style your instructor requires so that you can prepare the documentation properly.

## Documentation Within the Body of the Paper

Documentation is required in two places. The first place is in the body of the paper itself, directly after a quotation or use of a source. In-text citations are brief (usually the last name of the author followed by a page reference in parentheses), providing just enough information so that the reader can find the full documentation at the end of the paper.

## Documentation at the End of the Paper (Works Cited)

Full documentation must be provided at the end of the paper, on a page usually titled "Works Cited." Below are examples of how some typical sources would be documented using MLA style. A citation in MLA style has four basic parts: the author's name (followed by a period), the title of the work (followed by a period), the publishing information (followed by a period), and the medium of publication such as print, web, or radio (followed by a period). Keep these additional rules in mind as well:

1. The citations are given in alphabetical order, according to the author's last name.

2. Titles follow the standard rules. Titles of full-length works such as books are italicized or underlined, and titles of shorter works such as chapters, essays, short stories, and articles are placed within quotation marks.

3. If the place of publication is a well-known city such as Boston or New York, the state need not be given. If the place is less well known, however, both city and state should be given.

4. If the citation takes more than one line, additional lines are indented five spaces.

## SAMPLE ENTRIES FOR A WORKS-CITED PAGE IN MLA STYLE

**Books (Print)**

**A book by a single author**

Ehrenreich, Barbara. *Nickel and Dimed: On Not Getting By in America*. New York: Holt, 2001. Print.

**A book by two or three authors**

Mortenson, Greg, and David Oliver Relin. *Three Cups of Tea: One Man's Mission to Promote Peace One School at a Time*. New York: Penguin Books, 2007. Print.

### A book by four or more authors

Newman, Katherine S., et al. *Rampage: The Social Roots of School Shootings.* New York: Basic Books, 2004. Print.

**NOTE:** *et al.* means "and others."

### A book with a corporate author (authored by an organization)

Opposing Viewpoints Resource Center. *Teen Violence: Opposing Viewpoints Digest.* Farmington Hills, MI: Gale Group, 2003. Print.

### An anthology of writings with one or more editors rather than an author

Howell, James C., et al., eds. *Sourcebook on Serious, Violent, and Chronic Juvenile Offenders.* Thousand Oaks, CA: Sage, 1995. Print.

### An encyclopedia or dictionary entry with an author

Summers, William C. "Virology." *The Oxford Illustrated Companion to the History of Modern Science.* Ed. Edgar F. Borgatta et al. New York: Black Dog and Leventhal, 2008. Print.

**NOTE:** If material is arranged alphabetically, page numbers are not necessary.

### A chapter or essay from a book

Blankenhorn, David. *"Fatherless Society." Fatherless America: Confronting Our Most Urgent Social Problem.* New York: Harper Collins, 1995. 25–48. Print.

## Periodicals

Periodicals include newspapers, magazines, and journals.

### Article in a newspaper

Roth, Alex. "Dad Says Bullying Drove Son to Act." *San Diego Union Tribune* 6 Sept. 2001: A1. Print.

**NOTE:** Often a newspaper article does not give the name of the author. If the author is unknown, begin with the title of the article. Also, be sure to give the section in the newspaper where the article is found. (In the example above, the article was found in Section A, page 1.)

### Article in a magazine

Zakaria, Fared. "Free at Last: How to Achieve Genuine Energy Independence." *Newsweek* 13 Apr. 2009: 40–42. Print.

### Article in a scholarly journal

Wilkinson, Diane L., and Jeffrey Fagan. "What We Know About Gun Use Among Adolescents." *Clinical Child and Family Psychology Review* 4.2 (2001): 109–132. Print.

**NOTE:** If the journal is identified by its volume number, not by month or season, provide the volume and issue—in this case, volume 4, issue 2. Then give the year of publication in parentheses so as not to confuse the two sets of numbers.

## Web Publications

Documenting sources found on the web is often problematic. First of all, the information is often incomplete. You may not find page numbers, and it may be difficult to determine if the material is presented exactly as it was in the original (if it did occur in print). In the examples below, notice how the four items listed are included in the citation (whereas they would not be included in a print publication).

1. If no pages are given, use *n. pag.* to indicate that page numbers are not available.
2. If a database has been used, give the name of the database in italics.
3. Indicate that the publication was found on the web (to distinguish it from a print item).
4. Provide the date you accessed the site.

The practice of providing the URL is no longer necessary unless you think the site it difficult to locate. URLs are long and unwieldy, prone to error. Should you choose to include the URL, place it after the date of access. Be very careful. Since sites can change and even disappear, it would be wise to download any material you might want to use. This will ensure that you will be able to document the information even if it should later become unavailable.

### Article from a periodical found online

Krugman, Paul. "Stranded in America." n. pag. *New York Times* 19 May 2008. *LexisNexis*. Web. 16 Apr. 2009.

Crawford, Nicole. "New Ways to Stop Bullying." *Monitor*. 33.9 (2002). Web. 21 Aug. 2009. <http://www.apa.org/monitor/ oct02/bullying.html>.

### Study

University of California, *National Television Violence Study, Year Three*: 1996–1997. n. pag. Media Awareness Network. Web. 2 Mar. 2009.

### An encyclopedia or dictionary online

"Juvenile Justice." *Encyclopedia Britannica Online*. Encyclopedia Britannica, 2008. Web. 17 Apr. 2009.

## Miscellaneous Printed Material

This material might include speeches, lectures, letters, interviews, studies, reports, pamphlets, conference presentations, music, works of art, and government documents, including charts and graphs.

### Government document

United States Dept. of Health and Human Services. *The Course of Life, Vol. 2: Latency, Adolescence and Youth*. Washington: GPO, 1980. Print.

### Interview

Davies, Tristan. Interview by Neal Conan. *Talk of the Nation*. Natl. Public Radio. WYPR, Baltimore. 17 April 2008. Radio.

**Work of art**

Matisse, Henri. *Asia*. 1946. Oil on canvas. Kimbell Art Museum,
     Fort Worth.

**Music**

Beethoven, Ludwig van. *Symphony no. 6 in F Major "Pastoral."*
     Berlin Philharmonic Orchestra. Cond. Herbert von Karajan.
     Deutsche Grammophon, 1977. CD.

Should you need further information about documentation, a very good source is *The MLA Handbook for Writers of Research Papers* (seventh edition), published by the Modern Language Association of America (2009).

# HOW TO TAKE AN ESSAY EXAM: WRITING WELL UNDER PRESSURE

The first rule for doing well on any test is to come to the test well rested and well prepared. Research has shown that reviewing notes and reading assignments systematically throughout the semester is much more effective than cramming for a test the night before. You'll be greatly rewarded if you learn to use your time efficiently and wisely.

## COMING TO THE EXAM WELL PREPARED

1.  **Study the textbook chapters and your notes.** In your textbook, review headings and words in boldface type, as well as information you have highlighted or underlined. Look for chapter reviews and summaries at the ends of chapters. If you have already made an outline, study that too.

2.  **Avoid having to face any surprises when the exam is distributed.** When the test is first announced in class, ask whether it will include material from the textbook in addition to material covered in class. Also, find out the format of the test: how many essay questions will there be and how many points will each question be worth? Ask how much time you will have to complete the test.

3.  **Form a study group if you can.** One way a study group can work is as follows: The group meets to draw up the major questions they believe are likely to be on the test. Each person is then assigned one of the questions. He or she is responsible for preparing all the information needed for answering one of those questions and presenting it to the group at their next meeting. The other students take notes and add whatever additional information they can. Members of the group can also quiz each other on the information that is to be covered by the exam.

    If you are unable to be part of a study group, you should still try to predict what questions will be on the exam. Prepare an outline for study and then memorize your outline.

Remember that an essay test, unlike a multiple-choice test, requires more than simply recognizing information. In an essay exam, you must be able to recall ideas and specific details and present them quickly in your own words. Thus, for an essay exam some material needs to be memorized. Memorizing both concepts and factual information is quite a demanding task.

## FORMING A STRATEGY FOR SUCCESS

The smart test taker does not begin to answer the first question immediately. Instead, he or she takes a few moments to look over the test and form a strategy for tackling it. The following pointers will help you become "test smart."

1. **When you receive the exam, read over each essay question twice.** How many points is each question worth? A well-written test will give you this information. How you budget your time should depend heavily on the weight of each question. If, for example, one essay question is worth fifty points, you should spend approximately half your time planning and answering that question. However, if the test consists of ten shorter essay questions and you have a class period of one hundred minutes, you should spend no more than ten minutes on each question, keeping a careful watch on your time. Students often write too much for the first four or five questions and then panic because they have very little time left to answer the final questions.

2. **When you read an essay question, ask yourself what method of development is being asked for.** We all know stories of people who failed tests because they misunderstood the question. For example, if an exam question asks you to *compare or contrast*, you are being given a choice. If you are asked to *compare and contrast*, you are expected to do both.

3. **Use key words from the test question itself to compose your thesis statement.** In a test, the thesis statement should be the first sentence. Don't try to be too clever on a test. State your points as directly and clearly as possible.

4. **Answer the question by stating your basic point and then including as many specific details as you have time or knowledge to give.** The more specific names, dates, and places (all spelled correctly) you can provide, the more points will be added to your grade.

5. **If a question has more than one part, be sure you answer all the parts.** Check over the question to be sure your answer covers all the parts.

Study the following question to determine exactly what is being asked for:

> **What were the social changes that contributed to the rise of the feminist movement in the 1960s in the United States? Be specific.**

If the question were one of ten short essay questions on a ninety-minute final examination, the following answer would probably be adequate:

The feminist movement grew out of many social changes happening in the 1960s in the United States. In 1961, the President's Commission on the Status of Women documented discrimination against women in the workforce. The result of the Commission's report was a growing public awareness, which soon led to the enactment of two pieces of legislation: the Equal Pay Act of 1963 and the Civil Rights Act of 1964. In addition, the development of the birth-control pill brought the discussion of sexuality out into the open. It also lowered the birthrate, leaving more women looking to the world of work. A high divorce rate, as well as delayed marriages, further contributed to more women being concerned with feminist issues. Finally, in 1966 the National Organization for Women was formed, which encouraged women to share their experiences with each other and to organize in an effort to lobby for legislative change.

Notice that the first sentence uses the key words from the question to state the thesis. The answer gives not one but four examples of the changes that were taking place in the 1960s. These examples are very specific, naming a report, legislation, an organization, and giving dates whenever significant. Also, the examples are given in chronological order. Can you spot the transitional expressions the writer used to signal the movement from one example to the next?

## RECOGNIZING FREQUENTLY USED TERMS

Sometimes terms in the question indicate which method of development the instructor is looking for in your answer.

**Definition or Analysis:** A definition should give the precise meaning of a word or term. When you define something in an essay, you usually write an *extended definition* or *analysis*, in which you explain the significance of the term in the context of your work.

**Comparison/Contrast:** When you *compare* two people or things, you focus on the similarities between them. When you *contrast* two items, you point out the differences. Often you may find yourself using both comparison and contrast in an essay.

**Narration:** Narration is the telling of a story through the careful use of a sequence of events. The events are usually (but not always) presented in chronological order.

**Summary:** When you write a summary, you supply the main ideas of a longer piece of writing.

**Discussion:** The general term *discuss* is meant to encourage you to analyze a subject at length. Inviting students to discuss some aspect of a topic is a widely used method of constructing examination questions.

**Classification:** When you *classify* items of any kind, you place them into separate groups so that large amounts of material can be more easily understood.

**Cause and Effect:** When you deal with causes, you answer the question *why;* when you deal with effects, you show *results* or *consequences*.

**Process Analysis:** You are using process analysis when you give a step-by-step explanation of how something works or how something is (or was) done.

**EXERCISE** **2**   ## Methods of Development

**All of the following college essay questions deal with the topic of computers. Use the previous list of terms to decide which method of development is being called for in each case.**

1.  Trace the development of the computer, beginning in 1937. Be sure to include all significant developments discussed in class.

    Method of development: _____

2.  Choose two of the word-processing programs practiced in class and discuss the similarities and differences you encountered. What in your opinion were the advantages and disadvantages of each?

    Method of development: _____

3.  Explain the meaning of each of the following terms: *hard disk*, *memory*, *directory*, *menu*, and *software*.

    Method of development: _____

4.  We have discussed many of the common business applications for the computer. Select ten applications and group them according to the functions they perform.

    Method of development: _____

5.  Discuss the problems that have occurred in the typical office as a result of computer technology.

    Method of development: _____

**EXERCISE 3**

## Methods of Development/Parts of a Question

**Each of the following is an example of an essay question that could be asked in a college course. In the spaces provided after each question, indicate (a) what method of development (definition, comparison/contrast, narration, summary, discussion, classification, cause and effect, or process analysis) is indicated; and (b) how many parts there are to the question and of what do the parts consist. This dictates how many parts will be in your answer.**

1.  What does the term *sociology* mean? Include in your answer at least four different meanings the term *sociology* has had since this area of study began.

    Method of development: _____

    The different parts of the question: _____

    _____

2.  Compare and contrast the reasons the United States entered the Korean War with the reasons it entered the Vietnam War.

    Method of development: _____

    The different parts of the question: _____

    _____

3.  Trace the history of our knowledge of the planet Jupiter from the time it was first discovered until the present day. Include in your answer at least one nineteenth-century discovery and three of the most recent discoveries that have been made about Jupiter through the use of unmanned space vehicles sent near that planet.

    Method of development: _____

    The different parts of the question: _____

    _____

4.  In view of the dramatic increase in cases of contagious diseases, describe the types of precautions now required for medical personnel. What changes are likely to be required in the future?

Method of development: _____

The different parts of the question: _____

_____

5. Explain the three effects of high temperatures on space vehicles as they reenter the earth's atmosphere.

Method of development: _____

The different parts of the question: _____

_____

6. What was the complete process of restoring the Statue of Liberty to its original condition? Include in your answer six different aspects of the restoration, from the rebuilding of the inside supports to the treatment of the metal surface.

Method of development: _____

The different parts of the question: _____

7. Trace the history of the English language from its beginning to the present day. Divide the history of the language into at least three different parts, using Old English, Middle English, and Modern English as your main divisions.

Method of development: _____

The different parts of the question: _____

_____

8. Discuss the events that led up to World War II. Be sure to include the political and social problems of the time that directly and indirectly led to the war.

Method of development: _____

The different parts of the question: _____

_____

9. Summarize the four theories that have been proposed as to why dinosaurs became extinct sixty-five million years ago.

Method of development: _____

The different parts of the question: _____

10. Define the term *monarchy* and discuss the relevance or irrelevance of this form of government in today's world.

Method of development: _____

The different parts of the question: _____

_____

## COMPOSING A THESIS STATEMENT

One of the most effective ways to begin an essay answer is to write a thesis statement. Your thesis statement should include the important parts of the question and should give a clear indication of the approach you intend to take as you construct your answer. By writing your opening sentence in this way, you will give yourself a real advantage: as your professor begins to read your work, it will be clear what you are going to write about and how you intend to answer the question.

For example, suppose you had decided to write an essay answer to the following question:

> **Agree or disagree that doctors should be allowed to use germ-line gene therapy to alter a woman's egg, a man's sperm, or an embryo just a few days old to eliminate inherited diseases.**

An effective way to begin your essay would be the following thesis sentence:

> **A strong argument exists to support the view that doctors should be allowed to use germ-line therapy to alter the egg, the sperm, or the embryo if the purpose is to eliminate an inherited disease.**

The instructor would know that you clearly understand the test question and that you also have a plan how you intend to construct the answer.

**EXERCISE  4**

## Writing Thesis Statements

Rewrite each of the following essay questions in thesis-statement form. Read each question carefully and underline the word or phrase that indicates the method of development called for. An example has been done for you.

> **Essay question:**     <u>How</u> does one learn another language?
>
> **Thesis statement:**    **The process of learning another language is complicated but usually follows four distinct stages.**

1. Essay question: Discuss Thorstein Veblen's theory of the leisure class.

   Thesis statement: _____

   _____

2. Essay question: What are the effects of television violence on children?

   Thesis statement: _____

   _____

3. Essay question: Trace the development of portrait painting from the Middle Ages to today.

   Thesis statement: _____

   _____

4. Essay question: What are the major causes for the economic crisis facing the African nations today?

   Thesis statement: _____

   _____

5.    Essay question: What have been the most significant results of space exploration since the first moon landing?

Thesis statement: _____

_____

6.    Essay question: What are the problems when a couple adopts a child from one culture and raises that child in another culture?

Thesis statement: _____

_____

7.    Essay question: In what ways does the new Japan differ from the old Japan?

Thesis statement: _____

_____

8.    Essay question: What four countries depend on tourism for the major part of their national income, and why is this so?

Thesis statement: _____

_____

_____

9.    Essay question: What factors should a college use when judging the merits of a particular student for admission?

Thesis statement: _____

_____

10.   Essay question: Discuss the generally accepted definition of Alzheimer's disease, its sequence of characteristic symptoms, and the current methods of treatment.

Thesis statement: _____

_____

_____

## Exploring Online

Go to **www.cengage.com/devenglish/scarry/writersworkplace** to find the **Writer's Online Workplace,** a website designed for students using this book. You will find links to handouts, interactive quizzes, and other online resources as you explore the following topics:

• a comprehensive discussion of the research paper
• exploring the seven steps of the research process
• an essay exam tutorial

# Working Together

## INCORPORATING SOURCES: USING DIRECT AND INDIRECT QUOTATION, PARAPHRASING, AND SUMMARIZING

Many Americans believe the number of drunk drivers in the United States is a national disgrace. The following excerpt from a report by the National Transportation Safety Board gives these observations on the subject:

> Nationally, the confidence of the drunk driver remains almost unshaken. Amazingly, four out of every ten drivers admit to driving while under the influence of alcohol, while 10 percent of all drivers on weekend nights can be legally defined as intoxicated. There are good reasons for this, one of which is brought out by a recent report from the National Transportation Safety Board. It found that only one in 2,000 who drive while intoxicated will be pulled over. And even with the most thorough police control and rigorous administration, it doesn't rise to more than one in 200. Yet, all too often, those who do escape arrest do not live to get home. Every year, about 25,000 do not, including 4,000 teens.

### Working in Groups

Students should answer each question individually. Then together in your group, discuss the answers and agree on a single response for each question. Your instructor may expect the results to be submitted at the end of the class session.

1. Write a sentence of your own in which you give a *direct quote* from the second sentence of the excerpt above.

   _____

   _____

   _____

   _____

2. Write a sentence of your own in which you give an *indirect quote* from the second sentence of the excerpt above.

   _____

   _____

   _____

   _____

3. Write a *summary* of the paragraph. Remember that when you do this, you will be reducing the paragraph to one or two sentences that focus on the main ideas.

_____

_____

_____

_____

4. Write a *paraphrase* of the last two sentences.

_____

_____

_____

_____

## PORTFOLIO SUGGESTION

- Be careful to save all the copies of the articles and other materials you have used to write your research paper. You could be asked to refer to your sources again to make changes, or you might expand on your topic in the future.
- Study your own research papers to see if you are overusing quotations because you lack the confidence to write your own paraphrases and summaries of the source material. It is true that if you do not understand the source material, you will find it impossible to write a paraphrase or a summary.

# Part 6

# Further Readings For The College Writer

(continued on next page)

## CAUSE AND EFFECT

## DEFINITION AND ANALYSIS

## CLASSIFICATION

## ARGUMENTATION/PERSUASION

These selections show us professional writers at work, using the various methods of development studied in this textbook. A writer will sometimes use more than one method of development to construct a single piece of writing. For example, when Elaine Weiss defends her position on spousal abuse, she also uses elements of narration, details from her personal story, to support that position.

Each reading is introduced with a brief background note that provides a context for the piece and tells something about the author; marginal glosses are added to explain unfamiliar words or usages. Following each selection are two different sections. The first, "Questions for Critical Thinking," directs the reader to examine how each piece was constructed. The second section, "Writing in Response," invites student essays based on the themes found in each particular piece.

Before you approach the study of these readings, be sure to absorb the suggestions detailed in the following section, "Strategies for the Active Reader." Using these strategies in all of your college reading assignments will make you a more critical reader, one of the most important goals of an educated person.

# STRATEGIES FOR THE ACTIVE READER

Becoming an active and involved reader is an important key to success in college. When you become such a reader, you have a definite advantage in school and beyond. An active reader learns more, and learns more efficiently, absorbing the contents of books and essays with much greater awareness of their meaning.

Such awareness as a reader leads directly to a greater ability to compose effective college essays and term papers. When you study the models of writing contained in this book, you are doing what great writers like William Shakespeare and Charles Dickens did as they mastered their craft: turning to the best models they could find and using those models as their constant guides.

## PREVIEWING

Before you begin to read a selection, you should examine the title. What announcement is the writer making? Are there key words in the title that should be noted? Read the introductory paragraph and the concluding paragraph and then skim through the other paragraphs. Keep in mind that this first look at the various paragraphs is not to be thought of as speed reading. (Speed reading—an approach college students should not take—is a technique that helps busy executives and other people who are under pressure to review hundreds of pages of material as quickly as possible.) Are there any headings (usually in boldface type) announcing the different parts of the selection? In addition, you should note whether boxed features (often found in textbook chapters) give definitions of terms or other information in concise form. Also, look for key words or terms in boldface type, in addition to any sentences that are printed in italics. Words, headings, or sentences are presented in this way to emphasize their importance.

Another previewing technique is to read the first sentence of each paragraph. In many—but not all—cases, the first sentence is the topic sentence. Observing these key sentences before reading the entire piece is one of the best ways to get an overview of the material you are about to study.

## ANNOTATING/TAKING NOTES

> Why is marking up a book indispensable to reading? First, it keeps you awake. (And I don't mean merely conscious; I mean wide awake.) In the second place, reading, if it is active, is thinking, and thinking tends to express itself in words, spoken or written. The marked book is usually the thought-through book. Finally, writing helps you remember the thoughts you had, or the thoughts the author expressed.
>
> MORTIMER ADLER

Once you have previewed the text, you are ready to begin a careful reading. Being an active reader means interacting with the text you are studying. This involves some or all of the following activities:

- **Underlining key points.** Key points include the thesis, topic sentences, and major divisions of the essay.
- **Highlighting significant portions of the text.** Highlighting should be used to mark portions of the text that have enduring value for you or that you want to return to and remember. Some students make the mistake of highlighting too

much material because they do not have enough experience distinguishing main ideas from less critical points.

- **Making brief marginal comments.** Marginal comments might be as brief as a question mark to indicate a word or idea you don't understand, an X to indicate an important comment, or an exclamation mark to emphasize a statement you find surprising. Sometimes you will want to make longer notations about the contents or the author's point of view. You might also find yourself disagreeing with the author, or you might have a comment on how the writer's ideas do not agree with your own experience.

- **Using the dictionary.** If you cannot figure out the meaning of a word from its context or from a gloss that has been provided, you should look up the meaning in a dictionary.

After reading a selection, you should be able to answer these basic questions:

1. What was the author's **purpose** in creating the piece of writing? Was it written to entertain, inform, or persuade?
2. Who is the intended **audience** for the selection?
3. What is the **structure** of the selection? How many paragraphs make up the introduction? How has the author developed the points?
4. How does the author achieve **coherence?** For example, where does the author use transitions, repetition, and pronouns?
5. Does the writer present both **facts** and **opinions?** Do you find yourself agreeing or disagreeing with the writer's point of view?

## AN ANNOTATED TEXT

Below are a few paragraphs taken from the essay found on pages 674–678. Notice how the student has annotated the text.

*Controlling idea*

## The Changing American Family

*Topic*

*Thesis*  The American family is not dying. It is diversifying. This is the "secret" to understanding what is happening to ourselves, our children, and our society. Millions of people today are frightened about the future of the family. Dire predictions pour from the pulpit, the press, even from the White House. Emotional oratory about the need to "restore" the family is echoing through the nation.

? 

*Examples*

*why use quotation marks?*

*Topic sentence*

Because the economic and other conditions that made the nuclear family popular are changing, the nuclear family itself is less and less popular. America is no longer a nation of poorly educated blue-collar workers. Most of us work in service occupations or spend out time processing information. And today only some 7 percent of Americans still live in classical nuclear families.  The nuclear family is simply no longer the norm—and it is not likely to become the norm again, no matter how much pulpit-pounding or breast-beating we do about it. In its place, a new family system is emerging.

*What does "nuclear" mean here?*

*statistic hard to believe!*

*part 3 of the essay*

The Third Wave family: This new system is harder to describe because it is not based on a single dominant family form but on a dazzling diversity of household structures.

*Paragraph of example*

*use of statistics*

For example, look at what is happening to <u>single life</u>. Between 1970 and 1978 alone, the number of people aged 14 to 34 who live alone nearly tripled in the United States. Today fully one-fifth of all households are live-alones. Some are alone <u>out of necessity</u>; others prefer it. Then there are the child-free couples. As (James Ramey) of the Center for Policy Research has pointed out, we are seeing a massive shift from "child-centered" to "adult-centered" homes. The number of couples who deliberately decide not to have children—whether for economic, psychological, or ecological reasons—has increased dramatically.

*use of authority*

*why quotes?*

*why quotes?*

Next come the <u>single-parent households</u>. Divorce rates may be leveling out in this country, depending upon how they are measured, but broken nuclear households are so widespread that today as many <u>as one out</u> of <u>seven children are raised by a single parent</u>. In big cities that may run as high as one in four.

*When was this essay written? Are these statistics still accurate?*

*Although I was raised in a single parent household, I hope to marry and raise several children. Am I unusual?*

## REREADING

The pieces of writing we read as part of our day-to-day activities are generally read only once. For example, when we read an article in a newspaper or magazine to be informed or entertained, we seldom return to it. Reading in college is very different. As a college student who must read a great deal of material every semester, you will find yourself grateful to cover each reading assignment even once. However, you should try to review such material, if possible. For example, if you are studying difficult literary works or long chapters in a textbook, more than one reading may be needed before the meaning becomes clear. You have a very important reason for making sure you are in control of what you read: you will be tested and graded on that material. No matter what your reasons are for wanting to absorb written material, required or otherwise, if you are thoughtful in your reading, one of the great avenues to pleasure and meaning in life will be open to you.

# VISITING RITES

## Susan Musgrave

Susan Musgrave is the author of more than twenty books, including fiction, essays, and works for children, in addition to a great many poems. Born in California to Canadian parents, she has traveled internationally, giving poetry readings and workshops, in addition to holding writer-in-residence positions at more than one Canadian university. Since 1991, the author has worked online with over a thousand students across Canada, through the Writers in Electronic Residence Program. In the following essay, Susan Musgrave gives an open and honest account of a painful personal experience. In her hands, the grim reality of visiting her husband in prison takes on an almost poetic quality.

1      At first glance it looks like a fairy tale castle-hotel: parking lots shaded by endangered oaks, crewcut lawns, a stone wall running the length of the property. But when you look again you see it's a dungeon, with bars on every window and razor-wire surrounding the yard.

°**the poet Lovelace**
Richard Lovelace (1618–1657), British poet whose quoted words come from his lyric, "To Althea, from Prison"

2      The poet Lovelace° may have been right when he wrote, "stone walls do not a prison make," but razor-wire doesn't leave a doubt.

3      Visitors call it Wilkie, as if they feel some affection for the joint, or because Vancouver Island Regional Correction Centre is too much of a mouthful. Built on Wilkinson Road near Victoria after the turn of the century, it was a mental hospital before its present incarnation.° Two gold-painted lions lie in repose on either side of the steps leading up to the prison doors. I hand over my driver's licence and sign in at the front desk as though committing myself, as if shock treatment might be a relief after everything I've been through in the last two days, since my husband was arrested for bank robbery.

°**incarnation**
newly created reality

4      The newspapers say I am standing by my man. I'd rather be lying by him, I think, as I start to undress, taking off my wedding ring, my belt and sandals, before walking bare-soled through the metal detector. A guard inspects my Birkenstocks,° making sure I haven't concealed contraband—drugs, money, books—between the straps. I ask if I am allowed Kleenex—not that I plan to weep, but my motto has always been: if you want peace, prepare for war. The guard says he will "provide me with something."

°**Birkenstocks**
a brand of sandal

5      My visit is to take place "under glass." I enter the small Plexiglas and concrete booth, designed by someone who had the aesthetics° of the sensory-deprivation chamber in mind. The walls are off-cream, the trim around the windows a tinned-lima-bean green. All else is puce.°

°**aesthetics**
sense of good taste

°**puce**
a dark purple color

6      It's familiar decor. Stephen and I were married in prison, in 1986, when he was serving a twenty-year sentence for bank robbery. He was paroled a few months after we took our vows, twelve years ago almost to this day. But prison is not an easy place to escape, even if they release you. STEVE LOVES SUSAN FOREVER is etched into the Plexiglas. While I wait for my Stephen with a "ph," the guard brings me a roll of toilet paper and unwinds what he thinks I'll need. The $50,000 a year it costs to keep a man behind bars must not include the price of a box of Kleenex.

7    When the door to the prisoner's booth finally opens, the man I am supposed to be standing by is not the one standing before me. The guard picks up his telephone, I pick up mine. "He's refusing the visit," he says, point-blank.

8    I knew Stephen would be going through drug withdrawal, so I'm not surprised he can't keep our date. Part of me, though, feels betrayed. When we got married we vowed to be there for one another, in sickness and in health. The one-ply toilet paper, not meant for tears, is soon the size of a spitball in my fist.

9    I'm trying to leave when I am summoned to the office of the Director of Programs. He indicates a pile of papers on his desk and asks if I'm familiar with the "ion scanner." This device has detected microscopic particles of cocaine on my letters to Stephen; my driver's licence, too, is contaminated. Given that my husband has had a $1,000-a-day drug habit for the past six months, I expect my whole life is contaminated.

10    I ask why invisible drug particles could be a problem. "We don't want inmates in contact with individuals involved in drug-seeking activities," he explains. He will suspend my visits if I ever attempt to smuggle contraband to a prisoner. How could anyone smuggle anything through Plexiglas, over a phone? I ask. "Where there's a will, there's a way," he says.

11    Next time I visit, Stephen doesn't stand me up. I try to break the ice over the heavy telephone. "At least it's not long distance," I tell him. "It's not our dime."

**°accentuating**
emphasizing

12    Some previous visitor has severed the wires, and they have been repaired with electrician's tape. Our voices fade in and out, accentuating° the lonely long distance between us. Stephen says that just minutes before they fetched him for our visit, the wind slipped into his cell. He knew that meant I was near.

**°stutters**
making repeated reflections

13    My hand reaches out to the glass, and I see the reflection of my hand rest itself on Stephen's hands. My reflection travels up his arm, stutters° over the track-marks, and then moves sadly on. I stroke his trembling face. Where there's a will, there's a way. A way to touch, even if it's this way.

14    I don't cry until the visit is almost over, and this time I have nothing to wipe my nose on except my T-shirt sleeve.

15    They lead Stephen away though the puce-coloured doors. I wait to be released, and to book my next visit. But when I begin to spell my name for the new guard on shift, she stops me. "I know who you are," she says. "You've been an inspiration to me all my life."

16    She has taken me by surprise. I hadn't allowed myself to see past the uniform.

**°trite**
overused and not interesting

17    "I used to write poetry—at university," she says. "We all did. But you didn't stop like the rest of us—we had to get jobs." Her voice drops to a whisper. "I admire everything you've ever done. Except for one thing."

18    I expect her to say, "Marrying a criminal."

**°domesticity**
concerning the life of the home

19    "You know those essays you used to write for the newspapers—about family life? Well, I thought they were trite.°" She doesn't think domesticity° a subject worthy of my inspirational words. As Stephen would say, everyone's a critic.

20      Some days I feel lost. Other days life continues without Stephen, though he is here in every grain of wood, every dustball behind the wood stove, every fixed or broken thing. Words are what I know, and I have freedom in my love. All of him washes over me, like the mystery of wind.

## Questions for Critical Thinking

1.  Writers often take great care to compose an effective title. In this case, why is the use of the word "rites" such a good choice?

2.  In paragraph 2, the writer refers to a famous poem of the seventeenth century, "To Althea, from Prison" by Richard Lovelace. The poem contains the words "Stone walls do not a prison make/Nor iron bars a cage. . ." If stone and iron are indeed not the things that keep a person a prisoner, what are those things that do keep a person "in prison"?

3.  Susan Musgrave makes real the agony of so many people who have a loved one in prison. Make a list of several of the details of this narrative that give the essay its sad reality. One detail, the shedding of tears, can be traced in paragraphs 4, 6, 8, and 14.

4.  Narration achieves coherence by placing events in a time sequence. Divide the essay into parts according to the movement from one event to the next. Look for transitions of time that signal these movements.

5.  Narration should make a point. What do you think is the point of this essay? Point to the sentence or sentences that reflect the author's point of view.

## Writing in Response

1.  In paragraph 9, the writer tells us that because her husband had a "$1,000-a-day drug habit," she expects her "whole life is contaminated." Nearly everyone has known a member of a family who has done something to make the rest of the family suffer. Write an essay that tells the story of that family's unhappy experience.

2.  Visiting a family member who has moved away may bring back happy or sad memories from the past. Write an essay that explores the experience of visiting someone who no longer lives nearby.

3.  The dreams we have for our lives are often far from the reality of how we must live in the present. Susan Musgrave is visiting a husband in jail, an experience no wife would wish for. Write an essay that uses narration to illustrate this truth that we cannot always be masters of our fate, or write an essay that uses narration to illustrate another truth—that we are masters of our fate.

4.  The author reports in paragraph 4 that she is being described as "standing by" her man. Write an essay that discusses the complex problems that come with standing by someone who has committed a crime or betrayed a trust. What part does forgiveness play in such a situation? When is loyalty self-destructive?

# SUMMER READING

## Michael Dorris

Important events from childhood never fade from our minds. The late Native American novelist and essayist Michael Dorris (1945–1997) used his cultural background and his personal experience in many of his works. In the following essay, published in his book of collected writings, *Paper Trail*, the writer recalls a memorable summer during his adolescence when he was repaid a debt in an unexpected way. It was a repayment that profoundly changed his life.

°*clientele*
group of customers

1   When I was fourteen, I earned money in the summer by mowing lawns, and within a few weeks I had built up a regular clientele.° I got to know people by the flowers they planted that I had to remember not to cut down, by the things they lost in the grass or stuck in the ground on purpose. I reached the point with most of them when I knew in advance what complaint was about to be spoken, which particular request was most important. And I learned something about the measure of my neighbors by their preferred method of payment: by the job, by the month—or not at all.

2   Mr. Ballou fell into the last category, and he always had a reason why. On one day he had no change for a fifty, on another he was flat out of checks, on another, he was simply out when I knocked on his door. Still, except for the money part, he was a nice enough old guy, always waving or tipping his hat when he'd see me from a distance. I figured him for a thin retirement check, maybe a work-related injury that kept him from doing his own yard work. Sure, I kept a running total, but I didn't worry about the amount too much. Grass was grass, and the little that Mr. Ballou's property comprised didn't take long to trim.

°*muted*
soft

3   Then, one late afternoon in mid-July, the hottest time of the year, I was walking by his house and he opened the door, motioned me to come inside. The hall was cool, shaded, and it took my eyes a minute to adjust to the muted° light.

4   "I owe you," Mr. Ballou began, "but . . ."

5   I thought I'd save him the trouble of thinking up a new excuse. "No problem. Don't worry about it."

6   "The bank made a mistake in my account," he continued, ignoring my words. "It will be cleared up in a day or two. But in the meantime I thought perhaps you could choose one or two volumes for a down payment."

7   He gestured toward the walls and I saw that books were stacked everywhere. It was like a library, except with no order to the arrangement.

8   "Take your time," Mr. Ballou encouraged. "Read, borrow, keep. Find something you like. What do you read?"

9   "I don't know." And I didn't. I generally read what was in front of me, what I could snag from the paperback rack at the drugstore, what I found at the library, magazines, the back of cereal boxes, comics. The idea of consciously seeking out a special title was new to me, but, I realized, not without appeal—so I browsed through the piles of books.

10    "You actually read all of these?"

11    "This isn't much," Mr. Ballou said. "This is nothing, just what I've kept, the ones worth looking at a second time."

12    "Pick for me, then."

**°appraisingly**
with the intention
of making a judgment

13    He raised his eyebrows, cocked his head, regarded me appraisingly° as though measuring me for a suit. After a moment, he nodded, searched through a stack, and handed me a dark red hard-bound book, fairly thick.

14    *The Last of the Just,* I read. "By André Schwarz-Bart. What's it about?"

15    "You tell me," he said. "Next week."

**°oblivion**
total forgetfulness
of the world around

16    I started after supper, sitting outdoors on an uncomfortable kitchen chair. Within a few pages, the yard, the summer, disappeared, the bright oblivion° of adolescence temporarily lifted, and I was plunged into the aching tragedy of the Holocaust, the extraordinary clash of good, represented by one decent man, and evil. Translated from French, the language was elegant, simple, overwhelming. When the evening light finally failed I moved inside, read all through the night.

17    To this day, thirty years later, I vividly remember the experience. It was my first voluntary encounter with world literature, and I was stunned by the undiluted power a novel could contain. I lacked the vocabulary, however, to translate my feelings into words, so the next week, when Mr. Ballou asked, "Well?" I only replied, "It was good."

18    "Keep it, then," he said. "Shall I suggest another?"

19    I nodded, and was presented with the paperback edition of Margaret Mead's *Coming of Age in Samoa.°*

**°Coming of Age
in Samoa**
groundbreaking 1925
study of adolescent
behavior in the South
Pacific

20    To make two long stories short, Mr. Ballou never paid me a dime for cutting his grass that year or the next, but for fifteen years I taught anthropology at Dartmouth College. Summer reading was not the innocent pastime I had assumed it to be, not a breezy, instantly forgettable escape in a hammock (though I've since enjoyed many of those, too). A book, if it arrives before you at the right moment, in the proper season, at a point of intermission° in the daily business of things, will change the course of all that follows.

**°intermission**
a period between
events

# Questions for Critical Thinking

1.    The author uses narration as his method of developing ideas about the importance of reading. He orders the material by presenting a sequence of events. Summarize this narrative by listing the sequence of events. (Do not quote the conversations in the essay.)

2.    Review paragraphs 2 through 6 of the essay and decide why Mr. Ballou could not (or would not) pay Michael Dorris. Do you think he did not have enough money, or was he unwilling to spend money on something other than books?

3.    What were the author's reading habits before his encounter with Mr. Ballou? What do you think his reading habits were after this summer experience?

4. The second book Mr. Ballou gave the author was the anthropologist Margaret Mead's *Coming of Age in Samoa*, a book often assigned in college anthropology courses. In the next sentence, Michael Dorris tells us that "for fifteen years I taught anthropology at Dartmouth College." What connection does the writer want us to make?

5. When a person owes another person money, is it ever appropriate to repay the debt with something other than money—goods or services for example? When is it a good idea to settle a money debt in a non-money way?

6. In the first paragraph, the writer tells us that some of his clients did not pay him at all, and in his last paragraph mentions that Mr. Ballou also never gave him money for mowing his lawn. Nevertheless, the writer did receive payment for his work. Explain this seeming contradiction.

## Writing in Response

1. In this story an adolescent has a summer job that turns out to change his life. Write an essay in which you tell the story of yourself or someone else you know who had a part-time job while going to school. What happened? Were any lessons learned? You may want to use dialogue as part of your narration.

2. Write an essay in which you tell a story about a person in your neighborhood, a friend, or a relative. Remember that you will be relating a specific incident or a series of events to make a point. Your point might be what you learned from observing what happened to the person.

3. Michael Dorris concludes his essay by noting that if you come across a book "at the right moment," it could change the direction of your life. Write a narrative essay in which you tell the story of a life-changing event.

# MY DAUGHTER SMOKES

## Alice Walker

When a family passes down traditions from one generation to another, not all of these traditions are positive. In the following autobiographical essay, Alice Walker, the prize-winning author of *The Color Purple* and many other fiction and nonfiction works, writes about a deadly tradition in her family. Born the youngest of eight children in Georgia in 1944, Alice Walker was the child of sharecroppers. More than one of her childhood experiences have found their way into this essay. However, the essay goes far beyond that single childhood, as the writer shares her profound worldview and gives us her deep historical insights.

1    My daughter smokes. While she is doing her homework, her feet on the bench in front of her and her calculator clicking out answers to her algebra problems. I am looking at the half-empty package of Camels tossed carelessly close at hand. Camels. I pick them up, take them into the kitchen, where the light is better, and study them—they're filtered, for which I am grateful. My heart feels terrible. I want to weep. In fact, I do weep a little, standing there by the stove holding one of the instruments, so white, so precisely rolled, that could cause my daughter's death. When she smoked Marlboros and Players I hardened myself against feeling so bad; nobody I knew ever smoked these brands.

2    She doesn't know this, but it was Camels that my father, her grandfather, smoked. But before he smoked "ready-mades"—when he was very young and very poor, with eyes like lanterns—he smoked Prince Albert tobacco in cigarettes he rolled himself. I remember the bright-red tobacco tin, with a picture of Queen Victoria's° consort,° Prince Albert, dressed in a black frock coat and carrying a cane.

°*Queen Victoria*
queen of England, 1837–1901

°*consort*
the spouse of a king or queen

3    The tobacco was dark brown, pungent,° slightly bitter. I tasted it more than once as a child, and the discarded tins could be used for a number of things: to keep buttons and shoelaces in, to store seeds, and best of all, to hold worms for the rare times my father took us fishing.

°*pungent*
sharp and penetrating

4    By the late forties and early fifties no one rolled his own anymore (and few women smoked) in my hometown, Eatonton, Georgia. The tobacco industry, coupled with Hollywood movies in which both hero and heroine smoked like chimneys, won over completely people like my father, who were hopelessly addicted to cigarettes. He never looked as dapper° as Prince Albert, though; he continued to look like a poor, overweight, overworked colored man with too large a family; black, with a very white cigarette stuck in his mouth.

°*dapper*
stylish

5    I do not remember when he started to cough. Perhaps it was unnoticeable at first. A little hacking in the morning as he lit his first cigarette upon getting out of bed. By the time I was my daughter's age, his breath was a wheeze, embarrassing to hear; he could not climb stairs without resting every third or fourth step. It was not unusual for him to cough for an hour.

6    It is hard to believe there was a time when people did not understand that cigarette smoking is an addiction. I wondered aloud once to my sister—who is perennially° trying to quit—whether our father realized this. I wondered how she, a smoker since high school, viewed her own habit.

°*perennially*
continually; regularly

623

7    It was our father who gave her her first cigarette, one day when she had taken water to him in the fields.

8    "I always wondered why he did that," she said, puzzled, and with some bitterness.

9    "What did he say?" I asked.

10    "That he didn't want me to go to anyone else for them," she said, "which never really crossed my mind."

11    So he was aware it was addictive, I thought, though as annoyed as she that he assumed she would be interested.

12    I began smoking in eleventh grade, also the year I drank numerous bottles of terrible sweet, very cheap wine. My friends and I, all boys for this venture, bought our supplies from a man who ran a segregated bar and liquor store on the outskirts of town. Over the entrance there was a large sign that said colored. We were not permitted to drink there, only to buy. I smoked Kools, because my sister did. By then I thought her toxic darkened lips and gums glamorous. However, my body simply would not tolerate smoke. After six months I had a **chronic°** sore throat. I gave up smoking, gladly. Because it was a ritual with my buddies—Murl, Leon, and "Dog" Farley—I continued to drink wine.

**°chronic**
lasting a long time

13    My father died from "the poor man's friend," pneumonia, one hard winter when his bronchitis and emphysema had left him low. I doubt he had much lung left at all, after coughing for so many years. He had so little breath that, during his last years, he was always leaning on something. I remember once, at a family reunion, when my daughter was two, that my father picked her up for a minute— long enough for me to photograph them—but the effort was obvious. Near the very end of his life, and largely because he had no more lungs, he quit smoking. He gained a couple of pounds, but by then he was so **emaciated°** no one noticed.

**°emaciated**
unhealthily thin

14    When I travel to Third World countries I see many people like my father and daughter. There are large billboards directed at them both: the tough, "take-charge," or dapper older man, the glamorous, "worldly" young woman, both puffing away. In these poor countries, as in American ghettos and on reservations, money that should be spent for food goes instead to the tobacco companies; over time, people starve themselves of both food and air, effectively weakening and addicting their children, eventually **eradicating°** themselves. I read in the newspaper and in my gardening magazine that cigarette butts are so toxic that if a baby swallows one, it is likely to die, and that the boiled water from a bunch of them makes an effective insecticide.

**°eradicating**
getting rid of completely

15    My daughter would like to quit, she says. We both know the statistics are against her; most people who try to quit smoking do not succeed.*

16    There is a deep hurt that I feel as a mother. Some days it is a feeling of **futility.°** I remember how carefully I ate when I was pregnant, how patiently I taught my daughter how to cross a street safely. For what, I sometimes wonder; so that she can wheeze through most of her life feeling half her strength, and then die of self-poisoning, as her grandfather did?

**°futility**
uselessness

**°empathy for**
identification with

17    But, finally, one must feel **empathy for°** the tobacco plant itself. For thousands of years, it has been **venerated°** by Native Americans as a sacred medicine.

**°venerated**
treated with deep respect

*Three months after reading this essay my daughter stopped smoking.

They have used it extensively—its juice, its leaves, its roots, its (holy) smoke—to heal wounds and cure diseases, and in ceremonies of prayer and peace. And though the plant as most of us know it has been poisoned by chemicals and denatured° by intensive mono-cropping° and is therefore hardly the plant it was, still, to some modern Indians it remains a plant of positive power. I learned this when my Native American friends, Bill Wahpepah and his family, visited with me for a few days and the first thing he did was sow a few tobacco seeds in my garden.

**°denatured**
having its natural qualities changed

**°mono-cropping**
raising only one crop

18    Perhaps we can liberate tobacco from those who have captured and abused it, enslaving the plant on large plantations, keeping it from freedom and its kin, and forcing it to enslave the world. Its true nature suppressed, no wonder it has become deadly. Maybe by sowing a few seeds of tobacco in our gardens and treating the plant with the reverence it deserves, we can redeem tobacco's soul and restore its self-respect.

19    Besides, how grim, if one is a smoker, to realize one is smoking a slave.

20    There is a slogan from a battered women's shelter that I especially like: "Peace on earth begins at home." I believe everything does. I think of a slogan for people trying to stop smoking: "Every home a smoke-free zone." Smoking is a form of self-battering that also batters those who must sit by, occasionally cajole° or complain, and helplessly watch. I realize now that as a child I sat by, through the years, and literally watched my father kill himself; surely one such victory in my family, for the rich white men who own the tobacco companies, is enough.

**°cajole**
to gently urge

## Questions for Critical Thinking

1. On the basis of the first paragraph of the essay, construct a sentence that could be the thesis for this essay. Although Alice Walker does not directly provide her thesis in one sentence, you can find her controlling idea by reviewing her introductory paragraph. What do you think is implied by the title and the first sentence?

2. Review the essay and determine how many members of Alice Walker's family figure in this story.

3. The art of narration usually includes a sequence of events to tell a story. What is the sequence of events in Alice Walker's story?

4. To achieve coherence in narrative pieces, writers need to use transitions of time. Review the essay and underline all the transitional expressions you can find.

5. In the final paragraph of her essay, Alice Walker quotes the slogan "Peace on earth begins at home," and she adds, "I believe everything does." With your classmates, make a list of the kinds of problems that are best solved in the home. What problems cannot be solved in the home and require outside intervention?

6. When Alice Walker remembers the Prince Albert tobacco tin, with its picture of the elegant royal prince, she observes that her father "never looked as dapper as Prince Albert." Examine advertisements for widely used products that you consider harmful or dangerous. In your view, how far from these advertising images are the facts about the product?

## Writing in Response

1. Alice Walker describes a bad habit that has linked the generations of her family. Think about your own family. Looking back on your parents or grandparents and then considering yourself or your own children, can you find a habit (bad or good) that goes through more than one generation? If so, write an essay in which you trace how a habit has been passed down from one generation to another. These might include eating habits, work habits, sleep habits, or leisure-time habits.

2. Alice Walker tells us in a footnote that three months after reading her mother's essay, her daughter stopped smoking. How might Alice Walker's essay have played a part in that daughter's decision to quit smoking? Write an essay in which you deal with one of the following:

   - What would it take to break a bad habit of your own?
   - What are the ways to help someone break a bad habit?
   - Why do so many people persist in behaviors they know to be self-destructive?

3. Write an essay in which you discuss the possibility that some products on the market today are later found harmful. Your essay could include discussions of several products, or you could concentrate on one product and discuss your reservations about its safety.

4. Alice Walker gave up cigarettes because her throat hurt, but she continued to drink wine as a "ritual" with her "buddies." We all know that teenagers are likely to engage in harmful activities as a result of peer pressure. Tell a story from your experience that relates how one person you have known handled peer pressure.

# UNFORGETTABLE MISS BESSIE

## Carl T. Rowan

Carl T. Rowan (1925–2000) enjoyed a long and distinguished career as a journalist, commentator, and high government official. Born in Tennessee, he attended college and graduate school before starting to work at the *Minneapolis Tribune* in 1948. He worked in the U.S. Department of State under presidents John F. Kennedy and Lyndon B. Johnson, serving as ambassador to Finland and later as director of the United States Information Agency. In 1965 he returned to newspaper work and broadcast journalism, where he was seen and heard on national television and radio. In 1991, he published his autobiography, *Breaking Barriers: A Memoir*.

**°Beowulf**
early English epic poem

1    She was only about five feet tall and probably never weighed more than 110 pounds, but Miss Bessie was a towering presence in the classroom. She was the only woman tough enough to make me read *Beowulf* ° and think for a few foolish days that I liked it. From 1938 to 1942, when I attended Bernard High School in McMinnville, Tenn., she taught me English, history, civics—and a lot more than I realized.

2    I shall never forget the day she scolded me into reading *Beowulf*.

3    "But Miss Bessie," I complained, "I ain't much interested in it."

4    Her large brown eyes became daggerish slits. "Boy," she said, "how dare you say 'ain't' to me! I've taught you better than that."

5    "Miss Bessie," I pleaded, "I'm trying to make first-string end on the football team, and if I go around saying 'it isn't' and 'they aren't,' the guys are gonna laugh me off the squad."

6    "Boy," she responded, "you'll play football because you have guts. But do you know what *really* takes guts? Refusing to lower your standards to those of the crowd. It takes guts to say you've got to live and be somebody fifty years after all the football games are over."

7    I started saying "it isn't" and "they aren't," and I still made first-string end—and class valedictorian—without losing my buddies' respect.

8    During her remarkable 44-year career, Mrs. Bessie Taylor Gwynn taught hundreds of economically deprived black youngsters—including my mother, my brother, my sisters and me. I remember her now with gratitude and affection—especially in this era when Americans are so wrought-up about a "rising tide of mediocrity" in public education and the problems of finding competent, caring teachers. Miss Bessie was an example of an informed, dedicated teacher, a blessing to children and an asset to the nation.

9    Born in 1895, in poverty, she grew up in Athens, Ala., where there was no public school for blacks. She attended Trinity School, a private institution for blacks run

627

by the American Missionary Association, and in 1911 graduated from the Normal School (a "super" high school) at Fisk University in Nashville. Mrs. Gwynn, the essence of pride and privacy, never talked about her years in Athens; only in the months before her death did she reveal that she had never attended Fisk University itself because she could not afford the four-year course.

10      At Normal School she learned a lot about Shakespeare, but most of all about the profound importance of education—especially for a people trying to move up from slavery. "What you put in your head, boy," she once said, "can never be pulled out by the Ku Klux Klan, the Congress or anybody."

11      Miss Bessie's bearing of dignity told anyone who met her that she was "educated" in the best sense of the word. There was never a discipline problem in her classes. We didn't dare mess with a woman who knew about the Battle of Hastings,° the Magna Carta° and the Bill of Rights—and who could also play the piano.

12      This frail-looking woman could make sense of Shakespeare, Milton, Voltaire,° and bring to life Booker T. Washington° and W. E. B. DuBois.° Believing that it was important to know who the officials were that spent taxpayers' money and made public policy, she made us memorize the names of everyone on the Supreme Courts and in the President's Cabinet. It could be embarrassing to be unprepared when Miss Bessie said, "Get up and tell the class who Frances Perkins is and what you think about her."

13      Miss Bessie knew that my family, like so many others during the Depression, couldn't afford to subscribe to a newspaper. She knew we didn't even own a radio. Still, she prodded° me to "look out for your future and find some way to keep up with what's going on in the world." So I became a delivery boy for the Chattanooga *Times*. I rarely made a dollar a week, but I got to read a newspaper every day.

14      Miss Bessie noticed things that had nothing to do with schoolwork, but were vital° to a youngster's development. Once a few classmates made fun of my frayed, hand-me-down overcoat, calling me "Strings." As I was leaving school, Miss Bessie patted me on the back of that old overcoat and said, "Carl, never fret° about what you *don't* have. Just make the most of what you *do* have—a brain."

15      Among the things that I did not have was electricity in the little frame house that my father had built for $400 with his World War I bonus. But because of her inspiration, I spent many hours squinting beside a kerosene lamp reading Shakespeare and Thoreau,° Samuel Pepys° and William Cullen Bryant.°

16      No one in my family had ever graduated from high school, so there was no tradition of commitment to learning for me to lean on. Like millions of youngsters in today's ghettos and barrios, I needed the push and stimulation of a teacher who truly cared. Miss Bessie gave plenty of both, as she immersed° me in a wonderful world of similes,° metaphors° and even onomatopoeia.° She led me to believe that I could write sonnets as well as Shakespeare, or iambic-pentameter verse° to put Alexander Pope° to shame.

17      In those days the McMinnville school system was rigidly "Jim Crow," and poor black children had to struggle to put anything in their heads. Our high school was only slightly larger than the once-typical little red schoolhouse, and its library was outrageously inadequate—so small, I like to say, that if two students were in it and one wanted to turn a page, the other one had to step outside.

18      Negroes, as we were called then, were not allowed in the town library, except to mop floors or dust tables. But through one of those secret Old South arrangements

---

°**Battle of Hastings**
important English battle of 1066 that established William of Normandy as king

°**Magna Carta**
an English charter of political rights, from 1215

°**Voltaire**
French writer and philosopher (1694–1778)

°**Booker T. Washington**
African American educator (1856–1915)

°**W. E. B. DuBois**
African American civil rights leader, founder of the National Association for the Advancement of Colored People (NAACP)

°**prodded**
urged

°**vital**
essential

°**fret**
worry

°**Henry David Thoreau**
American writer (1817–1862)

°**Samuel Pepys**
famous English diary writer (1633–1703)

°**William Cullen Bryant**
American poet (1794–1878)

°**immersed**
completely involved

**°simile**
a figure of speech that compares two dissimilar things using the words *like* or *as*

**°metaphor**
a figure of speech that compares two dissimilar things

**°onomatopoeia**
the sound of a word suggesting its meaning as in *hiss* or *sizzle*

**°iambic-pentameter verse**
poetry of a particular meter

**°Alexander Pope**
English poet (1688–1744)

**°the Brontës**
family of 19th century British novelists

**°Byron, Coleridge, Keats**
19th century British Romantic poets

**°Tennyson**
British poet (1809–1892)

**°Henry Wadsworth Longfellow**
American poet (1824–1884)

**°osmotic**
absorbing

**°rippled**
flowed out in little waves

between whites of conscience and blacks of stature, Miss Bessie kept getting books smuggled out of the white library. That is how she introduced me to the Brontës,° Byron, Coleridge, Keats° and Tennyson.° "If you don't read, you can't write, and if you can't write, you might as well stop dreaming," Miss Bessie once told me.

19    So I read whatever Miss Bessie told me to, and tried to remember the things she insisted that I store away. Forty-five years later, I can still recite her "truths to live by," such as Henry Wadsworth Longfellow's° lines from "The Ladder of Augustine":

The heights by great men reached and kept

Were not attained by sudden flight.

But they, while their companions slept,

Were toiling upward in the night.

20    Years later, her inspiration, prodding, anger, cajoling and almost osmotic° infusion of learning finally led to that lovely day when Miss Bessie dropped me a note saying, "I'm so proud to read your column in the Nashville *Tennessean*."

21    Miss Bessie was a spry 80 when I went back to McMinnville and visited her in a senior citizens' apartment building. Pointing out proudly that her building was racially integrated, she reached for two glasses and a pint of bourbon. I was momentarily shocked, because it would have been scandalous in the 1930s and '40s for word to get out that a teacher drank, and nobody had ever raised a rumor that Miss Bessie did.

22    I felt a new sense of equality as she lifted her glass to mine. Then she revealed a softness and compassion that I had never known as a student.

23    "I've never forgotten that examination day," she said, "when Buster Martin held up seven fingers, obviously asking you for help with question number seven, 'Name a common carrier.' I can still picture you looking at your exam paper and humming a few bars of 'Chattanooga Choo Choo.' I was so tickled, I couldn't punish either of you."

24    Miss Bessie was telling me, with bourbon-laced grace, that I never fooled her for a moment.

25    When Miss Bessie died in 1980, at age 85, hundreds of her former students mourned. They knew the measure of a great teacher: love and motivation. Her wisdom and influence had rippled° out across generations.

26    Some of her students who might normally have been doomed to poverty went on to become doctors, dentists and college professors. Many, guided by Miss Bessie's example, became public-school teachers.

27    "The memory of Miss Bessie and how she conducted her classroom did more for me than anything I learned in college," recalls Gladys Wood of Knoxville, Tenn., a highly respected English teacher who spent 43 years in the state's school system. "So many times, when I faced a difficult classroom problem, I asked myself, *How would Miss Bessie deal with this?* And I'd remember how she could handle it with laughter and love.

28    No child can get all the necessary support at home, and millions of poor children get *no* support at all. This is what makes a wise, educated, warm-hearted teacher like Miss Bessie so vital to the minds, hearts and souls of this country's children.

## Questions for Critical Thinking

1. Carl Rowan's description of his beloved teacher Miss Bessie includes only a few physical descriptions of Miss Bessie. How many can you find? Why are these few details significant?

2. The picture we form of Miss Bessie is also created by the words that she spoke. Carl Rowan quotes Miss Bessie in several places in the essay. Find the important quotes that Carl Rowan remembers even now that he is an older man. Underline them. How might these quotes affect a person's life?

3. Carl Rowan uses many specific examples of the information he learned in Miss Bessie's class. Make a check beside the references he makes to historical people and events. Why do you think the writer included all this information?

4. When Miss Bessie pressured Carl Rowan into reading the ancient English poem *Beowulf,* she used her student's mistake in grammar to teach him another lesson. What was the lesson she taught him? What might one learn from reading literature or poetry from another time in history? In your opinion, was the lesson more important than what he could have learned from reading *Beowulf*?

5. In paragraph 5, Carl Rowan admits to his teacher that if he used proper grammar in front of other football players, they would laugh him off the team. To what extent is this a current attitude? In what circumstances is it not fashionable to be enthusiastic about learning?

## Writing in Response

1. Writing about his childhood, Carl Rowan tells us that his family could not afford "to subscribe to a newspaper" and "didn't even own a radio." Yet, Miss Bessie urged him to "find some way to keep up with what's going on in the world." She was not a person to give up. How did Carl Rowan solve his problem? In today's world, what are the best ways to keep up with "what's going on in the world"? If a person cannot afford to own the latest technology, what are the best ways to obtain current information? Write an essay in which you give examples of several specific obstacles and explain how it is possible to overcome each one.

2. Write an essay of description in which your sensory images reveal the character of someone you have known. How did that person's character touch your life?

3. Our society is very concerned with acquiring money and possessions. Miss Bessie told Carl Rowan not to worry about "what you don't have. Just make the most of what you do have." Write an essay in which you describe three "things" you do have and how you intend to make the most of these talents or assets.

4. Carl Rowan observes that no child "can get all the necessary support at home." How much support should we expect a child to get at home? What kind of support should a child receive outside the home? Where can a child find such support? Write an essay in which you describe the support systems for children that already do or should exist in your community. How can we be assured that the children in a community are having their basic needs met?

5. In paragraph 6, Miss Bessie points to what should be most important to a person—to "be somebody fifty years after all the football games are over." Miss Bessie is taking the long view on the subject of "being somebody." How difficult is it for a young person to take such a long-term view? Is it asking too much to expect a young person to plan for the future? Write an essay that points out the reasons why so many youth do not plan for their futures.

# A DAY AT THE THEME PARK

## W. Bruce Cameron

W. Bruce Cameron began an Internet-based humor column in 1995, and within a year, he was the most widely read humorist on the World Wide Web. Four years later, he began his newspaper columns for the Denver, Colorado, *Rocky Mountain News.* His pieces had such wide appeal that he expanded some of them into a book, *8 Simple Rules for Dating My Teenage Daughter.* The book quickly became a best-seller and later became the basis of a television show, *8 Simple Rules.*

When W. Bruce Cameron writes about the problems that parents encounter while raising their children, he speaks from authority: he is the father of three teenagers, two girls and a boy. The following essay, which originally appeared in the *Rocky Mountain News,* is clearly based on the author's personal experience. While his humor makes us smile, the essay carries with it an element of truth about how parents will make great sacrifices for the sake of their children.

°**endearing**
giving affection

°**utter**
complete

°**fiendish**
cruel

°**carnivorous**
flesh eating

°**DIA**
Denver International
Airport

1      One of the most endearing° traits of children is their utter° trust that their parents provide them with all life's necessities, meaning food, shelter, and a weekend at a theme park.

2      A theme park is a sort of artificial vacation, a place where you can enjoy all your favorite pastimes at once, such as motion sickness and heat exhaustion. Adult tolerance for theme parks peaks at about an hour, which is how long it takes to walk from the parking lot to the front gate. You fork over an obscene amount of money to gain entrance to a theme park, though it costs nothing to leave (which is odd because you'd pay anything to escape). The two main activities in a theme park are (a) standing in line, and (b) sweating. The sun reflects off the concrete with a fiendish° lack of mercy. You're about to learn the boiling point of tennis shoes. Your hair is sunburned, and when a small child in front of you gestures with her hand she smacks you in the face with her cotton candy; now it feels like your cheeks are covered with carnivorous° sand.

3      The ride your children have selected for you is a corkscrewing, stomach compressing roller coaster built by the same folks who manufactured the baggage delivery system at DIA.° Apparently the theme of this particular park is "Nausea." You sit down and are strapped in so tightly you can feel your shoulders grinding against your pelvis. Once the ride begins you are thrown about with such violence it reminds you of your teenager's driving. When the ride is over your children want to get something to eat, but first the ride attendants have to pry your fingers off the safety bar. "Open your eyes, please sir," they keep shouting. They finally persuade you to let go, though it seems a bit discourteous of them to have used pepper spray. Staggering, you follow your children to the Hot Dog Palace for some breakfast.

4      Food at a theme park is so expensive it would be cheaper to just eat your own money. Your son's meal costs a day's pay and consists of items manufactured of corn syrup, which is sugar; sucrose, which is sugar; fructose, which is sugar; and sugar, which is sugar. He also consumes large quantities of what in dog food

would be called "meat byproducts." When, after a couple of rides, he announces that he feels like he is going to throw up, you're very alarmed. Having seen this meal once, you're in no mood to see it again.

**°pummeling**
a beating

5    With the exception of that first pummeling,° you manage to stay off the rides all day, explaining to your children that it isn't good for you when your internal organs are forcibly rearranged. Now, though, they coax you back in line, promising a ride that doesn't twist, doesn't hang you upside down like a bat, doesn't cause your brain to flop around inside your skull; it just goes up and then comes back down. That's it, Dad, no big deal. What they don't tell you is HOW it comes back

**°acrophobia**
fear of heights

down. You're strapped into a seat and pulled gently up into acrophobia,° the city falling away from you. Okay, not so bad, and in the conversation you're having with God you explain that you're thankful for the wonderful view but would really like to get down now.

6    And that's just how you descend: NOW. Without warning, you plummet to the ground in an uncontrolled free fall. You must be moving faster than the speed of sound because when you open your mouth, nothing comes out. Your life passes before your eyes, and your one regret is that you will not have an opportunity to punish your children for bringing you to this hellish place. Brakes cut in and you slam to a stop. You gingerly touch your face to confirm it has fallen off. "Wasn't that fun, Dad?" your kids ask. "Why are you kissing the ground?"

**°impervious**
unaffected

7    At the end of the day, you let your teenager drive home. (After the theme park, you are impervious° to fear.)

## Questions for Critical Thinking

1.  Is the purpose of this essay to inform, to persuade, or to entertain?

2.  Explain what part of the one-sentence introduction is the topic.

3.  What word could the writer have used for his controlling idea if he had wanted to reveal that controlling idea in the beginning of his essay?

4.  Study the writer's two-sentence conclusion. What single word in that conclusion reveals the author's attitude toward theme parks and therefore gives us his controlling idea for the entire essay?

5.  Choose a sensory image from each of the five body paragraphs (paragraphs 2–6) that you find especially humorous. Although humor is hard to analyze, try to explain why you were amused by each image you have chosen.

6.  Underline the topic sentences of the body paragraphs.

## Writing in Response

1.  Many people have a dream to do something like go across the country on a motorcycle, visit Paris, or see the pyramids before they die. Write an essay that describes, either seriously or humorously, an activity that you want to do sometime during your lifetime.

2.  In paragraph 2, the writer describes going to a theme park as "a sort of artificial vacation." Describe your idea of a "real" vacation.

3.   We live in a permissive society. Write an essay that describes several situations in which a parent should say no.

4.   Write an essay that describes a form of entertainment that you believe has become too expensive for the average person or family to enjoy.

5.   Describe what you believe to be the best amusement or entertainment for children.

6.   If you have ever enjoyed a visit to a theme park, describe the three best rides you have ever experienced.

# MY HEROES

## Elizabeth Berg

Before she devoted herself to full-time writing, Elizabeth Berg worked in a number of professions, including that of a registered nurse. However, she came to the conclusion that writing was the most rewarding and creative outlet for her. Her success with fiction and nonfiction confirmed her choice. Her novel *Durable Goods,* published in 1993, was followed in 1997 by *Joy School.* Another novel, *Range of Motion,* appeared in 1995, and a television movie based on that story was produced five years later. A major theme in much of Elizabeth Berg's writing is the importance of celebrating the small things in life. As the author expresses it, "A lesson I learned from being a nurse is how important seemingly ordinary life is." Personal relationships are also at the center of much of this writer's fiction. The following essay shows her sensitivity to relationships among people and her focus on the common things of everyday life.

1    My eight-year-old daughter, Jenny, was given a school assignment not too long ago to write about a hero. "So who did you pick?" I asked her. I was imagining some possibilities: Rosa Parks, Christa McAuliffe, Sara Lee. But Jenny answered, "Laura."

2    "Who?" I asked.

3    "Laura," she said again.

4    "You mean your friend from across the street?" I asked.

5    "Yeah!" she said.

°**ultrapatient**
extremely patient

6    I was a little mystified. "How come you picked her?" I asked. "Because," Jenny answered in the ultrapatient° voice of Instructor of the Hopeless, "she is my hero."

7    "Oh," I said. "I see."

8    I must confess that at first I was disappointed. I thought that if her hero was only her friend, she had failed to appreciate the magnificent contributions that real heroes have made to the world. I thought I'd better go out that afternoon and buy some books about famous scientists, artists, athletes, world leaders. That would wise her up. Also, I'd have a look at what they were teaching her in school—didn't she have an appreciation for Martin Luther King?

9    But then I thought about who I would say my heroes are, and I realized that if I told the truth, they wouldn't be famous, either. For although it is undeniable that there have been outstanding people in history who have set glorious examples and inspired me mightily, the people who inspire me most tend to be those who touch me personally, and in quiet ways.

10    For example, I had an eighth-grade English teacher named Mrs. Zinz. She was demanding and rather straight-laced, I thought, but she taught us certain

critical skills for reading and writing. She was concerned not only with what we learned but also with what we were becoming: She put a premium on honesty and tried to get us to understand why it was important. She insisted that we always do our best, and in her class, we almost always did. She told me that I was a terrific creative writer and encouraged my every effort.

11      As payment for all her good work, I, along with my evil best friend, tortured her. We laughed at her in class, tried to pit our other teachers against her by telling them how unfairly she graded, and once, in a moment of extreme obnoxiousness,° called her on the telephone over and over, only to hang up when she answered. Mrs. Zinz was no dummy. She knew who was calling her. In turn she called my mother, who insisted that I call Mrs. Zinz and apologize. With my face aflame, and between clenched teeth, I muttered a grossly insincere "Sorry." She accepted my apology warmly and with a style so graceful that I was infuriated all the more. And though I sulked every day in her class for the rest of the year, she never bowed by reacting to it. I got an A for the term. I moved soon after and lost track of Mrs. Zinz. I never did apologize in any legitimate way to her. Ironically, she is still an inspiration to me, a lesson in how not to lower yourself to someone else's level, even when that person is doing everything she can to make you crazy. She is, in that way, a hero.

12      My grandfather, known to me as "Papa," was also a hero of mine. For one thing, he made all of us grandchildren laugh all of the time. He told riddles that were viewed by us as the essence° of sophisticated humor. When he greeted us, he shook our hands enthusiastically and at great length, shouting, "How do! How do!" We used to line up and sit on his lap and watch him pop his dentures in and out of his mouth, an astounding feat that thrilled and terrified us—especially before we realized that the teeth were false. He was unfailingly warm and kind and knew how to make a friend out of a stranger; he loved people. I saw him as a man who felt light inside, happy; and feeling that way is no small task in a world that often seems intent on taking two back for every one you get.

13      Then there is my mother-in-law, Sylvia, who at the age of retirement went back to school to pursue a lifetime dream: getting a college diploma. She bumped her bifocals into microscopes, suffered verbal abuse at the hands of an insensitive computer instructor, got used to being the last one to finish every exam, and worried about homework on weekends when she could have been luxuriating° in the fact that she had nothing to do. She says that she learned an awful lot, but if you ask me, it's she who did the teaching. I am honored that our family has her love of learning to inspire us.

14      Beyond that, there are people who are heroes to me because of what they do: mail carriers, who, on days when I stay inside hiding from the cold or heat, subject themselves to hours of it; nurses, who care for those who can't care for themselves every second of every day. I admire stay-at-home mothers for their patience and their creativity in the face of almost no thanks or recognition, and working mothers for the way they juggle an awesome load of responsibilities.

15      There are people with chronic illness, for whom getting through each day is heroic. There are people who have been married for sixty years, who have lessons to teach us all. There are those who are strong enough in heart and in spirit to speak up when something feels wrong to them, to go against the majority, and oftentimes to risk themselves for the sake of others. And then there are those whom I admire most: people who seem to have found the secret of calm and can relinquish° the race for the pleasure of seeing what's around them, right here, right now.

°**obnoxiousness**
being very offensive

°**essence**
the fundamental quality

°**luxuriating**
enjoying with great pleasure

°**relinquish**
give up

°**precipitated**
made to happen

16     I was thinking about all this when I saw Jenny and Laura come into the house. I wanted to know a little more about what had precipitated° Jenny's calling Laura a hero. Was it her sharing her brand-new toys? Being there to listen, to soothe, to make better a bad situation in the way that only good friends can? Well, as it happens, no. Jenny told me that Laura was her hero because Laura had saved her from drowning in a creek. *"What?"* I yelled.

17     Laura rolled her eyes. "Jenny, the water was only about an inch deep." Jenny shrugged and said, "So? You still saved me."

18     Laura and I let pass a certain look between us. Then she and Jenny went outside again to play.

19     If you're smart, I thought, you gratefully take your heroes where you find them. As it happens, they are everywhere. So what if the water was only an inch deep? Someone was there, caring about Jenny and showing that she did, a safe hand stretched out to another who was in trouble. This seemed heroic indeed, and later that night when I was tucking her in, I told Jenny that I thought her choice was perfect. "I know," she yawned. "Good night."

## Questions for Critical Thinking

1. You have to read more than one paragraph of this piece to find the writer's thesis statement. Underline what you believe is the thesis statement.

2. Choose one of the following introductory patterns as the best description of the introductory pattern used for this essay:

   a.  a general subject is narrowed down into a more specific topic

   b.  a well-known expression or familiar quotation is used

   c.  a definition of the concept to be discussed is given

   d.  a brief anecdote introduces the topic

   e.  classification indicates how the topic fits into a larger class

3. In which paragraph does the author list several examples in a single sentence?

4. In this essay of illustration, mark each example provided by the author. Circle transitions that signal an example.

5. Explain how the essay comes full circle. Where does the conclusion begin?

## Writing in Response

1. One of the author's heroes was a grade school teacher, Mrs. Zinz, who showed the young student how to act with dignity. Write an essay giving examples of lessons you have learned from teachers who provided more than academic instruction.

2. In paragraph 13, the author describes how her mother-in-law returns to school at a time in her life when she did not have to do so. Write an essay that gives examples of how some people continue to learn (whether they go back to school or not).

3.  Write an essay that gives examples of how retired people can still be productive and useful to society.

4.  Write an essay that gives examples of people whose heroic struggles with illnesses demand courage to get through every day.

# AMERICA'S GAMBLING CRAZE

## James Popkin with Katia Hetter

Gambling used to be classified as a vice, something to be warned against and eliminated. In recent years, however, many institutions in our society have welcomed the revenues that gambling can produce. The issue of gambling evokes strong feelings pro and con, as people argue the benefits and drawbacks of gambling in our society. In the following essay, written in 1994, we are given many different facts and statistics about gambling. This information educates us about a topic that remains controversial today.

1.     No one howled in protest last month when H&R Block set up makeshift tax-preparation offices in four Nevada casinos and offered gamblers same-day "refund-anticipation loans." And few people cared recently when a Florida inventor won a U.S. patent that could someday enable television audiences to legally bet on game shows, football games, and even beauty pageants from their homes.

2.     What's the deal? Not that long ago, Americans held gambling in nearly the same esteem as heroin dealing and applauded when ax-wielding police paid a visit to the corner dice room. But moral outrage has become as outmoded as a penny slot machine. In 1955, for example, baseball commissioner Ford Frick considered wagering so corrupt he prohibited major leaguers from overnighting in Las Vegas. Last year, by contrast, Americans for the first time made more trips to casinos than they did to Major League ballparks—some 92 million trips, according to one study.

3.     It took six decades for gambling to become America's Pastime, from the legalization of Nevada casinos in 1931 to April Fool's Day 1991, when Davenport, Iowa, launched the Diamond Lady, the nation's first legal riverboat casino. The gradual creation of 37 state lotteries broke down the public's mistrust, conveying a clear message that the government sanctioned° gambling; indeed, is even coming to depend on it as a tax-revenue source. Corporate ownership of casinos helped in its own way, too, replacing shady operators with trusted brand names like Hilton and MGM. Casinos now operate or are authorized in 23 states, and 95 percent of all Americans are expected to live within a three- or four-hour drive of one by the year 2000.

**°sanctioned**
gave approval to

4.     Today, the Bible Belt might as well be renamed the Blackjack Belt, with floating and land-based casinos throughout Mississippi and Louisiana and plans for more in Florida, Texas, Alabama and Arkansas. Meanwhile, the Midwest is overrun with slot hogs, none of the porcine variety.° Iowa, Illinois, Indiana and Missouri allow riverboat gambling, and a 50,000-square-foot land-based casino is scheduled to open in mid-May just outside Detroit, in Windsor, Ontario. Low-stakes casinos attract visitors to old mining towns in Colorado and South Dakota, and Indian tribes operate 225 casinos and high-stakes bingo halls nationwide. Add church bingo, card rooms, sports wagering, dog and horse racing, and jai alai° to the mix and it becomes clear why Americans legally wagered $330 billion in 1992—a 1,800 percent increase over 1976.

**°slot hogs**
people who take up multiple slot machines at once (not actual pigs)

**°jai alai**
a fast game similar to handball, played on a walled court

°**Prohibition**
the period from 1920
to 1930 in the United
States, when all
alcoholic beverages
were forbidden

5      Like the first bars that opened after Prohibition,° modern gambling halls are enormously successful. "It will be impossible not to make a lot of money," one executive in New Orleans bragged before his casino had even opened. "It's like spitting and missing the floor." Such boasts—and the real possibility that the boom will create 500,000 jobs nationwide this decade—have not been lost on federal, state, and local lawmakers. In the first six weeks of this year alone they introduced more than 200 bills regarding gambling.

6      But casinos and lotteries may not guarantee the jackpots many politicians expect. When urban-planning professor Robert Goodman reviewed the economic-impact studies that 14 government agencies relied upon before deciding to embrace casino gambling, he found that most were written with a pro-industry spin and only four were balanced and factored in° gambling's hidden costs. Goodman's two-year study, due out next week, concludes that newly opened casinos "suck money out of the local economy," away from existing movie theaters, car dealerships, clothing shops and sports arenas. In Atlantic City, for example, about 100 of 250 local restaurants have closed since the casinos debuted in 1978, says Goodman, who teaches at the University of Massachusetts at Amherst.

°**factored in**
considered as
elements

7      States that get hooked on gambling revenues soon suffer withdrawal symptoms when local competition kicks in. Although pioneering casinos and lotteries typically are profitable, gambling grosses decline when lotteries or casinos open in neighboring states. In Biloxi, Mississippi, for example, slot revenues at first topped about $207 per machine per day. A year later when competitors moved in, however, the daily win-per-machine figure dipped to $109.

8      States frequently overestimate the financial impact of gambling revenues, too. "Legalized gambling is never large enough to solve any social problems," says gambling-law professor and paid industry consultant I. Nelson Rose. In New Jersey, for example, horse racing alone accounted for about 10 percent of state revenue in the 1950s. Today, despite the addition of a lottery and 12 casinos, the state earns only 6 percent of its revenue through gambling. "Atlantic City used to be a slum by the sea," says Rose. "Now it's a slum by the sea with casinos."

9      America's love affair with dice and cards has always been a fickle romance, and some academics predict a breakup soon. Legalized gambling in America has been running on a 70-year boom-and-bust cycle since the colonists started the first lotteries. "We're now riding the third wave of legal gambling" that began with the Depression, says Rose, who has written extensively on the subject and teaches at Whittier Law School in Los Angeles. The trend self-destructs after a few decades, when the public simply gets fed up and embraces more conservative values. Rose believes a cheating or corruption scandal will trigger the next crash in about 35 years, an idea that most casino officials think is ludicrous.

10     The sky is not falling yet. Apart from a handful of academics and the odd politician, few Americans are seriously questioning the morality of an industry that is expected to help gamblers lose a record $35 billion in 1995 alone. Religious leaders have been oddly silent, perhaps because so many churches and synagogues rely on bingo revenues. "The biggest things we have to help people are churches and temples and the government," says Arnie Wexler, executive director of the Council on Compulsive Gambling of New Jersey. "And now they're all in the gambling business."

11     The consequences can be damaging. Wexler says he got a phone call late last week from a man in his 70s who ran up $150,000 in debt just by buying lottery

tickets. Although most gambling experts believe that only 1 percent to 3 percent of Americans have a serious gambling problem at any given time, a July 1993 Gallup Poll funded by Wexler's group suggests that the figure may be closer to 5 percent. Regardless, now that casinos are no longer located just in Atlantic City and Nevada it's reasonable to assume that the total number of problem gamblers will soar. "If you put a guy who wouldn't cheat on his wife in a room with a gorgeous nude woman, some guys would fall by the wayside," Wexler says. "When you make gambling legal and socially acceptable, people will try it and some of them will get hooked."

12      But try telling that to a gambler happily feeding a slot machine and waiting for a multimillion-dollar payoff. Fifty-one percent of American adults now find casino gambling "acceptable for anyone," and 35 percent describe it as "acceptable for others but not for me," according to a recent Yankelovich Inc. survey paid for by Harrah's Casinos. The attraction is simple. "The action for them is the thrill of what's going to happen in the next pull of that slot-machine handle," explains Harrah's president, Phil Satre.

## Questions for Critical Thinking

1. The purpose for an essay may be to entertain, to inform, or to persuade. Which of these do you believe is the authors' purpose?

2. The first paragraph does not present the thesis. Instead, it gives us two examples of how American attitudes about gambling have changed. After reading the essay, write what you believe is the authors' thesis.

3. Read paragraph 4. Write a topic sentence that expresses the main idea of this paragraph.

4. Most good writing includes illustrations of some kind to support the points being made. This essay is composed of one example after another. Go through the essay and find the four times the authors indicate an example by using the expression "for example."

5. Starting in paragraph 6, the authors use quotations from experts to support their points. Each person's qualification or position is carefully indicated within the text. Fill out the following chart to summarize these examples.

| Name of expert | Title/position | Idea presented in the quotation |
|---|---|---|
| 1. | | |
| 2. | | |
| 3. | | |
| 4. | | |

6    What are the major points the authors make about gambling? Be careful not to confuse main ideas with detailed examples.

7    This essay was published in 1994. If you were to write an updated version of this essay, you would want to find the latest facts or statistics that would make your essay timely. Review each paragraph of the essay and locate those facts or statistics you believe could be updated. Websites such as casinowatch.org may be helpful in researching information.

## Writing in Response

1.   Write an essay in which you present your personal position on gambling. Do you recognize different levels of gambling, or do all forms of gambling seem the same to you? For example, is buying a lottery ticket the same as gambling in a casino?

2.   Gambling revenues are widely advertised as helping communities pay for education and other needed social improvements. In many cases, this has not happened. Write an essay about a situation, an organization, or an activity that is supposed to offer a solution to a social problem but actually creates other, possibly more serious problems.

3.   In paragraph 2, the authors explain how in the past gambling was seen as a vice. People felt a "moral outrage" when they encountered any kind of gambling. What situation, practice, or failure in our society causes a feeling of "moral outrage" in you? Write an essay in which you argue your position on this topic.

4.   Over the years, people's attitudes toward certain social issues have changed. Gambling is just one example of such an issue. Identify one of the changes that you have observed in our society. Present an argument that claims this change has been positive or negative.

# SLICE OF LIFE

## Russell Baker

While Russell Baker may be best known for his sharp political and social commentaries, he is also well known as a humorist. After growing up in Baltimore, Maryland, during the Great Depression, his breakthrough in journalism came in 1962 when the *New York Times* gave him his "Observer" column. Until 1998, Russell Baker produced that column and numerous other essays, winning two Pulitzer prizes for his work. Many readers have had a good laugh enjoying the following essay. They can identify with the problems facing a person who tries to make a holiday go smoothly.

1    How to carve a turkey:

2    Assemble the following tools—carving knife, stone for sharpening carving knife, hot water, soap, wash cloth, two bath towels, barbells, meat cleaver. If the house lacks a meat cleaver, an ax may be substituted. If it is, add bandages, sutures,° and iodine to above list.

3    Begin by moving the turkey from the roasting pan to a suitable carving area, This is done by inserting the carving knife into the posterior° stuffed area of the turkey and the knife-sharpening stone into the stuffed area under the neck.

4    Thus skewered,° the turkey may be lifted out of the hot grease with relative safety. Should the turkey drop to the floor, however, remove the knife and stone, roll the turkey gingerly° into the two bath, towels, wrap them several times around it and lift the encased fowl to the carving place.

5    You are now ready to begin carving. Sharpen the knife on the stone and insert it where the thigh joins the torso.° If you do this correctly, which is improbable, the knife will almost immediately encounter a barrier of bone and gristle. This may very well be the joint. It could, however, be your thumb. If not, execute° a vigorous sawing motion until satisfied that the knife has been defeated. Withdraw the knife and ask someone nearby, in as testy° a manner as possible, why the knives at your house are not kept in better carving condition.

6    Exercise the biceps and forearms by lifting barbells until they are strong enough for you to tackle the leg joint with bare hands. Wrapping one hand firmly around the thigh, seize the turkey's torso in the other hand and scream. Run cold water over hands to relieve pain of burns.

7    Now, take a bath towel in each hand and repeat the above maneuver.° The entire leg should snap away from the chassis° with a distinct crack, and the rest of the turkey, obedient to Newton's Law° about equal and opposite reactions, should roll in the opposite direction, which means that if you are carving at the table the turkey will probably come to rest in someone's lap.

8    Get the turkey out of the lap with as little fuss as possible, and concentrate on the leg. Use the meat cleaver to sever° the sinewy° leather which binds the thigh to the drumstick.

°**sutures**
fine stitches to close surgical wounds

°**posterior**
the back side

°**skewered**
pierced by the knife

°**gingerly**
with great care

°**torso**
the human body minus the head and limbs

°**execute**
perform

°**testy**
irritated

°**maneuver**
a strategic action

°**chassis**
frame or skeleton

°**Newton's Law**
Isaac Newton (1642–1727), who discovered that every action has an equal and opposite reaction

**°sever**
to cut off

**°sinewy**
stringy and tough

**°compelled**
forced or pressured

9        If using the alternate, ax method, this operation should be performed on a cement walk outside the house in order to preserve the table.

10        Repeat the above operation on the turkey's uncarved side. You now have two thighs and two drumsticks. Using the wash cloth, soap and hot water, bathe thoroughly and, if possible, go to a movie. Otherwise, look each person in the eye and say, "I don't suppose anyone wants white meat.

11        If compelled° to carve the breast anyhow, sharpen the knife on the stone again with sufficient awkwardness to tip over the gravy bowl on the person who started the stampede for white meat.

12        While everyone is rushing about to mop the gravy off her slacks, hack at the turkey breast until it starts crumbling off the carcass in ugly chunks.

13        The alternative method for carving white meat is to visit around the neighborhood until you find someone who has a good carving knife and borrow it, if you find one, which is unlikely.

14        This method enables you to watch the football game on neighbors' television sets and also creates the possibility that somebody back at your table will grow tired of waiting and do the carving herself.

**°mutilations**
damages beyond repair

15        In this case, upon returning home, cast a pained stare upon the mound of chopped white meat that has been hacked out by the family carving knife and refuse to do any more carving that day. No one who cares about the artistry of carving can be expected to work upon the mutilations° of amateurs, and it would be a betrayal of the carver's art to do so.

## Questions for Critical Thinking

1.    Not everyone brings the same sense of humor to written material. Did you find this essay humorous? Why or why not? How would you describe Russell Baker's humor?

2.    Decide where in the essay you first realized the piece would be humorous. Mark that place.

3.    What makes the title effective?

4.    We have learned that one sentence is not an adequate paragraph. Why then has Russell Baker begun this essay with only one sentence in his first paragraph?

5.    Go through the essay and mark every transitional word that signals movement from one step to the next.

6.    Process writing can be directional or informational. Would you describe this essay as directional or informational?

7.    Although this is intended as a humorous essay, Russell Baker has probably lived long enough and served turkey enough times to have seen most of the problems that he describes with exaggerated drama. Review the essay and make a list of the mishaps that often happen when people try to carve a turkey or do some other household chore.

## Writing in Response

1. Write an essay in which you discuss a task you perform at holiday time. If you like, try your hand at humor.

2. Write a straightforward essay on how to carve a turkey (or how to prepare some other dish that calls for a special skill).

3. When a person lacks proper training to accomplish a particular task, the results can be disappointing. Write an essay in which you give several examples of processes that should be left to well-trained professionals. Point out the serious dangers of untrained persons attempting the tasks described in your essay.

4. Write a narrative essay telling of your attempt to perform a certain task for which you lacked the necessary skill. What was the final result?

# HOW TO MARK A BOOK

## Mortimer Adler

Mortimer Adler (1902–2001) dropped out of his New York City high school when he was fifteen, but later attended Columbia University. He failed to obtain his degree there, however, because he did not take the swimming test required for graduation. Despite this, he was given a teaching post at Columbia as an instructor in psychology, and in a few years he wrote a doctoral dissertation—the only student in the country to earn a PhD without the benefit of even a high school diploma. In 1983, Columbia finally excused Adler from the swimming requirement and gave him his BA—sixty years after he should have graduated.

Adler firmly believed that everyone can find a good education by studying areas of knowledge that help people think clearly and exercise their free will, and throughout his life, Adler worked toward proving his theory. In 1946, while he was at the University of Chicago, Adler was instrumental in starting the Great Books Program, which brought adults together regularly to discuss classic works of literature and philosophy. To support this program, *Encyclopaedia Britannica* printed a set of fifty-four books. The idea behind the Great Books Program spread throughout the country, influencing the lives of many people for years.

°**contend**
assert

°**bluntly**
frankly

°**mutilation**
damage beyond repair

°**prelude**
an introductory action

°**reverence**
deep respect

1    You know you have to read "between the lines" to get the most out of anything. I want to persuade you to do something equally important in the course of your reading. I want to persuade you to "write between the lines." Unless you do, you are not likely to do the most efficient kind of reading.

2    I contend,° quite bluntly,° that marking up a book is not an act of mutilation° but of love.

3    You shouldn't mark up a book which isn't yours. Librarians (or your friends) who lend you books expect you to keep them clean, and you should. If you decide that I am right about the usefulness of marking books, you will have to buy them. Most of the world's great books are available today, in reprint editions, at less than a dollar.°

4    There are two ways in which you can own a book. The first is the property right you establish by paying for it, just as you pay for clothes or furniture. But this act of purchase is only the prelude° to possession. Full ownership comes only when you have made it a part of yourself, and the best way to make yourself a part of it is by writing in it. An illustration may make the point clear. You buy a beefsteak and transfer it from the butcher's icebox to your own. But you do not own the beefsteak in the most important sense until you consume it and get it into your bloodstream. I am arguing that books, too, must be absorbed in your bloodstream to do you any good.

5    Confusion about what it means to *own* a book leads people to a false reverence° for paper, binding, and type—a respect for the physical thing—the craft of the printer rather than the genius of the author. They forget that it is possible for a man to acquire the idea, to possess the beauty, which a great book contains, without staking his claim by pasting his bookplate inside the cover.

°At today's prices, many of these books might be found for under five dollars.

Having a fine library doesn't prove that its owner has a mind enriched by books; it proves nothing more than that he, his father, or his wife, was rich enough to buy them.

6      There are three kinds of book owners. The first has all the standard sets and best-sellers—unread, untouched. (This deluded° individual owns woodpulp and ink, not books.) The second has a great many books—a few of them read through, most of them dipped into, but all of them as clean and shiny as the day they were bought. (This person would probably like to make books his own, but is restrained by a false respect for their physical appearance.) The third has a few books or many—every one of them dog-eared and dilapidated,° shaken and loosened by continual use, marked and scribbled in from front to back. (This man owns books.)

7      Is it false respect, you may ask, to preserve intact and unblemished° a beautifully printed book, an elegantly bound edition? Of course not. I'd no more scribble all over a first edition of *Paradise Lost°* than I'd give my baby a set of crayons and an original Rembrandt!° I wouldn't mark up a painting or a statue. Its soul, so to speak, is inseparable from its body. And the beauty of a rare edition or of a richly manufactured volume is like that of a painting or a statue.

8      But the soul of a book *can* be separated from its body. A book is more like the score of a piece of music than it is like a painting. No great musician confuses a symphony with the printed sheets of music. Arturo Toscanini° reveres Brahms,° but Toscanini's score of the C-minor Symphony is so thoroughly marked up that no one but the maestro° himself can read it. The reason why a great conductor makes notations on his musical scores—marks them up again and again each time he returns to study them—is the reason why you should mark your books. If your respect for magnificent binding or typography gets in the way, buy yourself a cheap edition and pay your respects to the author.

9      Why is marking up a book indispensable° to reading? First, it keeps you awake. (And I don't mean merely conscious; I mean wide awake.) In the second place, reading, if it is active, is thinking, and thinking tends to express itself in words, spoken or written. The marked book is usually the thought-through book. Finally, writing helps you remember the thoughts you had, or the thoughts the author expressed. Let me develop these three points.

10      If reading is to accomplish anything more than passing time, it must be active. You can't let your eyes glide across the lines of a book and come up with an understanding of what you have read. Now an ordinary piece of light fiction, like say, *Gone With the Wind,°* doesn't require the most active kind of reading. The books you read for pleasure can be read in a state of relaxation, and nothing is lost. But a great book, rich in ideas and beauty, a book that raises and tries to answer great fundamental questions, demands the most active reading of which you are capable. You don't absorb the ideas of John Dewey° the way you absorb the crooning of Mr. Vallee.° You have to reach for them. That you cannot do while you're asleep.

11      If, when you've finished reading a book, the pages are filled with your notes, you know that you read actively. The most famous active reader of great books I know is President Hutchins, of the University of Chicago. He also has the hardest schedule of business activities of any man I know. He invariably° reads with a pencil, and sometimes, when he picks up a book and a pencil in the

°**deluded**
self-deceived

°**dilapidated**
shabby

°**unblemished**
without a flaw

°**Paradise Lost**
epic poem by John Milton (1608–1674)

°**Rembrandt**
Dutch painter (1606–1669)

°**Toscanini**
Italian conductor (1867–1957)

°**Brahms**
German composer (1833–1897)

°**maestro**
master musician

°**indispensable**
essential

°**Gone with the Wind**
novel about the American Civil War

°**John Dewey**
American educator (1859–1952)

°**Mr. Vallee**
Rudy Vallee, popular singer (1901–1986)

°**invariably**
always

evening, he finds himself, instead of making intelligent notes, drawing what he calls "caviar factories" on the margins. When that happens, he puts the book down. He knows he's too tired to read, and he's just wasting time.

12    But, you may ask, why is writing necessary? Well, the physical act of writing, with your own hand, brings words and sentences more sharply before your mind and preserves them better in your memory. To set down your reaction to important words and sentences you have read, and the questions they have raised in your mind, is to preserve those reactions and sharpen those questions.

13    Even if you wrote on a scratch pad, and threw the paper away when you had finished writing, your grasp of the book would be surer. But you don't have to throw the paper away. The margins (top and bottom, as well as side), the end-papers, the very space between the lines, are all available. They aren't sacred. And, best of all, your marks and notes become an integral° part of the book and stay there forever. You can pick up the book the following week or year, and there are all your points of agreement, disagreement, doubt, and inquiry. It's like resuming an interrupted conversation with the advantage of being able to pick up where you left off.

**°integral**
essential

14    And that is exactly what reading a book should be: a conversation between you and the author. Presumably he knows more about the subject than you do; naturally, you'll have the proper humility as you approach him. But don't let anybody tell you that a reader is supposed to be solely on the receiving end. Understanding is a two-way operation; learning doesn't consist in being an empty receptacle.° The learner has to question himself and question the teacher. He even has to argue with the teacher, once he understands what the teacher is saying. And marking a book is literally° an expression of your differences, or agreements of opinion, with the author.

**°receptacle**
a container

**°literally**
really, exactly

15    There are all kinds of devices° for marking a book intelligently and fruitfully.° Here's the way I do it:

**°devices**
techniques

**°fruitfully**
producing results

1.    *Underlining:* of major points, of important or forceful statements.

2.    *Vertical° lines at the margin:* to emphasize a statement already underlined.

**°vertical**
up and down lines

3.    *Star, asterisk, or other doo-dad at the margin:* to be used sparingly, to emphasize the ten or twenty most important statements in the book. (You may want to fold the bottom corner of each page on which you use such marks. It won't hurt the sturdy paper on which most modern books are printed, and you will be able to take the book off the shelf at any time and, by opening it at the folded-corner page, refresh your recollection of the book.)

4.    *Numbers in the margin:* to indicate the sequence of points the author makes in developing a single argument.

5.    *Numbers of other pages in the margin:* to indicate where else in the book the author made points relevant to the point marked; to tie up the ideas in a book, which, though they may be separated by many pages, belong together.

6.    *Circling of key words or phrases.*

7. *Writing in the margin, or at the top or bottom of the page, for the sake of:* recording questions (and perhaps answers) which a passage raised in your mind; reducing a complicated discussion to a simple statement; recording the sequence of major points right through the books. I use the end-papers at the back of the book to make a personal index of the author's points in the order of their appearance.

16    The front end-papers are, to me, the most important. Some people reserve them for a fancy bookplate.° I reserve them for fancy thinking. After I have finished reading the book and making my personal index on the back end-papers, I turn to the front and try to outline the book, not page by page, or point by point (I've already done that at the back), but as an integrated structure, with a basic unity and an order of parts. This outline is, to me, the measure of my understanding of the work.

**°bookplate**
a label placed in a book, with the owner's name

17    If you're a die-hard anti-book-marker, you may object that the margins, the space between the lines, and the end-papers don't give you room enough. All right. How about using a scratch pad slightly smaller than the page-size of the book—so that the edges of the sheets won't protrude? Make your index, outlines, and even your notes on the pad, and then insert these sheets permanently inside the front and back covers of the book.

18    Or, you may say that this business of marking books is going to slow up your reading. It probably will. That's one of the reasons for doing it. Most of us have been taken in by the notion that the speed of reading is a measure of our intelligence. There is no such thing as the right speed for intelligent reading. Some things should be read quickly and effortlessly, and some should be read slowly and even laboriously. The sign of intelligence in reading is in the ability to read different things differently according to their worth. In the case of good books, the point is not to see how many of them you can get through, but rather how many can get through you—how many you can make your own. A few friends are better than a thousand acquaintances. If this be your aim, as it should be, you will not be impatient if it takes more time and effort to read a great book than it does a newspaper.

19    You may have one final objection to marking books. You can't lend them to your friends because nobody else can read them without being distracted by your notes. Furthermore, you won't want to lend them because a marked copy is a kind of intellectual diary, and lending it is almost like giving your mind away.

**°Plutarch's Lives**
famous biography of people from the ancient world

**°The Federalist Papers**
a series of articles published in 1787 urging the ratification of the U.S. Constitution

20    If your friend wishes to read your *Plutarch's Lives*,° *Shakespeare*, or *The Federalist Papers*,° tell him gently but firmly to buy a copy. You will lend him your car or your coat—but your books are as much a part of you as your head or your heart.

# Questions for Critical Thinking

1. Mortimer Adler begins his essay by quite clearly saying he will try to persuade us that we should mark our books when we read. This, of course, means he is writing an argument. Yet the title is the typical title of a process analysis essay. Scan the essay to find where he gets to the process part of the essay. What paragraphs tell us how to mark a book?

2.   Where in the essay does Mortimer Adler use classification?

3.   Mortimer Adler uses a simile to make clear what he thinks a book is like. What is the simile? Explain the simile in your own words.

4.   How would you define "active reading" using Mortimer Adler's viewpoint?

5.   Mortimer Adler begins by making some disclaimer about marking up books. What are the cases in which a book should not be marked?

6.   In paragraph 9, what are the three transitional words?

7.   According to paragraph 12, what is the relationship between writing and memory?

8.   In paragraph 14, Mortimer Adler claims that the reader or learner is not an "empty receptacle." Explain what he means by this.

## Writing in Response

1.   Our culture places a great deal of emphasis on owning things: fancy cars, beautiful jewelry, name-brand clothes. Mortimer Adler has a very different attitude about who owns a book. Explore his idea and expand it to look at other things. Who owns a college degree? Who owns a piece of property?

2.   Reread this essay. Using Mortimer Adler's advice, mark his essay.

3.   Using Mortimer Adler's ideas, write a guide for college students giving them advice on how to read a chapter in a textbook that they will be tested on.

4.   Write an essay about your own reading habits or study habits. What is the process you follow when you do homework or study for an exam?

5.   How important is it to have books in your home? Write an essay in which you give advice to someone how to begin collecting books for a home library.

# NEAT PEOPLE VS. SLOPPY PEOPLE

## Suzanne Britt

Sometimes we learn the most about ourselves when our shortcomings are pointed out in a humorous way. The author of the following essay does just this, as she divides the human population into two basic groups. Suzanne Britt teaches English literature and writing at Meredith College in Raleigh, North Carolina. Her writing has been widely published: her essay and articles have appeared in such periodicals as *Newsweek* and the *New York Times,* and her books have been well received by readers of popular fiction and by students working in college writing classrooms. As you read the following essay, decide which of the two groups described by the author is the better one for you—or which group is the one you would like to join.

1    I've finally figured out the difference between neat people and sloppy people. The distinction is, as always, moral. Neat people are lazier and meaner than sloppy people.

2    Sloppy people, you see, are not really sloppy. Their sloppiness is merely the unfortunate consequence of their extreme moral rectitude.° Sloppy people carry in their mind's eye a heavenly vision, a precise plan, that is so stupendous, so perfect, it can't be achieved in this world or the next.

°**rectitude**
correctness

3    Sloppy people live in Never-Never Land. Someday is their *métier.*° Someday they are planning to alphabetize all their books and set up home catalogues. Someday they will go through their wardrobes and mark certain items for tentative mending and certain items for passing on to relatives of similar shape and size. Someday sloppy people will make family scrapbooks into which they will put newspaper clippings, postcards, locks of hair, and the dried corsage from their senior prom. Someday they will file everything on the surface of their desks, including the cash receipts from coffee purchases at the snack shop. Someday they will sit down and read all the back issues of *The New Yorker.*

°**métier**
French for "a person's specialty"

4    For all these noble reasons and more, sloppy people never get neat. They aim too high and wide. They save everything, planning someday to file, order, and straighten out the world. But while these ambitious plans take clearer and clearer shape in their heads, the books spill from the shelves onto the floor, the clothes pile up in the hamper and closet, the family mementos accumulate in every drawer, the surface of the desk is buried under mounds of paper and the unread magazines threaten to reach the ceiling.

5    Sloppy people can't bear to part with anything. They give loving attention to every detail. When sloppy people say they're going to tackle the surface of the desk, they really mean it. Not a paper will go unturned; not a rubber band will go unboxed. Four hours or two weeks into the excavation, the desk looks exactly the same, primarily because the sloppy person is meticulously creating new piles of papers with new headings and scrupulously stopping to read all the old

book catalogs before he throws them away. A neat person would just bulldoze the desk.

°*cavalier*

very informal and offhand

6      Neat people are bums and clods at heart. They have cavalier° attitudes toward possessions, including family heirlooms. Everything is just another dust-catcher to them. If anything collects dust, it's got to go and that's that. Neat people will toy with the idea of throwing the children out of the house just to cut down on the clutter.

7      Neat people don't care about process. They like results. What they want to do is get the whole thing over with so they can sit down and watch the rasslin' on TV. Neat people operate on two unvarying principles: Never handle any item twice, and throw everything away.

8      The only thing messy in a neat person's house is the trash can. The minute something comes to a neat person's hand, he will look at it, try to decide if it has immediate use and, finding none, throw it in the trash.

9      Neat people are especially vicious with mail. They never go through their mail unless they are standing directly over a trash can. If the trash can is beside the mailbox, even better. All ads, catalogs, pleas for charitable contributions, church bulletins and money-saving coupons go straight into the trash can without being opened. All letters from home, postcards from Europe, bills and paychecks are opened, immediately responded to, then dropped in the trash can. Neat people keep their receipts only for tax purposes. That's it. No sentimental salvaging of birthday cards or the last letter a dying relative ever wrote. Into the trash it goes.

10     Neat people place neatness above everything, even economics. They are incredibly wasteful. Neat people throw away several toys every time they walk through the den. I knew a neat person once who threw away a perfectly good dish drainer because it had mold on it. The drainer was too much trouble to wash. And neat people sell their furniture when they move. They will sell a La-Z-Boy recliner while you are reclining in it.

11     Neat people are no good to borrow from. Neat people buy everything in expensive little single portions. They get their flour and sugar in two-pound bags. They wouldn't consider clipping a coupon, saving a leftover, reusing plastic non-dairy whipped cream containers or rinsing off tin foil and draping it over the unmoldy dish drainer. You can never borrow a neat person's newspaper to see what's playing at the movies. Neat people have the paper all wadded up and in the trash by 7:05 A.M.

12     Neat people cut a clean swath through the organic as well as the inorganic world. People, animals, and things are all one to them. They are so insensitive. After they've finished with the pantry, the medicine cabinet, and the attic, they will throw out the red geranium (too many leaves), sell the dog (too many fleas), and send the children off to boarding school (too many scuffmarks on the hardwood floors).

## Questions for Critical Thinking

1.  At what point in your reading of the essay did you become aware that this was a humorous piece of writing?

2.  What explanation does Suzanne Britt give for a sloppy person's behavior? Do you agree with her?

3.  In paragraph 3, what are the examples the writer lists when she presents the projects a sloppy person plans to do? Do these plans seem admirable to you?

4.  Does the author use the block method or the point-by-point method to contrast sloppy people with neat people?

5.  One of the reasons Suzanne Britt's writing is so appreciated is that readers recognize themselves in her essays. In paragraph 11, the author tells us that "neat people are no good to borrow from." What makes her supporting statements for this comment humorous?

6.  Review the concluding paragraph of the essay. Do you know anyone who acts in the ways listed in that paragraph? By the time you have finished the essay, have you come to your own conclusion as to which category the writer herself belongs to?

## Writing in Response

1.  Write an essay that takes the opposite viewpoint from the one given by Suzanne Britt. Defend the neat person and criticize the sloppy person.

2.  Describe two people you know who have very different approaches to being neat and organized. Explain what it is like to be with each of them.

3.  How would you describe the household in which you grew up? In what ways were your parents very organized? In what areas were they disorganized? What are the problems of growing up in a household that is extreme in one way or another?

4.  Write an essay in which you give advice to a young couple setting up a household. How would you advise them on being neat and organized?

5.  Suzanne Britt claims that sloppy people cannot part with anything. Write an essay in which you analyze your own attitude about possessions. What are the things you have a hard time parting with? What things do you especially like to collect and save?

# DREAM HOUSES

## Tenaya Darlington

When the author's parents move into a new house, she is confronted with the fact that although it is her parents' "dream house," it does not feel at all like home.

°**shag**
a rug with long fibers

1   The house I grew up in had one bathroom, a tub in it. No shower. The rooms were small, more like clubhouses than rooms, and the basement, which was divided into my father's music room on one side and our playroom on the other, had been decorated by the previous owners who were local football fans. Hence the red and yellow shag.° It was a make-do house. A small ranch-style with a high-sloping driveway on a corner lot. Every year there was talk of putting in a shower, taking down the foil wallpaper over the stove, getting rid of that awful paneling downstairs, and fixing the part of the ceiling that buckled. But every year, the same reply from my parents: *we're waiting for our dream house, we'll probably move next year.*

2   Three years ago, my parents finally moved. After twenty, yes, twenty temporary years, the perfect house in the woods came onto the market: a modern-looking flat-roof with wood siding stained a cool gray. Inside, the back wall is all glass and there are skylights. A huge stone fireplace pipes warmth into the heating ducts to warm the whole house. When my brother and I visit during the holidays we sleep in large rooms that overlook a wooded ravine, snow falling against timber, and somewhere in the distance, a barred owl croons for a matching call. It's the sort of house people smoke pipes in and writers write in. The low-slung pine beams on the upper floor make it feel less like a house real people live in and more like a ski lodge, a retreat for dreamers. And so we watch our parents float in front of the window, my mother in her wool clogs, my father in his moccasins, hands wrapped around chunky mugs of coffee. It feels like a commercial. When my brother and I swap hellos going in and out of the bathroom (with its massager shower and all-white matchingness), I can't help but think of Best Western.

3   In the afternoons at the dream house, we do dream things: walk down the ravine to where there is a river with a small island, find a swatch of fox fur on the path, climb a fallen tree that looks like a reclining woman (two big branches like her legs, two big knots like her breasts). My brother is in college now and I am several years out, yet we act like kids in those woods, running through the trees, skipping rocks, delighting in a nest or a set of deer prints, and dragging home a huge sheet of bark to plant in front of the house like a flag. We live on hot chocolate and hard cookies sent to us by an aunt in Switzerland, and in the evening, at my mother's insistence, we roast hot dogs and marshmallows in front of the fire and eat lying down.

4   My mother gets a little teary during these visits. *It's a shame,* she'll say, shaking her head, *that we didn't live here when you were children. Think how differently you'd look back on your childhood.* What she doesn't know is this: sometimes at night, my brother and I will go for a drive. We'll drive across town, sleet pressing itself against the windshield and the radio tuned to some eighties station, and we'll park in front of our old house. It's in a neighborhood of other small houses like it where, at one time, we knew all the families. Mrs. Berry in

°**divinity**
a soft, white candy
usually containing nuts

the pale blue house who used to give us divinity°; the Clarks in the white colonial with the playhouse and fish pond; the Phillips in the vanilla two-story who threw birthday parties for their bulldogs; the Zimmermans across from them who took us arrowhead-hunting on rainy Saturdays; Mr. Cook, diagonally, who helped my father on the car and had a cat lovingly named "Cat."

5      Our old house looks at us like a dejected pet in a pound. It knows we are sitting outside in the car, sharing a bag of Raisinets from the glove compartment. Lights are on in two windows, like eyes—figures passing in the hallway like our own shadows still lingering, still fighting over who gets to take the first bath. Our breath freezes like blank captions in a cartoon of ourselves, and I think of the one bathroom with the ledge where I used to sit and paint my toes. My mother would be taking a bubble bath, my father reading *Stereo Review* on his throne, my brother brushing his teeth and making faces at himself in the mirror while the dog slept on a pile of towels. The whole family crowded in one bathroom, its door never closed. It was the center of everything, the stage with the tubside seating where we watched my mother cut her hair, my father trim his beard. Aside from going to the mall two blocks east, it was the social hub. I can't imagine us like that now, hanging out, sharing gossip in one of the dream bathrooms with its three-way mirrors, fader switches, and cold floors.

6      My brother and I drive back across town, a trail of tire tracks in the snow connecting the old house with the new. *Remember the dent in the door from your moon boot? Remember the mark on the ceiling above the oven that we always thought was a trap door? Remember the space under the stairs where we hoarded Flintstones vitamins and ate them like candy?* When we return, the house is dark, our parents asleep at their end of the house. We pat the walls, hunting for a light switch.

°**grandiose**
great in scope or intent

°**combs (honeycombs)**
waxy structures
composed of walled
cells or rooms made by
honeybees for storing
honey and larvae

°**pervade**
to completely fill

7      The truth about dream houses, especially dream houses out in the woods that are purchased late in life, is that they are like empty beehives, grandiose° combs° with elaborate compartments but without the dreams to fill them. When I go home to visit, I enjoy the beautiful view, the way the seasons pervade° the living room—the changing leaves like changing wallpaper—and I love that raccoons come to the window in the den at night and look in, but they are no substitute for having neighbors. And when my brother and I leave after the holidays are over, I envision my parents rattling around in a house as empty as it is beautiful. I see them spread out in distant corners, my father downstairs in his office, my mother upstairs at her desk, both of them looking out through binoculars at a pheasant or a grouse and seeing only snowflakes magnified many times to look like moths. And beyond that: nothing, and more nothing, and beyond that, perhaps a dream, or the footprints of a dream leading to another house.

## Questions for Critical Thinking

1. In her essay, the author compares the bathrooms of the two houses (paragraphs 1 and 5) to discuss some larger truths about her family. Why does she focus on that room to illustrate her points?

2. In paragraph 2, we discover clues as to the author's attitude toward her parents' new house. Review the paragraph and underline those words and phrases that reveal the author's attitudes.

3. A place some people might consider a perfect home may be less than satisfactory to other people. Compare those aspects of a house that matter to the parents in this essay with those aspects that matter to the children.

4. The writer pays a good deal of attention to childhood memories and how we look back on our experiences during those years. Think back to your own childhood. What are some of the strongest memories you have from childhood?

## Writing in Response

1. What room was "the center of everything" in the home where you grew up? Write an essay in which you describe this memorable room and what took place there during your childhood years.

2. Recall a home you lived in as a child or one you visited often, and compare it with the home you live in now.

3. What is your own dream house like? Where is it located? How is it furnished? With whom would you share it?

4. At the conclusion of her essay, the writer emphasizes that, no matter how perfect a place might be to live, there is "no substitute for having neighbors." To what extent do neighbors make up an important part of the quality of life where you live? To what extent do you depend on your neighbors?

5. When people dream of material possessions—anything from a pair of sneakers to a car or a house—they often give these items an emotional significance. Write about a possession that holds emotional significance for you. Or describe a process you went through in attaining something you had wanted for a long time. Was it all you had hoped for?

# WHY MARRIAGES FAIL

## Anne Roiphe

Anne Roiphe is noted for her exploration of women's search for personal identity. Themes running through her fiction and nonfiction include feminism, marriage, family, and cultural identity. One commentator has referred to her writing as a "thoughtful and often provocative" analysis of history and of the forces that shape modern culture and society. Anne Roiphe's best-known novel is *Up the Sandbox!* She has also contributed to such magazines as *Redbook* and *Family Circle.* In the following essay, the writer examines one of the striking facts of our modern society, that is, the large number of marriages ending in divorce. As she explores this topic, we notice two impressive aspects of her writing: an analysis that is always clear and convincing, and a voice that is reasonable and calm.

**°obsolete**
no longer used

1    These days so many marriages end in divorce that our most sacred vows no longer ring with truth. "Happily ever after" and "Till death do us part" are expressions that seem on the way to becoming obsolete.° Why has it become so hard for couples to stay together? What goes wrong? What has happened to us that close to one-half of all marriages are destined for the divorce courts? How could we have created a society in which 42 percent of our children will grow up in single-parent homes? If statistics could only measure loneliness, regret, pain, loss of self-confidence and fear of the future, the numbers would be beyond quantifying.°

**°quantifying**
expressing an exact amount

2    Even though each broken marriage is unique, we can still find the common perils, the common causes for marital despair. Each marriage has crisis points and each marriage tests endurance, the capacity for both intimacy and change. Outside pressures such as job loss, illness, infertility,° trouble with a child, care of aging parents and all the other plagues of life hit marriage the way hurricanes blast our shores. Some marriages survive these storms and others don't. Marriages fail, however, not simply because of the outside weather but because the inner climate becomes too hot or too cold, too turbulent or too stupefying.°

**°infertility**
inability to conceive a child

**°stupefying**
amazing; astonishing

3    When we look at how we choose our partners and what expectations exist at the tender beginnings of romance, some of the reasons for disaster become quite clear. We all select with unconscious accuracy a mate who will recreate with us the emotional patterns of our first homes. Dr. Carl A. Whitaker, a marital therapist and emeritus° professor of psychiatry at the University of Wisconsin, explains, "From early childhood on, each of us carried models for marriage, femininity, masculinity, motherhood, fatherhood and all the other family roles." Each of us falls in love with a mate who has qualities of our parents, who will help us discover both the psychological happiness and miseries of our past lives. We may think we have found a man unlike Dad, but then he turns to drink or drugs, or loses his job over and over again or sits silently in front of the T.V. just the way Dad did. A man may choose a woman who doesn't like kids just like his mother or who gambles away the family life savings just like his mother. Or he may choose a slender wife who seems unlike his obese mother but then turns out to have other addictions that destroy mutual happiness.

**°emeritus**
retired keeping an honorary title

**°compulsively**
unable to resist acting

**°yearning**
a deep desire

4    A man and a woman bring to their marriage bed a blended concoction of conscious and unconscious memories of their parents' lives together. The human way is to compulsively° repeat and recreate the patterns of the past. Sigmund Freud so well described the unhappy design that many of us get trapped in: the unmet needs of childhood, the angry feelings left over from frustrations long ago, the limits of trust and the recurrence of old fears. Once an individual senses this entrapment, there may follow a yearning° to escape, and the result could be a broken, splintered marriage.

5    Of course people can overcome the habits and attitudes that developed in childhood. We all have hidden strengths and amazing capacities for growth and creative change. Change, however, requires work—observing your part in a rotten pattern, bringing difficulties out into the open—and work runs counter to the basic myth of marriage: "When I wed this person all my problems will be over. I will have achieved success and I will become the center of life for this other person and this person will be my center, and we will mean everything to each other forever." This myth, which every marriage relies on, is soon exposed. The coming of children, the pulls and tugs of their demands on affection and time, place considerable strain on that basic myth of meaning everything to each other, of merging together and solving all of life's problems.

6    Concern and tension about money take each partner away from the other. Obligations to demanding parents or still-depended-upon parents create further strain. Couples today must also deal with all the cultural changes brought on in recent years by the women's movement and the sexual revolution. The altering of roles and the shifting of responsibilities have been extremely trying for many marriages.

**°erode**
to diminish; to make disappear

**°euphoric**
extremely happy

7    These and other realities of life erode° the visions of marital bliss the way sandstorms eat at rock and the ocean nibbles away at the dunes. Those euphoric,° grand feelings that accompany romantic love are really self-delusions, self-hypnotic dreams that enable us to forge a relationship. Real life, failure at work, disappointments, exhaustion, bad smells, bad colds and hard times all puncture the dream and leave us stranded with our mate, with our childhood patterns pushing us this way and that, with our unfulfilled expectations.

8    The struggle to survive in marriage requires adaptability, flexibility, genuine love and kindness and an imagination strong enough to feel what the other is feeling. Many marriages fall apart because either partner cannot imagine what the other wants or cannot communicate what he or she needs or feels. Anger builds until it erupts into a volcanic burst that buries the marriage in ash.

9    It is not hard to see, therefore, how essential communication is for a good marriage. A man and a woman must be able to tell each other how they feel and why they feel the way they do; otherwise they will impose on each other roles and actions that lead to further unhappiness. In some cases, the communication patterns of childhood—of not talking, of talking too much, of not listening, of distrust and anger, of withdrawal—spill into the marriage and prevent a healthy exchange of thoughts and feelings. The answer is to set up new patterns of communication and intimacy.

10   At the same time, however, we must see each other as individuals. "To achieve a balance between separateness and closeness is one of the major psychological tasks of all human beings at every stage of life," says Dr. Stuart Bartle, a psychiatrist at the New York University Medical Center.

11      If we sense from our mate a need for too much intimacy, we tend to push him or her away, fearing that we may lose our identities in the merging of marriage. One partner may suffocate the other partner in a childlike dependency.

**°clings**
holds on tightly

12      A good marriage means growing as a couple but also growing as individuals. This isn't easy. Richard gives up his interest in carpentry because his wife, Helen, is jealous of the time he spends away from her. Karen quits her choir group because her husband dislikes the friends she makes there. Each pair clings° to each other and are angry with each other as life closes in on them. This kind of marital balance is easily thrown as one or the other pulls away and divorce follows.

13      Sometimes people pretend that a new partner will solve the old problems. Most often extramarital sex destroys a marriage because it allows an artificial split between the good and the bad—the good is projected on the new partner and the bad is dumped on the head of the old. Dishonesty, hiding and cheating create walls between men and women. Infidelity is just a symptom of trouble. It is a symbolic complaint, a weapon of revenge, as well as an unraveler of closeness. Infidelity is often that proverbial° last straw that sinks the camel to the ground.

**°proverbial**
a saying that expresses a basic truth

14      All right—marriage has always been difficult. Why then are we seeing so many divorces at this time? Yes, our modern social fabric is thin, and yes the permissiveness of society has created unrealistic expectations and thrown the family into chaos. But divorce is so common because people today are unwilling to exercise the self-discipline that marriage requires. They expect easy joy, like the entertainment on TV, the thrill of a good party.

15      Marriage takes some kind of sacrifice, not dreadful self-sacrifice of the soul, but some level of compromise. Some of one's fantasies, some of one's legitimate desires have to be given up for the value of the marriage itself. "While all marital partners feel shackled at times, it is they who really choose to make the marital ties into confining chains or supporting bonds," says Dr. Whitaker. Marriage requires sexual, financial and emotional discipline. A man and a woman cannot follow every impulse, cannot allow themselves to stop growing or changing.

**°devastation**
shock; destruction

16      Divorce is not an evil act. Sometimes it provides salvation for people who have grown helplessly apart or were frozen in patterns of pain or mutual unhappiness. Divorce can be, despite its initial devastation,° like the first cut of the surgeon's knife, a step toward new health and a good life. On the other hand, if the partners can stay past the breaking up of the romantic myths into the development of real love and intimacy, they have achieved a work as amazing as the greatest cathedrals of the world. Marriages that do not fail but improve, that persist despite imperfections, are not only rare these days but offer a wondrous shelter in which the face of our mutual humanity can safely show itself.

## Questions for Critical Thinking

1.  When an essay is concerned with answering the question why, we know the method of development is cause and effect. There are many ways to write an introductory paragraph; describe how Anne Roiphe chose to introduce her topic.

2.  Certain transitional words in a piece of writing are used to help the reader understand how one idea connects to another. In paragraph 2, find two words that signal contrast, two words that signal cause, and one expression that signals to us that examples will follow.

3. Find at least two examples of the author's use of simile or metaphor.

4. Mark any place in the essay where the author uses an authority to support a point.

5. In paragraph 3, Anne Roiphe claims that "Each of us falls in love with a mate who has the qualities of our parents." Do you agree or disagree with this claim? Do you have any counterevidence?

6. Summarize this essay by making a list of reasons why marriages fail, according to Anne Roiphe.

# Writing in Response

1. Anne Roiphe provides a list of major problems that often occur in a person's life: loss of a job, serious illness, infertility, trouble with a child, or caring for an aging parent. Write an essay discussing how the occurrence of even one of these events can affect many of the relationships in a person's life.

2. Many couples go to therapists hoping to work out their problems. Write an essay in which you discuss the benefits of having a third person listen to a couple explaining their problems.

3. In your view, does going through hard times help or hurt a person's ability to sustain relationships? Write an essay answering this question by using your own experience and observations.

4. Many people believe that if they make a change (such as getting married, having a child, moving to another place) they will fix something that is broken in their lives. Write an essay in which you discuss the extent to which a major change can be a benefit for a person, and to what extent making a change will not really solve any of that person's problems.

5. The old expression "Money comes between friends" can also be applied to family relationships. Write an essay in which you discuss how issues of money can have negative effects on people's relationships. How can money issues create several kinds of problems in people's lives?

## REQUIEM° FOR THE CHAMP

**June Jordan**

°**requiem**
a composition (musical or literary) for the dead

Many sports figures become heroes, but when one of these heroes falls from grace, a feeling of disillusionment inevitably follows. In the following essay, the late African American poet, essayist, and professor June Jordan reflects on the life and career of one of these heroes, the boxer Mike Tyson. In the process of examining the tragedy of this fighter, who suffered his greatest defeat outside the ring, the writer makes some harsh observations, and even harsher judgments, on American society.

1.    Mike Tyson comes from Brooklyn. And so do I. Where he grew up was about a twenty-minute bus ride from my house. I always thought his neighborhood looked like a war zone. It reminded me of Berlin—immediately after World War II. I had never seen Berlin except for black-and-white photos in *Life* magazine, but that was bad enough: Rubble. Barren. Blasted. Everywhere you turned your eyes recoiled from the jagged edges of an office building or a cathedral, shattered, or the tops of apartment houses torn off, and nothing alive even intimated,° anywhere. I used to think, "This is what it means to fight and really win or really lose. War means you hurt somebody, or something, until there's nothing soft or sensible left."

°**intimated**
hinted at

2    For sure I never had a boyfriend who came out of Mike Tyson's territory. Yes, I enjoyed my share of tough guys and/or gang members who walked and talked and fought and loved in quintessential° Brooklyn ways: cool, tough, and deadly serious. But there was a code as rigid and as romantic as anything that ever made the pages of traditional English literature. A guy would beat up another guy or, if appropriate, he'd kill him. But a guy talked different to a girl. A guy made other guys clean up their language around "his girl." A guy brought ribbons and candies and earrings and tulips to a girl. He took care of her. He walked her home. And if he got serious about that girl, and even if she was only twelve years old, then she became his "lady." And woe betide any other guy stupid enough to disrespect that particular young Black female.

°**quintessential**
the most typical

3    But none of the boys—none of the young men—none of the young Black male inhabitants of my universe and my heart ever came from Mike Tyson's streets or avenues. We didn't live someplace fancy or middle-class, but at least there were ten-cent gardens, front and back, and coin Laundromats, and grocery stores, and soda parlors, and barber shops, and Holy Roller churchfronts, and chicken shacks, and dry cleaners, and bars-and-grills, and a takeout Chinese restaurant, and all of that usable detail that does not survive a war. That kind of seasonal green turf and daily-life supporting pattern of establishments to meet your needs did not exist inside the gelid° urban cemetery where Mike Tyson learned what he thought he needed to know.

°**gelid**
very cold or icy

4    I remember when the City of New York decided to construct a senior housing project there, in the childhood world of former heavyweight boxing champion Mike Tyson. I remember wondering, "Where in the hell will those old people have to go in order to find food? And how will they get there?"

°**diadems**
crowns

5    I'm talking godforsaken. And much of living in Brooklyn was like that. But then it might rain or it might snow and, for example, I could look at the rain forcing forsythia into bloom or watch how snowflakes can tease bare tree limbs into temporary blossoms of snow dissolving into diadems° of sunlight. And what did Mike Tyson ever see besides brick walls and garbage in the gutter and disintegrating concrete steps and boarded-up windows and broken car parts blocking the sidewalk and men, bitter, with their hands in their pockets, and women, bitter, with their heads down and their eyes almost closed?

6    In his neighborhood, where could you buy ribbons for a girl, or tulips?

°**intimidating**
making afraid

°**adversaries**
enemies

7    Mike Tyson comes from Brooklyn. And so do I. In the big picture of America, I never had much going for me. And he had less. I only learned, last year, that I can stop whatever violence starts with me. I only learned, last year, that love is infinitely more interesting, and more exciting, and more powerful, than really winning or really losing a fight. I only learned, last year, that all war leads to death and that all love leads you away from death. I am more than twice Mike Tyson's age. And I'm not stupid. Or slow. But I'm Black. And I come from Brooklyn. And I grew up fighting. And I grew up and I got out of Brooklyn because I got pretty good at fighting. And winning. Or else, intimidating° my would-be adversaries° with my fists, my feet, and my mouth. And I never wanted to fight. I never wanted anybody to hit me. And I never wanted to hit anybody. But the bell would ring at the end of another dumb day in school and I'd head out with dread and a nervous sweat because I knew some jackass more or less my age and more or less my height would be waiting for me because she or he had nothing better to do than to wait for me and hope to kick my butt or tear up my books or break my pencils or pull hair out of my head.

8    This is the meaning of poverty: when you have nothing better to do than to hate somebody who, just exactly like yourself, has nothing better to do than to pick on you instead of trying to figure out how come there's nothing better to do. How come there's no gym/no swimming pool/no dirt track/no soccer field/no ice-skating rink/no bike/no bike path/no tennis courts/no language arts workshop/no computer science center/no band practice/no choir rehearsal/no music lessons/no basketball or baseball team? How come neither one of you has his or her own room in a house where you can hang out and dance and make out or get on the telephone or eat and drink up everything in the kitchen that can move? How come nobody on your block and nobody in your class has any of these things?

9    I'm Black. Mike Tyson is Black. And neither one of us was ever supposed to win anything more than a fight between the two of us. And if you check out the mass-media material on "us," and if you check out the emergency-room reports on "us," you might well believe we're losing the fight to be more than our enemies have decreed. Our enemies would deprive us of everything except each other: hungry and furious and drug-addicted and rejected and ever convinced we can never be beautiful or right or true or different from the beggarly monsters our enemies envision and insist upon, and how should we then stand, Black man and Black woman, face to face?

10   Way back when I was born, Richard Wright had just published *Native Son* and, thereby, introduced white America to the monstrous product of its racist hatred.

11    Poverty does not beautify. Poverty does not teach generosity or allow for sucker attributes of tenderness and restraint. In white America, hatred of Black-folks has imposed horrible poverty upon us.

12    And so, back in the thirties, Richard Wright's Native Son, Bigger Thomas, did what he thought he had to do: he hideously murdered a white woman and he viciously murdered his Black girlfriend in what he conceived° as self-defense. He did not perceive° any options to these psychopathic,° horrifying deeds. I do not believe he, Bigger Thomas, had any other choices open to him. Not to him, he who was meant to die like the rat he, Bigger Thomas, cornered and smashed to death in his mother's beggarly clean space.

13    I never thought Bigger Thomas was okay. I never thought he should skate back into my, or anyone's community. But I did and I do think he is my brother. The choices available to us dehumanize.° And any single one of us, Black in this white country, we may be defeated, we may become dehumanized, by the monstrous hatred arrayed° against us and our needy dreams.

14    And so I write this requiem for Mike Tyson: international celebrity, millionaire, former heavyweight boxing champion of the world, a big-time winner, a big-time loser, an African-American male in his twenties, and, now, a convicted rapist.

15    Do I believe he is guilty of rape?

16    Yes I do.

17    And what would I propose as appropriate punishment?

18    Whatever will force him to fear the justice of exact retribution,° and whatever will force him, for the rest of his damned life, to regret and to detest the fact that he defiled,° he subjugated,° and he wounded somebody helpless to his power.

19    And do I therefore rejoice in the jury's finding?

20    I do not.

21    Well, would I like to see Mike Tyson a free man again?

22    He was never free!

23    And I do not excuse or condone° or forget or minimize or forgive the crime of his violation of the young Black woman he raped!

24    But did anybody ever tell Mike Tyson that you talk different to a girl? Where would he learn that? Would he learn that from U.S. Senator Ted Kennedy? Or from hotshot/scot-free movie director Roman Polanski?° Or from rap recording star Ice Cube? Or from Ronald Reagan and the Grenada escapade?° Or from George Bush in Panama? Or from George Bush and Colin Powell in the Persian Gulf? Or from the military hero flyboys who returned from bombing the shit out of civilian cities in Iraq and then said, laughing and proud, on international TV: "All I need, now, is a woman"? Or from the hundreds of thousands of American football fans? Or from the millions of Americans who would, if they could, pay surrealistic° amounts of money just to witness, up close, somebody like Mike Tyson beat the brains out of somebody?

---

**°conceived**
imagined

**°perceive**
gain understanding

**°psychopathic**
perverted or criminal

**°dehumanize**
deprive of dignity

**°arrayed**
set

**°retribution**
appropriate punishment

**°defiled**
ruined or made unclean

**°subjugated**
conquered or controlled

**°condone**
to forgive or overlook

**°Roman Polanski**
indicted for rape
of a minor

**°Granada escapade**
refers to the 1983 United
States invasion of the
Caribbean island

**°surrealistic**
fantastic; unreal;
dreamlike

**°citadel**
a fortress or other place
of control

**°stigma**
a mark of disgrace

**°a priori**
existing from the start
and based on belief, not
fact

**°refurbish**
to make clean and fresh

**°nurture**
to help grow and
develop

25      And what could which university teach Mike Tyson about the difference between violence and love? Is there any citadel° of higher education in the country that does not pay its football coach at least three times as much as the chancellor and six times as much as its professors and ten times as much as its social and psychological counselors?

26      In this America where Mike Tyson and I live together and bitterly, bitterly, apart, I say he became what he felt. He felt the stigma° of a priori° hatred and intentional poverty. He was given the choice of violence or violence: the violence of defeat or the violence of victory. Who would pay him to rehabilitate inner-city housing or to refurbish° a bridge? Who would pay him what to study the facts of our collective history? Who would pay him what to plant and nurture° the trees of a forest? And who will write and who will play the songs that tell a guy like Mike Tyson how to talk to a girl?

27      What was America willing to love about Mike Tyson? Or any Black man? Or any man's man?

28      Tyson's neighborhood and my own have become the same no-win battleground. And he has fallen there. And I do not rejoice. I do not.

## Questions for Critical Thinking

1. In paragraph 1, June Jordan compares the neighborhood of Mike Tyson's childhood with that of Berlin after World War II. What three words does she use that she wants us to remember? How does she make these three words stand out?

2. In paragraph 2, the author contrasts her own neighborhood in Brooklyn with Tyson's neighborhood. What are the differences?

3. What is June Jordan's definition of poverty? Do you believe her definition is correct?

4. In paragraph 8, June Jordan refers to people who occupy their time by fighting with each other, "instead of trying to figure out how come there's nothing better to do." What are the results when people struggle against each other instead of struggling against their negative circumstances?

5. In paragraph 22, the writer states that Mike Tyson was never free. What does she mean?

6. In paragraph 7, what does June Jordan tell us she has learned during the past year?

7. What should be the social responsibility of a government toward its citizens who are struggling with poverty and lack of opportunity? What mistakes were made by government agencies in the past and continue to be made even now?

## Writing in Response

1. Compare and contrast two neighborhoods with which you are familiar. How are they alike? How are they different? How do the physical and social environments of these places play a role in how the people behave?

2. June Jordan points out the historical forces that have conspired against her people. What are these forces? Discuss these forces and the extent to which they continue to influence the direction of our society.

3. Write an essay in which you discuss the social conditions that lead women to be victimized by men.

4. Write an essay in which you propose how children could be better protected from destructive or threatening forces in our society today.

5. How can two people from similar backgrounds turn out so differently?

# WHAT IS THIS THING CALLED FAMILY?

## Lee Herrick

Poet Lee Herrick has been published in many literary journals including *Berkeley Poetry Review, Hawaii Pacific Review,* and the *Willow Review*. In 2000 he was nominated for a prestigious Pushcart Prize. Currently teaching at Fresno City College, he is the founding editor of the literary magazine called *In the Grove*. In the following essay, the poet explores the definition of *family*. He has experienced the special issues of living in a multi-cultural family. Born in South Korea in 1970, he was adopted at less than a year old and raised in California. His perspective may offer insight to all of us about what it means to be part of a family.

**°perspective**
a mental outlook

**°disdain**
contempt

**°quirks**
odd mannerisms

**°sibling rivalry**
competition between brothers and sisters

**°taunting**
making insulting comments

**°wary**
on guard; cautious

**°inquisitive**
questioning

1     As a Korean adoptee raised by Caucasian parents, I have a unique perspective° on the notion of family. It is not defined by physical similarity. I look nothing like them. I am Asian and they are Caucasian, as is my sister (adopted as well, from Alameda). But the subtle similarities one acquires through family are inevitable—the sighs, the way one lifts her eyebrows in curiosity or disdain.° We joke about having each others' traits, but they are habits or quirks,° not the same shape of nose or chin.

2     My sister and I were raised in California's East Bay Area and later in the Central Valley. In the 1970's, the towns weren't as diverse as they are now. But we had great childhoods. We had a sibling rivalry° for the ages, but deep down there was a whole lot of love. I remember her defending me when racial slurs would come my way.

3     "He's Korean," Holly would say, when the other kids would tell me "Go back to where you came from, Chinaman." She would intervene and change the subject when I was asked irritating questions like "What *are* you?" and "How can *she* be your sister?" I think of my sister like a defender, a protector. I also now realize that as much as she was defending me, she was defending herself and her right as an adoptee to have a brother who looked like me.

4     I remember an incident when I came home from grade school one day, sniffling and trying to conceal my tears after a day of particularly aggressive taunting—the subject at hand was my "flat face." It was hurtful and brought me to tears on the long walk home after the bus dropped me off. But it was also very strange to me because I was raised in a Caucasian family, so the boy taunting° me looked like my cousins . . . why was he so mean? It was also confusing because I didn't have an Asian accent, nor did I speak Korean or any other Asian language. My favorite baseball team was the Oakland A's, my favorite player Reggie Jackson. I loved Star Wars, Batman, and eventually Atari—all things 70's. I felt normal (whatever that is). Many well-intentioned people also told me "you're so American!" or "you're not like other Asians I've met." To this day I am wary° of all these suspect declarations.

5     I walked in the front door, Phil Donahue's inquisitive° lisp coming from the television. My mother noticed I had been crying. She bent down like a baseball

catcher and took my face into her open hands, wiping my tears with her thumbs. "Oh, honey, what's *wrong*?" she asked.

6    I sniffed and wiped my nose with the back of my hand. "Nothing," I said.

7    "Honey, I'm your mom. You can tell me," she said.

8    "My face isn't flat, is it?" I asked, feeling the small mound of my nose on my face, proving it wasn't flat. I was still sniffling.

9    I can still remember the hurt look on her face, the sadness. I can't remember exactly what she said, but it was something about how some people are just ignorant and to let it "roll right off my back." I felt better that day, and time after time throughout my life as I encountered difficult times I would often repeat her mantra° in my head. She gave me something to use. Years later, as I was defining the term *idiot* in high school, acting out some of my anger, she would often be the one to spell out the conditions of my grounding. Of course, years later I came to appreciate the support (and discipline) she and my father gave me. Some things just take a while.

°**mantra**
a repeated verbal word
or phrase

10    My father is a quiet man. I think of him as the model for giving of yourself as much as you can. Once, when I was fifteen or sixteen, at the height of my selfish teen years, he asked me if I wanted to help him volunteer serving hot dogs at the local Peach Fair.

11    "Do I get paid?" I asked, clearly not hearing the word *volunteer*.

12    "No," he said. He left, no doubt wondering what kind of person I was becoming.

13    He is also the kindest, most soft-spoken, modest person I know. I have never heard him scream, not even when my sister and I were raising all kinds of hell as teenagers. Sure, he gets mad, but his calm demeanor° is a trait I have always admired (and probably never successfully emulated°).

°**demeanor**
the way a person
behaves

°**emulated**
imitated

14    Being a Korean adoptee has been wonderful but undoubtedly challenging. Anger, kindness, and forgiveness have all been a part of my life. To varying degrees I have to believe they are a part of all families. To say the least, being separated from one's birth mother is not easy to come to terms with, and it is complicated further by being in an interracial family. But that is what we are—a family.

15    I have come to believe that family goes far beyond a child's eyes looking like her mother and father's, or a child having the same mannerisms as her parents (which we do, in fact, have). It is more than a name or the number of bedrooms in a home. I have come to believe that family is about love and struggle and adapting. That there are many different types of family and that they evolve—2.5 kids and a white fence, single parent families, those involving incarceration,° illness (or a combination of all of these)—family is a wide term with plenty of room for interpretation.

°**incarceration**
imprisonment

16    Yes, I think about my birth parents from time to time, although I have not met them. But several years ago I returned to Seoul, the capital city where I was born. It felt like going home—no one staring at me because I was the only Asian in a room, eating barbecued squid and kimchi° from the street vendor, shopping in Lotte World and the Namdaemun Market, seeing the ancient temples and modern skyscrapers downtown.

°**kimchi**
a spicy Korean dish

17    But while it felt like home, it really wasn't. Home is about family, the people who will stand up for you and say "He's Korean." It is about people who comfort you and tell you that your face is not flat. It is *not* about perfection; it is about trying to be a good person (I realize this now when I am volunteering). It is about getting opportunities and support, discipline and the chance to fail and be responsible. No family member, no matter how present or absent, fills just one role. 'My sister is the protector but also an inspiration for kindness. My mother is a support system but also the creative force. My father is a role model but also a support system. They are all hilarious and have great work ethics. I can only hope just an ounce of this rubbed off on me.

18    I still find it interesting when children look just like their parents. Of course biology dictates that likelihood, but not in my family. It is second nature that we don't look the same. Currently, my wife (part German-Irish, part Filipina) and I are adopting. We will soon welcome our daughter into our lives (and vice-versa), aware of some of the many challenges of an international adoption, the beauty and hard work involved in family, and a foundation of unconditional love from which we should always begin.

## Questions for Critical Thinking

1.    Underline the thesis. What is the topic? What is the controlling idea?

2.    What paragraph gives the author's clearest definition of the term *family*?

3.    The author provides several anecdotes, each one portraying the character of a different member of his family. Find each anecdote in the essay and explain how the anecdote reveals something important about that family member. How has that person influenced Lee Herrick's life?

4.    Throughout the essay, the writer reports various examples of the ignorance shown by others when it comes to his racial background. Review the essay and trace these examples of ignorant thinking. In your view, which one strikes you as the worst?

5.    In paragraph 9, the author tells us how words from his mother helped him get through a hard time, and in fact became a mantra that helped him overcome some difficult experiences he had to endure later in life. What is a *mantra* and what are some examples of mantras that can be helpful in people's lives?

## Writing in Response

1.    What is your own definition of *family*? Give several examples of families you have known. In your opinion, what groupings could not be called families?

2.    Lee Herrick admits about his sister and himself, "We had a sibling rivalry for the ages." Write an essay using extended definition to explore the meaning of *sibling rivalry*. Are there times when sibling rivalry can be constructive? When is sibling rivalry destructive?

3.    What are the responsibilities family members should have for each other? Write an essay that presents several situations you have observed over the years and give your expectations of how family members should treat each other.

4.  What are the unique issues of the adopted child? Write an essay that gives several examples of the problems adopted children face. Conclude with advice as to how these problems should be handled.

5.  More than once in the essay, the writer looks back critically at different periods in his life. In paragraph 10, he refers to a period in his adolescence as "the height of my selfish teen years. . ." Many of us look back to our adolescence with some sense of regret for moments of selfishness. Write an essay that explores the concept of *selfishness*. In what circumstances does one need to be "selfish"? What are some examples of the selfishness typical of adolescence?

# WHAT IS INTELLIGENCE, ANYWAY?

## Isaac Asimov

Isaac Asimov (1920–1992) was one of the most prolific writers of his time and is still remembered as an author who educated the reading public with books and essays devoted to history and science. His work reached an even wider public with the popularity of his many stories of science fiction.

In the following essay, Asimov asks a question that people always find provocative. His common sense answer draws on his own experience and combines it with methods of scientific observation, an area in which he was well trained. The result is an essay that helps us reshape our definition of intelligence and leads us to a new view of ourselves.

**°aptitude**
ability

**°KP**
kitchen duty

**°complacent**
self-satisfied

**°bents**
inclinations; tendencies

**°vitals**
essential parts

**°oracles**
sources of wisdom

**°academician**
teacher

**°foist**
to force others to accept

**°arbiter**
judge

1    What is intelligence, anyway? When I was in the Army, I received a kind of aptitude° test that all soldiers took and, against a normal of 100, scored 160. No one at the base had ever seen a figure like that, and for two hours they made a big fuss over me. (It didn't mean anything. The next day I was still a buck private with KP° as my highest duty.)

2    All of my life I've been registering scores like that, so that I have the complacent° feeling that I'm highly intelligent, and I expect other people think so, too. Actually, though, don't such scores simply mean that I am very good at answering the type of academic questions that are considered worthy of answers by the people who make up the intelligence tests—people with intellectual bents° similar to mine?

3    For instance, I had an auto repairman once, who, on these intelligence tests, could not possibly have scored more than 80, by my estimate. I always took it for granted that I was far more intelligent than he was. Yet, when anything went wrong with my car, I hastened to him with it, watched him anxiously as he explored its vitals,° and listened to his pronouncements as though they were divine oracles°—and he always fixed my car.

4    Well, then, suppose my auto repairman devised questions for an intelligence test. Or suppose a carpenter did, or a farmer, or, indeed, almost anyone but an academician.° By every one of those tests, I'd prove myself a moron. And I'd *be* a moron, too. In a world where I could not use my academic training and my verbal talents but had to do something intricate or hard, working with my hands, I would do poorly. My intelligence, then, is not absolute but is a function of the society I live in and of the fact that a small subsection of that society has managed to foist° itself on the rest as arbiter° of such matters.

5    Consider my auto repairman, again. He had a habit of telling me jokes whenever he saw me. One time he raised his head from under the automobile hood to say, "Doc, a deaf-and-dumb guy went into a hardware store to ask for some nails. He put two fingers together on the counter and made hammering motions with the other hand. The clerk brought him a hammer. He shook his head and

°**indulgently**
in a spirit of cooperation

°**raucously**
in a loud, harsh manner

pointed to the two fingers he was hammering. The clerk brought him nails. He picked out the sizes he wanted, and left. Well, doc, the next guy who came in was a blind man. He wanted scissors. How do you suppose he asked for them?"

6    Indulgently,° I lifted my right hand and made scissoring motions with my first two fingers. Whereupon my auto repairman laughed raucously° and said, "Why, you dumb jerk, he used his *voice* and asked for them." Then he said, smugly, "I've been trying that on all my customers today." "Did you catch many?" I asked. "Quite a few," he said, "but I knew for sure I'd catch *you*." "Why is that?" I asked. "Because you're so goddamned educated, doc, I *knew* you couldn't be very smart."

7    And I have an uneasy feeling he had something there.

## Questions for Critical Thinking

1.    What is the point of the author's first paragraph? How is it made more effective by his use of personal experience?

2.    Isaac Asimov uses the extended example of the auto mechanic to point out the difference between practical intelligence and the more theoretical or abstract academic intelligence. Why is the auto mechanic such a good example for the writer to use? What other examples could the writer have used to make an effective distinction between the different kinds of intelligence?

3.    How would the author define "intelligence"? How do you think the author would define the terms "smart" and "educated"?

## Writing in Response

1.    Write an essay in which you classify the different types of intelligence as you have observed them. You might want to choose among the following categories: artistic intelligence, social intelligence, emotional intelligence, verbal intelligence, mathematical intelligence, and practical intelligence.

2.    Before the Industrial Revolution, most of the people in the United States lived on farms. Their lives were centered around caring for animals, crops, and family. For most people today, the world is very different. Write an essay in which you compare the skills you imagine were needed to survive in yesterday's rural setting with the skills you know are needed to survive in today's more urban, industrialized, and technological environment. How do people acquire the necessary skills? What happens to people who lack such skills?

3.    In paragraph 1, the writer tells us that when he achieved a high score on a traditional intelligence test at the army base, "for two hours they made a big fuss over me." When a person achieves something that can be measured in numbers, what does that achievement signify? What does it not signify? Consider SAT scores or exam scores in a college course. In what ways can a score be misleading? Write an essay in which you try to explain the significance of test scores, when they are useful and when they are not useful.

4.    We have all known people who are very educated but who seem to be very ignorant in some important ways. Write an essay on this topic. You might use narration and/or example to develop your thesis.

# THE WAYS OF MEETING OPPRESSION

## Martin Luther King Jr.

Martin Luther King Jr. (1929–1968) earned his BA degree from Morehouse College in Atlanta, Georgia, and finished his graduate studies in theology in Boston, in 1953. It was also in Boston that he met and married Coretta Scott.

The following year, the young minister accepted a position in a church in Montgomery, Alabama. It was in Montgomery, in 1955, that the Reverend King headed the famous boycott that lasted for more than a year in that city. The boycott had been sparked by the refusal of Rosa Parks to give up her seat on one of the Montgomery buses. When at last the Supreme Court declared segregation laws unconstitutional, Martin Luther King instantly became a national figure in the struggle for civil rights.

Throughout the ten-year period that began in 1957, Martin Luther King traveled six million miles and spoke more than twenty-five hundred times, all in the fight to end injustice and inequality. His most famous public moment came in 1963, when he directed a peaceful march on Washington, D.C., and where he delivered his memorable I Have a Dream speech. Five years later, he was assassinated.

In the following essay, the civil rights activist looks at the situation of oppressed people everywhere, from the ancient world to modern American society, and gives us his insights into the different ways subjugated people deal with the unjust situations in which they find themselves.

---

°**tacitly**
with silent acceptance

°**see Hamlet, act 3, scene 1**
°**emancipation**
freedom from bondage

1    Oppressed people deal with their oppression in three characteristic ways. One way is acquiescence: the oppressed resign themselves to their doom. They tacitly° adjust themselves to oppression, and thereby become conditioned to it. In every movement toward freedom some of the oppressed prefer to remain oppressed. Almost 2800 years ago Moses set out to lead the children of Israel from the slavery of Egypt to the freedom of the promised land. He soon discovered that slaves do not always welcome their deliverers. They become accustomed to being slaves. They would rather bear those ills they have, as Shakespeare pointed out, than flee to others that they know not of.° They prefer the "fleshpots of Egypt" to the ordeals of emancipation.°

°**yoke**
instrument of bondage

°**engulfs**
overwhelms

2    There is such a thing as the freedom of exhaustion. Some people are so worn down by the yoke° of oppression that they give up. A few years ago in the slum areas of Atlanta, a Negro guitarist used to sing almost daily: "Been down so long that down don't bother me." This is the type of negative freedom and resignation that often engulfs° the life of the oppressed.

3    But this is not the way out. To accept passively an unjust system is to cooperate with that system; thereby the oppressed become as evil as the oppressor. Noncooperation with evil is as much a moral obligation as is cooperation with good. The oppressed must never allow the conscience of the oppressor to

slumber. Religion reminds every man that he is his brother's keeper. To accept injustice or segregation passively is to say to the oppressor that his actions are morally right. It is a way of allowing his conscience to fall asleep. At this moment the oppressed fails to be his brother's keeper. So acquiescence—while often the easier way—is not the moral way. It is the way of the coward. The Negro cannot win the respect of his oppressor by acquiescing; he merely increases the oppressor's arrogance and contempt. Acquiescence is interpreted as proof of the Negro's inferiority. The Negro cannot win the respect of the white people of the South or the peoples of the world if he is willing to sell the future of his children for his personal and immediate comfort and safety.

°**corroding**
gradually destructive

4    A second way that oppressed people sometimes deal with oppression is to resort to physical violence and corroding° hatred. Violence often brings about momentary results. Nations have frequently won their independence in battle. But in spite of temporary victories, violence never brings permanent peace. It solves no social problem; it merely creates new and more complicated ones.

5    Violence as a way of achieving racial justice is both impractical and immoral. It is impractical because it is a descending spiral ending in destruction for all. The old law of an eye for an eye leaves everybody blind. It is immoral because it seeks to humiliate the opponent rather than win his understanding; it seeks to annihilate° rather than to convert. Violence is immoral because it thrives on hatred rather than love. It destroys community and makes brotherhood impossible. It leaves society in monologue° rather than dialogue. Violence ends by defeating itself. It creates bitterness in the survivors and brutality in the destroyers. A voice echoes through time saying to every potential Peter, "Put up your sword."° History is cluttered with the wreckage of nations that failed to follow this command.

°**annihilate**
destroy completely

°**monologue**
a speech by one person

°**see Christ's words to Peter in John 18:11 of the Christian Bible**

°**succumb**
give in to

6    If the American Negro and other victims of oppression succumb° to the temptation of using violence in the struggle for freedom, future generations will be the recipients of a desolate° night of bitterness, and our chief legacy to them will be an endless reign of meaningless chaos.° Violence is not the way.

°**desolate**
dreary; dismal

°**chaos**
total confusion

7    The third way open to oppressed people in their quest for freedom is the way of nonviolent resistance. Like the synthesis° in Hegelian philosophy,° the principle of nonviolent resistance seeks to reconcile the truths of two opposites— the acquiescence and violence—while avoiding the extremes and immoralities of both. The nonviolent resister agrees with the person who acquiesces that one should not be physically aggressive toward his opponent; but he balances the equation by agreeing with the person of violence that evil must be resisted. He avoids the nonresistance of the former and the violent resistance of the latter. With nonviolent resistance, no individual or group need to submit to any wrong.

°**synthesis**
combination of elements

°**Hegelian philosophy**
Hegel's belief that we arrive at truth by combining theories

°**perpetrators**
those responsible for an act

8    It seems to me that this is the method that must guide the actions of the Negro in the present crisis in race relations. Through nonviolent resistance the Negro will be able to rise to the noble height of opposing the unjust system while loving the perpetrators° of the system. The Negro must work passionately and unrelentingly° for full stature° as a citizen, but he must not use inferior methods to gain it. He must never come to terms with falsehood, malice, hate, or destruction.

°**unrelentingly**
without lessening in force

°**stature**
status

9    Nonviolent resistance makes it possible for the Negro to remain in the South and struggle for his rights. The Negro's problem will not be solved by running away. He cannot listen to the glib° suggestion of those who would urge him to migrate en masse° to other sections of the country. By grasping his

**°glib**
superficial

**°en masse**
French for "all together"

**°sublime**
noble; majestic

**°banner**
a flag

great opportunity in the South he can make a lasting contribution to the moral strength of the nation and set a sublime° example of courage for generations yet unborn.

10      By nonviolent resistance, the Negro can also enlist all men of good will in his struggle for equality. The problem is not a purely racial one, with Negroes set against whites. In the end, it is not a struggle between people at all, but a tension between justice and injustice. Nonviolent resistance is not aimed against oppressors but oppression. Under its banner° consciences, not racial groups, are enlisted.

## Questions for Critical Thinking

1.  Martin Luther King Jr. begins his essay with an extended reference to the situation Moses and the Israelites faced in Egypt nearly three thousand years ago. Why does the author begin his essay with this reminder of the ancient world?

2.  How many ways does Martin Luther King give for meeting oppression? Mark each place in the essay where a category or "way" is first presented.

3.  To what extent do you agree with Martin Luther King's statement in paragraph 2 that some people "are so worn down by the yoke of oppression that they give up"?

4.  When, in paragraph 3, Martin Luther King states, "Nations have frequently won their independence in battle," he adds, almost immediately, that "violence never brings permanent peace." Can you give an example of this seeming paradox?

5.  In paragraph 9, Martin Luther King notes that the problem of injustice faced by the African American "will not be solved by running away." What examples do you have, from your own observations of others and from your awareness of history, of people who ran away from their problems? In each case, what were the consequences?

6.  In paragraph 10, Martin Luther King stresses that the struggle for equality is not a struggle between people but rather "between justice and injustice." Do you agree with him? Is it not true that the problems people face are created by other people and not by some abstract concept?

## Writing in Response

1.  Write an essay of persuasion that seeks to convince your classmates that they should participate in a current social issue.

2.  Write an essay in which you classify people into types according to how they react to situations that call for a response.

3.  Different situations call for different responses. Write an essay in which you suggest which kinds of situations would belong in each of the following categories: (1) those situations where a person should do nothing, (2) those situations where a person should act in a limited or guarded way, (3) those situations where a person has an ethical or legal duty to act, and (4) those extreme cases (if there are any) where a person should act even if it means disobeying a law.

# THE CHANGING AMERICAN FAMILY

## Alvin and Heidi Toffler

No one denies that the American family has changed and will continue to evolve. Researchers Alvin and Heidi Toffler have concluded that not all of these changes are necessarily negative. As they share the results of their research, the Tofflers not only provide a broad historical review of some of the most striking changes the family has undergone but also classify families according to different types.

1    The American family is not dying. It is diversifying. This is the "secret" to understanding what is happening to ourselves, our children, and our society. Millions of people today are frightened about the future of the family. Dire° predictions pour from the pulpit, the press, even from the White House. Emotional oratory about the need to "restore" the family is echoing through the nation.

°**dire**
desperate; urgent;
warning of disaster

2    Unfortunately, our attempts to strengthen family life are doomed unless we first understand what is happening. And all the evidence suggests we don't.

3    Despite misconceptions, the American family system is not falling apart because of immoral television programs or permissive child-rearing or because of some sinister conspiracy. If that were the problem, the solutions would be simpler.

4    To begin with, it is worth noticing that whatever is happening to family life is *not* just happening in the United States. Many of today's trends in divorce, remarriage, new family styles, and attitudes toward children are present in Britain, France, Sweden, Germany, Canada, even in the Soviet Union and Eastern Europe. Something is happening to families in all these countries at once.

°**fracturing**
breaking up

5    What is happening is that the existing family system is fracturing°—and taking on a new, more diversified form—because of powerful pressures arising from revolutionary changes in energy, technology, work, economics, and communications. If permissiveness and immorality play a role, they are far less important than these other, larger pressures.

6    The whole world is changing rapidly, and it seems reasonable that you cannot have a revolution in all these fields without expecting a revolution in family life as well.

7    Human history has gone through successive phases—each characterized by a certain kind of family. In greatly simplified terms we can sketch these:

8    The First Wave family: Ten thousand years ago, the invention of agriculture launched the First Wave of change in history. As people shifted from hunting, fishing, and foraging, the typical peasant-style family spread: a large household, with grandparents and children, uncles and aunts and sometimes nonblood relatives, as well as neighbors, boarders or others, all living together and—most important—working together as a production team in the fields.

674

9      This kind of "extended" family was found all over the world, from Japan to Eastern Europe to France to the American colonies. It is still the dominant type of family in the nonindustrial, agricultural countries today.

10     The Second Wave family: Three hundred years ago, the Industrial Revolution exploded in England and triggered the Second Wave of change.

11.    The old style family which worked so well as a production team in the fields did not fit well in the new evolving world of factories and offices. The elderly couldn't keep up with the clattering machines. Children were too undisciplined to be really efficient factory hands. And the industrial economy needed workers who could move from city to city as jobs opened up or closed. That was hard to do with a big family.

12     Gradually, under these pressures, families became smaller, more streamlined, with the husband going out to work in a factory or office, the wife staying home, and the kids marching off to school. Old folks were farmed out to their own apartments or nursing homes. Young people moved into their own apartments as soon as they could afford it. The family adapted to the new conditions and the so-called "nuclear" family became the most popular model.

13     This is the type of family that most of today's evangelists, politicians, and others have in mind when they say we must "protect" the family or "restore" it. They act as though the nuclear family were the only acceptable form of family life.

14     Yet today, as society is struck by a new shock-wave of technological, economic, ecological, and energy changes, the family system is adapting once more, just as it did three hundred years ago.

15     Because the economic and other conditions that made the nuclear family popular are changing, the nuclear family itself is less and less popular. America is no longer a nation of poorly educated blue-collar workers. Most of us work in service occupations or spend our time processing information. And today only some 7 percent of Americans still live in classical nuclear families. The nuclear family is simply no longer the norm—and it is not likely to become the norm again, no matter how much pulpit-pounding or breast-beating we do about it. In its place, a new family system is emerging.

16     The Third Wave family: This new system is harder to describe because it is not based on a single dominant family form but on a dazzling diversity of household structures.

17     For example, look at what is happening to single life. Between 1970 and 1978 alone, the number of people aged 14 to 34 who live alone nearly tripled in the United States. Today fully one-fifth of all households are live-alones. Some are alone out of necessity, others prefer it. Then there are the child-free couples. As James Ramey of the Center for Policy Research has pointed out, we are seeing a massive shift from "child-centered" to "adult-centered" homes. The number of couples who deliberately decide not to have children—whether for economic, psychological, or ecological reasons—has increased dramatically.

18     Next come the single-parent households. Divorce rates may be leveling out in this country, depending upon how they are measured, but broken nuclear households are so widespread that today as many as one out of seven children are raised by a single parent. In big cities that may run as high as one in four.

19    In many countries at once, the single-parent household is becoming a key family form. Sweden gives one-parent households first crack at nursery and day-care facilities. Germany is building special blocks of apartments for them.

20    Then there is what we have called the "aggregate family." That's where two divorced people—each with kids—marry, and the kids from both sides come to know each other and form a kind of tribe. Often the kids get on better than the parents. It has been estimated that, before long, 25 percent of American kids may be part of such "aggregate families."

21    Trial marriages . . . single-sex households . . . communes . . . all can be found as people struggle to find alternatives to the nuclear model. Some of these will turn out to be workable alternatives; others will fall by the wayside.

22    We can also expect to see an increasing number of "electronic cottage" families—families in which one or both spouses work at home instead of commuting to the job. As the cost of gasoline skyrockets and the cost of computers and communication plummets, companies will increasingly supply their employees with simple work-at-home electronic equipment.

23    In such homes, we may well find husband and wife sharing the same work. Even children and old folks might pitch in, as they once did in the agricultural household. In our day, such "electronic cottage" families are as much an outgrowth of changes in energy, technology, and communications, as the nuclear family was a response to the factory system at the time of the Industrial Revolution.

24    In the new environment, nuclear households will no doubt continue to survive. For many people, they work. But this Second Wave family form will hardly dominate the future, as it did the recent past.

25    What we are seeing today, therefore, is not the death of the family, but the rapid emergence of a Third Wave family system based on many different types of family.

26    This historic shift to new, more varied and flexible family arrangements is rooted in and related to parallel changes now fast developing in other fields. In fact, we find the same push toward diversity at every level.

27    The energy system is diversifying, shifting from a near-total reliance on fossil fuels to new, alternative sources of energy. In the world of work, we see a similar trend: Older Second Wave industries engaged in mass production—turning out millions of identical items. Newer Third Wave industries, based on computers, numerical controls, and robots, custom-tailor their goods and turn them out in small runs. At the consumer level, we see an increasing variety of products.

28    The same shift toward diversity is even stronger in communications where the power of the great mass media is increasingly challenged by new "mini-media"—cable television, satellite-based networks, special-interest magazines. This shift toward diversity amounts to the demassification of the media.

29    In short, the whole structure of society is moving toward increased diversity. It is hardly surprising that the family system is in tune with this shift. The recent startling changes in American family structure are part of this larger move from a mass society to one that offers a far greater variety of life choice.

30      Any attempt to go backward to a simpler system dominated by the nuclear family—or by any one model—will fail, just as our attempts to save the economy by "reindustrializing" have failed. For in both cases we are looking backward rather than forward.

31      To help families adapt to the new Third Wave society, with its diversified energy, production, communications, and politics, we should encourage innovations that permit employees to adjust their work hours to personal needs. We should favor "flex-time," part-time work arrangements, job-sharing. We should eliminate housing tax and credit regulations that discriminate against non-nuclear families. We need more imaginative day-care facilities.

32      An idea put forward by one businesswoman: a bank of word-processors and a nursery located in a suburban shopping center, so that busy housewives or husbands can put in an hour or two of paid work whenever it is convenient for them, and actually have their kids right there with them.

33      In short, anything that makes it easier to combine working and self-help, job-work with housework, easier to enter and leave the labor force, could smooth the transition for millions of people who are now caught, as it were, between the old, Second Wave, family arrangements and the fast-emerging Third Wave family system.

**°wallowing**
surrendering
to an emotion

34      Rather than wallowing° in nostalgia and praising the "good old days"—which were never as good as they may seem in retrospect—we ought to be finding ways to make the new system more decent, responsible, morally satisfying, and humane. The first step is an understanding of the Third Wave.

## Questions for Critical Thinking

1.  The Tofflers argue that people should not be so upset about the changing American family. Find the paragraph where they begin using classification as a method of developing their argument.

2.  Explain each of the three distinct categories, or "waves," described by the authors. Do you agree with this historical classification? Can you think of other ways to classify the family?

3.  In paragraphs 16 through 24, find the nine types of families suggested for the Third Wave. Discuss the conditions of our modern world that make these "new" family groupings possible.

4.  The Tofflers point out that only 7 percent of Americans still live in classic nuclear families. This fact frightens many people, even some who themselves are outside a nuclear family. What are some of the reasons for these fears? Do these reasons make you less optimistic than the Tofflers about the new family structures?

5.  In paragraph 30, the writers point out that any "attempt to go backward to a simpler system dominated by the nuclear family . . . will fail" because that would mean looking backward instead of ahead. Do you agree or disagree, and why?

6. The Tofflers suggest we need to understand the Third Wave to make the new system "more decent, responsible, morally satisfying and humane." What are some of their suggestions? Do you think American society is moving toward greater understanding of the Third Wave family? Discuss.

## Writing in Response

1. An often-repeated saying is "The only thing you can be sure of in life is change." Most people have trouble adapting to change in their lives. Write an essay in which you classify the types of changes that can happen to a person during the course of a lifetime. You may want to include categories such as physical change, economic change, and social change. Be sure to provide good examples within each category.

2. Write an essay in which you classify the different types of relationships you have known. Explain what is unique about each type you select. Devote at least one well-developed paragraph to each category.

3. The Tofflers suggest that employers need to make innovations that will permit workers to adjust working hours to their personal needs. Write an essay in which you classify the kinds of innovations that could be made by employers to make life better for families. What is the likelihood that your suggestions will actually be put into effect? Why or why not?

# GET A KNIFE, GET A DOG, BUT GET RID OF GUNS

## Molly Ivins

One of the most popular and colorful journalists of recent years was Molly Ivins (1944–2007). Her syndicated columns appeared in over three hundred newspapers nationwide. It has been said that while Molly Ivins wrote on many topics and worked for newspapers in several cities, including New York, Denver, and Minneapolis, it was Texas that was her favorite topic and her spiritual home. When she took aim at a current topic, she always hit her target!

The following essay finds Molly Ivins at her most independent and most confrontational. The subject of gun control divides many Americans, but from the moment you read her title, Molly Ivins tells you her position on the topic is uncompromising. She presents her argument in a voice that is feisty and irreverent.

1    Guns. Everywhere guns

2    Let me start this discussion by pointing out that I am not antigun. I'm proknife. Consider the merits of the knife.

3    In the first place, you have to catch up with someone in order to stab him. A general substitution of knives for guns would promote physical fitness. We'd turn into a whole nation of great runners. Plus, knives don't ricochet.° And people are seldom killed while cleaning their knives.

4    As a civil libertarian, I, of course, support the Second Amendment. And I believe it means exactly what it says:

5    *A well-regulated militia being necessary to the security of a free state, the right of the people to keep and bear arms shall not be infringed.°* Fourteen-year-old boys are not part of a well-regulated militia. Members of wacky° religious cults are not part of a well-regulated militia. Permitting unregulated citizens to have guns is destroying the security of this free state.

6    I am intrigued by the arguments of those who claim to follow the judicial doctrine of original intent. How do they know it was the dearest wish of Thomas Jefferson's heart that teenage drug dealers should cruise the cities of this nation perforating° their fellow citizens with assault rifles? Channeling?°

7    There is more hooey° spread about the Second Amendment. It says quite clearly that guns are for those who form part of a well-regulated militia, that is, the armed forces, including the National Guard. The reasons for keeping them away from everyone else get clearer by the day.

8    The comparison most often used is that of the automobile, another lethal° object that is regularly used to wreak° great carnage.° Obviously, this society is full of people who haven't enough common sense to use an automobile properly. But we haven't outlawed cars yet.

°**ricochet**
bounce back

°**infringed**
violated

°**wacky**
crazy

°**perforating**
making holes through

°**channeling**
supposed communication with a spirit world

°**hooey**
nonsense

°**lethal**
deadly

°**wreak**
cause

°**carnage**
bloody slaughter

**°sober**
serious

9     We do, however, license them and their owners, restrict their use to presumably sane and sober° adults, and keep track of who sells them to whom. At a minimum, we should do the same with guns.

10     In truth, there is no rational argument for guns in this society. This is no longer a frontier nation in which people hunt their own food. It is a crowded, overwhelmingly urban country in which letting people have access to guns is a continuing disaster. Those who want guns—whether for target shooting, hunting, or potting rattlesnakes (get a hoe)—should be subject to the same restrictions placed on gun owners in England, a nation in which liberty has survived nicely without an armed populace.

**°patent**
obvious

11     The argument that "guns don't kill people" is patent° nonsense. Anyone who has ever worked in a cop shop knows how many family arguments end in murder because there was a gun in the house. Did the gun kill someone? No. But if there had been no gun, no one would have died. At least not without a good foot race first. Guns do kill. Unlike cars, that is all they do.

12     Michael Crichton makes an interesting argument about technology in his thriller *Jurassic Park.* He points out that power without discipline is making this society into a wreckage. By the time someone who studies the martial arts becomes a master—literally able to kill with bare hands—that person has also undergone years of training and discipline. But any fool can pick up a gun and kill with it.

**°taunting**
ridiculing

**°psychosexual**
the mental aspects
of sexuality

**°NRA**
The National Rifle
Association

**°psyches**
ways of thinking

13     "A well-regulated militia" surely implies both long training and long discipline. That is the least, the very least, that should be required of those who are permitted to have guns, because a gun is literally the power to kill. For years I used to enjoy taunting° my gun-nut friends about their psychosexual° hang-ups—always in a spirit of good cheer, you understand. But letting the noisy minority in the NRA° force us to allow this carnage to continue is just plain insane.

14     I do think psyches gun nuts have a power hang-up. I don't know what is missing in their psyches° that they need to feel they have the power to kill. But no sane society would allow this to continue.

15     Ban the damn things. Ban them all.

16     You want protection? Get a dog.

# Questions for Critical Thinking

1.  Explain the tone that Molly Ivins establishes in the opening three paragraphs of the essay.

2.  Where in the essay is there a clearly stated thesis? Underline it.

4.  In paragraph 4, the author refers to the Second Amendment. In what historical document is this Second Amendment found?

5.  Why is the first sentence of paragraph 5 in italics? Much of the debate around the right to buy and own guns is centered around the interpretation of this sentence. How do you interpret this sentence?

6.  What does Molly Ivins mean when she refers in paragraph 6 to the "judicial doctrine of original intent"? What is the very convincing example she provides that our founding fathers could never have imagined?

7.  In your own words, list each piece of evidence Molly Ivins presents against civilians owning guns.

## Writing in Response

1.  Molly Ivins thinks the right of civilians to buy guns in this country is "insane." Write an argument about another situation in this country that you think is insane. Be sure to present your reasons for this choice and provide what you believe would be the solution to the situation.

2.  Write your own argument on gun ownership. In your opinion, who should be able to own a gun and what laws should regulate the sale of guns?

3.  Write an essay using *example* as the method of development. Give examples of the misuse of guns and examples of the proper use of guns.

# WHY DON'T THESE WOMEN JUST LEAVE?

## Elaine Weiss

One of our society's most serious problems is spousal abuse. Elaine Weiss uses her own painful experience as an abused wife to discuss this problem in a direct and compelling way. Her essay argues against the commonly held belief that the problem could be solved if only the abused partner would simply leave the relationship. The writer does not support her argument with any outside facts or statistics, nor does she quote any experts on the matter. All she does is give us a clear and convincing personal history, one that is impossible to contradict.

1      Last May, Neal and I celebrated our sixteenth wedding anniversary. This is his first marriage; my second. Ours is a fine, strong partnership, filled with shared interests, mutual respect, and ever-deepening intimacy. That's not the point of this story. This story is about my first marriage. But to tell the story of my first marriage is to take a risk—and I feel I have to start by establishing that I am capable of a good marriage.

2      I've spent nineteen years trying to make sense of my first marriage: the one that began in 1967 and ended when I left in 1976. I've spent nineteen years trying to unravel the tightly-woven threads of physical and verbal abuse that made up the fabric° of that marriage. I've spent nineteen years, and I may spend nineteen more. Why bother? Why not just be grateful that I found the strength to leave—that I didn't simply become a statistic in a "Domestic Violence" docudrama? Because, I still have nightmares, sometimes. Because, beautiful though *Carousel*° is, I can't watch Billy Bigelow hit Julie Jordan and watch her forgive him. Because when I see Charles Boyer° methodically driving Ingrid Bergman° slowly mad in *Gaslight*,° I cry, and then feel silly for overreacting. And because after O. J. Simpson's arrest, during the brief spasm of media interest in domestic violence, I overheard a woman in the beauty parlor proclaim, "You know, the women who let themselves be abused are just as sick as the men who abuse them. She should have walked out the very first time he raised a hand to her. That's what I would have done."

3      She should have . . . our glib° answer to women who are physically and emotionally abused. These days we're far too sophisticated to directly blame the woman for the man's behavior; we no longer say, "Well, if he beat her up, she must have done something to deserve it." Instead, we say, "She should have been more assertive." "She should have been more accommodating." "She should have left." "She should have gotten therapy." "She should have called the police."

4      So, as if the pain of the abusive relationship weren't enough, we tell women that this pain is their fault. They hear *she should*—never *he should*. They hear, "She should have stood up to him"—which, ideally, she should—but they never hear, "He should have stopped being abusive."

°**fabric**
the underlying structure

°**Carousel**
a 1945 Broadway musical composed by Richard Rodgers

°**Charles Boyer and Ingrid Bergman**
screen actors who appeared together in the 1944 film drama °**Gaslight**

°**glib**
offhand; slick

682

5    I know it's not as simple as that. I've read all the books and articles. I know that men who batter their partners are themselves in pain. I know that their behavior is a desperate attempt to make themselves feel in control. I know that many of them were once victims of abuse. I know they can't just stop—that they need professional help. And I sympathize—just as I sympathize with alcoholics and drug addicts. I'm no longer angry with my former husband (though this took me years to accomplish). But I am angry—hotly, fiercely angry—when I hear "Why don't these women just leave?"

6    To me, this question is as meaningless as asking the victim of a train wreck "Why didn't you just drive to work that morning?" Nevertheless, I'm going to tell you why I didn't leave; or, rather, why it took me eight years, seven months, and twenty-one days to leave. This is what I wish I had said to the woman in the beauty parlor.

7    I didn't leave . . . because abuse wasn't supposed to happen to people like me. I was only nineteen when I married, halfway through college, with little experience of the world. This was 1967; the term "spouse abuse" didn't exist: No one thought to join those two words, since no one accepted that it happened. Or, if it did, it happened only to impoverished, uneducated women married to men with names like Billy Bob, who turned into mean drunks on Saturday nights. It certainly didn't happen to nice Jewish girls from upper-middle-class families; they went to college, married nice boys, taught school for a while, and then started a family. This is what my friends and I were raised to believe, and this is how I thought the world worked. So when the abuse started, within a week of the wedding, I had no way to frame° what was happening.

°**frame**
to put into words

8    I didn't leave . . . because I thought it was my fault. My only experience of marriage was the seventeen years I had spent in my parents' home, and there I saw warmth, kindness, and love. If my marriage looked nothing like theirs, I assumed that I must be doing something wrong. My husband would become angry and throw me against a wall—then berate° me for "egging him on." Lying in bed that night, I would replay the scene, trying to pinpoint the exact moment where I had gone wrong. I always found it, too: "I should have laughed it off when he told me the dinner was disgusting." "I should have ignored it when he called me a 'fat dummy, too useless to live.'" "I shouldn't have cried when he announced that he wanted to have affairs with other women—and that if I didn't like it, I was being too possessive."

°**berate**
to scold angrily

9    I didn't leave . . . because I believed I could fix it. During our courtship, he was tender and affectionate. He told me I was the most wonderful girl in the world (in 1967 we were all "girls"—as were our mothers and grandmothers). So I held on to the image of the man who was once my loving boyfriend, and was now my menacing husband. He told me I had changed—that I was no longer the cute, bright girl he had married—and I imagined he must be right. Since rational people don't suddenly turn violent without provocation,° I must be provoking him. I thought that if I could just get it right, he would be nice to me again.

°**provocation**
something that causes a person to become angry

10   I didn't leave . . . because I told myself that I was overreacting. Yes, he would occasionally punch me in the stomach or choke me—but at least he never gave me a black eye or a broken arm. Yes, he would delight in pointing out an obese woman on the street and saying "Your ass is even bigger than hers"—but perhaps I did need to lose weight (I was then, as I am now, a size six). Yes, he would indicate another woman, tall, blond, buxom and leggy, and scold "Why

can't you look like that?"—but this was the 1960s, when the Beach Boys wished we all could be California Girls, and maybe a petite brunette couldn't hope to be seen as attractive. Yes, he would occasionally put a pillow over my face while I slept, then watch with detached interest as I woke up half-smothered—but I had to be imagining that, didn't I?

11      I didn't leave . . . because there was no support for women like me. There was no place I could tell my story and be told "It's not you—it's him. There's no way you can 'get it right,' because he desperately needs you to get it wrong." I convinced my husband to enter couple therapy, and tried to find the words to pin down my husband's actions. "If he goes through a door ahead of me, he gives it an extra push to let it swing back and hit me." "He tells me I'm so ugly that his new nickname for me is 'uggles'." "I feel like I'm constantly walking on eggshells." The therapist's response was to insist that I had an obligation to stay in the marriage because my husband couldn't function without me. He also insisted that if I stopped being my father's Little Girl and became my husband's Adult Wife, my problems would be solved. Since this advice came from a professional, I assumed it had to be correct. We spent two years in weekly visits to this man, after which I was discharged with the admonition° to put my energy into supporting my husband.

12      I didn't leave . . . because I grew accustomed to living a lie. He treated me well in public. To our friends, we were the perfect couple. Maintaining our outward loving appearance became an unspoken conspiracy between us. He called it "not airing our dirty linen in public," and I agreed. Of course I agreed. I was to blame for his behavior, and I couldn't manage to figure out how to be the sort of wife he cherished.° Which, he assured me, he surely would—if I could just learn how to make him happy. A wife who can't make her husband happy—why would I want that to become public knowledge? I agreed to the charade,° and I played my part well. Which probably explains why, when I finally left, he got to keep the friends; no one could see why I'd want to escape such a wonderful marriage.

13      I didn't leave . . . and then one day I left. Why? It sounds so trivial in retrospect,° but it was triggered by an encounter with an unknown woman in New York City. This was in 1974, shortly after my husband and I moved to Manhattan. He had taken a job with a prestigious° corporate law firm and, after five years as a schoolteacher, I was beginning graduate school at Columbia University. One afternoon, as we stood on a street corner at a downtown crosswalk, I looked up to see a particularly lovely old building with a magnificent garden on its terraced roof. I pointed and said, "Isn't that building beautiful?" "Which one," sneered my husband, "you mean the one up there that looks exactly like every other building on the street?" A woman standing beside us turned abruptly. "She's right, you know. The building is beautiful—and you are a horse's ass." As the light changed and she stalked off, something shifted inside me. I finally realized that this man was never going to change, and that I deserved better. Within a year I announced that I was leaving.

14      Yes, of course it took more than this one encounter. My professors at Columbia told me I was a talented instructional designer, and encouraged me to enter the doctoral program. Fellow students became close friends. Many of them had never met my husband—I was more than half a couple. With professional and personal successes, I stopped caring about, hardly noticed, my husband's abuse. Ironically, the more I ignored him, the nicer he acted. The day I told him the marriage was over (my twenty-eighth birthday), he cried and begged

**°admonition**
piece of cautionary advice

**°cherished**
held dear

**°charade**
a pretense in which people act out parts

**°in retrospect**
in looking back

**°prestigious**
having a high standing or reputation

**°idyllic**
simple and carefree

me to stay. He told me how much he needed me. He said he couldn't imagine life without me. He swore he would change. He painted an idyllic° picture of the new life we would build. I barely heard him.

15      And so I left. I am one of the lucky ones. He didn't threaten me. He didn't physically try to stop me. He didn't stalk me. He didn't murder me. Some men do. I am one of the lucky ones. The impact on the rest of my life has been minimal. I didn't become homeless. I didn't turn to drugs or alcohol. I didn't enter into a series of abusive relationships. I didn't commit suicide. Some women do.

16      Instead, I went on to earn a doctorate, develop a successful consulting practice, and build a strong marriage. Life is good. But I still have nightmares, sometimes. I still walk out of movies that show acts of violence against women. And I still, and probably always will, feel anguish° when I hear someone ask "Why don't these women just leave?"

**°anguish**
agonizing mental pain

## Questions for Critical Thinking

1.  The author presents the opposing point of view to her own argument when she reports a conversation she once overheard in a beauty salon. Find the quote, underline it, and label it "opposing viewpoint" in the margin of the essay.

2.  An author's thesis is usually found in the opening paragraph of a piece of writing, but that is not the case in this essay. Nevertheless, the writer's thesis is still very clear. We come to realize what that thesis is from the essay's contents, beginning with the title. Using your own words, write a sentence that will provide the thesis of this essay.

3.  Why does the author begin her essay with a picture of her present marriage? What effect does this positive opening have on us as we read the rest of the essay?

4.  In the first six paragraphs, the author presents the traditional thinking about women who find themselves in abusive relationships. What are some of those traditional ideas?

5.  The heart of a persuasive essay is the evidence an author uses to support the essay's thesis. In this selection, which paragraphs present the evidence for the author's thesis? Find these paragraphs and underline the six reasons the writer gives for having stayed in her abusive relationship.

6.  What are the words the author repeats as she introduces each new reason? What is the writer's reason for this repetition?

7.  Paragraphs 11, 13, and 14 point out the roles that other people played in the author's struggle to understand her marriage. Explain the role of each of these persons and the degree of influence each one had on the author's thinking.

8.  What are all the elements that make this essay a convincing argument? Can you find any weak points in the writer's approach? Refer to the guidelines for writing a persuasive essay given in Chapter 32.

## Writing in Response

1. Recall a relationship you remember well. Why did that relationship succeed or fail? Using the Weiss essay as your model, tell the story of that relationship. As you tell that story, make an argument to convince your reader as to why that relationship did or did not work.

2. Write an essay in which you classify marriages according to their degree of success. Give each of your categories a heading. For instance, one category could be called "marriages doomed to failure."

3. In this essay, we learn that the image a family member presents in public may be very different from the reality the rest of the family experiences at home. Write an essay that describes someone you have observed whose actions at home are very different from that person's public image.

4. In paragraph 13 of the essay, Elaine Weiss presents a seemingly unimportant event that turns out to be an epiphany (an incident that is suddenly and profoundly revealing). Write your recollection of an experience you had or a moment in your own life that was an epiphany for you. Explain the effects of this moment of revelation on your life.

5. Many people seek the advice of counselors, therapists, and other experts to help them with their problems. In paragraph 10 of the essay, Elaine Weiss tells us that she received some unfortunate advice from a therapist, advice she assumed had to be correct because it came from a professional. Use your personal experience or experiences of others you know to make an argument for seeking help from experts. How can a person judge the advice of a professional?

6. Write a helpful letter to a friend who has been suffering in an abusive relationship. Advise that person what to do and give the person a step-by-step plan to follow. (Use process as the letter's method of development.)

7. In paragraph 14, the author mentions the people who supported her during a difficult period in her life. Write an essay in which you discuss how the support of other people can be important when an individual is in distress. Your essay could be a *narration* of your personal experience; it could include *classification* of the types of individuals who can be helpful to people in need; or it could present an *argument* that many people need much more support than they are presently receiving.

# MY BODY IS MY OWN BUSINESS

## Naheed Mustafa

The wearing of the hijab, the headscarf for Muslim women, has become a controversial issue in several countries today. In the following essay, originally published in the *Toronto Globe and Mail*, the Canadian-born Muslim journalist and freelance broadcaster Naheed Mustafa argues for the use of this distinctive item of clothing. Contrary to commonly held belief, the writer sees the use of the hijab as an indication of female liberation.

Naheed Mustafa graduated from the University of Toronto in 1992 with an honors degree in political science and history. She has been nominated for more than one award, including recognition for a Canadian radio broadcast she made from Afghanistan.

1    I often wonder whether people see me as a radical, fundamentalist Muslim terrorist packing an AK-47 assault rifle inside my jean jacket. Or maybe they see me as the poster girl for oppressed womanhood everywhere. I'm not sure which it is.

°**gamut**
a complete range

°**covert**
not openly shown

2    I get the whole gamut° of strange looks, stares and covert° glances. You see, I wear the *hijab,* a scarf that covers my head, neck and throat. I do this because I am a Muslim woman who believes her body is her own private concern.

3    Young Muslim women are reclaiming the *hijab,* reinterpreting it in light of its original purpose—to give back to women ultimate control of their own bodies.

°**the Koran**
the sacred text of Islam

4    The Koran° teaches us that men and women are equal, that individuals should not be judged according to gender, beauty, wealth or privilege. The only thing that makes one person better than another is her or his character.

5    Nonetheless, people have a difficult time relating to me. After all, I'm young, Canadian born and raised, university-educated—why would I do this to myself, they ask.

°**charades**
a game where words are represented by gestures

6    Strangers speak to me in loud, slow English and often appear to be playing charades.° They politely inquire how I like living in Canada and whether or not the cold bothers me. If I'm in the right mood, it can be very amusing.

7    But why would I, a woman with all the advantages of a North American upbringing, suddenly, at 21, want to cover myself so that with the *hijab* and the other clothes I choose to wear, only my face and hands show?

°**abstract**
removed from concrete existence

8    Because it gives me freedom.

°**futile**
useless

9    "Women are taught from early childhood that their worth is proportional° to their attractiveness. We feel compelled to pursue abstract° notions of beauty, half realizing that such a pursuit is futile.°

**°unconscionable**
beyond a reasonable limit

**°militancy**
combative aggression

**°realm**
area

**°bulimic**
a person with bulimia,
an eating disorder

**°Cindy Crawford**
a fashion model

**°waifish**
small and forlorn
looking

**°objectification**
making a person an
object

10    When women reject this form of oppression, they face ridicule and contempt. Whether it's women who refuse to wear makeup or to shave their legs or to expose their bodies, society, both men and women, have trouble dealing with them.

11    In the Western world, the *hijab* has come to symbolize either forced silence or radical, unconscionable° militancy.° Actually, it's neither. It is simply a woman's assertion that judgment of her physical person is to play no role whatsoever in social interaction.

12    Wearing the *hijab* has given me freedom from constant attention to my physical self. Because my appearance is not subjected to public scrutiny, my beauty, or perhaps lack of it, has been removed from the realm° of what can legitimately be discussed.

13    No one knows whether my hair looks as if I just stepped out of a salon, whether or not I can pinch an inch, or even if I have unsightly stretch marks. And because no one knows, no one cares.

14    Feeling that one has to meet the impossible male standards of beauty is tiring and often humiliating. I should know, I spent my entire teenage years trying to do it. I was a borderline bulimic° and spent a lot of money I didn't have on potions and lotions in hopes of becoming the next Cindy Crawford.°

15    The definition of beauty is ever-changing; waifish° is good, waifish is bad, athletic is good—sorry, athletic is bad. Narrow hips? Great. Narrow hips? Too bad.

16    Women are not going to achieve equality with the right to bare their breasts in public, as some people would like to have you believe. That would only make us party to our own objectification.° True equality will be had only when women don't need to display themselves to get attention and won't need to defend their decision to keep their bodies to themselves.

# Questions for Critical Thinking

1.  In paragraph 1, the author suggests that a woman wearing a hijab is often judged unfairly, both from a political point of view and from a feminist point of view. What are the political and feminist judgments that non-Muslim people are likely to make?

2.  Discuss how a person coming from a different culture with its own customs or practices can often be viewed with suspicion from the dominant culture. Are there any circumstances that justify such attitudes?

3.  The author believes that men hold women to a standard of beauty that these women can never hope to achieve. Compose a list of the author's examples showing how women try to make themselves beautiful (paragraphs 10, 13, 14, 15, and 16).

4.  According to the author, what are the advantages of wearing the hijab?

5.  Which of the following would be the best thesis for this essay?

    (a)  Most women's attempts to reach the current standard for beauty are doomed to failure.

    (b)  Wearing the hijab should be seen as a liberating choice rather than a sign of oppression.

    (c)  We should never judge people from other cultures by their appearance.

6.  Is Naheed Mustafa's argument convincing? Can you think of any counterarguments?

# Writing in Response

1.  Write an essay in which you provide examples of a culture's innocent customs or practices that are sometimes judged unfairly by today's society.

2.  Write an essay providing examples of the customs or practices of a culture, other than your own, that you believe should be viewed with alarm.

3.  Write an essay in which you discuss the recent trend of women to wear revealing clothing in public. Do you believe this trend is liberating?

4.  Write an essay in which you argue for our society's more balanced attitude toward a woman's physical appearance. What can be done to encourage our society to help young girls gain a healthier attitude about their appearance?

5.  The author states, "The only thing that makes one person better than another is her or his character." Write an essay in which you offer parents specific guidelines that will help them instill better character traits in their children.

# REFERENCE GUIDE FOR THE ESOL STUDENT

Many students in the United States today have a first language that is not English. These students share similar problems with spoken and written English. The following appendix reviews some of the more common difficulties faced by these students.

## USING THE ARTICLES *A*, *AN*, AND *THE*

### HOW DO YOU KNOW WHEN TO USE THE ARTICLE *A* OR *AN* BEFORE A NOUN?

- Most English nouns are **count nouns;** that is, they can be counted:

  one town          two towns

  one orange        two oranges

> Use *a* or *an* with single count nouns when the noun has not been specifically identified. (Perhaps the noun is being introduced for the first time to the reader.)
>
> *A town* in Georgia was struck by a tornado.
>
> *An orange* contains vitamin C.

- **Noncount nouns** cannot be counted easily:

  courage          homework          sugar

> Do *not* use *a* or *an* with noncount nouns.
>
> We admire people with *courage.*
>
> Do you have *homework* tonight?
>
> I like *sugar* in my coffee.

**NOTE:** Never add *s* to make a noncount noun plural. Noncount nouns have no plural form.

- Learn to recognize common noncount nouns:

| | |
|---|---|
| **Abstract nouns:** | beauty, courage, health, information, knowledge |
| **Areas of study:** | astronomy, biology, history, math, music |
| **Diseases:** | diabetes, measles |
| **Games:** | football, soccer |
| **Nouns that indicate a mass of something:** | advice, clothing, entertainment, equipment, furniture, homework, jewelry, luggage, machinery, mail, money, news, research, traffic |
| **Food and drink:** | flour, sugar, rice, salt, water, coffee, tea, milk, butter, oil |
| **Natural substances:** | air, blood, cotton, silk, coal, gasoline, ice, snow |

- Some nouns can be countable or uncountable, depending on the context:

| | |
|---|---|
| **Count noun:** | There is *a time* for work and *a time* for play. |
| **Noncount noun:** | *Time* is passing. |
| **Count noun:** | He found *a hair* on the lens of the camera. |
| **Noncount noun:** | She cuts *hair* for a living. |

## HOW DO YOU KNOW WHEN TO USE THE ARTICLE *THE* BEFORE A NOUN?

> Use *the* with both count and noncount nouns when the noun is specifically identified by its context. Do *not* use *the* if the noun has not been clearly identified or if the meaning carries the idea of *all* or in *general*.

| **Examples of nouns that are identified** | | **Examples of nouns that are not identified or whose meaning carries the idea of *all* or *in general*** |
|---|---|---|
| *The city of Macon* was struck by a tornado. | but | *A city in Georgia* was struck by a tornado. |
| *The cities of Macon and Savannah* were struck by tornadoes. | | *Cities in Georgia* were struck by tornadoes. |
| *The jacket with the hood* is mine. | but | I would like *a jacket with a hood.* |
| *The jackets with the hoods* are new. | | *Jackets with hoods* are popular. |
| The soldier spoke of *the courage that his platoon displayed* in the battle. | but | The soldier spoke of *courage.* |

> **Most singular proper nouns do not take the article *the*.**
> **I live on Walnut Street in Buffalo, New York.**

The following categories of proper nouns do *not* take the article *the:*

| | |
|---|---|
| **Countries of one word:** | Canada, Mexico |
| **Continents:** | Asia, Africa |
| **States:** | New Jersey, Arizona |
| **Cities:** | Miami, Detroit |
| **Streets:** | Elm Street, Rodeo Drive |
| **Parks:** | Central Park |
| **Lakes:** | Lake Michigan |
| **Persons:** | Mayor Fernandez, Captain Cook |
| **Days of the week:** | Monday, Tuesday |
| **Months of the year:** | January, February |

There are many exceptions to this rule, so it is important to learn the following list of categories of nouns that *do* require the article *the.*

The following categories of proper nouns take the article *the.*

**Most bodies of water, including oceans, seas, canals, gulfs, and rivers:**

the Indian Ocean, the Panama Canal, the Ohio River    but    Lake Louise

**Deserts and mountain ranges:**

the Sonoma Desert, the Rocky Mountains    but    Mount Everest

**Countries whose names suggest plural units:**

the United States, the United Arab Emirates,

the Virgin Islands    but    Puerto Rico

**Geographical regions and areas:**

the Ukraine, the Mississippi Delta, the Northwest Territory

**Historical periods and events:**

the Depression, the French Revolution, the Civil War

**Buildings, bridges, hotels, and highways:**

the Sears Tower, the Delaware Memorial Bridge, the Marriott Hotel, the Dixie Highway

**Groups:**

the Rotary, the Shriners, the Red Cross

## WHAT ARE THE OTHER DETERMINERS BESIDES *A, AN,* AND *THE?*

**Determiners** are those adjectives that identify and quantify nouns. In a series of adjectives before a noun, these determiners always come first.

For count nouns, you can choose from the following determiners:

| | |
|---|---|
| **Singular:** | a, one, each, every, this, that |
| **Plural:** | the, these, those, few, a few, many, more, most, some, several, any, two, three, and so on. |

Thus,

I have *one book* to read.

I have *many books* to read.

For noncount nouns, you can choose from somewhat different determiners:

the, this, that, some, little, a little, much, more, any

Thus,

I have *much homework* to do.

Notice you cannot use specific numbers.

| | |
|---|---|
| **Incorrect:** | I have *five homeworks* to do. |
| **Correct:** | I have *some homework* to do. |

or

| | |
|---|---|
| **Correct:** | I have *five assignments* to do. |

(Changing to the count noun *assignment* allows you to use the number *five.*)

# ENGLISH WORD ORDER

## WORD ORDER FOR ADJECTIVES

When more than one adjective is used to modify a noun, use the conventional order:

| | |
|---|---|
| **Determiner:** | a, each, the, this (see previous list) |
| **Judgment:** | friendly, stunning |
| **Size:** | tiny, petite |
| **Shape:** | round, slender |
| **Age:** | young, elderly |
| **Color:** | yellow, green |
| **Nationality:** | Korean, Nigerian |
| **Material:** | wax, wood |

Thus,

**I found a beautiful, antique, silver bracelet.**

**She purchased two large, oval, linen tablecloths.**

## WORD ORDER FOR ADVERBS

Adverbs showing frequency (*always, often, usually, sometimes, never*) come after forms of the verb *be*, but before other verbs.

**My aunt *is usually* on time.**

**My aunt *usually brings* us candy.**

## WORD ORDER FOR NEGATION

*Not* is placed after the first helping verb. When there is no helping verb, insert a form of the verb *do* before *not*.

| | |
|---|---|
| **Statement:** | **The patient *has been taking* the medicine.** |
| **Negation:** | **The patient *has not been taking* the medicine.** |
| **Statement:** | **The patient *takes* the medicine every day.** |
| **Negation:** | **The patient *does not take* the medicine every day.** |

# THE IDIOMATIC USE OF PREPOSITIONS

Learning to choose the correct preposition comes mostly from reading and listening to the idiomatic use of prepositions. Some expressions should be carefully studied. Learn these idiomatic uses of prepositions for expressing time.

| Use *on* for a specific day or date | Use *in* for a period of time | Use *at* for a specific time |
|---|---|---|
| on Thursday | in the morning | at 12 noon |
| on Friday afternoon | in the afternoon | at 3 a.m. |
| on August 25, 2010 | in the evening (but *at* night) | at dawn |
| | in 2010 | at dusk |
| | in the summer | at night |
| | in August | |
| | in six hours | |

# SPECIAL PROBLEMS WITH ENGLISH VERBS

## THE FIVE FORMS OF ENGLISH VERBS

Most English verbs have five forms. One exception is the verb *be*, which has eight forms.

|  | Regular | Irregular | Verb *be* |
|---|---|---|---|
| **Base form** (used for first person, second person, and third-person plural) | walk | go | be (am, are) |
| ***-s* form** (present third-person singular) | walks | goes | is |
| ***-ing* form** (present participle) | walking | going | being |
| **Past tense form** | walked | went | was, were |
| **Past participle form** | walked | gone | been |

## THE MEANINGS OF ENGLISH HELPING VERBS

Of the twenty-three helping verbs (including forms of *do, have,* and *be*), nine are called **modals.** These modals function only as helping verbs. They do not have the five forms of the main verbs. They are used to form tenses and to add shades of meaning to the main verb. Be sure you know these meanings. Notice that in some cases a modal may have an alternate expression that has the same meaning. (See *can, must,* and *should* in the following chart.)

| Verb | Meaning | Example |
|---|---|---|
| 1. can is able to (another option for *can*) | ability | I *can* paint this room. I *am able* to paint this room. |
| 2. could (after a past tense) | ability | He said I *could* paint this room. |
| 3. will | intention | I *will* paint this room. |
| 4. shall | usually used for questions | *Shall* I paint this room? |
| 5. would | intention (after a past tense) | I promised him that I *would* paint this room. |
| 6. may | permission | *May* I paint this room? |
| 7. might | possibility | I *might* paint this room if you buy the paint. |
| 8. must | necessity | I *must* paint this room before we move in. |
| have to (another option for *must*) | | I *have* to paint this room before we move in. |
| must | probability | He *must* be ill; he didn't show up for work. |
| 9. should | advisability | The room is shabby; I *should* paint it. |
| ought to (another option for *should*) | | The room is shabby; I *ought* to paint it. |
| should ought to | expectation | He *should* arrive soon. He *ought* to arrive soon. |

## VERBS THAT DO NOT OCCUR IN THE CONTINUOUS FORM

The continuous form indicates an ongoing activity:

**Continuous form:**          The chef is *learning* to make pastry.

Some English verbs cannot occur in the continuous form, even though they indicate an ongoing activity. These verbs are called **stative verbs.**

**Incorrect:**          The chef is understanding today's demonstration.

**Correct:**          The chef *understands* today's demonstration.

**Incorrect:**          He is knowing how to make pie crust.

**Correct:**          He *knows* how to make pie crust.

**Do not use the continuous form with stative verbs.**

## Verbs with Stative Meanings

| State of being | Mental activity | Sensory perception | Measurement | Relationship |
|---|---|---|---|---|
| be | believe | appear | cost | belong |
|  | doubt | feel | equal | contain |
| **Emotion** | know | hear | measure | entail |
| desire | remember | see | weigh | have |
| dislike | think | seem |  | own |
| hate | understand | smell |  |  |
| like |  | taste |  |  |
| love |  |  |  |  |
| want |  |  |  |  |

Note that in some cases a verb may have both a stative meaning and an active meaning.

**Stative verb:**          The child *weighs* sixty pounds.

     but

**Active verb:**          The grocer is *weighing* the fruit.

## THE VERB FORMS *BEEN* AND *BEING*

Although *been* and *being* may sound similar in speech, in writing there is an important difference. Use *been* when a past participle is needed. *Been* will follow *has, have,* or *had.*

| | |
|---|---|
| **Active voice:** | **The actress *has been studying* her part.** |
| **Passive voice:** | **The part *has been studied* by the actress.** |

Use *being* when a present participle is needed. *Being* will follow some form of the helping verb *be (am, is, are, was, were)*.

| | |
|---|---|
| **Active voice:** | **The scientists *are being* observant.** |
| **Passive voice:** | **The experiment *is being observed* by the scientist.** |

## IDIOMATIC EXPRESSIONS USING *DO* OR *MAKE*
Following are some of the many idiomatic expressions using *do* or *make*.

| | |
|---|---|
| *do* the wash | *make* the bed |
| *do* the dishes | *make* a pie, cake, meal |
| *do* your homework | *make* a decision |
| *do* a job | *make* a mistake |
| *do* the shopping | *make* a deal |
| *do* the laundry | *make* progress |
| *do* someone a favor | *make* a speech |
| *do* your hair | *make* a living |

## VERB-PREPOSITION COMBINATIONS
The uses and meanings of prepositions in the English language are very difficult to master. When they are part of two-word and three-word combinations with verbs, the prepositions are called **particles,** and the combinations are called **phrasal verbs.** Some of these particles may be separated from the verb, and others may not be separated. Since there is no clear rule, each one must be learned the same way you would learn a new vocabulary word. Below are a few common verb-preposition combinations.

**Separable phrasal verbs**

| | |
|---|---|
| ask out (invite on a date) | **He *asked out* the older girl.**<br>**He *asked* the older girl *out*.** |
| call off (cancel) | **Let's *call off* the party.**<br>**Let's *call* the party *off*.** |
| call up (telephone) | **The officer *called up* the applicant.**<br>**The officer *called* the applicant *up*.** |
| clear up (solve) | **Can you *clear up* this problem?**<br>**Can you *clear* this problem *up*?** |
| fill out (complete) | **Please *fill out* these forms.**<br>**Please *fill* these forms *out*.** |

| | |
|---|---|
| get back (recover) | The student *got back* the test results.<br>The student *got* the test results *back.* |
| leave out (omit) | Don't *leave out* any answers.<br>Don't *leave* any answers *out.* |
| look over (review) | *Look over* this paper for any errors.<br>*Look* this paper *over* for any errors. |
| look up (research, check) | *Look up* the number in the telephone book.<br>*Look* the number *up* in the telephone book. |
| make up (create, invent, lie) | Do you think he *made up* the story?<br>Do you think he *made* the story *up?* |
| turn down (refuse) | She *turned down* our generous offer.<br>She *turned* our generous offer *down.* |
| turn off (switch off) | *Turn off* the light.<br>*Turn* the light *off.* |

## Nonseparable phrasal verbs

| | |
|---|---|
| call on (visit; choose) | Doctors used to *call on* patients in their homes.<br>The teacher *called on* me for the answer. |
| get away with (escape the consequences of) | Our dog always tries to *get away with* something when we are out. |
| get along with (be on good terms with) | The new employee *gets along with* all her coworkers. |
| get over (recover from) | We took a long time to *get over* the loss of our pet. |
| get at (hint, suggest) | What do you think the editorial was *getting at?* |
| get after (scold) | The mother will *get after* the child for being disobedient. |
| go over (review) | Please *go over* the chapter before taking the test. |
| let up (diminish in force) | The storm will soon *let up.* |
| look in on (visit) | Joshua *looks in on* his elderly mother at least twice a week. |

| | |
|---|---|
| look into (investigate) | The federal agents will *look into* the case. |
| run into (meet) | I always *run into* someone I know at the supermarket. |
| run out of (become used up) | The printer will soon *run out of* paper. |
| speak up (talk in a louder voice) | Please *speak up* so that I can hear you. |
| turn up (appear) | Has the lost child *turned up* yet? |
| wear out (become unusable through long use) | He *wore out* five pairs of jeans this season. |

## VERBS FOLLOWED BY GERUNDS OR INFINITIVES

Some verbs may be followed by gerunds (*-ing* form of the verb). Others are followed by infinitives (*to* plus the base form of the verb). Still others may be followed by either a gerund or an infinitive. Because this is a challenging aspect of becoming fluent in English, begin by learning the most commonly used expressions. Then gradually increase your correct usage of these many expressions. Look for them as you read and try to incorporate them into your speaking and writing.

### Verbs followed by gerunds

| | | | |
|---|---|---|---|
| admit | deny | imagine | practice |
| appreciate | discuss | keep | quit |
| avoid | enjoy | miss | risk |
| consider | finish | postpone | suggest |

I *imagined going* on a cruise.

I *quit eating* junk food.

### Verbs followed by infinitives

| | | | |
|---|---|---|---|
| agree to | decide to | mean to | promise to |
| ask to | expect to | need to | refuse to |
| beg to | have to | offer to | want to |
| choose to | hope to | plan to | |
| claim to | manage to | pretend to | |

I *expect to visit* you by the end of the summer.

### Verbs followed by either gerunds or infinitives

| | | | |
|---|---|---|---|
| begin | hate | remember | try |
| continue | like | start | |
| forget | love | stop | |

Stuart *began reading* at age four.

or

Stuart *began to read* at age four.

# ESOL WORD CONFUSIONS

## WHEN DO YOU USE *NO* AND WHEN DO YOU USE *NOT*?

Use *no* before a noun. *No* is an adjective.

I have *no food* in the house.

Use *not* before a verb, adverb, or adjective. *Not* is an adverb.

I am *not going.*

They were *not very* satisfied.

We are *not unhappy.*

## WHAT IS THE DIFFERENCE BETWEEN *A FEW* AND *FEW* AND BETWEEN *A LITTLE* AND *LITTLE*?

Use *a few* and *a little* to mean *some:*

| | |
|---|---|
| **With count nouns:** | We have *a few cans* on the shelf, maybe five or six. |
| **With noncount nouns:** | We have *a little money* in the bank. |

Use *few* and *little* to mean *not many* or *not much:*

| | |
|---|---|
| **With count nouns:** | We have *few cans* left, two or three at most. |
| **With noncount nouns:** | We have *little money* in the bank. |

# OTHER ESOL CONCERNS ADDRESSED I*N THE WRITER'S WORKPLACE*

# PARTS OF SPEECH

Words can be divided into categories called **parts of speech.** Understanding these categories will help you work with language more easily, especially when it comes to revising your own writing.

## NOUNS

> A **noun** is a word that names a person, place, or thing.

| Common nouns | Proper nouns |
|---|---|
| officer | Michael Johnson |
| station | Grand Central Station |
| magazine | *Newsweek* |

Nouns are said to be **concrete** if they name things you can see or touch.

window    paper    river

Nouns are said to be **abstract** if they name things you cannot see or touch. These words may express concepts, ideas, or qualities.

marriage    democracy    honesty

To find out whether a word is a noun, it may help to ask one or more of these questions:

- Can I make the word plural? (Most nouns have a plural form.)
- Can I put the article *the* in front of the word?
- Is the word used as the subject or object of the sentence?

## PRONOUNS

> A **pronoun** is a word that takes the place of a noun. Like a noun, a pronoun can be a subject or an object in a sentence. It can also be used to show possession.

Pronouns can be divided into eight classes. Four of these are given in the following chart: *personal pronouns, relative pronouns, demonstrative pronouns, and indefinite pronouns.*

## Classes of Pronouns

### PERSONAL PRONOUNS

| | Subjective | | Objective | | Possessive | |
|---|---|---|---|---|---|---|
| | **Singular** | **Plural** | **Singular** | **Plural** | **Singular** | **Plural** |
| 1st Person | I | we | me | us | my (mine) | our (ours) |
| 2nd Person | you | you | you | you | your (yours) | your (yours) |
| 3rd Person | he<br>she<br>it | they | him<br>her<br>it | them | his (his)<br>her (hers)<br>its (its) | their (theirs) |

### RELATIVE PRONOUNS
### (CAN INTRODUCE NOUN CLAUSES AND ADJECTIVE CLAUSES)

who    what    whose    which    that    what    whoever    whichever    whatever

### DEMONSTRATIVE PRONOUNS
### (CAN POINT OUT THE ANTECEDENT)

this    these    that    those

### INDEFINITE PRONOUNS
#### Singular

| | | | | | |
|---|---|---|---|---|---|
| another | someone | everyone | no one | each | much |
| anyone | somebody | everybody | nobody | either | one |
| anybody | something | everything | nothing | neither | such |
| anything | | | | | |

#### Plural

both    few    many    several

#### Singular or Plural
#### (depending on meaning)

all    any    more    most    none    some

# ADJECTIVES

> An **adjective** is a word that modifies, describes, or limits a noun or a pronoun. Adjectives usually come directly before the nouns they modify, but they can also appear later in the sentence.

Here the adjective comes directly in front of the noun it modifies:

**The *unusual* package was placed on my desk.**

Here the adjective occurs later but refers back to the noun it modifies:

**The package felt *cold*.**

# VERBS

> A ***verb*** is a word that shows action or expresses being. It can change form to show the time (past, present, or future) of that action or being.

Verbs can be divided into three classes: action verbs, linking verbs, and helping verbs.

## ACTION VERBS

> An ***action verb*** tells us what the subject is doing and when the action occurs.

In this sentence, the action takes place in the present:

**The athlete *runs* five miles every morning.**

In this sentence, the action takes place in the past:

**The crowd *cheered* for the oldest runner.**

## LINKING VERBS

> A ***linking verb*** joins the subject of a sentence to one or more words that describe or identify the subject.

Here the linking verb *was* identifies *he* with the noun *dancer*:

**He *was* a dancer in his twenties.**

Here the linking verb *seemed* describes *she* as *disappointed*:

**She *seemed* disappointed with her job.**

## Common Linking Verbs

| | | | |
|---|---|---|---|
| act | become | look | sound |
| appear | feel | remain | taste |
| be (am, is, are, was, were, | get | seem | turn |
| has been, have been, had been) | grow | smell | |

## HELPING VERBS (ALSO CALLED AUXILIARIES)

> A **helping verb** combines with the main verb to form a verb phrase. It always comes before the main verb.

The helping verb could show the *tense* of the verb:

**It *will* rain tomorrow.**

The helping verb could show the *passive voice:*

**The new civic center *has been* finished.**

The helping verb could give a *special meaning* to the verb:

**Barry Manilow *may be* singing here tonight.**

## Common Helping Verbs

|       |        | Forms of *be* |      | Forms of *have* | Forms of *do* |
|-------|--------|---------------|------|-----------------|---------------|
| can   | shall  | being         | are  | has             | does          |
| could | should | been          | was  | have            | do            |
| may   | will   | am            | were | had             | did           |
| might | would  | is            |      |                 |               |
| must  |        |               |      |                 |               |

# ADVERBS

> An **adverb** is a word that modifies a verb, an adjective, or another adverb. It often ends in *-ly*, but a better test is to ask yourself if the word answers one of the questions *how, when,* or *where.*

The adverb could modify a *verb:*

**The student walked *happily* into the classroom.**

The adverb could modify an *adjective:*

**It will be *very* cold tomorrow.**

The adverb could modify another *adverb:*

**Winter has come *too* early.**

Learn to recognize the common adverbs in the following list.

## Common Adverbs

| Adverbs of frequency | | Adverbs of degree | |
|---|---|---|---|
| always | often | even | only |
| ever | seldom | extremely | quite |
| never | sometimes | just | surely |
| | | more | too |
| | | much | very |

# PREPOSITIONS

A **preposition** is a word that may be used to relate a noun or pronoun to some other word in the sentence. The preposition with its noun or pronoun and any modifiers is called a **prepositional phrase.**

**The letter is *from* my father.**

**The envelope is addressed *to* my sister.**

Read through the following list of prepositions several times so that you will be able to recognize them. Your instructor may ask you to memorize them.

## Common Prepositions

| | | | | |
|---|---|---|---|---|
| about | behind | except | onto | toward |
| above | below | for | out | under |
| across | beneath | from | outside | underneath |
| after | beside | in | over | unlike |
| against | between | inside | past | until |
| along | beyond | into | regarding | up |
| among | by | like | since | upon |
| around | concerning | near | through | with |
| as | despite | of | throughout | within |
| at | down | off | till | without |
| before | during | on | to | |

# CONJUNCTIONS

> A **conjunction** is a word that joins or connects words, phrases, or clauses.

A conjunction may connect *two words:*

**Sooner *or* later, you will have to pay.**

A conjunction may connect *two phrases:*

**The story was on the radio *and* in the newspaper.**

A conjunction may connect *two clauses:*

**Dinner was late *because* I had to work overtime.**

## Conjunctions

### Coordinating conjunctions

| | |
|---|---|
| and | yet |
| but | so |
| or | |
| nor | |
| for (meaning *because*) | |

### Subordinating conjunctions

| | |
|---|---|
| after | if, even if | though |
| although | in order that | unless |
| as, as if, as though | provided | until |
| as long as | that | when, whenever |
| because | rather than | where, wherever |
| before | since | whether |
| even though | so that | while |
| how | that | |

### Correlative conjunctions

either . . . or
neither . . . nor
both . . . and
not only . . . but
also

### Adverbial conjunctions
### (also known as conjunctive adverbs)

| | | | |
|---|---|---|---|
| *To add an idea:* | furthermore | *To show an alternative:* | otherwise |
| | moreover | | instead |
| | likewise | | on the other |
| | in addition | *To show likeness:* | hand |
| | also | | likewise |
| | besides | *To show emphasis:* | similarly |
| *To contrast:* | however | *To show time:* | indeed |
| | nevertheless | | in fact |
| | nonetheless | | meanwhile |
| | consequently | | |
| *To show results:* | therefore | | |
| | accordingly | | |
| | hence | | |
| | thus | | |

# INTERJECTIONS

> An *interjection* is a word that expresses a strong feeling and is not connected grammatically to any other part of the sentence.

**Oh, I forgot my keys.**

***Well*, that means I'll have to sit here all day.**

# STUDYING THE CONTEXT

Because one word may function differently or have different forms or meanings in different sentences, you must often study the context in which the word is found to be sure of its part of speech. In the following sentence, *for* functions as a preposition:

**The parent makes sacrifices *for* the good of the children.**

But in this next sentence, *for* functions as a conjunction, meaning *because:*

**The parent worked two jobs, *for* her child needed a good education.**

# IRREGULAR VERBS

Following is an alphabetical listing of the principal parts of common irregular verbs.

| Base form | Past tense | Past participle |
| --- | --- | --- |
| arise | arose | arisen |
| bear | bore | borne |
| beat | beat | beat, beaten |
| become | became | become |
| begin | began | begun |
| bend | bent | bent |
| bet | bet | bet |
| bind | bound | bound |
| bite | bit | bitten, bit |
| bleed | bled | bled |
| blow | blew | blown |
| break | broke | broken |
| breed | bred | bred |
| bring | brought | brought |
| build | built | built |
| burst | burst | burst |
| buy | bought | bought |
| cast | cast | cast |
| catch | caught | caught |
| choose | chose | chosen |
| cling | clung | clung |
| come | came | come |
| cost | cost | cost |
| creep | crept | crept |
| cut | cut | cut |
| deal | dealt | dealt |
| dig | dug | dug |
| dive | dived, dove | dived |

| Base form | Past tense | Past participle |
| --- | --- | --- |
| do | did | done |
| draw | drew | drawn |
| drink | drank | drunk |
| drive | drove | driven |
| eat | ate | eaten |
| fall | fell | fallen |
| feed | fed | fed |
| feel | felt | felt |
| fight | fought | fought |
| find | found | found |
| fit | fit | fit |
| flee | fled | fled |
| fling | flung | flung |
| fly | flew | flown |
| forbid | forbade, forbad | forbidden |
| forget | forgot | forgotten |
| forgive | forgave | forgiven |
| freeze | froze | frozen |
| get | got | gotten |
| give | gave | given |
| go | went | gone |
| grind | ground | ground |
| grow | grew | grown |
| hang | hung, hanged* | hung, hanged |
| have | had | had |
| hear | heard | heard |
| hide | hid | hidden |
| hit | hit | hit |
| hold | held | held |
| hurt | hurt | hurt |
| keep | kept | kept |
| kneel | knelt | knelt |
| know | knew | known |
| lay (to put) | laid | laid |
| lead | led | led |
| leave | left | left |
| lend | lent | lent |

*See the dictionary to clarify usage.

| Base form | Past tense | Past participle |
| --- | --- | --- |
| let | let | let |
| lie (to recline) | lay | lain |
| lose | lost | lost |
| make | made | made |
| mean | meant | meant |
| meet | met | met |
| mistake | mistook | mistaken |
| pay | paid | paid |
| plead | pleaded, pled | pleaded, pled |
| prove | proved | proved, proven |
| put | put | put |
| quit | quit | quit |
| read | read* | read* |
| ride | rode | ridden |
| ring | rang | rung |
| rise | rose | risen |
| run | ran | run |
| say | said | said |
| see | saw | seen |
| seek | sought | sought |
| sell | sold | sold |
| send | sent | sent |
| set | set | set |
| sew | sewed | sewn, sewed |
| shake | shook | shaken |
| shave | shaved | shaved, shaven |
| shed | shed | shed |
| shine | shone | shone |
| shoot | shot | shot |
| show | showed | shown, showed |
| shrink | shrank, shrunk | shrunk, shrunken |
| shut | shut | shut |
| sing | sang | sung |
| sink | sank | sunk |
| sit | sat | sat |
| slay | slew | slain |
| sleep | slept | slept |
| slide | slid | slid |

*Pronunciation changes in past and past participle forms.

| Base form | Past tense | Past participle |
| --- | --- | --- |
| sling | slung | slung |
| slink | slunk | slunk |
| slit | slit | slit |
| sow | sowed | sown, sowed |
| speak | spoke | spoken |
| speed | sped, speeded | sped, speeded |
| spend | spent | spent |
| spin | spun | spun |
| spit | spat | spat |
| split | split | split |
| spread | spread | spread |
| spring | sprang | sprung |
| stand | stood | stood |
| steal | stole | stolen |
| stick | stuck | stuck |
| sting | stung | stung |
| stink | stank, stunk | stunk |
| stride | strode | stridden |
| strike | struck | struck |
| string | strung | strung |
| swear | swore | sworn |
| sweep | swept | swept |
| swim | swam | swum |
| swing | swung | swung |
| take | took | taken |
| teach | taught | taught |
| tear | tore | torn |
| tell | told | told |
| think | thought | thought |
| throw | threw | thrown |
| wake | woke, waked | woken, waked |
| wear | wore | worn |
| weave | wove | woven |
| weep | wept | wept |
| wet | wet | wet |
| win | won | won |
| wind | wound | wound |
| wring | wrung | wrung |
| write | wrote | written |

# SPELLING

## FORMING THE PLURALS OF NOUNS

Almost all nouns can be made plural by simply adding *s* to the singular form:

| | |
|---|---|
| girl | girls |
| dinner | dinners |

However, each of the following groups of words has its own special rules for forming the plural.

1. **Words ending in -y.** For words ending in *-y* preceded by a *consonant*, change the *y* to *i* and add *es*.

| | |
|---|---|
| la*dy* | lad*ies* |
| ceremo*ny* | ceremon*ies* |

Words ending in *-y* preceded by a *vowel* form their plurals in the regular way, by just adding *s*.

| | |
|---|---|
| d*ay* | days |
| monk*ey* | monkeys |
| vall*ey* | valleys |

2. **Words ending in -o.** Most words ending in *-o* preceded by a *consonant* add *es* to form the plural.

| | |
|---|---|
| he*ro* | hero*es* |
| pota*to* | potato*es* |
| ec*ho* | echo*es* |

However, musical terms or names of musical instruments add only *s*.

| | |
|---|---|
| pian*o* | pianos |
| sol*o* | solos |
| sopran*o* | sopranos |

Words ending in *-o* preceded by a *vowel* add *s*.

| | |
|---|---|
| pat*io* | patios |
| rad*io* | radios |
| rod*eo* | rodeos |

Some words ending in *-o* may form their plural with *s* or *es*.

| memento | mementos | or | mementoes |
| pinto | pintos | or | pintoes |
| zero | zeros | or | zeroes |

If you are uncertain about the plural ending of a word ending in *-o,* it is best to consult a dictionary. The dictionary gives all the endings of irregular plurals. If no plural form is given, you know the word forms its plural in the regular way, by adding only *s*.

3. **Words ending in -ch, -sh, -s, -x, and -z.** For words ending in *-ch, -sh, -s, -x,* and *-z*, add *es*.

| witches | dresses | buzzes |
| dishes | taxes | |

4. **Words ending in -fe or -f.** For some words ending in *-fe* or *-f*, change the *f* to *v* and add *es*. You can hear the change from the *f* sound to the *v* sound in the plural.

| wife | wives |
| leaf | leaves |

For other words ending in *-fe* or *-f*, keep the *f* and just add *s*.

| sheriff | sheriffs |
| belief | beliefs |

Again, you can hear that the *f* sound is kept in the plural. Some words can form their plural either way. If so, the dictionary will give the preferred way first.

5. **Foreign words.** Some words borrowed from other languages use the plurals from those other languages.

| crisis | crises |
| phenomenon | phenomena |
| alumnus (masc.) | alumni |
| alumna (fem.) | alumnae |
| alga | algae |

6. **Compound nouns.** Plurals of compound nouns are formed by putting *s* on the end of the main word.

| brother-in-law | brothers-in-law |
| passer-by | passers-by |

7. **Irregular plurals.** Some nouns in English have irregular plurals.

| child | children |
| deer | deer |
| foot | feet |
| goose | geese |

| | |
|---|---|
| man, woman | men, women |
| moose | moose |
| mouse | mice |
| ox | oxen |
| sheep | sheep |
| tooth | teeth |

## ADDING ENDINGS TO WORDS ENDING IN -Y

1.  When a *y* at the end of a word is preceded by a consonant, change *y* to *i* and add the ending. (After you have studied the examples, write the other words on the blanks.)

| Word | | Ending | | New word |
|---|---|---|---|---|
| carry | + | er | = | carri*er* |
| merry | + | ment | = | merri*ment* |
| funny | + | er | = | _____ |
| busy | + | ness | = | _____ |
| vary | + | es | = | _____ |

**Exceptions:** Do not change the y to i if the ending starts with i. In English, we seldom have two i's together.

| study | + | ing | = | stud*ying* (not studiing) |
|---|---|---|---|---|
| ready | + | ing | = | _____ |

Some long words drop the y when the ending is added. You can hear that the y syllable is missing when you pronounce the word correctly.

| military | + | ism | = | militarism |
|---|---|---|---|---|
| accomp*any* | + | *ist* | = | _____ |

2.  When a *y* at the end of a word is preceded by a vowel, do *not* change the *y* when adding the ending. Simply add the ending.

| survey | + | s | = | surve*ys* |
|---|---|---|---|---|
| enjo*y* | + | ment | = | _____ |

# LEARNING TO SPELL *IE* OR *EI* WORDS

Use this rhyme to help you remember how to spell most *ie* and *ei* words:

> **i before e**
>
> **except after c**
>
> **or when sounded like ā**
>
> **as in *neighbor* or *weigh*.**

*i* before *e* (*ie* is much more common than *ei*):

| | | |
|---|---|---|
| believe | friend | yield |
| chief | shriek | |

except after *c*:

| | | |
|---|---|---|
| ceiling | conceive | receive |
| conceit | receipt | |

or when sounded like *ā* as in **n*ei*ghbor** or **w*ei*gh**:

| | | |
|---|---|---|
| beige | reins | vein |
| eight | sleigh | |

Once you have learned the rhyme, concentrate on learning the following groups of words, which are exceptions to the rhyme.

**Exceptions to the *ie/ei* rule**

| | | | | |
|---|---|---|---|---|
| caffeine | leisure | ancient | either | counterfeit |
| codeine | seize | conscience | neither | Fahrenheit |
| protein | seizure | efficient | sheik | foreign |
| | | sufficient | stein | height |
| | | | their | |
| | | | weird | |

# WHEN SHOULD THE FINAL CONSONANT OF A WORD BE DOUBLED?

When you add an ending that begins with a vowel (*-ed, -er, -est, -ing*) to a word, how do you know whether you should double the final consonant of that word? The answer to this question involves a complicated spelling rule. However, the rule is well worth learning because once you know it, you will suddenly be able to spell scores of words correctly.

In the examples below, can you explain why the word *trap* doubles its *p* but the word *turn* does not double its *n*?

**The final *p* doubles:**           trap + ing = tra**pp**ing

**The final *n* does not double:**  turn + ing = tur**n**ing

Because the last three letters (*rap*) in the word *trap* are a consonant-vowel-consonant combination, you double the final consonant in this one-syllable word (when adding an ending beginning with a vowel). Since the last three letters (*urn*) in the word *turn* are a vowel-consonant-consonant combination, you do not double the final consonant in this one-syllable word (when adding an ending beginning with a vowel).

> Double the final consonant of a one-syllable word when adding an ending that begins with a vowel only if the last three letters of the word end with a consonant-vowel-consonant combination.

**Practice**  **Study the list of words that follows. For each of these one-syllable words, decide whether to double the final consonant when adding an ending beginning with a vowel.**

| One-syllable word | Consonant-vowel-consonant combination? | Double? | Word with -ing ending |
|---|---|---|---|
| 1. drag | _____ | _____ | _____ |
| 2. drain | _____ | _____ | _____ |
| 3. slip | _____ | _____ | _____ |
| 4. crack | _____ | _____ | _____ |
| 5. broil | _____ | _____ | _____ |
| 6. win | _____ | _____ | _____ |

**NOTE:** In words with *qu*, like *quit* or *quiz*, think of the *qu* as a consonant: *quit* + ing = quitting. The *u* does have a consonant *w* sound.

**For words of more than one syllable, the rule has one more condition: If the first syllable in the newly formed word is accented, do not double the final consonant.**

Thus,

**pre fer´ + ed = pre ferred´**

(The new word *preferred* maintains the accent on the second syllable, so the final *r* is doubled.) However,

**pre fer´ + ence = pref´ er ence**

(In the new word *preference*, the accent is on the first syllable, so the final consonant *r* is not doubled.)

## IS IT ONE WORD OR TWO?

Deciding whether certain words should be joined to form compound words is difficult. To avoid confusion, study the following three groups of words.

These words are always written as one word:

| | | |
|---|---|---|
| another | good-bye, | playroom |
| bathroom | or good-by | roommate |
| bedroom | grandmother | schoolteacher |
| bookkeeper | nearby | southeast, northwest, and so on |
| cannot | nevertheless | yourself |
| downstairs | newspaper | |

These words are always written as two words:

| | | | |
|---|---|---|---|
| a lot | dining room | high school | no one |
| all right | good night | living room | |

The following words may be written as one or two words depending on their use. After you have studied the spellings and definitions, write the proper words on the blanks in the sample sentences.

**all ready (pron, adj):**   completely prepared

**already (adv):** previously; before

He was _____there by the time I arrived.

I have_____read that book.

We were_____for the New Year's Eve party.

**all together (pron, adj):**   in a group

**altogether (adv):**        completely

Our family was_____at Thanksgiving.

I am _____too upset to concentrate.

Have you gathered your papers _____?

**all ways (adj, noun):**     every road or path

**always (adv):**        on every occasion

Be sure to check _____before you cross that intersection.

_____look both ways before you cross that intersection.

She _____figures out the homework.

**any one (adj, pron):**        one person or thing in a specific group

**anyone (indefinite pron):**   any person at all

Did _____ever find my gloves?

She will talk to_____ who will listen to her.

I would choose_____ of those sweaters if I had the money.

**every one (adj, pron):**      every person or thing in a specific group

**everyone (indefinite pron):**    all of the people

_____of the books we wanted was out of stock.

_____was so disappointed.

_____of the workers disapproved of the new rules.

**may be (verb):**               might be

**maybe (adv):**                 perhaps

The news broadcast said that there_____ a storm tomorrow.

If it's bad, _____ I won't go to work.

_____my car won't start.

# SPELLING COMMONLY MISPRONOUNCED WORDS

Several common English words are often mispronounced or pronounced in such a way that the result is incorrect spelling. Below are sixty common words that are often misspelled. As you study them, be careful to spell each of the underlined syllables correctly.

1.  Remember the *a* in each underlined syllable:

    | | |
    |---|---|
    | accidentally | literature |
    | basically | miniature |
    | boundary | separate |
    | extraordinary | temperament |
    | incidentally | temperature |

2.  Remember the *e* in each underlined syllable:

    | | |
    |---|---|
    | considerable | mathematics |
    | difference | numerous |
    | funeral | scenery |
    | interesting | |

Notice, however, that the words below in column 1, which end in -*er*, drop the *e* when they change to the new form in column 2.

| | |
|---|---|
| disaster | disastrous |
| enter | entrance |
| hinder | hindrance |

> hunger       hungry
>
> launder      laundry
>
> monster      monstrous
>
> remember     remembrance

3. Remember the *i* in each underlined syllable:

   aspirin       family     similar

4. Remember the *o* in each underlined syllable:

   chocolate     humorous
   environment   laboratory
   favorite      sophomore

5. Remember the *u* in each underlined syllable:

   luxury        accuracy

6. Remember the *y* in each underlined syllable:

   studying      carrying

7. Remember the underlined consonant in each of the following words:

   **b**                    **n**

   probably                 government

   **c**                    **r**

   arctic                   February

                            library

   **d**                    surprise

   candidate

   handkerchief             **t**

   supposed to              authentic

   used to                  identical

                            partner

   **g**                    promptly

   recognize                quantity

8. Do not add an extra *e* after the *th:*

   athlete                  athletic

9. Do not transpose the underlined letters:

   tragedy

   persuade                 prefer

   perform                  prescription

# SPELLING TWO HUNDRED TOUGH WORDS

## Word List 1: Silent Letters

**b**

climb

crumb

debt

doubt

**c**

indict

**d**

knowledge

Wednesday

**h**

exhibit

rhetoric

rhythm

schedule

**l**

colonel

**n**

autumn

column

condemn

**p**

pneumonia

psychology

**s**

aisle

debris

island

**t**

depot

listen

mortgage

**w**

answer

## Word List 2: Double Letters

| | | | |
|---|---|---|---|
| accidentally | committee | possession | suggest |
| accommodate | exaggerate | preferred | summarize |
| across | finally | questionnaire | tomorrow |
| annual | guarantee | recommend | written (but writing) |
| apparently | necessary | succeed | |
| arrangement | occasionally | success | |

## Word List 3: -*able* or -*ible*

**-able.** Usually, when you begin with a complete word, the ending is -*able*.

acceptable          agreeable

These words keep the *e* when the ending is added:

knowledgeable      noticeable

manageable          peaceable

These words drop the *e* when the ending is added:

conceivable         imaginable

desirable           indispensable

**-ible.** Usually, if you start with a root that is not a word, the ending is *-ible*.

| | | |
|---|---|---|
| audible | illegible | possible |
| compatible | incredible | susceptible |
| eligible | permissible | tangible |
| feasible | plausible | |

## Word List 4: *de-* or *di-*

**de-**

| | |
|---|---|
| decide | despise |
| decision | despite |
| delinquent | despondent |
| descend | destructive |
| describe | develop |
| despair | device |
| despicable | |

**di-**

| | |
|---|---|
| dilemma | dispense |
| dilute | dispute |
| discipline | dissent |
| discuss | divide |
| disease | divine |
| disguise | division |

## Word List 5: The *-er* Sound

Most words ending with the *-er* sound are spelled with *-er,* like the words *prisoner, customer,* and *hunger.* Words that are exceptions to this should be learned carefully.

| **-ar** | **-or** | **-ur** |
|---|---|---|
| beggar | actor | murmur |
| burglar | author | |
| calendar | bachelor | **-yr** |
| cellar | doctor | martyr |
| dollar | emperor | |
| grammar | governor | |
| pillar | humor | |
| polar | labor | |
| similar | motor | |
| vulgar | neighbor | |
| | professor | |
| | sailor | |
| | scissors | |

## Word List 6: *-ance* or *-ence*

Most words with the *-ence* sound at the end are spelled *-ence*. Here are a few examples:

| | |
|---|---|
| audience | intelligence |
| correspondence | presence |
| excellence | reference |
| existence | |

Learn these exceptions:

| **-ance** | | **-ense** | **-eance** |
|---|---|---|---|
| allowance | guidance | license | vengeance |
| ambulance | ignorance | | |
| appearance | nuisance | | |
| assistance | observance | | |
| attendance | resistance | | |
| balance | significance | | |
| dominance | tolerance | | |

## Word List 7: Problems with *s, c, z, x,* and *k*

| | | | |
|---|---|---|---|
| absence | concede | exceed | prejudice |
| alcohol | consensus | exercise | recede |
| analyze | criticize | fascinate | sincerely |
| auxiliary | ecstasy | magazine | supersede |
| awkward | emphasize | medicine | vacillate |
| biscuit | especially | muscle | vicious |
| complexion | | | |

## Word List 8: Twenty-Five Demons

| | | | |
|---|---|---|---|
| acquire | corroborate | judgment | privilege |
| argument | courageous | lightning | ridiculous |
| benefit | extremely | ninety | secretary |
| cafeteria | frightening | ninth | truly |
| category | grateful | occurred | until |
| cemetery | inoculate | occurrence | village |
| conquer | | | |

# TRANSITIONS

Transitions are words or phrases that take the reader from one idea to another. Here are some of the most commonly used transitional expressions. They are especially useful when you want to make the connections between ideas clear to your readers.

### Transitions for description—to show place

| | |
|---|---|
| above, on top of | to the left, to the right |
| beneath, under | beside, near, close by, at hand, next to |
| ahead, in front of, | across from, nearby, |
| in the distance | in the neighborhood |
| behind, in back of | between, in the middle, in the center |
| toward, away from | |

### Transitions for narration—to show a shift in time

| | | |
|---|---|---|
| recently | suddenly | then |
| previously | immediately | next, the next day |
| earlier | meanwhile | several weeks later |
| in the past | at the same time | the following month |
| a few days ago | within a few minutes | finally |
| a hundred years ago | soon, soon afterward | eventually |
| now, by now | later, later on | in the end |
| at once | after a little while | |

### Transitions to show examples

| | | |
|---|---|---|
| for example | a case in point is. . . | specifically |
| another example is. . . | one such case | for instance |
| to illustrate | a typical case | such as |
| an illustration of this is. . . | consider the case of. . . | |

### Transitions for process

| | | |
|---|---|---|
| the first step | while you are. . . | the last step |
| in the beginning | as you are. . . | the final step |
| to start with | next | finally |

to begin with　　　　then　　　　　　at last

first of all　　　　　the second step　　eventually

　　　　　　　　　　after you have. . .

## Transitions for comparison

| | |
|---|---|
| again | like |
| also | likewise |
| as well as | moreover |
| both | the same |
| equally | similar to |
| furthermore | similarly |
| just as | so |
| just like | too |

## Transitions for contrast

| | |
|---|---|
| although | nevertheless |
| and | on the contrary |
| but | on the other hand |
| despite | otherwise |
| different from | still |
| even though | though |
| except for | unlike |
| however | whereas |
| in contrast with | yet |
| instead | |

## Transitions for cause

because

caused by

results from

the reason is that

since

## Transitions for effect

accordingly

as a result, resulted in

consequently

for this reason

so, so that

then, therefore, thus

## Terms that signal classification

divisions, divided into

categories, categorized by

types, kinds

groups, groupings, grouped into

areas, fields

## Phrases that signal definition

is defined as

is understood to be

means that

is sometimes thought to be

signifies that

## Transitions for persuasion

*To signal the thesis:*

I agree (disagree)

I (do not) support

I am (not) in favor of

. . .should (not) be changed

. . .should (not) be adopted

I propose

*To signal a reason:*

a convincing piece of evidence

an additional reason

because

in view of this fact

*To admit an opponent's viewpoint:*

while it is true

although there are those who. . .

the opposition would have you believe. . .

of course,

some may claim

we have been told that. . .

popular thought is that. . .

most people assume that. . .

*To signal a conclusion:*

therefore

consequently

as a result

# CHAPTER 1: GATHERING IDEAS FOR WRITING

## Activity 5: Preparing Questions for an Interview (page 15)

1. What is a typical day at work like?
2. What is the range of salaries that a person could expect to earn as a lawyer?
3. What are the different areas of law practice, and how did you choose which one you wanted to pursue?
4. What is the most interesting case you have ever had?
5. What are some of your greatest challenges, and how do you handle them?

# CHAPTER 2: RECOGNIZING THE ELEMENTS OF GOOD WRITING

## Activity 1: Providing Examples for Different Approaches to a Subject (page 21, sample answers)

1. *A personal story:* the story of my unusual part-time job.
2. *Effects:* the hidden costs of having a job while going to school
3. *How to do something:* how to succeed in school while holding a job.
4. *Comparison/contrast:* the contrast between students who hold a job while going to school and students who can devote all their time to school
5. *Persuasion:* three good reasons why you should not work while you are going to school

## Activity 3: Identifying an Audience and a Purpose (page 23, sample answers)

1. *Audience:* first-aid class; *Purpose:* information
2. *Audience:* town council; *Purpose:* information and persuasion
3. *Audience:* owners; *Purpose:* information
4. *Audience:* community; *Purpose:* persuasion
5. *Audience:* classmates; *purpose:* entertainment

# CHAPTER 3: FINDING SUBJECTS AND VERBS IN SIMPLE SENTENCES

## Practice (page 35)

1. gym   2. coach   3. He   4. athletes
5. People

## Practice (page 36)

1. morning, June   2. flowers, grass   3. people, village, square   4. lottery, Mr. Sommers
5. man, time, energy, activities

## Practice (pages 36–37)

1. They   2. It   3. They   4. She   5. We
6. Nobody or No one

## Practice (pages 37–38)

1. The, confident
2. Her, long, strenuous (*her* is a possessive pronoun used as an adjective)
3. Several, the, finish
4. a, terrible, one
5. A, disappointing, the
  Note: *A, an,* and *the* are usually called *articles* or *noun determiners.*

## Practice (page 38)

1. Exercise, diet   2. Mothers, fathers
3. factors, factors

## Practice (page 38)

1. child: concrete common noun
2. Helen Keller: concrete proper noun
3. She: personal pronoun
4. park: concrete common noun

5. leaves: concrete common noun
6. thought: abstract common noun
7. parents, teacher: compound subject; concrete common nouns

## Exercise 1: Finding the Subject of a Sentence (page 39)

1. train    2. Steven Laye    3. He
4. Everything    5. man    6. tunnel
7. Buses, cars  8. People    9. noise
10. Loneliness

## Exercise 5: Recognizing Prepositions (page 42)

1. on    2. at    3. about    4. of    5. in
6. as    7. for fear of    8. According to
9. to    10. Without

## Exercise 7: Finding Subjects in Sentences with Prepositional Phrases (pages 42–43)

1. On Friday, January 27, 2006, Western Union sent its last telegram.
2. With the ascendancy of modern technology, the telegram is no longer needed.
3. In 1851 in Rochester, New York, Western Union had its beginings.
4. Messages were transmitted by Morse code over the wires and delivered by couriers.
5. Eventually, telegraph service drove the pony express out of business.
6. Until the emergence of the telegraph, the average delivery time for a message by pony express took ten days.
7. At the height of the telegram business, in 1929, two hundred million telegrams were sent around the world.
8. Now for Western Union, money transfers, bill payment, and products such as telephone service and Internet access will form the core of their business.
9. In the past, families sent messages of births, deaths, birthdays, and weddings by telegram.
10. In the present era, e-mail and fax messages have taken the place of the telegram.

## Practice (pages 43–44)

1. Alex Harkavy, a high school senior, has an auditory-processing disorder.

2. Marcia Rubinstein, an educational consultant, can help him find the right college.
3. For instance, Landmark, a college in Putney, Vermont, specializes in programs for students with learning disabilities.
4. A federal law, the Americans with Disabilities Act, was enacted in 1990.
5. Now many colleges, both public and private ones, offer support for learning-disabled students.
6. One particular guidebook, *Peterson's Colleges with Programs for Students with Learning Disabilities or Attention Deficit Disorders,* is especially helpful.

## Practice (page 45)

1. Here in America the sale of human organs for transplant is against the law.
2. Unfortunately, there is a disturbing illegal market in the sale of these organs.
3. Where do some people desperately look for kidneys?
4. Why are so many donors exploited and unprotected?
5, Get involved.
6. Work toward a solution to this tragic social problem.

## Exercise 8: Finding Subjects in Simple Sentences (page 45)

1. child    2. motion    3. mother    4. lights
5. passengers    6. silence    7. people
8. children    9. woman    10. man

## Practice (page 47)

1. is    2. has    3. comes

## Exercise 11: Finding Action Verbs (page 48)

1. Collectors enjoy    2. people collect

3. collection will give   4. man saved

5. group trades    6. Members  gather

7. person   kept    8. Arthur Fiedler  hung

9. Tom Bloom  finds   10. Collections will entertain

## Exercise 13: Finding Linking Verbs (page 50)

1. My dream last night was wonderful.

2. I had been transformed.

3. I looked young again.

4. The house was empty and quiet.

5. In a sunlit kitchen with a book in hand, I appeared relaxed and happy.

6. In the morning light, the kitchen felt cozy.

7. It seemed safe.

8. The brewing coffee smelled delicious.

9. The bacon, my usual Sunday morning treat, never tasted better.

10. In this dreamworld, life felt satisfying.

## Exercise 15: Finding Helping Verbs (pages 52–53)

1. Graduation from high school does not signal the end of one's learning.
2. In today's world, workers must adjust to many changes in the workplace.
3. They will need to understand new technologies.
4. Can they recognize the difference between facts and opinions in news articles?
5. All citizens would benefit from annual refresher courses in their fields.
6. Everyone should read a daily newspaper.
7. Senior citizens might take courses at local community colleges.
8. Also, they could keep their minds active with crossword puzzles and other games.
9. Have people learned to try new recipes from television cooking programs?
10. Do we take responsibility for keeping our minds curious and engaged?

## Exercise 17: Identifying Parts of Speech (page 54)

1. e   2. d   3. c   4. a   5. b   6. f   7. c
8. f   9. d   10. a

## CHAPTER 4: MAKING SUBJECTS AND VERBS AGREE

### Practice (page 60)

1. barks    2. wakes    3. become    4. deserve
5. throw

### Practice (page 61)

1. doesn't    2. were    3. doesn't    4. Were
5. doesn't

### Exercise 1: Making the Subject and Verb Agree (page 62)

1. writers present    2. They nominate
3. writer lives    4. He doesn't    5. we see
6. He wears    7. books center    8. book is
9. He was    10. We don't

### Exercise 4: Agreement with Hidden Subjects (page 64)

1. plan is    2. busywork prevents    3. period is
4. People do    5. breaks are    6. clutter causes
7. perfectionists do    8. habit is    9. activities are
10. Children need

### Exercise 6: Agreement with Collective Nouns (pages 66–67)

1. crew is    2. union accuses    3. group files
4. team are    5. public voice    6. crowd grows
7. audience interrupt    8. jury hears
9. group have    10. crowd sit

### Exercise 8: Agreement with Indefinite Pronouns (page 68)

1. One was        2. Each is
3. Few deny       4. Nobody has
5. Many show      6. Others depict
7. Some are       8. Most was
9. All were        10. Anything has

## Exercise 10: Subject-Verb Agreement with Compound Subjects (page 70)

1. Macaroni and cheese is
2. meal (and) others have
3. mother (and) father enjoy
4. habits (or) routine needs
5. salad (or) vegetable is
6. Adults (and) children do
7. pizzas (and) sodas are
8. lack (or) eating causes
9. chips (nor) popcorn is
10. apple (or) grapes make

# CHAPTER 5: UNDERSTANDING FRAGMENTS AND PHRASES

## Exercise 1: Putting a Conversation into Complete Sentences (pages 79–80)

1. Do you have everything?
2. I have everything but the new flight plan.
3. We have twenty minutes until takeoff.
4. It looks like nasty weather.
5. Hopefully, there won't be any flocks of birds in our flight path.
6. Have they deiced the wings?
7. It has just been done!
8. We will have a full plane today.
9. Are you ready?
10. We are good to go.

## Exercise 3: Correcting Fragments That Belong to Other Sentences (page 83)

1. Fishing is one of the oldest sports in the world **and can be one of the most relaxing.** A person with a simple wooden pole and line can have as much fun as a sportsman **with expensive equipment. For busy executives, overworked teachers, and even presidents of nations,** fishing can be a good way to escape from the stress of demanding jobs.
2. The first electric car was built in 1887. It was sold commercially **six years later.** At the turn of the century, people had great faith in new technology. In fact, three hundred electric taxicabs were operating in New York City by 1900. However, electric cars soon lost their popularity. The new

gasoline engine became more widely used. **With our concern over pollution,** perhaps electric cars will become desirable once again.
3. Tiger Woods is famous for his success as a championship golfer. He is also known for his work with children. In Anaheim, California, Tiger has recently opened a learning center **for fourth to twelfth graders.** Children can apply for a wide range of classes **including robotics, creative writing, forensics, and photography.** Eventually, the center will serve five thousand children. Tiger is planning the construction of other centers around the country **at a cost of five million dollars apiece.** He is grateful for his loving and supportive family **and wants to help less fortunate children.**

## Practice (page 85)

1. INF 2. PP 3. INF 4. INF 5. PP

## Practice (page 86)

1. P 2. G 3. G 4. P 5. P

## Exercise 5: Identifying Phrases (page 87)

1. prepositional phrase
2. infinitive phrase
3. prepositional phrase
4. prepositional phrase
5. verb phrase
6. participial phrase
7. infinitive phrase
8. prepositional phrase
9. noun phrase
10. verb phrase

## Exercise 11: Correcting the Fragment That Contains a Participle (page 91, sample answers)

Walking through the deserted apartment building, I poked around in piles of junk. Broken furniture had been left behind. The brick walls were crumbling. Water dripped from an overhead pipe. Two children were playing in the dismal hallways. We are waiting for someone to restore the building to its former glory.

## Exercise 13: Correcting Fragments (pages 92–93, sample answers )

1. Early morning is a time of peace in my neighborhood.
2. The gray mist covers up all but the faint outlines of nearby houses.

3. I can barely make out the shapes of cars in the streets and driveways.
4. Often if I have the time, I sit and look out the window.
5. Holding a steaming cup of coffee, I slowly wake up.
6. The only sound to be heard is the rumbling of a truck.
7. It is passing by on the highway a quarter mile away.
8. Children are all tucked in their beds.
9. No barking dogs can be heard.
10. I love to sit by the window in this soft, silent dreamworld.

# CHAPTER 6: COMBINING SENTENCES USING THREE OPTIONS FOR COORDINATION

## Practice (page 102)

1. The audience was packed, for this was a man with an international reputation.

2. He could have told about all his successes, but instead he spoke about his disappointments.

3. His words were electric, so the crowd was attentive.

4. I should have brought a tape recorder, or at least I should have taken notes.

## Exercise 1: Combining Sentences Using Coordinating Conjunctions (pages 102–103)

1. *contrast:* but
2. *adds an idea:* and
3. *result:* so
4. *adds an idea when both clauses are in the negative:* nor
5. *reason:* for
6. *result:* so
7. *contrast:* but
8. *choice:* or
9. *contrast:* but
10. *choice:* or

## Practice (page 107)

1. The restaurant is always too crowded on Saturdays; nevertheless, it serves the best food in town.

2. The land was not for sale; however, the house could be rented.

3. The lawsuit cost the company several million dollars; consequently, the company went out of business a short time later.

4. The doctor told him to lose weight; furthermore, she instructed him to stop smoking.

## Exercise 4: Combining Sentences Using Adverbial Conjunctions (page 108)

1. *contrast:* however    2. *result:* therefore
3. *contrast:* nonetheless
4. *contrast:* on the other hand
5. *contrast:* however    6. *emphasis:* indeed
7. *emphasis:* in fact    8. *adds and idea:* in addition
9. *adds an idea:* furthermore
10. *result:* accordingly

## Exercise 7: Combining Sentences Using the Semicolon (page 112)

1. The assistant wrote the speech; the manager delivered it at the national meeting.
2. The man stood in front of me; the others stood to the side.
3. The apartment was light and airy; the property was neat and clean.
4. Shoppers were pushing grocery carts down the aisles; workers were stocking the shelves.
5. no semicolon required
6. He worked in the stockroom counting inventory; his coworker handled the customers.
7. He tried to explain; nobody gave him a chance.
8. Many teenagers spend hours playing video games; they neglect their studies.
9. no semicolon required
10. Ming-Na agreed to take the teaching position; she turned down a job singing backup in a rock band.

# CHAPTER 7: COMBINING SENTENCES USING SUBORDINATION

## Exercise 1: Identifying Dependent and Independent Clauses (pages 121–122)

1. IC    2. DC    3. DC    4. IC    5. IC
6. DC    7. DC    8. IC    9. IC    10. DC

## Practice (page 124)

1. DC    2. PP    3. PP    4. DC    5. PP
6. DC

## Practice (page 125)

1. a. Calvin went out to celebrate after he won the wrestling match.
   b. After he won the wrestling match, Calvin went out to celebrate.
2. a. The family was excited when Carla returned from Venezuela this spring.
   b. When Carla returned from Venezuela this spring, the family was excited.

## Exercise 4: Combining Sentences Using Subordination (page 126, sample answers)

1. While he was eating breakfast, the results of the election came over the radio.
2. The town council voted against the plan because they believed the project was too expensive.
3. I will see Maya Angelou tonight because she is speaking at the university.
4. The worker hoped for a promotion even though not one person in the department had received a promotion last year.
5. Because the worker hoped for a promotion, he did all his work accurately and on time.

## Practice (page 129)

1. The chemistry lab that I attend is two hours long.
2. The student assistant who is standing by the door is very knowledgeable.
3. The equipment that was purchased last year will make possible some important new research.

## Practice (page 131)

1. no commas
2. no commas
3. Her biology course, which met four times a week for two hours each session, was extremely demanding.
4. no commas
5. My own poetry, which has improved over the semester, has brought me much satisfaction.

## Exercise 8: Combining Sentences Using Relative Pronouns (pages 132–133)

1. Stress, which we experience every day, can do a great deal of harm.
2. People whose jobs are demanding often use food to help them cope. (no commas)
3. The practice of eating to cope with stress, which usually goes back to childhood, is often automatic.

4. Some foods that people turn to in times of stress can actually increase tension. (no commas)
5. Sweet foods, which are popular with people who need a lift, are actually not energy boosters.
6. Another substance that people use to get an energy boost is caffeine. (no commas)
7. One of the biggest mistakes is to use alcohol, which is really a depressant, as an aid to achieving calm.
8. People who want to feel a sense of calm should eat three light meals a day and two small snacks. (no commas)
9. Getting enough protein is also important in keeping an adequate energy level, which will get you through the day.
10. A person should eat regularly to avoid binges, which put on pounds and drain one's energy.

# CHAPTER 8: CORRECTING FRAGMENTS AND RUN-ONS

## Exercise 1: Recognizing Fragments (page 144)

1. b   2. c   3. a   4. c   5. d   6. c
7. a   8. d   9. b   10. d

## Practice (page 147, sample answers)

1. In recent years, several celebrities, including Michael J. Fox, Lance Armstrong, and Melissa Etheridge, have shared their health situations with the public. This has had a beneficial effect.
2. In 1995, Christopher Reeve became a quadriplegic after a horse riding accident. He and his wife worked tirelessly until their untimely deaths to draw attention to the need for better treatments and cures for spinal cord injuries.
3. Katie Couric, the American media personality, lost her husband to colon cancer in 1998. After his death, Katie became a spokeswoman for colon cancer awareness.
4. In fact, Katie had a colonoscopy on the air in March of 2000, **and** she inspired many to follow her example.
5. Katie Couric's efforts have become known as the "Couric effect;" we now know a celebrity can draw significant attention and support to worthwhile causes.

## Exercise 4: Recognizing and Correcting Run-Ons (pages 147–148, sample answer)

I was driving along on Route 80 when my daughter asked my wife to change the radio station. My wife told my daughter to do it herself, so my daughter unhooked her seatbelt and reached over from the back seat to change the station. However, just then her brother tickled her, and she lost her balance and fell on the gear shift. The gear shift was pushed into neutral, causing the car to lose power instantly. That's when we were hit by the van behind us.

# CHAPTER 9: CHOOSING CORRECT PRONOUNS

## Practice (page 159–160)

1. I    2. me    3. me

## Practice (page 161)

1. he    2. me

## Practice (page 163)

1. whom    2. who    3. whoever
4. who    5. who

## Exercise 3: Choosing the Correct Pronoun Using *Who/Whom* (pages 163–164)

1. who    2. whom    3. who    4. Whom
5. who's    6. whom    7. who    8. whose
9. who    10. whom

## Exercise 5: Choosing Correct Pronoun Forms (page 165)

1. she    2. me    3. whoever    4. she
5. Whoever    6. Who    7. they    8. ours
9. him    10. I

## Practice (page 167, sample answers)

1. Everyone should bring suggestions to the meeting.
2. These sorts of clothes are popular now.
3. The students didn't know what they were doing.
4. If the bird watchers hope to see anything, they must get up early.
5. This type of book appeals to me.

## Practice (page 168, sample answers)

1. I enjoy math exams because I can show what I know.
2. When I took geometry, I discovered that frequent review of past assignments helped make the course seem easy.
3. People always need to practice their skills to not forget them.

4. Math games can be fun for a student if he or she has a spirit of curiosity.
5. When studying math, you must remember that you have to "use it or lose it."

## Practice (page 169, sample answers)

1. The biologist asked the director to bring back the biologist's microscope.
2. The report says that the number of science and engineering students seeking doctoral degrees has fallen 50 percent since the mid-1960s.
3. At the laboratory, the scientists said the research had run into serious difficulties.
4. The testing equipment, which was accidentally dropped onto the aquarium, was badly damaged.
5. I don't watch the 10 o'clock news anymore because the programs have become too slick.

## Exercise 7: Making Pronouns and Antecedents Agree (pages 169–170)

1. The father mailed his son the son's high school yearbook.
2. No one wants his or her income reduced.
3. When a company fails to update its equipment, it often pays a price in the long run.
4. Women today have many more options open to them than ever before.
5. Everybody knows his or her own strengths best.
6. All of the workers anticipate their summer vacations.
7. If the campers want to eat quickly, they should help themselves.
8. This sort of bathing suit looks ridiculous on me.
9. The application says you must pay a registration fee of thirty-five dollars.
10. The doctor said that those types of diseases are rare here.

# CHAPTER 10: WORKING WITH ADJECTIVES, ADVERBS, AND PARALLEL STRUCTURE

## Practice (pages 178–179)

1. <u>also</u> known: *adverb*

2. <u>mild</u> form: *adjective*

3. <u>more</u> severe: *adverb*

4. <u>very</u> high: *adverb*

5. occur <u>regularly</u>: *adverb*

6. <u>anxious</u> people: *adjective*

7. <u>starchy</u> foods: *adjective*

8. <u>helpful</u> walk: *adjective*

Note: In #8, the word *walk* functions as a noun.

## Exercise 1: Adjectives and Adverbs Used in Comparisons (pages 181–182)

1. easier     2. tallest     3. more easily
4. better     5. most famous     6. most helpful
7. more slowly     8. worst     9. worse
10. most delicious

## Practice (page 184)

1. awfully     2. bad     3. well     4. quickly
5. really

## Exercise 3: Revising Misplaced Modifiers (page 187)

1. I gave the puppy with the white paws to my sister.
2. I am looking for the missing keys to the filing cabinets.
3. We decided to buy better sleeping bags before the camping trip.
4. The pilot always put passenger safety first.
5. They need to go directly home immediately after the party.
6. Watching the faces of the judges, the dance contestants waited eagerly.
7. The jeweler wanted to design a special charm bracelet for his new customer.
8. I took my daughter, who loved a day off from school, to my office.
9. The accountant almost forgot to tell his client about the change in the law.
10. There are exactly five tablets in this medicine bottle.

## Exercise 4: Revising Dangling Modifiers (pages 188–189)

1. Wearing his tuxedo, Victor fed the dog.
2. While we were visiting Yellowstone National Park, Old Faithful entertained us by performing on schedule.
3. Hoping to see the news, I turned on the television set at seven o'clock.
4. Although I ran up the stairs, the train had already left for Philadelphia.
5. After running over the hill, I could see the farm in the valley below.

6. I thought my son, dressed in a Dracula costume, looked perfect for Halloween.
7. She saw three spiders hanging from the ceiling in her bedroom.
8. After I wiped my glasses, the redbird flew away.
9. We listened to the neighbor's dog howling all evening without a stop.
10. After I had painted my room all afternoon, my cat demanded her dinner.

## Practice (page 190, sample answers)

1. A person should never (or shouldn't ever) go out with something cooking on the stove.
2. You have neither a bike nor a car (or You haven't either a bike or a car).
3. I don't want anything (or I want nothing).
4. I will never (or won't ever) break my promise.
5. I can't (or can hardly) wait until summer.

## Practice (page 191)

1. dirty
2. sewing her own clothes
3. willingly explain the lesson more than once

## Exercise 6: Revising Sentences for Parallel Structure (page 192)

1. bitterly cold     2. fixing an old car
3. a dedicated father     4. dark     5. graceful
6. sunny     7. to work out at the gym
8. work on my term paper for political science
9. imagination     10. head for the homestretch

# CHAPTER 11: MASTERING IRREGULAR VERB FORMS

## Practice (page 202)

1. cost     2. quit     3. spread     4. hit
5. become

## Practice (pages 203–204)

1. bought     2. spent     3. bled
4. kept     5. thought     6. sought
7. fought     8. taught     9. led     10. sent

## Practice (pages 204–205)

1. known     2. began     3. sang
4. grew     5. drove     6. rose     7. rode
8. flown     9. sprung     10. written

## Exercise 1: Practicing Irregular Verb Forms (pages 205–206)

1. began    2. written    3. knew
4. bet    5. hit    6. threw
7. kept    8. come    9. shrunk    10. hidden

## Exercise 4: Practicing More Irregular Verb Forms (page 207)

1. shot    2. built    3. fled    4. burst
5. mistook    6. slid    7. dealt    8. drawn
9. frozen    10. wrung

# CHAPTER 12: USING VERB TENSES CORRECTLY

## Practice (page 217)

1. went    2. have gone    3. has studied
4. took    5. has been

## Practice (pages 218–219)

1. has fascinated    2. has become, have watched
3. have replaced, had existed
4. had lived    5. has built

## Exercise 1: Practicing with Sequence of Tenses (page 220)

1. have stopped    2. would have
3. will buy    4. had never been    5. liked
6. will soon be    7. are    8. knew    9. would go
10. had gone

## Exercise 3: Correcting Unnecessary Shifts in Verb Tense (page 223)

1. completed    2. was    3. doesn't    4. came
5. didn't    6. continues    7. has    8. came
9. prefers    10. arrived

## Exercise 6: Forming Active Voice and Passive Voice (page 226)

1. *Active voice:* The child dialed the wrong number.
2. *Active voice:* My grandmother very carefully crocheted the sweater.
3. *Passive voice:* Cherry Creek was struck by a tornado last spring.
4. *Passive voice:* The leaves were blown across the yard (by the wind).
5. *Active voice:* In the seventies, many fashionable young men and women wore platform shoes.

## Practice (page 228)

1. When President Roosevelt died in 1945, the law required that Vice President Truman take over immediately.
2. It was essential that President Truman act quickly and decisively.
3. Truman must have wished that he were able to avoid using the atomic bomb to bring an end to World War II.
4. He felt it was necessary that the United States help Europe recover from the destruction of World War II.
5. President Truman always insisted that other countries be economically strong.

# CHAPTER 13: LEARNING THE RULES FOR CAPITALIZATION AND PUNCTUATION

## Exercise 1: Capitalization (page 237)

1. We    2. Winter Solstice
3. General Motors    4. Old Testament
5. Louisiana Purchase, France
6. Southwest
7. Automobile Workers Union, President Obama
8. Dominican    9. *Lost, Law and Order*
10. Judge Johnson

## Practice (page 240)

1. On November 14, 1977, officials discovered a major body of polluted water in Oswego, New York.
2. Problems with the water supply of the United States, Europe, Canada, and other parts of the world are growing.
3. Water is colorless, tasteless, odorless, and free of calories.
4. You will use on an average day twenty-four gallons of water for flushing, thirty-two gallons for bathing and washing clothes, and twenty-five gallons for other uses.
5. It took 120 gallons of water to create the eggs you ate for breakfast, 3,500 gallons for the steak you might eat for dinner, and more than 60,000 gallons to produce the steel used to make your car.

## Practice (page 241)

1. The most overused bodies of water are our rivers, but they continue to serve us daily.
2. American cities often developed next to rivers, and industries followed soon after in the same locations.
3. The people of the Industrial Age can try to clean the water they have used, or they can watch pollution take over.
4. The Great Lakes are showing signs of renewal, yet the struggle against pollution there must continue.
5. Many people have not yet been educated about the dangers to our water supply, nor are all our legislators fully aware of the problem.

## Practice (page 242)

1. To many people from the East, the plans to supply more water to the western states seem unnecessary.
2. However, people in the West know that they have no future without a good water supply.
3. When they entered Salt Lake Valley in 1847, the Mormons found dry soil that needed water before crops could be grown.
4. Confidently, the new settlers dug ditches that brought the needed water.
5. Learning from the past, modern farmers are trying to cooperate with nature.

## Practice (page 243)

1. Some parts of our country, I believe, do not have ample supplies of water.
2. The rocky soil of Virginia, for example, cannot absorb much rainwater.
3. Johnstown, Pennsylvania, an industrial city of forty-eight thousand, is situated in one of the most flood-prone valleys of America.
4. It is not, therefore, a very safe place to live.
5. The Colorado, which is one of our longest rivers, gives up most of its water to farmers and cities before it reaches the sea.

## Practice (page 243)

1. Dear, your tea is ready now.
2. I wonder, Jason, if the game has been canceled.
3. Dad, could I borrow five dollars?
4. I insist, sir, on speaking with the manager.
5. Kim, is that you?

## Practice (page 244)

1. 4,876,454    2. 87,602    3. 156,439,600
4. 187,000    5. 10,000,000,000,000

## Practice (page 244)

1. "I won't," he insisted, "be a part of your scheme."
2. He mumbled, "I plead the Fifth Amendment."
3. "I was told," the defendant explained, "to answer every question."
4. "The court case," the judge announced, "will be televised."
5. "The jury," said Al Tarvin of the press, "was hand-picked."

## Practice (pages 244–245)

1. Kicking, the child was carried off to bed.
2. To John, Russell Baker is the best columnist.
3. When you can, come and visit us.
4. We surveyed the students in the class; out of the twenty, seven were married.
5. Some types of skin cancers can kill, doctors say.

## Exercise 4: Using the Comma Correctly (page 245)

1. In Weaverville, California, the local high school administrators made an interesting discovery.
2. At a cost of four hundred dollars a year per student, a private company was offering college-level advanced placement courses on the web.
3. Because some students need these courses to get into more competitive colleges, everyone thought this would be a perfect way to take advantage of the new technology.
4. The problems, however, soon became apparent when two students signed up for a government course.
5. Brian Jones, a senior who wants to be a record producer, and Jeremy Forbes, a classmate who dreams of being a cartoonist, found these problems very frustrating.
6. Their worst problems were long delays getting online, many technical glitches, and the absence of a teacher to encourage persistence.
7. Out of six hundred students who enrolled in one of the company's online courses last year, two-thirds did not complete enough course work to take the final exam.
8. Government officials have praised the use of this electronic support for schools, but others say online courses are a poor replacement for the 180,000 new teachers the country really needs.
9. Still others worry that too many cyberspace offerings provide only supplemental services such as SAT training, college counseling, and virtual field trips.

10. Francisco J. Hernandez, an educator at the University of California at Santa Cruz, says, "Our intent is not to be an alternative to a high-quality teacher and classroom but to be an alternative to nothing because that's what students are getting right now."

## Exercise 7: Using the Apostrophe (page 249)

1. sun's   2. press's   3. room's
4. Anthony and Maria's   5. nobody's
6. his   7. Queen Elizabeth's reign
8. That's   9. boys'   10. book's

## Practice (page 252)

1. "The Gift of the Magi" is one of the short stories in O. Henry's book *The Four Million*.
2. Franklin Delano Roosevelt said, "We have nothing to fear but fear itself."
3. no quotation marks with indirect speech
4. The term "reggae" refers to a popular musical style originating in Jamaica.
5. She read the article "Can Empathy Be Taught?" in a recent issue of *Academe*.

## Practice (pages 252–253)

1. One of the best ways to remember a vacation is to take numerous photos; one of the best ways to recall the contents of a book is to take notes.
2. The problem of street crime must be solved; otherwise, the number of vigilantes will increase.
3. The committee was made up of Kevin Corey, a writer; Anita Poindexter, a professor; and Jorge Rodriguez, a politician.
4. The bank president was very cordial; however, he would not approve the loan.
5. The retailer wants higher profits; the customer wants lower cost.

## Practice (page 254)

1. Three vocalists performed in Los Angeles recently: Natalie Cole, Bruce Springsteen, and Sheryl Crow.
2. The official has one major flaw in his personality: greed.
3. no colon
4. The college offers four courses in English literature: Romantic Poetry, Shakespeare's Plays, The British Short Story, and The Modern Novel.
5. Arriving at 6:15 in the morning, Marlene brought me a sausage and cheese pizza, soda, and a gallon of ice cream.

## Practice (page 255)

1. Herbert Simon is—and I don't think this is an exaggeration—a genius.
2. George Eliot (her real name was Mary Ann Evans) wrote *Silas Marner*.
3. You should—in fact, I insist—see a doctor.
4. Unemployment brings with it a number of other problems (see the study by Brody, 2010).
5. Mass media (television, radio, movies, magazines, and newspapers) are able to transmit information over a wide range and to a large number of people.

## Exercise 10: Other Marks of Punctuation (pages 255–256)

1. To measure crime, sociologists have used three different techniques: official statistics, victimization surveys, and self-report studies.
2. "The Bells" is one of the best-loved poems of Edgar Allan Poe.
3. The lake has one major disadvantage to swimmers this summer: weeds.
4. E. B. White wrote numerous essays for adults; however, he also wrote some very popular books for children.
5. Tuberculosis (also known as consumption) has once again become a serious health issue.
6. The Victorian Period (1837–1901) saw a rapid expansion of industry.
7. He promised me—I know he promised—that he would come to my graduation.
8. Do you know what the French expression "déjà vu" means?
9. She wanted to go to the movies; he wanted to stay home and watch a movie on the DVD player.
10. She has the qualifications needed for the job: a teaching degree, a pleasant personality, two years' experience, and a love of children.

# CHAPTER 14: CHOOSING WORDS THAT WORK

## Exercise 1: Using Words Rich in Meaning (page 267)

Thin: 1. c   2. e   3. d   4. a   5. b

Eat: 1. d   2. f   3. a   4. e   5. b   6. c

## Exercise 3: Denotation/Connotation (pages 269–270, sample answers)

1. farmhouse
2. trudge
3. lady
4. packages
5. in her eighties
6. wrinkles
7. converse
8. drab
9. mumbling
10. relaxing

## Exercise 6: Revising Wordy Sentences (pages 272–273, sample answers)

1. The deadline for your project is May 18, or Your project is due May 18.
2. The thought of the exam is stressful for her.
3. The best place to study is our library.
4. Some people believe that astrology is a science.
5. We all need better organizational skills.
6. Mike is very handy mechanically.
7. She is cooking dinner.
8. The game will be canceled because of the rain.
9. The reasons for unemployment are complex.
10. The box was oblong.

## Exercise 8: Recognizing Language Inappropriate for Formal Writing (page 276)

1. *stop beating around the bush:* get to the point
2. *chill out:* calm down; relax
3. *a bummer:* a disappointment; unpleasant
4. *businessmen:* businesspeople
5. *come clean:* speak honestly
6. *a downer:* a disappointment
7. *guts:* courage; determination
8. *a dump:* a mess
9. *guys:* men
10. *crash:* rest; go to bed

# CHAPTER 15: PAYING ATTENTION TO LOOK-ALIKES AND SOUND-ALIKES

## Group I (pages 285–288)

oral, aural; By, buy, by; capital, capitol; clothes, close; course, coarse; complement, compliment; forward, foreword; past, passed, past; plain, plane; presence, presents

## Exercise 1: Group I Words (pages 288–289)

1. aural, oral
2. By, buy

3. capital, capital
4. cloth, clothes, close
5. course, coarse
6. complement, compliment
7. forward, foreword
8. past, passed
9. plain, plane
10. presents, presents

## Group II (pages 290–293)

principal, principal, principles; reign, rain; site, sight, cited; stationary, stationery; two, to, too; vain, vein; waist, waste; whether, weather; hole, whole; write, right, rite

## Exercise 3: Group II Words (page 293)

1. principal, principle
2. rein, reign
3. cite, sight
4. stationery, stationary
5. to, to, too
6. vain, vein
7. waste, waist
8. weather, whether
9. whole, hole
10. right, rite

## Group III (pages 294–295)

It's, its; They're, there, their; where, Were, we're; Whose, who's; your, you're

## Exercise 5: Group III Words (pages 295–296)

1. It's, its
2. its, it's
3. they're, their, there
4. they're, their, there
5. We're, were, where
6. Where, we're
7. Whose, who's
8. Who's, whose
9. you're, your
10. your, you're

## Group IV (pages 296–299)

accept, except; advise, advice; affect, effect; breath, breathe; choose, chose; conscience, conscious, conscientious; custom, costume; council, counsel, consul; desert, dessert; diner, dinner, diners

## Exercise 7: Group IV Words (pages 299–300)

1. accept, except
2. advice, advise
3. affect, effect
4. breathe, breath
5. choose, chose
6. conscious, conscience
7. customs, costumes
8. council, counsel
9. dessert, desert
10. dinner, diner

## Group V (pages 300–303)

emigrate, immigrate, emigrants, immigrants; further, farther; loose, lose; personal, personnel; quite, quiet, quit; receipt, recipe; special, especially; than, then; thought, thorough, though, threw, through; used to, used, use

## Exercise 9: Group V Words (page 303)

1. emigrated    2. farther    3. loose
4. personnel    5. quiet    6. receipt
7. special    8. than    9. through, though
10. used

## Practice Group VI (pages 305–306, sample answers)

1. laid the package
2. raised his son
3. set the groceries
4. laying down the new floor
5. lay out my clothes
6. raises many questions
7. set the timer
8. laid the ground rules
9. setting the table
10. raised a substantial amount of money

## Practice Group VI (page 307)

1. rising
2. lie
3. sitting
4. lay
5. rose
6. lying
7. sat
8. risen
9. lain
10. sat

## Exercise 11: Group VI Words (pages 307–308)

1. laid
2. sitting
3. sit
4. raised
5. rose
6. rose
7. raised
8. lie
9. lying
10. laid

# CHAPTER 16: WORKING WITH PARAGRAPHS: TOPIC SENTENCES AND CONTROLLING IDEAS

## Exercise 2: Finding the Topic Sentence of a Paragraph (pages 318–320)

1. We are the great "Let's junk it" society!
2. Today, the hospital nurse has one of the hardest jobs of all.
3. Anything can happen at a county agricultural fair.
4. This was one of the worst situations I had ever been in.
5. In order to shop wisely, several basic rules should be kept in mind.

## Exercise 5: Distinguishing a Topic Sentence from a Title (pages 323–324)

1. T    2. T    3. TS    4. T    5. TS
6. T    7. T    8. TS    9. T    10. TS

## Exercise 8: Finding the Topic in a Topic Sentence (page 325)

1. Remodeling an old house
2. two-part topic: College work and high school work
3. A well-made suit
4. Growing up near a museum
5. My favorite room in the house
6. The huge trade imbalance of the United States
7. One of the disadvantages of skiing
8. Spanking
9. An attractive wardrobe
10. first year

## Exercise 11: Finding the Controlling Idea (pages 327–328)

1. *Topic:* vigorous exercise; *controlling idea:* a good way to reduce the effects of stress on the body
2. *Two-part topic:* Buffalo and Toronto; *controlling idea:* differ
3. *Topic:* television violence; *controlling idea:* causes aggressive behavior
4. *Topic:* athletic scholarships available to women; *controlling idea:* increasing
5. *Topic:* caffeine; *controlling idea:* several adverse effects on the body
6. *Topic:* Serena Williams and her sister Venus; *controlling idea:* have dominated the world of women's tennis
7. *Topic:* training a parakeet to talk; *controlling idea:* takes great patience
8. *Topic:* babysitting for a family with four preschool children; *controlling idea:* difficult
9. *Topic:* the hours between five and seven in the morning; *controlling idea:* productive
10. *Topic:* the foggy night; *controlling idea:* spooky

# CHAPTER 17: WORKING WITH PARAGRAPHS: SUPPORTING DETAILS

## Practice (page 339)

*Topic sentence:* Everyone has heard of surefire formulas to prevent getting a cold.

*Examples of home remedies:* a cold shower, exercise, hot rum toddy, cod-liver oil, tea with honey, citrus fruit juices, keeping one's feet dry

*Examples of over-the-counter remedies:* vitamins, alkalizers, lemon drinks, antihistamines, decongestants, timed-release capsules, antibiotics, antiseptic gargles, bioflavonoids, nose drops and sprays

*Fact:* Americans average two or three colds a year, each lasting about a week.

*Expert and statistic:* U.S. Public Health Service; 50 percent of the population experiences a common cold during winter and 20 percent has a cold during the summer.

## Exercise 1: Finding the Topic Sentence and Supporting Details (page 340)

Paragraph 1

*Topic sentence:* Heroes in American movies usually fall into types.

*First type:* the tight-lipped loner man like Clint Eastwood or Humphrey Bogart

*Second type:* the quiet, shy, fumbling type like Jimmy Stewart

*Third type:* the superman type like Sylvester Stallone

Paragraph 2

*Topic sentence:* Blue jeans have become a tradition, and along the way have acquired a history of their own.

*First historical example:* the trainman who replaced a faulty coupling with a pair of jeans

*Second historical example:* the Wyoming man who used his jeans as a towrope to haul his car out of a ditch

*Third historical example:* the Californian who found several 63-year-old pairs of jeans in a mine and they were as good as new

*Fourth historical example:* the construction worker who dangled fifty-two stories above the street, supported only his Levi's belt loop

## Exercise 4: Distinguishing a Supporting Detail from a Restatement of the Main Idea (pages 344–345)

1. a. SD  b. R  c. SD  d. SD
2. a. SD  b. SD  c. R  d. SD
3. a. R  b. SD  c. SD  d. SD
4. a. SD  b. SD  c. R  d. SD
5. a. SD  b. SD  c. SD  d. R

# CHAPTER 18: DEVELOPING PARAGRAPHS: ILLUSTRATION

## Exercise 1: The Sources for Illustrations (pages 354–355)

1. information from a survey
2. hypothetical example
3. example from personal experience

## Exercise 4: Analyzing Paragraphs That Use Examples (pages 356–357)

1. *Example of the main idea in one's own words:* As a lover of junk, I have a happily messed-up life.
2. 17
4. yes (the word *list*, line 3)
5. Like the junk itself, the examples have no obvious order.

# CHAPTER 19: DEVELOPING PARAGRAPHS: NARRATION

## Exercise 4: Placing Details in Order of Time Sequence (pages 372–373)

3, 1, 4, 2, 5

## Exercise 7: Working with Transitions (pages 375–376, sample answers)

*The author's choice of transitions:*

1. A few months ago     2. Then
3. A few weeks later     4. Twenty-four hours later
5. the next three months     6. Today
7. from time to time

# CHAPTER 20: DEVELOPING PARAGRAPHS: DESCRIPTION

## Exercise 1: Selecting the Dominant Impression (pages 389–390, sample answers)

1. transformed     2. well lit     3. cluttered
4. well stocked     5. dusty     6. busy
7. overcrowded     8. raucous     9. welcoming
10. bright

## Exercise 3: Revising Vague Dominant Impressions (page 391, sample answers)

1. a brilliant blue
2. cool
3. energizing
4. destructive
5. clean and well-lighted
6. bustling
7. creamy
8. his happy self again
9. comfortable
10. satisfying for now

## Practice (page 393)

1. *Hearing:* loud humming; *touch:* cool; *sight:* large refrigerator case, milk, cream, soda, beer
2. *Smell:* onion, caraway seed, pumpernickel
3. *Sight, smell, and taste:* cheese, smoked meat

## Exercise 6: Recognizing Sensory Images (page 393)

*Sight:* room: wide, dirty, disheveled; ancient typewriters; copyeditors at coffee-stained desks; crumpled paper on floor; green, grimy walls
*Sound:* clatter from old typewriters; voice of the boss, L. L. Engelking
*Smell:* smoke from cigarettes and cigars

## Exercise 12: Using Spatial Order (pages 398–399)

1. 3, 1, 5, 4, 2     2. 4, 5, 2, 1, 3     3. 2, 3, 1, 4

# CHAPTER 21: DEVELOPING PARAGRAPHS: PROCESS ANALYSIS

## Exercise 1: Is the Process Complete? (page 413)

*Missing steps in the recipe for the Swedish spice cake:* a list of ingredients, directions to separate the eggs yolks from the egg whites (saving the egg whites until later), temperature of the oven, how long to bake the cake

## Exercise 4: Ordering in Logical Sequence (page 415)

4, 8, 7, 10, 1, 3, 6, 9, 5, 2

# CHAPTER 22: DEVELOPING PARAGRAPHS: COMPARISON/ CONTRAST

## Exercise 1: Evaluating the Two-Part Topic (page 429)

Answers could vary depending on explanation.

1. too broad     2. suitable     3. suitable
4. suitable     5. too broad     6. suitable
7. too broad     8. suitable     9. too broad
10. too broad

## Exercise 4: Recognizing the Two Approaches to Ordering Material (pages 433–434)

1. Block, differences
2. Point-by-point, similarities

3. Block, differences
4. Point-by-point, similarities

## Exercise 7: Using Transitions in Comparisons and Contrasts (pages 436–437, sample answers)

1. Dr. Rappole has an excellent bedside manner, but Dr. Connolly is very withdrawn.
2. The first apartment had almost no furniture, was badly in need of painting, and felt dark and cheerless; likewise, the second apartment was equally bare, felt totally neglected, and looked out onto a brick wall.
3. In the United States, interest in soccer has become apparent only in recent years; however, in Brazil, soccer has always been immensely popular.
4. Unlike the French Revolution, which was directed by the common people, the Russian Revolution was directed by an elite group of thinkers.
5. Whereas Amy is carefree and fun loving, with little interest in school, Noreen, Amy's sister, is so studious and hardworking that she is always on the honor roll.

# CHAPTER 23: DEVELOPING PARAGRAPHS: CAUSE AND EFFECT

## Exercise 1: Finding Causes and Effects in Paragraphs (pages 453–454)

*Causes of headaches:*

1. nervous tension
2. dietary factors
   a. dependency on caffeine
   b. allergy to salt
   c. low blood sugar
3. environmental factors—chemicals
   a. polishes
   b. waxes
   c. bug killers
   d. paint

*Effects of headaches:*

1. nausea
2. interrupted sleep, which can worsen the physical and emotional state
3. reliance on drugs with negative side effects
4. reduced productivity on the job, even absences
5. interruption of family life

## Exercise 3: Looking for the Causal Relationship (page 456)

1. U   2. C   3. U   4. C   5. C
6. U   7. C   8. U   9. C   10. U

# CHAPTER 24: DEVELOPING PARAGRAPHS: DEFINITION AND ANALYSIS

## Exercise 1: Defining by Class (page 472)

1. Mythology is one form of a culture's literature.
2. Nylon is a strong resilient synthetic material.
3. An amoeba is a protozoan.
4. A tricycle is a vehicle.
5. Cabbage is a plant.
6. Democracy is a form of government.
7. Asbestos is a fibrous mineral.
8. A piccolo is a musical instrument.
9. Poetry is a division of literature.
10. A university is an institution of learning.

# CHAPTER 26: MOVING FROM THE PARAGRAPH TO THE ESSAY

## Practice (page 499)

1. F   2. TH   3. TH   4. T   5. F

## Exercise 1: Recognizing a Thesis Statement (page 500)

1. F   2. TH   3. F   4. F   5. T   6. F
7. T   8. TH   9. TH   10. T

## Exercise 6: The Thesis Statement: Adding the Strategy of Development (page 504)

1. The effects of gambling are disastrous.

   Strategy of Development: effects

2. Learning how to do your own tax return can be frustrating.

   Strategy of Development: process

3. The sight of our neighborhood park is dismaying.

   Strategy of Development: description

4. The meaning of the term *patriotism* is often controversial.

   Strategy of Development: definition

5. Which type of loan a person takes out is very consequential.

   Strategy of Development: classification

## Exercise 9: Identifying Common Introductory Patterns (pages 508–509)

1. 3. Definition of the concept to be discussed
2. 7. A number of descriptive images leading to the thesis
3. 1. Begins with a general subject (farm work); then narrows down to the topic of the essay (cidering).

## Exercise 12: Finding Transitional Expressions (pages 513–514)

*Transitional expressions:* In the past, Sometimes, many times, For one thing, For another, For example, Naturally, Then, after a short while, Of course, Finally

*Pronouns:* They, they, it, it, we, all this, we, we, no one, they both, we, itself, ourselves

*Repeated terms:* appear/disappear/reappear, reasons, geopolitical/geopolitically, supported, ally, bases, ties, moved into, both sides

# CHAPTER 33: OTHER COLLEGE WRITING: THE RESEARCH PAPER AND THE ESSAY EXAM

## Exercise 2: Methods of Development (pages 605–606)

1. summary
2. comparison/contrast
3. definition
4. classification
5. cause and effect

# CREDITS

## PHOTOS

**Chapter 1. 5:** Denis Vrublevski/Shutterstock **18:** Winston Davidian/iStockPhoto.com

**Chapter 2. 21:** Olga Besnard/Shutterstock **30:** Splitcast/iStockPhoto.com

**Chapter 3. 34:** digitalskillet/iStockPhoto.com **54:** Dan Kite/iStockPhoto.com **57:** Katherine Moffitt/iStockPhoto.com

**Chapter 4. 68:** Image courtesy of the Walter Anderson Museum of Art Ocean Springs, Mississippi **76:** © Jose Luis Pelaez, Inc./CORBIS

**Chapter 5. 82:** Used with permission from the author **87:** John Pitcher/iStockPhoto.com

**Chapter 6. 114:** © 2008 The Record **119:** LeggNet/iStockPhoto.com

**Chapter 7. 122:** Photo by Arnold Slater / Rex USA / Courtesy Everett Collection **133:** Susan Stewart/iStockPhoto.com **136:** © Frymire Archive / Alamy **137:** © North Wind Picture Archives / Alamy **140:** © Beryl Goldberg

**Chapter 8. 144:** Michael Krinke/iStockPhoto.com **153:** Terrance Emerson/iStockPhoto.com **156:** Riche Legg/iStockPhoto.com

**Chapter 9. 164:** Guy Le Querrec/Magnum Photos **173:** © Classic Image / Alamy

**Chapter 10. 179:** Lise Gagne/iStockPhoto.com

**Chapter 11. 205:** © Pictorial Press Ltd / Alamy **213:** © Jose Luis Palez, Inc. / Corbis

**Chapter 12. 222:** © Associated Press **233:** ArtisticCaptures/iStockphoto.com

**Chapter 13. 246:** DaddyBit/iStockphoto.com **260:** © Photos.com Select/IndexOpen

**Chapter 14. 278:** Photograph Perspectives-Jeff Smith/Shutterstock **283:** Ryan McVay / Photo Library

**Chapter 15. 289:** HultonArchive/iStockPhoto.com

**Chapter 16. 317:** © 2005 Getty Images News **336:** © Tony Lathan/CORBIS

**Chapter 17. 339:** Tarabura/iStockPhoto.com **343:** Anyka/iStockPhoto.com **350:** © Dewitt Jones/CORBIS

**Chapter 18. 360:** © Mike Kezar/Stone/Getty Images **368:** Gene Chatka/iStockPhoto.com

**Chapter 19. 378:** Ann Marie Kurtz/iStockPhoto.com **386:** Kevin Miller/iStockPhoto.com

**Chapter 20. 402:** Used with permission from the author **410:** © Digital Vision/Getty Images

**Chapter 21. 418:** stray_cat/iStockPhoto.com **426:** Bob Thomas/iStockPhoto.com

**Chapter 22. 440:** Monkey Business Images/Shutterstock **449:** © 2000 Gigi Cohen/Network Photographers

**Chapter 23. 462:** Willie B. Thomas/iStockPhoto.com **468:** © Bettmann/CORBIS

**Chapter 24. 472:** digitalskillet/iStockPhoto.com **483:** © Mark M. Lawrence/CORBIS

**Chapter 25. 492:** Gene Chutka/iStockPhoto.com **495:** Rene Marsi/iStockPhoto.com

**Chapter 26. 508:** Joseph Gareri/iStockPhoto.com **517:** Tom Toles in the *Buffalo News* © 1997

**Chapter 27. 520:** Used with permission from the author **533:** Alberto L. Pomares/iStockPhoto.com

**Chapter 28. 535:** © Jim Craigmyle/First Light/Getty Images **544:** Nancy Louie/iStockPhoto.com

**Chapter 29. 545:** © Cengage Learning **554:** Achim Prill/iStockPhoto.com

**Chapter 30. 556:** Sharon Dominick/iStockPhoto.com **564:** Don Bayley/iStockPhoto.com

**Chapter 31. 567:** © VStock LLC/IndexOpen **577:** Sean Locke/iStockPhoto.com

**Chapter 32. 580:** Monkey Business Images/Shutterstock **590:** Tommr/iStockPhoto.com

**Chapter 33. 610:** Peter Chen/iStockPhoto.com

## READINGS

**Chapter 5.** Copyright © Bankers Trust Company. All rights reserved. Reproduced by permission.

**Chapter 7.** © 2000 The New York Times Co. Reprinted with permission.

**Chapter 9.** "Princess Must Face Immigration Charges," The Associated Press, July 18, 2000, Copyright © 2000 The Associated Press. Reprinted by permission.

**Chapter 23.** From Jessie Carney Smith. *Notable Black American Women.* Copyright © 2002 Gale, a part of Cengage Learning, Inc. Reproduced by permission. www.cengage.com/permissions

**Chapter 28.** © 1976 by The New York Times Co. Reprinted with permission.

**Chapter 29.** "Salvation" from *The Big Sea* by Langston Hughes. Copyright © 1940 by Langston Hughes. Copyright renewed 1968 by Arna Bontemps and George Houston Bass. Reprinted by permission of Hill and Wang, a division of Farrar, Straus and Giroux, LLC. and Harold Ober Associates Incorporated.

**Chapter 30.** Copyright © 1997 from *T+D* by Richard Koonce. Reprinted with permission of American Society for Training & Development.

**Further Readings.** "A Day at a Theme Park," by W. Bruce Cameron, *Rocky Mountain News*, August 22, 1999. Copyright © W. Bruce Cameron. Reproduced by permission of W. Bruce Cameron and Creators Syndicate, Inc.; "My Daughter Smokes" from *Living by the Word: Selected Writings 1973–1987*, published by Harcourt, first appeared in *In These Hard Times*, copyright © 1987 by Alice Walker, reprinted by permission of Houghton Mifflin Harcourt Publishing Company, The Wendy Weil Agency, Inc., and David Higham Associates; "My Heroes," by Elizabeth Berg, *Parents Magazine*, 1992. Reprinted by permission of International Creative Management, Inc. Copyright © 1992 by Elizabeth Berg; "Summer Reading", pp. 282–285 from *Paper Trail* by Michael Dorris. Copyright © 1994 by Michael Dorris. Reprinted by permission of HarperCollins Publishers; "Unforgettable Miss Bessie" by Carl T. Rowan (March 1985). Reprinted with permission from *The Reader's Digest*, March 1985. Copyright © 1985 by The Reader's Digest Assn., Inc.; "Why Marriages Fail" by Anne Roiphe, *Parents*

*Magazine,* 1992. Copyright © Anne Roiphe. All rights reserved. Reproduced with permission of the author; Copyright © 1994 U.S. News & World Report, L.P. Reprinted with permission; From "Get a Knife, Get a Dog, but Get Rid of Guns" from *Nothin' But Good Times Ahead* by Molly Ivins, copyright © 1993 by Molly Ivins. Used by permision of Random House, Inc.; Isaac Asimov, "What Is Intelligence, Anyway?" Copyright © Issac Asimov, published by permission of the Estate of Issac Asimov, c/o Ralph M. Vicinanza, Ltd. New York; Lee Herrick, "What Is This Thing Called Family?" Copyright © Lee Herrick. All rights reserved. Reproduced by permission; Naheed Mustafa, "My Body Is My Own Business" in *The Globe and Mail,* 1993. Copyright © Naheed Mustafa. All rights reserved. Reproduced by permission; Reprinted by arrangement with the Estate of Martin Luther King Jr., c/o Writers House as agent for the proprietor New York, NY. Copyright © 1958 Dr. Martin Luther King Jr., copyright renewed 1986 Coretta Scott King; Russell Baker, "Slice of Life," in *New York Times,* November 24, 1974. Copyright © 1974 by The New York Times Company. All rights reserved. Reproduced by permission; Susan Musgrave, "Visiting Rites." Copyright © 1999 by Susan Musgrave. First published in Canada by Saturday Night. Reprinted by permission of the author.

# INDEX